Selected Verb Forms

Regular Verbs — Simple Tenses and Present Perfect (Indicative)

	PRESENT	PRETERITE	IMPERFECT	PRESENT PERFECT
hablar	hablo	hablé	hablaba	he hablado
comer	como	comí	comía	he comido
vivir	vivo	viví	vivía	he vivido

Common Irregular Verbs — Present and Preterite (Indicative)

caer	caigo	caí	**poner**	pongo	puse
dar	doy	di	**querer**	quiero	quise
decir	digo	dije	**saber**	sé	supe
estar	estoy	estuve	**ser**	soy	fui
hacer	hago	hice	**tener**	tengo	tuve
ir	voy	fui	**traer**	traigo	traje
oír	oigo	oí	**venir**	vengo	vine
poder	puedo	pude	**ver**	veo	vi

Irregular Verbs — Imperfect (Indicative)

ir	iba	**ser**	era	**ver**	veía

Regular Verbs — Simple Tenses and Present Perfect (Subjunctive)

	PRESENT	IMPERFECT	PRESENT PERFECT
hablar	hable	hablara	haya hablado
comer	coma	comiera	haya comido
vivir	viva	viviera	haya vivido

Regular and Irregular Verbs — Future and Conditional

hablar	hablaré	hablaría
comer	comeré	comería
vivir	viviré	viviría

decir	diré	diría	**querer**	querré	querría
hacer	haré	haría	**saber**	sabré	sabría
poder	podré	podría	**tener**	tendré	tendría
poner	pondré	pondría	**venir**	vendré	vendría

Puntos de partida

Puntos de partida

AN INVITATION TO SPANISH

SIXTH EDITION
ANNIVERSARY EDITION

Marty Knorre

Thalia Dorwick

Ana María Pérez-Gironés
Wesleyan University

William R. Glass

Hildebrando Villarreal
California State University, Los Angeles

Boston   Burr Ridge, IL   Dubuque, IA   Madison, WI   New York   San Francisco   St. Louis
Bangkok   Bogotá   Caracas   Lisbon   London   Madrid
Mexico City   Milan   New Delhi   Seoul   Singapore   Sydney   Taipei   Toronto

McGraw-Hill Higher Education

*A Division of The **McGraw-Hill** Companies*

This is an  book.

Puntos de partida
An Invitation to Spanish

Published by McGraw-Hill, an imprint of The McGraw-Hill Companies, Inc., 1221 Avenue of the Americas, New York, NY 10020. Copyright © 2001, 1997, 1993, 1989, 1985, 1981 by The McGraw-Hill Companies, Inc. All rights reserved. No part of this publication may be reproduced or distributed in any form or by any means, or stored in a database or retrieval system, without the prior written consent of The McGraw-Hill Companies, Inc., including, but not limited to, in any network or other electronic storage or transmission, or broadcast for distance learning.

This book is printed on acid-free paper.

1 2 3 4 5 6 7 8 9 0 VNH VNH 9 0 9 8 7 6 5 4 3 2 1 0

ISBN 0-07-232071-0 (Student's Edition)
ISBN 0-07-238261-9 (Instructor's Edition)

Editor-in-chief: *Thalia Dorwick*
Executive editor: *William R. Glass*
Development editor: *Ina Cumpiano*
Senior marketing manager: *Nick Agnew*
Project manager: *David M. Staloch*
Senior production supervisor: *Pam Augspurger*
Designer: *Francis Owens*
Freelance designer (front and end matter): *Andrew Ogus*
Freelance design coordinator: *Mary L. Christianson*
Cover image: *WOODS+WOODS*
Art editor: *Nora Agbayani*
Compositor: *York Graphic Services, Inc.*
Supplements coordinator: *Louis Swaim*
Typeface: *Palatino*
Printer and binder: *Von Hoffmann Press*

Because this page cannot legibly accommodate all the copyright notices, credits are listed after the index and constitute an extension of the copyright page.

Library of Congress Cataloging-in-Publication Data

Puntos de partida: An Invitation to Spanish / Marty Knorre ... [et al.] 6th ed.
        p. cm
        Includes index
        ISBN 0-07-232071-0
        1.   Spanish language—Textbooks for foreign speakers—English.

PC4129.E5 P86 2000
468.2'421—dc21

00-064753

http://www.mhhe.com

BRIEF TABLE OF CONTENTS

CONTENTS

In this chapter, you will be introduced to the Spanish language and the Spanish-speaking world at large. You will learn some useful greetings and other expressions of courtesy, as well as begin to learn to count in Spanish.

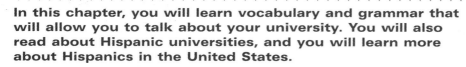

Capítulo 1

En la universidad 32

In this chapter, you will learn vocabulary and grammar that will allow you to talk about your university. You will also read about Hispanic universities, and you will learn more about Hispanics in the United States.

Capítulo 2

La familia 64

In this chapter, you will learn vocabulary and grammar that will allow you to talk about your family. You will also read about the family unit, and you will learn about Mexico.

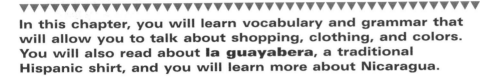

Capítulo 3

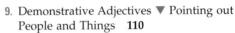

De compras 100

In this chapter, you will learn vocabulary and grammar that will allow you to talk about shopping, clothing, and colors. You will also read about **la guayabera**, a traditional Hispanic shirt, and you will learn more about Nicaragua.

Capítulo 4

En casa 130

In this chapter, you will learn vocabulary and grammar that will allow you to talk about your house and its furnishings. You will read about houses in the Hispanic world, in addition to reviewing some advertisements for homes for sale. You will also learn more about Costa Rica.

Capítulo 5

Las estaciones, el tiempo y un poco de geografía   158

▼▼

In this chapter, you will learn vocabulary and grammar that will allow you to talk about the seasons and the weather. You will read about the tropics and the biodiversity of that region. You will also learn more about Guatemala.

 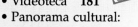
Capítulo 6

¿Qué le gusta comer?   190

▼▼

In this chapter, you will learn vocabulary and grammar that will allow you to talk about food and beverages. You will also read about Spanish cuisine and learn more about Panama.

 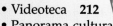

Capítulo 7

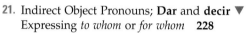

De vacaciones 222

In this chapter, you will learn vocabulary and grammar that will allow you to talk about travel, vacations, and modes of transportation. You will also read about tourist attractions in Mexico and learn more about Honduras and El Salvador.

Capítulo 8

Los días festivos 252

In this chapter, you will learn vocabulary and grammar that will allow you to talk about holidays and celebrations. You will also read about different ways of celebrating New Year's Eve and learn more about Cuba.

Capítulo 9

El tiempo libre   278

In this chapter, you will learn vocabulary and grammar that will allow you to talk about your free time and about various pastimes and sports. You will also read about the Hispanic music scene in Canada and learn more about Colombia.

Capítulo 10

La salud   306

In this chapter, you will learn vocabulary and grammar that will allow you to talk about your health and well-being. You will read about medicine in Hispanic countries, as well as about health and vitamins. You will also learn more about Venezuela.

Capítulo 11

Presiones de la vida moderna   336

▼▼

In this chapter, you will learn vocabulary and grammar that will allow you to talk about the pressures and stress that you might endure as a student. You will read about how different aspects of modern life affect our health, and you will also learn more about Puerto Rico.

Capítulo 12

La calidad de la vida   364

▼▼

In this chapter, you will learn vocabulary and grammar that will allow you to talk about the things that affect your quality of life. You will read an article about hand-held electronic appointment books, and you will also learn more about Peru.

Capítulo 13

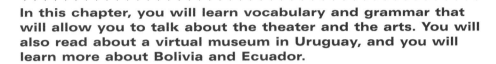

El arte y la cultura   396

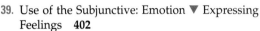

In this chapter, you will learn vocabulary and grammar that will allow you to talk about the theater and the arts. You will also read about a virtual museum in Uruguay, and you will learn more about Bolivia and Ecuador.

Capítulo 14

El medio ambiente   424

In this chapter, you will learn vocabulary and grammar that will allow you to talk about the environment and ecology. You will also read about the Amazon and learn more about Argentina.

Capítulo 15

La vida social y la vida afectiva 450

In this chapter, you will learn vocabulary and grammar that will allow you to talk about your social life and personal relationships. You will read an article about wedding ceremonies, and you will also learn more about Chile.

Capítulo 16

¿Trabajar para vivir o vivir para trabajar? 472

In this chapter, you will learn vocabulary and grammar that will allow you to talk about your job and various professions. You will read a poem about a fig tree, and you will also learn more about Uruguay and Paraguay.

Capítulo 17

En la actualidad   500

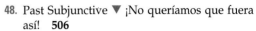

In this chapter, you will learn vocabulary and grammar that will allow you to talk about the news, government, and civic responsibilities. You will read a poem about an aspect of Cuban culture in this country, and you will also learn more about the Dominican Republic.

Capítulo 18

En el extranjero   524

In this chapter, you will learn vocabulary and grammar that will allow you to talk about traveling abroad. You will also read a poem about the paths of life, and you will also learn more about Spain.

Appendices   547

▼▼▼

Vocabularies   569

▼▼▼

Index   605

▼▼▼

About the Authors   615

▼▼▼

PREFACE

> ▶ " . . . to help students develop proficiency
> ▶ in the four language skills essential to
> ▶ truly communicative language teaching
> ▶ . . . "
>
> from the preface to *Puntos de partida,*
> first edition, 1981

In the twenty years since the publication of the first edition of *Puntos de partida* (or *Puntos,* as the series has come to be called), more than a million students have studied Spanish using *Puntos.* The coauthors of *Puntos de partida* are grateful for this tremendous and positive response to its goals and approach.

The goal of the coauthors—cited above—has remained constant since the first edition. As for the text's approach, we believe that it has evolved, keeping pace in its own way with technological advances and with our increasing knowledge of how languages are learned. The ancillary package for the first edition of *Puntos,* excellent for its time, seems small in comparison to the plethora of materials that are available to instructors today. We remember our excitement as we worked hard to develop what we felt was a truly creative audio program (available for copying on large reels!) for the first edition. We have been delighted to feel that same excitement over the years as we have used new technologies to create video programs, computer programs, CD-ROMs, and other electronic supplements. In the context of language learning, these supplements are not window dressing; they are true enhancements that make Spanish come alive for students in ways that a classroom instructor alone cannot do.

In addition to those new technologies, instructors will find in the sixth edition, a special Anniversary Edition, those features that they have come to know and trust over the years and that have made the text one of the most widely adopted in the country. These features include:

- an abundance of practice material, ranging from form-focused exercises to communicative activities

- vocabulary, grammar, and culture that work together as interactive units

- an emphasis on meaningful use of Spanish

- a positive portrayal of Hispanic cultures

- supplementary materials that are carefully coordinated with the core text and that actually "work" with it.

Here are some of the most important features of the Anniversary Edition.

- a special Annotated Instructor's Edition that includes a larger trim size to accommodate a wrap-around design. The result is an AIE that is not only easier to read but one that includes special recurring features, including notes and special activities for Heritage Speaker students, comments on the National Standards, and suggestions for integrating multimedia.

- a redesigned two-page chapter-opening spread that introduces students to the chapter theme through engaging questions and also serves to preview the integrated multimedia components

- a new **Panorama cultural** page in each chapter that focuses on individual countries of the Spanish-speaking world

- a revised **En los Estados Unidos y el Canadá...** feature, which now includes cultural information about the Hispanic community in Canada

- a revised **Un paso más** section at the end of each chapter, including new readings and writing activities in almost all chapters

- a new text-specific, integrated video (**En contexto**) filmed on location in Costa Rica, Mexico, and Peru. Integrated in the new **Videoteca** section of each chapter, this video illustrates functional language for the learner.

- a completely revised interactive CD-ROM that reviews and practices vocabulary, grammar, and skills in an engaging, meaningful way

- a new Online Learning Center Website that provides important resources and materials for instructors and students

- additional innovative multimedia products

A GUIDED TOUR

CHAPTER-OPENING SPREAD

Each chapter opens with a two-page spread that provides an engaging and purposeful introduction to the chapter for both the instructor and the student. On the left-hand page of each spread a photo depicts the chapter theme, followed by a series of questions (¿Qué opina Ud.?) that encourage students to reflect on the theme. A corresponding feature on the *Puntos* Website provides responses from a Spanish-speaker to the same questions, allowing students to compare and contrast their own responses with those of a native speaker.

The right-hand page of the spread provides a brief overview of the chapter objectives, including vocabulary, grammar, and cultural topics (in the **En este capítulo...** section). In addition, the right-hand page also includes a preview of the integrated multimedia components of the chapter (**Puntos interactivo**), including the two videos presented in the **Videoteca** section and the CD-ROM.

VOCABULARIO: PREPARACIÓN

This section presents and practices the chapter's thematic vocabulary. The lexical lists in these sections are recorded on the Listening Comprehension Cassette (or CD) that accompanies the student textbook and are signaled by a headphone icon. Each new lexical list is followed by a **Conversación** section that practices the new vocabulary in context.

PRONUNCIACIÓN

This section, a feature of the first seven chapters, focuses on individual sounds that are particularly difficult for native speakers of English.

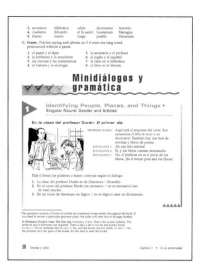

MINIDIÁLOGOS Y GRAMÁTICA

This section presents two to four grammar points. Each point is introduced by a minidialogue, a cartoon or drawing, realia, or a brief reading that presents the grammar topic in context. Grammar explanations, in English, appear in the left-hand column of the two-column design; paradigms and sample sentences appear in the right-hand column. Each grammar presentation is followed by a series of contextualized exercises and activities that progress from more controlled (**Práctica**) to open-ended (**Conversación**). The **Conversación** sections especially contain many partner-pair activities.

VIDEOTECA

This section presents the two functional/situational videos that accompany *Puntos*. The first video, **Minidramas**, consists of three ongoing story lines that take place in Mexico, Spain, and Ecuador, respectively. The textbook offers sections of dialogues taken directly from these video segments, which illustrate situations related to the chapter theme. Follow-up activities ask students to practice an aspect of language featured in the dialogue. In addition, backstory information is presented about characters from the video in a feature called **Un poco más sobre...**

The second video, called **En contexto**, provides brief functional vignettes (e.g., asking for directions, making an appointment) filmed on location in Costa Rica, Mexico, and Peru. Follow-up activities ask students to work individually and with partners to check comprehension and practice language. In addition, a corresponding feature on the *Puntos* CD-ROM allows students to recreate these vignettes by participating in a "video dialogue" with characters from the **En contexto** video.

UN POCO DE TODO

The exercises and activities in this section combine and review grammar presented in the chapter as well as important grammar from previous chapters. Major topics that are continuously spiraled in this section include **ser** and **estar**, preterite and imperfect, gender and number agreement, and indicative and subjunctive.

PANORAMA CULTURAL

This new cultural section focuses on an individual country of the Spanish-speaking world (or in a few instances, two countries presented together). This in-depth look at the Hispanic world features information about prominent figures, the arts, cuisine, politics, history, and so forth.

VOCABULARIO

The end-of-chapter vocabulary lists include all important words and expressions from the chapter that are considered active.

UN PASO MÁS

At the end of each chapter, this optional supplementary section presents tasks and activities that further develop learners' reading and writing skills and complement the chapter theme.

At the beginning of each **Un paso más** section is the **Lectura**. Each reading is accompanied by a reading strategy (**Estrategia**). Readings are author-written in the early chapters and realia-based or completely authentic in later chapters. Authentic readings have been culled from Spanish language magazines and journals and include literary selections in the final three chapters. Some readings have been edited for length but not for content or language.

Following the reading is **Escritura**, comprised of writing tasks that vary from writing simple sentences to extended narrations.

ADDITIONAL FEATURES

Other important features that appear throughout the text include:

▶ **Nota cultural** features that highlight an aspect of Hispanic cultures throughout the world

▶ **En los Estados Unidos y el Canadá...** sections that focus on U.S. and Canadian Hispanics and communities

▶ **Nota communicativa** sections that provide additional information and strategies for communicating in Spanish

▶ **Vocabulario útil** boxes that give additional vocabulary that may be necessary to work through specific activities

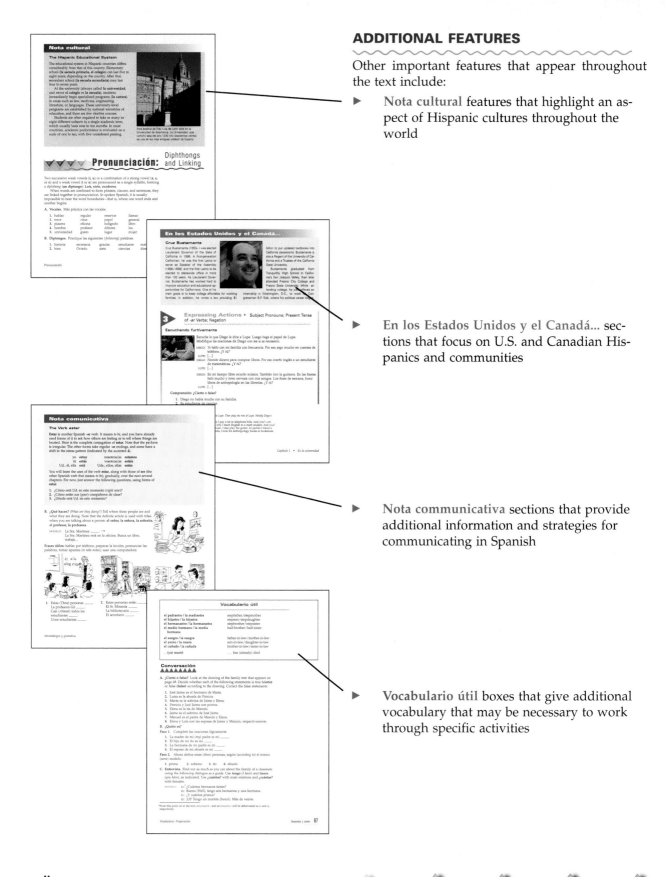

WHAT'S NEW TO THE SIXTH EDITION?

CHAPTER THEMES

The positive response from adopters of the fifth edition confirmed that the chapter themes found in *Puntos* provide engaging and relevant content for exploration and discussion. Naturally, in the sixth edition, theme vocabulary for all chapters has been updated to reflect changes in the areas of technology, recreational activities, and so forth. In addition, instructors familiar with previous editions will notice that the theme of **Capítulo 11** has been revised and now focuses on pressures of modern life, with a particular emphasis on student experiences.

NEW CHAPTER-OPENING SPREAD

Many comments from adopters of the fifth edition revealed that the chapter-opener page was often skipped in class, which led us to reexamine all aspects of this page: the intended purpose, the content, and the design. Informed by useful suggestions and feedback from professors across the country, we completely redesigned and restructured the opening page, converting it into a two-page spread. The result, we believe, is an introduction to the chapter that is more engaging and more purposeful to the instructor and the student. Spending class time on the chapter opener will provide a useful introduction to the chapter for the student and set the stage for a more successful experience with the chapter content. (A visual presentation of the new Chapter Opener is provided in the Guided Tour presented earlier in this Preface.)

SCOPE AND SEQUENCE OF GRAMMAR

Numerous comments from adopters and potential adopters of the fifth and earlier editions have guided the authors in modifying the presentation of grammar. This feedback has resulted in a grammatical scope and sequence in the sixth edition that we believe is in sync with how *Puntos* is actually used in the classroom. The modifications to the sixth edition include the following:

▶ Unstressed possessive adjectives are now introduced in **Capítulo 2** rather than in **Capítulo 3**.

▶ Demonstrative adjectives are now introduced in **Capítulo 3** rather than in **Capítulo 4**.

▶ The verbs **hacer**, **oír**, **poner**, **salir**, **traer**, and **ver** are now presented as a separate grammar point in **Capítulo 4** instead of as a vocabulary note, as in previous editions.

▶ An introduction to the subjunctive, which was presented for recognition in **Capítulo 6** of the fifth edition, is now treated as a **Nota comunicativa**.

PANORAMA CULTURAL

In the fifth edition of *Puntos*, extensive cultural content was covered in a section called **El mundo hispánico de cerca**, which focused on broad regions of the Spanish-speaking world. While adopters had many positive things to say about that section, many also noted that a country-specific rather than regional focus would be of interest. In response, we have replaced the cultural spreads found in the fifth edition with the new **Panorama cultural** page now found in every chapter. This page, which focuses on one country (or in a few chapters, two countries), provides interesting information about customs, traditions, people, and so forth. A corresponding feature is also found on the *Puntos* Website.

VIDEOTECA

New to the sixth edition is a section called **Videoteca**, which includes the **Minidramas** and **En contexto** videos. Both videos are text specific, the former filmed on location in Ecuador, Mexico, and Spain, and the latter in Costa Rica, Mexico, and Peru. This section provides information and activities that will facilitate the viewing experience for students, as well as postviewing comprehension questions. In addition, a new feature called **Un poco más sobre...** offers more backstory detail about the characters from the **Minidramas** video, with a corresponding feature on the *Puntos* Website.

UN PASO MÁS: READING AND WRITING

Instructors familiar with the previous edition of *Puntos* will notice a revised **Un paso más** section fol-lowing each chapter. This section, which has traditionally provided optional content to develop learners' reading and writing skills, continues to serve this important function. More than half of the readings are new to the sixth edition, and all of these are authentic readings culled from sources written for heritage speakers of Spanish. We believe it is crucial that students be exposed to authentic written language not only for the development of reading skills but also for the acquisition of language. Students also feel a tremendous sense of accomplishment knowing that they have read (and understood!) a text written for native speakers.

In addition, the reading selections in the final three chapters (Capítulos 16–18) are authentic poems that provide an introduction to literature for beginning students of Spanish. These selections represent works from Spain and Latin America. We believe that a structured and guided introduction to literature at the beginning level of study will facilitate the transition to intermediate and upper-division courses that emphasize literature.

As in the previous edition, all readings highlight a particular reading strategy that serves to assist students, thus making their task more enjoyable and more successful. For example, in one passage we bring to the students' attention the function that cognates can play in the reading process; in another passage we underscore the importance of rhetorical structure and organization. These strategies, which are informed by second-language reading research, can be carried from one reading to the next, as well as to texts that students might read on their own outside of class.

In addition to revising the reading passages for the sixth edition, we also revised the accompanying writing activities, now called **Escritura**. These activities serve to introduce students to the writing process and range from brief tasks such as filling out a form to longer tasks such as writing a letter, a descriptive paragraph, an essay, and so forth. The theme of the writing tasks is related to the theme of the reading passage, thereby integrating and uniting the two skills in a purposeful way.

USING PUNTOS DE PARTIDA IN THE CLASSROOM

DEVELOPING LANGUAGE PROFICIENCY

The authors believe that students' (and instructors') class time is best spent using Spanish: listening to and speaking with their instructor and classmates, listening and viewing audiovisual materials of many kinds, and reading in-text and supplementary materials. For that reason, grammar explanations have been written to be self-explanatory, and sample answers for many exercises are provided in the back of the book so that students can check their work before coming to class. Thus, instructors can spot-check exercises as needed in class but devote more time to the multitude of extensions, follow-up suggestions, and special activities offered in the Annotated Instructor's Edition. Consequently, class time can be focused on new material and novel language experiences that will maintain student interest and provide more exposure to spoken and written Spanish. Research in second-language acquisition has revealed that environments that expose learners to the language and also offer them opportunities to use the language in meaningful ways provide an optimal learning situation. Students make few gains in language learning when all of their class time is spent correcting exercises.

The preceding comments underscore the authors' conceptualization of *Puntos* throughout its many editions as a text that fosters students' proficiency in Spanish. The following features help realize this objective:

► a focus on the acquisition of vocabulary during the early stages of language learning (**Ante todo**) and then in each chapter throughout the text

► an emphasis on meaningful and creative use of language

► careful attention to skills development rather than grammatical knowledge alone

► a cyclical organization in which vocabulary, grammar, and language functions are consistently reviewed and reentered

► an integrated cultural component that embeds practice in a wide variety of culturally significant contexts

► content that aims to raise student awareness of the interaction of language, culture, and society

The overall text organization progresses from a focus on formulaic expressions, to vocabulary and structures relevant to the "here and now" (student life, family life), to survival situations (ordering a meal, travel-related activities), and to topics of broader interest (current events, social and environmental issues). This breadth of thematic diversity—coupled with the focus on vocabulary, grammatical structures, and language functions—helps develop students' language proficiency, thus preparing them to function in Spanish in situations that they are most likely to encounter outside the classroom.

PUNTOS DE PARTIDA AND THE NATIONAL STANDARDS

In response to the *Goals 2000: Educate America Act,* the American Council on the Teaching of Foreign Languages (ACTFL) received funding to develop K-12 content standards for foreign language education. Working in collaboration with professional organizations such as the American Association of Teachers of Spanish and Portuguese, among others,[1] ACTFL launched the National Standards in its 1996 volume *Standards for Foreign Language Learning: Preparing for the 21st Century.* The Standards and their challenging vision of educational reform have been embraced by government, business, and over fifty professional and state organizations.

The Standards are organized into five goal areas: Communication, Cultures, Connections, Comparisons, and Communities. These "five Cs" are symbolized by five interlocking circles, representing the close interrelationship among these goals. Each includes two or three content standards that describe what students should know and be able to use as a result of their language study. The Standards differ from a skill-based paradigm, where listening, speaking, reading, and writing are divorced from content and communication. Rather, the Standards emphasize these four skills as instruments for acquiring cross-disciplinary knowledge as well as developing critical thinking skills and communicative strategies. While the Standards do not prescribe curriculum, they necessarily influence pedagogical approaches and performance outcomes.

More specifically, the Standards ask us to reconceptualize our approach to culture. As Phillips notes: "In spite of much lip service over the years, culture remained at the periphery of instruction, most frequently referred to as a fifth skill, a capsule, a cultural note at the bottom of a textbook page, or a Friday "fun" activity. . . . Teachers taught the culture as they knew it; students learned items randomly, not as connected threads or themes. In most courses, no systemic process was visible that enabled students to observe cultural manifestations; to analyze the patterns of behavior; to hypothesize about origins, usage, or context; and to understand the perspectives of the people in the target cultures. In sum, most cultural content learned was fact or act in isolation from how it related to the values and attitudes of a person or a people."[2]

With its integrated approach to culture, *Puntos* exemplifies the spirit of the Standards. Culture is organized thematically by chapter. Then, within each chapter of the text and via the various multimedia supplements (video, CD-ROM, Website), students are exposed to a multiplicity of *products*, *processes*, and *perspectives*. From interviews with native speakers, to in-depth cultural commentary on the countries of the Spanish-speaking world, to reflections on the Hispanic community in the United States and Canada, *Puntos* provides sustained opportunities for hypothesis and analysis, inviting students to make connections between beliefs, behaviors, and cultural artifacts.

In addition to **culture**, *Puntos* integrates the four additional goal areas described in the National Standards. Through its presentation of functional language, role play activities, and personalized activities, *Puntos* emphasizes **communication**. The readings and other exploratory activities help students make **connections** among discipline areas. Ample opportunities are provided for cross-cultural **comparisons** in the **¿Qué opina Ud.?** activities that begin each chapter and that are continued on the *Puntos* Website. Finally, Internet-based and experiential activities allow students to explore **communities**. Throughout the Instructor's Edition, a special recurring feature devoted to the National Standards indicates how and in what manner the Standards are represented in the content of the material.

[1]The other organizations included in this project were the American Association of Teachers of French and the American Association of Teachers of German.

[2]June K. Phillips, ed., *Foreign Language Standards: Linking Research, Theories, and Practices* (Lincolnwood: NTC, 1999), p. 8.

SUPPLEMENTARY MATERIALS

A variety of additional components are available to support *Puntos de partida*. Many are free to adopting institutions. Please content your local McGraw-Hill representative for details on policies, prices, and availability.

The *Instructor's Edition*, which has always been regarded as a principal teaching resource for both novice and experienced instructors, celebrates the Anniversary Edition of *Puntos* with an enlarged trim size and additional instructional ideas and activities. Revised by Ana María Pérez-Gironés (Wesleyan University) and A. Raymond Elliott (University of Texas, Arlington), this unparalled supplement contains suggestions for implementing activities, supplementary exercises for developing listening and speaking skills, and abundant variations and follow-ups on student text materials. In addition, special new features found in the wrap-around annotation space include a recurring Resources note at the beginning of each chapter identifying key supplements and resources for that chapter, notes and suggestions for adapting certain activities to accommodate Heritage Speaker students, and notes that identify activities that support the National Standards. There are also additional exercises for the **Vocabulario: Preparación** sections, the **Minidramas** video, and the **Lectura** and **Escritura** sections. In addition, instructors will also find a recurring reference to the **Tesoros** CD-ROM, a new interactive mystery story line CD-ROM that also provides complete presentation of core vocabulary and grammatical structures. This engaging CD-ROM is discussed in greater detail in the Video and Multimedia section of this Preface.

The *Workbook*, by Alice Arana (formerly of Fullerton College) and Oswaldo Arana (formerly of California State University, Fullerton), continues the successful format of previous editions by providing additional practice with vocabulary and structures through a variety of input-based, controlled, and open-ended activities and guilded compositions. Retained from the fifth edition is the **Prueba corta**, now preceded by a new grammar self-check feature called **A ver si sabe...**, which allows students to quickly assess their knowledge of grammatical structures before completing the final quiz. The new **Panorama cultural** section offers focused vocabulary and fact-based activities related to the same feature found in the student textbook.

The *Laboratory Manual* and *Audio Program*, by María Sabló-Yates (Delta College), continue to emphasize listening comprehension activities as well as cultural listening passages with listening strategies. Chapters offer form-focused speaking practice as well as interview and dialogue-based activities, including activities that correspond to the **Videoteca** section of the student textbook. New to the sixth edition is **Prueba corta**, a chapter-ending self-quiz that allows students to assess their language development before moving on to the next chapter. Audiocassettes or CDs are free to adopting institutions and are also available for student purchase upon request. An Audioscript is also available.

The *Instructor's Manual and Resource Kit* offers an extensive introduction to teaching techniques, general guidelines for instructors, suggestions for lesson planning in semester and quarter schedules, and additional pre- and postviewing activities for the **Minidramas** video. Also included are a wide variety of interactive and communicative games for practicing vocabulary and grammar.

The *Testing Program* reflects the revisions in the student text for the sixth edition. It also includes sections for testing reading and listening comprehension, as well as tests for oral proficiency and sections designed to test cultural material presented in the program.

Packaged with every new student text is a free *Listening Comprehension Cassette* (or *CD*) that provides additional vocabulary practice for the **Vocabulario**: **Preparación** sections of the text. This audio supplement was designed to meet the needs of individual students and can be used to review and practice vocabulary as well as to practice pronunciation.

A set of *Overhead Transparencies*, most in full color, contains drawing from the text and supplementary drawings for use with vocabulary and grammar presentation. An electronic online version of the Transparencies is available to instructors on the *Puntos* Online Learning Center Website.

Also available are *Supplemental Materials to accompany Puntos de partida*, by Sharon Foerster and Jean Miller (University of Texas, Austin). Comprised of a worktext and a teacher's guide, these two supplements are a compilation of materials that include short pronunciation practice, listening exercises, grammar worksheets, integrative communication-building activities, comprehensive chapter reviews, and language games.

The *McGraw-Hill Electronic Language Tutor (MHELT)*, available in both IBM and Macintosh formats, offers most of the more controlled exercises from the student text as well as some supplementary mechanical practice. A parsing tool provides students with guided feedback while they complete the exercises and keeps track of their work.

A *training/orientation manual* for use with teaching assistants, by James F. Lee (Indiana University), offers practical advice for beginning language instructors and language coordinators.

Also available for use with *Puntos de partida* is a software program called *Spanish Partner*, developed by Monica Morley and Karl Fisher (Vanderbilt University). This user-friendly program helps students master first-year vocabulary and grammar topics. Available for student purchase, Spanish Partner also offers clear feedback that helps students learn from their errors.

The *Destinos Video Modules* are also available for use with the sixth edition of *Puntos*. Containing footage from the popular "Destinos" telecourse series, as well as from original footage shot on location, the modules offer high-quality video segments that enhance learning of vocabulary, functional language, situational language, and culture.

The *Rand-McNally / McGraw-Hill World Map on CD-ROM*, available for student purchase, contains numerous detailed maps along with visuals and textual information (in English) about key events in history, famous figures, important cities, and so on. The detail and information provided significantly enhance the foreign language experience from a cultural, historical, and geographical perspective.

A *Practical Guide to Language Learning*, by H. Douglas Brown (San Francisco State University), provides beginning foreign language students with a general introduction to the language-learning process. This guide is free to adopting institutions, and it can also be made available for student purchase.

VIDEO AND MULTIMEDIA

These video and multimedia supplements are currently available. Please contact your McGraw-Hill representative for information about electronic supplements that may be available in the future.

THE VIDEO

The Anniversary Edition of *Puntos* is accompanied by a culturally rich and engaging video whose three distinct parts offer interesting story lines, illustrate functional language, and take viewers on a cultural tour of the countries of the Spanish-speaking world. The video segments are integrated within each chapter of the textbook.

The first two segments, **Minidramas** and **En contexto**, are presented in the **Videoteca** section. **Minidramas**, which was filmed on location in Ecuador, Mexico, and Spain, provides a story line built around a cast of characters in each of those countries, respectively. **En contexto**, filmed on location in Costa Rica, Mexico, and Peru, offers brief vignettes that illustrate functional language, such as making a hotel reservation, opening a bank account, and so on. The textbook provides accompanying activities, as does the Laboratory Manual. Additional information on using the **Minidramas** and **En contexto** segments in the classroom, as well as pre- and postviewing activities and a complete videoscript, are also included in the Instructor's Manual.

A third brief video segment is integrated within the new **Panorama cultural** section of each chapter. These segments offer an engaging visual tour and overview of each of the countries of the Spanish-speaking world and highlight major cities, monuments, festivals, traditions, and so on.

THE CAST OF CHARACTERS

Featured throughout the **Minidramas** segment are many main and supporting characters. Here are some of the main characters you will meet.

Diego González, a U.S. graduate student living in Mexico

Lupe Carrasco, an anthropology student from Mexico City

Antonio Sifuentes, a graduate student from Mexico City

Elisa Velasco, a travel writer from Quito

José Miguel Martin Velasco, son of Elisa and a student

Paloma Velasco, José Miguel's cousin, also a university freshman

Manolo Durán García, a university professor of literature in Seville

Lola Benítez Guzmán, a Spanish professor for American students

THE *PUNTOS DE PARTIDA* CD-ROM

Available in multiplatform format, the *Puntos* CD-ROM continues the emphasis on the meaningful use of Spanish that characterizes the student text. Correlated with the textbook by chapter and by major sections within chapters, the CD-ROM offers multiple opportunities for learners to review and practice vocabulary and grammar in a meaningful, interactive format. A video segment in each lesson invites learners to "participate" in a dialogue with a native speaker of Spanish and further practice the language functions presented in the **En contexto** video. In addition, learners continue their development of reading, writing, listening, and speaking skills through interaction with textual passages and other engaging content. Cultural themes introduced in the textbook are further discussed in the CD-ROM, and a link from the CD-ROM takes the user directly to the *Puntos* Online Learning Center Website. The inclusion of additional learning resources, including the McGraw-Hill Electronic Language Tutor program, a "talking" glossary of terms, and verb reference charts, makes the *Puntos de partida* CD-ROM a unique multimedia learning tool for the student of Spanish.

THE *TESOROS* CD-ROM

The new *Tesoros* CD-ROM, which can be used independently for self-study or in conjunction with *Puntos de partida* (or other texts), introduces a new experience in interactive multimedia language study. Organized into sixteen lessons, this CD-ROM involves users in a mystery treasure hunt adventure that takes them through the Spanish-speaking world and involves each participant as a character in the story line. Animated storyboards bring this virtual adventure to life for the user. In addition, the *Tesoros* CD-ROM offers a complete presentation and practice of first-year grammar (correlated to the *Puntos* textbook) in an interactive format that includes audio segments. An interactive city map serves as the vehicle for presenting thematic vocabulary. In each lesson, users click on different city buildings for a presentation of vocabulary terms followed by practice exercises. An extensive bilingual illustrated dictionary, accompanied by audio segments, makes the *Tesoros* CD-ROM a unique supplement to *Puntos*.

THE ONLINE LEARNING CENTER WEBSITE

The new Online Learning Center (OLC) Website brings the Spanish-speaking world directly into students' lives and their language-learning experience through a myriad of resources and activities. Resources for students include vocabulary and grammar activities for each chapter, cultural Internet links and activities, and vocabulary flashcards. For instructors, the OLC provides grammar PowerPoint slides, online transparencies, and links to professional organizations and other resources. The *Puntos* OLC can be accessed at **www.mhhe.com/puntos**.

ACKNOWLEDGMENTS

The suggestions, advice, and work of the following friends and colleagues are gratefully acknowledges by the authors of the sixth edition.

▶ Dr. Bill VanPatten (University of Illinois, Chicago), whose creativity has been an inspiration to us for a number of editions and from whom we have learned so very much about language teaching and about how students learn

▶ Dr. A. Raymond Elliott (University of Texas, Arlington) and Ana María Pérez-Gironés (Wesleyan University), whose contributions to the Instructor's Edition have served to make that supplement an even more invaluable teaching resource

▶ Dr. Gail Fenderson (Brock University, St. Catherines, Ontario), whose work on the revised **En los Estados Unidos y el Canadá...** sections has expanded our knowledge of the Hispanic community in Canada

▶ Dr. Manuela González-Bueno (University of Kansas), whose thoughtful suggestions on the **Pronunciación** sections in the fifth edition are retained in the sixth edition

▶ Laura Chastain (El Salvador), whose invaluable contributions to the text range from language usage to suggestions for realia

In addition, the publisher wishes to acknowledge the suggestions received from the following instructors and professional friends across the country. The feedback we received through their formal reviews of the fifth edition and through their participation in focus groups was instrumental in shaping the revision of the sixth edition. The appearance of their names in this list does not necessarily constitute their endorsement of the text or its methodology.

FOCUS GROUP PARTICIPANTS

Ezequiel Cárdenas
Cuyamaca College

Cristina Cordero
North Harris College

David Detwiler
Cuyamaca College

Margaret Eomurian
Houston Community College

Sharon Foerster
University of Texas–Austin

María Grana
Houston Community College

María Louise Hams
San Diego City College

Janett Hillar
Houston Community College

Ana Hnat
Houston Community College

Paul Jacques
Grossmont College

John Kellogg
Golden West College

Teresa López
University of San Diego

Américo López-Rodríguez
Golden West College

Janine Mendis
Grossmont College

Dan McLean
North Harris College

Virginia Naters
Grossmont College

David Nielson
University of San Diego

Bertha I. Parle
Montgomery College

Dennis Parle
University of Houston

Judy Penate
Golden West College

María Clara Romero-Huerte
San Diego City College

América Salazar
Grossmont College

Patricia Santana
Cuyamaca College

Catalina Segovia Case
University of San Diego

Wayne Stromberg
University of San Diego

Carlos Villacis
Houston Community College

Paul Vincent
Grossmont College

Larissa Watkins
University of San Diego

Simi Windward Smith
University of San Diego

Gloria Yamprey-Jorg
Houston Community College

REVIEWERS

Yaw Agawu-Kakraba
Grand Valley State University

Delmar Asbill
Northeastern State University

Frank Attoon
College of the Desert

Deborah A. Dougherty
Alma College

Phillip P. Flahive
North Central College

Marianne Franco
Modesto Junior College

Javier Alejandro Galván
Santa Ana College

Gilberto Gómez
Wabash College

Edna Greenway
Calvin College

Rebecca Harclerode
Drexel University

Caroline Kreide
Merced College

Barbara Lingo
Baptist Bible College

Patricia A. Marshall
Brown University

Olga Marina Moran
Cypress College

Duane Nelson
Cloud County Community College

Comfort Pratt-Panford
Northwestern State University of Louisiana

Diane Rosner
Lake Tahoe Community College

Cynthia Slagter
Calvin College

Gerald R. St. Martin
Salisbury State University

Jim Swann
Northeast Texas Community College

Lynn Walford
Louisiana State University

Alex Whitman
Lower Columbia College

Simi Windward Smith
University of San Diego

Many other individuals deserve our thanks and appreciation for their help and support. Among them are the people who, in addition to authors, read the sixth edition at various stages of development to ensure its linguistic and cultural authenticity and pedagogical accuracy: Alice Arana (United States), Oswaldo Arana (Peru), Laura Chastain (El Salvador), and María Sabló-Yates (Panama). Thanks also to Ana María Pérez-Gironés for her help in creating the original concepts and characters for the **Minidramas** video segments.

Within the McGraw-Hill family, we would like to acknowledge the contributions of the following individuals: Diane Renda and the McGraw-Hill production group, especially Francis Owens for his inspired work on the design of the sixth edition, David Staloch for his invaluable assistance as Project Manager, and Pam Augspurger and Louis Swaim for their work on various aspects of production. We would also like to thank Horacio Durazo and Fionnuala McEvoy for their helpful editorial assistance.

Special thanks are due to Eirik Børve, who originally brought some of us together, and to Nick Agnew and the McGraw-Hill marketing and sales staff for their constant support and efforts. Finally, we would like to thank the development editors whose thoughtful and patient editorial talents are seen in the textbook and other parts of the *Puntos* package: Dr. Ina Cumpiano, Max Ehrsam, and Dr. Pennie Alem.

The only reasons for publishing a new textbook or to revise an existing one are to help the profession evolve in meaningful ways and to make the task of daily classroom instruction easier and more enjoyable for experienced instructors and teaching assistants alike. Language teaching has changed in important ways in the twenty years since the publication of the first edition of *Puntos de partida*. We are delighted to have been—and to continue to be—agents of that evolution. And we are grateful to McGraw-Hill for its continuing support of our ideas.

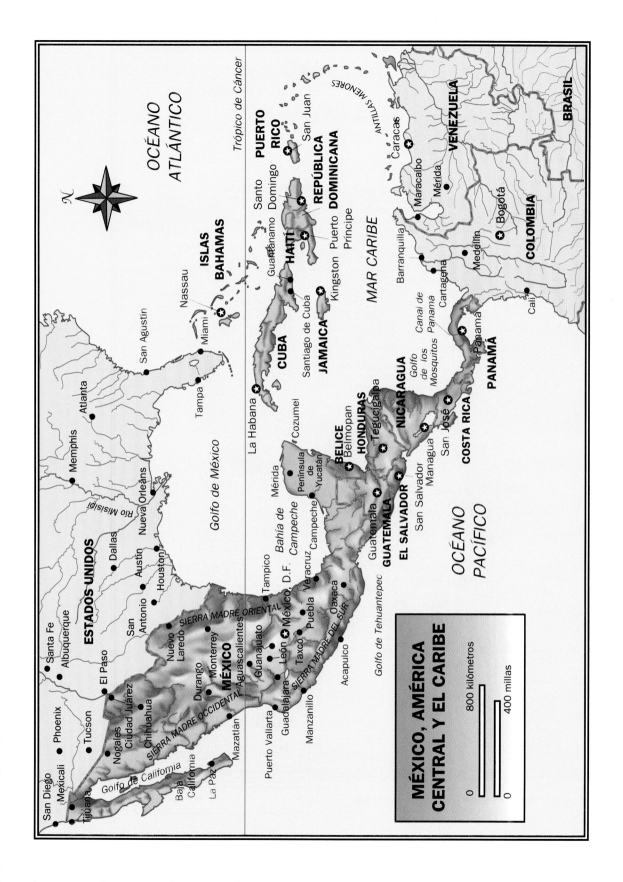

MÉXICO, AMÉRICA CENTRAL Y EL CARIBE

OCÉANO ATLÁNTICO

Trópico de Cáncer

ANTILLAS MENORES

PUERTO RICO
San Juan

REPÚBLICA DOMINICANA
Santo Domingo

HAITÍ
Puerto Príncipe
Guantánamo

ISLAS BAHAMAS
Nassau

VENEZUELA
Caracas

BRASIL

COLOMBIA
Bogotá
Maracaibo
Mérida
Medellín
Barranquilla
Cartagena
Cali

MAR CARIBE

Kingston
JAMAICA
Santiago de Cuba

CUBA
La Habana

Miami
Tampa
San Agustín

Atlanta
Memphis

Nueva Orleans

Golfo de México

OCÉANO PACÍFICO

PANAMÁ
Canal de Panamá
Golfo de los Mosquitos
Panamá

COSTA RICA
San José

NICARAGUA
Managua

HONDURAS
Tegucigalpa

EL SALVADOR
San Salvador

GUATEMALA
Guatemala

BELICE
Belmopan

Cozumel
Península de Yucatán
Campeche
Bahía de Campeche
Mérida

Veracruz
Tampico

México, D.F.
Puebla
Oaxaca
Golfo de Tehuantepec
Acapulco

MÉXICO
SIERRA MADRE ORIENTAL
SIERRA MADRE DEL SUR
SIERRA MADRE OCCIDENTAL

Aguascalientes
Guanajuato
León
Taxco
Guadalajara
Manzanillo
Puerto Vallarta
Mazatlán
Durango
Monterrey
Nuevo Laredo
Chihuahua
Ciudad Juárez

ESTADOS UNIDOS
El Paso
Nogales
Tucson
Phoenix
Mexicali
San Diego
Tijuana
Santa Fe
Albuquerque
Dallas
Austin
San Antonio
Houston

Golfo de California
Baja California
La Paz

Río Misisipí

N

0   800 kilómetros
0   400 millas

XXXV

MAR CARIBE

OCÉANO
ATLÁNTICO

Barranquilla
Maracaibo
PANAMÁ
Caracas
Panamá
Medellín
VENEZUELA
GUYANA
Georgetown
Paramaribo
Cayena
Río Orinoco
Bogotá
Cali
COLOMBIA
SURINAME
GUYANA FRANCESA
Quito
Ecuador
ECUADOR
Río Amazonas
Belém
Guayaquil
Manaus
PERÚ
BRASIL
Recife
CORDILLERA DE LOS ANDES
Cuzco
Lima
La Paz
Brasília
Arequipa
BOLIVIA
Sucre
Antofagasta
PARAGUAY
Río de Janeiro
CHILE
Asunción
Trópico de Capricornio
San Miguel
de Tucumán
São Paulo
La Serena
OCÉANO
PACÍFICO
Córdoba
Rosario
URUGUAY
OCÉANO
ATLÁNTICO
Valparaíso
Santiago
ARGENTINA
Concepción
Buenos Aires
Montevideo
Río de la Plata
Bahía Blanca
Puerto Montt
Bariloche
Chiloé
AMÉRICA DEL SUR
0   1500 kilómetros
Islas Malvinas
Estrecho de Magallanes
0   1000 millas
Punta Arenas
Tierra del Fuego
Cabo de Hornos

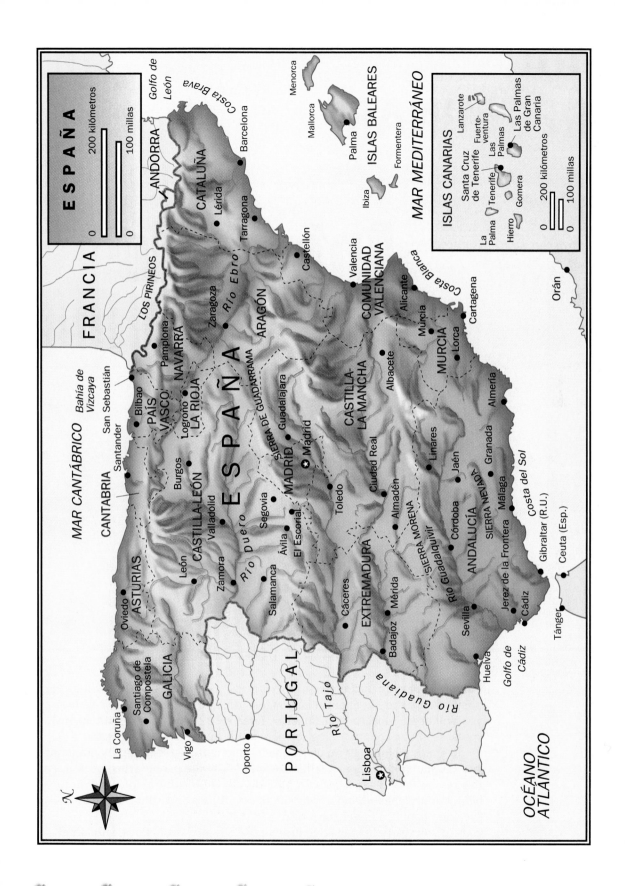

ESPAÑA

MAR CANTÁBRICO
Bahía de Vizcaya
Golfo de León
Costa Brava

FRANCIA
ANDORRA
LOS PIRINEOS

CATALUÑA
Barcelona
Lérida
Tarragona
Castellón

Río Ebro
ARAGÓN
Zaragoza

NAVARRA
Pamplona
PAÍS VASCO
Bilbao
San Sebastián
Santander
CANTABRIA

LA RIOJA
Logroño

COMUNIDAD VALENCIANA
Valencia
Alicante
Costa Blanca
Cartagena

MURCIA
Murcia
Lorca
Almería

CASTILLA-LA MANCHA
Guadalajara
Albacete
Ciudad Real
Linares

ESPAÑA
MADRID
Madrid
SIERRA DE GUADARRAMA
Segovia
Ávila
El Escorial
Toledo

ASTURIAS
Oviedo
GALICIA
Santiago de Compostela
La Coruña
Vigo

CASTILLA-LEÓN
Burgos
Valladolid
León
Zamora
Salamanca
Río Duero

Cáceres
EXTREMADURA
Mérida
Badajoz

PORTUGAL
Río Tajo
Río Guadiana
Lisboa
Oporto

SIERRA MORENA
Almadén
Córdoba
Jaén
Río Guadalquivir
ANDALUCÍA
SIERRA NEVADA
Granada
Málaga
Costa del Sol
Gibraltar (R.U.)
Ceuta (Esp.)
Sevilla
Jerez de la Frontera
Cádiz
Huelva
Golfo de Cádiz
Tánger
Orán

OCÉANO ATLÁNTICO

ISLAS BALEARES
Menorca
Mallorca
Palma
Ibiza
Formentera
MAR MEDITERRÁNEO

ISLAS CANARIAS
Lanzarote
Fuerteventura
Las Palmas
Las Palmas de Gran Canaria
Santa Cruz de Tenerife
Tenerife
La Palma
Gomera
Hierro
200 kilómetros
100 millas
0

200 kilómetros
100 millas
0

xxxvii

PRELIMINAR

Ante todo

North and Central American students get to know each other in Costa Rica.

Puntos de partida means *points of departure* in Spanish. This book will be your point of departure in Spanish language and culture. With *Puntos de partida* you will begin to learn Spanish and get ready to communicate with Spanish speakers in this country and elsewhere in the Spanish-speaking world.

To speak a language involves much more than just learning its grammar and vocabulary; to know a language is to know the people who speak it. For this reason *Puntos de partida* will provide you with cultural information to help you understand and appreciate the traditions and values of Spanish-speaking people all over the world.

Are you ready for the adventure of learning Spanish? **Pues, ¡adelante!** (*Well, let's go!*)

En este capítulo...

In this section, you will find a brief overview of the vocabulary and grammar that will be covered in the chapter. By reading this section before you begin, you will be able to anticipate and prepare for the chapter. Beginning with **Capítulo 1,** this overview will also help you understand how the language and culture content introduced in a given chapter compliment the information from earlier chapters.

- The vocabulary in this **Capítulo preliminar** will show you how to greet people you know well and people with whom you have formal relationships. You will also learn some polite expressions, like **muchas gracias** and **¿qué tal?. (Primera parte)**
- You will learn some forms of the verb **ser** (*to be*), which will allow you to describe people and things. **(Segunda parte)**
- You will learn the numbers 1 to 30 **(Segunda parte)** and practice telling time. **(Tercera parte)**
- You will become familiar with ways to express your likes and dislikes. **(Segunda parte)**
- You will learn how to ask questions in Spanish. **(Tercera parte)**

P U N T O S   I N T E R A C T I V O

Videoteca

◀ Minidramas
In this episode Diego, an American graduate student studying in Mexico, meets one of his professors and another student. Do you greet your professors in the same way you greet your fellow students?

En contexto ▶
In this episode, Mariela moves into a new apartment in Costa Rica and meets her new neighbors. How do you greet people you've never met before?

CD-ROM
In addition to completing vocabulary and grammar activities, you will have the opportunity to "greet" and "introduce" yourself to a Spanish speaker.

Internet
In the **Ante todo** section of the *Puntos de partida* Website you can access links to sites that will acquaint you with the Spanish-speaking world at **www.mhhe.com/puntos**.

Primera parte

Saludos° y expresiones de cortesía

Greetings

Here are some words, phrases, and expressions that will enable you to meet and greet others appropriately in Spanish.

1. MANOLO: ¡Hola, Maricarmen!
    MARICARMEN: ¿Qué tal, Manolo? ¿Cómo estás?
    MANOLO: Muy bien. ¿Y tú?
    MARICARMEN: Regular. Nos vemos, ¿eh?
    MANOLO: Hasta mañana.

2. ELISA VELASCO: Buenas tardes, señor Gómez.
    MARTÍN GÓMEZ: Muy buenas, señora Velasco. ¿Cómo está?
    ELISA VELASCO: Bien, gracias. ¿Y usted?
    MARTÍN GÓMEZ: Muy bien, gracias. Hasta luego.
    ELISA VELASCO: Adiós.

¿Qué tal?, **¿Cómo estás?**, and **¿Y tú?** are expressions used in informal situations with people you know well, on a first-name basis.

¿Cómo está? and **¿Y usted?** are used to address someone with whom you have a formal relationship.

3. LUPE: Buenos días, profesor.
    PROFESOR: Buenos días. ¿Cómo te llamas?
    LUPE: Me llamo Lupe Carrasco.
    PROFESOR: Mucho gusto, Lupe.
    LUPE: Igualmente. likewise

¿Cómo se llama usted? is used in formal situations. **¿Cómo te llamas?** is used in informal situations—for example, with other students. The phrases **mucho gusto** and **igualmente** are used by both men and women when meeting for the first time. In response to **mucho gusto**, a woman can also say **encantada;** a man can say **encantado**. (delighted)

1.
Sevilla, España

2.
Quito, Ecuador

3.
La Ciudad de México, México

---

1. MANOLO: Hi, Maricarmen! MARICARMEN: How's it going, Manolo? How are you? MANOLO: Very well. And you? MARICARMEN: OK. See you around, OK? MANOLO: See you tomorrow.
2. ELISA VELASCO: Good afternoon, Mr. Gómez. MARTÍN GÓMEZ: Afternoon, Mrs. Velasco. How are you? ELISA VELASCO: Fine, thank you. And you? MARTÍN GÓMEZ: Very well, thanks. See you later. ELISA VELASCO: Bye.
3. LUPE: Good morning, professor. PROFESSOR: Good morning. What's your name? LUPE: My name is Lupe Carrasco. PROFESSOR: Nice to meet you, Lupe. LUPE: Likewise.

4 Cuatro

Capítulo preliminar • Ante todo

Nota comunicativa

Otros saludos y expresiones de cortesía

buenos días	good morning (*used until the midday meal*)
buenas tardes	good afternoon (*used until the evening meal*)
buenas noches	good evening; good night (*used after the evening meal*)
señor (Sr.)	Mr., sir
señora (Sra.)	Mrs., ma'am
señorita (Srta.)	Miss (**¡OJO!*** *There is no Spanish equivalent for Ms. Use* **Sra.** *or* **Srta.** *as appropriate.*)
gracias	thanks, thank you
muchas gracias	thank you very much
de nada, no hay de qué	you're welcome
por favor	please (*also used to get someone's attention*)
perdón	pardon me, excuse me (*to ask forgiveness or to get someone's attention*)
con permiso	pardon me, excuse me (*to request permission to pass by or through a group of people*)

Conversación

▲▲▲▲▲▲▲▲

A. **Cortesía.** How many different ways can you respond to the following greetings and phrases?

1. Buenas tardes.
2. Adiós.
3. ¿Qué tal?
4. Hola.
5. ¿Cómo está?
6. Buenas noches.
7. Muchas gracias.
8. Hasta mañana.
9. ¿Cómo se llama usted?
10. Mucho gusto.

B. **Situaciones.** If the following persons met or passed each other at the times given, what might they say to each other? Role-play the situations with a classmate.

1. Mr. Santana and Miss Pérez, at 5:00 P.M. *Buenas tardes*
2. Mrs. Ortega and Pablo, at 10:00 A.M. *buenos días*
3. Ms. Hernández and Olivia, at 11:00 P.M. *buenas noches*
4. you and a classmate, just before your Spanish class *Hola*

C. **Más** (*More*) **situaciones.** Are these people saying **por favor, con permiso,** or **perdón**?

Watch out!, Careful!* **¡OJO! will be used throughout *Puntos de partida* to alert you to pay special attention to the item that follows.

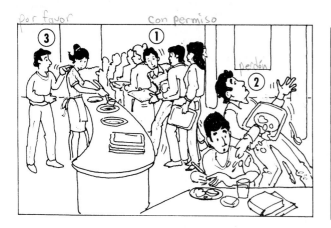

D. Entrevista (*Interview*). Turn to a person sitting next to you and do the following.

- Greet him or her appropriately, that is, with informal forms.
- Find out his or her name.
- Ask how he or she is.
- Conclude the exchange.

Now have a similar conversation with your instructor, using the appropriate formal forms.

El alfabeto español

There are twenty-eight letters in the Spanish alphabet (**el alfabeto**)—two more than in the English alphabet. The two additional letters are the **ñ** and **rr** (considered one letter even though it is a two-letter group). The letters **k** and **w** appear only in words borrowed from other languages.

Until recently, the **Real Academia Española** (*Royal Spanish Academy*), which establishes many of the guidelines for the use of Spanish throughout the world, considered the **ch** (**che**) and **ll** (**elle**) to be separate letters of the Spanish alphabet. In *Puntos de partida*, you will not see them listed as separate letters. However, the **ch** and **ll** *do* maintain a distinct pronunciation.*

Listen carefully as your instructor pronounces the names listed with the letters of the alphabet.

---

*The **ch** is pronounced with the same sound as in English *cherry* or *chair,* as in **nachos** or **muchacho**. The **ll** is pronounced as a type of *y* sound. Spanish examples of this sound that you may already know are **tortilla** and **Sevilla**.

Letters	Names of Letters	Examples		
a	a	Antonio	Ana	(la) Argentina
b	be	Benito	Blanca	Bolivia
c	ce	Carlos	Cecilia	Cáceres
d	de	Domingo	Dolores	Durango
e	e	Eduardo	Elena	(el) Ecuador
f	efe	Felipe	Francisca	Florida
g	ge	Gerardo	Gloria	Guatemala
h	hache	Héctor	Hortensia	Honduras
i	i	Ignacio	Inés	Ibiza
j	jota	José	Juana	Jalisco
k	ca (ka)	(Karl)	(Kati)	(Kansas)
l	ele	Luis	Lola	Lima
m	eme	Manuel	María	México
n	ene	Nicolás	Nati	Nicaragua
ñ	eñe	Íñigo	Begoña	España
o	o	Octavio	Olivia	Oviedo
p	pe	Pablo	Pilar	Panamá
q	cu	Enrique	Raquel	Quito
r	ere	Álvaro	Clara	(el) Perú
rr	erre *or* ere doble	Rafael	Rosa	Monterrey
s	ese	Salvador	Sara	San Juan
t	te	Tomás	Teresa	Toledo
u	u	Agustín	Lucía	(el) Uruguay
v	ve *or* uve	Víctor	Victoria	Venezuela
w	doble ve, ve doble, *or* uve doble	Oswaldo	(Wilma)	(Washington)
x	equis	Xavier	Ximena	Extremadura
y	i griega	Pelayo	Yolanda	(el) Paraguay
z	ceta (zeta)	Gonzalo	Esperanza	Zaragoza

Práctica

A. **¡Pronuncie!** The letters and combinations of letters listed on the following page represent the Spanish sounds that are the most different from English. You will practice the pronunciation of some of these letters in upcoming chapters of *Puntos de partida*. For the moment pay particular attention to their pronunciation when you see them. Can you match the Spanish letters with their equivalent pronunciation?

EXAMPLES/SPELLING

1. mucho: **ch** c
2. Geraldo: **ge** (also: **gi**)
   Jiménez: **j** e
3. hola: **h** i
4. gusto: **gu** (also: **ga, go**) A
5. me llamo: **ll** f
6. señor: **ñ** h
7. profesora: **r** b
8. Ramón: **r** (to start a
   word) g
   Monterrey: **rr**
9. nos vemos: **v** D

PRONUNCIATION

a. like the *g* in English *garden*
b. similar to *tt* of *butter* when
   pronounced very quickly
c. like *ch* in English *cheese*
d. like Spanish **b**
e. similar to a "strong" English *h*
f. like *y* in English *yes* or like the
   li sound in *million*
g. a trilled sound, several Spanish **r**'s in a row
h. similar to the *ny* sound in
   canyon
i. never pronounced

B. Deletreo (*Spelling*)

Paso (*Step*) **1.**   Pronounce these U.S. place names in Spanish. Then spell
aloud the names in Spanish. All of them are of Hispanic origin: **Toledo, Los
Ángeles, Texas, Montana, Colorado, El Paso, Florida, Las Vegas, Amarillo,
San Francisco.**

Paso 2.   Spell your own name aloud in Spanish, and listen as your classmates
spell their names. Try to remember as many of their names as you can.

MODELO: Me llamo María: **M** (eme) **a** (a) **r** (ere) **í** (i acentuada) **a** (a).

Los cognados

Many Spanish and English words are similar or identical
in form and meaning. These related words are called
cognates (**los cognados**). Spanish and English share so
many cognates because a number of words in both
languages are derived from the same Latin root words—
and also because
Spanish and English are "language neighbors," especially in the
southwestern United States. Each language has borrowed words from the
other and adapted them to its own sound system.

Many cognates are used in **Ante todo.** Don't try to memorize all of
them—just get used to the sound of them in Spanish.

Here are some Spanish adjectives that are cognates of English words.
These adjectives can be used to describe either a man or a woman.

arrogante	importante	pesimista
cruel	independiente	realista
eficiente	inteligente	rebelde
egoísta	interesante	responsable
elegante	liberal	sentimental
emocional	materialista	terrible
flexible	optimista	valiente
idealista	paciente	vulnerable

Cognados
leader → **el líder**
el lagarto (*the lizard*) →
alligator

adjectives = words
used to describe
people, places,
and things

The following adjectives change form. Use the **-o** ending when describing a man, the **-a** ending when describing a woman.

extrovertido/a	religioso/a	serio/a
generoso/a	reservado/a	sincero/a
impulsivo/a	romántico/a	tímido/a

¿Cómo es usted?°

¿Cómo... What are you like?

You can use these forms of the verb **ser** (*to be*) to describe yourself and others.

(yo)	**soy**	I am
(tú)	**eres**	you (*familiar*) are
(usted)	**es**	you (*formal*) are
(él, ella)	**es**	he/she is

—¿Cómo es usted?
—Bueno...° Yo soy moderna, urbana, sofisticada...

Well . . .

Yo soy impulsiva, flexible, independiente

Conversación

A. Descripciones

Paso 1. With a classmate, describe the famous Hispanic people in these photos, using cognate adjectives (see page 10 and above). **¡OJO!** Remember that some adjectives can end in **-o** or **-a**, such as **romántico/a**, **serio/a**, **tímido/a**. Use the **-o** ending when describing a male and the **-a** ending when describing a female.

MODELOS: ESTUDIANTE 1: ¿Cómo es Ricky Martin?
ESTUDIANTE 2: (Ricky Martin) Es importante, romántico y serio.

ESTUDIANTE 1: ¿Cómo es Cameron Diaz?
ESTUDIANTE 2: (Cameron Diaz) Es elegante y extrovertida.

1. Ricky Martin

extrovertido
romántico

2. Sammy Sosa

es

3. Cameron Díaz

4. Jennifer López

egoísta
arrogante

Primera parte

Paso 2. Now describe yourself to your classmate.

MODELO: Yo soy muy sentimental y sincero/a. Yo no soy pesimista.

B. Reacciones

Paso 1. Use the following adjectives, or any others you know, to create one sentence about a classmate. You can begin with **Creo que...** (*I think that . . .*). Your classmate will listen to your sentences, then tell you if you are right.

Adjetivos: eficiente, emocional, generoso/a, inteligente, impulsivo/a, liberal, sincero/a

MODELO: ESTUDIANTE 1: Alicia, (creo que) eres generosa.
ESTUDIANTE 2: Sí, soy generosa. (Sí, soy muy generosa.) (No, no soy generosa.)

Paso 2. Now find out what kind of person your instructor is, using the same adjectives. Use the appropriate formal forms.

MODELO: **¿Es usted** optimista (generoso/a...)?

Spanish in the United States and in the World

Although no one knows exactly how many languages are spoken around the world, linguists estimate that there are between 3,000 and 6,000. Spanish, with 332 million native speakers, is among the top five languages. It is the language spoken in Spain, in Mexico, in all of South America (except Brazil and the Guianas), in most of Central America, in Cuba, in Puerto Rico, and in the Dominican Republic—in approximately twenty countries in all. It is also spoken by a great number of people in the United States and Canada.

Like all languages spoken by large numbers of people, modern Spanish varies from region to region. The Spanish of Madrid is different from that spoken in Mexico City, Buenos Aires, or Los Angeles, just as the English of London differs from that of Chicago or Toronto. Although these differences are most noticeable in pronunciation ("accent"), they are also found in vocabulary and special expressions used in different geographical areas. In Great Britain one hears the word *lift*, but the same apparatus is called an *elevator* in the United States. What is called an **autobús** (*bus*) in Spain may be called a **guagua** in the Caribbean. Although such differences are noticeable, they result only rarely in misunderstandings among native speakers, since the majority of structures and vocabulary are common to the many varieties of each language.

You don't need to go abroad to encounter people who speak Spanish on a daily basis. The Spanish language and people of Hispanic descent have been an integral part of United States and Canadian life for centuries. In fact, the United States is now the fifth largest Spanish-speaking country in the world!

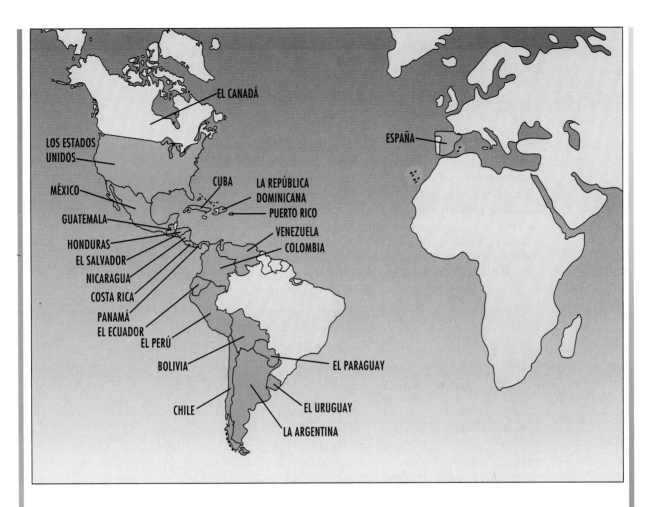

EL CANADÁ

ESPAÑA

LOS ESTADOS UNIDOS

MÉXICO

CUBA
LA REPÚBLICA DOMINICANA
PUERTO RICO

GUATEMALA

VENEZUELA
COLOMBIA

HONDURAS
EL SALVADOR
NICARAGUA
COSTA RICA
PANAMÁ
EL ECUADOR
EL PERÚ
BOLIVIA
EL PARAGUAY

CHILE
EL URUGUAY
LA ARGENTINA

Who are the over 31 million people of Hispanic descent living in the United States today? For one thing, not all Hispanics are similar. They are characterized by great diversity, the result of their ancestors' or their country of origin, socioeconomic and professional factors, and, of course, individual talents and aspirations.

There is also great regional diversity among U.S. Hispanics. Many people of Mexican descent inhabit the southwestern part of the United States, including populations as far north as Colorado. Large groups of

Comparing origins of U.S. Hispanic population

Total population based on U.S. census, 1999 estimates*
31.7 million

Percentages:

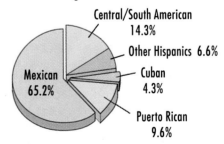

Central/South American 14.3%

Other Hispanics 6.6%

Cuban 4.3%

Mexican 65.2%

Puerto Rican 9.6%

* Does not include Puerto Ricans residing in Puerto Rico.

Puerto Ricans can be found in New York, while Florida is host to a large Cuban and Central American population. More recent immigrants include Nicaraguans and Salvadorans, who have established large communities in many U.S. cities, among them San Francisco and Los Angeles.

Although not all people of Hispanic origin speak Spanish, many are in fact bilingual and bicultural. This dual cultural identity is being increasingly recognized by the media and business community. Many major U.S. cities have one or more Spanish-language newspapers as well as television and radio stations. A wide variety of businesses are owned and operated by Hispanics, and major corporations in the food, clothing, entertainment, and service fields appeal to Hispanic clients . . . in both English and Spanish!

As you will discover in subsequent chapters of *Puntos de partida*, the Spanish language and people of Hispanic descent have been and will continue to be an integral part of the fabric of this country. Take special note of **En los Estados Unidos y el Canadá...**, a routinely occurring section of *Puntos de partida* that profiles Hispanics in these two countries.

Mural de la Pequeña Habana, el barrio cubano de Miami

Más cognados

^aSu... *(Here is) Your dinner (lit. little piece of lettuce).*

Although some English and Spanish cognate nouns are spelled identically (*idea, general, gas, animal, motor*), most will differ slightly in spelling: *position* / **posición**, *secret* / **secreto**, *student* / **estudiante**, *rose* / **rosa**, *lottery* / **lotería**, *opportunity* / **oportunidad**, *exam* / **examen**.

The following exercises will give you more practice in recognizing and pronouncing cognates. Remember: Don't try to learn all of these words. Just get used to the way they sound.

> **noun** = person, place, or thing

Práctica

A. **Categorías.** Pronounce each of the following cognates and give its English equivalent. You will also recognize the meaning of most of the categories (**Naciones, Personas**, ...). Based on the words listed in the group, can you guess the meaning of the categories indicated with a gloss symbol (°)?

Naciones: el Japón, Italia, Francia, España, el Brasil, China, el Canadá, Rusia

Personas: líder, profesor, actriz, pintor, político, estudiante

Lugares:° restaurante, café, museo, garaje, bar, banco, hotel, oficina, océano, parque

Conceptos: libertad, dignidad, declaración, cooperación, comunismo

Cosas:° teléfono, fotografía, sofá, televisión, radio, bomba, novela, diccionario, dólar, lámpara, yate

Animales: león, cebra, chimpancé, tigre, hipopótamo

Comidas y bebidas:° hamburguesa, cóctel, patata, café, limón, banana

Deportes:° béisbol, tenis, vólibol, fútbol americano

Instrumentos musicales: guitarra, piano, flauta, clarinete, trompeta, violín

> **OJO**
>
> In **Práctica B**, note that Spanish has two different ways to express *a (an)*: **un** and **una**. All nouns are either masculine (*m.*) or feminine (*f.*)

in Spanish. **Un** is used with masculine nouns, **una** with feminine nouns. You will learn more about this aspect of Spanish in **Capítulo 1**.

Don't try to learn the gender of nouns now. You do not have to know the gender of nouns to do **Práctica B**.

B. **¿Qué es esto?** (*What is this?*) Being able to tell what something is or to identify the group to which it belongs is a useful conversation strategy. Begin to practice this strategy by pronouncing these cognates and identifying the category from **Práctica A** to which they belong. Use the following sentences as a guide.

Es **un** lugar (concepto, animal, deporte, instrumento musical).*
Es **una** nación (persona, cosa, comida, bebida).*

MODELO: béisbol → Es un deporte.

1. calculadora
2. burro
3. sándwich
4. golf
5. México

6. actor
7. clase
8. limonada
9. elefante
10. refrigerador

11. universidad
12. fama
13. terrorista
14. acordeón
15. democracia

Conversación

▲▲▲▲▲▲▲▲

Identificaciones. With a classmate, practice identifying words, using the categories given in **Práctica A**.

MODELO: ESTUDIANTE 1: ¿Qué es un hospital?
ESTUDIANTE 2: Es un lugar.

1. un saxofón
2. un autobús
3. un rancho

4. un doctor
5. Bolivia
6. una Coca-Cola

7. una enchilada
8. una jirafa
9. una turista

Pronunciación

You have probably already noted that there is a very close relationship between the way Spanish is written and the way it is pronounced. This makes it relatively easy to learn the basics of Spanish spelling and pronunciation.

Many Spanish sounds, however, do not have an exact equivalent in English, so you should not trust English to be your guide to Spanish pronunciation. Even words that are spelled the same in both languages are usually pronounced quite differently. It is important to become so familiar with Spanish sounds that you can pronounce them automatically, right from the beginning of your study of the language.

---

*The English equivalent of these sentences is *It is a place (concept, . . .); It is a country (person, . . .).*

Las vocales (*Vowels*): *a, e, i, o, u*

Unlike English vowels, which can have many different pronunciations or may be silent, Spanish vowels are always pronounced, and they are almost always pronounced in the same way. Spanish vowels are always short and tense. They are never drawn out with a *u* or *i* glide as in English: **lo** ≠ *low;* **de** ≠ *day.*

a: pronounced like the *a* in *father,* but short and tense
e: pronounced like the *e* in *they,* but without the *i* glide
i: pronounced like the *i* in *machine,* but short and tense*
o: pronounced like the *o* in *home,* but without the *u* glide
u: pronounced like the *u* in *rule,* but short and tense

OJO

The *uh* sound or schwa (which is how most unstressed vowels are pronounced in English: *canal, waited, atom*) does not exist in Spanish.

A. Sílabas. Pronounce the following Spanish syllables, being careful to pronounce each vowel with a short, tense sound.

1. ma fa la ta pa
2. me fe le te pe
3. mi fi li ti pi
4. mo fo lo to po
5. mu fu lu tu pu
6. mi fe la tu do
7. su mi te so la
8. se tu no ya li

B. Palabras (*Words*). Repeat the following words after your instructor.

1. hasta tal nada mañana natural normal fascinante
2. me qué Pérez Elena rebelde excelente elegante
3. sí señorita permiso terrible imposible tímido Ibiza
4. yo con como noches profesor señor generoso
5. uno usted tú mucho Perú Lupe Úrsula

C. Trabalenguas (*Tongue-twister*)

Paso 1. Here is a popular nonsense rhyme, the Spanish version of "Eeny, meeny, miney, moe." (*Note:* The person who corresponds to **fue** is "it.") Listen as your instructor pronounces it.

> Pin, marín
> de don Pingüe
> cúcara, mácara
> títere, fue.

Paso 2. Now pronounce the vowels clearly as you repeat the rhyme.

D. Naciones

Paso 1. Here is part of a rental car ad in Spanish. Say aloud the names of the countries where you can find this company's offices. Can you recognize all of the countries?

---

*The word **y** (*and*) is also pronounced like the letter **i**.

Paso 2. Find the following information in the ad.

1. How many cars does the agency have available?
2. How many offices does the agency have?
3. What Spanish word expresses the English word *immediately*?

Los números 0-30; *hay*

Canción infantil

Dos y dos son cuatro,
cuatro y dos son seis,
seis y dos son ocho,
y ocho dieciséis.

0	cero				
1	uno	11	once	21	veintiuno
2	dos	12	doce	22	veintidós
3	tres	13	trece	23	veintitrés
4	cuatro	14	catorce	24	veinticuatro
5	cinco	15	quince	25	veinticinco
6	seis	16	dieciséis*	26	veintiséis
7	siete	17	diecisiete	27	veintisiete
8	ocho	18	dieciocho	28	veintiocho
9	nueve	19	diecinueve	29	veintinueve
10	diez	20	veinte	30	treinta

The number *one* has several forms in Spanish. **Uno** is the form used in counting. **Un** is used before masculine singular nouns, **una** before feminine singular nouns: **un señor, una señora.** Also note that the number **veintiuno** becomes **veintiún** before masculine nouns and **veintiuna** before feminine nouns: **veintiún señores, veintiuna señoras.**

> **OJO**
>
> **uno,** dos, tres,... veintiuno, veintidós,...
>   *but*
> **un** señor, veintiún señores
> **una** señora, veintiuna señoras

Use the word **hay** to express both *there is* and *there are* in Spanish. **No hay** means *there is not* and *there are not.* **¿Hay... ?** asks *Is there . . . ?* or *Are there . . . ?*

> **hay =**
> there is /
> there are

—¿Cuántos estudiantes **hay** en la clase?	*How many students are there in the class?*
—**(Hay)** Treinta.	*(There are) Thirty.*
—¿**Hay** pandas en el zoo?	*Are there any pandas at the zoo?*
—**Hay** veinte osos, pero **no hay** pandas.	*There are twenty bears, but there aren't any pandas.*

A children's song   Two and two are four, four and two are six, six and two are eight, and eight (makes) sixteen.

*The numbers 16 to 19 and 21 to 29 can be written as one word (**dieciséis... veintiuno...**) or as three (**diez y seis... veinte y uno...**).

Práctica

▲▲▲▲▲▲

A. Los números. Practique los números según (*according to*) el modelo.

MODELO: 1 señor → Hay un señor.

1. 4 señoras
2. 12 pianos
3. 1 café (*m.*)
4. 21 cafés (*m.*)
5. 14 días
6. 1 clase (*f.*)
7. 21 ideas (*f.*)
8. 11 personas
9. 15 estudiantes
10. 13 teléfonos
11. 28 naciones
12. 5 guitarras
13. 1 león (*m.*)
14. 30 señores
15. 20 oficinas

B. Problemas de matemáticas. Do the following simple mathematical equations in Spanish. *Note:* + (**y**), − (**menos**), = (**son**).

MODELO: 2 + 2 = 4 → Dos y dos son cuatro.
4 − 2 = 2 → Cuatro menos dos son dos.

1. 2 + 4 = ?
2. 8 + 17 = ?
3. 11 + 1 = ?
4. 3 + 18 = ?
5. 9 + 6 = ?
6. 5 + 4 = ?
7. 1 + 13 = ?
8. 15 − 2 = ?
9. 9 − 9 = ?
10. 13 − 8 = ?
11. 14 + 12 = ?
12. 23 − 13 = ?

Conversación

▲▲▲▲▲▲▲

Preguntas (*Questions*)

1. ¿Cuántos estudiantes hay en la clase de español? ¿Cuántos estudiantes hay en clase hoy (*today*)? ¿Hay tres profesores o un profesor?
2. ¿Cuántos días hay en una semana (*week*)? ¿Hay seis? (No, no hay...) ¿Cuántos días hay en un fin de semana (*weekend*)? Hay cuatro semanas en un mes. ¿Qué significa **mes** en inglés? ¿Cuántos días hay en el mes de febrero? ¿en el mes de junio? ¿Cuántos meses hay en un año?
3. Hay muchos edificios (*many buildings*) en una universidad. En esta (*this*) universidad, ¿hay una cafetería? ¿un teatro? ¿un cine (*movie theater*)? ¿un laboratorio de lenguas (*languages*)? ¿un bar? ¿una clínica? ¿un hospital? ¿un museo? ¿muchos estudiantes? ¿muchos profesores?

▶ ## Gustos° y preferencias   *Likes*

〜〜〜〜〜〜〜〜〜〜〜〜〜〜〜〜〜〜〜〜〜〜〜〜〜〜〜〜〜〜

¿Te gusta el fútbol? →

- Sí, me gusta mucho el fútbol.
- No, no me gusta el fútbol.
- Sí, me gusta, pero me gusta más el fútbol americano.

Do you like soccer? → • Yes, I like soccer very much. • No, I don't like soccer. • Yes, I like soccer, but I like football more.

To indicate that you like something in Spanish, say **Me gusta** _____. To indicate that you don't like something, use **No me gusta** _____. Use the question **¿Te gusta** _____? to ask a classmate if he or she likes something. Use **¿Le gusta** _____? to ask your instructor the same question.

In the following conversations, you will use the word **el** to mean *the* with masculine nouns and the word **la** with feminine nouns. Don't try to memorize which nouns are masculine and which are feminine. Just get used to using the words **el** and **la** before nouns.

You will also be using a number of Spanish verbs in the infinitive form, which always ends in **-r**. Here are some examples: **estudiar** = *to study;* **comer** = *to eat.* Try to guess the meanings of the infinitives used in these activities from context. If someone asks you, for instance, **¿Te gusta** *beber* **Coca-Cola?**, it is a safe guess that **beber** means *to drink.*

En español, **fútbol** = *soccer* y **fútbol americano** = *football.*

verb = a word that describes an action or a state of being

Conversación

A. Gustos y preferencias

Paso 1. Make a list of six things you like and six things you don't like, following the model. If you wish, you may choose items from the **Vocabulario útil** box below. All words are provided with the appropriate definite article.

MODELO: Me gusta *la clase de español.* No me gusta *la clase de matemáticas.*

Vocabulario útil*

el café, el té, la limonada, la cerveza (*beer*)
la música moderna, la música clásica, el rap, la música *country*
la pizza, la pasta, la comida mexicana, la comida de la cafetería (*cafeteria food*)
el actor _____, la actriz _____
el/la cantante (*singer*) _____ (**¡OJO!** cantante is used for both men *and* women)
el cine (*movies*), el teatro, la ópera, el arte abstracto

---

1. Me gusta _____. No me gusta _____.
2. Me gusta _____. No me gusta _____.
3. _____

4. _____
5. _____
6. _____

---

*The material in **Vocabulario útil** lists is not active, that is, it is not part of what you need to focus on learning at this point. You may use these words and phrases to complete exercises or to help you converse in Spanish, if you need them.

Paso 2. Now ask a classmate if he or she shares your likes and dislikes.

MODELO: ¿Te gusta la clase de español? ¿y la clase de matemáticas?

B. Más (More) gustos y preferencias

Paso 1. Here are some useful verbs and nouns to talk about what you like. For each item, combine a verb (shaded) with a noun to form a sentence that is true for you. Can you use context to guess the meaning of verbs you don't know?

MODELO: Me gusta _____. → Me gusta estudiar inglés.

1. **beber**   café   té   limonada   chocolate
2. **comer**   pizza   enchiladas   hamburguesas   pasta
3. **estudiar** español   matemáticas   historia
   computación   (computer science)
4. **hablar**   español   con mis amigos (with my friends)
   por teléfono (on the phone)
5. **jugar**   al tenis   al fútbol   al fútbol americano   al béisbol
   al basquetbol
6. **tocar**   la guitarra   el piano   el violín

Paso 2. Ask a classmate about his or her likes using your own preferences as a guide.

MODELO: ¿Te gusta comer enchiladas?

Paso 3. Now ask your professor if he or she likes certain things.
¡OJO! Remember to address your professor in a formal manner.

MODELO: ¿Le gusta jugar al tenis?

LECTURA

El mundo hispánico (Parte 1)

Estrategia:° Recognizing Interrogative Words and *estar*

Strategy

In the following brief reading, note that the word **está** means *is located;* **está** and other forms of the verb **estar** (*to be*) are used to tell where things are. You will learn more about the uses of **estar** in **Capítulo 5.**

The reading also contains a series of questions with interrogative words. You are already familiar with **¿cómo?, ¿qué?,** and **¿cuántos?** (and should be able to guess the meaning of **¿cuántas?** easily). The meaning of other interrogatives may not be immediately obvious to you, but the sentences in which the words appear may offer some clues to meaning. You probably do not know the meaning of **¿dónde?** and **¿cuál?,** but you should be able to guess their meaning in the following sentences.

Cuba está en el Mar Caribe. ¿Dónde está la República Dominicana?
Managua es la capital de Nicaragua. ¿Cuál es la capital de México?

Note that the reading has been divided into four very short parts. Each part corresponds to a map that offers geographical and population information about the countries of the Spanish-speaking world. Use the statements in the short parts as models to answer the questions.

Las naciones del mundo hispánico

Parte 1 México y Centroamérica

Hay casi noventa y siete (*almost 97*) millones de habitantes en México. ¿Cuántos millones de habitantes hay en Guatemala? ¿en El Salvador? ¿en las demás[a] naciones de Centroamérica? ¿En cuántas naciones de Centroamérica se habla español? México es parte de Norteamérica. ¿En cuántas naciones de Norteamérica se habla español? ¿Cuál es la capital de México? ¿de Costa Rica?

Parte 2 El Caribe

Cuba está en el Mar Caribe. ¿Dónde está la República Dominicana? ¿Qué parte de los Estados Unidos está también[b] en el Mar Caribe? ¿Dónde está el Canal de Panamá?

Parte 3 Sudamérica

¿En cuántas naciones de Sudamérica se habla español? ¿Se habla español o portugués en el Brasil? ¿Cuántos millones de habitantes hay en Venezuela? ¿en Chile? ¿en las demás naciones? ¿Cuál es la capital de cada[c] nación?

[a]las... *the other* [b]*also* [c]*each*

Parte 4 España

España está en la Península Ibérica. ¿Qué otra nación está también en esa^d península? ¿Cuántos millones de habitantes hay en España? No se habla español en Portugal. ¿Qué lengua se habla allí^e? ¿Cuál es la capital de España? ¿Está en el centro de la península?

^d*that*   ^e*there*

Tercera parte

¿Qué hora es?

Es la una.   **Son** las dos.   **Son** las cinco.

¿Qué hora es? is used to ask *What time is it?* In telling time, one says *Es la una* but *Son las dos* (**las tres, las cuatro,** and so on).

Es la una y $\begin{cases} \textbf{cuarto.} \\ \textbf{quince.} \end{cases}$ Son las dos y $\begin{cases} \textbf{media} \\ \textbf{treinta.} \end{cases}$

Son las cinco **y diez.**   Son las ocho **y veinticinco.**

Note that from the hour to the half-hour, Spanish, like English, expresses time by adding minutes or a portion of an hour to the hour.

Son las dos **menos** {cuarto. / quince.}

Son las ocho **menos diez.**

Son las once **menos veinte.**

From the half-hour to the hour, Spanish usually expresses time by subtracting minutes or a part of an hour from the *next* hour.

Nota comunicativa

Para expresar° la hora

Para... To express

de la mañana	A.M., in the morning
de la tarde	P.M., in the afternoon (*and early evening*)
de la noche	P.M., in the evening
en punto	exactly, on the dot, sharp
¿a qué hora?	(at) what time?
a la una (las dos,...)	at 1:00 (2:00, ...)

Son las cuatro de la tarde **en punto.**

It's exactly 4:00 P.M.

¿A qué hora es la clase de español?

(At) What time is Spanish class?

Hay una recepción **a las once** de la mañana.

There is a reception at 11:00 A.M.

 Don't confuse **Es/Son la(s)...** with **A la(s)...** The first is used for telling time, the second for telling at what time something happens (at what time class starts, at what time one arrives, and so on).

Práctica

A. **¡Atención!** Listen as your instructor says a time of day. Find the clock or watch face that corresponds to the time you heard and say its number in Spanish. (Note the sun or the moon that accompanies each clock to indicate whether the time shown is day or night.)

1.   **2.**   **3.**   **4.**   **5.**   **6.**   **7.**   **8.**

B. ¿Qué hora es? Express the time in full sentences in Spanish.

1. 1:00 P.M.
2. 6:00 P.M.
3. 11:00 A.M.
4. 1:30

5. 3:15
6. 6:45
7. 4:15

8. 11:45 exactly
9. 9:10 on the dot
10. 9:50 sharp

Conversación

▲▲▲▲▲▲▲

A. Entrevista

Paso 1. Ask a classmate at what time the following events or activities take place. He or she will answer according to the cue or will provide the necessary information.

> MODELO: la clase de español (10:00 A.M.) →
> ESTUDIANTE 1: ¿A qué hora es la clase de español?
> ESTUDIANTE 2: A las diez de la mañana... ¡en punto!

1. la clase de francés (1:45 P.M.)
2. la sesión de laboratorio (3:10 P.M.)
3. la excursión (8:45 A.M.)
4. el concierto (7:30 P.M.)

Paso 2. Now ask what time your partner likes to perform these activities. He or she should provide the necessary information.

> MODELO: cenar (*to have dinner*) →
> ESTUDIANTE 1: ¿A qué hora te gusta cenar?
> ESTUDIANTE 2: Me gusta cenar a las ocho de la noche.

1. almorzar (*to have lunch*)
2. mirar (*to watch*) la televisión
3. ir (*to go*) al laboratorio de lenguas
4. ir al cine

B. Situaciones. How might the following people greet each other if they met at the indicated time? With a classmate, create a brief dialogue for each situation.

> MODELO: Jorge y María, a las once de la noche →
> JORGE: Buenas noches, María.
> MARÍA: Hola, Jorge. ¿Cómo estás?
> JORGE: Bien, gracias. ¿Y tú?
> MARÍA: ¡Muy bien!

1. el profesor Martínez y Gloria, a las diez de la mañana
2. la Sra. López y la Srta. Luna, a las cuatro y media de la tarde
3. usted y su (*your*) profesor(a) de español, en la clase de español

Palabras interrogativas

You have already used a number of interrogative words and phrases to get information. Some other useful ones are listed here, along with the ones you already know, and you will learn more in later chapters. Be sure you know the meaning of all these words before you begin the activities in the **Práctica** section.

¿a qué hora?	¿A qué hora es la clase?
¿cómo?	¿Cómo estás? ¿Cómo es Gloria Estefan? ¿Cómo te llamas?
¿cuál?*	¿Cuál es la capital de Colombia?
¿cuándo?	¿Cuándo es la fiesta?
¿cuánto?	¿Cuánto es?
¿cuántos?, ¿cuántas?	¿Cuántos días hay en una semana? ¿Cuántas naciones hay en Sudamérica?
¿dónde?	¿Dónde está España?
¿qué?*	¿Qué es un hospital? ¿Qué es esto? ¿Qué hora es?
¿quién?	¿Quién es el presidente?

Note that in Spanish the voice falls at the end of questions that begin with interrogative words.

¿Qué es un tren?   ¿Cómo estás?

---

*Use **¿qué?** to mean *what?* when you are asking for a definition or an explanation. Use **¿cuál?** to mean *what?* in all other circumstances. See also Grammar Section 29 in **Capítulo 9**.

Práctica

▲▲▲▲▲

Preguntas y respuestas (*Questions and answers*)

Paso 1. What interrogative words do you associate with the following information?

1. ¡A las tres en punto!
2. En el centro de la península.
3. Soy profesor.
4. Muy bien, gracias.
5. ¡Es muy arrogante!
6. Hay 5 millones (de habitantes).
7. Dos pesos.
8. (La capital) Es Caracas.
9. Es un instrumento musical.
10. Mañana, a las cinco.
11. Son las once.
12. Soy Roberto González.

Paso 2. Now ask the questions that would result in the answers given in **Paso 1.**

Conversación

▲▲▲▲▲▲▲

Más preguntas. What questions are being asked by the indicated persons? More than one answer is possible for some items. Select questions from the following list or create your own questions.

PREGUNTAS

¿A qué hora es el programa sobre (*about*) México?

¿Cómo estás?

¿Cuál es la capital de Colombia?

¿Cuándo es la fiesta?

¿Cuántas personas hay en la fiesta?

¿Dónde está Buenos Aires?

¿Dónde está el diccionario?

¿Qué es esto?

¿Qué hay en la televisión hoy?

¿Quién es?

Videoteca

In this section of each chapter of *Puntos de partida* you will find two video segments to help you practice your listening comprehension as well as your ability to communicate effectively in Spanish. Both videos offer dialogues with very functional, everyday language that will provide useful models for interacting with native speakers of Spanish, wherever you may meet them. Your instructor may show these video segments in class or ask you to watch them in the language lab or media center.

Minidramas

The characters of the **Minidramas** video segments live in Mexico City, Mexico; Quito, Ecuador; and Seville, Spain. For these segments, there is always a transcript of part of the dialogue as it appears in the video.

MÉXICO

In this episode, a professor at the **Universidad Nacional Autónoma de México**, most commonly referred to as "**la UNAM**," in Mexico City, is speaking with a student when another student joins them. You should be able to get the gist of the dialogue easily, as it contains many cognates as well as a lot of vocabulary that you already know.

Diego se acerca al[a] profesor Salazar.

DIEGO: Perdón. ¿Es usted el profesor Salazar?
PROFESOR: Sí, yo soy.
DIEGO: Buenas tardes. Me llamo Diego González. Soy el estudiante de la Universidad de California.

[a]se... *approaches*

Un poco más sobre[a]... Diego González

Diego González es un estudiante norteamericano, de California. Estudia[b] en la Universidad Nacional Autónoma de México (la UNAM), en la Ciudad de México.[c] Habla[d] español muy bien: es de ascendencia hispana.[e] Está orgulloso[f] de su herencia[g] lingüística y cultural.

[a]Un... *A little more about. . .* [b]*He studies* [c]*Ciudad... Mexico City* [d]*He speaks* [e]ascendencia... *Hispanic ancestry* [f]Está... *He's proud* [g]*heritage*

To read more about the characters from this video, visit the *Puntos de partida* Website at **www.mhhe.com/puntos**

PROFESOR: Ah, sí. El estudiante de Los Ángeles. Mucho gusto.

DIEGO: Igualmente.

PROFESOR: ¡Bienvenido[b] a México! Él es Antonio Sifuentes. Es estudiante posgraduado en la facultad.[c]

ANTONIO: ¿Qué tal, Diego?

DIEGO: Muy bien, gracias. ¿Y tú?

ANTONIO: Muy bien. Mucho gusto.

DIEGO: Igualmente, Antonio.

[b]*Welcome*   [c]*department*

Con un compañero / una compañera

With a partner, practice greeting one another. In your conversation, you should try to ask and answer the following information:

your name   where you are from   how you are doing

En contexto

The **En contexto** segments represent highly functional contexts and language that you are likely to encounter in your interactions with Spanish speakers.

COSTA RICA

The scenes have been filmed in San Jose, Costa Rica; Lima, Peru; and Mexico City, Mexico.

In this chapter's episode, Mariela Castillo, who is moving to a new apartment, meets her neighbors. Pay attention to the greetings and introductions used in the segment.

A. Lluvia de ideas (*Brainstorm*)

This recurring activity will direct your attention to a topic or topics featured in the **En contexto** video segment, in order to help you understand it more fully.

- How would you introduce yourself to a new neighbor? What if the neighbor were older than you? What if the neighbor were younger than you?
- How do these greetings differ in English and Spanish?

B. Dictado (*Dictation*)

This recurring activity requires that you complete part of the dialogue in the video in order to help you focus on the specific language used by the video characters.

Fill in the missing portions of the dialogue. (There is an underlined space for each word.)

MARIELA: ¿Cómo te llamás?*

RICARDO: Me llamo Ricardo. ¿Cómo _____ _____ usted?

*Note that Mariela says **llamás** instead of **llamas**, with the stress on the last syllable of the word. This is known as **voseo**, a common dialectical feature of Spanish in Costa Rica and other Spanish-speaking countries. **Voseo** forms will not be actively taught or practiced in *Puntos de partida*. For now you just need to know that Mariela is asking the young boy's name.

MARIELA: _____ _____ _____ Mariela Castillo. _____ _____, Ricardo.

RICARDO: _____, Sra. Castillo.

MARIELA: _____ soy _____, soy _____. Por el momento.[a]

[a]Por... *At this time.*

C. Un diálogo original

Paso 1. In groups of three, re-enact the situation between Mariela, Ricardo, and his mom (**mamá**). Don't forget to say **bienvenido** or **bienvenida** (*welcome*) to the new neighbor!

Paso 2. With a different classmate, role-play a situation similar to the one in the video. Each of you should choose one of the following two roles:

ESTUDIANTE 1: You are a new student moving into a dormitory.

ESTUDIANTE 2: You are a returning student at the dormitory. You want to greet and welcome the new student.

LECTURA

El mundo hispánico (Parte 2)

Estrategia: Guessing Meaning from Context

You will recognize the meaning of a number of cognates in the following reading about the geography of the Hispanic world. In addition, you should be able to guess the meaning of the underlined words from the context (the words that surround them); they are the names of geographical features. The photo captions will also be helpful. You have learned to recognize the meaning of the word **¿qué?** in questions; in this reading, **que** (with no accent mark) means *that* or *which*.

Note also that a series of headings divides the reading into brief parts. It is always a good idea to scan such headings before starting to read, in order to get a sense of a reading's overall content.

La geografía del mundo hispánico

Introducción

La geografía del mundo hispánico es impresionante y muy variada. En algunas[a] regiones hay de todo.[b]

En las Américas

En la Argentina hay <u>pampas</u> extensas en el sur[c] y la <u>cordillera</u> de los Andes en el oeste. En partes de Venezuela, Colombia y el Ecuador, hay regiones tropicales de densa <u>selva</u>. En el Brasil está el famoso <u>Río</u> Amazonas. En el centro de México y también en El Salvador, Nicaragua y Colombia, hay <u>volcanes</u> activos. A veces[d] producen erupciones catastróficas. El Perú y Bolivia comparten[e] el enorme <u>Lago</u> Titicaca, situado en una <u>meseta</u> entre los dos países.[f]

[a]*some* [b]de... *a bit of everything* [c]*south* [d]A... *Sometimes* [e]*share* [f]naciones

La cordillera de los Andes, Chile

La isla de Caja de Muertos, Puerto Rico

Una selva tropical en Colombia

Una meseta de La Mancha, España

En las naciones del Caribe

Cuba, Puerto Rico y la República Dominicana son tres <u>islas</u> situadas en el <u>Mar</u> Caribe. Las bellas playas[g] del Mar Caribe y de la <u>península</u> de Yucatán son populares entre[h] los turistas de todo el mundo.

En la Península Ibérica

España, que comparte la Península Ibérica con Portugal, también tiene[i] una geografía variada. En el norte están los Pirineos, la <u>cordillera</u> que separa a España del[j] resto de Europa. Madrid, la capital del país, está situada en la <u>meseta</u> central. En las <u>costas</u> del sur y del este hay playas tan bonitas como las de[k] Latinoamérica y del Caribe.

La ciudad de Montevideo, Uruguay

[g]bellas... *beautiful beaches* [h]*among* [i]*has* [j]*from the* [k]tan... *as pretty as those of*

¿Y las <u>ciudades</u>?

Es importante mencionar también la gran[1] diversidad de las ciudades del mundo hispánico. En la Argentina está la gran ciudad de Buenos Aires. Muchos consideran a Buenos Aires «el París» o «la Nueva York» de Sudamérica. En Venezuela está Caracas, y en el Perú está Lima, la capital, y Cuzco, una ciudad antigua de origen indio.

Conclusión

En fin,[m] el mundo hispánico es diverso respecto a la geografía. ¿Y Norteamérica? ●

[1]great   [m]En... *In short*

Comprensión

Demonstrate your understanding of the words underlined in the reading and other words from the reading by giving an example of a similar geographical feature found in this country or close to it. Then give an example from the Spanish-speaking world.

MODELO: un río → *the Mississippi*, el Río Orinoco

1. un lago
2. una cordillera
3. un río
4. una isla
5. una playa
6. una costa
7. un mar
8. un volcán
9. una península

Vocabulario

Although you have used and heard many words in this preliminary chapter of *Puntos de partida*, the following words are the ones considered to be active vocabulary. Be sure that you know all of them before beginning **Capítulo 1**.

Saludos y expresiones de cortesía

Buenos días. Buenas tardes. Buenas noches.
Hola. (Muy) Buenas. ¿Qué tal? ¿Cómo está(s)?
Regular. (Muy) Bien.
¿Y tú? ¿Y usted?
Adiós. Hasta mañana. Hasta luego. Nos vemos.

¿Cómo te llamas? ¿Cómo se llama usted?
  Me llamo _____.

señor (Sr.), señora (Sra.), señorita (Srta.)

(Muchas) Gracias.
De nada. No hay de qué.
Por favor. Perdón. Con permiso.
Mucho gusto. Igualmente. Encantado/a.

¿Cómo es usted?

soy, eres, es

Los números

cero, uno, dos, tres, cuatro, cinco, seis, siete, ocho, nueve, diez, once, doce, trece, catorce, quince, dieciséis, diecisiete, dieciocho, diecinueve, veinte, treinta

Gustos y preferencias

¿Te gusta _____? ¿Le gusta _____? Sí, me gusta _____. No, no me gusta _____.

¿Qué hora es?

es la... , son las... y/menos cuarto (quince), y
media (treinta), en punto, de la mañana
(tarde, noche), ¿a qué hora?, a la(s)...

Palabras interrogativas

¿cómo?	how?; what?
¿cuál?	what?, which?
¿cuándo?	when?
¿cuánto?	how much?
¿cuántos/as?	how many?
¿dónde?	where?
¿qué?	what?, which?
¿quién?	who?, whom?

Palabras adicionales

sí	yes
no	no
está	is (located)
hay	there is/are
no hay	there is not / are not
hoy	today
mañana	tomorrow
y	and
o	or
a	to; at (*with time*)
de	of; from
en	in; on; at
pero	but
también	also

Vocabulario

En la universidad

Estudiantes hispanoamericanos charlan (*chat*) en la cafetería de la universidad.

¿Qué opina usted?

Answer these questions based on your own life. Do you think that your answer is typical of answers that other students in this country might give? Visit the *Puntos de partida* Website to read how a Hispanic-American student answered the same questions.

1. Are you a full-time or part-time student?
2. How old were you when you started your university studies?
3. Is your campus large or small? Is it urban or set apart from the city?
4. Do most students on your campus live in a dorm? Off-campus?
5. When will you select your major? If you've already selected one, what is it?

En este capítulo...

- You will study vocabulary related to the university. Does your school have a **cafetería**? Is your Spanish instructor a **profesor** or a **profesora**?
- You will learn how to identify people, places, and things by gender and number and how to assign the appropriate article. Did you know that most words in Spanish are considered either feminine or masculine? Can you guess the gender of **la secretaria**? **los secretarios**? (Grammar 1, 2)
- In this chapter you will expand your growing knowledge of Spanish grammar by studying verbs that end with **–ar**. (Grammar 3)
- You know how to use interrogative words such as **¿cuándo?** and **¿dónde?** You will now practice two more ways of asking questions and getting information. (Grammar 4)
- The **Panorama cultural** section of this chapter will focus on the growing Hispanic population in this country.

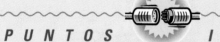

PUNTOS INTERACTIVO

Videoteca

◀ **Minidramas**
Diego y Lupe casually meet in the bookstore and talk about their classes. What classes are you currently taking?

En contexto ▶
Juan Carlos goes to his economics class and meets a classmate. How do you introduce yourself to other people?

CD-ROM

In addition to completing vocabulary and grammar activities, you will have the opportunity to "converse" with someone about your class schedule.

WEB

Internet

In the **Capítulo 1** section of the *Puntos de partida* Website, you can access links to Spanish resources and educational Websites at **www.mhhe.com/puntos**.

En la clase

la ventana
la puerta
el papel
la pizarra
el cuaderno
la silla
el escritorio
la mesa
la mochila

¿Dónde? Lugares en la universidad

la biblioteca	the library
la cafetería	the cafeteria
la clase	the class
el edificio	the building
la librería	the bookstore
la oficina	the office
la residencia	the dormitory

¿Qué? Cosas

el bolígrafo	the pen
la calculadora	the calculator
el diccionario	the dictionary
el dinero	the money
el lápiz	the pencil
el libro	the book
el libro de texto	the textbook

¿Quién? Personas

el bibliotecario	the (male) librarian
la bibliotecaria	the (female) librarian
el compañero de clase	the (male) classmate
la compañera de clase	the (female) classmate
el compañero de cuarto	the (male) roommate
la compañera de cuarto	the (female) roommate
el consejero	the (male) advisor
la consejera	the (female) advisor
el estudiante	the (male) student
la estudiante	the (female) student
el hombre	the man
la mujer	the woman
el profesor	the (male) professor
la profesora	the (female) professor
el secretario	the (male) secretary
la secretaria	the (female) secretary

Conversación

▲▲▲▲▲▲▲

A. ¿Dónde están ahora (*are they now*)**?** Tell where these people are. Then identify the numbered people and things: 1 = **la mesa**, 3 = **el consejero**, and so on. Refer to the drawing and lists on page 36 as much as you need to.

1. Están en _____.

2. Están en _____.

3. Están en _____.

4. Están en _____.

B. Identificaciones. ¿Es hombre o mujer?

MODELO: ¿La consejera? → Es mujer.

1. ¿El profesor?   **4.** ¿El estudiante?
2. ¿La estudiante?   **5.** ¿La bibliotecaria?
3. ¿El secretario?   **6.** ¿El compañero de cuarto?

Las materias

The names for most of these subject areas are cognates. See if you can recognize their meaning without looking at the English equivalent. You should learn in particular the names of subject areas that are of interest to you.

la administración de empresas	business	**la computación**	computer science
		las comunicaciones	communications
el arte	art	**la economía**	economics

el español	Spanish
la filosofía	philosophy
la física	physics
la historia	history
el inglés	English
la literatura	literature
las matemáticas	mathematics
la química	chemistry
la sicología	psychology
la sociología	sociology
las ciencias	sciences
las humanidades	humanities
las lenguas extranjeras	foreign languages

Conversación

▲▲▲▲▲▲▲

A. Asociaciones. ¿Con qué materia(s) asocia usted a... ?

1. Louis Pasteur, Marie Curie *la química*
2. la doctora Joyce Brothers, B. F. Skinner *la sicología*
3. Barbara Walters, Peter Jennings *las comunicaciones*
4. Aristóteles, Confucio *la filosofía*
5. Mark Twain, Toni Morrison *la literatura*
6. Frida Kahlo, Pablo Picasso *el arte*
7. Microsoft, IBM *la computación*
8. Isaac Newton, Stephen Hawking *la física*

B. ¿Qué estudias? (*What are you studying?*) The right-hand column lists a number of university subjects. Tell about your academic interests by creating sentences using one word or phrase from each column. You can tell what you *are* studying (**Estudio...**), *want* to study (**Deseo estudiar...**), *need* to study (**Necesito estudiar...**), and *like* to study (**Me gusta estudiar...**). Using the word **no** makes the sentence negative.

(No) Estudio _____.	español, francés, inglés
(No) Deseo estudiar _____.	arte, filosofía, literatura, música
(No) Necesito estudiar _____.	ciencias políticas, historia
(No) Me gusta estudiar _____.	antropología, sicología, sociología
	biología, física, química
	matemáticas, computación
	¿ ?

The Hispanic Educational System

The educational system in Hispanic countries differs considerably from that of this country. Elementary school (**la escuela primaria, el colegio**) can last five to eight years, depending on the country. After that, secondary school (**la escuela secundaria**) may last four to seven years.

At the university (always called **la universidad**, and never **el colegio** or **la escuela**), students immediately begin specialized programs (**la carrera**) in areas such as law, medicine, engineering, literature, or languages. These university-level programs are established by national ministries of education, and there are few elective courses.

Students are often required to take as many as eight different subjects in a single academic term, which usually lasts nine to ten months. In most countries, academic performance is evaluated on a scale of one to ten, with five considered passing.

Esta estatua de Fray Luis de León está en la Universidad de Salamanca. La Universidad, que (*which*) data del año 1220 (mil doscientos veinte), es una de las más antiguas (*oldest*) de España.

Pronunciación: Diphthongs and Linking

Two successive weak vowels (**i, u**) or a combination of a strong vowel (**a, e,** or **o**) and a weak vowel (**i** or **u**) are pronounced as a single syllable, forming a *diphthong* (**un diptongo**): L**ui**s, s**ie**te, c**ua**derno.

When words are combined to form phrases, clauses, and sentences, they are linked together in pronunciation. In spoken Spanish, it is usually impossible to hear the word boundaries—that is, where one word ends and another begins.

A. Vocales. Más práctica con las vocales.

1. hablar	regular	reservar	llamar
2. trece ı3	clase	papel	general
3. pizarra	oficina	bolígrafo	libro
4. hombre	profesor	dólares	los
5. universidad	gusto	lugar -place	mujer

B. Diptongos. Practique las siguientes (*following*) palabras.

1. historia	secretaria	gracias	estudiante	materia
2. bien	Oviedo	siete	ciencias	diez

3. secretario   biblioteca   adiós   diccionario   Antonio
4. cuaderno   Eduardo   el Ecuador   Guatemala   Managua
5. bueno   nueve   luego   pueblo   Venezuela

C. Frases. Practice saying each phrase as if it were one long word, pronounced without a pause.

1. el papel y el lápiz
2. la profesora y la estudiante
3. las ciencias y las matemáticas
4. la historia y la sicología
5. la secretaria y el profesor
6. el inglés y el español
7. la clase en la biblioteca
8. el libro en la librería

Minidiálogos y gramática

Identifying People, Places, and Things •
Singular Nouns: Gender and Articles*

En *la clase* del *profesor* Durán: *El primer día*

PROFESOR DURÁN: Aquí está *el programa* del *curso*. Son necesarios *el libro de texto* y *un diccionario*. También hay *una lista* de novelas y libros de poesía.

ESTUDIANTE 1:   ¡Es *una lista* infinita!

ESTUDIANTE 2:   Sí, y los libros cuestan demasiado.

ESTUDIANTE 1:   No, *el problema* no es *el precio* de los libros. ¡Es *el tiempo* para leer los libros!

Elija (*Choose*) las palabras o frases correctas según el diálogo.

1. La clase del profesor Durán es de (literatura / filosofía).
2. En el curso del profesor Durán (es necesario / no es necesario) leer (*to read*) mucho.
3. En un curso de literatura (es lógico / no es lógico) usar un diccionario.

---

*The grammar sections of *Puntos de partida* are numbered consecutively throughout the book. If you need to review a particular grammar point, the index will refer you to its page number.

In Professor Durán's class: The first day PROFESSOR DURÁN: Here's the course syllabus. The textbook and a dictionary are required. There is also a list of novels and poetry books. STUDENT 1: It's an immense list! STUDENT 2: Yes, and the books cost too much, STUDENT 1: No, the problem isn't the price of the books. It's the time to read the books!

To name persons, places, things, or ideas, you need to be able to use nouns. In Spanish, all *nouns* (**los sustantivos**) have either masculine or feminine *gender* (**el género**). This is a purely grammatical feature of nouns; it does not mean that Spanish speakers perceive things or ideas as having male or female attributes.

Since the gender of all nouns must be memorized, it is best to learn the definite article along with the noun; that is, learn **el lápiz** rather than just **lápiz**. The definite article will be given with nouns in vocabulary lists in this book.

	Masculine Nouns		Feminine Nouns	
Definite Articles	**el** hombre **el** libro	*the man* *the book*	**la** mujer **la** mesa	*the woman* *the table*
Indefinite Articles	**un** hombre **un** libro	*a (one) man* *a (one) book*	**una** mujer **una** mesa	*a (one) woman* *a (one) table*

Gender

A. Nouns that refer to male beings and most nouns that end in **-o** are *masculine* (**masculino**) in gender.

sustantivos masculinos: hombre, libro

B. Nouns that refer to female beings and most nouns that end in **-a, -ción, -tad**, and **-dad** are *feminine* (**femenino**) in gender.

sustantivos femeninos: mujer, mesa, nación, libertad, universidad

C. Nouns that have other endings and that do not refer to either male or female beings may be masculine or feminine. The gender of these words must be memorized.

el lápiz, la clase, la tarde, la noche

D. Many nouns that refer to persons indicate gender

   1. by changing the last vowel

el compañero ⟶ la compañe**ra**
el bibliotecario ⟶ la bibliotecar**ia**

   2. by adding **-a** to the last consonant of the masculine form to make it feminine

un profesor ⟶ una profeso**ra**

E. Many other nouns that refer to people have a single form for both masculine and feminine genders. Gender is indicated by an article.

el estudiante (*the male student*) ⟶ **la** estudiante (*the female student*)
el cliente (*the male client*) ⟶ **la** cliente (*the female client*)
el dentista (*the male dentist*) ⟶ **la** dentista (*the female dentist*)

However, a few nouns that end in **-e** also have a feminine form that ends in **-a**.

el presidente → la presidenta
el dependiente (*the male clerk*) → la dependienta
(*the female clerk*)

A common exception to the normal rules of gender is the word **el día**, which is masculine in gender. Many words ending in **-ma** are also masculine: **el problema, el programa, el sistema,** and so on. Watch for these exceptions as you continue your study of Spanish.

Articles

A. In English, there is only one *definite article* (**el artículo definido**): *the.* In Spanish, the definite article for masculine singular nouns is **el**; for feminine singular nouns it is **la**.

definite article: *the*
m. sing. → **el**
f. sing. → **la**

B. In English, the singular *indefinite article* (**el artículo indefinido**) is *a* or *an*. In Spanish, the indefinite article, like the definite article, must agree with the gender of the noun: **un** for masculine nouns, **una** for feminine nouns. **Un** and **una** can mean *one* as well as *a* or *an*. Context determines meaning.

indefinite article: *a, an*
m. sing. → **un**
f. sing. → **una**

Práctica

A. Artículos

Dé (*Give*) el artículo definido apropiado (**el, la**).

1. escritorio	**5.** hombre	**9.** mujer
2. biblioteca	**6.** diccionario	**10.** nación
3. bolígrafo	**7.** universidad	**11.** bibliotecario
4. mochila	**8.** dinero	**12.** calculadora

Ahora (*Now*) dé el artículo indefinido apropiado (**un, una**).

1. día	**4.** lápiz	**7.** papel
2. mañana	**5.** clase	**8.** condición
3. problema	**6.** noche	**9.** programa

B. Escenas de la universidad

Paso 1. Haga una oración con las palabras (*words*) indicadas.

MODELO: estudiante / librería → Hay un estudiante en la librería.

1. consejero / oficina	**6.** bolígrafo / silla
2. profesora / clase	**7.** palabra / papel
3. lápiz / mesa	**8.** oficina / residencia
4. cuaderno / escritorio	**9.** compañero / biblioteca
5. libro / mochila	

Paso 2. Now create new sentences by changing one of the words in each item in **Paso 1**. If you do this with a partner, try to come up with as many variations as possible.

MODELO: Hay un estudiante en *la residencia*. (Hay *una profesora* en la librería.)

Conversación

A. **Definiciones.** Con un compañero / una compañera, definan estas palabras en español según el modelo.

MODELO: biblioteca / edificio → ESTUDIANTE 1: ¿La biblioteca?
ESTUDIANTE 2: Es un edificio.

Categorías: cosa, edificio, materia, persona

1. cliente / persona
2. bolígrafo / cosa
3. residencia / edificio
4. dependiente / ¿ ?
5. hotel (*m.*) / ¿ ?
6. calculadora / ¿ ?
7. computación / ¿ ?
8. inglés / ¿ ?
9. ¿ ?

B. **Asociaciones.** Identifique dos cosas y dos personas que usted asocia con los siguientes lugares.

MODELO: la clase → la silla, el libro de texto
el profesor, el estudiante

1. la biblioteca
2. la librería
3. una oficina
4. la residencia

Identifying People, Places, and Things •
Nouns and Articles: Plural Forms

- You should be able to find many nouns in these ads. Can you guess the meaning of most of them?
- Many of the nouns in these ads are plural. Can you tell how to make nouns plural in Spanish, based on these nouns?
- Look for the Spanish equivalent of the following words.

  intensive   centers
  group   emphasis

- Can you recognize any other cognates in the ads? What are they?

	Singular	Plural	
Nouns Ending in a Vowel	**el** libro **la** mesa **un** libro **una** mesa	**los** libros **las** mesas **unos** libros **unas** mesas	*the books* *the tables* *some books* *some tables*
Nouns Ending in a Consonant	**la** universidad **un** papel	**las** universidad**es** **unos** papel**es**	*the universities* *some papers*

A. Spanish nouns that end in a vowel form plurals by adding **-s**. Nouns that end in a consonant add **-es**. Nouns that end in the consonant **-z** change the **-z** to **-c** before adding **-es: lápiz → lápices**.

Plurals in Spanish:
- vowel + **s**
- consonant + **es**
- **-z → -ces**

B. The definite and indefinite articles also have plural forms: **el → los, la → las, un → unos, una → unas. Unos** and **unas** mean *some, several,* or *a few.*

- **el → los**
- **la → las**
- **un → unos**
- **una → unas**

C. In Spanish, the masculine plural form of a noun is used to refer to a group that includes both males and females.

los amig**os**
the friends (both male and female)

unos extranjer**os**
some foreigners (both male and female)

Práctica

A. Singular → plural. Dé la forma plural

1. la mesa
2. el papel
3. el amigo
4. la oficina
5. un cuaderno
6. un lápiz
7. una universidad
8. un bolígrafo
9. un edificio

B. Plural → singular. Dé la forma singular.

1. los profesores
2. las calculadoras
3. las bibliotecarias
4. los estudiantes
5. unos hombres
6. unas tardes
7. unas residencias
8. unas sillas
9. unos escritorios

Conversación

▲▲▲▲▲▲▲

A. Identificaciones. Identifique las personas, las cosas y los lugares.

MODELO: Hay _____ en _____ . → Hay unos estudiantes en la clase.

Palabras útiles: la computadora, el experimento, la planta, el teléfono

1.

2.

B. Semejanzas (*Similarities*) **y diferencias**

Paso 1. ¿Cuáles son las semejanzas y las diferencias entre los dos cuartos? Hay por lo menos (*at least*) seis diferencias.

MODELO: En el dibujo A, hay _____.
En el dibujo B, hay sólo (*only*) _____.
En el escritorio del dibujo A, hay _____.
En el escritorio del dibujo B, hay _____.

Palabras útiles: la cama (*bed*), la computadora, el estante (*bookshelf*), la lámpara, la planta

Paso 2. Ahora indique qué hay en su propio (*your own*) cuarto. Use palabras del **Paso 1.**

MODELO: En mi cuarto hay _____. En mi escritorio hay _____.

Cruz Bustamante

Cruz Bustamante (1953–) was elected Lieutenant Governor of the State of California in 1998. A first-generation Californian, he was the first Latino to serve as Speaker of the Assembly (1996–1998), and the first Latino to be elected to statewide office in more than 120 years. As Lieutenant Governor, Bustamante has worked hard to improve education and educational opportunities for Californians. One of his main goals is to keep college affordable for working families. In addition, he wrote a law providing $1 billion to put updated textbooks into California classrooms. Bustamante is also a Regent of the University of California and a Trustee of the California State University.

Bustamante graduated from Tranquillity High School in California's San Joaquín Valley, then later attended Fresno City College and Fresno State University. While attending college, he was offered an internship in Washington, D.C., to work for Congressman B.F. Sisk, where his political career began.

---

3 Expressing Actions • Subject Pronouns; Present Tense of -ar Verbs; Negation

Escuchando furtivamente

Escuche lo que Diego le dice a Lupe. Luego haga el papel de Lupe. Modifique las oraciones de Diego con **no** si es necesario.

DIEGO: *Yo hablo* con mi familia con frecuencia. Por eso *pago* mucho en cuentas de teléfono. ¿Y *tú?*

LUPE: […]

DIEGO: *Necesito* dinero para comprar libros. Por eso *enseño* inglés a un estudiante de matemáticas. ¿Y *tú?*

LUPE: […]

DIEGO: En mi tiempo libre *escucho* música. También *toco* la guitarra. En las fiestas *bailo* mucho y *tomo* cerveza con mis amigos. Los fines de semana, *busco* libros de antropología en las librerías. ¿Y *tú?*

LUPE: […]

Comprensión: ¿Cierto o falso?

1. Diego no habla mucho con su familia.
2. Es estudiante de ciencias.

Eavesdropping   *Listen to what Diego is saying to Lupe. Then play the role of Lupe. Modify Diego's sentences with* **no** *if neccessary.*
DIEGO: I speak often with my family. That's why I pay a lot in telephone bills. And you? LUPE: […] DIEGO: I need money to buy books. That's why I teach English to a math student. And you? LUPE: […] DIEGO: In my spare time I listen to music. I also play the guitar. At parties I dance a lot and drink beer with my friends. On weekends, I look for anthropology books in bookstores. And you? LUPE: […]

3. No le gusta la música.
4. Es una persona introvertida y solitaria.
5. Habla francés.

Subject Pronouns

Singular		Plural	
yo	I	**nosotros / nosotras**	we
tú	you *(fam.)*	**vosotros / vosotras**	you *(fam. Sp.)*
usted (Ud.)*	you *(form.)*	**ustedes (Uds.)***	you *(form.)*
él	he	**ellos / ellas**	they
ella	she		

A. Several *subject pronouns* (**los pronombres personales**) have masculine and feminine forms. The masculine plural form is used to refer to a group of males as well as to a group of males and females.

> **pronoun** = a word that takes the place of a noun
> Ted → *he*
> Martha and Ted → *they*

ellos = *they* (all males; males and females)
ellas = *they* (all females)

B. Spanish has different words for *you*. In general, **tú** is used to refer to a close friend or a member of your family, while **usted** is used with people with whom the speaker has a more formal or distant relationship. The situations in which **tú** and **usted** are used also vary among different countries and regions.

tú → close friend, family member
usted (Ud.) → formal or distant relationship

C. In Latin America and in this country, the plural for both **usted** and **tú** is **ustedes**. In Spain, however, **vosotros/vosotras** is the plural of **tú**, while **ustedes** is used as the plural of **usted** exclusively.

Latin America, North America
tú ⎫
usted ⎭ ustedes

Spain
tú → vosotros/vosotras
usted (Ud.) → ustedes

D. Subject pronouns are not used as frequently in Spanish as they are in English and may usually be omitted. You will learn more about the uses of Spanish subject pronouns in **Capítulo 2**.

***Usted** and **ustedes** are frequently abbreviated in writing as **Ud.** or **Vd.**, and **Uds.** or **Vds.**, respectively.

Minidiálogos y gramática

A. The *infinitive* (**el infinitivo**) of a verb indicates the action or state of being, with no reference to who or what performs the action or when it is done (present, past, or future). In Spanish all infinitives end in **-ar**, **-er**, or **-ir**. Infinitives in English are indicated by *to: to* speak, *to* eat, *to* live.

-ar:	hablar	*to speak*
-er:	comer	*to eat*
-ir:	vivir	*to live*

B. To *conjugate* (**conjugar**) a verb means to give the various forms of the verb with their corresponding subjects: *I speak, you speak, she speaks,* and so on. All regular Spanish verbs are conjugated by adding *personal endings* (**las terminaciones personales**) that reflect the subject doing the action. These are added to the *stem* (**la raíz** or **el radical**), which is the infinitive minus the infinitive ending.

hablar → habl-
comer → com-
vivir → viv-

C. The right-hand column shows the personal endings that are added to the stem of all regular **-ar** verbs:

Regular **-ar** verb indings:
o, -as, -a, -amos, -áis, -an.

---

hablar (*to speak*): habl-

	Singular			**Plural**	
(yo)	hablo	*I speak*	(nosotros) (nosotras)	hablamos	*we speak*
(tú)	hablas	*you speak*	(vosotros) (vosotras)	habláis	*you speak*
(Ud.) (él) (ella)	habla	*you speak; he/she speaks*	(Uds.) (ellos) (ellas)	hablan	*you/they speak*

Some important **-ar** verbs in this chapter include those on the right.

bailar	to dance	**hablar**	to speak; to talk
buscar	to look for	**necesitar**	to need
cantar	to sing	**pagar**	to pay (for)
comprar	to buy	**practicar**	to practice
desear	to want	**regresar**	to return (*to a place*)
enseñar	to teach	**tocar**	to play (*a musical instrument*)
escuchar	to listen (to)	**tomar**	to take; to drink
estudiar	to study	**trabajar**	to work

O J O Note that in Spanish the meaning of the English word *for* is included in the verbs **buscar** (*to look for*) and **pagar** (*to pay for*); *to* is included in **escuchar** (*to listen to*).

D. As in English, when two Spanish verbs are used in sequence and there is no change of subject, the second verb is usually in the infinitive form.

Necesito llamar a mi familia.
I need to call my family.

Me gusta bailar.
I like to dance.

E. In both English and Spanish, conjugated verb forms also indicate the *time* or *tense* (**el tiempo**) of the action: *I speak* (present), *I spoke* (past).

Some English equivalents of the present tense forms of Spanish verbs are shown at the right.

hablo
- *I speak* — Simple present tense
- *I am speaking* — Present progressive (indicates an action in progress)
- *I will speak* — Near future action

Negation

In Spanish the word **no** is placed before the conjugated verb to make a negative sentence.

El estudiante **no** habla español.
The student doesn't speak Spanish.

No, **no** necesito dinero.
No, I don't need money.

Práctica

A. Mis compañeros y yo

Paso 1. Read the following statements and tell whether they are true for you and your classmates and for your classroom environment. If any statement is not true for you or your class, make it negative or change it in another way to make it correct.

MODELO: Toco el piano → Sí, toco el piano.
(No, no toco el piano. Toco la guitarra.)

1. Necesito dinero.
2. Trabajo en la biblioteca.
3. Tomo ocho clases este semestre/trimestre (*this term*).
4. En clase, cantamos en francés.
5. Deseamos practicar español.
6. Tomamos Coca-Cola en clase.
7. El profesor / La profesora enseña español.
8. El profesor / La profesora el alemán habla muy bien.

Paso 2. Now turn to the person next to you and rephrase each sentence, using **tú** forms of the verbs in all cases. Your partner will indicate whether the sentences are true for him or her.

MODELO: ¿Tocas el piano? → Sí, toco el piano. (No, no toco el piano.)

B. En una fiesta. The following paragraphs describe a party. Scan the paragraphs first, to get a general sense of their meaning. Then complete the paragraphs with the correct form of the numbered infinitives.

Esta noche[a] hay una fiesta en el apartamento de Marcos y Julio. Todos[b] los estudiantes (cantar[1]) y (bailar[2]). Una persona (tocar[3]) la guitarra y otras personas (escuchar[4]) la música.

Jaime (buscar[5]) un café. Marta (hablar[6]) con un amigo. María José (desear[7]) enseñarles a todos[c] un baile[d] de Colombia. Todas las estudiantes desean (bailar[8]) con el estudiante mexicano—¡él (bailar[9]) muy bien!

La fiesta es estupenda, pero todos (necesitar[10]) regresar a casa[e] o a su[f] cuarto temprano.[g] ¡Hay clases mañana!

[a]Esta... *Tonight*   [b]*All*   [c]enseñarles... *to teach everyone*   [d]*dance*   [e]a... *home*   [f]*their*   [g]*early*

Comprensión: ¿Cierto o falso?

1. Marcos es un profesor de español.
2. A Jaime le gusta la cerveza.
3. María José es de Colombia.
4. Los estudiantes desean bailar.

Conversación
▲▲▲▲▲▲▲▲

A. Oraciones lógicas. Form at least eight complete logical sentences by using one word or phrase from each column. The words and phrases may be used more than once, in many combinations. Be sure to use the correct form of the verbs. Make any of the sentences negative, if you wish.

MODELO: Yo no estudio francés.

yo	comprar	la guitarra, el piano, el violín
tú (estudiante)	regresar	el edificio de ciencias
nosotros (los miembros de esta clase)	buscar	en la cafetería, en la universidad
los estudiantes de aquí	trabajar	en una oficina, en una librería
el extranjero	hablar	a casa por la noche
	tocar	a la biblioteca a las dos
un secretario (no)	enseñar	francés, alemán (*German*)
un profesor de español	pagar	bien el español
un dependiente	tomar	los libros de texto con un cheque
	estudiar	libros y cuadernos en la librería
	desear	tomar una clase de computación
	necesitar	hablar bien el español
		estudiar más (*more*)
		comprar una calculadora, una mochila
		pagar la matrícula (*tuition*) en septiembre

The Verb *estar*

Estar is another Spanish **-ar** verb. It means *to be*, and you have already used forms of it to ask how others are feeling or to tell where things are located. Here is the complete conjugation of **estar**. Note that the **yo** form is irregular. The other forms take regular **-ar** endings, and some have a shift in the stress pattern (indicated by the accented **á**).

yo	**estoy**	nosotros/as	**estamos**
tú	**estás**	vosotros/as	**estáis**
Ud., él, ella	**está**	Uds., ellos, ellas	**están**

You will learn the uses of the verb **estar**, along with those of **ser** (the other Spanish verb that means *to be*), gradually, over the next several chapters. For now, just answer the following questions, using forms of **estar**.

1. ¿Cómo está Ud. en este momento (*right now*)?
2. ¿Cómo están sus (*your*) compañeros de clase?
3. ¿Dónde está Ud. en este momento?

B. ¿Qué hacen? (*What are they doing?*) Tell where these people are and what they are doing. Note that the definite article is used with titles when you are talking about a person: **el señor, la señora, la señorita, el profesor, la profesora**.

MODELO: La Sra. Martínez _____. →
La Sra. Martínez está en la oficina. Busca un libro, trabaja…

Frases útiles: hablar por teléfono, preparar la lección, pronunciar las palabras, tomar apuntes (*to take notes*), usar una computadora

1. Estas (*These*) personas *ellos* _____.
   La profesora Gil _____.
   Casi (*Almost*) todos los estudiantes _____.
   Unos estudiantes _____.

2. Estas personas están _____.
   El Sr. Miranda _____.
   La bibliotecaria _____.
   El secretario _____.

3. Estas personas _____.
   El cliente _____.
   La dependienta _____.

Nota comunicativa

Expressing the Time of Day

You can use the preposition **por** to mean *in* or *during* when expressing the time of day.

Estudio **por** la mañana y trabajo **por** la tarde. **Por** la noche, estoy en casa con la familia.
I study in the morning and I work in the afternoon. During the evening (At night), I'm at home with my family.

Remember that the phrases **de la mañana (tarde, noche)** are used when a specific hour of the day is mentioned.

C. Entrevista. Use the following questions as a guide to interview a classmate, and take notes on what he or she says. (Remember to write down the answers to your partner's questions using the **él/ella** form of the verbs.) Your instructor may want you to hand in your notes so that he or she can get to know the students better.

MODELO: ESTUDIANTE 1: Karen, ¿estudias filosofía?
ESTUDIANTE 2: No, no estudio filosofía. Estudio música.
ESTUDIANTE 1: (escribe [*writes*]): Karen no estudia filosofía. Estudia música.

1. ¿Estudias mucho o poco (*a lot or a little*)? ¿Dónde estudias, en casa (*at home*), en la residencia o en la biblioteca? ¿Cuándo estudias, por la tarde o por la noche?
2. ¿Cantas bien o mal (*poorly*)? ¿Tocas un instrumento musical? ¿Cuál es? (el piano, la guitarra, el violín...)
3. ¿Trabajas? ¿Dónde? ¿Cuántas horas a la semana (*per week*) trabajas?
4. ¿Quiénes pagan los libros de texto, tú o los profesores? ¿Qué más necesitas pagar? ¿diccionarios? ¿el alquiler (*rent*)? ¿ ?

Getting Information • Asking Yes/No Questions

En una universidad: La oficina de matrícula

ESTUDIANTE: Necesito una clase más por la mañana. *¿Hay sitio* en la clase de sicología 2?
CONSEJERO: Imposible, señorita. No hay.
ESTUDIANTE: *¿Hay un curso* de historia o de matemáticas?
CONSEJERO: Sólo por la noche. *¿Desea Ud. tomar* una clase por la noche?
ESTUDIANTE: Trabajo por la noche. Por eso necesito una clase por la mañana.

CONSEJERO: Pues… ¿qué tal el francés 10? Hay una clase a las diez de la mañana.

ESTUDIANTE: *¿El francés 10?* Perfecto. Pero, *¿no necesito tomar* primero el francés 1?

Comprensión

1. ¿Necesita la señorita dos clases más?
2. ¿Hay sitio en sicología 2?
3. ¿Hay cursos de historia o de matemáticas por la mañana?
4. ¿A qué hora es la clase de francés 10?
5. ¿Cuál es el problema con la clase de francés 10?

There are two kinds of questions: information questions and yes/no questions. Questions that ask for new information or facts that the speaker does not know often begin with *interrogative words* such as *who, what,* and so on. (You learned many interrogative words in **Ante todo**.) *Yes/no questions* are those that permit a simple *yes* or *no* answer.

Information questions:
¿Qué lengua habla Ud.? →
Hablo español.

Yes/no questions:
Habla Ud. francés? →
No (no hablo francés).

Rising Intonation

A common way to form yes/no questions in Spanish is simply to make your voice rise at the end of the question.

OJO
There is no Spanish equivalent to English *do* or *does* in questions. Note also the use of an inverted question mark (¿) at the beginning of a question.

STATEMENT: Ud. trabaja aquí todos los días.
You work here every day.

Arturo regresa a casa hoy.
Arturo is returning home today.

QUESTION: ¿Ud. trabaja aquí todos los días?
Do you work here every day?

¿Arturo regresa a casa hoy?
Is Arturo returning home today?

Inversion

Another way to form yes/no questions is to invert the order of the subject and verb, in addition to making your voice rise at the end of the question.

STATEMENT: **Ud.** trabaja aquí todos los días.

QUESTION: ¿Trabaja **Ud.** aquí todos los días?

STATEMENT: **Arturo** regresa a casa hoy.

QUESTION: ¿Regresa **Arturo** a casa hoy?

At a university: The registration office STUDENT: I need one more class in the morning. Is there space in Psychology 2? ADVISOR: Impossible, Miss. There's no room. STUDENT: Is there a history or math class? ADVISOR: Only at night. Do you want to take a night course? STUDENT: I work at night. That's why I need a class in the morning. ADVISOR: Well. . . what about French 10? There's a class at ten in the morning. STUDENT: French 10? Perfect. But don't I need to take French 1 first?

Práctica

Una conversación entre (*between*) **Diego y Lupe.** Diego and Lupe recently met each other. While having coffee, Lupe asks Diego some questions to find out more about him. Ask Lupe's questions that led to Diego's answers.

MODELO: Sí, estudio antropología. → ¿Estudias antropología?

1. Sí, soy norteamericano (*from the United States*).
2. Sí, estudio con frecuencia.
3. No, no toco el piano. Toco la guitarra clásica.
4. No, no deseo trabajar más horas.
5. No, no hablo francés, pero hablo un poco de (*a little bit of*) italiano.
6. ¡No, no soy reservado! Soy muy extrovertido.

Conversación

¿Qué haces? (*What do you do?*)

Paso 1. Use the following cues as a guide to form questions to ask a classmate. Of course, you may ask other questions as well. Write the questions on a sheet of paper first, if you like. (**¡OJO!** Use the **tú** form of the verbs with your partner.)

1. estudiar en la biblioteca por la noche
2. practicar español con un amigo / una amiga
3. tomar café por la mañana
4. bailar mucho en las fiestas
5. tocar un instrumento musical
6. regresar a casa muy tarde (*late*) a veces (*sometimes*)

Paso 2. Now use the questions to get information from your partner. Jot down his or her answers for use in **Paso 3**.

MODELO: ¿Estudias en la biblioteca… ?

Paso 3. With the information you gathered in **Paso 2**, report your partner's answers to the class. (You will use the **él/ella** form of the verbs when reporting.)

MODELO: Jenny no estudia en la biblioteca por la noche. Estudia en casa.

[a]¿Qué… *What the devil is that*   [b]vos = tú en la Argentina y el Uruguay   [c]*Do you understand?*

Capítulo 1   •   En la universidad

Videoteca

Minidramas

In this **Minidramas** dialogue, Diego González and Lupe Carrasco, two students at UNAM, run into each other at the campus bookstore. Pay close attention to the topic of their discussion. What are they talking about?

Diego y Lupe se tropiezan[a] en la librería.

DIEGO: ¡Ay, perdón!
LUPE: No hay por qué. ¡Ay, Diego!
DIEGO: ¡Lupe! ¿Qué haces?[b]
LUPE: Busco un libro para la clase de antropología.
DIEGO: ¿Te gusta la antropología?
LUPE: Sí, me gusta mucho. Sobre todo,[c] me gusta la antropología precolombina.
DIEGO: ¿En serio?[d] Es mi[e] materia favorita. ¿Qué clase tomas?
LUPE: Tomo la clase del profesor Salazar. Es una clase fascinante.
DIEGO: Yo tambien tomo esa[f] clase. Así que[g] somos compañeros… Bueno, Lupe, nos vemos[h] en clase.
LUPE: Sí, nos vemos.

F U N C T I O N

expressing likes and dislikes

---

[a]se… *bump into each other* [b]¿Qué… *What are you doing?* [c]Sobre… *Above all* [d]¿En… *Really?*
[e]*my* [f]*that* [g]Así… *So* [h]nos… *we'll see each other*

Con un compañero / una compañera

With a partner, practice telling each other what classes you are taking this semester/quarter. You should be able to give the following information:

- course names
- professor names
- which class is your favorite

Un poco más sobre… Lupe Carrasco

Lupe Carrasco es estudiante en la Universidad Nacional Autónoma de México (la UNAM), en la Ciudad de México. Este[a] semestre toma varias clases diferentes: antropología, literatura, sicología y otras más.[b] Es muy buena[c] estudiante: se dedica a sus estudios.[d]

[a]*This* [b]otras… *others*
[c]*good* [d]se… *she is dedicated to her studies*

To read more about the characters from this video, visit the *Puntos de partida* Website at **www.mhhe.com/puntos**

En contexto

In this video segment, Peruvian student Juan Carlos engages a fellow student in conversation. As you watch the segment, pay particular attention to the information they give. What classes are they taking? What do they like to do on weekends?

PERÚ

A. Lluvia de ideas

What usually happens when you attend a class for the first time? Do you talk to your fellow students? What do you talk about?

B. Dictado

Here is the second half of this segment's dialogue. Fill in the missing portions of Eduardo's dialogue. (There is an underlined space for each word.)

EDUARDO: … Oye, tomas también la clase de sociología con el profesor Ramón?

JUAN CARLOS: Sí, también tomo esa[a] clase.

EDUARDO: ¿_____ _____ _____ es la clase de _____?
¿Es a la una o _____ _____ _____ _____ _____?

JUAN CARLOS: Es a la una y media, creo[b]… Sí, a la una y media.

EDUARDO: Este_____ _____ _____.

JUAN CARLOS: Sí, escucho su[c] música con frecuencia. Me gusta mucho el jazz.

EDUARDO: ¿Ah, sí?_____ _____ _____ _____ Café Azul. Allí[d] _____ _____ _____ todos los fines de semana _____ _____ _____.

JUAN CARLOS: ¡Qué bacán![e] ¿A qué hora?

EDUARDO: _____ _____ _____.

JUAN CARLOS: ¡Perfecto! Entonces,[f] este[g] fin de semana escucho jazz en tu[h] café. Oye,[i] ¿qué hora es?

EDUARDO: Son _____ _____ _____. ¿Dónde _____ _____ _____? La clase es a las once…

[a]that [b]I think [c]their [d]There [e]Que... Cool! [f]Then [g]this [h]your [i]Hey

C. Un diálogo original

Paso 1. With a classmate, re-enact the situation between Eduardo and Juan Carlos.

Paso 2. With a different classmate, role-play a situation similar to the one in the video. Here are the roles:

ESTUDIANTE 1: You are a student coming into the classroom the first day of classes. You want to start a conversation with a classmate. As you sit down, you let your classmate see a CD (pronounced as the letters **c d** [**ce de**]), which you like a lot.

ESTUDIANTE 2: You are already sitting in class. You are also interested in making a new friend. One of your classmates has a CD of one of your favorite bands.

Un poco de todo

A. Conversaciones en la cafetería

Paso 1. Form complete questions and answers based on the words given, in the order given. Conjugate the verbs and add other words if necessary. Do not use the subject pronouns in parentheses.

PREGUNTAS

1. ¿buscar (tú) / libro de español?
2. ¿no trabajar / Paco / aquí / en / cafetería?
3. ¿qué más / necesitar / Uds. / en / clase de cálculo?
4. ¿dónde / estar / Juanita?
5. ¿no desear (tú) / estudiar / minutos / más?

RESPUESTAS

1. no, / (yo) necesitar / regresar / a casa
2. no, / (yo) buscar / mochila
3. (nosotros) necesitar / calculadora / y / cuaderno
4. no, / él / trabajar / en / biblioteca
5. ella / trabajar / en / residencia / por / tardes

Paso 2. Now match the answers with the questions to form short conversational exchanges, or practice them with a partner, if you wish.

B. Una carta (*letter*) **a una amiga.** Complete the following paragraphs from Angela's letter about college to a friend in her hometown. Give the correct form of the words in parentheses, as suggested by the context. When two possibilities are given in parentheses, select the correct word.

Mi amiga Kathy y yo estamos muy contentas. ¡Todo (ser[1]) fantástico! Kathy (tomar[2]) cuatro clases y yo, cinco. (*Nosotras:* Estudiar[3]) mucho. A mí (me/te[4]) gusta ir[a] temprano a la cafetería. A esas horas[b] hay unos donuts riquísimos.[c] (*Yo:* Comprar[5]) un café y dos donuts y (estudiar[6]) unos minutos o media hora, especialmente para[d] (el/la[7]) clase de español.

En la residencia hay (un/una[8]) estudiante de Puerto Rico, Luisa, que vive[e] en el cuarto de enfrente.[f] Con Luisa (*nosotras:* practicar[9]) (el/la[10]) pronunciación. Ella también nos[g] enseña canciones en español. Kathy (cantar[11]) muy mal, pero (bailar[12]) la salsa muy bien... o «chévere», como dice Luisa.[h]

Kathy y yo también (trabajar[13]). Yo trabajo en la biblioteca (por/de[14]) las tardes. Kathy no trabaja en (el/la[15]) universidad, pero su trabajo[i] no (ser[16]) muy diferente. Es (cliente/dependienta[17]) en una librería. ¡Las dos (*nosotras:* estar[18]) con libros todo (el/la[19]) día!

[a]*to go* [b]*A... At that hour* [c]*extremely delicious* [d]*for* [e]*que... who lives* [f]*de... in front (of us)* [g]*us* [h]*como... as Luisa says* [i]*su... her work*

Comprensión: ¿Cierto o falso? Which of these statements do you agree with after reading Ángela's letter? Change incorrect statements to make them true.

1. Ángela toma Español 1 en la universidad.
2. A Ángela no le gusta el español como materia.
3. Ángela no estudia con frecuencia.
4. Todos los amigos de Ángela son de habla inglesa (*English-speaking*).

C. ¿Qué pasa (*What's happening*) **en la fiesta?**

Paso 1. With a classmate, briefly describe what's going on in the following scene.

Paso 2. Now compare the scene above with parties *you* go to. You can use the **nosotros** form of verbs to describe what you and your friends do at these parties.

Vocabulario útil: descansar (*to rest*), escuchar, fumar (*to smoke*), mirar una película/la tele (*to watch a movie/TV*), tocar el piano/la guitarra, tomar cerveza/vino/refrescos (*beer/wine/soft drinks*)

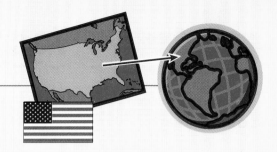

PANORAMA *cultural*

Los hispanos en los Estados Unidos

Datos[a] esenciales

- La población hispánica total de los Estados Unidos: más de 31 millones en 1999 (mil novecientos noventa y nueve), según el *Census Bureau*.

- Orígenes de la población hispánica en los Estados Unidos:
  México: 61% (sesenta y uno por ciento)
  Centroamérica, Sudamérica y otros países:[b] 23%
  Puerto Rico: 12%
  Cuba: 4%

[a]*Facts* [b]otros... *other countries*

¡Fíjese![a]

- En 1997 (mil novecientos noventa y siete) había[b] veintiún hispanos en el Congreso de los Estados Unidos. ¿Cuántos hay ahora? (www.house.gov)

- De los más de[c] 31 (treinta y un) millones de hispanos en los Estados Unidos (hay estimados de casi[d] 40 [cuarenta] millones), la mayoría[e] habla español (mucho o poco).

- Las palabras **hispano** e[f] **hispánico** se refieren al[g] idioma y a la cultura, no a la raza[h] o el grupo étnico. Originalmente, **hispano** e **hispánico** derivan de[i] la palabra *Hispania,* el nombre de España en latín. El idioma español es la clave[j] de la identidad cultural de los pueblos[k] hispánicos.

[a]*Check it out!* [b]*there were* [c]*De... Of the more than* [d]*almost* [e]*majority* [f]*y* [g]*Se... refer to the* [h]*the race* [i]*derivan... come from* [j]*key* [k]*peoples*

Conozca a[a]... César Chávez

La contribución de César Chávez (1927–1993 [mil novecientos veintisiete a mil novecientos noventa y tres]) al movimiento de los trabajadores agrícolas[b] es enorme. Hijo de campesinos migrantes,[c] la educación de Chávez sólo llega al séptimo grado.[d]

En 1962 (mil novecientos sesenta y dos), Chávez organiza a los campesinos que cosechan uvas.[e] Como resultado de las huelgas[f] y el boicoteo de las uvas de mesa,[g] los campesinos reciben contratos más favorables para ellos; el United Farm Workers se establece[h] como sindicato[i] oficial.

Hoy en día,[j] la vida,[k] los sacrificios y los ideales de Chávez sirven de[l] inspiración a muchas personas.

[a]*Conozca... Meet* [b]*trabajadores... agricultural workers* [c]*campesinos... migrant farm workers* [d]*llega... reaches the seventh grade* [e]*cosechan... harvest grapes* [f]*strikes* [g]*uvas... table grapes* [h]*se... is established* [i]*union* [j]*Hoy... Nowadays* [k]*life* [l]*sirven... serve as an*

 Capítulo 1 of the video to accompany *Puntos de partida* contains cultural footage of Hispanics in the United States.

 Visit the *Puntos de partida* Website at www.mhhe.com/puntos.

Vocabulario

Los verbos

bailar	to dance
buscar	to look for
cantar	to sing
comprar	to buy
desear	to want
enseñar	to teach
escuchar	to listen (to)
estar (*irreg.*)	to be
estudiar	to study
hablar	to speak; to talk
hablar por teléfono	to talk on the phone
necesitar	to need
pagar	to pay (for)
practicar	to practice
regresar	to return (*to a place*)
regresar a casa	to go home
tocar	to play (*a musical instrument*)
tomar	to take; to drink
trabajar	to work

Los lugares

el apartamento	apartment
la biblioteca	library
la cafetería	cafeteria
la clase	class
el cuarto	room
el edificio	building
la fiesta	party
la librería	bookstore
la oficina	office
la residencia	dormitory
la universidad	university

Las personas

el/la amigo/a	friend
el/la bibliotecario/a	librarian
el/la cliente	client
el/la compañero/a (de clase)	classmate
el/la compañero/a de cuarto	roommate
el/la consejero/a	advisor
el/la dependiente/a	clerk
el/la estudiante	student
el/la extranjero/a	foreigner
el hombre	man
la mujer	woman
el/la profesor(a)	professor
el/la secretario/a	secretary

Las lenguas (extranjeras)

el alemán	German
el español	Spanish
el francés	French
el inglés	English
el italiano	Italian

Otras materias

la administración de empresas, el arte, las ciencias, la computación, las comunicaciones, la economía, la filosofía, la física, la historia, las humanidades, la literatura, las matemáticas, la química, la sicología, la sociología

Las cosas

el bolígrafo	pen
la calculadora	calculator
el cuaderno	notebook
el diccionario	dictionary
el dinero	money
el escritorio	desk
el lápiz (*pl.* lápices)	pencil
el libro (de texto)	(text)book
la mesa	table
la mochila	backpack
el papel	paper

la pizarra	chalkboard
la puerta	door
la silla	chair
la ventana	window

Otros sustantivos

el café	coffee
la cerveza	beer
el día	day
la matrícula	tuition

¿Cuándo?

ahora	now
con frecuencia	frequently
el fin de semana	weekend
por la mañana	in the morning
(tarde, noche)	(afternoon, evening)
tarde/temprano	late/early
todos los días	every day

Pronombres personales

yo, tú, usted (Ud.), él/ella, nosotros/nosotras, vosotros/vosotras, ustedes (Uds.), ellos/ellas

Palabras adicionales

aquí	here
con	with
en casa	at home
mal	poorly
más	more
mucho	much; a lot
muy	very
poco	little; a little bit
por eso	therefore
sólo	only

Un paso más 1

LECTURA

Estrategia: More on Guessing Meaning from Context

As you learned in **El mundo hispánico (Ante todo)**, you can often guess the meaning of unfamiliar words from the context (the words that surround them) and by using your knowledge about the topic in general. Making "educated guesses" about words in this way will be an important part of your reading skills in Spanish.

What is the meaning of the underlined words in these sentences?

1. En una lista alfabetizada, la palabra **grande** aparece <u>antes de</u> **grotesco.**
2. El edificio no es moderno; es <u>viejo.</u>
3. Me gusta estudiar español, pero detesto la biología. En general, <u>odio</u> las ciencias como materia.

Some words are underlined in the following reading (and in the readings in subsequent chapters). Try to guess their meaning from context.

Like the passages in **Ante todo** and some others in subsequent chapters, this reading contains section subheadings. Scanning these subheadings in advance will help you make predictions about the reading's content, which will also help to facilitate your overall comprehension. Another useful way to manage longer passages is to read section by section. At this point, don't try to understand every word. Your main objective should be to understand the general content of the passage.

▶ **Sobre la lectura...** This reading was written by the authors of *Puntos de*
▶ *partida* for students of Spanish like you. Later on in this text, you will have
▶ the chance to read more "authentic" selections.

Las universidades hispánicas

Introducción
En el mundo hispánico—y en los Estados Unidos y el Canadá—hay universidades grandes[a] y <u>pequeñas</u>; públicas, religiosas y privadas; modernas y antiguas. Pero el concepto de «vida[b] universitaria» es diferente.

El campus
Por ejemplo, en los países[c] hispánicos la universidad no es un centro de actividad social.

No hay muchas residencias estudiantiles. En general, los estudiantes <u>viven</u> en pensiones[d] o en casas particulares[e] y <u>llegan</u> a la universidad en coche o en autobús. En algunas[f] universidades hay un *campus* similar a los de[g] las universidades de los Estados Unidos y el Canadá. En estos casos se habla[h] de la «ciudad[i] universitaria». Otras universidades ocupan sólo un edificio grande, o posiblemente varios edificios, pero no hay zonas verdes.[j]

[a]*large* [b]*life* [c]*naciones* [d]*boarding houses* [e]*private* [f]*some* [g]*los... those of* [h]*se... one speaks* [i]*city* [j]*green*

Estudiantes de Medicina en Caracas, Venezuela

Los deportes

Otra diferencia es que en la mayoría de las universidades hispánicas los <u>deportes</u> no son muy importantes. Si los estudiantes desean practicar un deporte—el tenis, el fútbol o el béisbol—hay clubes deportivos, pero estos[k] no forman parte de la universidad.

Las diversiones[l]

Como se puede ver,[m] la forma y la organización de la universidad son diferentes en las dos culturas. Pero los estudiantes estudian y se divierten[n] en todas partes.[o] A los estudiantes hispanos—así como[p] a los estadounidenses* y canadienses[q] les gusta mucho toda clase de música: la música moderna—la nacional[r] y la <u>importada</u> (y hay para todos: Madonna, N Sync, R.E.M., …)—la música clásica y la música con raíces[s] tradicionales. Otras diversiones preferidas por los estudiantes son las discotecas y los cafés. Hay cafés ideales para hablar con los amigos. También hay exposiciones de arte, <u>obras</u> de teatro y películas[t] interesantes.

Conclusión

Los días favoritos de muchos jóvenes[u] hispánicos son los fines de semana. ¿Realmente son muy distintos los estudiantes hispanos? ●

[k]*they* (lit. *these*)   [l]Las… *Entertainment*   [m]Como… *As you can see*   [n]*se… have a good time*   [o]*en… everywhere*
[p]*así… like*   [q]*estadounidenses… people from the U.S. and Canadians*   [r]*la… (music) from their own country*   [s]*roots*
[t]*movies*   [u]*young people*

*Although, technically, **norteamericano** refers to all North Americans, the term is sometimes used to refer soley to people from the United States of America. In this book, **estadounidenses** will refer to people of The United States and **norteamericanos** to North Americans.

Comprensión

A. ¿Cierto o falso? Indique si las siguientes oraciones son ciertas o falsas.

1. En los países hispánicos, la mayoría de los estudiantes vive en residencias.
2. En las universidades hispánicas, los deportes ocupan un lugar esencial en el programa de estudios del estudiante.
3. En una universidad hispánica, no hay mucho tiempo para asistir a (*time for attending*) conciertos y exposiciones de arte.
4. No hay mucha diferencia entre (*between*) una universidad hispánica y una universidad norteamericana con respecto al *campus*.
5. La música es una diversión para los estudiantes en todas partes.

B. ¿Qué universidad? Indique si las siguientes oraciones son de un estudiante de la Universidad de Sevilla o de un estudiante de la Universidad de Michigan… ¡o de los dos!

	SEVILLA	MICHIGAN	LOS DOS
1. «Me gusta jugar al Frisbee en el *campus*.»	☐	☐	☐
2. «La casa es muy cómoda (*comfortable*) y tengo derecho a usar la cocina (*I have kitchen privileges*).»	☐	☐	☐
3. «Después de mi clase, ¿qué tal si tomamos un café?»	☐	☐	☐
4. «El sábado (*Saturday*) hay un partido de basquetbol. ¿Deseas ir (*to go*)?»	☐	☐	☐

ESCRITURA

A. Una comparación. Compare su propia (*your own*) universidad con una universidad hispánica, completando (*by completing*) la siguiente tabla con información de la lectura.

	La universidad hispánica	Mi universidad
Alojamiento (*Housing*)	pensiones, casas particulares	
El *campus*		
Deportes		
Diversiones	música, discotecas, cafés, películas, exposiciones de arte	

B. In light of what you now know about some differences and similarities between universities in this country and in Hispanic countries, what information do you think would be important to share with a Hispanic student planning on studying at *your* university? In a brief paragraph, describe your university to such a student. Use the information from the table above as well as other facts: **el número de residencias; si la universidad es grande/pequeña, pública/privada; el edificio más grande** (*biggest*); and so on.

Mi universidad…

La familia

Una familia hispana. Los hispanos de hoy, especialmente en las zonas urbanas, prefieren tener (*to have*) familias pequeñas (*small*).

¿Qué opina Ud.?

Answer the following questions based on your own life. Do you think that your answer is typical of answers other students in this country might give? Visit the *Puntos de partida* Website to read how a student from Mexico answered the same questions.

1. Do you live near other members of your family?
2. When did you leave home? Do you expect to leave home in the future? If so, when?
3. What expectations does/did your family have in regards to marriage and a family? Do you share those opinions?
4. Where do/did your grandparents live?

64

En este capítulo...

- You will study vocabulary related to the family. Can you guess what **el esposo** means? Or **la madre**? Who do you think your **prima** is?
- You will also learn adjectives that will help you describe people. What does **simpático/a** mean? Or **bueno/a**?
- In the **Capítulo preliminar,** you learned how to use **soy, eres,** and **es.** In this chapter, you will study other forms of the verb **ser.** (Grammar 5)
- You will begin to use possessive adjectives to tell what belongs to you and others. (Grammar 6)
- Additionally, you will learn how to use adjectives to describe people and things, depending on their gender and number. (Grammar 7)
- In **Capítulo 1**, you learned the endings of **-ar** verbs. Now you will study verbs whose infinitives have **-er** and **-ir** endings. (Grammar 8)
- The **Panorama cultural** section of this chapter will focus on Mexico.

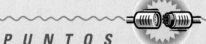

PUNTOS *INTERACTIVO*

Videoteca

◀ **Minidramas**
José Miguel and Elisa look at old family photos to put them in an album. Do you like looking at old family pictures?

En contexto ▶
Roberto and Martín look for Roberto's cousin in the park. Roberto describes her to Martín. What adjectives do you use when you describe a person physically?

 CD-ROM

In addition to completing vocabulary and grammar activities, you will have the opportunity to "converse" with Roberto and describe your family and friends.

 Internet

In the **Capítulo 2** section of the *Puntos de partida* Website, you can access links to Spanish resources about the Hispanic family at **www.mhhe.com/puntos**.

La familia y los parientes° *relatives*

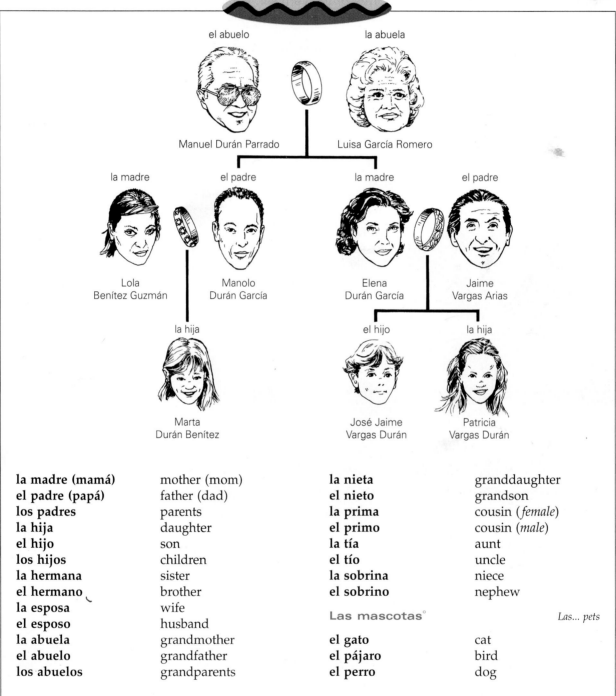

el abuelo — Manuel Durán Parrado

la abuela — Luisa García Romero

la madre — Lola Benítez Guzmán

el padre — Manolo Durán García

la madre — Elena Durán García

el padre — Jaime Vargas Arias

la hija — Marta Durán Benítez

el hijo — José Jaime Vargas Durán

la hija — Patricia Vargas Durán

la madre (mamá)	mother (mom)	**la nieta**	granddaughter
el padre (papá)	father (dad)	**el nieto**	grandson
los padres	parents	**la prima**	cousin (*female*)
la hija	daughter	**el primo**	cousin (*male*)
el hijo	son	**la tía**	aunt
los hijos	children	**el tío**	uncle
la hermana	sister	**la sobrina**	niece
el hermano	brother	**el sobrino**	nephew
la esposa	wife	**Las mascotas**°	*Las... pets*
el esposo	husband		
la abuela	grandmother	**el gato**	cat
el abuelo	grandfather	**el pájaro**	bird
los abuelos	grandparents	**el perro**	dog

Vocabulario útil

el padrastro / la madrastra	stepfather/stepmother
el hijastro / la hijastra	stepson/stepdaughter
el hermanastro / la hermanastra	stepbrother/stepsister
el medio hermano / la media hermana	half-brother/half-sister
el suegro / la suegra	father-in-law/mother-in-law
el yerno / la nuera	son-in-law/daughter-in-law
el cuñado / la cuñada	brother-in-law/sister-in-law
…(ya) murió	. . . has (already) died

Conversación

▲▲▲▲▲▲▲▲▲

A. ¿Cierto o falso? Look at the drawing of the family tree that appears on page 68. Decide whether each of the following statements is true **(cierto)** or false **(falso)** according to the drawing. Correct the false statements.

1. José Jaime es el hermano de Marta.
2. Luisa es la abuela de Patricia.
3. Marta es la sobrina de Jaime y Elena.
4. Patricia y José Jaime son primos.
5. Elena es la tía de Manolo.
6. Jaime es el sobrino de José Jaime.
7. Manuel es el padre de Manolo y Elena.
8. Elena y Lola son las esposas de Jaime y Manolo, respectivamente.

B. ¿Quién es?

Paso 1. Complete las oraciones lógicamente.

1. La madre de mi (*my*) padre es mi _____.
2. El hijo de mi tío es mi _____.
3. La hermana de mi padre es mi _____.
4. El esposo de mi abuela es mi _____.

Paso 2. Ahora defina estas (*these*) personas, según (*according to*) el mismo (*same*) modelo.

1. prima   **2.** sobrino   **3.** tío   **4.** abuelo

C. Entrevista. Find out as much as you can about the family of a classmate using the following dialogue as a guide. Use **tengo** (*I have*) and **tienes** (*you have*), as indicated. Use **¿cuántos?** with male relations and **¿cuántas?** with females.

MODELO: E1:* ¿Cuántos hermanos tienes?
         E2: Bueno (*Well*), tengo seis hermanos y una hermana.
         E1: ¿Y cuántos primos?
         E2: ¡Uf! Tengo un montón (*bunch*). Más de veinte.

---

*From this point on in the text, ESTUDIANTE 1 and ESTUDIANTE 2 will be abbreviated as E1 and E2, respectively.

Vocabulario: Preparación

Adjetivos

guapo handsome, good-looking
bonito pretty
feo ugly

grande   pequeño

casado married
soltero single
simpático nice, likeable
antipático unpleasant

rubio   moreno

alto   bajo

corto short (*in length*)
largo long
bueno good
malo bad
listo smart, clever
tonto silly, foolish

trabajador   perezoso

joven   nuevo   viejo

rico rich
pobre poor
delgado thin, slender
gordo fat

To describe a masculine singular noun, use **alto**, **bajo**, and so on; use **alta**, **baja**, and so on for feminine singular nouns.

Conversación

A. Preguntas. Conteste según los dibujos.

1. Einstein es listo.
   ¿Y el chimpancé?

2. Roberto es trabajador.
   ¿Y José?

3. Pepe es bajo.
   ¿Y Pablo?

Satanás

el ángel

Ramón Ramírez

Paco Pereda

el libro

el lápiz

4. El ángel es bueno y simpático. También es guapo. ¿Y el demonio?

5. Ramón Ramírez es casado. También es viejo. ¿Y Paco Pereda?

6. El libro es viejo y corto. ¿Y el lápiz?

B. ¿Cómo es? Describe a famous personality, using as many adjectives as possible so that your classmates can guess who the person is. Don't forget to use cognate adjectives that you have seen in **Ante todo** and **Capítulo 1**.

MODELO: Es un hombre importante; controla una gran compañía de *software*. Es muy trabajador y muy rico. (Bill Gates)

Los números 31–100

Continúe la secuencia:

treinta y uno, treinta y dos. . .
ochenta y cuatro, ochenta y cinco...

31	treinta y uno	36	treinta y seis	50	cincuenta
32	treinta y dos	37	treinta y siete	60	sesenta
33	treinta y tres	38	treinta y ocho	70	setenta
34	treinta y cuatro	39	treinta y nueve	80	ochenta
35	treinta y cinco	40	cuarenta	90	noventa
				100	cien, ciento

¿Qué cuenta (*counts*) el perro?

Beginning with 31, Spanish numbers are *not* written in a combined form; **treinta y uno,*** **cuarenta y dos, sesenta y tres,** and so on must be three separate words.

Cien is used before nouns and in counting.

cien casas
noventa y ocho, noventa y nueve, **cien**

a (one) hundred houses
ninety-eight, ninety-nine, one hundred

---

*Remember that when **uno** is part of a compound number (**treinta y uno, cuarenta y uno,** and so on), it becomes **un** before a masculine noun and **una** before a feminine noun: **cincuenta y *una* mesas; setenta y *un* coches.**

Conversación

A. Más problemas de matemáticas. Recuerde: + **y**, − **menos**, = **son**.

1. 30 + 50 = ?	**4.** 77 + 23 = ?	**7.** 84 − 34 = ?
2. 45 + 45 = ?	**5.** 100 − 40 = ?	**8.** 78 − 36 = ?
3. 32 + 58 = ?	**6.** 99 − 39 = ?	**9.** 88 − 28 = ?

Nota cultural

Hispanic Last Names

In many Hispanic countries, people are given two last names
(**apellidos**) such as in the case of **Amalia *Lázaro Aguirre***. The first last
name (**Lázaro**) is that of Amalia's father; the second (**Aguirre**) is her
mother's. This system for assigning last names is characteristic of all
parts of the Spanish-speaking world, although it is not widely used by
Hispanics living in this country.

B. Los números de teléfono

Paso 1. Here are parts of several pages from Hispanic telephone books.
What can you tell about the names? (See the **Nota cultural** above.)

Paso 2. With a classmate, practice giving telephone numbers at random
from the list. Your partner will listen and identify the person. **¡OJO!** In many
Hispanic countries phone numbers are said differently than in this country.
Follow the model.

> MODELO: 4 – 15 – 00 – 46 →
>
> E1: Es el *cuatro-quince-cero cero-cuarenta y seis.*
> E2: Es el número de *A. Lázaro Aguirre.*

Paso 3. Now give your classmate your phone number and get his or hers.

> MODELO: Mi número es el...

```
LAZARO AGUIRRE, A. –Schez Pacheco, 17    415 0046
LAZCANO DEL MORAL, A. –E. Larreta, 14     215 8194
LAZCANO DEL MORAL, A. –Ibiza, 8 . . . .   274 6868
LEAL ANTON, J. –Pozo, 8 . . . . . . . . . . . . .  222 3894
LIEBANA RODRIGUEZ, A.
    Guadarrama, 10 . . . . . . . . . . . . . . . . .  463 2593
LOPEZ BARTOLOME, J. –Palma, 69 . . . . .  232 2027
LOPEZ CABRA, J. –E. Solana, 118 . . . . . .  407 5086
LOPEZ CABRA, J. –L. Van, 5 . . . . . . . . . .  776 4602
LOPEZ GONZALEZ, J. A. –Ibiza, 27 . . . . .  409 2552
LOPEZ GUTIERREZ, G. –S. Cameros, 7 . . .  478 8494
LOPEZ LOPEZ, J. –Alamedilla, 21 . . . . . .  227 3570
LOPEZ MARIN, V. –Illescas, 53 . . . . . . . . .  218 6630
LOPEZ MARIN, V. –N. Rey, 7 . . . . . . . . . .  463 6873
LOPEZ MARIN, V. –Valmojado, 289 . . . . .  717 2823
LOPEZ NUÑEZ, J. –Pl. Pinazo, s/n . . . . . .  796 0035
LOPEZ NUÑEZ, J. –Rocafort, Bl. 321 . . . . .  796 5387
LOPEZ RODRIGUEZ, C. –Pl. Jesus, 7 . . . . .  429 3278
LOPEZ RODRIGUEZ, J. –Pl. Angel, 15 . . . .  239 4323
LOPEZ RODRIGUEZ, M. E.
    B. Murillo, 104 . . . . . . . . . . . . . . . . .  233 4239
LOPEZ TRAPERO, A. –Cam. Ingenieros, 1 .  462 5392
LOPEZ VAZQUEZ, J. –A. Torrejón, 17 . . . .  433 4646
LOPEZ VEGA, J. –M. Santa Ana, 5 . . . . . .  231 2131
LORENTE VILLARREAL, G. –Gandia, 7 . . .  252 2758
LORENZO MARTINEZ, A. –Moscareta, 5 . .  479 6282
LORENZO MARTINEZ, A. –P. Laborde, 21   778 2800
LORENZO MARTINEZ, A.
    Av. S. Diego, 116 . . . . . . . . . . . . . . .  477 1040
LOSADA MIRON, M. –Padilla, 31 . . . . . . .  276 9373
LOSADA MIRON, M. –Padilla, 31 . . . . . . .  431 7461
LOZANO GUILLEN, E.
    Juan H. Mendoza, 5 . . . . . . . . . . . . . .  250 3884
LOZANO PIERA, F. J. –Pinguino, 8 . . . . . .  466 3205
LUDEÑA FLORES, G. –Lope Rueda, 56 . . .  273 3735
LUENGO CHAMORRO, J.
    Gral Ricardos, 99 . . . . . . . . . . . . . . .  471 4906
LUQUE CASTILLO, J. –Pto Arlaban, 121 . .  478 5253
LUQUE CASTILLO, L. –Cardeñosa, 15 . . . .  477 6644
```

Expressing Age

NIETA: ¿Cuántos años tienes, abuela?
ABUELA: Setenta y tres, Nora.
NIETA: ¿Y cuántos años tiene el abuelo?
ABUELA: Setenta y cinco, mi amor (*love*). Y ahora, dime (*tell me*), ¿cuántos años tienes tú?
NIETA: Tengo tres.

In Spanish, age is expressed with the phrase **tener** _____ **años** (literally, *to have. . . years*). You have now seen all the singular forms of **tener** (*to have*): **tengo, tienes, tiene.**

C. ¡Seamos (*Let's be*) **lógicos!** Complete las oraciones lógicamente.

1. Un hombre que (*who*) tiene noventa años es muy ~~viejo~~.
2. Un niño (*small child*) que tiene sólo un año es muy ~~joven~~.
3. La persona más vieja (*oldest*) de mi familia es mi ~~abuela~~. Tiene ~~ochenta y cinco~~ años.
4. La persona más joven de mi familia es mi _____. Tiene ~~nueve~~ años.
5. En mi opinión, es ideal tener ~~veinte~~ años. ~~sobrino~~
6. Cuando una persona tiene ~~18 tres~~ años, ya es adulta. ~~dieciocho~~
7. Para (*In order to*) tomar cerveza en este estado, es necesario tener ~~21~~ años. ~~veintiuno~~
8. Para mí (*for me*), ¡la idea de tener ~~70~~ años es inconcebible (*inconceivable*)! ~~setenta~~

Pronunciación: Stress and Written Accent Marks (Part 1)

By now you will have noticed that some Spanish words have *written accent marks* over one of the vowels. That mark is called **el acento** (**ortográfico**). It means that the syllable containing the accented vowel is stressed when the word is pronounced, as in the word **bolígrafo** (**bo-LI-gra-fo**), for example.

Although all Spanish words of more than one syllable have a stressed vowel, most words do not have a written accent mark. Most words have the spoken stress exactly where native speakers of Spanish would predict it. These two simple rules tell you which syllable is accented when a word does not have a written accent.

> In this chapter you will learn predictable patterns of stress. In the next chapter, you will learn when the written accent mark is needed.

- Words that end in a vowel, or **-n,** or **-s** are stressed on the next-to-last syllable.

co-sa	e-**xa**-men	i-ta-**lia**-no
gra-cias	**e**-res	**len**-guas

- Words that end in any other consonant are stressed on the last syllable.

us-**ted**	es-pa-**ñol**	doc-**tor**
na-tu-**ral**	pro-fe-**sor**	es-**tar**

A. Sílabas. The following words have been separated into syllables for you. Read them aloud, paying careful attention to where the spoken stress should fall.

1. Stress on the next-to-last syllable

chi-no	me-sa	li-bro	cien-cias
ar-te	si-lla	con-se-je-ra	o-ri-gen
cla-se	Car-men	li-te-ra-tu-ra	com-pu-ta-do-ra

2. Stress on the last syllable

se-ñor	ac-tor	li-ber-tad	lu-gar
mu-jer	co-lor	ge-ne-ral	u-ni-ver-si-dad
fa-vor	po-pu-lar	sen-ti-men-tal	con-trol

B. Vocales. Indicate the stressed vowel in each of the following words.

1. mo-chi-la	**4.** i-gual-men-te	**7.** li-be-ral
2. me-nos	**5.** E-cua-dor	**8.** hu-ma-ni-dad
3. re-gu-lar	**6.** e-le-gán-te	

Minidiálogos y gramática

¿Recuerda Ud.?

Before beginning Grammar Section 5, review the forms and uses of **ser** that you have already learned by answering these questions.

1. ¿Es Ud. estudiante o profesor(a)?

2. ¿Cómo es Ud.? ¿Es una persona sentimental? ¿inteligente? ¿paciente? ¿elegante?

3. ¿Qué hora es? ¿A qué hora es la clase de español?

4. ¿Qué es un hospital? ¿Es una persona? ¿una cosa? ¿un edificio?

5 Expressing *to be* • Present Tense of *ser;* Summary of Uses

Presentaciones

— Hola. Me llamo Manolo Durán.

- *Soy* profesor en la universidad.
- *Soy* alto y moreno.
- *Soy* de Sevilla, España.

— ¿Y Lola Benítez, mi esposa? Complete la descripción de ella.

Es ___ (profesión).
Es ___ y ___ (descripción).
Es de ___ (origen).

Málaga, España
bonita
profesora
delgada

As you know, there are two Spanish verbs that mean *to be:* **ser** and **estar.** They are not interchangeable; the meaning that the speaker wishes to convey determines their use. In this chapter, you will review the uses of **ser** that you already know and learn some new ones. Remember to use **estar** to express location and to ask how someone is feeling. You will learn more about the uses of **estar** in **Capítulo 5.**

A. Here are some basic language functions of **ser.** You have used or seen all of them already in this and previous chapters.

ser (*to be*)			
yo	**soy**	nosotros/as	**somos**
tú	**eres**	vosotros/as	**sois**
Ud.		Uds.	
él	**es**	ellos	**son**
ella		ellas	

- To *identify* people and things

  [Práctica A]

  When you see a note in brackets [**Práctica A**] here, it refers you to that exercise for the grammar point. In this case, Exercise A (page 76) in the next **Práctica** section will allow you to practice this point.

Yo soy **estudiante.**
Alicia y yo somos **amigas.**
La doctora Ramos es **profesora.**
Esto (*This*) es **un libro.**

- To *describe* people and things*

Soy **sentimental.**
I'm sentimental (a sentimental person).

El coche es **muy viejo.**
The car is very old.

- With **de,** to express *origin*

[Práctica B–C]

Somos **de los Estados Unidos,** pero nuestros padres son **de la Argentina. ¿De dónde** es Ud.?
We're from the United States, but our parents are from Argentina. Where are you from?

- To express *generalizations* (only **es**)

[Conversación B]

Es **importante** estudiar, pero no es **necesario** estudiar todos los días.
It's important to study, but it's not necessary to study every day.

B. Here are two basic language functions of **ser** that you have not yet practiced.

- With **de,** to express *possession*

[Práctica D]

Es el perro **de Carla.**
It's Carla's dog.

Note that there is no **'s** in Spanish.

Son las gatas **de Jorge.**
They're Jorge's (female) cats.

OJO

The masculine singular article **el** contracts with the preposition **de** to form **del.** No other article contracts with **de.**

Es la casa **del** profesor.
It's the (male) professor's house.

Es la casa **de la** profesora.
It's the (female) professor's house.

de + el → del

- With **para,** to tell for whom or what something *is intended*

[Conversación A]

¿*Romeo y Julieta?* Es **para** la clase de inglés.
Romeo and Juliet? It's for English class.

_____ ¿**Para** quién son los regalos?
_____ (Son) **Para** mi nieto.
Who are the presents for?
(They're) For my grandson.

Práctica

▲▲▲▲▲

A. Los parientes de Manolo. Look back at the family tree on page 68. Then tell whether the following statements are true **(cierto)** or false **(falso)** from Manolo's standpoint. Correct the false statements.

*You will practice this language function of **ser** in Grammar 7 in this chapter and in subsequent chapters.

1. Lola y yo somos hermanos.
2. Mi esposa es la prima de Patricia.
3. Manuel y Luisa son mis (*my*) padres.
4. José Jaime es mi sobrino.
5. Mi hermana es la esposa de Jaime.
6. Mi padre no es abuelo todavía (*yet*).
7. Mi familia no es muy grande.

B. Nacionalidades

Paso 1. ¿De dónde son, según los nombres y apellidos?

Naciones: Francia, México, Italia, los Estados Unidos, Inglaterra (*England*), Alemania (*Germany*)

1. John Doe	3. Graziana Lazzarino	5. Claudette Moreau
2. Karl Lotze	4. María Gómez	6. Timothy Windsor

Paso 2. Ahora, ¿de dónde es Ud.? ¿de este estado? ¿de una metrópoli? ¿de un área rural? ¿Es Ud. de una ciudad (*city*) que tiene un nombre hispano? ¿Es de otro país (*another country*)?

C. Personas extranjeras

Paso 1. ¿Quiénes son, de dónde son y dónde trabajan ahora?

MODELO: Teresa: actriz / de Madrid / en Cleveland →
Teresa es actriz. Es de Madrid. Ahora trabaja en Cleveland.

1. Carlos Miguel: médico (*doctor*) / de Cuba / en Milwaukee
2. Maripili: profesora / de Burgos / en Miami
3. Mariela: dependienta / de Buenos Aires / en Nueva York
4. Juan: dentista* / de Lima / en Los Ángeles

Paso 2. Ahora hable sobre (*about*) un amigo o pariente suyo (*of yours*) según el **Paso 1**.

D. ¡Seamos (*Let's be*) **lógicos!** ¿De quién son estas cosas? Con un compañero/una compañera, haga y conteste preguntas (*ask and answer questions*) según el modelo.

MODELO: E1: ¿De quién es el perro?
E2: Es de…

Personas: las estudiantes, la actriz, el niño, la familia con diez hijos, el estudiante extranjero, los señores Schmidt

¿De quién es/son. . .?

1. la casa en Beverly Hills	4. el perro
2. la casa en Viena	5. las fotos de la Argentina
3. la camioneta (*station wagon*)	6. las mochilas con todos los libros

---

*A number of professions end in **-ista** in both masculine and feminine forms. The article indicates gender: **el/la dentista, el/la artista,** and so on.

Explaining Your Reasons

In conversation, it is often necessary to explain a decision, tell why someone did something, and so on. Here are some simple words and phrases that speakers use to offer explanations.

porque because

— ¿Por qué necesitamos un televisor nuevo?

— Pues... **para** mirar el partido de fútbol... ¡Es el campeonato!

— ¿Por qué trabajas tanto?

— ¡**Porque** necesitamos el dinero!

para in order to

Why do we need a new TV set?

Well . . . (in order) to watch the soccer game . . . It's the championship!

Why do you work so much?
Because we need the money!

Note the differences between **porque** (one word, no accent) and the interrogative **¿por qué?**

Conversación

▲▲▲▲▲▲▲

A. **El regalo ideal.** The first column below lists gifts that Diego would like to give to certain members of his family, listed in the second column. For him, money is no object! Decide who receives each gift, and explain your decisions by using the additional information included about the family members.

MODELO: _____ es para _____ →
    El dinero es para Carmina, la hermana. Ella desea estudiar en otro estado. Por eso necesita el dinero.

REGALOS

1. la calculadora
2. los libros de literatura clásica
3. los discos compactos de Andrés Segovia
4. el televisor
5. el radio
6. el dinero

MIEMBROS DE LA FAMILIA

a. José, el padre: Le gusta escuchar las noticias (*news*).
b. Julián y María, los abuelos: Les gusta mucho la música de guitarra clásica.
c. Carmen, la madre: Le gusta mirar programas cómicos.
d. Joey, el hermano: Le gustan mucho las historias viejas.
e. Carmina, la hermana: Desea estudiar en otro estado.
f. Raulito, el primo: Le gustan las matemáticas.

B. ¿Qué opinas? Exprese opiniones originales, afirmativas o negativas, con estas palabras.

(No)
- Es importante
- Es muy práctico
- Es necesario
- Es tonto (*foolish*)
- Es fascinante
- Es una lata (*pain, drag*)
- Es posible

- mirar la televisión todos los días
- hablar español en la clase
- tener muchas mascotas
- llegar (*to arrive*) a clase puntualmente
- tomar cerveza en clase
- hablar con los animales / las plantas
- tomar mucho café y fumar cigarrillos
- trabajar dieciocho horas al día
- tener muchos hermanos
- ser amable con todos los miembros de la familia
- estar en las fiestas familiares
- pasar mucho tiempo con la familia

6 Expressing Possession • Possessive Adjectives (Unstressed)*

La familia de Carlos IV (cuarto)

La familia de Carlos IV, un rey español del siglo XVIII. En el cuadro están su esposa, sus hijos… ¿y sus padres y sus abuelos? ¿Quiénes son las personas a la izquierda del rey?

¿Tiene Ud. una foto reciente de su familia? ¿Quiénes están en la foto?

You have already seen and used several possessive adjectives in Spanish. Here is the complete set.

Possessive Adjectives

my	**mi** libro/mesa **mis** libros/mesas	*our*	nuestro libro nuestra mesa nuestros libros nuestras mesas
your	**tu** libro/mesa **tus** libros/mesas	*your*	vuestro libro vuestra mesa vuestros libros vuestras mesas
your, his, *her, its*	**su** libro/mesa **sus** libros/mesas	*your,* *their*	**su** libro/mesa **sus** libros/mesas

---

Carlos IV's Family   The family of Carlos IV, an 18th century Spanish king. In the painting are his wife, his children… and his parents and grandparents? Who are the people to the left of the king?

*Another kind of possessive is called the stressed possessive adjective. It can be used as a noun. You will learn more about using stressed possessive adjectives in Grammar 49.

In Spanish, the ending of a possessive adjective agrees in form with the person or thing possessed, not with the owner or possessor. Note that these possessive adjectives are placed before the noun.

The possessive adjectives **mi(s)**, **tu(s)**, and **su(s)** show agreement in number only with the nouns they modify **Nuestro/a/os/as** and **vuestro/a/os/as**, like all adjectives that end in **-o**, show agreement in both number and gender.

The possessive adjectives **vuestro/a/os/as** are used extensively in Spain, but are not common in Latin America.

OJO

Su(s) can have several different equivalents in English: *your* (*sing.*), *his*, *her*, *its*, *your* (*pl.*), and *their*. Usually its meaning will be clear in context. When context does not make the meaning of **su(s)** clear, **de** and a pronoun are used instead, to indicate the possessor.

Son $\begin{Bmatrix} mis \\ tus \\ sus \end{Bmatrix}$ cuadernos.

Es $\begin{Bmatrix} nuestra \\ vuestra \\ su \end{Bmatrix}$ casa.

el coche
la casa $\Big\}$ de él (de ella, de Ud., de
los libros   ellos, de ellas, de Uds.)
las mesas

¿Son jóvenes los hijos **de él?**
Are his children young?

¿Dónde vive el abuelo **de ellas?**
Where does their grandfather live?

Práctica

▲▲▲▲▲▲

A. Posesiones. Which nouns can these possessive adjectives modify without changing form?

1. su: problema primos dinero tías escritorios familia
2. tus: perro idea hijos profesoras abuelo examen
3. mi: ventana médicos cuarto coche abuela gatos
4. sus: animales oficina nietas padre hermana abuelo
5. nuestras: guitarra libro materias lápiz sobrinas tía
6. nuestro: gustos consejeros parientes puerta clase residencia

B. ¿Cómo es la familia de Carlos IV?

Paso 1. Mire la ilustración de Carlos IV y su familia en la página 77. Conteste según el modelo.

MODELO: familia / grande →
Su familia es grande

1. hijo pequeño / guapo
2. esposa / fea
3. retrato (*portrait*) / bueno
4. hijas / solteras
5. familia / importante y rica

Paso 2. Imagine que Ud. es Carlos IV. Cambie las respuestas (*answers*) del 1 al 3.

MODELO: hijo pequeño / guapo → Mi hijo pequeño es guapo.

Paso 3. Imagine que Ud. es la esposa de Carlos IV y hable por (*for*) Ud. y por su esposo. Cambie las respuestas del 3 al 5.

MODELO: retrato / bueno →
Nuestro retrato es bueno.

Conversación
▲▲▲▲▲▲▲

A. **Entrevista.** You have already learned a great deal about the families of your classmates and instructor. This interview will help you gather more information. Use the questions as a guide to interview your instructor or a classmate and take notes on what he or she says. (Use **tu[s]** when interviewing a classmate.) Then report the information to the class.

1. ¿Cómo es su familia? ¿grande? ¿pequeña? ¿Cuántas personas viven (*live*) en su casa?
2. ¿Son simpáticos sus padres? ¿generosos? ¿cariñosos (*caring*)?
3. ¿Cuántos hijos tienen (*have*) sus padres? ¿Cuántos años tienen?
4. ¿Cómo son sus hermanos? ¿inteligentes? ¿traviesos (*mischievous*)? ¿trabajadores? Si (*If*) son muy jóvenes, ¿prefieren (*do they prefer*) estudiar o mirar la televisión? Si son mayores (*older*), ¿trabajan o estudian? ¿Dónde?
5. ¿Tiene Ud. (*Do you have*) esposo/a (compañero/a de cuarto)? ¿Cómo es? ¿Trabaja o estudia?

B. **Asociaciones.** Working with several classmates, see how many words you can associate with the following phrases. Everyone in the group must agree with the associations decided on. Remember to use the words and phrases you know to agree or disagree with the suggestions of others.

MODELO: nuestro país →
Nuestro país es _____. (En nuestro país hay _____. En nuestro país uno puede [*can*] _____.)

1. nuestro país
2. nuestra clase de español
3. nuestra universidad (librería)
4. nuestra ciudad (nuestro estado)
5. el centro de nuestra ciudad

Describing • Adjectives: Gender, Number, and Position

Un poema sencillo

Amigo		Amiga
Fiel		Fiel
Amable		Amable
Simpático		Simpática
¡Lo admiro!		¡La admiro!

According to their form, which of the adjectives below can be used to describe each person? Which can refer to you?

Marta:
Mario: { fiel   amable   simpática   simpático

Adjectives (**Los adjetivos**) are words used to talk about nouns or pronouns. Adjectives may describe or tell how many there are.

You have been using adjectives to describe people since **Ante todo**. In this section, you will learn more about describing the people and things around you.

 adjective = a word used to describe a noun or pronoun

large desk   *few* desks
tall woman   *several* women

Adjectives with *ser*

In Spanish, forms of **ser** are used with adjectives that describe basic, inherent qualities or characteristics of the nouns or pronouns they modify.

Tú **eres amable.**
You're nice. (You're a nice person.)

El diccionario **es barato.**
The dictionary is inexpensive.

A simple poem Friend Loyal Kind Nice I admire him/her!

Spanish adjectives agree in gender and number with the noun or pronoun they modify. Each adjective has more than one form.

A. Adjectives that end in **-o (alto)** have four forms, showing gender and number.*

	Masculine	Feminine
Singular	amigo al**to**	amiga al**ta**
Plural	amigos al**tos**	amigas al**tas**

B. Adjectives that end in **-e (inteligente)** or in most consonants (**fiel**) have only two forms, a singular and a plural form. The plural of adjectives is formed in the same way as that of nouns.

[Práctica A–D]

	Masculine	Feminine
Singular	amigo inteligent**e**	amiga inteligent**e**
	amigo fiel	amiga fiel
Plural	amigos inteligent**es**	amigas inteligent**es**
	amigos fiel**es**	amigas fiel**es**

C. Most adjectives of nationality have four forms.

The names of many languages—which are masculine in gender—are the same as the masculine singular form of the corresponding adjective of nationality **el español, el inglés, el alemán, el francés,** and so on.

[Práctica E]

Note that in Spanish the names of languages and adjectives of nationality are not capitalized, but the names of countries are: **español, española,** but **España.**

	Masculine	Feminine
Singular	el doctor mexicano	la doctora mexicana
	español	española
	alemán	alemana
	inglés	inglesa
Plural	los doctores mexicanos	las doctoras mexicanas
	españoles	españolas
	alemanes	alemanas
	ingleses	inglesas

As you have probably noticed, adjectives do not always precede the noun in Spanish as they do in English. Note the following rules for adjective placement.

A. Adjectives of quantity, like numbers, *precede* the noun, as do the interrogatives **¿cuánto/a?** and **¿cuántos/as?**

Hay **muchas** sillas y **dos** escritorios.
There are many chairs and two desks.

¿Cuánto dinero necesitas?
How much money do you need?

---

*Adjectives that end in **-dor, -ón, -án,** and **-ín** also have four forms: **trabajador, trabajadora, trabajadores, trabajadoras.**

Otro/a by itself means *another* or *other*. The indefinite article is never used with **otro/a**.	Busco **otro** coche *I'm looking for another car.*

B. Adjectives that describe the qualities of a noun and distinguish it from others generally *follow* the noun. Adjectives of nationality are included in this category.

un perro **bueno**
un dependiente **trabajador**
una joven **delgada** y **morena**
un joven **español**

C. The adjectives **bueno** and **malo** may precede or follow the noun they modify. When they precede a masculine singular noun, they shorten to **buen** and **mal** respectively.

[Práctica D]

un **buen** perro / un perro **bueno**
una **buena** perra / una perra **buena**
un **mal** día / un día **malo**
una **mala** noche / una noche **mala**

D. The adjective **grande** may also precede or follow the noun. When it precedes a singular noun—masculine or feminine—it shortens to **gran** and means *great* or *impressive*. When it follows the noun, it means *large* or *big*.

[Conversación]

Nueva York es una ciudad **grande**.
New York is a large city.
Nueva York es una **gran** ciudad.
New York is a great (impressive) city.

Forms of *this/these*

A. The demonstrative adjective *this/these* has four forms in Spanish.* Learn to recognize them when you see them.

este hijo	*this son*
esta hija	*this daughter*
estos hijos	*these sons*
estas hijas	*these daughters*

B. You have already seen the neuter demonstrative **esto**. It refers to something that is as yet unidentified.

¿Qué es esto?
What is this?

Práctica
▲▲▲▲▲▲

A. La familia de José Miguel. The following incomplete sentences describe some members of the family of José Miguel Martín Velasco, a student from Quito, Ecuador. For each item, scan through the adjectives to see which ones can complete the statement. Pay close attention to the form of each adjective.

   1. El tío Miguel es _____ (trabajador / alto / nueva / grande / fea / amable)

---

*You will learn all forms of the Spanish demonstrative adjectives (*this, that, these, those*) in Grammar 9.

2. Los abuelos son _____. (rubio / antipático / inteligentes / viejos / religiosos / sinceras)
3. La madre de José Miguel es _____. (rubio / elegante /sentimental / buenas / casadas / simpática)
4. Las primas son _____. (solteras / morenas / lógica / bajos / mala)

Vocabulario útil

Here are some additional adjectives to use in this section. You should be able to guess the meaning of some of them.

agresivo/a	¿ ?	**difícil**	difficult
amistoso/a	friendly	**encantador(a)**	delightful
animado/a	lively	**fácil**	easy
atrevido/a	daring	**sensible**	sensitive
cariñoso/a	affectionate	**suficiente**	¿ ?
chistoso/a	amusing	**tolerante**	¿ ?
comprensivo/a	understanding	**travieso/a**	mischievous

B. **Hablando** (*Speaking*) **de la universidad.** Tell what you think about aspects of your university by telling whether you agree (**Estoy de acuerdo.**) or disagree (**No estoy de acuerdo.**) with the statements. If you don't have an opinion, say **No tengo opinión.**

1. Hay suficientes actividades sociales.
2. Los profesores son excelentes.
3. Las residencias son buenas.
4. Hay suficientes gimnasios.
5. Es fácil aparcar el coche.
6. Es fácil llegar a la universidad en autobús.
7. Hay suficientes zonas verdes.
8. Los restaurantes, cafeterías y cafés son buenos.
9. En la librería, los precios son bajos.
10. Los bibliotecarios son cooperativos.

C. **Descripciones.** Describa a su familia, haciendo oraciones completas con estas palabras.

Mi familia		interesante, importante,
Mi padre/madre		amable, (im)paciente,
Mi ¿ ? (otro pariente)	(no) es	grande, ¿ ?
Mi perro/gato		intelectual, fiel, ¿ ?
		nuevo, viejo, pequeño, bueno,
		malo, famoso, ¿ ?
	tiene	…años

D. **¡Dolores es igual!** Cambie Diego → Dolores.

Diego es un buen estudiante. Es listo y trabajador y estudia mucho. Es estadounidense de origen mexicano, y por eso habla español. Desea ser profesor de antropología. Diego es moreno, guapo y atlético. Le gustan las fiestas grandes y tiene buenos amigos en la universidad. Tiene parientes estadounidenses y mexicanos

E. Nacionalidades. Tell what nationality the following persons could be and where they might live: **Portugal, Alemania, China, Inglaterra, España, Francia, Italia.**

1. Monique habla francés; es _____ y vive (*she lives*) en _____.
2. José habla español; es _____ y vive en _____.
3. Greta y Hans hablan alemán; son _____ y viven en _____.
4. Gilberto habla portugués; es _____ y vive en _____.
5. Gina y Sofía hablan italiano; son _____ y viven en _____.
6. Winston habla inglés; es _____ y vive en _____.
7. Hai (*m.*) y Han (*m.*) hablan chino; son _____ y viven en _____.

Conversación

Asociaciones: With several classmates, how many names can you associate with the following phrases? To introduce your suggestions, you can say **Creo que (_____ es un gran hombre).** To express agreement or disagreement, use **(No) Estoy de acuerdo.**

1. un mal restaurante
2. un buen programa de televisión
3. una gran mujer, un gran hombre
4. un buen libro (¿una novela?), un libro horrible

En los Estados Unidos y el Canadá...

La famosa familia Iglesias

Two generations of the Iglesias family now live in the United States: Julio Iglesias, who moved to the U.S. in the early 1980's, and all his children. Like their father, Julio's eldest children, Chabeli (Isabel), Julio, and Enrique, were born in Spain. They started spending most of the year in the U.S. when their father moved to Miami in 1982.

Some people consider Julio Iglesias (1943–) to be one of the most famous singers in the world. In countries that speak Spanish, English, and Portuguese, he has been a major celebrity for almost 20 years. His crossover to the English language musical scene happened in 1984.

Now his oldest sons are following his steps. Enrique (1975–) started his own career at age 20, and has already won a Grammy for the best Latin pop singer. His older brother, Julio Jr. (1973–), recently began singing professionally, after having worked as an actor and a model. Their sister Chabeli is a TV host for the Univision channel.

8 Expressing Actions • Present Tense of *-er;* and *-ir* Verbs; More About Subject Pronouns

Diego se presenta.

Hola. Me llamo Diego González. Soy estudiante de UCLA, pero este
año *asisto* a la Universidad Nacional Autónoma de México. *Vivo* con mi
tía Matilde en la Ciudad de México. *Como* pizza con frecuencia y *bebo*
cerveza en las fiestas. Me gusta la ropa de moda; por eso *recibo* varios
catálogos. *Leo* muchos libros de antropología para mi especialización.
También *escribo* muchas cartas a mi familia. *Creo* que una educación
universitaria es muy importante. Por eso estudio y *aprendo* mucho.
¡Pero *comprendo* también que es muy importante estar con los amigos
y con la familia!

¿Es Diego un estudiante típico? ¿Cómo es Ud.? Adapte las oraciones
de Diego a su conveniencia.

Verbs That End in *-er* and *-ir*

A. The present tense of **-er** and **-ir** verbs is
formed by adding personal endings to the
stem of the verb (the infinitive minus its **-er/
-ir** ending). The personal endings for **-er** and
-ir verbs are the same except for the first and
second person plural.

comer (*to eat*)		vivir (*to live*)	
como	comemos	vivo	vivimos
comes	coméis	vives	vivís
come	comen	vive	viven

Diego introduces himself. Hello. My name is Diego González. I'm a student at UCLA, but this
year I attend the Universidad Nacional Autónoma de México. I live with my aunt Matilde in
Mexico City. I eat pizza frequently and I drink beer at parties. I like the latest fashions; that's why I
receive various catalogues. I read lots of anthropology books for my major. I also write a lot of
letters to my family. I think that a university education is very important. That's why I study and
learn a lot. But I also understand that it's very important to be with friends and family!

B. Some frequently used -**er** and -**ir** verbs in this chapter include those on the right.

-er verbs		*-ir* verbs	
aprender	to learn	abrir	to open
beber	to drink	asistir (a)	to attend, go to
comer	to eat		(*a class, function*)
comprender	to understand	escribir	to write
creer (en)	to think, believe (in)	recibir	to receive
deber (+ *inf.*)	should, must, ought	vivir	to live
	to (*do something*)		
leer	to read		
vender	to sell		

Remember that the Spanish present tense has a number of present tense equivalents in English and can also be used to express future meaning.

como = *I eat, I am eating, I will eat*

Use and Omission of Subject Pronouns

In English, a verb must have an expressed subject (a noun or pronoun): *she says,* **the train** *arrives.* In Spanish, however, as you have probably noticed, an expressed subject is not required. Verbs are accompanied by a subject pronoun only for clarification, emphasis, or contrast.

- *Clarification:* When the context does not make the subject clear, the subject pronoun is expressed. This happens most frequently with third person singular and plural verb forms.

Ud./él/ella vende
Uds./ellos/ellas venden

- *Emphasis:* Subject pronouns are used in Spanish to emphasize the subject when in English you would stress it with your voice.

—¿Quién debe pagar?
—¡**Tú** debes pagar!
Who should pay?
You *should pay!*

- *Contrast:* Contrast is a special case of emphasis. Subject pronouns are used to contrast the actions of two individuals or groups.

Ellos leen mucho; **nosotros** leemos poco.
They *read a lot;* ***we*** *read little.*

Práctica

▲▲▲▲▲▲

A. En la clase de español

Paso 1. Read the following statements and tell whether they are true for your classroom environment. If any statement is not true for you or your class, make it negative or change it in another way to make it correct.

MODELO: Bebo café en clase. → Sí, bebo café en clase.
(No, no bebo café en clase. Bebo café en casa.)

1. Debo estudiar más para esta clase.
2. Leo todas las partes de las lecciones.
3. Comprendo bien cuando mi profesor / profesora habla.
4. Asisto al laboratorio con frecuencia.
5. Debemos abrir más los libros en clase.
6. Escribimos mucho en esta clase.
7. Aprendemos a hablar español en esta clase.*
8. Vendemos nuestros libros al final del año (*year*).

Paso 2. Now turn to the person next to you and rephrase each sentence, using **tú** forms of the verbs. Your partner will indicate whether the sentences are true for him or her.

MODELO: Debes estudiar más para esta clase, ¿verdad (*right*)? →
Sí, debo estudiar más.
(No, no debo estudiar más.)
(No. Debo estudiar más para la clase de matemáticas.)

B. Diego habla de su padre. Complete este párrafo con la forma correcta de los verbos entre paréntesis.

Mi padre (vender[1]) coches y trabaja mucho. Mis hermanos y yo (aprender[2]) mucho de papá. Según mi padre, los jóvenes (deber[3]) (asistir[4]) a clase todos los días, porque es su[a] obligación. Papá también (creer[5]) que no es necesario mirar la televisión por la noche. Es más interesante (leer[6]) el periódico[b] o un buen libro. Por eso nosotros (leer[7]) o (escribir[8]) por la noche y no miramos la televisión mucho. Yo admiro mucho a[†] mi papá y (creer[9]) que él (comprender[10]) la importancia de la educación.

[a]*their* [b]*newspaper*

C. Un sábado (*Saturday*) en Sevilla. Using all the cues given, form complete sentences about Manolo's narration about a certain Saturday at home with his family. Make any changes and add words when necessary. When the subject pronoun is in parentheses, do not use it in the sentence.

1. yo / leer / periódico
2. mi hija, Marta / mirar / televisión
3. también / (ella) escribir / composición
4. mi esposa, Lola / abrir / y / leer / cartas
5. ¡hoy / (nosotros) recibir / carta / tío Ricardo!
6. (él) ser de / España / pero / ahora / vivir / México
7. ¡ay! / ser / dos / de / tarde
8. ¡(nosotros) / deber / comer / ahora!

---

*Note: **aprender** + **a** + infinitive = to learn how to (*do something*)

[†]Note the use of **a** here. In this context, the word **a** has no equivalent in English. It is used in Spanish before a direct object that is a specific person. You will learn more about this use of **a** in **Capítulo 6.** Until then, the exercises and activities in *Puntos de partida* will indicate when to use it.

Conversación

Telling How Frequently You Do Things

Use the following words and phrases to tell how often you perform an activity. Some of them will already be familiar to you.

todos los días, siempre	every day, always
con frecuencia	frequently
a veces	at times
una vez a la semana	once a week
casi nunca	almost never
nunca	never

Hablo con mis amigos **todos los días**. Hablo con mis padres **una vez a la semana**. **Casi nunca** hablo con mis abuelos. Y **nunca** hablo con mis tíos que viven en Italia.

For now, use the expressions **casi nunca** and **nunca** only at the beginning of a sentence. You will learn more about how to use them in Grammar 19.

A. ¿Con qué frecuencia?

Paso 1. How frequently do you do the following things?

	CON FRECUENCIA	A VECES	CASI NUNCA	NUNCA
1. Asisto al laboratorio de lenguas (o uso las cintas [*tapes*]).	☐	☐	☒	☐
2. Recibo cartas.	☐	☐	☒	☐
3. Escribo poemas.	☐	☐	☐	☒
4. Leo novelas románticas.	☐	☐	☒	☐
5. Como en una pizzería.	☐	☒	☐	☐
6. Recibo y leo catálogos.	☐	☒	☐	☐
7. Aprendo palabras nuevas en español.	☒	☐	☐	☐
8. Asisto a todas las clases.	☒	☐	☐	☐
9. Compro regalos para los amigos.	☐	☒	☐	☐
10. Vendo los libros al final del semestre/trimestre.	☒	☐	☐	☐

Paso 2. Now compare your answers with those of a classmate. Then answer the following questions. (*Note:* **los/las dos** = *both* [*of us*]; **ninguno/a** = *neither*)

	YO	MI COMPAÑERO/A	LOS/LAS DOS	NINGUNO/A
1. ¿Quién es muy estudioso/a?	☒	☐	☐	☐
2. ¿Quién come mucha pizza?	☐	☐	☒	☐
3. ¿Quién compra muchas cosas?	☐	☐	☐	☒
4. ¿Quién es muy romántico/a?	☐	☐	☒	☐
5. ¿Quién recibe mucho (*a lot*) por correo (*by mail*)?	☐	☐	☐	☒

B. ¿Qué hacen? (*What do they do?*) Form complete sentences using one word or phrase from each column. Be sure to use the correct form of the verbs. Make any of the sentences negative if you wish.

yo	abrir	novelas de ciencia ficción/de horror
tú, estudiante	leer	la situación/los problemas de los estudiantes
Ud., profesor(a)	escribir	el periódico/una revista (*magazine*) todos los días
los estudiantes de aquí	beber	Coca-Cola/café/cerveza antes de (*before*) la clase
los hombres / las mujeres	vender	mi ropa (*clothing*), un estéreo viejo
un consejero	comprender	la puerta para las mujeres / los hombres
mis padres/hijos	recibir	
me gusta	vivir	mucho/poco
	deber	
	¿ ?	muchas/pocas cartas, novelas, revistas
		muchos/pocos ejercicios, libros, regalos

en una casa / un apartamento / una residencia
en otra ciudad, en otro estado/país
en un cuaderno / con un bolígrafo / con un lápiz

mirar mucho la televisión
llegar a casa temprano

Videoteca

ECUADOR

Minidramas

In this **Minidramas** dialogue, which takes place in Quito, Ecuador, Paloma Velasco introduces her boyfriend Gustavo to her aunt Elisa. How do you greet your friends' parents?

Suena el timbre[a] *en casa de Elisa Velasco. La criada*[b] *contesta la puerta y Paloma entra.*

FUNCTION

introductions

PALOMA: ¡Buenas tardes, tía Elisa!
ELISA: ¡Hola! ¡Adelante![c]
PALOMA: Tía, quiero presentarte a mi novio,[d] Gustavo. Gustavo, esta es mi tía, Elisa Velasco.
GUSTAVO: Mucho gusto en conocerla,[e] señora.
ELISA: El gusto es mío,[f] Gustavo.
PALOMA: Y ya conoces a[g] mi primo José Miguel.
JOSÉ MIGUEL: ¿Qué tal?
GUSTAVO: ¡Hola!

[a]Suena... *The doorbell rings* [b]*maid* [c]*Come on in!* [d]quiero... *I'd like to introduce you to my boyfriend* [e]en... *to meet you* [f]*mine*
[g]ya... *you already know*

Con un compañero / una compañera

With other students, practice making the following introductions, using formal or informal phrases, as appropriate. Tell something about the person you are introducing.

1. You are at home, and a good friend stops by for a few minutes. Introduce him or her to your family.
2. You are in the library and happen to run into two of your professors at the circulation desk. Introduce them to each other.
3. You are at a party. Introduce one good friend to another.
4. Introduce the student next to you to another student.

MÉXICO

En contexto

In this video segment, Roberto and Martín are walking in the park, looking for Roberto's cousin Sabina. As you watch the segment, pay particular attention to the words the characters use to describe Sabina. How does Roberto describe her? Is this accurate?

A. Lluvia de ideas

- What words do you use most often to describe people physically? Do you generally describe their height or weight? Their eye and hair color? Other qualities?
- If you are arranging to meet someone you don't know in a public place, how do you describe yourself? What do

you do to make sure that the two of you recognize each other? Do you wear a flower in your lapel? Do you identify yourself in some other way?

B. Dictado

Here is the first part of this segment's dialogue. Fill in the missing portions of Roberto's dialogue.

ROBERTO: No entiendo.[a] Ya _____ las tres. Mi prima Sabina _____ estar aquí.

MARTÍN: No, todavía no[b] son las tres. _____ temprano. Yo tengo las tres menos cinco.

ROBERTO: Ah, bueno.

[a]comprendo   [b]todavía... *not yet*

Un poco más sobre... José Miguel Martín Velasco

José Miguel Martín Velasco es un estudiante universitario de primer año.[a] Vive en Quito con su madre, Elisa. Quito, la capital de Ecuador y situada en las montañas,[b] es una ciudad hermosa.[c] Como[d] muchos estudiantes, José Miguel sale[e] con frecuencia con sus amigos.

[a]de... *freshman*   [b]*mountains*
[c]*bonita*   [d]*Like*   [e]*goes out*

To read more about the characters in this video, visit the *Puntos de partida* Website at **www.mhhe.com/puntos**

MARTÍN: ¿Cómo es tu prima?

ROBERTO: Es una chica _____; tiene _____ años.

MARTÍN: Mira… la chica allí es joven. ¿Es Sabina?

ROBERTO: No, no es _____. Esa chica es _____. Sabina es _____.

MARTÍN: Ajá.

C. Un diálogo original

Paso 1. With a classmate, re-enact the situation between Roberto and Martín.

Paso 2. Then, imagine that you and a different classmate are looking for someone during a crowded party at your school. These are the roles:

ESTUDIANTE 1: You are looking for a friend that you are supposed to meet at the party.

ESTUDIANTE 2: You don't know the person that **Estudiante 1** is looking for. You ask questions about that person's appearance, to help find him or her.

Un poco de todo

A. La familia del nuevo nieto

Paso 1. The following sentences will form a description of a family in which there is a new grandchild. The name of the person described is given in parentheses after each description when necessary. Form complete sentences based on the words given, in the order given. Conjugate the verbs and add other words if necessary. Be sure to pay close attention to adjective endings.

As you create the sentences, complete the family tree given below with the names of the family members. *Hint:* Hispanic families pass on first and middle names just as families in this country do.

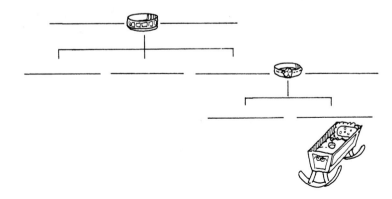

1. yo / ser/ abuela / panameño (Anita)
2. nuevo / nieto / ser / de / Estados Unidos (Juan José)
3. Juan José / ser / padre / nieto
4. Juan José / también / ser / hijo / abuelo / panameño
5. uno / de / tías / de/ nieto / ser / médico (Pilar)
6. otro / tía / ser / profesor / famoso (Julia)
7. madre / niño / ser / norteamericano (Paula)
8. hermana / niño / se llama / Concepción

Paso 2. Ahora conteste estas preguntas según la descripción de la familia.

1. ¿De dónde son los abuelos y tíos?
2. ¿De dónde es la madre del niño?
3. ¿Cómo se llama el abuelo de la familia?

B. ¿Existe la familia hispánica típica? Complete the following paragraphs about families. Give the correct form of the words in parentheses, as suggested by the context.

Muchas personas (creer[1]) que (todo[2]) las familias (hispánico[3]) son (grande[4]). Pero el concepto de la familia (ser[5]) diferente ahora, sobre todo[a] en las ciudades (grande[6]).

(Ser[7]) cierto que la familia rural (típico[8]) es grande, pero es así[b] en casi (todo[9]) las sociedades rurales del mundo.[c] Muchos hijos (trabajar[10]) la tierra[d] con sus padres. Por eso es bueno y (necesario[11]) tener muchos niños.

Pero en los grandes centros (urbano[12]) las familias con sólo dos o tres hijos (ser[13]) más comunes. Es difícil[e] tener (mucho[14]) hijos en una sociedad (industrializado[15]). Y cuando los padres (trabajar[16]) fuera de[f] casa, ellos (pagar[17]) mucho para cuidar a[g] los niños. Esto pasa especialmente en las familias de la clase media.[h]

Pero es realmente difícil (hablar[18]) de una familia (hispánico[19]) típica. ¿Hay una familia (norteamericano[20]) típica?

[a]sobre… *above all* [b]es… *that's the way it is* [c]*world* [d]*land* [e]*difficult* [f]fuera… *outside of the* [g]cuidar… *care for* [h]*middle*

Comprensión: ¿Cierto o falso? Corrija las oraciones falsas.

1. Todas las familias hispánicas son iguales.
2. Las familias rurales son grandes en casi todas partes del mundo.
3. Las familias rurales necesitan muchos niños.
4. Por lo general (*Generally*), las familias urbanas son más pequeñas.

PANORAMA *cultural*

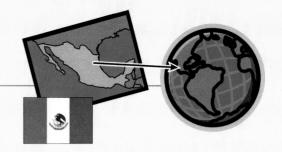

México

Datos esenciales

Nombre oficial: Estados Unidos Mexicanos
Capital: la Ciudad de México, o México, Distrito Federal (el D.F.)
Población: 94.000.000 (noventa y cuatro millones) de habitantes
Moneda:[a] el nuevo peso
Idiomas:[b] el español (oficial), el zapoteca, el mixteca, el náhuatl, varios dialectos mayas

[a]*Currency* [b]*Languages*

¡Fíjese!

- México tiene 31 estados y el Distrito Federal.

- La población de México es aproximadamente: 25% indígena, 15% blanca y 60% mestiza (que se refiere a las personas de padres de razas indígena y blanca).

- Los indígenas mexicanos pertenecen a[a] grupos diversos: aztecas, mayas, zapotecas, mixtecas, olmecas y otros. La influencia de estas culturas indígenas contribuye a la diversidad y la riqueza de la cultura mexicana actual.[b]

- La ciudad de México ocupa el lugar del antiguo[c] Lago Texcoco. En el centro del lago estaba[d] Tenochtitlán, la capital del imperio azteca. Tenochtitlán era[e] una de las ciudades más grandes del mundo en el siglo XVI.[f]

- La Universidad Autónoma de México es una de las universidades más antiguas[g] de las Américas: es del año[h] 1551 (mil quinientos cincuenta y uno).

[a]*pertenecen... belong to* [b]*current* [c]*old, ancient* [d]*was* [e]*was*
[f]*siglo... 16th century* [g]*más... oldest* [h]*es... it dates from the year*

Conozca a... los grandes muralistas mexicanos

El muralismo es el estilo de pintura[a] que decora las paredes[b] de edificios públicos. Con su obra,[c] los muralistas desean enseñar la historia y la cultura de su país, y con frecuencia sus murales representan sus ideales políticos también.

Tres pintores mexicanos—Diego Rivera (1886–1957 [mil ochocientos ochenta y seis a mil novecientos cincuenta y siete]), José Clemente Orozco (1883–1949 [mil ochocientos ochenta y tres a mil novecientos cuarenta y nueve]) y David Alfaro Siqueiros (1898–1974 [mil ochocientos noventa y ocho a mil novecientos setenta y cuatro])—son probablemente los muralistas más famosos de hoy. Hay muchos murales de estos tres grandes muralistas por todo México.

[a]*painting* [b]*walls* [c]*work*

The Epic of American Civilization es un mural de Orozco. Está en Dartmouth College.

 Capítulo 2 of the video to accompany *Puntos de partida* contains cultural footage of Mexico.

 Visit the *Puntos de partida* Website at www.mhhe.com/puntos.

Vocabulario

Los verbos

abrir	to open
aprender	to learn
asistir (a)	to attend, go to (*a class, function*)
beber	to drink
comer	to eat
comprender	to understand
creer (en)	to think, believe (in)
deber (+ *inf.*)	should, must, ought to (*do something*)
escribir	to write
leer	to read
llegar	to arrive
mirar	to look at, watch
mirar la televisión	to watch television
recibir	to receive
ser (*irreg.*)	to be
vender	to sell
vivir	to live

La familia y los parientes

el/la abuelo/a	grandfather/grandmother
los abuelos	grandparents
el/la esposo/a	husband/wife
el/la hermano/a	brother/sister
el/la hijo/a	son/daughter
los hijos	children
la madre (mamá)	mother (mom)
el/la nieto/a	grandson/granddaughter
el/la niño/a	small child; boy/girl
el padre (papá)	father (dad)
los padres	parents
el/la primo/a	cousin
el/la sobrino/a	niece/nephew
el/la tío/a	uncle/aunt

Las mascotas

el gato	cat
el pájaro	bird
el perro	dog

Otros sustantivos

la carta	letter
la casa	house, home
la ciudad	city
el coche	car
el estado	state
el/la médico/a	(medical) doctor
el país	country
el periódico	newspaper
el regalo	present, gift
la revista	magazine

Los adjetivos

alto/a	tall
amable	kind; nice
antipático/a	unpleasant
bajo/a	short (*in height*)
bonito/a	pretty
buen, bueno/a	good
casado/a	married
corto/a	short (*in length*)
delgado/a	thin, slender
este/a	this
estos/as	these
feo/a	ugly
fiel	faithful
gordo/a	fat
gran, grande	large, big; great
guapo/a	handsome; good-looking
inteligente	intelligent
joven	young
largo/a	long
listo/a	smart; clever
mal, malo/a	bad
moreno/a	brunet(te)
mucho/a	a lot
muchos/as	many
necesario/a	necessary
nuevo/a	new
otro/a	other, another
pequeño/a	small
perezoso/a	lazy
pobre	poor
posible	possible

rico/a	rich
rubio/a	blond(e)
simpático/a	nice; likeable
soltero/a	single (*not married*)
todo/a	all; every
tonto/a	silly, foolish
trabajador(a)	hardworking
viejo/a	old

Los adjetivos de nacionalidad

alemán/alemana, español(a), francés/francesa, inglés/inglesa, mexicano/a, norteamericano/a

Los adjetivos posesivos

mi(s)	my
tu(s)	your (*inform. sing.*)
nuestro/a(s)	our
vuestro/a(s)	your (*inform. pl. Sp.*)
su(s)	his, hers, its, your (*form. sing.*); their, your (*form. pl.*)

Los números

treinta, cuarenta, cincuenta, sesenta, setenta, ochenta, noventa, cien (ciento)

¿Con qué frecuencia... ?

a veces	sometimes, at times
casi nunca	almost never
con frecuencia	frequently
nunca	never
siempre	always
una vez a la semana	once a week

Palabras adicionales

bueno...	well...
¿de dónde es Ud.?	where are you from?
¿de quién?	whose?
del	of the, from the
(no) estoy de acuerdo	I (don't) agree
para	(intended) for; in order to
¿por qué?	why?
porque	because
que	that; who
según	according to
si	if
tener (*irreg.*) ... años	to be... years old

Un paso más 2

LECTURA

Estrategia: Connecting Words; A Reminder About Cognates

Some words or phrases indicate what kind of information they introduce. For example, as you know, **por eso** (*for that reason, that's why*) is a signal that the information following it is a justification or a reason for the information that came before.

> Necesito dinero. **Por eso** trabajo en la librería.

What kinds of clues do these words give you about the information that follows?

1. Por otra parte,... (*On the other hand, . . .*)
2. También...
3. En cambio,... (*On the other hand, . . .*)
4. ... porque...

5. Por ejemplo,...
6. Por lo general,...
7. ¡Hasta... ! (*Even . . . !*)

Scan the following reading to see if you can find any of the preceding connectors. You may wish to circle them in the reading so that you pay particular attention to them when you get to them.

Note: The following reading contains a number of cognates that you should be able to guess in context, including some verb forms with endings different from those you have learned about. You will recognize the meaning of most of those verbs easily, however.

▶ **Sobre la lectura...** This reading was written by the authors of *Puntos de*
▶ *partida* for language learners like you. Do you think that the authors were
▶ being completely serious when they presented this contrast between fami-
▶ lies in this country and in Spanish-speaking countries?

La unidad familiar: ¿Perspectivas culturales válidas o estereotipadas?

Tamalada (*Making Tamales*), por Carmen Lomas Garza (estadounidense)

La familia estadounidense y canadiense

Cuando un hispano observa la estructura de la familia estadounidense o canadiense, puede[a] llegar muy pronto a esta conclusión: La familia ya no[b] existe en estos países. ¿Por qué podría creer[c] esto?

Los padres e hijos estadounidense o canadiense no se quieren.[d] Cuando los hijos tienen unos 18 años, sus padres los mandan[e] a vivir a otra parte. A veces[f] los hijos trabajan en otras ciudades y a veces abandonan la casa familiar sólo porque sí.[g] Los padres ancianos viven <u>solos</u> porque cuando sus hijos ya tienen otra familia los padres son para ellos una gran <u>molestia.</u> ¡Hasta hay <u>hospicios</u> para los viejos! No están en casa, que es donde deberían[h] estar.

La familia hispánica

Por otra parte, un estadounidense o un canadiense que mira la estructura de la familia hispánica puede <u>concluir</u> lo siguiente: La influencia de la familia es demasiado fuerte.[i] ¿Por qué podría creer esto?

Los padres no confían[j] en sus hijos, y no los[k] preparan para la vida. Por ejemplo, hay hijos ya <u>mayores</u> —de 30 años o más— que todavía viven en la casa de sus padres. Estos hijos tienen buenos trabajos y suficiente dinero para vivir aparte. Obviamente los padres no desarrollan[l] en ellos la capacidad de vivir independientemente y por eso los hijos no dejan el nido.[m]

Culturas diferentes

¿Son válidas estas conclusiones? El concepto de la unidad familiar existe en las dos culturas. En los Estados Unidos y el Canadá, la independencia personal tiene gran importancia social. Es una gran responsabilidad de los padres el hacer[n] independientes a sus hijos. La integridad de la familia

[a]*he can* [b]*ya… no longer* [c]*podría… might he think* [d]*no… don't love each other* [e]*los… send them off* [f]*A… Sometimes* [g]*sólo… just because they want to* [h]*they should*

[i]*demasiado… too strong* [j]*trust* [k]*them* [l]*develop* [m]*dejan… leave the nest* [n]*el… to make*

depende menos de la cercanía° física y geográfica.

En cambio, en la cultura hispánica es muy importante <u>mantener</u> intacto el grupo familiar. En muchos casos, los hijos dejan la casa cuando <u>contraen</u> matrimonio y no cuando terminan sus estudios o <u>comienzan</u> a trabajar. Las dos sociedades tienen perspectivas diferentes; es imposible evaluar una cultura según las normas de otra. ●

°*closeness*

Comprensión

A. ¿Opinión o hecho (*fact*)**?** Indique si las siguientes oraciones representan una opinión o un hecho.

	OPINIÓN	HECHO
1. A veces los hijos estadounidenses y canadienses trabajan en otras ciudades porque sus padres no los quieren (*don't love them*).	☐	☐
2. En muchos casos, los hijos hispanos viven con su familia aun (*even*) cuando tienen buenos trabajos.	☐	☐
3. La proximidad geográfica de los parientes es muy importante para la familia hispana.	☐	☐
4. Los padres ancianos representan una molestia para los hijos estadounidenses y canadienses.	☐	☐

B. ¿Quién habla? Indique quién habla en las siguientes oraciones. **¡OJO!** Hay diferentes normas culturales.

	UN HISPANO/ UNA HISPANA	UN(A) ESTADOUNIDENSE O CANADIENSE
1. «Tengo 28 años. Soy soltero y vivo con mis padres.»	☐	☐
2. «Necesito visitar a mi madre. Tiene 79 años y vive sola (*alone*).»	☐	☐
3. «La independencia es muy importante en mi vida. No deseo depender de mis padres el resto de mi vida (*life*).»	☐	☐
4. «Mi hija tiene un buen trabajo en una gran compañía. Vive con una amiga en la ciudad y yo vivo aquí, en el pueblo.»	☐	☐

ESCRITURA

A. **Ud. y su familia.** ¿Cómo son sus relaciones con su familia? ¿Es Ud. como el típico hijo estadounidense o canadiense de la lectura? ¿Es Ud. independiente o todavía vive con sus padres? ¿Por qué? ¿Tiene relaciones estrechas (*close*) con su familia? ¿O son un poco distantes? Conteste en un breve párrafo (*paragraph*). Trate de (*Try to*) usar palabras y frases de la Estrategia (p. 96).

B. **¿Quién es Ud.?** You have already learned enough Spanish to be able to say a lot about yourself and your family. Answer the following questions. Then rewrite them in the form of one or two brief paragraphs that tell as much about you as possible.

1. ¿Cómo se llama Ud.?
2. ¿Cuántos años tiene Ud.?
3. ¿Qué profesión tiene? (¿Es estudiante?)
4. ¿Dónde estudia Ud.? ¿Qué estudia?
5. ¿Vive Ud. solo/a, con amigos o con la familia? ¿En qué ciudad vive?
6. Económicamente, ¿es Ud. completamente independiente de sus padres? ¿O depende en parte o mucho de ellos?

De compras

Estos mexicanos van de compras (*go shopping*) en el centro comercial Plaza del Sol, en Guadalajara, México.

WEB

¿Qué opina Ud.?

Answer the following questions according to your own life. Do you think a person from a different country might give similar answers? Visit the *Puntos de partida* Website to read how a person from Nicaragua answered the same questions.

1. How often do you shop at a mall?
2. What shopping do you do in your neighborhood? For example, do you shop for clothing there?
3. How do you generally get to the place where you shop?
4. Have you ever done any shopping on the Internet?
5. With the exception of food and entertainment, how do you spend most of your money?

En este capítulo...

- In this chapter, you will study vocabulary related to shopping, clothing, and colors. Can you guess what the word **mercado** means?
- In **Capítulo 2**, you learned to use possessive articles to indicate to whom things belonged (**mi, tu, su,** and so on). In this chapter, you will learn demonstrative adjectives that will allow you to point out things near and far from you. (Grammar 9)
- You studied regular verbs in **Capítulo 1** and **Capítulo 2**. In this chapter, you will study some irregular ones and practice some common phrases that use the verb **tener** (*to have*). (Grammar 10). You will also learn the verb **ir** (*to go*), which you can use to tell both where you are going and what will happen in the future. (Grammar 11)
- The **Panorama cultural** section will focus on Nicaragua.

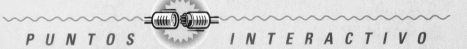

PUNTOS INTERACTIVO

Videoteca

◀ **Minidramas**
José Miguel and Elisa and his cousin are going shopping. Do you enjoy shopping? Is shopping for clothing harder or easier for you than other kinds of shopping? Why?

En contexto ▶
Mariela wants to buy something from a street vendor. Are there street vendors where you live? Is it possible to bargain with them?

CD-ROM

In addition to completing vocabulary and grammar activities, you will have the opportunity to "barter" with a vendor about a virtual sale.

Internet

In the **Capítulo 3** section of the *Puntos de partida* Website you can access links to Spanish resources related to shopping at **www.mhhe.com/puntos**.

Vocabulario: Preparación

De compras: La ropa°

De... Shopping: Clothing

el impermeable · el reloj · la camisa · la chaqueta · el suéter · el abrigo · el sombrero · la blusa · los calcetines · la falda · la camiseta · los *jeans** · las medias · los pantalones · los zapatos · la ropa interior · el cinturón · la corbata

Los verbos

comprar	to buy
llevar	to wear; to carry; to take
regatear	to haggle, bargain
usar	to wear; to use
vender	to sell
venden de todo	they sell (have) everything

Los lugares

el almacén	department store
el centro	downtown
el centro comercial	shopping mall
el mercado	market(place)
la tienda	shop, store

¿Cuánto cuesta?

la ganga	bargain
el precio	price
el precio fijo	fixed (set) price
las rebajas	sales
barato/a	inexpensive
caro/a	expensive

Otras expresiones útiles

un par de (zapatos, medias,...)	a pair of (shoes, stockings, . . .)
es de (lana, algodón, seda)[†]	it is made of (wool, cotton, silk)
¡Es de última moda!	It's the latest style!

---

*The influx of U.S. goods to Latin America and Spain has affected common language. *Jeans* is one example of an English word that is commonly used in Spanish-speaking countries.

[†]Note another use of **ser** + **de**: to tell what material something is made of.

la bolsa	purse	el traje	suit
las botas	boots	el traje de baño	swimsuit
la cartera	wallet	el vestido	dress
las sandalias	sandals	los zapatos de tenis	tennis shoes

Conversación

A. La ropa. ¿Qué ropa llevan estas personas?

1. El Sr. Rivera lleva _un_ traje _una corbata_

2. La Srta. Alonso lleva _los pantalones y la chaqueta_ El perro lleva _un suéter_

3. Sara lleva _____. _la falda y unas medias_

4. Alfredo lleva _____. Necesita comprar _____.

De estas personas, ¿quién trabaja hoy? ¿Quién va a (*is going to*) una fiesta? ¿Quién no trabaja en este momento?

B. Asociaciones. Complete las oraciones lógicamente.

1. Un _almacén_ es una tienda grande.
2. No es posible _regatear_ cuando hay precios fijos.
3. En la librería, _venden_ de todo: textos y otros libros, cuadernos, lápices, cintas (*tapes*). Hay grandes _rebajas_ al final del semestre/trimestre, en los cuales (*in which*) todo es muy barato.
4. Siempre hay *boutiques* en los _centros comerciales_
5. El _centro_ de una ciudad es la parte céntrica.
6. Estos artículos de ropa no son para hombres: _faldas y vestidos_
7. Estos artículos de ropa son para hombres y mujeres: _pantalones_
8. La ropa de _seda_ (*material*) es muy elegante.
9. La ropa de _algodón_ es muy práctica.

Vocabulario: Preparación

C. ¿Qué lleva Ud.? Para hablar de Ud. y de la ropa, complete estas oraciones lógicamente.

1. Para ir (*go*) a la universidad, me gusta usar _____.
2. Para ir a las fiestas con los amigos, me gusta usar _____.
3. Para pasar un día en la playa (*beach*), me gusta llevar el traje de baño.
4. Cuando estoy en casa todo el día, llevo _____.
5. Nunca uso _____.
6. _____ es un artículo / son artículos de ropa absolutamente necesario(s) para mí.

Nota comunicativa

More About Getting Information

Tag phrases can change statements into questions.

Venden de todo aquí,	{ **¿no?** ¿verdad?**	*They sell everything here, right?* (*don't they?*)
No necesito impermeable hoy, ¿verdad?		*I don't need a raincoat today, do I?*

¿Verdad? is found after affirmative or negative statements; **¿no?** is usually found after affirmative statements only. Note that the inverted question mark comes immediately before the tag question, not at the beginning of the statement.

D. Preguntas. Using tag questions, ask a classmate questions based on the following statements. He or she will answer based on general information—or as truthfully as possible—if the question is about aspects of his or her life.

MODELO: E1: Estudias en la biblioteca por la noche, ¿verdad?
       E2: No. Estudio en la biblioteca por la mañana. (No, no estudio en la biblioteca. Me gusta estudiar en casa.)

1. En un almacén hay precios fijos.
2. Regateamos mucho en los Estados Unidos.
3. No hay muchos mercados en esta ciudad.
4. Los *jeans* Gap son muy baratos.
5. Es necesario llevar traje y corbata a clase.
6. Eres una persona muy independiente.
7. Tienes una familia muy grande.
8. No hay examen (*test*) mañana.

¿De qué color es?

Here are colors and other helpful phrases you can use to describe clothing and other objects.

amarillo/a	yellow	**negro/a**	black
anaranjado/a	orange	**pardo/a**	brown
azul	blue	**rojo/a**	red
blanco/a	white	**rosado/a**	pink
gris	gray	**verde**	green
morado/a	purple		

¿Cuántos colores hay en este cuadro (*painting*) de Gonzalo Endara Crow? ¿Cuáles son?

Después de (After) *la noche,* por Gonzalo Endara Crow (ecuatoriano)

Otras frases útiles

de cuadros	plaid
de lunares	polka-dotted
de rayas	striped

 Note that some colors only have one form for masculine and feminine nouns.

el traje **azul,** la camisa **azul**

La guayabera

In the Caribbean and other warm parts of Latin America, it is common for men to wear an article of clothing called **una guayabera**. It's an elegant short-sleeved shirt, often embroidered or with pleats, that is worn outside the pants (not tucked in). It is ideal for warm, humid climates and can be worn in formal and informal situations. The famous Colombian writer Gabriel García Márquez even wore a similar shirt, a **liquelique**, when he accepted the Nobel Prize for literature in 1982.

Gabriel García Márquez acepta el Premio Nóbel.

Conversación

A. ¿Escaparates idénticos? These showcase windows are almost alike . . . but not quite! Can you find at least eight differences between them? In Spanish, activities like this one are often called **¡Ojo alerta!** (*Eagle eye!*).

MODELO: En el dibujo A hay _____, pero en el dibujo B hay _____.

A.

B.

B. ¿De qué color es?

Paso 1.   Tell the color of things in your classroom, especially the clothing your classmates are wearing.

MODELO: El bolígrafo de Anita es amarillo. Roberto lleva calcetines
azules, una camisa de cuadros morados y azules, *jeans*...

Paso 2. Now describe what someone in the class is wearing, without
revealing his or her name. Using your clues, can your classmates guess
whom you are describing?

C. Asociaciones. ¿Qué colores asocia Ud. con... ?

1. el dinero   *verde*
2. la una de la mañana   *negra*
3. una mañana bonita   *azul*
4. una mañana fea   *gris*
5. el demonio   *rojo*
6. los Estados Unidos   *rojo, blanco y azul*
7. una jirafa   *parda, anaranjada*
8. un pingüino   *negro y blanco*
9. un limón   *amarillo*
10. una naranja   *anaranjada*
11. un elefante   *gris*
12. las flores (*flowers*)   *rosada, amarilla, morada*

Más alla del° número 100

Más... *Beyond the*

Continúe la secuencia:

noventa y nueve, cien, ciento uno,...
mil, dos mil,...
un millón, dos millones,...

100	cien, ciento	700	setecientos/as
101	ciento uno/una	800	ochocientos/as
200	doscientos/as	900	novecientos/as
300	trescientos/as	1.000*	mil
400	cuatrocientos/as	2.000	dos mil
500	quinientos/as	1.000.000	un millón
600	seiscientos/as	2.000.000	dos millones

- **Ciento** is used in combination with numbers from 1 to 99 to express the numbers 101 through 199: **ciento uno, ciento dos, ciento setenta y nueve,** and so on. **Cien** is used in counting and before numbers greater than 100: **cien mil, cien millones.**
- When the numbers 200 through 900 modify a noun, they must agree in gender: **cuatrocientas niñas, doscientas dos casas.**
- **Mil** means *one thousand* or *a thousand.* It does not have a plural form in counting, but **millón** does. When used with a noun, **millón** (**dos millones,** and so on) must be followed by **de.**

3.000 habitantes	tres mil habitantes
14.000.000 **de** habitantes	catorce millones de habitantes

- Note how years are expressed in Spanish.

1899	mil ochocientos noventa y nueve
2002	dos mil dos

*In many parts of the Spanish-speaking world, a period in numerals is used where English uses a comma, and a comma is used to indicate the decimal where English uses a period: **$10,45; 65,9%.**

Conversación

▲▲▲▲▲▲▲

A. ¿Cuánto pesan? (*How much do they weigh?*)

Paso 1. Estos son los animales terrestres más grandes. ¿Cuánto pesan en kilos? **¡OJO!** (*Watch out!*) Use el artículo masculino para todos los nombres, menos para (*except for*) los nombres que terminan (*that end*) en **-a**.

Paso 2. Pregunte (*Ask*) a un compañero / una compañera aproximadamente cuánto pesa en libras:

1. su perro/gato
2. su mochila con los libros para hoy
3. su coche
4. su libro de español
5. el animal más grande del mundo (*world*)

B. ¿Cuánto es? Diga los precios.

el dólar (los Estados Unidos, el Canadá, Puerto Rico)
el nuevo peso (México)
el bolívar (Venezuela)
la peseta (España)
el quetzal (Guatemala)

1. 7.345 pesetas
2. $100
3. 5.710 quetzales
4. 670 bolívares
5. $1.000.000

6. 528 nuevos pesos
7. 836 bolívares
8. 101 pesetas
9. $4.000.000,00
10. 6.000.000 quetzales

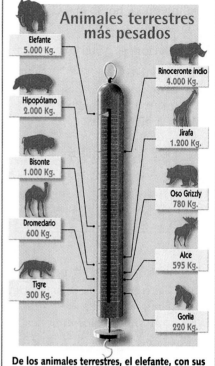

Animales terrestres más pesados

Elefante 5.000 Kg.
Hipopótamo 2.000 Kg.
Bisonte 1.000 Kg.
Dromedario 600 Kg.
Tigre 300 Kg.
Rinoceronte indio 4.000 Kg.
Jirafa 1.200 Kg.
Oso Grizzly 780 Kg.
Alce 595 Kg.
Gorila 220 Kg.

De los animales terrestres, el elefante, con sus 5.000 kilos de peso medio entre todas sus especies, es sin duda el mamífero más pesado. El hipopótamo y el rinoceronte son los siguientes en la lista, y el hombre, ni aparece.

C. Compras personales

Paso 1. With a classmate, determine how much the following items probably cost, using **¿Cuánto es... ?** or **¿Cuánto cuesta(n)... ?** Keep track of the prices that you decide on.

1. una calculadora pequeña
2. un coche nuevo/usado
3. una computadora Mac o IBM
4. un reloj Timex / de oro (*gold*)
5. unos zapatos de tenis
6. una casa en esta ciudad

Paso 2. Now compare the prices you selected with those of others in the class. What is the most expensive thing on the list? **(¿Cuál es la cosa más cara?)** What is the least expensive? **(¿Cuál es la cosa más barata?)**

The written accent mark is used in the following situations.

- A written accent mark is needed when a word does not follow the two basic rules presented. Look at the words in this group.

  ta-bú   a-le-mán   na-ción   in-glés   es-tás

  These words end in a vowel, **-n**, or **-s**, so one would predict that they would be stressed on the next-to-last syllable. But the written accent mark shows that they are in fact accented on the last syllable.

  Now look at the words in this group.

  lá-piz   dó-lar   ál-bum   á-gil   dó-cil

  These words end in a consonant (other than **-n** or **-s**), so one would predict that they would be stressed on the last syllable. But the written accent mark shows that they are in fact accented on the next-to-last syllable.

- All words that are stressed on the third-to-last syllable must have a written accent mark.

  bo-lí-gra-fo   ma-trí-cu-la   ma-te-má-ti-cas

- When two consecutive vowels do not form a diphthong (see **Capítulo 1**), the vowel that receives the spoken stress will have a written accent mark. This pattern is very frequent in words that end in **-ía**.

  Ma-rí-a   dí-a   po-li-cí-a   bio-lo-gí-a   as-tro-no-mí-a

  Contrast the pronunciation of those words with the following words in which the vowels **i** and **a** *do* form a diphthong: **Patricia, Francia, infancia, distancia.**

- Some one-syllable words have accents to distinguish them from other words that sound like them. For example:

  él (*he*)/el (*the*)   tú (*you*)/tu (*your*)
  sí (*yes*)/si (*if*)   mí (*me*)/mi (*my*)

- Interrogative and exclamatory words have a written accent on the stressed vowel. For example:

  ¿quién?   ¿dónde?   ¡Qué ganga! (*What a bargain!*)

A. Sílabas. The following words have been separated into syllables for you.

> As you know, most Spanish words do not need a written accent mark because their pronunciation is completely predictable by native speakers. Here are the two basic rules.
> - A word that ends in a vowel, **-n,** or **-s** is stressed on the next-to-last syllable.
> - A word that ends in any other consonant is stressed on the last syllable.

Read them aloud, paying careful attention to where the spoken stress should fall. Don't worry about the meanings of words you haven't heard before. The rules you have learned will help you pronounce them correctly.

1. a-quí	pa-pá	a-diós	bus-qué
2. prác-ti-co	mur-cié-la-go	te-lé-fo-no	ar-chi-pié-la-go
3. Ji-mé-nez	Ro-drí-guez	Pé-rez	Gó-mez
4. si-co-lo-gí-a	so-cio-lo-gí-a	sa-bi-du-rí-a	e-ner-gí-a
5. his-to-ria	te-ra-pia	Pre-to-ria	me-mo-ria

B. Reglas (*Rules*). Indicate the stressed vowel of each word in the list that follows. Give the rule that determines the stress of each word.

1. exámenes	**7.** dólares	**12.** mujer
2. lápiz	**8.** francés	**13.** plástico
3. necesitar	**9.** están	**14.** María
4. perezoso	**10.** hombre	**15.** Rodríguez
5. actitud	**11.** peso	**16.** Patricia
6. acciones		

Minidiálogos y gramática

¿Recuerda Ud.?

You have already used the forms of **este** (*this*), one of the Spanish demonstrative adjectives. Review them by describing objects near you and the clothes you are wearing.

MODELO: Esta camisa es de rayas. Estos lápices son amarillos.

9 Pointing Out People and Things • Demonstrative Adjectives

Suéteres a buenos precios

VENDEDOR: *Estos* suéteres de aquí cuestan 150 pesos y *ese* suéter en su mano cuesta 250 pesos.

SUSANA: ¿Por qué es más caro *este*?

VENDEDOR: Porque *esos* son de pura lana virgen, de excelente calidad.

SUSANA: ¿Y *aquellos* suéteres de rayas?

VENDEDOR: *Aquellos* cuestan cien pesos solamente; son acrílicos.

Sweaters at good prices SALESMAN: These sweaters here cost 150 pesos and that sweater in your hand costs 250 pesos. SUSANA: Why is this one more expensive? SALESMAN: Because those are of pure virgin wool, of excellent quality. SUSANA: What about those striped sweaters over there? SALESMAN: Those cost only one hundred; they are acrylic.

Susana

Jorge

Vendedor

¿Quién habla, Susana, Jorge o el vendedor?

1. Me gustan estos suéteres de rayas, y sólo cuestan cien pesos.
2. Señores, miren (*look at*) estos suéteres en mi mesa. Cuestan 150 pesos.
3. Voy a (*I am going to*) comprar este suéter. Me gusta la ropa de lana.
4. Este suéter acrílico es más barato que aquel suéter de lana.

Singular			Plural		
this	este libro	esta mesa	*these*	estos libros	estas mesas
that	ese libro	esa mesa	*those*	esos libros	esas mesas
	aquel libro	aquella mesa		aquellos libros	aquellas mesas
	(allí)	(allí)		(allí)	(allí)

OJO

est**e** *but* est**os**, es**e** *but* es**os** (no **o** in the masculine singular forms)

est**e** cuaderno	*this notebook*
es**a** cas**a**	*that house*
aquell**os** chic**os**	*those boys (over there)*

Demonstrative adjectives (**los adjetivos demostrativos**) are used to point out or indicate a specific noun or nouns. In Spanish, demonstrative adjectives precede the nouns they modify. They also agree in number and gender with the nouns.

- There are two ways to say *that/those* in Spanish. Forms of **ese** refer to nouns that are not close to the speaker in space or in time. Forms of **aquel** are used to refer to nouns that are even farther away.

Este niño es mi hijo. **Ese** joven es mi hijo también. Y **aquel** señor allí es mi esposo.
This boy is my son. That young man is also my son. And that man over there is my husband.

- To express English *this one* (*that one*), just drop the noun.

este coche y **ese**	aquella casa y **esta***
this car and that one	*that house (over there) and this one*

- Use the neuter demonstratives **esto, eso,** and **aquello** to refer to as yet unidentified objects or to a whole idea, concept, or situation.

¿Qué es **esto?**
What is this?

Eso es todo.
That's it. That's all.

¡Aquello es terrible!
That's terrible!

Práctica

A. Comparaciones

Paso 1. Restate the sentences, changing forms of **este** to **ese** and adding **también,** following the model.

MODELO: Este abrigo es muy grande. →
Ese abrigo también es muy grande.

1. Esta falda es muy pequeña.
2. Estos pantalones son muy largos.
3. Este libro es muy bueno.
4. Estas corbatas son muy feas.

Paso 2. Now change the forms of **este** to **aquel.**

MODELO: Este abrigo es muy grande. →
Aquel abrigo también es muy grande.

B. Situaciones. Find an appropriate response for each situation.

Posibilidades: ¡Eso es un desastre!, ¿Qué es esto?, ¡Eso es magnífico!, ¡Eso es terrible!

1. Aquí hay un regalo para Ud.
2. Ocurre un accidente en la cafetería: Ud. tiene tomate en su camisa favorita.
3. No hay clases mañana.
4. La matrícula cuesta más este semestre/trimestre.
5. Ud. tiene una A en su examen de español.

---

*Some Spanish speakers prefer to use accents on these forms: **este coche y ése, aquella casa y ésta.** However, it is acceptable in modern Spanish, per the **Real Academia Española** in Madrid, to omit the accent on these forms when context makes the meaning clear and no ambiguity is possible. To learn more about these forms, consult Appendix 2, Using Adjectives as Nouns.

Conversación

▲▲▲▲▲▲

Una tarde en un patio mexicano

Paso 1. ¿A qué parte del dibujo se refieren las siguientes oraciones? Habla la mujer de los zapatos verdes.

1. Aquella mujer es de Cuernavaca.
2. Estas plantas son un regalo de un amigo chileno.
3. Ese pájaro habla inglés y español.
4. Aquel joven es un primo de Taxco.

Paso 2. Ahora, con un compañero/una compañera, imaginen que Uds. son otras personas en el dibujo e inventen oraciones sobre el dibujo.

En los Estados Unidos y el Canadá...

Diseñadores de moda° famosos

Two Hispanic designers have led the American fashion industry for more than twenty years: the Venezuelan Carolina Herrera and the Dominican Óscar de la Renta. One, Óscar de la Renta, has the distinction of being the first high-fashion designer whose business ventures were publicly traded on the U.S. stock market.

Narciso Rodríguez

Now a young Cuban-American from New Jersey has joined the fashion limelight. Narciso Rodríguez has been highly sought after since designing Carolyn Bessette Kennedy's wedding gown in 1996. Rodríguez likes designs that include intricate beadwork and embroidery, an influence he attributes to his Cuban roots.

Diseñadores... *Fashion designers*

Expressing Actions and States • *Tener, venir, preferir, querer,* and *poder;* Some Idioms with *tener*

Una gorra para José Miguel, después de mirar en tres tiendas

ELISA:	¿Qué gorra *prefieres*, José Miguel?
JOSÉ MIGUEL:	*Prefiero* la gris.
ELISA:	¡Pero ya *tienes* una gris, y es casi idéntica!
JOSÉ MIGUEL:	Pues, no *quiero* esas otras gorras. ¿*Podemos* mirar en la tienda anterior otra vez?
ELISA:	¿Otra vez? Bueno, si realmente insistes…

Comprensión: ¿Sí o no?

1. José Miguel quiere comprar una corbata.
2. Él prefiere la gorra azul.
3. No puede decidir entre las gorras.
4. Parece que (*It seems that*) Elisa tiene mucha paciencia.

tener (*to have*)	**venir** (*to come*)	**preferir** (*to prefer*)	**querer** (*to want*)	**poder** (*to be able, can*)
tengo	vengo	prefiero	quiero	puedo
tienes	vienes	prefieres	quieres	puedes
tiene	viene	prefiere	quiere	puede
tenemos	venimos	preferimos	queremos	podemos
tenéis	venís	preferís	queréis	podéis
tienen	vienen	prefieren	quieren	pueden

- The **yo** forms of **tener** and **venir** are irregular.

- In other forms of **tener, venir, preferir,** and **querer,** when the stem vowel **e** is stressed, it becomes **ie**.

- Similarly, the stem vowel **o** in **poder** becomes **ue** when stressed. In vocabulary lists these changes are shown in parentheses after the infinitive: **poder (ue).** You will learn more verbs of this type in Grammar Section 11.

- **O J O** **Nosotros** and **vosotros** forms for these verbs do not have irregular changes.

Irregularities:
tener: yo tengo, tú tienes (e → ie)…
venir: yo vengo, tú vienes (e → ie)…
preferir, querer: (e → ie)
poder: (o → ue)

A cap for José Miguel, after looking in three stores ELISA: Which cap do you prefer, José Miguel? JOSÉ MIGUEL: I prefer the gray one. ELISA: But you already have a gray one, and it's almost identical! JOSÉ MIGUEL: Well, I don't want those other caps. Can we look in the previous store again? ELISA: Again? Well, if you really insist . . .

A. Many ideas expressed in English with the verb *to be* are expressed in Spanish with *idioms* (**los modismos**) using **tener.** You have already used one **tener** idiom: **tener... años.** At the right are some additional ones. Note that they describe a condition or state that a person can experience.

tener miedo (de)	to be afraid (of)
tener prisa	to be in a hurry
(no) tener razón	to be right (wrong)
tener sueño	to be sleepy

> Idiomatic expressions are often different from one language to another. For example, in English, *to pull Mary's leg* usually means *to tease her*, not *to grab her leg and pull it*. In Spanish, *to pull Mary's leg* is **tomarle el pelo a Mary** (literally, *to take hold of Mary's hair*).

B. Other **tener** idioms include **tener ganas de** (*to feel like*) and **tener que** (*to have to*). The infinitive is always used after these two idiomatic expressions.

Tengo ganas de **comer.**
I feel like eating.

¿No tiene Ud. que **leer** este capítulo?
Don't you have to read this chapter?

> Note that the English translation of one of these examples results in a verb ending in *-ing*, not the infinitive.

Práctica

A. ¡Sara tiene mucha tarea (*homework*)!

Paso 1. Haga oraciones con las palabras indicadas. Añada (*Add*) palabras si es necesario.

1. Sara / tener / muchos exámenes
2. (ella) venir / a / universidad / todos los días
3. hoy / trabajar / hasta (*until*) / nueve / de / noche
4. preferir / estudiar / en / biblioteca
5. querer / leer / más / pero / no poder
6. por eso / regresar / a / casa
7. tener / ganas de / leer / más
8. pero / unos amigos / venir a mirar / televisión
9. Sara / decidir / mirar / televisión / con ellos

Paso 2. Now retell the same sequence of events, first as if they had happened to you, using **yo** as the subject of all but sentence number 8, then as if they had happened to you and your roommate, using **nosotros/as.**

B. Situaciones. Expand the situations described in these sentences by using an appropriate idiom with **tener**. There is often more than one possible answer.

MODELO: Tengo un examen mañana. Por eso… → Por eso tengo que estudiar mucho.

1. ¿Cuántos años? ¿Cuarenta? No, yo…
2. Un perro grande y feo vive en esa casa. Por eso yo…
3. ¿Ya son las tres de la mañana? Ah, por eso…
4. No, dos y dos no son cinco. Son cuatro. Tú…
5. Tengo que estar en el centro a las tres. Ya (*Already*) son las tres menos cuarto. Yo…
6. Cuando hay un terremoto (*earthquake*), todos…
7. ¿Los exámenes de la clase de español? ¡Esos son siempre muy fáciles! Yo no…
8. Sí, la capital de la Argentina es Buenos Aires. Tú…

Conversación

A. Estereotipos. Draw some conclusions about Isabel based on this scene. Think about things that she has, needs to or has to do or buy, likes, and so on. When you have finished, compare your predictions with those of others in the class. Did you all reach the same conclusions?

Palabras útiles: los aretes (*earrings*), el juguete (*toy*), hablar por teléfono, los muebles (*furniture*), el sofá, tener alergia a (*be allergic to*)

Nota comunicativa

Using *mucho* and *poco*

In the first chapters of *Puntos de partida*, you have used the words **mucho** and **poco** as both adjectives and adverbs. *Adverbs* **(Los adverbios)** are words that modify verbs, adjectives, or other adverbs: *quickly, very smart, very quickly*. In Spanish and in English, adverbs are invariable in form. However, in Spanish adjectives agree in number and gender with the word they modify.

> **adverb** = a word that modifies a verb, adjective, or another adverb

ADVERB

Rosario estudia **mucho** hoy.	*Rosario is studying a lot today.*
Julio come **poco**.	*Julio doesn't eat much.*

ADJECTIVE

Rosario tiene **mucha** ropa. Sobre todo tiene **muchos** zapatos.	*Rosario has a lot of clothes. She especially has a lot of shoes.*
Julio come **poca** carne. Come **pocos** postres.	*Julio doesn't eat much meat. He eats few desserts.*

B. Entrevista: Preferencias. Try to predict the choices your instructor will make in each of the following cases. Then, using tag questions, find out if you are correct.

MODELO: El profesor / La profesora tiene…
(muchos libros) / pocos libros →
Ud. tiene muchos libros, ¿verdad?

1. El profesor / La profesora tiene…
   mucha ropa / poca ropa
   sólo un coche / varios coches
2. Prefiere…
   los gatos / los perros
   la ropa elegante / la ropa informal
3. Quiere comprar…
   un coche deportivo (*sports car*), por ejemplo, un Porsche / una
       camioneta (*station wagon*)
   un abrigo / un impermeable
4. Viene a la universidad…
   todos los días / sólo tres veces a la semana
   en coche / en autobús / en bicicleta / a pie (*on foot*)
5. Esta noche tiene muchas ganas de…
   mirar la televisión / leer
   comer en un restaurante / comer en casa

C. Entrevista: Más preferencias. With a classmate, explore preferences in a number of areas by asking and answering questions based on the following cues. Form your questions with expressions like these:

¿Prefieres… o… ?
¿Te gusta más (*infinitive*) o (*infinitive*)?

If you have no preference, express that by saying **No tengo preferencia.** Be prepared to report some of your findings to the class. If you both agree, you will express this by saying **Preferimos...** or **No tenemos preferencia.** If you do not agree, give the preferences of both persons: **Yo prefiero..., pero Cecilia prefiere...**

1. Los animales: ¿los gatos siameses o los persas? ¿los perros pastores alemanes o los perros de lanas (*poodles*)?
2. El color de la ropa informal: ¿el color negro o el blanco? ¿el rojo o el azul?
3. La ropa informal: ¿las camisas de algodón o las de seda? ¿los *jeans* de algodón o los pantalones de lana?
4. La ropa de mujeres: ¿las faldas largas o las minifaldas? ¿los pantalones largos o los pantalones cortos?
5. La ropa de hombres: ¿las camisas de cuadros o las de rayas? ¿las camisas de un solo (*single*) color? ¿chaqueta y pantalón o un traje formal?
6. Las actividades en casa: ¿mirar la televisión o leer una novela? ¿escribir cartas o hablar con unos amigos?

11 Expressing Destination and Future Actions • *ir*; *ir* + *a* + Infinitive; The Contraction *al*

¿Qué *va a* hacer Ud. este fin de semana?

- ¿*Va a ir al* centro?   Sí, *voy a ir al* centro.
- ¿*Va a ir* de compras?   No, no *voy a ir* de compras.
- ¿*Va a* hablar con sus amigos?   Sí, *voy a* hablar con mis amigos.
- ¿*Va a* estudiar español?   ¡Claro que sí!

Si quiere añadir (*add*) otras actividades a la lista, use la frase **También voy a** + *infinitive.*

Ir is the irregular Spanish verb used to express *to go.*

ir (*to go*)	
voy	vamos
vas	vais
va	van

The first person plural of **ir, vamos** (*we go, are going, do go*), is also used to express *let's go.*

Ir + **a** + infinitive is used to describe actions or events in the near future.

Vamos a clase ahora mismo.
Let's go to class right now.

Van a venir a la fiesta esta noche.
They're going to come to the party tonight.

Voy a ir de compras esta tarde.
I'm going to go shopping this afternoon.

In **Capítulo 2** you learned about the contraction **del (de + el → del)**. The only other contraction in Spanish is **al (a + el → al)**. ¡OJO! Both **del** and **al** are obligatory contractions.

a + el → al

Voy **al** centro comercial.
I'm going to the mall.

Vamos **a la** tienda.
I'm going to the store.

Práctica
▲▲▲▲▲▲

A. ¿Adónde van de compras? Haga oraciones completas usando **ir.**

Recuerde: **a + el = al.**

MODELO: Marta / el centro → Marta *va al* centro.

1. Ud. / una *boutique*
2. Francisco / el almacén Goya
3. Jorge y Carlos / el centro comercial
4. tú / un mercado
5. nosotros / una tienda pequeña
6. yo / ¿ ?

B. ¡Vamos de compras en Sevilla! Describa el día, desde el punto de vista (*from the point of view*) de Lola Benítez. Use **ir** + **a** + el infinitivo, según el modelo.

MODELO: Manolo compra un regalo para su madre. →
Manolo *va a comprar* un regalo para su madre.

1. Llegamos al centro a las diez de la mañana.
2. La niña quiere comer algo (*something*).
3. Compro unos chocolates para Marta.
4. Manolo busca una blusa de seda.
5. No compras esta blusa de rayas, ¿verdad?
6. Buscamos algo más barato.
7. ¿Vas de compras mañana también?

Conversación
▲▲▲▲▲▲▲▲

A. ¿Adónde vas si... ? ¿Cuántas oraciones puede hacer Ud.?

Me gusta {
leer novelas.
ir de compras —y ¡no regateo!
buscar gangas y regatear.
hablar con mis amigos.
comer en restaurantes elegantes.
mirar programas de detectives.
} Por eso voy a _____.

B. Entrevista: El fin de semana

Paso 1. Interview a classmate about his or her plans for the weekend. Try to "personalize" the interview by asking additional questions. For example, if your partner is going to read a novel, ask questions like **¿Qué novela?** or **¿Quién es el autor?**

¿Vas a... ?   SÍ   NO
   1. ir de compras   ☐   ☐
   2. leer una novela   ☐   ☐
   3. asistir a un concierto   ☐   ☐
   4. estudiar para un examen   ☐   ☐
   5. ir a una fiesta   ☐   ☐
   6. escribir una carta   ☐   ☐
   7. ir a bailar   ☐   ☐
   8. escribir los ejercicios para la clase de español   ☐   ☐
   9. practicar un deporte (*sport*)   ☐   ☐
   10. mirar mucho la televisión   ☐   ☐

Paso 2. En general, ¿es muy activo/a su compañero/a? ¿O prefiere la
tranquilidad? En el **Paso 1,** los números pares (2, 4, 6,...) son actividades
más o menos pasivas o tranquilas. Los números impares (1, 3, 5,...)
representan actividades más activas. ¿Cómo es su compañero/a?

Videoteca

ECUADOR

Minidramas

In this **Minidramas** dialogue, José Miguel Martín Velasco goes shopping
for clothes in his hometown of Quito, Ecuador. What similarities are
there between shopping in an Hispanic country, such as Ecuador, and
in this country? What differences do you notice?

F U N C T I O N
shopping for clothes

José Miguel está en una tienda de ropa. Una empleada[a]
se acerca a[b] *él.*

EMPLEADA: Buenos días. ¿En qué puedo servirle?[c]
JOSÉ MIGUEL: ¿Qué precio tienen estas camisas?
EMPLEADA: Están en rebaja. Cuestan 40.000 sucres[d] cada
una.
JOSÉ MIGUEL: Es un precio excelente.

EMPLEADA: Sí. Las camisas son de puro algodón, y las tenemos de[e] muchos
colores. Aquí tiene una verde, otra roja, otra amarilla y otra azul.
¿Qué talla[f] usa?
JOSÉ MIGUEL: La 38, por lo general.

[a]*employee*   [b]*se... approaches*   [c]¿*En... How may I help you?*   [d]*monetary unit of Ecuador*   [e]*las... we
have them in*   [f]*size*

EMPLEADA: Mire. Estos pantalones son perfectos para esta camisa. Con este pantalón negro y esta camisa azul, Ud. está a la última moda.

JOSÉ MIGUEL: Me gustan mucho los pantalones. Y la camisa también. ¿Me los puedo probar?[g]

EMPLEADA: Sí, cómo no. Por allí[h] están los probadores.[i]

[g]¿Me... *May I try them on?* [h]*Por... Over there* [i]*fitting rooms*

Con un compañero / una compañera

Although it is often possible—and lots of fun—to bargain over the price of an item in a shop or open-air market, merchandise is normally sold at a fixed price in many, if not most, Hispanic stores.

With your instructor acting as the salesperson, try to make the purchases described in one of the following situations. Use the phrases and expressions from the previous dialogue as a model.

1. Ud. está en una *boutique*. Desea comprar un suéter. Quiere un color y un estilo específico.
2. Ud. está en un almacén. Necesita comprar un traje formal / un vestido de noche para asistir a una fiesta muy elegante.

En contexto

In this video segment, which takes place in Costa Rica, Mariela bargains with a street vendor for a very special item. As you watch this segment, pay particular attention to the words that the salesperson uses to convince Mariela to buy. Do they both agree on prices? Who "wins"?

COSTA RICA

A. Lluvia de ideas

- ¿Hay mercados al aire libre en su ciudad? ¿Qué venden? ¿Compra Ud. en ellos con frecuencia?
- En este país, ¿son normales los precios fijos? ¿Hay alguna (*any*) ocasión en que Ud. regatea?

Un poco más sobre...Paloma Velasco

Como Ud. sabe,[a] Paloma Velasco es prima de José Miguel y sobrina de Elisa. Vive en Quito, Ecuador, donde es estudiante universitaria. Paloma es buena estudiante, y le gusta estudiar. Toma muchas clases diferentes: la historia latinoamericana, el francés y la filosofía.

[a]*know*

To read more about the characters from this video, visit the *Puntos de partida* Website at **www.mhhe.com/puntos**

B. Dictado

Here is the first part of this segment's dialogue. Fill in the missing portions of the dialogue.

MARIELA: Buenos días, señora. ¿ _____ _____ son las chaquetas?

VENDEDORA: Las chaquetas son _____, _____ _____. Son muy bonitas, ¿_____?

MARIELA: Sí, son bonitas. ¿Cuánto cuestan?

VENDEDORA: Cuestan _____ _____ colones. Son muy buenas chaquetas.

MARIELA: No estoy segura… Es _____.

VENDEDORA: Pero ¡el precio es _____ _____! Son realmente buenas.

MARIELA: Sí, Ud. tiene razón. Son chaquetas muy bonitas, pero de todos modos son un _____ caras.

C. Un diálogo original

Paso 1. Con un compañero/una compañera, dramaticen la escena de Mariela con la vendedora.

Paso 2. Imagine que Ud. y su compañero/a están de compras en casa de una persona que va a mudarse (*move*).

ESTUDIANTE 1: You want to buy some old clothes that are for sale. You want a cheaper price because you want to buy several items.

ESTUDIANTE 2: You are selling household items. You are willing to lower your prices, but not too much. Your items are high-quality.

Un poco de todo

A. ¿Qué prefieren? Forme oraciones completas usando una palabra o frase de cada (*each*) columna. Si quiere, las oraciones pueden ser negativas también.

1. yo	poder	estudiar en la biblioteca
2. mi mejor (*best*) amigo/a	tener que	visitar mi universidad
3. mis padres / hijos	tener ganas de	ir de compras en el centro
4. nuestro profesor / nuestra (no)	querer	comprar cuando hay rebajas
profesora	preferir	escribir un informe (*report*) para la clase de ¿ ?
5. mi familia	ir (a)	ir al cine (*movies*)
6. tú y yo		llevar ropa informal
		leer novelas de ciencia ficción / terror / ¿ ?

B. Pero, ¿no se puede (*can't one*) **regatear?** Complete the following paragraph with the correct form of the words in parentheses, as suggested by the context. When two possibilities are given in parentheses, select the correct word.

En (los/las[1]) ciudades hispánicas, hay una (grande[2]) variedad de tiendas para (ir[3]) de compras. Hay almacenes, centros comerciales y *boutiques* (elegante[4]), como en (los/las[5]) Estados Unidos, donde los precios son siempre (fijo[6]).

También hay tiendas (pequeño[7]) que venden un solo[a] producto. Por ejemplo,[b] en una zapatería sólo hay zapatos. En español el sufijo **-ería** se usa[c] para (formar[8]) el nombre de la tienda. ¿Dónde (creer[9]) Ud. que venden papel y (otro[10]) artículos de escritorio? ¿A qué tienda (ir[11]) a ir Ud. a comprar fruta?

Si Ud. (poder[12]) pagar el precio que piden,[d] (deber[13]) comprar los recuerdos[e] en (los/las[14]) almacenes o *boutiques*. Pero si (tener[15]) ganas o necesidad de regatear, tiene (de/que[16]) ir a un mercado: un conjunto[f] de tiendas o locales[g] donde el ambiente[h] es más (informal[17]) que[i] en los (grande[18]) almacenes. Ud. no (deber[19]) pagar el primer[j] precio que menciona el vendedor.[k] ¡Casi siempre va (a/de[20]) ser muy alto!

[a]*single* [b]*Por... For example* [c]*se... is used* [d]*they ask* [e]*souvenirs* [f]*group* [g]*stalls* [h]*atmosphere* [i]*than* [j]*first* [k]*seller*

Comprensión: ¿Cierto o falso? Corrija las oraciones falsas.

1. En el mundo hispánico, todas las tiendas son similares.
2. Uno puede regatear en un almacén hispánico.
3. Es posible comprar limones en una papelería.
4. En un mercado, el vendedor siempre ofrece un precio bajo al principio (*beginning*).

C. ¿Somos tan diferentes?

Paso 1. Answer the following questions. Then ask the same questions of other students in the class to try to find at least one person who answered a given question the way you did.

1. De la siguiente lista, ¿qué cosa tienes ganas de tener? ¿Por qué? (**¡OJO!** También es posible contestar: **No quiero tener ninguna.**)
   _____ un abrigo de pieles (*fur*)
   _____ unas botas de cuero (*leather*)
   _____ unos aretes de oro (*gold*)
   _____ un reloj de diamantes
2. ¿Cuál de las siguientes cosas que dicta la moda es la más tonta, en tu opinión?
   _____ llevar aretes en la nariz (*nose*)
   _____ llevar las gorras (*caps*) de atrás para delante (*backward*)
   _____ los *jeans* de los grandes diseñadores como Calvin Klein y Guess
   _____ la ropa de estilo rap
3. ¿Cierto o falso?
   _____ Las personas mayores (*older*) deben llevar siempre ropa de colores oscuros, como negro, gris, etcétera.
   _____ Una mujer que tiene más de 30 años nunca debe llevar minifalda.
   _____ Sólo las mujeres deben usar arete(s).
   _____ Cuando la moda cambia (*changes*), es necesario comprar mucha ropa nueva.

Paso 2. Now ask a classmate his or her opinion about the following items. You can start your questions with the phrases **¿Qué opinas de... ?** or **¿Qué piensas de... ?** Your partner can begin his or her questions with **Creo que...** or **Pienso que...**

1. las personas que sólo llevan ropa oscura
2. las personas que llevan los *jeans* rotos en las rodillas (*torn at the knees*)
3. la ropa de los diseñadores famosos que vemos (*we see*) en las revistas como *Elle, Vogue,* etcétera

PANORAMA *cultural*

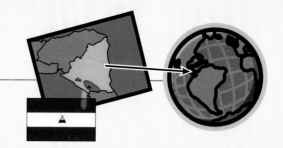

Nicaragua

Datos esenciales

Nombre oficial: República de Nicaragua
Capital: Managua
Población: 4.000.000 de habitantes
Moneda: el córdoba
Idiomas: el español (oficial), el misquito, el sumo*

¡Fíjese!

- En 1856, un norteamericano, William Walker, se declaró[a] presidente de Nicaragua. Dos años después, fue derrotado por[b] los nicaragüenses, liberales y conservadores que se unieron[c] para expulsarlo[d] del país.

- El Lago de Nicaragua es el lago más grande de Centroamérica. Hay más de 300 islas en el lago. En «las Isletas», hay pequeñas comunidades agrícolas[e] y, en algunas,[f] casas de personas ricas.

Violeta Barrios de Chamorro.

- Violeta Barrios de Chamorro fue[g] presidenta de Nicaragua de 1990 a 1997. Fue la primera[h] presiden**ta** en Centroamérica. En 1997, Arnaldo Alemán Lacayo fue elegido[i] presidente.

[a]se... *declared himself* [b]*fue... he was defeated by* [c]*se... joined together* [d]*expel him* [e]*agricultural* [f]*some* [g]*was* [h]*first* [i]*fue... was elected*

Nota histórica

Cristóbal Colón llegó[a] a las costas de Nicaragua en 1502, pero la región no fue colonizada[b] hasta[c] 1524.

Nicaragua tiene una historia turbulenta por las luchas[d] entre las fuerzas conservadoras y las fuerzas liberales. La lucha se complicó[e] por la intervención de los Estados Unidos en la política del país. En 1990 terminó[f] una época[g] difícil de dictadura y lucha: hubo[h] una revolución y un movimiento en contra de la revolución. Esta lucha fue entre los somozistas (revolucionarios marxistas) y los «contras», (antirrevolucionarios).

[a]*arrived* [b]*no... was not colonized* [c]*until* [d]*struggles* [e]*se... was complicated* [f]*ended* [g]*time* [h]*there was*

 Capítulo 3 of the video to accompany *Puntos de partida* contains cultural footage of Nicaragua.

 Visit the *Puntos de partida* Website at www.mhhe.com/puntos.

---

*En la costa oeste (*west coast*) de Nicaragua, también se habla un dialecto criollo (*creole*) que está basado en el inglés.

Vocabulario

Los verbos

ir (*irreg.*)	to go
ir a + *inf.*	to be going to (*do something*)
ir de compras	to go shopping
llevar	to wear; to carry; to take
poder (ue)	to be able, can
preferir (ie)	to prefer
querer (ie)	to want
regatear	to haggle, bargain
tener (*irreg.*)	to have
usar	to wear; to use
venir (*irreg.*)	to come

Repaso: comprar, vender

La ropa

el abrigo	coat
los aretes	earrings
la blusa	blouse
la bolsa	purse
la bota	boot
los calcetines	socks
la camisa	shirt
la camiseta	T-shirt
la cartera	wallet
la chaqueta	jacket
el cinturón	belt
la corbata	tie
la falda	skirt
el impermeable	raincoat
los *jeans*	jeans
las medias	stockings
los pantalones	pants
el par	pair
el reloj	watch
la ropa interior	underwear
la sandalia	sandal
el sombrero	hat
el suéter	sweater
el traje	suit
el traje de baño	swimsuit
el vestido	dress
el zapato (de tenis)	(tennis) shoe

Los colores

amarillo/a	yellow
anaranjado/a	orange
azul	blue
blanco/a	white
gris	gray
morado/a	purple
negro/a	black
pardo/a	brown
rojo/a	red
rosado/a	pink
verde	green

De compras

de cuadros	plaid
de lunares	polka-dotted
de rayas	striped
de última moda	the latest style
la ganga	bargain
el precio (fijo)	(fixed) price
las rebajas	sales, reductions
¿cuánto cuesta?	how much does it cost?
¿cuánto es?	how much is it?

Los materiales

es de...	it is made of...
algodón (*m.*)	cotton
lana	wool
seda	silk

Los lugares

el almacén	department store
el centro	downtown
el centro comercial	shopping mall
el mercado	market(place)
la tienda	shop, store

Otros sustantivos

la cinta	tape
el ejercicio	exercise
el examen	exam, test

Los adjetivos

barato/a	inexpensive
caro/a	expensive
poco/a	little

Los números

doscientos/as, trescientos/as, cuatrocientos/as, quinientos/as, seiscientos/as, setecientos/as, ochocientos/as, novecientos/as, mil, un millón (de)

Repaso: cien(to)

Formas demostrativas

aquel, aquella, aquellos/as	that, those (over there)

ese/a, esos/as	that, those
esto, eso, aquello	this, that, that (over there)

Repaso: este/a, estos/as

Palabras adicionales

¿adónde?	where (to)?
al	to the
algo	something
allí	(over) there
de todo	everything

tener...	
ganas de + *inf.*	to feel like (*doing something*)
miedo (de)	to be afraid (of)
prisa	to be in a hurry
que + *inf.*	to have to (*do something*)
razón	to be right
sueño	to be sleepy
no tener razón	to be wrong
¿no?, ¿verdad?	right?, don't they (you, etc.)?

Un paso más 3

LECTURA

Estrategia: Using Visuals and Graphics to Predict Content

In **Capítulo 1** you learned that you can use section subheadings to help you better understand a passage. Another useful strategy is to use photographs and other visual clues (charts, drawings, graphic images, and so on) that accompany the reading as tools to help you predict the content of the passage. A successful reader is able to make predictions about content in advance, and then confirms or rejects these predictions while reading.

Before reading the article below, look at the subheadings. What predictions can you make based on the visual presentation of the subheadings?

▶ **Sobre la lectura...** This reading is adapted from an article that appeared
▶ in *Quo*, a magazine published in Spain that is comparable to *Vanity Fair, De-*
▶ *tails*, and other glossy general interest magazines. *Quo* publishes articles
▶ about topics ranging from diet and health to fashion to politics.

La psicología de los colores

«Está demostrado[a] que los colores percibidos[b] por la vista[c] <u>provocan</u> una reacción psicológica sobre nuestro estado de ánimo[d]», asegura Carlos Obelleiro, <u>experto</u> en la utilización de color. Y de un buen estado de ánimo depende mucho la salud física. Según expertos en psicología de los colores, cada uno indica una actitud en quien lo lleva puesto[e].

Rojo
Es el color que produce mayor impacto visual. Actúa como un estimulante psíquico, pero activa la <u>agresividad</u> y si alguien lo lleva puede incomodar a los demás.[f]

Amarillo
Está íntimamente relacionado con la autoestima[g] y <u>estimula</u> la creatividad, pero puede resultar agresivo para gente emocionalmente <u>frágil.</u>

Azul
Favorece la calma y la concentración en trabajos que exigen[h] esfuerzo[i] mental. Tranquiliza, pero puede dar imagen de frialdad.[j] Cuanto más oscuro es,[k] más idea da[l] de eficiencia y autoridad.

Verde
Es el color más relajante y suele[m] provocar una sensación de <u>equilibrio</u> y de tranquilidad personal.

Blanco
Aunque[n] es muy higiénico, puede resultar muy severo y dar la impresión de que la persona que lo lleva quiere crear una barrera.[o]

[a]Está... *It has been shown* [b]*perceived* [c]*sight* [d]estado... *state of mind* [e]quien... *the person who wears it* [f]incomodar... *make others uncomfortable* [g]*self esteem* [h]*demand* [i]*effort* [j]*coldness* [k]Cuanto... *The darker it is* [l]*it gives* [m]*it tends to* [n]*Although* [o]crear... *to create a barrier*

Rosa

Es la más pura expresión de la <u>feminidad</u>. Utilizado en decoración actúa como relajante, pero en exceso causa debilitamiento.[p]

Negro

Es elegante, pero puede resultar amenazador[q] y, como el blanco, crear barreras entre la persona que lo lleva y el resto de la gente.

Violeta

Es el color de la introversión. Puede transmitir la sensación de que quien lo viste[r] quiere estar solo, sin intromisiones.[s]

Gris

Se trata del único color totalmente <u>neutro</u>, con lo que no tiene apenas[t] propiedades psicológicas. A veces puede indicar falta[u] de confianza en uno mismo. ●

[p]*debilitation, weakness*   [q]*threatening*   [r]*quien... the person who wears it*   [s]*sin... without intrusions*
[t]*hardly any*   [u]*a lack*

Comprensión

A. ¿Qué color? Identify the color (or colors!) that corresponds to each psychological trait below, according to the reading.

1. Este color no se asocia con la extroversión, sino lo contrario (*but rather the opposite*).
   violeta

2. A veces este color se asocia con la frigidez.
   azul

3. Estos dos colores dan la impresión de crear obstáculos.
   blanco
   negro

4. Este color provoca reacciones muy agresivas.
   rojo + amarillo

5. Este color provoca la creatividad.
   amarillo

B. ¿Qué color recomienda Ud. (*do you recommend*)**?** Which color do you recommend a person wear in order to make the following impressions or provoke the following reactions?

1. Una persona desea dar una impresión de control y poder (*power*). _azul oscuro_
2. Una persona quiere expresar su confianza en sí misma (*confidence in him or herself*).
3. Una persona no quiere producir ningún (*any*) impacto. _gris_

ESCRITURA

Mi ropa favorita. In a brief paragraph, write a description of your favorite article of clothing. You will want to include information such as the material that it is made of, why you like it, and so on. And be sure to identify the color! How do you feel when you wear it? Does the color provoke certain reactions in you, similar to those described in the reading? What reactions? Your instructor can help you with words or constructions that are unfamiliar to you.

En casa

¿Cómo es su casa? ¿Es moderna y urbana o es antigua (*old*) y rural como esta en Guadalajara, México?

¿Qué opina Ud.?

Conteste según su propia vida (*Answer according to your own life*). ¿Cree Ud. que una persona de otro país diría (*would say*) algo similar? Visite (*Visit*) el sitio Web de *Puntos de partida* para leer las respuestas a estas preguntas que da (*are given by*) una persona de Costa Rica.

1. ¿Vive Ud. en una casa, en una residencia o en un apartamento? ¿Cómo es?
2. ¿Es grande? ¿Cuántos cuartos tiene? ¿Qué **muebles** tiene Ud. en su casa?
3. ¿Tiene Ud. un cuarto favorito? ¿Qué **hace** Ud. en ese cuarto?
4. ¿Qué parte de la casa es **la más** importante para Ud.?
5. ¿Hay tiendas cerca de (*near*) su casa, residencia o apartamento? ¿Qué venden?

En este capítulo...

- In this chapter you will study vocabulary related to the day of the week and to the parts and furnishings of a house.
- In **Capítulo 3**, you learned several irregular verbs. In this chapter, you will learn some additional ones that will help you express actions such as *to do*, *to hear*, *to bring*, and so on. (Grammar 12)
- You will also practice some verbs that have the same stem-changes as **querer** and **poder**, which you also learned in **Capítulo 3**. (Grammar 13)
- Spanish has a way of changing a verb to indicate an action that you do to yourself or for yourself (bathing yourself, for example). In this chapter you will learn how to do that by using reflexive pronouns. (Grammar 14)
- The **Panorama cultural** section will focus on Costa Rica.

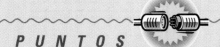

P U N T O S   I N T E R A C T I V O

Videoteca

◀ **Minidramas**
Diego va a vivir con su amigo Antonio. ¿Vive Ud. con un amigo / una amiga? ¿Le gusta a Ud. el lugar donde vive?

En contexto ▶
Juan Carlos busca un apartamento y habla con una agente de inmobiliaria (*real estate agent*). ¿Con quién habla Ud. cuando tiene que mudarse (*move*)?

 CD-ROM

In addition to completing vocabulary and grammar activities, you will have the opportunity to role-play the part of an apartment-seeker "talking" to a real estate agent.

 Internet

In the **Capítulo 4** section of the *Puntos de partida* Website you can access links to Spanish-language resources about homes at **www.mhhe.com/puntos**.

Vocabulario: Preparación

¿Qué día es hoy?

lunes	Monday		
martes	Tuesday		
miércoles	Wednesday		
jueves	Thursday		
viernes	Friday		
sábado	Saturday		
domingo	Sunday		

agosto

lunes 14	jueves 17
martes 15	viernes 18
miércoles 16	sábado 19 domingo 20

el lunes, el martes...	on Monday, on Tuesday . . .
los lunes, los martes...	on Mondays, on Tuesdays . . .
Hoy (Mañana) es viernes.	Today (Tomorrow) is Friday.
Ayer fue miércoles.	Yesterday was Wednesday.
el fin de semana	(on) the weekend
pasado mañana	the day after tomorrow
el próximo (martes, miércoles,...)	next (Tuesday, Wednesday, . . .)
la semana que viene	next week

- Except for **el sábado / los sábados** and **el domingo / los domingos**, all the days of the week use the same form for the plural as they do for the singular.
- The definite articles are used to express *on* with the days of the week.
- The days are not capitalized in Spanish.
- In Spanish-speaking countries, the week usually starts with **lunes**.

Conversación

A. Preguntas

1. ¿Qué día es hoy? ¿Qué día es mañana? Si hoy es sábado, ¿qué día es mañana? Si hoy es jueves, ¿qué día es mañana? ¿Qué día fue ayer?
2. ¿Qué días de la semana tenemos clase? ¿Qué días no?
3. ¿Estudia Ud. mucho durante (*during*) el fin de semana? ¿y los domingos por la noche?
4. ¿Qué le gusta hacer (*to do*) los viernes por la tarde? ¿Le gusta salir (*to go out*) con los amigos los sábados por la noche?

B. Mi semana

Indique una cosa que Ud. quiere, puede o tiene que hacer cada (*each*) día de esta semana.

MODELO: El lunes tengo que (puedo, quiero) ir al laboratorio de lenguas.

Palabras útiles: dormir (*to sleep*) hasta muy tarde, jugar (*to play*) al tenis (al golf, al vólibol, al…), ir al cine (*movies*), ir al bar (al parque, al museo, a…)

Los muebles,° los cuartos y otras partes de la casa

Los... *Furniture*

la alcoba*	bedroom	**la cama (de agua)**	(water) bed
el baño	bathroom	**la cómoda**	bureau; dresser
la cocina	kitchen	**el escritorio**	desk
el comedor	dining room	**el estante**	bookshelf
el garaje	garage	**la lámpara**	lamp
el jardín	yard	**el lavabo**	(bathroom) sink
la pared	wall	**la mesa**	table
el patio	patio; yard	**la mesita**	end table
la piscina	swimming pool	**los platos**	dishes; plates
la sala	living room	**la silla**	chair
		el sillón	armchair
la alfombra	rug	**el sofá**	sofa
el armario	closet	**el televisor**	television set
la bañera	bathtub		

Note: This is the first group of words you will learn for talking about where you live and the things found in your house or apartment. You will learn additional vocabulary for those topics in **Capítulos 9**, **12**, and **14**.

Conversación

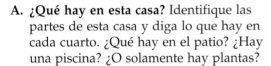

A. ¿Qué hay en esta casa? Identifique las partes de esta casa y diga lo que hay en cada cuarto. ¿Qué hay en el patio? ¿Hay una piscina? ¿O solamente hay plantas?

B. Asociaciones

Paso 1. ¿Qué muebles o partes de la casa asocia Ud. con las siguientes actividades?

1. estudiar para un examen
2. dormir la siesta (*taking a nap*) por la tarde

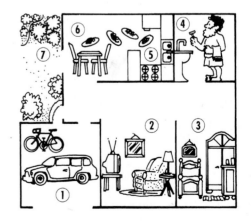

---

*Other frequently used words for *bedroom* include **el dormitorio** and **la habitación**.

---

3. pasar una noche en casa con la familia
4. celebrar con una comida (*meal*) especial
5. tomar el sol (*sunbathing*)
6. hablar de temas (*topics*) serios con los amigos (padres, hijos)

Paso 2. Ahora compare sus asociaciones con las (*those*) de otros estudiantes. ¿Tienen todos las mismas costumbres (*customs*)?

¿Cuándo? • Preposiciones

Prepositions express relationships in time and space.	The book is *on* the table. The homework is *for* tomorrow.
Some common prepositions you have already used include **a, con, de, en, para,** and **por.** Here are some prepositions that express time relationships.	**antes de** *before* **durante** *during* **después de** *after* **hasta** *until*
The infinitive is the only verb form that can follow a preposition.	¿Adónde vas **después de estudiar**? *Where are you going after studying (after you study)?*

Conversación

A. ¿Antes o después?   Complete las oraciones lógicamente, con **antes de** o **después de.**

1. Voy a la clase de español _____ preparar la lección.
2. Por lo general, prefiero estudiar _____ mirar un poco la televisión.
3. Los viernes siempre descanso (*I rest*) _____ salir para una fiesta.
4. Me gusta investigar un tema _____ escribir una composición.
5. Prefiero comer fuera (*to eat out*) _____ ir al cine.
6. Tengo que estudiar mucho _____ tomar un examen.

B. Preguntas

1. ¿Estudia Ud. durante su programa favorito de televisión? ¿Qué más hace (*do you do*) cuando estudia?
2. ¿Habla por teléfono antes o después de estudiar? ¿Dónde habla por teléfono, en la sala o en su cuarto?
3. ¿Hasta qué hora estudia, generalmente? ¿Estudia hasta dormirse (*you fall asleep*)?

4. ¿Lee durante las conferencias (*lectures*) en una clase? ¿Lee la lección antes o después de la explicación (*explanation*) del profesor / de la profesora?
5. ¿Trabaja durante las vacaciones? ¿Cuántas horas? ¿Trabaja por la noche hasta muy tarde?

Nota cultural

Houses in the Hispanic World

There is no such thing as a typical Hispanic house. Often, the style of housing depends on geographic location. For example, in hot regions, many houses are built around a central interior patio. These patios are filled with plants, and some even have a fountain.

However, the population in Hispanic countries tends to be centered in urban areas. That's why the majority of people that live in a city live in apartments, like people in larger cities in this country. Here are some more details about Hispanic houses.

El balcón de una casa en San Juan, Puerto Rico

- While the Spanish word **hogar** literally means *home,* Hispanics often speak of a **casa**, whether they live in an actual house or an apartment.

    Voy a casa.   *I'm going home.*

- Hispanics are generally more concerned with the appearance of the inside of their homes than the outside.
- A balcony or terrace is a very desirable feature in an apartment.
- Many houses are also homes to birds. They are normally small birds that sing beautifully, such as canaries.

Pronunciación: b and v

In Spanish, the pronunciation of the letters **b** and **v** is identical. At the beginning of a phrase or sentence—that is, after a pause—or after **m** or **n,** the letters **b** and **v** are pronounced just like the English stop [b]. Everywhere else they are pronounced like the fricative [b̄], produced by creating friction when pushing the air through the lips. This sound has no equivalent in English.

A. Práctica. Practique las siguientes palabras y frases.

1. [b]　　bueno viejo verde venir barato Vicente viernes también hombre sombrero
2. [b̶]　　nueve llevar libro pobre abrir abrigo universidad abuelo
3. [b/b̶]　bueno / es bueno　busca / Ud. busca　bien / muy bien
　　　　　en Venezuela / de Venezuela　vende / se vende
　　　　　en Bolivia / de Bolivia
4. [b/b̶]　beber bebida vivir biblioteca Babel vívido

B. Adivinanza (*Riddle*).　Practice saying the following riddle aloud. Pay special attention to the pronunciation of the **b** sound.

Busca, busca, estoy abajo;
busca, busca, estoy arriba;
busca, busca, en la cabeza,
busca, busca, en la barriga.

¿No me encuentras? Busca, busca,
que me doblo en las bombillas.

Look, look, I'm below;
look, look, I'm above;
look, look, in your head,
look, look, in your belly.

You can't find me? Look, look,
because I appear twice in
*　lightbulbs.*

Minidiálogos y gramática

12　**Expressing Actions** • *Hacer, oír, poner, salir, traer,* and *ver*

Los jóvenes de hoy

«¡Estos muchachos sólo quieren *salir*! No *ponen* sus cosas en orden en sus cuartos... Los jóvenes de hoy día no *hacen* nada bien; no son responsables... ¡Hasta quieren *traer* muchachas a sus cuartos!»

¿Son estos comentarios típicos de las personas mayores (*elderly*) de su país?
¿Cree Ud. que tienen razón?
¿Tienen los jóvenes algunos (*any*) estereotipos sobre (*about*) las personas mayores?

Today's young people These boys only want to go out! They don't put things in order in their rooms. . . Today's young people don't do anything right; they are not responsible people . . . They even want to bring girls to their rooms!

hacer (to do; to make)		oír (to hear)		poner (to put; to place)		salir (to leave; to go out)		traer (to bring)		ver (to see)	
hago	hacemos	oigo	oímos	pongo	ponemos	salgo	salimos	traigo	traemos	veo	vemos
haces	hacéis	oyes	ois	pones	ponéis	sales	salís	traes	traéis	ves	veis
hace	hacen	oye	oyen	pone	ponen	sale	salen	trae	traen	ve	ven

- **hacer**

  Some common idioms with **hacer** are **hacer ejercicio** (*to exercise*), **hacer un viaje** (*to take a trip*), and **hacer una pregunta** (*to ask a question*).

  ¿Por qué no **haces** los ejercicios?
  Why aren't you doing the exercises?

  Quieren **hacer un viaje** al Perú.
  They want to take a trip to Peru.

  Los niños siempre **hacen muchas preguntas.**
  Children always ask a lot of questions.

- **oír**

  The command forms of **oír**—**oye (tú), oiga (Ud.),** and **oigan (Uds.)**—are used to attract someone's attention in the same way that English uses *Listen!* or *Hey!*

  No **oigo** bien por el ruido.
  I can't hear well because of the noise.

  Oye, Juan, ¿vas a la fiesta?
  Hey, Juan, are you going to the party?

  ¡Oigan! ¡Silencio, por favor!
  Listen! Silence, please!

- **poner**

  Many Spanish speakers use **poner** with appliances to express *to turn on.*

  Siempre **pongo** leche y mucho azúcar en el café.
  I always put milk and a lot of sugar in my coffee.

  Voy a **poner** el televisor.
  I'm going to turn on the TV.

- **salir**

  Note that **salir** is always followed by **de** to express leaving a place. **Salir con** can mean *to go out with, to date.*

  Use **salir para** to indicate destination.

  Salen de la clase ahora.
  They're leaving class now.

  Salgo con el hermano de Cecilia.
  I'm going out with Cecilia's brother.

  Salimos para la sierra pasado mañana.
  We're leaving for the mountains the day after tomorrow.

- **traer**

  ¿Por qué no **traes** la radio a la cocina?
  Why don't you bring the radio to the kitchen?

- **ver**

  No **veo** bien sin mis lentes de contacto.
  I can't see well without my contact lenses.

Minidiálogos y gramática

Práctica

Cosas rutinarias

Paso 1. ¿Cierto o falso?

1. Hago ejercicio en el gimnasio con frecuencia.
2. Siempre veo la televisión por la noche.
3. Nunca salgo con mis primos por la noche.
4. Siempre hago los ejercicios para la clase de español.
5. Salgo para clase a las ocho de la mañana.
6. Nunca pongo la ropa en la cómoda o en el armario.
7. Siempre traigo todos los libros necesarios a clase.
8. Siempre oigo todo lo que dice (*says*) el profesor / la profesora de español.

Paso 2. Now rephrase each sentence in **Paso 1** as a question and interview a classmate. Use the **tú** form of the verb.

Conversación

A. Consecuencias lógicas. Con un compañero / una compañera, indiquen una acción lógica para cada situación, usando (*using*) las siguientes frases.

Frases útiles: poner el televisor / el estéreo, oír al profesor / a la profesora,* salir con/de/para… , hacer un viaje / una pregunta, traer el libro a clase, ver mi programa favorito.

1. Me gusta esquiar en las montañas. Por eso…
2. En la clase de español usamos este libro todos los días. Por eso…
3. Mis compañeros de cuarto hacen mucho ruido en la sala. Por eso…
4. El televisor no funciona. Por eso no…
5. Hay mucho ruido en la clase. Por eso no…
6. Estoy en la biblioteca y ¡no puedo estudiar más! Por eso…
7. Queremos bailar y necesitamos música. Por eso…
8. No comprendo la lección. Por eso…

B. Preguntas

1. ¿Qué pone Ud. en el armario? ¿en la cómoda? ¿Qué pone en su mochila o bolsa todos los días para ir a clase? Generalmente, ¿qué más trae a clase?
2. ¿Qué quiere hacer esta noche (*tonight*)? ¿Qué necesita hacer? ¿Qué va a hacer? ¿Va a salir con sus amigos (con su familia)? ¿Adónde van?
3. ¿A qué hora sale Ud. de la clase de español? ¿de las otras clases? ¿A veces sale tarde de clase? ¿Por qué?

---

*Remember that the word **a** is necessary in front of a human direct object. You will study this usage of **a** in **Capítulo 6**. For now, you can answer following the pattern of the **frase útil**.

4. ¿Oye Ud. las noticias (*news*) todos los días? ¿Pone Ud. la radio o el televisor para oír las noticias? ¿Y para oír música? ¿Qué programa ve en la televisión todas las semanas?

¿Recuerda Ud.?

The change in the stem vowels of **querer** and **poder** (**e** and **o**, respectively) follows the same pattern as that of the verbs presented in the next section. Review the forms of **querer** and **poder** before beginning that section.

querer: **e** → ¿?   qu ____ ro   queremos
                   qu ____ res   queréis
                   qu ____ re   qu ____ ren

poder: **o** → ¿?   p ____ do   podemos
                 p ____ des   podéis
                 p ____ de   p ____ den

13   Expressing Actions • Present Tense of Stem-Changing Verbs

¡Nunca más!

ALICIA: ¡No *vuelvo* a comprar en la papelería Franco!
ARMANDO: Yo también *empiezo* a cansarme de esa tienda. Nunca *tienen* los materiales que les *pido*.
ALICIA: ¿No *piensas* que los precios son muy caros? Yo creo
que siempre *perdemos* dinero cuando compramos allí.
ARMANDO: Te *entiendo* perfectamente. Los precios son horribles. Como la papelería está tan cerca de la facultad, ¡*piensan* que *pueden* pedir mucho dinero por todo!

¿Quién piensa que…

1. los precios de la papelería son muy caros?
2. la papelería no tiene muchas cosas necesarias?
3. pueden pedir mucho dinero porque la papelería está muy cerca de la facultad?
4. los estudiantes pierden dinero cuando compran en la papelería Franco?

▲▲▲▲▲

Never again! ALICIA: I'm not going to shop at Franco's stationery store again! ARMANDO: I'm also beginning to get fed up with that store. They never have the things I ask them for. ALICIA: Don't you think that the prices are very expensive? I think that we always lose money when we buy there. ARMANDO: I understand you perfectly. The prices are awful. Since the stationery store is so close to the campus, they think that they can ask a lot of money for everything!

e → ie **pensar (ie)** (*to think*)		o (u) → ue **volver (ue)** (*to return*)		e → i **pedir (i)** (*to ask for; to order*)	
pienso	pensamos	vuelvo	volvemos	pido	pedimos
piensas	pensáis	vuelves	volvéis	pides	pedís
piensa	piensan	vuelve	vuelven	pide	piden

A: You have already learned five *stem-changing verbs* (**los verbos que cambian el radical**): **querer, preferir, tener, venir,** and **poder.** In these verbs the stem vowels **e** and **o** become **ie** and **ue,** respectively, in stressed syllables. The stem vowels are stressed in all present tense forms except **nosotros** and **vosotros.** All three classes of stem-changing verbs follow this regular pattern in the present tense. In vocabulary lists, the stem change will always be shown in parentheses after the infinitive: **volver (ue).**

Stem vowel changes:

e → ie
e → i
o → ue

Nosotros and **vosotros** forms do not have a stem vowel change.

B: Some stem-changing verbs practiced in this chapter include the following.

e → ie		o (u) → ue		e → i	
cerrar (ie)	*to close*	almorzar (ue)	*to have lunch*	pedir (i)	*to ask for; to order*
empezar (ie)	*to begin*	dormir (ue)	*to sleep*	servir (i)	*to serve*
entender (ie)	*to understand*	jugar (ue)*	*to play* (a game, sport)		
pensar (ie)	*to think*				
perder (ie)	*to lose; to miss (a function)*	volver (ue)	*to return (to a place)*		

- When used with an infinitive, **empezar** is followed by **a.**

Uds. **empiezan a hablar** muy bien el español.
You're beginning to speak Spanish very well.

- When used with an infinitive, **volver** is also followed by **a.** The phrase then means *to do (something) again.*

¿Cuándo **vuelves a jugar** al tenis?
When are you going to play tennis again?

---

*Jugar is the only **u → ue** stem-changing verb in Spanish. **Jugar** is often followed by **al** when used with the name of a sport: **Juego** *al* **tenis.** Some Spanish speakers, however, omit the **al**.

- When followed directly by an infinitive, **pensar** means *to intend, plan to.*

  The phrase **pensar en** can be used to express *to think about.*

¿Cuándo **piensas contestar** la carta?
When do you intend to answer the letter?

—¿**En** qué **piensas**?
What are you thinking about?

—**Pienso en** la tarea para la clase de física.
I'm thinking about the homework for physics class.

Práctica

▲▲▲▲▲▲

A. **¿Dónde están Diego y Antonio?** Tell in what part of Antonio's apartment the following things are happening. More than one answer is possible in some cases.

MODELO: Diego y Antonio empiezan a hacer la tarea. → Están en la alcoba.

1. Antonio sirve el desayuno (*breakfast*).
2. Antonio cierra la revista y pone el televisor.
3. Los dos almuerzan con un compañero de la universidad.
4. Los dos juegan al ajedrez (*chess*), y Diego pierde.
5. Diego piensa en las cosas que tiene que hacer hoy.
6. Antonio vuelve a casa después de las clases.
7. Antonio duerme la siesta.
8. Diego pide una pizza por teléfono.

B. **Una tarde típica en casa.** ¿Cuáles son las actividades de todos? Haga oraciones completas con una palabra o frase de cada grupo. Use sólo los nombres que son apropiados para Ud.

yo			
mi padre/madre		almorzar	descansar, dormir
mi esposo/a		volver	en un sillón / en el patio / en la cocina
los niños		preferir	toda la tarde
		perder	su pelota (*ball*)
mi amigo/a ____ y yo	(no)	pensar	muchos refrescos (*soft drinks*)
el perro/gato		jugar	tarde / temprano a casa
mi compañero/a		pedir	afuera (*outside*)
		dormir	la siesta
		¿ ?	en el patio / en la piscina
			al golf (tenis, vólibol…)
			las películas (*movies*) viejas/recientes
			¿ ?

C. Hoy queremos comer paella

Paso 1. Using the following cues as a guide, tell about the visit of Ismael's family to a restaurant that specializes in Hispanic cuisine. Use **ellos** as the subject except where otherwise indicated.

Minidiálogos y gramática

1. familia / de / Ismael / tener ganas / comer / paella
2. volver / a / su / restaurante / favorito
3. pensar / que / paella / de / restaurante / ser / estupendo
4. pedir / paella / para / seis / persona
5. pero / hoy / sólo / servir / menú (*m.*) / mexicano
6. por eso / pedir / tacos / y / guacamole (*m.*)

Paso 2. Now retell the story as if it were your family, using **nosotros** as the subject, except in item 5, where you will use **ellos**.

Conversación
▲▲▲▲▲▲▲

Preguntas

1. ¿A qué hora cierran la biblioteca? ¿A qué hora cierran la cafetería? Y durante la época de los exámenes finales, ¿a qué hora cierran?
2. ¿A qué hora almuerza Ud., por lo general? ¿Dónde le gusta almorzar? ¿Con quién? ¿Dónde piensa Ud. almorzar hoy? ¿mañana?
3. ¿Es Ud. un poco olvidadizo/a? Es decir (*That is*), ¿pierde las cosas con frecuencia? ¿Qué cosa pierde Ud.? ¿el dinero? ¿su cuaderno? ¿su mochila? ¿sus llaves (*keys*)?

14 **Expressing -self/selves** • Reflexive Pronouns

La rutina diaria de Diego

1.

2.

3.

4.

5.

6.

7.

Me despierto a las siete y media y *me levanto* en seguida (1). Primero, *me ducho* (2) y luego *me cepillo* los dientes (3). *Me peino* (4), *me pongo* la bata (5) y voy al cuarto a *vestirme* (6). Por fin, salgo para mis clases (7). No tomo nada antes de salir para la universidad porque, por lo general, ¡tengo prisa!

Diego's daily routine I wake up at seven-thirty and I get up right away. First, I take a shower and then I brush my teeth. I comb my hair, I put on my robe, and I go to my room to get dressed. Finally, I leave for my classes. I don't eat or drink anything before leaving for the university because I'm generally in a hurry!

¿Cómo es la rutina diaria de Ud.?

1. Yo me levanto a las _____.
2. Me ducho por la (mañana/noche).
3. Me visto en (el baño/mi cuarto).
4. Me peino (antes de/después de) vestirme.
5. Antes de salir para las clases, (tomo/no tomo) el desayuno.

Uses of Reflexive Pronouns

bañarse (*to take a bath*)

(yo)	**me** baño	*I take a bath*
(tú)	**te** bañas	*you take a bath*
(Ud.)		*you take a bath*
(él)	**se** baña	*he takes a bath*
(ella)		*she takes a bath*
(nosotros)	**nos** bañamos	*we take baths*
(vosotros)	**os** bañáis	*you take baths*
(Uds.)		*you take baths*
(ellos)	**se** bañan	*they take baths*
(ellas)		*they take baths*

A. The pronoun **se** at the end of an infinitive indicates that the verb is used reflexively. The reflexive pronoun in Spanish reflects the subject doing something to or for himself, herself, or itself. When the verb is conjugated, the reflexive pronoun that corresponds to the subject must be used.

Many English verbs that describe parts of one's daily routine—to get up, to take a bath, and so on—are expressed in Spanish with a reflexive construction.

Reflexive Pronouns

me	myself
te	yourself (*fam, sing.*)
se	himself, herself, itself; yourself (*form. sing.*)

nos	ourselves
os	yourselves (*fam. pl. Sp.*)
se	themselves; yourselves (*form. pl.*)

me baño = I take a bath (bathe myself)

B. Here are some reflexive verbs you will find useful as you talk about daily routines. Note that some of these verbs are also stem-changing.

acostarse (ue)	to go to bed	**levantarse**	to get up; to stand up
afeitarse	to shave		
bañarse	to take a bath	**ponerse**	to put on (*clothing*)
despertarse (ie)	to wake up		
divertirse (ie)	to have a good time, enjoy oneself	**quitarse**	to take off (*clothing*)
dormirse (ue)	to fall asleep	**sentarse (ie)**	to sit down
ducharse	to take a shower	**vestirse (i)**	to get dressed

Note also the verb **llamarse** (*to be called*), which you have been using since **Ante todo: Me llamo**_____. **¿Cómo se llama Ud.?**

All of these verbs can also be used nonreflexively, often with a different meaning. Some examples of this appear at the right:

O J O

After **ponerse** and **quitarse**, the definite article, not the possessive as in English, is used with articles of clothing.

[Práctica A–B]

dormir = to sleep   **dormirse** = to fall asleep
poner = to put, place   **ponerse** = to put on

Se pone **el** abrigo.
He's putting on his coat.

Se quitan **el** sombrero.
They're taking off their hats.

Placement of Reflexive Pronouns

Reflexive pronouns are placed before a conjugated verb but after the word **no** in a negative sentence: **No** *se* **bañan.** They may either precede the conjugated verb or be attached to an infinitive.

[Práctica C]

Me tengo que levantar temprano.
Tengo que levantar**me** temprano.
I have to get up early.

Práctica

A. Su rutina diaria

Paso 1.   ¿Hace Ud. lo mismo (*the same thing*) todos los días? Conteste con sí o no.

	LOS LUNES		LOS SÁBADOS	
	SÍ	NO	SÍ	NO
1. Me levanto antes de las ocho.	☐	☒	☐	☒
2. Siempre me baño o me ducho.	☒	☐	☒	☐
3. Siempre me afeito.	☒	☐	☒	☐
4. Me pongo un traje / un vestido / una falda.	☐	☒	☐	☒

5. Me quito los zapatos después de
llegar a casa. ☒ ☐ ☒ ☐

6. Me acuesto antes de las once de la noche. ☐ ☒ ☐ ☒

Paso 2. ¿Tiene Ud. una rutina diferente los sábados? ¿Qué día prefiere? ¿Por qué?

B. La rutina diaria de los Durán

Paso 1. ¿Qué acostumbran hacer los miembros de la familia Durán? Conteste, imaginando (*imagining*) que Ud. es Manolo Durán. Use el sujeto pronominal cuando sea (*whenever it is*) necesario.

1. yo / levantarse / a las siete
2. mi esposa Lola / levantarse / más tarde
3. nosotros / ducharse / por la mañana
4. por costumbre / nuestro / hija Marta / bañarse / por la noche
5. yo / vestirse / antes de tomar el desayuno
6. Lola / vestirse / después de tomar un café
7. por la noche / Marta / acostarse / temprano
8. yo / acostarse / más tarde, a las once
9. por lo general / Lola / acostarse / más tarde que (*than*) yo

Paso 2. En la familia Durán, ¿quién… ?
1. se levanta primero Manolo 3. no se baña por la mañana Marta
2. se acuesta primero Marta 4. se viste antes de tomar el desayuno Manolo

C. Un día típico

Paso 1. Complete las siguientes oraciones lógicamente para describir su rutina diaria. Use el pronombre reflexivo cuando sea necesario. **¡OJO!** Use el infinitivo después de las preposiciones.

1. Me levanto después de _____.
2. Primero (yo) _____ y luego _____.
3. Me visto antes de / después de _____.
4. Luego me siento a la mesa para _____.
5. Me gusta estudiar antes de _____ o después de _____.
6. Por la noche me divierto un poco y luego _____.
7. Me acuesto antes de / después de _____ y finalmente _____.

Paso 2. Con las oraciones del **Paso 1,** describa los hábitos de su esposo/a, su compañero/a de cuarto/casa, sus hijos…

Conversación
▲▲▲▲▲▲▲

A. Entrevista: ¿Cómo es tu rutina diaria?

Paso 1. Ahora, con un compañero / una compañera, hagan y contesten preguntas breves sobre su rutina diaria. Anote (*Jot down*) las respuestas de su compañero/a.

1. Los días de semana (*weekdays*), ¿te levantas temprano? ¿antes de las siete de la mañana? ¿A qué hora te levantas los sábados?
2. ¿Te bañas o te duchas? ¿Cuándo lo haces (*do you do it*), por la mañana o por la noche?
3. ¿Te afeitas todos los días? ¿Usas una afeitadora eléctrica? ¿Prefieres no afeitarte los fines de semana?
4. Por lo general, ¿te vistes con elegancia o informalmente? ¿Qué ropa te pones cuando quieres estar elegante? ¿cuando quieres estar muy cómodo/a (*comfortable*)? ¿Qué te pones para ir a la universidad?
5. ¿A qué hora vuelves a casa, generalmente? ¿Qué haces cuando regresas? ¿Te quitas los zapatos? ¿Te pones ropa más cómoda? ¿Estudias? ¿Miras la televisión? ¿Preparas la cena (*dinner*)?
6. ¿A qué hora te acuestas? ¿Cuál es la última (*last*) cosa que haces antes de acostarte? ¿Cuál es la última cosa o persona en que piensas antes de dormirte?

Paso 2. Ahora, describa la rutina de su compañero/a a la clase, usando las respuestas del **Paso 1.** ¿Cuántos estudiantes de la clase tienen rutinas parecidas (*similar*)?

En los Estados Unidos y el Canadá...

Vicente Wolf

As a boy in Cuba, designer Vicente Wolf spent hours in architects' studios and at construction sites. The visits he paid to museums in Havana when he was a teenager awakened his love for art. The experience of being a Cuban refugee who moved to Miami at age 14 and was forced to begin a new life in a foreign country also drove him in his determination to succeed.

Una sala decorada por Vicente Wolf

the Design and Decoration Building in Manhattan. He successfully completed several commissions and then became a business associate of the Spanish designer Robert Patino, a partnership that lasted for sixteen years.

Currently, Wolf runs his own business and lectures at the Parsons School of Design. He believes that it is important for Hispanics to hear about the

Wolf never formally studied interior design, but rather learned it on the job. When he was 18, he moved from Miami to New York and found work at

success that other Hispanic immigrants have had in this country, with the hope that it will instill in them the desire to succeed as he has done.

B. **Hábitos.** ¿Dónde hace Ud. lo siguiente? Indique el cuarto o la parte de la casa donde Ud. hace cada actividad. Debe indicar también los muebles y otras cosas que usa.

MODELO: estudiar →
Cuando estudio, prefiero estar (por lo general estoy) en la
alcoba. Uso el escritorio, una silla, los libros y la computadora.

1. estudiar
2. dormir la siesta
3. quitarse los zapatos
4. bañarse o ducharse
5. despertarse
6. tomar el desayuno
7. sentarse a almorzar
8. vestirse
9. divertirse
10. acostarse

Videoteca

MÉXICO

Minidramas

In this **Minidramas** dialogue,
Diego decides to move out of his aunt Matilde's
house and into an apartment with Antonio,
his friend from the university. Here they are
talking about their daily routines. Are these
routines similar to yours, or different?

F U N C T I O N

*talking about daily
routines*

*Diego acaba de mudarse[a] al apartamento de su amigo
Antonio. Los dos hablan de su rutina diaria*

DIEGO: Dime,[b] Antonio, ¿cómo es el horario de
Uds.?

ANTONIO: Normalmente, yo me levanto a las siete y
Juan se levanta a las seis y media. ¿A qué
horas te levantas tú?

DIEGO: Si tengo clases, me levanto a las siete y
media.

ANTONIO: ¡Perfecto! Primero Juan se baña y se afeita,
después yo y por último tú.

DIEGO: ¿Y vuelven Uds. a casa para almorzar?

ANTONIO: Bueno, los lunes, miércoles y viernes sí
vuelvo a casa para almorzar, porque no tengo clases por la tarde.
Pero los martes y jueves almuerzo en la cafetería de la
universidad. Juan no vuelve a casa para almorzar. Come en casa
de su novia.[c]

DIEGO: Muy bien. Entonces, los lunes, miércoles y viernes podemos
almorzar aquí tú y yo. Antonio, creo que sí me va a gustar mucho
vivir aquí.

[a]acaba... *has just moved in* [b]*Tell me* [c]*girlfriend*

Con un compañero / una compañera

Find a classmate with whom you have not yet spoken about your daily
schedule. Take turns repeating the dialogue with real information about your

routines. Take notes about what the other person says. Then, report your
information to the class.

En contexto

In this video segment, Juan Carlos, the Peruvian
student, talks to a real estate agent about an
apartment. As you watch the segment, pay particular
attention to the questions that the agent asks and to
Juan Carlos' answers. What kind of apartment does
Juan Carlos want? What rooms would he like?

PERÚ

A. Lluvia de ideas

- ¿Vive Ud. en un apartamento o en una casa? ¿Con quién vive? ¿Le gusta
  a Ud. su vivienda (*home*)? ¿Por qué?
- ¿Cambia Ud. de vivienda con frecuencia? ¿Qué hace para buscar una
  nueva vivienda? ¿Usa los servicios de un(a) agente de inmobiliaria (*real
  estate agent*)?
- ¿Piensa cambiar de vivienda en un futuro próximo (*in the near future*)?
  ¿Qué tipo de vivienda va a buscar?

B. Dictado

Here is the first part of this segment's dialogue. Fill in the missing portions
of the dialogue.

AGENTE: ¿Juan Carlos Alarcón?
JUAN CARLOS: ¿Sí?
AGENTE: _____ _____. Yo soy Amanda Villanueva, la agente.
JUAN CARLOS: Es un placer,[a] _____.
AGENTE: _____. ¿Así que Ud. busca _____?
JUAN CARLOS: Sí._____ _____ en un apartamento cerca del[b] centro.
AGENTE: ¿Y qué tipo de apartamento _____? Tenemos
muchísimos[c]…

[a]*pleasure* [b]*cerca... near to the* [c]*lots*

Un poco más sobre... Antonio Sifuentes

Antonio Sifuentes es un
estudiante graduado en
la UNAM, donde es
amigo de Diego
González. De hecho,[a]
no sólo son amigos.
También son
compañeros de casa.
Antonio invita a Diego
a compartir[b] su
apartamento porque
Diego no está contento
en casa de su tía
Matilde. Diego, como
muchos estudiantes,
quiere ser
independiente.

[a]*De... In fact* [b]*share*

To read more about the
characters from this
video visit the *Puntos
de partida* Website at
www.mhhe.com/puntos

C. Un diálogo original

Paso 1. Con un compañero / una compañera dramaticen la escena de Juan Carlos con la agente.

Paso 2. Imagine que Ud. y su compañero/a van a buscar un apartamento juntos/as (*together*). Pero primero (*first*) deben decidir lo que necesitan y pueden pagar

ESTUDIANTE 1: You want at least two bedrooms and no more housemates. You can afford $500/month (**al mes**).

ESTUDIANTE 2: Location is important for you, but you don't have a lot of money (only $400/month). For this reason, you prefer to share (**compartir**) a bedroom or get another housemate.

Un poco de todo

A. Un día normal. Ángela es dependienta en una tienda de ropa para jóvenes en El Paso. ¿Cómo es un día normal de trabajo para ella? Complete la narración en la página 150 con los verbos apropiados, según los dibujos.

Vocabulario útil

These adverbs will help you understand the sequence of events.

primero	first		**luego**	then, afterward
entonces	then, next		**finalmente**	finally

1.

2.   3.

4.   **5.**   **6.**

Verbos: almorzar, cerrar, comer, dormir, empezar, hablar, ir, pedir, ser, volver

1. Llego a la tienda a las 9:50 de la mañana con mis compañeras de trabajo. Primero (yo) _____ a ordenar (*put in order*) la ropa. La ropa de la tienda _____ bonita.
2. A las 10 abren la tienda y entonces los clientes _____ a llegar.
3. Mis compañeras no _____ español. Por eso yo siempre atiendo a los clientes hispanos.
4. (Yo) _____ a las 12:30 con mi amiga Susie, que trabaja en una zapatería. Generalmente (nosotras) _____ en la pizzería San Marcos y casi siempre _____ pizza.
5. Luego, (yo) _____ a la tienda y _____ a trabajar. Nunca _____ la siesta.
6. Finalmente, la supervisora _____ la tienda a las 6:00 en punto. Entonces yo _____ a casa.

B. De compras y amistades (*friendships*). Complete the following paragraphs with the correct forms of the words in parentheses, as suggested by the context. When two possibilities are given in parentheses, select the correct word. In addition to reviewing vocabulary from previous chapters, these paragraphs ask you to choose between **ser** and **estar** in several situations that you should already know well. You will learn more about **ser** and **estar** in **Capítulo 5**.

(Me/Mi[1]) gusta ir de (comprar/compras[2]) con mi amiga Margarita cuando ella tiene (gangas/ganas[3]) de acompañarme.[a] (Este/Esta[4]) fin de semana, necesito (buscar[5]) unos regalos para los hijos (de el / del[6]) Sr. Suárez. Él (trabajar[7]) con mi madre en el hospital. (Mi[8]) padres (ser/estar[9]) muy buenos amigos de los Suárez, aunque[b] no (ser/estar[10]) siempre de acuerdo con sus opiniones (político[11]). La familia Suárez (venir[12]) a (nuestro[13]) casa con frecuencia.

Este mes[c] todos los niños de los Suárez (celebrar[14]) su cumpleaños.[d] Por (ese/eso[15]) tengo que (ir[16]) de compras antes (de/en[17]) su visita. La hija mayor,[e] Ana, (ser/estar[18]) una chica muy simpática que (asistir[19]) a la secundaria. (*Yo:* Querer[20]) comprarle[f] un vestido de cuadros o de

[a]*going with me* [b]*although* [c]*month* [d]*birthday* [e]*oldest* [f]*to buy her*

(rayos/rayas²¹). Ya tiene (tres/trece²²) años y (empezar²³) a tener interés en (vestirse²⁴) con más elegancia. (Su²⁵) hermanos son muy jóvenes todavía—casi siempre (llevar²⁶) camisetas y pantalones cortos. Por eso no (*yo:* ir²⁷) a comprarles^g ropa. Creo que (*ellos: divertirse*²⁸) más con los juguetes.^h

Más tarde, por teléfono

—¿Diga?^i
—Margarita, ¿eres tú?
—Sí, chica. ¿Qué hay?^j ¿Cómo (*tú:* ser/estar²⁹)?
—Muy bien. Oye, ¿qué (hacer³⁰) ahora?
—(*Yo:* Leer³¹) una novela para la clase de literatura (inglés³²). ¿Por qué?
—¿Qué te parece si^k (*nosotros:* ir³³) al centro? Hay (mucho³⁴) gangas en las tiendas (este³⁵) días y tengo que comprar unos regalos.
—¡(Encantado³⁶)! Voy a (ponerse³⁷ el abrigo y (salir³⁸) de casa en unos minutos.
　　　　　　　　　　　ponerme　　　　　salgo

^g*buy them*　^h*toys*　^i*Hello?* (on the telephone, *Spain*)　^j*¿Qué… What's up?*　^k*¿Qué… What if*

C. **Comprensión.** Who might have said the following? Look for possible names in the story. Call the person who is telling the story **la persona que narra la historia.** *Hint:* More than one answer is possible for some items.

1. Tengo que comprar muchos regalos esta semana.　*la persona*
2. Voy a leer toda la tarde.　*Margarita*
3. ¡Necesitamos más juguetes!　*los hijos*
4. Trabajo con el Sr. Suárez. Es simpático, pero… sus ideas políticas son otra cosa.　*la madre*
5. Antes no necesitaba (*I didn't used to need*) mucha ropa, pero ahora sí.　*Ana*
6. Paso por tu casa en unos minutos.　*Margarita*
7. Celebro mi cumpleaños este mes.　*los hijos*

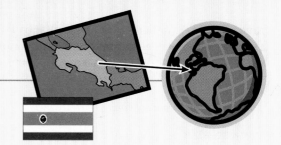

PANORAMA *cultural*

Costa Rica

Datos esenciales

Nombre oficial: República de Costa Rica
Capital: San José
Población: 3.534.174 de habitantes
Moneda: el colón
Idioma oficial: el español

¡Fíjese!

El ecoturismo es importante para la economía de Costa Rica y para la preservación de la biodiversidad y la belleza[a] natural que existe en el país. El ecoturismo tiene como propósito[b] controlar la entrada[c] de turistas en regiones protegidas[d] y, a la vez,[e] obtener fondos[f] para continuar con la protección de las regiones naturales. Aproximadamente un treinta por ciento (%) del territorio costarricense está cubierto de selvas o bosques.[g] En total, más de un cuarto[h] del territorio del país ha sido destinado[i] para la preservación.

[a]*beauty* [b]*purpose* [c]*entrance* [d]*protected* [e]*a... at the same time* [f]*funds* [g]*está... is covered with jungles or forests* [h]*fourth* [i]*ha... has been set aside*

Conozca a... Óscar Arias Sánchez

Óscar Arias Sánchez (1941–), presidente de Costa Rica de 1986 a 1990, asistió a[a] la Universidad de Costa Rica, a Boston University y a otras universidades en Inglaterra.[b] En 1987, Arias recibió[c] el Premio Nóbel de la Paz[d] por sus esfuerzos[e] por aliviar las tensiones entre el gobierno sandinista de Nicaragua y los Estados Unidos. El acuerdo de paz[f] de Arias se firmó[g] en 1986. Desde 1990, se encarga de[h] la Fundación Arias para la paz y el progreso humano.

[a]*asistió... attended* [b]*England* [c]*received* [d]*Premio... Nobel Peace Prize* [e]*efforts* [f]*acuerdo... peace agreement* [g]*se... was signed* [h]*se... he has been running*

Óscar Arias Sánchez

Capítulo 4 of the video to accompany *Puntos de partida* contains cultural footage of Costa Rica.

Visit the *Puntos de partida* Website at www.mhhe.com/puntos.

Vocabulario

Los verbos

almorzar (ue)	to have lunch
cerrar (ie)	to close
contestar	to answer
descansar	to rest
dormir (ue)	to sleep
dormir la siesta	to take a nap
empezar (ie)	to begin
entender (ie)	to understand
hacer (*irreg.*)	to do; to make
hacer ejercicio	to exercise
hacer un viaje	to take a trip
hacer una pregunta	to ask a question
jugar (ue)(al)	to play (*a game, sport*)
oír (*irreg.*)	to hear
pedir (i)	to ask for; to order
pensar (ie)	to think; to intend
perder (ie)	to lose; to miss (*a function*)
poner (*irreg.*)	to put; to place
salir (*irreg.*) (de)	to leave; to go out
servir (i)	to serve
traer (*irreg.*)	to bring
ver (*irreg.*)	to see
volver (ue)	to return (*to a place*)
volver a + *inf.*	to (*do something*) again

Los verbos reflexivos

acostarse (ue)	to go to bed
afeitarse	to shave
bañarse	to take a bath
cepillarse los dientes	to brush one's teeth
despertarse (ie)	to wake up
divertirse (ie)	to have a good time, enjoy oneself
dormirse (ue)	to fall asleep
ducharse	to take a shower
levantarse	to get up; to stand up
llamarse	to be called
peinarse	to comb one's hair
ponerse (*irreg.*)	to put on (*clothing*)
quitarse	to take off (*clothing*)
sentarse (ie)	to sit down
vestirse (i)	to get dressed

Los cuartos y otras partes de una casa

la alcoba	bedroom
el baño	bathroom
la cocina	kitchen
el comedor	dining room
el garaje	garage
el jardín	yard
la pared	wall
el patio	patio; yard
la piscina	swimming pool
la sala	living room

Los muebles y otras cosas de una casa

la alfombra	rug
el armario	closet
la bañera	bathtub
la cama (de agua)	(water) bed
la cómoda	bureau; dresser
el estante	bookshelf
la lámpara	lamp
el lavabo	(bathroom) sink
la mesita	end table
los platos	dishes; plates
el sillón	armchair
el sofá	sofa
el televisor	television set

Repaso: el escritorio, la mesa, la silla

Otros sustantivos

el ajedrez	chess
el cine	movies, movie theater
el desayuno	breakfast
el/la muchacho/a	boy/girl
la película	movie

el ruido	noise
la rutina diaria	daily routine
la tarea	homework

Los adjetivos

cada (*inv.*)	each, every
cómodo/a	comfortable

Preposiciones

antes de	before
después de	after
durante	during
hasta	until
por	during; for
sin	without

¿Cuándo?

ayer fue (miércoles)	yesterday was (Wednesday)
pasado mañana	the day after tomorrow
el próximo (martes)	next (Tuesday)
la semana que viene	next week

Los días de la semana: lunes, martes, miércoles, jueves, viernes, sábado, domingo

Repaso: el fin de semana, hoy, mañana

Palabras adicionales

por fin	finally
por lo general	generally
primero	first

Un paso más 4

LECTURA

Estrategia: **Recognizing Cognate Patterns**

You already know that cognates are words that are similar in form and meaning from one language to another: for example, English *poet* and Spanish **poeta**. The more cognates you can recognize, the more easily you will read Spanish.

The endings of many Spanish words correspond to English word endings according to fixed patterns. Learning to recognize these patterns will increase the number of close and not-so-close cognates that you can recognize. Here are a few of the most common.

-dad → *-ty*	-ción → *-tion*	-ico → *-ic, -ical*
-mente → *-ly*	-sión → *-sion*	-oso → *-ous*

What are the English equivalents of these words?

1. unidad
2. reducción
3. explosión
4. idéntico
5. estudioso
6. frecuentemente

Now try to deduce the meaning of the following words, which are taken from the reading in this section.

1. totalmente
2. transportación
3. espaciosa
4. información
5. conveniente

Try to spot additional cognates in the following reading and remember that you should be able to guess the meaning of underlined words from context.

▶ **Sobre la lectura...** The reading on the following page is adapted from
▶ real estate ads in a Puerto Rican newspaper. Since Puerto Rico is part of the
▶ United States, you will find examples of English or the influence of English
▶ scattered throughout the ads.

❶ Alto Apolo
Bonito «townhouse», área exclusiva. 3 dorms., 3 baños. Equipado. «Family», tres terrazas. Cerca centros comerciales, transportación. Bajos $80s. Hipoteca $57.250 al 8½%. Mens. $478. 790-6811, 789-9331.

❷ LOMAS DEL SOL
Hermosa res. 3 dorms., 2 baños. Fabulosa vista con lago en el patio. Gallinero, árboles frutales, marq. doble. 2.179 mts. de solar. Hip. $64.000 al 8%. Mens. $489. Pronto $36.000. Información 725-0773.

❸ Borinquen Gardens
Con un poquito de amor usted arregla esta amplia casa de 4 dorms., 2 baños. Su precio en los $60s.

❹ TORRIMAR I
Recién remodelada con buen gusto, casa de 5 dorms., 4 baños, en calle tranquila. Dueños bajan precio para venta rápida. Haga un cita exclusiva, hoy.

❺ Sta. María
Preciosa residencia de ejecutivo con:
• 4 dorms
• 3 baños
• cuarto de servicio
• amplia terraza
• barra
• piscina
• y mucho más.
Haga su cita exclusiva, hoy.

❻ Santa Paula
Amplísima residencia 4 dorms., 4 baños. Moderna fachada, espaciosa cocina. Inmenso cuarto de juego. Estudio, «family». Piscina. Solar sobre 1.000 metros. Medios $100s. Financiamiento especial. 790-6811, 789-9331.

❼ CAPARRA HILLS
Atractiva res. de 2 años construida, moderna, sencilla. Perfecta para familia pequeña. Con doble garaje, patio interior, terraza cubierta, en más de 650 m.s. Con hipoteca alta. En los medios $100s. Llama ahora. UNIVERSAL HOMES (Selected Homes Specialista) 781-7605.

❾ Villa Ávila. Encantadora residencia totalmente redecorada. 3 dorms., 2 baños. Cocina y equipos nuevos. Toda empapelada y alfombrada. «Family». Preciosa piscina. Cable TV. Bajos $100s con términos. Conveniente mensualidad $509. 790-6811, 789-9331.

Comprensión

A. El inglés en Puerto Rico. ¿Ve Ud. la influencia lingüística del inglés en el español en estos anuncios de Puerto Rico? A veces se «copian» algunas palabras directamente. Por ejemplo, la palabra *family* aparece en tres anuncios. ¿A qué tipo de cuarto se refiere? ¡Es muy fácil de deducir!

B. La casa perfecta. Vuelva a leer los anuncios rápidamente e indique cuáles de las siguientes casas serían (*would be*) apropiadas para los Juárez, una familia «extendida» que consiste en los padres, cuatro hijos y una abuela.

	SÍ	NO
Número 4, Torrimar I	☒	☐
Número 7, Caparra Hills	☐	☒
Número 8, Villa Ávila	☒	☐
Número 2, Lomas del Sol	☒	☐

ESCRITURA

Los clientes. Lea los anuncios en la lectura para encontrar la mejor casa para los siguientes clientes. Escriba por qué a estos clientes les gustaría (*would like*) esa casa.

1. Pedro Aquino, un carpintero a quien le gusta el trabajo manual.
2. Los Pino, un matrimonio mayor (*elderly couple*) que no tiene coche pero que le gusta ir de compras.
3. Óscar Sifuentes, un banquero por vocación pero mecánico por diversión. Los fines de semana repara su coche antiguo, llueva o no llueva (*rain or shine*).
4. Los Pérez, una familia con cuatro hijos muy activos. Desean una casa espaciosa donde los hijos puedan jugar sin molestar (*bothering*) a los adultos.

5 Las estaciones, el tiempo y un poco de geografía

Estos pingüinos viven en la Patagonia, en el extremo sur de la Argentina.

WEB

¿Qué opina Ud.?

Conteste según su propia vida. ¿Cree Ud. que una persona de otro país diría (*would say*) algo similar? Visite el sitio Web de *Puntos de partida* para leer las respuestas a estas preguntas que da una persona de Guatemala.

1. ¿Cómo es **el clima** en su país?
2. ¿Son extremas **las estaciones** en su país? ¿Cuál es su estación favorita?
3. ¿Cómo afecta su vida el clima de su país?
4. ¿Qué tipo de clima prefiere para sus vacaciones? ¿Por qué?
5. ¿Qué sabe Ud. (*do you know*) del clima de la Argentina? ¿de España?

158

En este capítulo...

- You will study vocabulary related to the weather and the seasons. You will also learn the names of the months of the year.
- In **Capítulo 4**, you learned some prepositions that allowed you to express relationships in time. This chapter will present other prepositions, which allow you to indicate location.
- In this chapter, you will study the present progressive, a verb form that you can use to describe an action that is happening right now. (Grammar 15)
- You began to use the verbs **ser** and **estar** in a limited way in the **Capítulo preliminar**. Now you will learn more about when to use each. (Grammar 16)
- You will learn how to express comparisons (bigger than, as good as, and so on). (Grammar 17)
- The **Panorama cultural** section will focus on Guatemala.

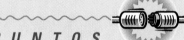

PUNTOS INTERACTIVO

Videoteca

◀ **Minidramas**
Manolo no puede encontrar algo. ¿Pierde Ud. las cosas con facilidad (*easily*)? O, por lo general, ¿recuerda Ud. dónde pone las cosas? Manolo y su esposa Lola también hacen planes para el fin de semana. ¿Tiene Ud. planes para el fin de semana?

En contexto ▶
Roberto va a una agencia de viajes (*travel agency*). Tiene que decidir adónde desea ir. Cuando Ud. quiere planear un viaje, ¿va a una agencia de viajes?

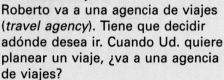

CD-ROM

In addition to completing vocabulary and grammar activities, you will have the opportunity to "converse" with someone about the weather.

Internet

In the **Capítulo 5** section of the *Puntos de partida* Website you can access links to Spanish-language resources about the weather in the Caribbean at www.mhhe.com/puntos.

Vocabulario: Preparación

¿Qué tiempo hace hoy?°   *¿Qué… What's the weather like today?*

Hace frío.

Hace calor.

Hace viento.

Hace sol.

Está (muy) nublado.

Llueve.

Nieva.

Hay mucha/poca contaminación.

Hace (mucho) frío (calor, viento, sol).   It's (very) cold (hot, windy, sunny).

Hace fresco.   It's cool.
Hace (muy) buen/mal tiempo.   It's (very) good/bad weather. The weather is (very) good/bad.

> In Spanish, many weather conditions are expressed with **hace**. The adjective **mucho** is used with the nouns **frío, calor, viento,** and **sol** to express *very*.

Pronunciation hint: Remember that, in most parts of the Spanish-speaking world, **ll** is pronounced exactly like **y: llueve.**

Conversación

A. El tiempo y la ropa. Diga qué tiempo hace, según la ropa de cada persona.

1. San Diego: María lleva pantalones cortos y una camiseta.
2. Madison: Juan lleva suéter, pero no lleva chaqueta.
3. Toronto: Roberto lleva suéter y chaqueta.
4. San Miguel de Allende: Ramón lleva impermeable y botas y también tiene paraguas (*umbrella*).
5. Buenos Aires: Todos llevan abrigo, botas y sombrero.

B. Consejos (*Advice*) para Joaquín. Joaquín es de Valencia, España. El clima (*climate*) allí es mediterráneo: hace mucho sol y las temperaturas son moderadas. No hay mucha contaminación.

Paso 1. Joaquín tiene una lista de lugares que desea visitar en los Estados Unidos. Ayúdelo (*Help him*) con información sobre el clima. Como Joaquín no sabe (*As Joaquín doesn't know*) en qué estación va a viajar (*travel*), es bueno ofrecerle información sobre el clima de todo el año.

1. Seattle, Washington
2. Los Ángeles, California
3. Phoenix, Arizona
4. Nueva Orleans, Louisiana
5. Buffalo, New York

Paso 2. Es obvio que la lista de Joaquín no está completa. ¿Qué otros tres lugares cree Ud. que debe visitar? ¿Qué clima hace allí?

C. El tiempo y las actividades. Haga oraciones completas, indicando una actividad apropiada para cada situación.

cuando llueve	me quedo (*I stay*) en cama/casa
cuando hace buen tiempo	juego al basquetbol/vólibol
cuando hace calor	con mis amigos
cuando hace frío	almuerzo afuera (*outside*) /
cuando nieva	en el parque
cuando hay mucha contaminación	me divierto en el parque / en
	la playa (*beach*) con mis
	amigos
	no salgo de casa
	vuelvo a casa y trabajo o estudio

Nota comunicativa

More *tener* Idioms

Several other conditions expressed in Spanish with **tener** idioms—not with *to be*, as in English—include the following.

tener (mucho) calor	to be (very) warm, hot
tener (mucho) frío	to be (very) cold

These expressions are used to describe people or animals only. To be comfortable—neither hot nor cold—is expressed with **estar bien**.

D. ¿Tienen frío o calor? ¿Están bien? Describe the following weather conditions and tell how the people pictured are feeling.

Los meses y las estaciones° del año

seasons

septiembre⎫
octubre ⎬ **el otoño**
noviembre ⎭

marzo ⎫
abril ⎬ **la primavera**
mayo ⎭

enero							abril						
	1	2	3	4	5	6		1	2	3	4	5	6	7
7	8	9	10	11	12	13	8	9	10	11	12	13	14
14	15	16	17	18	19	20	15	16	17	18	19	20	21
21	22	23	24	25	26	27	22	23	24	25	26	27	28
28	29	30	31				29	30					

diciembre⎫
enero ⎬ **el invierno**
febrero ⎭

junio ⎫
julio ⎬ **el verano**
agosto ⎭

febrero							mayo						
					1	2	3			1	2	3	4	5
4	5	6	7	8	9	10	6	7	8	9	10	11	12
11	12	13	14	15	16	17	13	14	15	16	17	18	19
18	19	20	21	22	23	24	20	21	22	23	24	25	26
25	26	27	28				27	28	29	30	31		

¿Cuál es la fecha de hoy? What is today's date?
(Hoy) Es el primero de abril. (Today) It is the first of April.

(Hoy) Es el cinco de febrero. (Today) It is the fifth of February.

marzo							junio						
					1	2	3						1	2
4	5	6	7	8	9	10	3	4	5	6	7	8	9
11	12	13	14	15	16	17	10	11	12	13	14	15	16
18	19	20	21	22	23	24	17	18	19	20	21	22	23
25	26	27	28	29	30	31	24	25	26	27	28	29	30

- The ordinal number **primero** is used to express the first day of the month. Cardinal numbers (**dos, tres,** and so on) are used for other days.
- The definite article **el** is used before the date. However, when the day of the week is expressed, **el** is omitted: **Hoy es jueves, tres de octubre.**
- As you know, **mil** is used to express the year after 999.

1950 mil novecientos cincuenta   2003 dos mil tres

Conversación

A. El mes de noviembre. Mire este calendario para el mes de noviembre. ¿Qué día de la semana es el 12 (1, 20, 16, 11, 4, 29) de noviembre?

B. Fechas

Paso 1. Exprese estas fechas en español. ¿En qué estación caen (*do they fall*)?

1. March 7
2. August 24
3. December 1
4. June 5

5. September 19, 1997
6. May 30, 1842
7. January 31, 1660
8. July 4, 1776

Paso 2. ¿Cuándo se celebran?

1. el Día de la Raza (*Columbus Day*)
2. el Día del Año Nuevo
3. el Día de los Enamorados (de San Valentín)
4. el Día de la Independencia de los Estados Unidos

Note that the word **se** before a verb changes the verb's meaning slightly. **¿Cuándo se celebran?** = *When are they celebrated?* You will see this construction throughout *Puntos de partida.* Learn to recognize it, for it is frequently used in Spanish.

5. el Día de los Inocentes (*Fools*), en los Estados Unidos
6. la Navidad (*Christmas*)
7. su cumpleaños (*birthday*)

Nota cultural

The Southern Hemisphere

Seasons are reversed in the Southern Hemisphere, where many Spanish-speaking countries are located. This means, of course, that when it is summer in this country, it is winter in Argentina, and vice versa. You may never have thought about the effect of this phenomenon on the celebration of many traditional holidays. Christmas and New Year's Eve, winter holidays for residents of this country, are generally associated with snow and ice, snow figures, winter sports, and so on.

C. ¿En qué año... ? Lea los siguientes años en español. ¿A qué hecho (*event*) corresponden?

1. 1492 c   **a.** la Declaración de la Independencia
2. 1776 A   **b.** el asesinato de John F. Kennedy
3. 1945 D   **c.** Cristóbal Colón llega a América
4. 2001   **d.** la bomba atómica
5. 1963 b   **e.** una película famosa
6. 1984 F   **f.** la novela de George Orwell
7. ¿ ?   **g.** este año

D. ¡Feliz (*Happy*) cumpleaños!

Paso 1. Entreviste a un compañero / una compañera de clase acerca de (*about*) su cumpleaños. Use las siguientes preguntas.

1. ¿Cuál es la fecha de tu cumpleaños?
2. ¿En qué estación es?
3. Generalmente, ¿qué tiempo hace en tu ciudad el día de tu cumpleaños?
4. ¿Cómo celebras tu cumpleaños? (por lo menos tres actividades)
5. ¿Con quién(es) prefieres celebrar tu cumpleaños?

Paso 2. Su profesor(a) o un(a) estudiante va a escribir en la pizarra los nombres de los meses del año. Luego cada estudiante va a escribir la fecha de su cumpleaños en la columna apropiada. ¿En qué mes son la mayoría de los cumpleaños de los estudiantes de la clase? ¿Qué signo del horóscopo tienen?

Los signos: Aries, Tauro, Géminis, Cáncer, Leo, Virgo, Libra, Escorpión, Sagitario, Capricornio, Acuario, Piscis

¿Dónde está España? Está *en* la Península Ibérica, *al lado de* Portugal. *Al norte* está Francia, y el continente de Africa está *al sur*. *Al oeste* está el Océano Atlántico y *al este* está el Mar Mediterráneo. La capital de España es Madrid. *Cerca de* la Península Ibérica están las Islas Baleares, que son parte de España. Las Islas Canarias, también parte de España, están *al oeste de* África. Gibraltar está *entre* España y África. No es parte de España. Pertenece (*It belongs*) a Inglaterra.

cerca de	close to	**delante de**	in front of
lejos de	far from	**detrás de**	behind
encima de	on top of	**a la izquierda de**	to the left of
debajo de	below	**a la derecha de**	to the right of
al lado de	alongside of		
entre	between, among		

al este / oeste / norte / sur de   to the east / west / north / south of

In Spanish, the pronouns that serve as objects of prepositions are identical in form to the subject pronouns, except for **mí** and **ti**.

Julio está delante de **mí**.	*Julio is in front of me.*
María está detrás de **ti**.	*María is behind you.*
Me siento a la izquierda de **ella**.	*I sit on her left.*

OJO Note that **mí** has a written accent, but **ti** does not. This is to distinguish the object of a preposition (**mí**) from the possessive adjective (**mi**).

Conversación

A. ¿De qué país se habla?

Paso 1. Escuche la descripción que da (*gives*) su profesor(a) de un país de Sudamérica. ¿Puede Ud. identificar el país?

Paso 2. Ahora describa un país de Sudamérica. Sus compañeros de clase van a identificarlo. Siga el modelo, usando (*using*) todas las frases que sean (*are*) apropiadas.

MODELO: Este país está al norte/sur/este/oeste de _____.
También está cerca de _____.
Pero está lejos de _____. Está entre _____ y
_____. ¿Cómo se llama?

Paso 3. Ahora trate de (*try to*) emparejar los nombres de estas capitales de Sudamérica con sus países.

MODELO: _____ es la capital de _____.

Capitales: Brasilia, Buenos Aires, Bogotá, La Paz, Santiago, Asunción, Quito, Caracas, Montevideo, Lima

B. ¿De dónde es Ud.? Give as much information as you can about the location of your hometown or state, or about the country you are from. You should also tell what the weather is like there.

MODELO: Soy del pueblo (de la ciudad) de _____. Está cerca de la ciudad de _____. En verano hace _____. En invierno _____. (No) Llueve mucho en primavera.

Pronunciación: r and rr

Spanish has two **r** sounds, one of which is called a *flap*, the other a *trill*. The rapid pronunciation of *tt* and *dd* in the English words *Betty* and *ladder* produces a sound similar to the Spanish flap **r:** The tongue touches the alveolar ridge (behind the upper teeth) once. Although English has no trill, when English speakers imitate a motor they often produce the Spanish trill, which is a rapid series of flaps.

The trilled **r** is written **rr** between vowels (**carro, correcto**) and **r** at the beginning of a word (**rico, rosa**). Any other **r** is pronounced as a flap. Be careful to distinguish between the flap **r** and the trilled **r**. A mispronunciation will often change the meaning of a word—for example, **pero** (*but*) versus **perro** (*dog*).

A. Comparaciones

inglés:	*potter*	*ladder*	*cotter*	*meter*	*total*	*motor*
español:	para	Lara	cara	mire	toro	moro

B. Práctica

1. rico
2. ropa
3. roca
4. Roberto
5. Ramírez
6. rebelde
7. reportero
8. real

C. ¡Necesito compañero/a! With a classmate, pronounce one word from the following pairs of words, alternatively choosing one containing **r** or **rr.** Your partner will pronounce the one that you did not.

1. coro/corro
2. coral/corral
3. pero/perro
4. vara/barra
5. ahora/ahorra
6. caro/carro
7. cero/cerro
8. para/parra

D. Pronuncie.

1. el nombre correcto
2. un corral grande
3. una norteamericana
4. Puerto Rico
5. rosas amarillas
6. un libro negro y rojo
7. una mujer refinada
8. Enrique, Carlos y Rosita

9. El perro está en el corral.
10. Estos errores son raros.
11. Busco un carro caro
12. Soy el primo de Roberto Ramírez.

E. Trabalenguas (*Tongue-twister*)

Paso 1. Listen as your instructor says the following tongue-twister.

Erre con erre, guitarra,
Erre con erre, barril;[a]
¡qué rápido corren[b] los carros
del ferrocarril[c]!

[a]*barrel* [b]*run* [c]*train*

Paso 2. Now repeat the tongue-twister, paying special attention to the pronunciation of the trilled **r** sound.

Minidiálogos y gramática

15 ¿Qué están haciendo? • Present Progressive: *estar + -ndo*

¿Qué están haciendo en Quito, Ecuador?

José Miguel juega al tenis y levanta pesas con frecuencia. Ahora no *está jugando al tenis*. Tampoco *está levantando* pesas. ¿Qué *está haciendo*? Está _jugando_ football.

Elisa es periodista. Por eso escribe mucho y habla mucho por teléfono. Pero ahora, no *está escribiendo*. Tampoco *está hablando* por teléfono. ¿Qué *está haciendo*? Está _____.

¿Y Ud.? ¿Qué está haciendo Ud. en este momento?

1. ¿Está estudiando en casa? ¿en clase? ¿en la cafetería?
2. ¿Está leyendo? ¿Está mirando la tele al mismo (*same*) tiempo?
3. ¿Está escuchando al profesor / a la profesora?

Uses of the Progressive

In Spanish, you can use special verb forms to describe an action in progress—that is, something actually happening at the time it is being described. These Spanish forms, called **el progresivo,** correspond in form to the English *progressive: I am walking, we are driving, she is studying.* But their use is not identical. Compare the Spanish and English verb forms in the sentences at the right.

In Spanish, the present progressive is used primarily to describe an action that is actually *in progress,* as in the first example. The simple Spanish present is used in other cases where English would use the present progressive: to tell what is going to happen (the second sentence), and to tell what someone is doing over a period of time but not necessarily at this very moment (the third sentence).

1. Ramón **está comiendo** ahora mismo. *Ramón is eating right now.*
2. **Compramos** la casa mañana. *We're buying the house tomorrow.*
3. Adelaida **estudia** química este semestre. *Adelaida is studying chemistry this semester.*

Formation of the Present Progressive

A. The Spanish present progressive is formed with **estar** plus the *present participle* (**el gerundio**), which is formed by adding **-ando** to the stem of **-ar** verbs and **-iendo** to the stem of **-er** and **-ir** verbs.* The present participle never varies; it always ends in **-o.**

tomar → **tomando**	*taking; drinking*
comprender → **comprendiendo**	*understanding*
abrir → **abriendo**	*opening*

OJO

Unaccented **i** represents the sound [y] in the participle ending **-iendo: comiendo, viviendo.** Unaccented **i** between two vowels becomes the letter **y: leyendo, oyendo.**

B. The stem vowel in the present participle of **-ir** stem-changing verbs also shows a change. From this point on in *Puntos de partida,* both stem changes for **-ir** verbs will be given with infinitives in vocabulary lists.

preferir (ie, i) → prefiriendo   *preferring*
pedir (i, i) → pidiendo   *asking*
dormir (ue, u) → durmiendo   *sleeping*

Using Pronouns with the Present Progressive

Reflexive pronouns may be attached to a present participle or precede the conjugated form of

---

*Ir, poder,** and **venir** have irregular present participles: **yendo, pudiendo, viniendo.** These three verbs, however, are seldom used in the progressive.

estar. Note the use of a written accent mark when pronouns are attached to the present participle.

Pablo **se** está bañando.
Pablo está bañándo**se.** } *Pablo is taking a bath.*

Práctica

▲▲▲▲▲▲

A. Un sábado típico. Indique lo que Ud. está haciendo a las horas indicadas en un sábado típico. En algunos (*some*) casos hay más de una respuesta (*answer*) posible.

A las ocho de la mañana...

	SÍ	NO
1. estoy durmiendo	☒	☐
2. estoy tomando el desayuno	☐	☒
3. estoy mirando los dibujos animados (*cartoons*) en la tele	☒	☐
4. estoy duchándome	☐	☒
5. estoy trabajando	☐	☒
6. estoy _____	☐	☐

A mediodía (*noon*)...

	SÍ	NO
1. estoy durmiendo	☒	☐
2. estoy almorzando	☒	☐
3. estoy estudiando	☒	☐
4. estoy practicando algún deporte	☒	☐
5. estoy trabajando	☐	☒
6. estoy _____	☐	☐

A las diez de la noche...

	SÍ	NO
1. estoy durmiendo	☐	☒
2. estoy preparándome para salir	☐	☒
3. estoy mirando un programa en la tele	☒	☐
4. estoy bailando en una fiesta o en una discoteca	☐	☒
5. estoy trabajando	☐	☒
6. estoy hablando por teléfono con un amigo / una amiga	☐	☒
7. estoy _____	☐	☐

B. Un día especial. Ricardo Guzmán Rama, el tío de Lola Benítez, acaba de llegar (*has just arrived*) de México para visitar a su familia en Sevilla. Por eso, hoy es un día especial. Complete las siguientes oraciones para indicar lo que (*what*) está pasando en este momento en la familia de Lola.

1. Generalmente, Lola está en la universidad toda la mañana. Hoy Lola… (hablar con su tío Ricardo)

2. Casi siempre, Lola va a casa después de sus clases. Hoy Lola y su tío... (tomar un café en la universidad)

3. De lunes a viernes, la hija Marta va al colegio por la tarde. Ahora, a las dos de la tarde ella... (jugar con Ricardo)

4. Generalmente, la familia come a las dos. Hoy todos... (comer a las tres)

C. En casa con la familia Duarte

Paso 1. The Duarte family leads a busy life. Each picture sequence shows what the parents, the teen-age daughter, and the twins are doing at a particular time of their day. Read the following sentences and tell to which drawing each refers.

MODELO: Se está duchando. Dibujo A.

1. Está levantándose.
2. Está escribiendo cartas.
3. Está vistiéndose.
4. Está preparando la cena (*dinner*).
5. Está leyendo el periódico.
6. Están durmiendo.
7. Está trabajando.
8. Están jugando con el perro.
9. Están comiendo.
10. Está quitándose los zapatos.

A.

B.

C.

Paso 2. Now tell what is happening in each drawing.

MODELO: Dibujo A. Son las seis. Los niños están...

Conversación

▲▲▲▲▲▲▲

Preguntas

1. ¿Pasa Ud. más tiempo leyendo o viendo la televisión? ¿tocando o escuchando música? ¿trabajando o estudiando? ¿estudiando o viajando?
2. ¿Cómo se divierte Ud. más, viendo la tele o bailando en una fiesta? ¿practicando un deporte o leyendo una buena novela? ¿haciendo un *picnic* o preparando una cena elegante en casa? ¿mirando una película en casa o en el cine?

¿Recuerda Ud.?

You have been using forms of **ser** and **estar** since **Ante todo,** the preliminary chapter of *Puntos de partida*. The following section will help you consolidate everything you know so far about these two verbs, both of which express *to be* in Spanish. You will learn a bit more about them as well.

Before you begin, think in particular about the following questions: **¿Cómo está Ud.? ¿Cómo es Ud.?** What do these questions tell you about the difference between **ser** and **estar**?

---

16 ◢ ¿Ser o estar? • Summary of the Uses of *ser* and *estar*

Una conversación por larga distancia

Aquí hay un lado de la conversación entre una esposa que *está* en un viaje de negocios y su esposo, que *está* en casa. Habla el esposo. ¿Qué contesta la esposa?

Aló. [...¹] ¿Cómo *estás*, mi amor? [...²] ¿Dónde *estás* ahora? [...³] ¿Qué hora *es* allí? [...⁴] ¡Huy!, *es* muy tarde. Y el hotel, ¿cómo *es*? [...⁵] Oye, ¿qué *estás* haciendo ahora? [...⁶] Ay, pobre, lo siento. *Estás* muy ocupada. ¿Con quién *estás* citada mañana? [...⁷] ¿Quién *es* el dueño de la compañía? [...⁸] Ah, él *es* de Cuba, ¿verdad? [...⁹] Bueno, ¿qué tiempo hace allí? [...¹⁰] Muy bien, mi vida. Hasta luego, ¿eh? [...¹¹] Adiós.

A long-distance conversation Here is one side of a conversation between a wife who is on a business trip and her husband, who is at home. The husband is speaking. What does the wife answer? Hello... How are you, dear?... Where are you now?... What time is it there?... Boy, it's very late. And how's the hotel?... Hey, what are you doing now?... You poor thing, I'm sorry. You're very busy. Who are you meeting with tomorrow?... Who's the owner of the company?... Ah, he's from Cuba, isn't he?... Well, what's the weather like? Very well, sweetheart. See you later, OK?... Goodbye.

Aquí está el otro lado de la conversación... pero las respuestas no están en orden. Ponga las respuestas en el orden apropiado.

a. __5__ Es muy moderno. Me gusta mucho.
b. __9__ Sí, pero vive en Nueva York ahora.
c. __4__ Son las once y media.
d. __1__ Hola, querido (*dear*). ¿Qué tal?
e. __8__ Es el Sr. Cortina.
f. __6__ Pues, todavía (*still*) tengo que trabajar.
g. __11__ Sí, hasta pronto.
h. __3__ Estoy en Nueva York.
i. __2__ Un poco cansada, pero estoy bien.
j. __10__ Pues, hace buen tiempo, pero está un poco nublado.
k. __7__ Con un señor de Computec, una nueva compañía de computadoras.

Summary of the Uses of *ser*

• To *identify* people and things	Ella **es doctora**.
• To express *nationality*; with **de** to express *origin*	**Son cubanos. Son de** La Habana.
• With **de** to tell of what *material* something is made.	Este bolígrafo **es de plástico**.

• With **para** to tell *for whom something is intended*	El regalo **es para Sara**.
• To tell *time*	**Son las once. Es la una y media.**
• With **de** to express *possession*	**Es de** Carlota.
• With *adjectives* that describe *basic, inherent characteristics*	Ramona **es inteligente**.
• To form many *generalizations*	**Es necesario** llegar temprano. **Es importante** estudiar.

Summary of the Uses of *estar*

• To tell *location*	El libro **está en la mesa**.
• To describe *health*	**Estoy** muy **bien**, gracias.
• With *adjectives* that describe *conditions*	**Estoy** muy **ocupada**.
• In a number of *fixed expressions*	**(No) Estoy de acuerdo. Está bien.**
• With *present participles* to form the *progressive tense*	**Estoy estudiando** ahora mismo.

A. Ser is used with adjectives that describe the fundamental qualities of a person, place, or thing.

Esa mujer es muy **baja.**
That woman is very short.

Sus calcetines son **morados.**
His socks are purple.

Este sillón es **cómodo.**
This armchair is comfortable.

Sus padres son **cariñosos.**
Their parents are affectionate people.

B. Estar is used with adjectives to express conditions or observations that are true at a given moment but that do not describe inherent qualities of the noun. The following adjectives are generally used with **estar.**

abierto/a	open	**limpio/a**	clean
aburrido/a	bored	**loco/a**	crazy
alegre	happy	**nervioso/a**	nervous
cansado/a	tired	**ocupado/a**	busy
cerrado/a	closed	**ordenado/a**	neat
congelado/a	frozen; very cold	**preocupado/a**	worried
contento/a	content, happy	**seguro/a**	sure, certain
desordenado/a	messy	**sucio/a**	dirty
enfermo/a	sick	**triste**	sad
furioso/a	furious, angry		

C. Many adjectives can be used with either **ser** or **estar**, depending on what the speaker intends to communicate. In general, when *to be* implies *looks, feels,* or *appears,* **estar** is used. Compare the following pairs of sentences.

Daniel **es** guapo.
Daniel is handsome. (He is a handsome person.)

Daniel **está** muy guapo esta noche.
Daniel looks very nice (handsome) tonight.

—¿Cómo **es** Amalia?
—**Es** simpática.
What is Amalia like (as a person)?
She's nice.

—¿Cómo **está** Amalia?
—**Está** enferma todavía.
How is Amalia (feeling)?
She's still sick.

Práctica

A. Un regalo especial. Hay algo nuevo en el comedor. Es una computadora. ¿Qué puede Ud. decir de ella (*say about it*)? Haga oraciones completas con **es** o **está**.

La computadora es / está...
1. en la mesa del comedor
2. un regalo de cumpleaños

3. para mi compañero de cuarto
4. de la tienda Computec
5. en una caja (*box*) verde
6. de los padres de mi compañero
7. un regalo muy caro pero estupendo
8. de metal y plástico gris
9. una IBM, el último (*latest*) modelo
10. muy fácil (*easy*) de usar

Vocabulario útil

Por often expresses *because of or about*, especially with adjectives such as **preocupado, nervioso, contento,** and **furioso.**

Amalia está preocupada **por** los exámenes finales.
Amalia is worried about her final exams.

B. ¿Quiénes son? Ahora identifique a los jóvenes que aparecen en esta foto.

Los jóvenes son/están...

1. mis primos argentinos
2. de Buenos Aires
3. aquí este mes para visitar a la familia
4. al lado de los abuelos en la foto
5. muy simpáticos
6. muy contentos con el viaje en general
7. un poco cansados por el viaje

C. Actividades sociales. Complete the following description with the correct form of **ser** or **estar,** as suggested by the context.

Las fiestas
Las fiestas (ser/estar[1]) populares entre los jóvenes de todas partes del mundo. Ofrecen una buena oportunidad para (ser/estar[2]) con los amigos y conocer[a] a nuevas personas. Imagine que Ud. (ser/estar[3]) en una fiesta con unos amigos hispanos en este momento: todos (ser/estar[4]) alegres, comiendo, hablando y bailando... ¡Y (ser/estar[5]) las dos de la mañana!

La pandilla[b]
Ahora en el mundo hispánico no (ser/estar[6]) necesario tener chaperona. Muchas de las actividades sociales se dan[c] en grupos. Si Ud. (ser/estar[7]) miembro de una pandilla, sus amigos (ser/estar[8]) el centro de su vida social y Ud. y su novio[d] o novia salen frecuentemente con otras parejas[e] o personas del grupo.

[a]*to meet* [b]*group of friends* [c]*se... occur* [d]*boyfriend* [e]*couples*

Comprensión: ¿Sí o no? ¿Son estas las opiniones de un joven hispano?

1. Me gustan mucho las fiestas.
2. Nunca bailamos en las fiestas.
3. Es necesario salir con chaperona.
4. La pandilla tiene poca importancia para mí.

D. Una tarde terrible

Paso 1. Describa lo que (*what*) pasa hoy por la tarde en esta casa, cambiando por antónimos las palabras indicadas.

1. No hace *buen* tiempo; hace _mal_.
2. El bebé no está *bien*; está _mal_.
3. El gato no está *limpio*; está _sucio_.
4. El esposo no está *tranquilo*; está _preocupado_ por el bebé.
5. El garaje no está *cerrado*; está _abierto_.
6. Los niños no están *ocupados*; están _____. _aburridos_
7. La esposa no está *contenta*; está _preocupada_ por el tiempo.
8. La casa no está *ordenada*; está _desordenada_.

Paso 2. Ahora imagine que son las 6:30 de la tarde. Exprese lo que están haciendo los miembros de la familia en este momento. Use su imaginación y diga también lo que generalmente hacen estas personas a esa hora.

> MODELO: Hoy, a las seis y media, la madre está conduciendo su coche a casa. Generalmente está preparando la comida a esa hora.

Palabras útiles: cenar (*to have dinner*), conducir (*to drive*), ladrar (*to bark*), llorar (*to cry*)

Conversación

▲▲▲▲▲▲▲▲

Ana   Estela

A. Ana y Estela. Describa este dibujo de un cuarto típico de la residencia. Invente los detalles necesarios. ¿Quiénes son las dos compañeras de cuarto? ¿De dónde son? ¿Cómo son? ¿Dónde están en este momento? ¿Qué hay en el cuarto? ¿En qué condición está el cuarto? ¿Son ordenadas o desordenadas las dos?

Palabras útiles: el cartel (*poster*), la foto

B. Sentimientos. Complete the following sentences by telling how you feel in the situations described. Then ask questions of other students in the class to find at least one person who completed a given sentence the way you did.

MODELO: Cuando saco (*I get*) una «A» en un examen, estoy *alegre.* →
¿Cómo te sientes (*do you feel*) cuando sacas una «A» en un examen?

1. Cuando el profesor da una tarea difícil, estoy _____.
2. Cuando tengo mucho trabajo, estoy _loca_.
3. En otoño generalmente estoy _____ porque _____.
4. En verano estoy _____ porque _____.
5. Cuando llueve (nieva), estoy _____ porque _____.
6. Los lunes por la mañana estoy _cansada_
7. Los viernes por la noche estoy _contenta_
8. Cuando me acuesto muy tarde, estoy _____ al día siguiente (*the next day*). _me siento enferma_

En los Estados Unidos y el Canadá...

Alfredo Jaar

Upon arriving in the United States, Chilean artist Alfredo Jaar was surprised to learn that English speakers generally don't think of Canadians, Mexicans, Colombians, and so forth as "Americans." It bothered him that he was perceived as "Hispanic" or "Latin" but not as "American." "This country has co-opted the word *America*," he claimed.

So, Jaar used his artistic talents in an effort to enlighten people in the United States about the true meaning of the word *America*. He created a computerized animation that appeared on a sign board above New York City's Times Square in April of 1987. The computer animation depicted a lighted map of the United States with the statement "This is not America" written across it. Slowly the word *America* grew larger and larger until it filled the entire sign. At the same time,

El arte electrónico de Alfredo Jaar

the letter R transformed itself into a map of North and South America. This use of *America* is the meaning used in Spanish, the meaning that Jaar had known.

The message that Jaar was trying to send was that *America* does not belong only to the United States. Another thirty-three nations say that they are a part of America and that their approximately 500 million inhabitants are also Americans.

Jaar was also trying to combat the stereotype that all Hispanics are alike and that all the inhabitants of South America are Hispanics. For one thing, many inhabitants of South America are Brazilians, and thus of Portuguese rather than of Spanish heritage. In addition, there are many indigenous peoples throughout Latin America that have traditions, cultures, and languages that precede Columbus' arrival in this hemisphere.

Dos ciudades

México, D.F. (Distrito Federal)

Ricardo, el tío de Lola Benítez, hace comparaciones entre la Ciudad de México, o el D.F. (Distrito Federal), y Sevilla.

«De verdad, me gustan las dos ciudades.

- La Ciudad de México es *más* grande *que* Sevilla.
- Tiene *más* edificios altos *que* Sevilla.
- En el D.F. no hace *tanto* calor *como* en Sevilla.

Pero...

- Sevilla es *tan* bonita *como* la Ciudad de México.
- No tiene *tantos* habitantes *como* el D.F.
- Sin embargo, los sevillanos son *tan* simpáticos *como* los mexicanos.

En total, ¡me gusta Sevilla *tanto como* la Ciudad de México!»

El barrio de Santa Cruz, Sevilla, España

Ahora, hable Ud. de su ciudad o pueblo.

Mi ciudad/pueblo...

- (no) es tan grande como Chicago
- es más/menos cosmopolita que Quebec

Me gusta _____ (nombre de mi ciudad/pueblo)

- más que _____ (nombre de otra ciudad)
- menos que _____ (nombre de otra ciudad)
- tanto como _____ (nombre de otra ciudad)

Two Cities   Ricardo, Lola Benítez's uncle, makes comparisons between Mexico City, or D.F. (Federal District), and Seville. Really, I like both cities.
- Mexico City is bigger than Seville.
- It has more tall buildings than Seville.
- It is not as hot in Mexico City as it is in Seville.

But...
- Seville is as beautiful as Mexico City.
- It doesn't have as many inhabitants as Mexico City.
- Nevertheless, the people from Seville are as nice as those from Mexico City.

All told, I like Seville as much as Mexico City!

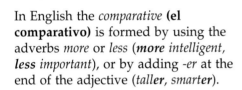

	Unequal Comparisons	Equal Comparisons
With Adjectives or Adverbs	más/menos _____ que	tan _____ como
With Nouns		tanto/a/os/as _____ como
With Verbs	_____ más/menos que	_____ tanto como

Comparison of Adjectives

EQUAL COMPARISONS

tan + *adjective* + como
(*as*)   (*as*)

Enrique es **tan** trabajador **como** Amalia.
Enrique is as hardworking as Amalia.

> In English the *comparative* **(el comparativo)** is formed by using the adverbs *more* or *less* (**more** *intelligent,* **less** *important*), or by adding *-er* at the end of the adjective (*tall**er**, smart**er***).

UNEQUAL COMPARISONS (REGULAR)

más + *adjective* + que
(*more*)   (*than*)

Alicia es **más** perezosa **que** Marta.
Alicia is lazier than Marta.

menos + *adjective* + que
(*less*)   (*than*)

Julio es **menos** listo **que** Jaime.
Julio is not as bright as Jaime.

UNEQUAL COMPARATIVES WITH IRREGULAR FORMS

bueno/a → mejor

Estos coches son **buenos,** pero esos son **mejores.**
These cars are good, but those are better.

malo/a → peor

Mi lámpara es **peor que** esta.
My lamp is worse than this one.

mayor (*older*)

Mi hermana es **mayor que** yo.
My sister is older than I (am).

menor (*younger*)

Mis primos son **menores que** yo.
My cousins are younger than I (am).

Comparison of Nouns

Tanto must agree in gender and number with
the noun it modifies.

> tanto/a/os/as + *noun* + como
> (*as much/many*)　　　　(*as*)

Alicia tiene **tantas** bolsas **como** Pati.
Alicia has as many purses as Pati (does).

Pablo tiene **tanto** dinero **como** Sergio.
Pablo has as much money as Sergio (does).

> más/menos + *noun* + que
> (*more/less*)　　　　(*than*)

The preposition **de** is used when the comparison
is followed by a number.

> más/menos de + *noun*
> (*more/less than*)

[Práctica A–C]

Alicia tiene **más / menos** bolsas **que** Susana.
Alicia has more/fewer purses than Susana (does).

Alicia tiene **más de** cinco bolsas.
Alicia has more than five purses.

Comparison of Verbs

Note that **tanto** is invariable is this construction.

> tanto como
> (*as much as*)

Yo estudio **tanto como** mi hermano mayor.
I study as much as my older brother (does).

> más/menos que
> (*more/less than*)

Yo duermo **más que** mi hermano menor.
I sleep more than my younger brother (does).

Comparison of Adverbs

> tan + *adverb* + como

Yo juego al tenis **tan** bien **como** mi hermano.
I play tennis as well as my brother (does).

> más/menos + *adverb* + que

> mejor/peor que

[Práctica D]

Yo como **más** rápido **que** mi padre.
I eat faster than my father (does).

Yo juego al tenis **peor que** mi hermana.
I play tennis worse than my sister (does).

Capítulo 5　•　Las estaciones, el tiempo y un poco de geografía

Práctica

A. ¿Es Ud. sincero/a?

Paso 1. Conteste las preguntas lógicamente. ¿Es Ud… ?

1. tan guapo/a como Antonio Banderas/Jennifer López
2. tan rico como Bill Gates
3. tan fiel como su mejor amigo/a
4. tan inteligente como Einstein
5. tan honesto/a como su padre/madre (novio/a…)

Paso 2. ¿Tiene Ud… ?

1. tantos tíos como tías
2. tantos amigos como amigas
3. tanto talento como Carlos Santana
4. tanta sabiduría (*knowledge*) como su profesor(a)

B. Opiniones.
Cambie las siguientes oraciones para expresar su opinión personal: **tan _____ como** → **más/menos _____ que.** Si está de acuerdo con la oración tal como está (*just as it is*), diga (*say*) **Estoy de acuerdo.**

1. Mi casa (apartamento/residencia) es tan grande como la casa del presidente de la universidad.
2. El fútbol (*soccer*) es tan popular como el fútbol americano.
3. Las artes son tan importantes como las ciencias.
4. Los estudios son menos importantes que los deportes.
5. La comida (*food*) de la cafetería es tan buena como la de mi mamá/papá (esposo/a, compañero/a…)

C. Alfredo y Gloria.
Compare la casa y las posesiones que tienen Alfredo y Gloria, haciendo oraciones con **más/menos _____ que** o **tanto/a/os/as _____ como.**

	ALFREDO	GLORIA
cuartos en total	8	6
baños	2	1
alcobas	3	3
camas	3	5
coches	3	1
dinero en el banco	$500.000	$5.000

D.
Cambie, indicando su opinión personal: **tanto como** → **más/menos que,** o vice versa. O, si es apropiado, diga **Estoy de acuerdo.**

1. Los profesores trabajan más que los estudiantes.
2. Me divierto tanto con mis amigos como con mis parientes.
3. Los niños duermen tanto como los adultos.
4. Aquí llueve más en primavera que en invierno.
5. Necesito más el dinero que la amistad.

Conversación

A. La familia de Amalia y Sancho Jordán

Paso 1. Mire la siguiente foto e identifique a los miembros de esta familia. Luego compárelos (*compare them*) con otro pariente. **¡OJO!** Amalia tiene dos hermanos y un sobrino.

> MODELO: Amalia es la hermana de Sancho. Ella es menor que Sancho, pero es más alta que él.

Ramón (24)
Amalia (19)
Sancho (20)
Ramoncito (1)
Lucía (43)   Miguel (45)   Sarita (25)   Laura (75)   Javier (80)

Paso 2. Su familia. Now compare the members of your own family, making ten comparative statements.

> MODELO: Mi hermana Mary es mayor que yo, pero yo soy más alto/a que ella.

Paso 3. Now read your sentences from **Paso 2** to a classmate, who should not take notes on them. Ask him or her questions about your comparisons and see if he or she remembers the details of your family.

> MODELO: ¿Qué miembro de mi familia es mayor que yo?

B. La rutina diaria… en invierno y en verano

Paso 1. ¿Es diferente nuestra rutina diaria en las diferentes estaciones? Complete las siguientes oraciones sobre su rutina.

Palabras útiles: el gimnasio, el parque, afuera

EN INVIERNO…

1. me levanto a _____ (hora)
2. almuerzo en _____
3. me divierto con mis amigos en _____
4. estudio _____ horas todos los días
5. estoy / me quedo en _____ (lugar) por la noche
6. me acuesto a _____

EN VERANO…

me levanto a _____
almuerzo en _____
me divierto con mis amigos en _____
(no) estudio _____ horas todos los días
estoy / me quedo en _____ por la noche
me acuesto a _____

Paso 2. Ahora compare sus actividades en invierno y en verano, según el modelo.

> MODELO: En invierno me levanto más temprano/tarde que en verano.
> (En invierno me levanto a la misma hora que en verano.)
> (En invierno me levanto tan temprano como en verano.)

Minidramas

In this **Minidramas** dialogue, Manolo Durán, from Seville, Spain, takes a phone call for his daughter Marta. Do you think brief phone conversations like this one in Spain are more or less formal than in this country?

Suena[a] el teléfono. Manolo lo contesta.[b]

MANOLO: ¿Diga?[c]

CAROLINA: Buenos días. Habla Carolina Díaz. ¿Está Marta?

MANOLO: No, Carolina. Marta no está en este momento. Está en el parque con su tío abuelo.[d] ¿Quieres dejarle un recado?[e]

CAROLINA: Sí, muchas gracias. Me gustaría decirle[f] que si quiere venir esta tarde a jugar conmigo.[g] Hace buen tiempo y podríamos[h] ir a jugar afuera.

MANOLO: Muy bien, Carolina. Yo le doy[i] el recado. Saluda a tus padres de mi parte,[j] por favor.

CAROLINA: Sí. Adiós.

MANOLO: Adiós.

[a]*Rings* [b]*lo... answers it* [c]*Hello? (Spain)* [d]*tío... great uncle* [e]*dejarle... to leave a message for her* [f]*Me... I'd like to ask for her* [g]*with me* [h]*we could* [i]*Yo... I'll give her* [j]*Saluda... Say "hi" to your folks for me*

Con un compañero / una compañera

In the preceding dialogue, note the different expressions that are used to get and give information when talking on the phone. Then, with a partner, take turns acting out the following situations.

1. Ud. llama a un amigo / una amiga por teléfono para ver si quiere estudiar esta noche con Ud. El compañero / La compañera de cuarto de su amigo/a contesta el teléfono. Desafortunadamente (*Unfortunately*), su amigo/a no está en casa.
2. Suena el teléfono y Ud. lo contesta. Habla la madre de su mejor amigo/a. Ella quiere saber (to *find out*) si su hijo/a está en casa de Ud.

FUNCTION

using the telphone

Un poco más sobre... Manolo Durán García

Manolo Durán García es profesor de literatura en una universidad sevillana, donde se especializa en la novela española. Aunque[a] es muy intelectual y estudioso, su interés principal es su familia: su esposa Lola y su hijita Marta.

[a]*Although*

To read more about the characters from this video, visit the *Puntos de partida* Website at **www.mhhe.com/puntos**

En contexto

MÉXICO

In this video segment, Roberto makes plans to travel outside of his native Mexico on vacation. As you watch the segment, pay particular attention to the information he gives the travel agent. What kind of a vacation would Roberto prefer? What suggestions does the agent make?

A. Lluvia de ideas

- ¿Le gusta a Ud. hacer viajes? ¿Con quién? ¿Adónde le gusta ir? ¿En qué estación del año prefiere ir?
- Cuando Ud. desea o necesita viajar, ¿va a una agencia de viajes? ¿Por qué?
- Imagine Ud. que una persona quiere visitar su ciudad o su estado. ¿En qué estación debe ir? ¿Qué se puede hacer allí?

B. Dictado

Here is the first part of this segment's dialogue. Fill in the missing portions of the dialogue.

ROBERTO: Quiero _____ un viaje este año, pero no sé _____ ni _____ todavía. Quiero bucear[a].

AGENTE: Bueno, tiene _____ _____ diferentes. ¿Adónde _____ _____?

ROBERTO: _____ viajar a una isla.

AGENTE: Bien… Dicen que bucear en las islas del Caribe _____ maravilloso.

ROBERTO: ¿Es caro el _____?

AGENTE: Depende de la _____. En el invierno, cuesta _____. En el verano, cuesta _____.

ROBERTO: Claro. ¿Y qué _____ hace en el Caribe durante el _____?

[a]to scuba dive

C. Un diálogo original

Paso 1. Con un compañero/una compañera, dramaticen la escena de Roberto con la agente.

Paso 2. Imagine que Ud. y su compañero/a desean hacer un viaje juntos (*together*). Pero primero deben decidir adónde quieren ir.

ESTUDIANTE 1: You like warm weather and exotic places. You don't have money to go to Europe.

ESTUDIANTE 2: You like both eco-tourism (**ecoturismo**) as well as visiting important cities. You wouldn't mind going to Europe, but are willing to entertain other options.

A. ¿Qué están haciendo? Diga qué están haciendo las siguientes personas, usando una palabra o frase de cada columna y la forma progresiva. Si Ud. no sabe (*know*) exactamente qué están haciendo esas personas, ¡use su imaginación!

yo	jugar (al)	fútbol/basquetbol
mi mejor amigo/a	dormir(se)	un libro / una novela
mis padres	leer	la radio
los Bills de Buffalo / los Bulls de Chicago	descansar	a los estudiantes / a sus consejeros
el presidente / la presidenta de la universidad	viajar	un informe
el presidente de los Estados Unidos	escuchar	ejercicio físico
el profesor / la profesora de español	trabajar	¿ ?
_____ (un compañero / una compañera de la clase de español que está ausente hoy)	practicar hacer	
mi consejero/a	¿ ?	

B. Dos hemisferios. Complete the following paragraphs with the correct forms of the words in parentheses, as suggested by the context. When two possibilities are given in parentheses, select the correct word.

Hay (mucho[1]) diferencias entre el clima del hemisferio norte y el del hemisferio sur. Cuando (ser/estar[2]) invierno en este país, por ejemplo, (ser/estar[3]) verano en la Argentina, en Bolivia, en Chile... Cuando yo (salir[4]) para la universidad en enero, con frecuencia tengo que (llevar[5]) abrigo y botas. En (los/las[6]) países del hemisferio sur, un estudiante (poder[7]) asistir (a/de[8]) clases en enero llevando sólo pantalones (corto[9]), camiseta y sandalias. En muchas partes de este país, (antes de / durante[10]) las vacaciones en diciembre, casi siempre (hacer[11]) frío y a veces (nevar[12]). En (grande[13]) parte de Sudamérica, al otro lado del ecuador, hace calor y (muy/mucho[14]) sol durante (ese[15]) mes. A veces en enero hay fotos, en los periódicos, de personas que (tomar[16]) el sol y nadan[a] en las playas sudamericanas.

   Tengo un amigo que (ir[17]) a (hacer/tomar[18]) un viaje a Buenos Aires. Él me dice[b] que allí la Navidad[c] (ser/estar[19]) una fiesta de verano y que todos (llevar[20]) ropa como la que[d] llevamos nosotros en julio. Parece[e] increíble, ¿verdad?

[a]*are swimming*   [b]*Él... He tells me*   [c]*Christmas*   [d]*la... that which*   [e]*It seems*

Comprensión: ¿Probable o improbable?

1. Los estudiantes argentinos van a la playa en julio.
2. Muchas personas sudamericanas hacen viajes de vacaciones en enero.
3. Hace frío en Santiago (Chile) en diciembre.

C. Las comparaciones son odiosas (*despicable*)**... ¡pero interesantes!**

Paso 1. Complete estas oraciones con información verdadera (*true*) para Ud.

1. Tomo _____ cursos, que hacen un total de _____ créditos.
2. Generalmente, me levanto a las _____ y me acuesto a las _____.
   Duermo _____ horas diarias, aproximadamente.
3. Tengo _____ años.
4. Tengo _____ hermanos. (No tengo hermanos. Soy hijo único/hija
   única [*only child*].)
5. Trabajo _____ horas a la semana, en _____.

Paso 2. Usando las oraciones de arriba (*above*) como guía (*as a guide*), haga preguntas a uno o dos compañeros. Anote (*Jot down*) sus respuestas.

MODELO: ¿Cuántos cursos tomas?

Paso 3. Ahora haga comparaciones entre sus compañeros y Ud.

MODELOS: Mike toma más cursos que yo, pero yo tomo más cursos que Susie.

PANORAMA *cultural*

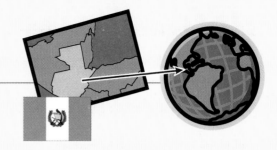

Guatemala

Datos esenciales

Nombre oficial: República de Guatemala
Capital: la Ciudad de Guatemala
Población: 12.007.580 de habitantes
Moneda: el quetzal
Idiomas: el español (oficial), 23 lenguas indígenas
(que incluyen el quiché, el cakchiquel y el kekchi)

¡Fíjese!

Más del cincuenta por ciento de los habitantes de
Guatemala son descendientes de los antiguos[a]
mayas. Esta civilización antigua tenía[b] un sistema
de escritura jeroglífica que usaban[c] para
documentar su historia, sus costumbres[f]
religiosas y su mitología. El calendario maya,
base del famoso calendario azteca, era[f] el
calendario más exacto de su época. Los mayas
también tenían un sistema político y social muy
desarrollado.[f] Tikal, en Guatemala, fue[g] una de
las ciudades mayas más importantes y también
una de las más grandes. Las ruinas de Tikal son
muestra[h] de la grandeza de la civilización maya.
Hoy día,[i] son un lugar turístico muy visitado.

[a]*ancient* [b]*had* [c]*they used* [d]*customs* [e]*was* [f]*developed* [g]*was*
[h]*an example* [i]*Hoy… Nowadays*

Conozca a... Rigoberta Menchú

Al período entre los años 1978 y 1985 en
Guatemala se le llama[a] con frecuencia «La
violencia». Durante este tiempo el ejército
guatemalteco[b] empieza una campaña[c] violenta
contra la población indígena[d] del norte del país.

　　Rigoberta Menchú, mujer de la región
indígena y de lengua[e] quiché (un grupo étnico de
la familia de los mayas) pierde a sus padres y
dos hermanos, todos asesinados por el ejército.

Menchú describe esta tragedia durante «La
violencia» en su famosa autobiografía
Yo, Rigoberta Menchú.

　　El trabajo de Menchú a favor de los derechos
humanos[f] y del pluralismo étnico de Guatemala
le otorgó[g] el Premio Nóbel de la Paz en 1992,
exactamente quinientos años después de la
llegada[h] de Cristóbal Colón a América.

[a]*Al… The period between 1978 and 1985 in Guatemala is called*
[b]*ejército… Guatemalan army* [c]*campaign* [d]*población…*
indigenous population [e]*language* [f]*a… on behalf of human rights*
[g]*le… won her* [h]*arrival*

Tikal, Guatemala

Capítulo 5 of the video to accompany
Puntos de partida contains cultural
footage of Guatemala.

Visit the *Puntos de partida* Website at
www.mhhe.com/puntos.

Vocabulario

Los verbos

celebrar	to celebrate
pasar	to spend (*time*); to happen
quedarse	to stay, remain (*in a place*)

¿Qué tiempo hace?

está (muy) nublado	it's (very) cloudy, overcast
hace...	it's . . .
buen/mal tiempo	good/bad weather
calor	hot
fresco	cool
frío	cold
sol	sunny
viento	windy
hay (mucha)	there's (lots of)
contaminación	pollution
llover (ue)	to rain
llueve	it's raining
nevar (ie)	to snow
nieva	it's snowing

Los meses del año

enero, febrero, marzo, abril, mayo, junio, julio,
agosto, septiembre, octubre, noviembre,
diciembre

Las estaciones del año

la primavera	spring
el verano	summer
el otoño	fall, autumn
el invierno	winter

Los lugares

la capital	capital city
la isla	island
el parque	park
la playa	beach

Otros sustantivos

el clima	climate
el cumpleaños	birthday
la fecha	date (*calendar*)
el/la novio/a	boyfriend/girlfriend
la respuesta	answer

Los adjetivos

abierto/a	open
aburrido/a	bored
alegre	happy
cansado/a	tired
cariñoso/a	affectionate
cerrado/a	closed
congelado/a	frozen; very cold
contento/a	content, happy
desordenado/a	messy
difícil	hard, difficult
enfermo/a	sick
fácil	easy
furioso/a	furious, angry
limpio/a	clean
loco/a	crazy
nervioso/a	nervous
ocupado/a	busy
ordenado/a	neat
preocupado/a	worried
querido/a	dear
seguro/a	sure, certain
sucio/a	dirty
triste	sad

Las comparaciones

más/menos... que	more/less . . . than
tan... como	as . . . as
tanto/a(s)... como	as much/many . . . as
tanto como	as much as
mayor	older
mejor	better; best
menor	younger
peor	worse

Las preposiciones

a la derecha de	to the right of
a la izquierda de	to the left of
al lado de	alongside of
cerca de	close to
debajo de	below
delante de	in front of
detrás de	behind
encima de	on top of
entre	between, among
lejos de	far from

Los puntos cardinales

el norte, el sur, el este, el oeste

Palabras adicionales

afuera	outdoors
¿Cuál es la fecha de hoy?	What's today's date?
esta noche	tonight
estar (*irreg.*) **bien**	to be comfortable (*temperature*)
mí (*obj. of prep.*)	me
el primero de	the first of (*month*)
siguiente	following
tener (*irreg.*) **(mucho) calor**	to be (very) warm, hot
tener (*irreg.*) **(mucho) frío**	to be (very) cold
ti (*obj. of prep.*)	you
todavía	still

Un paso más 5

LECTURA

Estrategia: Forming a General Idea About Content

Before starting a reading, it is a good idea to try to form a general sense of the content. The more you know about the reading before you begin to read, the easier it will seem to you. Here are some things you can do to prepare yourself for reading. You have already applied some of these strategies to the readings thus far in *Puntos de partida*.

1. Make sure you understand the title. Think about what it suggests to you and what you already know about the topic. Do the same with any subtitles in the reading.
2. Look at the drawings, photos, or other visual clues that accompany the reading. What do they indicate about the content?
3. Read the comprehension questions before starting to read the selection. They will direct you to the kind of information you should be looking for.

You should be able to determine the general message of the reading if you apply the preceding strategies.

- **The title.** The reading, **"Todos juntos en los trópicos,"** contains a key word in the title: **trópicos.** It is a cognate. Can you guess what it means?
- **The art.** The reading is accompanied by a photograph and caption. What additional information do these tell you about the reading?
- **The comprehension questions.** Scan the questions in **Comprensión.** What additional clues do they give you about the content of the passage?

▶ **Sobre la lectura...** This reading is taken from the magazine *Muy intere-*
▶ *sante,* which generally contains articles about popular science and related
▶ topics. Remember that knowing the source of a passage can also help you
▶ formulate hypotheses about the reading before you begin to read.

Todos juntos en los trópicos

Los trópicos son las regiones biológica-mente más diversas del planeta y cuen-tan con[a] el triple de <u>especies</u> que en cualquier otra zona. Pero, ¿por qué? Los bió-logos no han sido capaces[b] de dar una respuesta unívoca.[c] Es más, las diferentes teo-rías que se han propuesto[d] tienen todos sus puntos débiles.[e]

En resumen, existen tres <u>razones</u> expues-tas para esta riqueza.[f] La primera teoría fue

[a]cuentan... tienen [b]no... *have not been able* [c]respuesta... *unambiguous answer* [d]que... *that have been proposed* [e]puntos... *weak points*
[f]expuestas... *given for this wealth*

No hay una teoría única para explicar la exuberancia natural que se produce en los trópicos.

diseñada^g hace 20 años^h por Michael Rosenzweigh, de Arizona. Según él, en los trópicos hay más especies, sencillamente^i porque se cuenta con más espacio geográfico <u>habitable</u>.

La segunda es de los últimos años 80 y fue diseñada por George Stevens, de Nuevo México: las especies tropicales son esclavas^j de sus condiciones térmicas;^k por eso no pueden <u>colonizar</u> nuevos territorios menos cálidos^l y se concentran como un gueto^m en el trópico.

La tercera es una teoría histórica y explica que los trópicos fueron^n las áreas de la Tierra que escaparon al efecto destructor del aumento^o de las regiones heladas^p durante las <u>glaciaciones</u>.

Ninguna de las tres ha sido confirmada.^q ●

^g fue... *was outlined* ^h hace... *20 years ago* ^i *simply* ^j *slaves* ^k *thermal* ^l *hot* ^m *ghetto* ^n *were* ^o *increase* ^p *frozen*
^q ha... *has been confirmed*

Comprensión

A. **¿Se menciona o no?** ¿Cuáles de los siguientes temas se mencionan en la lectura?

	SÍ	NO
1. Información sobre la gente (*people*) indígena de los trópicos.	☐	☐
2. Teorías que explican (*explain*) la biodiversidad de los trópicos.	☐	☐
3. Información sobre la deforestación de los trópicos.	☐	☐
4. Teorías que explican la climatología de los trópicos.	☐	☐

B. **Resumen** (*Summary*). En inglés, escriba un breve resumen de las tres teorías presentadas en la lectura. Compare su resumen con el de otro estudiante. ¿Cuál de las teorías parece más factible (*feasible*)?

ESCRITURA

La biodiversidad local. La lectura comenta la gran biodiversidad de los trópicos, y propone teorías que explican este fenómeno. ¿Cómo es la biodiversidad en la región donde Ud. vive? ¿Hay muchos animales y plantas indígenas? ¿Cuál es la relación entre el clima de la región y la flora y la fauna? Escriba un breve ensayo (*essay*) que comente cómo es el clima donde Ud. vive y qué animales y plantas habitan la zona. (Consulte un diccionario bilingüe si es necesario.)

¿Qué le gusta comer?

Este carrito en el viejo San Juan, Puerto Rico, está lleno de (*is full of*) frutas tropicales.

¿Qué opina Ud.?

Conteste según su propia vida. ¿Cree Ud. que una persona de otro país diría (*would say*) algo similar? Visite el sitio Web de *Puntos de partida* para leer las respuestas a estas preguntas que da una persona de Panamá.

1. ¿Qué **comidas** hispanas le gustan?
2. ¿Cree que la comida hispana es más o menos picante (*spicy*) que la estadounidense o la canadiense?
3. ¿Qué es una tortilla? (Puede contestar en inglés, si prefiere.) **¿Conoce** otro tipo de tortilla? ¿Tiene equivalente la tortilla en la comida de este país?
4. Si en general come **carne,** ¿hay partes del animal que no come nunca? el cerebro (*brain*)? ¿la sangre (*blood*)? ¿los intestinos?
5. ¿A qué hora **cena**? ¿Cuándo come la comida más **fuerte** del día?

En este capítulo...

- In this chapter, you will study vocabulary related to foods and food preferences. Two new verbs, **saber** and **conocer**, will also allow you to talk about what and whom you know.
- You have been using subject pronouns (**yo, él/ella, Ud.,** and so on) since **Capítulo 1**. In this chapter, you will begin to use object pronouns to avoid repeating the object of the verb. (Grammar 18)
- In this chapter you will learn other indefinite and negative words. (Grammar 19)
- You will begin to use formal commands to tell others what to do. (Grammar 20)
- The **Panorama cultural** section will focus on Panamá.

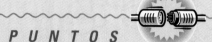

P U N T O S   I N T E R A C T I V O

Videoteca

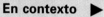

◀ **Minidramas**
Lola y Manolo van a cenar a un restaurante para celebrar su aniversario. ¿Celebra Ud. las fechas importantes de este modo?

En contexto ▶
Mariela compra verduras (*vegetables*) en el mercado para hacer una cena especial. ¿Compra Ud. toda la comida en el supermercado?

 CD-ROM

Además de completar el vocabulario y las actividades de gramática, Ud. va a tener la oportunidad de «hablar» con un vendedor acerca de (*about*) las verduras que quiere comprar.

 Internet

En la sección del **Capítulo 6** en el sitio Web de *Puntos de partida* aparecen enlaces que Ud. puede usar para conseguir información en español sobre la comida. Use la dirección www.mhhe.com/puntos para llegar al sitio Web.

La comida

Las comidas

el desayuno → desayunar
breakfast → to have (eat) breakfast

el almuerzo → almorzar (ue)
lunch → to have (eat) lunch

la cena → cenar
dinner → to have (eat) dinner, supper

Otras bebidas

el refresco	soft drink
el té	tea
el vino tinto	red wine

Otras verduras

el champiñón	mushroom
los espárragos	asparagus
los frijoles	beans

---

*The noun **agua** (*water*) is feminine, but the masculine articles are used with it in the singular: *el* **agua.** This occurs with all feminine nouns that begin with a stressed **a** sound, for example, *el* (*un*) **ama de casa** (*homemaker*).

Otras frutas		Otros postres	
la banana	banana	**el flan**	(baked) custard
la naranja	orange	**la galleta**	cookie
		el helado	ice cream

Otras carnes		Otras comidas	
el bistec	steak	**el arroz**	rice
la chuleta (de cerdo)	(pork) chop	**el huevo**	egg
la hamburguesa	hamburger	**el queso**	cheese
el jamón	ham	**el sándwich**	sandwich
el pavo	turkey	**el yogur**	yogurt
la salchicha	sausage; hot dog		

Otros pescados y mariscos	
el atún	tuna
los camarones	shrimp
la langosta	lobster
el salmón	salmon

Conversación

▲▲▲▲▲▲▲▲

A. **¿Qué quiere tomar?** Match the following descriptions of meals with these categories: **un menú ligero** (*light*) **para una dieta, una comida rápida, una cena elegante, un desayuno estilo norteamericano.**

1. una sopa fría, langosta, espárragos, una ensalada de lechuga y tomate, todo con vino blanco y, para terminar, un pastel
2. jugo de fruta, huevos con jamón, pan tostado y café
3. pollo asado, arroz, arvejas, agua mineral y, para terminar, una manzana
4. una hamburguesa con patatas fritas, un refresco y un helado

B. **Definiciones.** ¿Qué es?

1. un plato de lechuga y tomate
2. una bebida alcohólica blanca o roja
3. un líquido caliente (*hot*) que se toma* con cuchara (*spoon*)
4. una verdura anaranjada
5. la carne típica para la barbacoa en este país
6. una comida muy común en la China y en el Japón
7. la comida favorita de los ratones
8. una verdura frita que se come con las hamburguesas
9. una fruta roja o verde
10. una fruta amarilla de las zonas tropicales

---

*Placing **se** before a verb form can change its English equivalent slightly: **usa** (*he/she/it uses*) ⟶ **se usa** (*is used*).

More *tener* Idioms

Here are two additional **tener** idioms that you can use to talk about foods and eating.

tener (mucha) hambre	to be (very) hungry
tener (mucha) sed	to be (very) thirsty

C. Consejos (*Advice*) **a la hora de comer.** ¿Qué debe Ud. comer o beber en las siguientes situaciones?

1. Ud. quiere comer algo ligero porque no tiene hambre.
2. Ud. quiere comer algo fuerte (*heavy*) porque tiene mucha hambre.
3. Ud. tiene un poco de sed y quiere tomar algo antes de la comida.
4. Ud. quiere comer algo antes del plato principal.
5. Ud. quiere comer algo después del plato principal.
6. Ud. está a dieta.
7. Ud. está de vacaciones en Maine (o Boston).
8. Después de levantarse, Ud. no está completamente despierto/a (*awake*).

Nota cultural

Meals in the Spanish-Speaking World

Although Hispanic eating habits are becoming more and more like ours in this country, there are still many significant differences. Not only does the food itself differ somewhat, but the meals occur at different times.

There are three fundamental meals: **el desayuno, la comida / el almuerzo** (*midday meal*), and **la cena** (*supper*). Breakfast, which is generally eaten between 7:00 and 9:00, is a very simple meal, frugal by most U.S. or Canadian standards: **café con leche** or **chocolate** (*hot chocolate*) with a plain or sweet roll or toast; that is all. The **café con leche** is heated milk with very strong coffee to add flavor and color.

The main meal of the day, **la comida / el almuerzo**, is frequently eaten as late as 3:00 P.M., and it is a much heartier meal than our average lunch. It might consist of soup, a meat or fish dish with vegetables and potatoes or rice, a green salad, and then dessert (often fruit or cheese). Coffee is usually served after the meal.

The evening meal, **la cena**, is somewhat lighter than the noon meal. It is rarely eaten before 8:00, and in Spain it is commonly served as late as 10:00 or 11:00 P.M. Because the evening meal is served at such a late hour, it is customary to eat a light snack, or **merienda**, about 5:00 or 6:00 P.M. The **merienda** might consist of a sandwich or other snack with **café con leche** or **chocolate.** Similarly, a snack is often eaten in the morning between breakfast and the midday meal.

D. Preferencias gastronómicas

Paso 1. Haga una lista de sus tres platos favoritos y de sus tres lugares preferidos para comer en la ciudad donde Ud. vive.

Paso 2. Entreviste (*Interview*) a cinco compañeros de clase para averiguar (*find out*) cuáles son sus platos y lugares favoritos para comer.

MODELO: ¿Cuáles son tus tres lugares favoritos para comer?

Paso 3. Estudie los resultados de su encuesta (*survey*) para averiguar si hay gustos comunes entre todos de la clase. Después, comparta (*share*) con el resto de la clase sus observaciones.

¿Qué sabe Ud. y a quién conoce? *Saber* and *conocer*; Personal *a*

¿Le importa (*Does it matter to you*) mucho la comida? Si son ciertas para Ud. tres de las siguientes oraciones, sí le importa muchísimo (*a lot*).

1. Sé preparar muchos platos diferentes.
2. Conozco al dueño / a la dueña (*owner*) de mi restaurante favorito.
3. Sé el número de teléfono de mi restaurante favorito.
4. Sé cuánto cuesta, aproximadamente, una docena de huevos y un litro de leche.
5. Conozco muchos restaurantes en esta ciudad.

Saber and *conocer*

Two Spanish verbs express *to know*: **saber** and **conocer.**

saber (to know)		conocer (to know)	
sé	sabemos	conozco	conocemos
sabes	sabéis	conoces	conocéis
sabe	saben	conoce	conocen

saber

- to know facts or pieces of information

Ud. **sabe** su número de teléfono, ¿verdad?
You know her phone number, right?

saber + *infinitive*

- to know how to (*do something*)

conocer

- to know or be acquainted (familiar) with a person, place, or thing

¿Sabes jugar al ajedrez?
Do you know how to play chess?

¿Conoces a la nueva estudiante francesa?
Do you know the new French student?

Conozco un buen restaurante cerca de aquí.
I know (am familiar with) a good restaurant nearby.

| • to meet | ¿Quieres **conocer** al nuevo profesor?
Do you want to meet the new professor? |

Personal *a*

In Spanish, the word **a** immediately precedes the direct object* of a sentence when the direct object refers to a specific person or persons. This **a,** called the **a personal,** has no equivalent in English.[†]

¿Conoces **a** María?
Do you know María?

Llamo **a** mis padres con frecuencia.
I call my parents often.

OJO

The personal *a* is used before the interrogative words **¿quién?** and **¿quiénes?** when they function as direct objects.

¿**A quién** llamas?
Whom are you calling?

OJO

The verbs **buscar** (*to look for*), **escuchar** (*to listen to*), **esperar** (*to wait for*), and **mirar** (*to look at*) include the sense of the English prepositions *for, to,* and *at.* These verbs take direct objects in Spanish (not prepositional phrases, as in English).

Busco **mi abrigo.**
I'm looking for my overcoat.

Espero **a mi hijo.**
I'm waiting for my son.

Conversación

▲▲▲▲▲▲▲▲

A. Personas famosas

Paso 1. ¿Qué saben hacer estas personas?

Gloria Estefan		jugar al béisbol
Mikhail Baryshnikov		montar en (*to ride a*) bicicleta
José Canseco		cantar (en español)
Lance Armstrong	sabe	cocinar (*to cook*) bien
Michael Crichton		jugar al tenis
Arantxa Sánchez Vicario		escribir novelas
Julia Child		bailar

Paso 2. ¿Quién conoce a quién?

Adán		Martha
Napoleón		Cleopatra
Romeo		Eva
Rhett Butler	conoce a	Julieta
Marco Antonio		Scarlett O'Hara
George Washington		Josefina

---

*The *direct object* (**el complemento directo**) is the part of the sentence that indicates to whom or to what the verb is directed or upon whom or what it acts. In the sentence *I saw John,* the direct object is *John.*

[†]The personal **a** is not generally used with **tener: Tengo cuatro hijos.**

B. ¿Dónde cenamos? En esta escena del video, Lola y Manolo quieren cenar fuera. Pero, ¿dónde? Complete el diálogo con la forma correcta de **saber** o **conocer.**

LOLA: ¿(Sabes/Conoces[1]) adónde quieres ir a cenar?

MANOLO: No (sé/conozco[2]). ¿Y tú?

LOLA: No. Pero hay un restaurante nuevo en la calle Betis. Creo que se llama Guadalquivir. ¿(Sabes/Conoces[3]) el restaurante?

MANOLO: No, pero (sé/conozco[4]) que tiene mucha fama. Es el restaurante favorito de Virginia. Ella (sabe/conoce[5]) al dueño.

LOLA: ¿(Sabes/Conoces[6]) qué tipo de comida tienen?

MANOLO: No (sé/conozco[7]). Pero podemos llamar a Virginia. ¿(Sabes/Conoces[8]) su teléfono?

LOLA: Está en mi guía telefónica. Y pregúntale[a] a Virginia si ella (sabe/conoce[9]) si aceptan reservas con anticipación[b] o no.

MANOLO: De acuerdo.[c]

[a]*ask*   [b]con... *in advance*   [c]De... *OK.*

C. ¡Qué talento!

Paso 1. Invente oraciones sobre tres cosas que Ud. sabe hacer.

MODELO: Sé tocar el acordeón.

Paso 2. Ahora, en grupos de tres estudiantes, pregúnteles a sus compañeros si saben hacer esas actividades. Escriba sí o no, según sus respuestas.

MODELO: ¿Sabes tocar el acordeón?

Paso 3. Ahora describa las habilidades de los estudiantes en su grupo.

MODELO: Marta y yo sabemos tocar el acordeón, pero Elena no. (En el grupo, sólo yo sé tocar el acordeón.)

D. Preguntas

1. ¿Qué restaurantes conoce Ud. en esta ciudad? ¿Cuál es su restaurante favorito? ¿Por qué es su favorito? ¿Es buena la comida de allí? ¿Qué tipo de comida sirven? ¿Le gusta el ambiente (*atmosphere*)? ¿Come Ud. allí con frecuencia? ¿Llama primero para hacer reservaciones?

2. ¿Conoce Ud. a alguna persona famosa? ¿Quién es? ¿Cómo es? ¿Qué detalles sabe Ud. de la vida de esta persona?

3. ¿Qué platos sabe Ud. preparar? ¿tacos? ¿enchiladas? ¿pollo frito? ¿hamburguesas? ¿Le gusta cocinar? ¿Cocina con frecuencia?

4. ¿Espera Ud. a alguien para ir a la universidad? ¿Espera a alguien después de la clase? ¿A quién busca cuando necesita ayuda (*help*) con el español? ¿Dónde busca a sus amigos por la noche? ¿Dónde busca a sus hijos/amigos cuando es hora de comer?

Pronunciación: d and t

Some sounds, such as English [b], are called *stops* because, as you pronounce them, you briefly stop the flow of air and then release it. Other sounds, such as English [f] and [v], pronounced by pushing air out with a little friction, are called *fricatives*.

- Spanish **d** has two basic sounds. At the beginning of a phrase or sentence or after **n** or **l,** it is pronounced as a stop [d] (similar to English *d* in *dog*). Like the Spanish [t], it is produced by putting the tongue against the back of the upper teeth. In all other cases, it is pronounced as a fricative [đ], that is, like the *th* sound in English *they* and *another*.

- The main difference in the pronunciation of Spanish **t** and English **t** is that in English the tip of the tongue is placed against the top of the mouth, while in Spanish it is placed against the upper teeth. In addition, Spanish **t** is not pronounced with as much aspiration (pushing air out of the mouth) as in English. Spanish **t** sounds more like the **t** in the English word *star*. When it appears between two vowels, Spanish **t** uses full dental pronunciation, not a short pronunciation as occurs in English *matter*.

A. Práctica. Practique las siguientes palabras y frases.

1. [d]	diez	dos	doscientos	doctor
	¿dónde?	el doctor	el dinero	venden
2. [đ]	mucho dinero	adiós	usted	seda
	ciudad	la doctora	cuadros	todo

B. Pronuncie.

1. ¿Dónde está el dinero?
2. David Dávila es doctor.
3. Dos y diez son doce.
4. ¿Qué estudia Ud.?
5. Venden de todo, ¿verdad?

C. Más práctica. Practique las siguientes palabras y frases.

1.	traje	todo	mantequilla
	trimestre	patata	pastel
	zapatos	cartera	tenis
	necesito	tomate	tinto
	tres	trabajo	

2. ¿Cómo te llamas?
3. ¿Cuánto cuesta?
4. Mi tío trabaja en una tienda.

Expressing *what or whom* • Direct Object Pronouns

De compras en el supermercado

Indique cuáles de estas afirmaciones son verdaderas para Ud.

1. la leche
   - ☐ *La* bebo todos los días. Por eso tengo que comprar*la* con frecuencia.
   - ☒ *La* bebo de vez en cuando (*once in a while*). Por eso no *la* compro a menudo (*often*).
   - ☐ Nunca *la* bebo. No necesito comprar*la*.

2. el café
   - ☐ *Lo* bebo todos los días. Por eso tengo que comprar*lo* con frecuencia.
   - ☐ *Lo* bebo de vez en cuando. Por eso no *lo* compro a menudo.
   - ☒ Nunca *lo* bebo. No necesito comprar*lo*.

3. los huevos
   - ☐ *Los* como todos los días. Por eso tengo que comprar*los* con frecuencia.
   - ☒ *Los* como de vez en cuando. Por eso no *los* compro a menudo.
   - ☐ Nunca *los* como. No necesito comprar*los*.

4. las bananas
   - ☐ *Las* como todos los días. Por eso tengo que comprar*las* con frecuencia.
   - ☒ *Las* como de vez en cuando. Por eso no *las* compro a menudo.
   - ☐ Nunca *las* como. No necesito comprar*las*.

Direct Object Pronouns

me	me		**nos**	us
te	you (*fam. sing.*)		**os**	you (*fam. pl.*)
lo*	you (*form. sing.*), him, it (*m.*)		**los**	you (*form. pl.*), them (*m., m. + f.*)
la	you (*form. sing.*), her, it (*f.*)		**las**	you (*form. pl.*), them (*f.*)

A. Like direct object nouns, *direct object pronouns* (**los pronombres del complemento directo**) are the first recipient of the action of the verb. Direct object pronouns are placed before a conjugated verb and after the word **no** when it appears. Third person direct object pronouns are used only when the direct object noun has already been mentioned.

[Práctica A]

¿El libro? Diego no **lo** necesita.
The book? Diego doesn't need it.

¿Dónde están el libro y el periódico? **Los** necesito ahora.
Where are the book and the newspaper? I need them now.

Ellos **me** ayudan.
They're helping me.

B. The direct object pronouns may be attached to an infinitive or a present participle.

[Práctica B]

Las tengo que leer.
Tengo que leer**las**. } *I have to read them.*

Lo estoy comiendo.
Estoy comiéndo**lo**. } *I am eating it.*

C. Note that many verbs commonly used with reflexive pronouns can also be used with direct object nouns and pronouns when the action of the verb is directed at someone other than the subject of the sentence. The meaning of the verb will change slightly.

[Práctica C]

Generalmente me despierto a las ocho. La radio **me** despierta.
I generally wake up at eight. The radio wakes me.

En un restaurante, el camarero **nos** sienta.
In a restaurant, the waiter seats us.

D. Note that the direct object pronoun **lo** can refer to actions, situations, or ideas in general. When used in this way, **lo** expresses English *it* or *that*.

Lo comprende muy bien.
He understands it (that) very well.

No **lo** creo.
I don't believe it (that).

Lo sé.
I know (it).

---

*In Spain and in some other parts of the Spanish-speaking world, **le** is frequently used instead of **lo** for the direct object pronoun *him*. This usage will not be followed in *Puntos de partida*.

Práctica

A. ¿Qué comen los vegetarianos?

Paso 1. Aquí hay una lista de diferentes comidas. ¿Van a former parte de la dieta de un vegetariano? Conteste según los modelos.

MODELOS: el bistec → No *lo* va a comer.
la banana → *La* va a comer.

1. las patatas
2. el arroz
3. las chuletas de cerdo
4. los huevos
5. la zanahoria
6. la manzana
7. los camarones
8. el pan
9. el pan
10. los frijoles
11. la ensalada

Paso 2. Si hay un estudiante vegetariano / una estudiante vegetariana en la clase, pídale que verifique (*ask him or her to verify*) las respuestas de Ud.

B. La cena de Lola y Manolo.
La siguiente descripción de la cena de Lola y Manolo es muy repetitiva. Combine las oraciones, cambiando los nombres de complemento directo por pronombres cuando sea (*whenever it is*) necesario.

MODELO: El camarero (*waiter*) trae un menú. Lola lee el menú. →
El camarero trae un menú y Lola *lo* lee.

1. El camarero trae una botella de vino tinto. Pone la botella en la mesa.
2. El camarero trae las copas (*glasses*) de vino. Pone las copas delante de Lola y Manolo.
3. Lola quiere la especialidad de la casa. Va a pedir la especialidad de la casa.
4. Manolo prefiere el pescado fresco (*fresh*). Pide el pescado fresco.
5. Lola quiere una ensalada también. Por eso pide una ensalada.
6. El camerero trae la comida. Sirve la comida.
7. Manolo necesita otra servilleta (*napkin*). Pide otra servilleta.
8. «¿La cuenta (*bill*)? El dueño está preparando la cuenta para Uds.»
9. Manolo quiere pagar con tarjeta (*card*) de crédito. No trae su tarjeta.
10. Por fin, Lola toma la cuenta. Paga la cuenta.

C. ¿Quién o qué lo hace?
Indique a la persona o cosa que hace lo siguiente. Hay más de una respuesta posible.

Palabras útiles: el barbero, los (buenos) amigos, el camarero / la camarera, mi compañero/a, el despertador (*alarm clock*), el doctor / la doctora, el dueño / la dueña, los esposos, mi esposo/a, los estudiantes, mi padre/madre, los padres, los profesores, la radio

1. Por la mañana, _____ me despierta.
2. En un restaurante, _____ nos sienta.
3. En una barbería (*barber shop*), _____ nos afeita.
4. En un hospital, _____ nos examina.

5. _____ nos escuchan cuando necesitamos hablar.

6. _____ nos esperan cuando vamos a llegar tarde.

7. Generalmente los niños no se acuestan solos (*by themselves*). _____ los acuesta. _____ también los baña y los viste.

8. En una clase, _____ hacen las preguntas y _____ las contestan.

Nota comunicativa

Talking About What You Have Just Done

To talk about what you have *just* done, use the phrase **acabar** + **de** with an infinitive.

Acabo de almorzar con Beto.	*I just had lunch with Beto.*
Acabas de celebrar tu cumpleaños, ¿verdad?	*You just celebrated your birthday, didn't you?*

Note that the infinitive follows **de.** As you already know, the infinitive is the only verb form that can follow a preposition in Spanish.

D. ¡Acabo de hacerlo! Imagine that a friend is pressuring you to do the following things. With a classmate, tell him or her that you just did each one, using either of the forms in the model.

MODELO: E1: ¿Por qué no estudias la lección? →
E2: Acabo de estudiar*la.* (*La* acabo de estudiar.)

1. ¿Por qué no escribes las composiciones para tus clases?
2. ¿Vas a comprar el periódico hoy?
3. ¿Por qué no pagas los cafés?
4. ¿Vas a preparar la comida para la fiesta?
5. ¿Puedes pedir la cuenta?
6. ¿Tienes hambre? ¿Por qué no comes los tacos que preparé (*I made*)?

Conversación

A. ¿Quién ayuda? Todos necesitamos la ayuda de alguien en diferentes circunstancias. ¿Quién los/las ayuda a Uds. con lo siguiente? Use **nos** en sus respuestas.

Palabras útiles: nuestros padres (compañeros, consejeros, amigos, …)

1. con las cuentas **2.** con la tarea **3.** con la matrícula
4. con el horario de clases **5.** con los problemas personales

C. Una encuesta sobre la comida. Hágales (*Ask*) preguntas a sus compañeros de clase para saber si toman las comidas o bebidas indicadas y con qué frecuencia. Deben explicar también por qué toman o *no* toman cierta cosa.

MODELO: la carne → E1: ¿Comes carne?
E2: No *la* como casi nunca porque tiene mucho colesterol.

Palabras útiles: la cafeína, las calorías, el colesterol, la grasa (*fat*)

Frases útiles: estar a dieta, ser alérgico/a a, ser bueno/a para la salud (*health*), me pone (*it makes me*) nervioso/a, me da asco (*it makes me sick*) / me dan asco (*they make me sick*), lo/la/los/las detesto

1. la carne
2. los mariscos
3. el yogur
4. la pizza
5. las hamburguesas
6. el pollo
7. el café
8. los dulces (*sweets; candy*)
9. el alcohol
10. el atún
11. los espárragos
12. el hígado (*liver*)

19   Expressing Negation • Indefinite and Negative Words

En la cocina de Diego y Antonio

DIEGO: Quiero comer *algo*, pero *no* hay *nada* de comer en esta casa. Y no tengo ganas de ir de compras. Y además, ¡*no* tengo *ni* un centavo!

ANTONIO: ¡Ay! *Siempre* eres así. Tú *nunca* tienes ganas de ir de compras. Y lo del dinero… ¡esa ya es otra historia!

¿Quién… ?

1. tiene hambre
2. nunca tiene dinero
3. critica a su amigo
4. no quiere ir de compras

A. Here is a list of the most common indefinite and negative words in Spanish. You have been using many of them since the first chapters of *Puntos de partida*.

algo	something, anything	**nada**	nothing, not anything
alguien	someone, anyone	**nadie**	no one, nobody, not anybody
algún (alguno/a/os/as)	some, any	**ningún (ninguno/a)**	no, none, not any
siempre	always	**nunca, jamás**	never
también	also	**tampoco**	neither, not either

Pronunciation hint: Remember to pronounce the *d* in *nada* and *nadie* as a fricative, that is, like a *th* sound: *na da, na die.*

In Diego and Antonio's kitchen DIEGO: I want to eat something, but there's nothing to eat in this house. And I don't feel like going shopping. And furthermore, I don't have a cent! ANTONIO: Ah! You're always like that. You never feel like going shopping. And that bit about the money …, that's another story!

B. Pay particular attention to the following aspects of using negative words.

- When a negative word comes after the main verb, Spanish requires that another negative word—usually **no**—be placed before the verb. When a negative word precedes the verb, **no** is not used.

¿**No** estudia **nadie**? }
¿**Nadie** estudia? } *Isn't anyone studying?*

No estás en clase **nunca**. }
Nunca estás en clase. } *You're never in class.*

No quieren cenar aquí **tampoco**. }
Tampoco quieren cenar aquí. } *They don't want to have dinner here, either.*

- The adjectives **alguno** and **ninguno** shorten to **algún** and **ningún**, respectively, before a masculine singular noun—just as **uno** shortens to **un**, **bueno** to **buen**, and **malo** to **mal**. The plural forms **ningunos** and **ningunas** are rarely used.

—¿Hay **algunos** recados para mí hoy?
—Lo siento, pero hoy no hay **ningún** recado para Ud.
Are there any messages for me today?
I'm sorry, but there are no messages for you today.
  (There is not a single message for you today.)

Práctica

A. ¡Por eso no come nadie allí! Exprese negativamente, usando la negativa doble.

1. Hay algo interesante en el menú.
2. Tienen algunos platos típicos.
3. El profesor cena allí también.
4. Mis amigos siempre almuerzan allí.
5. Preparan algo especial para grupos grandes.
6. Siempre hacen platos nuevos.
7. Y también sirven paella, mi plato favorito.

B. Manolo está de mal humor (*in a bad mood*).

Paso 1. Lola y su esposo Manolo son profesores en la Universidad de Sevilla. Hoy Manolo está de mal humor y tiene una actitud muy negativa. ¿Qué opina Manolo de las afirmaciones de Lola sobre las clases y la vida universitaria en general?

MODELO: LOLA: Tengo algunos estudiantes excelentes este año.
MANOLO: Pues, yo *no* tengo *ningún* estudiante excelente este año.

LOLA:

1. Hay muchas clases interesantes en el departamento.
2. Me gusta tomar café con mis estudiantes con frecuencia.
3. Hay algunas personas buenas en la administración.
4. También hay un candidato bueno para el puesto (*position*) de rector de la facultad (*department*).
5. Hay muchas personas inteligentes en la universidad.
6. Me gustan algunas conferencias (*lectures*) que están planeadas para este mes.

Capítulo 6 • ¿Qué le gusta comer?

Paso 2. Ahora imagine las preguntas que hace Lola, según las respuestas de Manolo.

> MODELO: MANOLO: No, no hay nada interesante en el periódico.
> LOLA: ¿Hay *algo* interesante en el periódico?

MANOLO:

1. No, no hay nada interesante en la tele esta noche.
2. No, no hay nadie cómico en el programa.
3. No, no hay ninguna película buena en el cine esta semana.
4. No, no como nunca en la facultad.
5. Tampoco almuerzo entre clases.

C. **¿Qué pasa esta noche en casa?** Tell whether the following statements about what is happening at this house are true (**cierto**) or false (**falso**). Then create as many additional sentences as you can about what is happening, following the model of the sentences.

1. No hay nadie en el baño.
2. En la cocina, alguien está preparando la cena.
3. No hay ninguna persona en el patio.
4. Hay algo en la mesa del comedor.
5. Algunos amigos se están divirtiendo en la sala.
6. Hay algunos platos en la mesa del comedor.
7. No hay ningún niño en la casa.

Conversación

▲▲▲▲▲▲▲

Preguntas

1. ¿Vamos a vivir en la luna (*moon*) algún día? ¿Vamos a viajar (*to travel*) a otros planetas? ¿Vamos a vivir allí algún día? ¿Vamos a establecer contacto con seres (*beings*) de otros planetas algún día?
2. ¿Algunos de los estudiantes de esta universidad son de países extranjeros? ¿De dónde son? ¿Algunos de sus amigos son de habla española (*Spanish-speaking*)? ¿De dónde son?
3. En esta clase, ¿quién...

siempre tiene algunas buenas ideas?	nunca tiene tiempo para divertirse?
tiene algunos amigos españoles?	nunca ve la televisión?
siempre lo entiende todo?	no practica ningún deporte?
nunca contesta ninguna pregunta?	siempre invita a los otros a comer?
va a ser muy rico/a algún día?	

Felipe Rojas-Lombardi

El cocinero[a] **peruano Felipe Rojas-Lombardi** es autor del libro de cocina *The Art of South American Cooking.* Rojas-Lombardi presenta **la cocina**[b] **tradicional latinoamericana** a los norteamericanos en su restaurante The Ballroom en Nueva York.

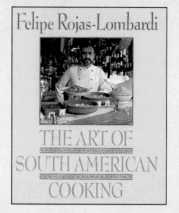

Felipe Rojas-Lombardi

THE ART OF SOUTH AMERICAN COOKING

La cocina de su familia, como la[c] del Perú, combina varios elementos. Primero tiene **los ingredientes nativos** y las combinaciones hechas por[d] **los quechuas** (los descendientes de los antiguos incas). Los quechuas cultivaban[e] más de cien tipos de patata, maíz[f] y ají[g] de distintas variedades. La cocina de la mayoría[h] de las naciones sudamericanas se basa en estos ingredientes.

El pescado y **los mariscos** también son una parte importante de la cocina peruana. Algunos consideran que **el cebiche,** pescado crudo[i] con jugo de limón, es el plato nacional del Perú.

Otra influencia importante es **la cocina española.** Los españoles introdujeron[j] en América ingredientes como el trigo,[k] además de animales de corral, como el cerdo, la vaca[l] y el pollo.

En la cocina de cada nación sudamericana hay también **influencias de los distintos grupos de inmigrantes.** La abuela de Rojas-Lombardi, por ejemplo, es **chilena.** En Chile el número elevado de **inmigrantes alemanes** significa que la cocina alemana tiene una importante influencia en la chilena. La familia **italiana** de su madre usa elementos de la cocina italiana, como la pasta y los tomates (los tomates son nativos de México). Rojas-Lombardi combina todos estos elementos para ofrecer[m] una aventura culinaria—¡e internacional!

[a]*chef* [b]*cuisine* [c]*la cocina* [d]*hechas... made by* [e]*grew* [f]*corn* [g]*chile* [h]*majority* [i]*raw* [j]*introduced* [k]*wheat* [l]*cow* [m]*offer*

---

20   Influencing Others • Formal Commands

Receta para guacamole

El guacamole

Ingredientes:
1 aguacate[a]
1 diente de ajo,[b] prensado[c]
1 tomate
jugo de un limón
sal
un poco de cilantro fresco[d]

Cómo se prepara
Corte el aguacate y el tomate en trozos[e] pequeños. *Añada* el jugo del limón, el ajo, el cilantro y la sal a su gusto. *Mezcle* bien todos los ingredientes y *sírvalo* con tortillas fritas de maíz.[f]

En español, los mandatos se usan con frecuencia en las recetas. Estos verbos se usan en forma de mandato en esta receta. ¿Puede encontrarlos?

añadir	to add
cortar	to cut
mezclar	to mix
servir (i, i)	to serve

[a]*avocado* [b]*diente... clove of garlic* [c]*crushed* [d]*fresh* [e]*pieces* [f]*corn*

---

*From this point on in *Puntos de partida,* the **En los Estados Unidos y el Canadá...** sections will be written in Spanish. Important words will be in boldface type. Scanning those words before you begin to read will help you get the gist of the passage.

In *Puntos de partida* you have seen commands throughout the direction lines of exercises: **haga, complete, conteste,** and so on.

Commands (imperatives) are verb forms used to tell someone to do something. In Spanish, *formal commands* **(los mandatos formales)** are used with people whom you address as **Ud.** or **Uds.** Here are some of the basic forms.

	hablar	**comer**	**escribir**	**volver**	**decir**
Ud.	hable	coma	escriba	vuelva	diga
Uds.	hablen	coman	escriban	vuelvan	digan
English	*speak*	*eat*	*write*	*come back*	*tell*

A. Almost all formal commands are based on the **yo** form of the present tense. Replace the **-o** with **-e** or **-en** for **-ar** verbs; replace the **-o** with **-a** or **-an** for **-er** and **-ir** verbs.

hablo → hable
como → coma
escribo → escriba

B. Formal commands of stem-changing verbs will show the stem change.

p**ie**nse Ud.
v**ue**lva Ud.
p**i**da Ud.

C. Verbs ending in **-car, -gar,** and **-zar** have a spelling change to preserve the **-c-, -g-,** and **-z-** sounds.

c → qu   buscar: bus**que** Ud.
g → gu   pagar: pa**gue** Ud.
z → c   empezar: empie**ce** Ud.

D. The **Ud./Uds.** commands for verbs that have irregular **yo** forms will reflect the irregularity.

conocer	→ **conozca** Ud.
decir* (*to say, tell*)	→ **diga** Ud.
hacer	→ **haga** Ud.
oír	→ **oiga** Ud.
poner	→ **ponga** Ud.
salir	→ **salga** Ud.
tener	→ **tenga** Ud.
traer	→ **traiga** Ud.
venir	→ **venga** Ud.
ver	→ **vea** Ud.

E. A few verbs have irregular **Ud./Uds.** command forms.

dar* (*to give*)	→ **dé** Ud.
estar	→ **esté** Ud.
ir	→ **vaya** Ud.
saber	→ **sepa** Ud.
ser	→ **sea** Ud.

*****Decir** and **dar** are used primarily with indirect objects. Both of these verbs and indirect object pronouns will be formally introduced in **Capítulo 7.**

Minidiálogos y gramática

Position of Pronouns with Formal Commands

- Direct object pronouns and reflexive pronouns must follow affirmative commands and be attached to them. In order to maintain the original stress of the verb form, an accent mark is added to the stressed vowel if the original command has two or more syllables.

Lé**alo** Ud.	*Read it.*
Sién**tese**, por favor.	*Sit down, please.*

- Direct object and reflexive pronouns must precede negative commands.

No lo lea Ud.	*Don't read it.*
No se siente.	*Don't sit down.*

Práctica

A. Una cena en casa. Los siguientes mandatos describen las acciones posibles cuando se prepara una cena elegante en casa. Póngalos en orden cronológico, del 1 al 8.

a. __2__ Vaya a la tienda para comprar comida y bebidas.
b. __7__ Abra la puerta cuando lleguen los invitados.
c. __4__ Prepare algunos platos especiales.
d. __1__ Haga una lista de invitados.
e. __8__ Diviértase con sus amigos.
f. __5__ Ponga (*Set*) la mesa.
g. __3__ Llame a los amigos para invitarlos.
h. __6__ Póngase ropa elegante.

B. Profesor(a) por un día. Imagine que Ud. es el profesor / la profesora hoy. ¿Qué mandatos debe dar a la clase?

MODELOS: hablar español → Hablen Uds. español.
hablar inglés → No hablen Uds. inglés.

1. llegar a tiempo
2. leer la lección
3. escribir una composición
4. abrir los libros

5. estar en clase mañana
6. traer los libros a clase
7. estudiar los verbos nuevos
8. ¿ ?

C. ¡Pobre Sr. Casiano!

Paso 1. El Sr. Casiano no se siente (*feel*) bien. Lea la descripción que él da de algunas de sus actividades.

«*Trabajo* muchísimo[a] —¡me gusta trabajar! En la oficina, *soy* impaciente y *critico* bastante[b] a los otros. En mi vida personal, a veces *soy* un poco

[a]*a great deal* [b]*a good deal*

impulsivo. *Fumo* bastante y también *bebo* cerveza y otras bebidas alcohólicas, a veces sin moderación… *Almuerzo* y *ceno* fuerte, y casi nunca *desayuno*. Por la noche, con frecuencia *salgo* con los amigos—me gusta ir a las discotecas— y *vuelvo* tarde a casa.»

Paso 2. ¿Qué *no* debe hacer el Sr. Casiano para estar mejor? Aconséjele (*Advise him*) sobre lo que (*what*) no debe hacer. Use los verbos indicados o cualquier (*any*) otro, según los modelos.

MODELOS: Trabajo → Sr. Casiano, no trabaje tanto.
soy → Sr. Casiano, no sea tan impaciente.

D. Situaciones. El Sr. Casiano quiere adelgazar (*to lose weight*). ¿Debe o no debe comer o beber las siguientes cosas? Con otro/a estudiante, haga y conteste preguntas según los modelos:

MODELOS: ensalada → E1: ¿Ensalada?
E2: Cómala.
postres → E1: ¿Postres?
E2: No los coma.

1. alcohol (*m.*)
2. verduras
3. pan
4. dulces
5. leche
6. hamburguesas con queso
7. frutas
8. refrescos dietéticos
9. pollo
10. carne
11. pizza
12. jugo de fruta

E. Consejos. Su vecino Pablo es una persona muy perezosa y descuidada (*careless*). No estudia mucho y tampoco hace sus quehaceres (*chores*) en el apartamento donde vive con un compañero. Déle (*Give him*) consejos lógicos usando estos verbos, según el modelo.

MODELO: afeitarse → ¡Aféitese!

1. despertarse más temprano
2. levantarse más temprano
3. bañarse más
4. quitarse esa ropa sucia
5. ponerse ropa limpia
6. vestirse mejor
7. estudiar más
8. no divertirse tanto con los amigos
9. ir más a la biblioteca
10. no acostarse tan tarde
11. ayudar con los quehaceres
12. ¿ ?

Nota comunicativa

El subjuntivo

Except for the command form, all verb forms that you have learned thus far in *Puntos de partida* have been part of what is called the *indicative mood* (**el modo indicativo**). In both English and

Spanish, the indicative is used to state facts and to ask questions. It objectively expresses most real-world actions or states of being.

Both English and Spanish have another verb system called the *subjunctive mood* (**el modo subjuntivo**). The **Ud./Uds.** command forms that you have just learned are part of the subjunctive system. You will not use the subjunctive actively until it is introduced (in **Capítulo 12**). But from this point on in *Puntos de partida* you will see the subjunctive used where it is natural to use it. What follows is a brief introduction to the subjunctive that will make it easy for you to recognize it when you see it.

Here are some examples of the forms of the subjunctive. The **Ud./Uds.** forms (identical to the **Ud./Uds.** command forms) are highlighted.

hablar		comer		servir		salir	
hable	hablemos	coma	comamos	sirva	sirvamos	salga	salgamos
hables	habléis	comas	comáis	sirvas	sirváis	salgas	salgáis
hable	hablen	coma	coman	sirva	sirvan	salga	salgan

The subjunctive is used to express more subjective or conceptualized states, in contrast to the indicative, which reports facts, information that is objectively true. Here are just a few of the situations in which the subjunctive is used in Spanish.

- to express what the speaker wants others to do (I want you to . . .)

- to express emotional reactions (I'm glad that . . .)

- to express probability or uncertainty (it's likely that . . .)

F. El cumpleaños de María. Fíjese en (*Notice*) los verbos subrayados (*underlined*). Diga por qué razón están subrayados. (Use la lista de la **Nota comunicativa**.)

En el parque

RAÚL: Como hoy es tu cumpleaños, quiero invitarte a cenar. ¿En qué restaurante quieres que <u>cenemos</u>?

MARÍA: Prefiero que tú me[a] <u>prepares</u> una de tus espléndidas cenas.

RAÚL: ¡Con mucho gusto!

En casa de María

MADRE: (*Hablando por teléfono.*) No, lo siento,[b] pero María no está en casa.

LUISA: ¿Es posible que <u>esté</u> en la biblioteca?

MADRE: No. Sé que ella y Raúl están cenando en casa de él.

LUISA: Ah, sí. Bueno, ¿puede pedirle a ella que <u>llame</u> a Luisa cuando regrese?

MADRE: Sí, cómo no,[c] Luisa. Adiós.

LUISA: Hasta luego.

[a]*for me* [b]lo... *I'm sorry* [c]cómo... *of course*

Conversación

Nota comunicativa

"Softening" Commands

In both English and Spanish, commands can be a very blunt way of requesting things. Here are some ways you can soften your requests.

- using polite expressions

favor de + *inf.*	please (*do something*)
por favor	please
si me hace (Ud.) el favor	if you would do me the favor
si es (Ud.) tan amable	if you would be so kind

- using a question in the present tense, as well as using an expression from the previous list

  ¿Me trae otra cerveza, **por favor?**
  Will you bring me another beer, please?

- using the verb **poder** to increase your politeness

  Por favor, ¿**puede** traerme más pan?
  Could you please bring me more bread?

Can you think of situations in which softer requests might be more appropriate than direct commands?

En la oficina del consejero. Imagine that you are a guidance counselor. Students consult you with all kinds of questions, some trivial and some important. Offer advice to them in the form of affirmative or negative commands, or softened requests. How many different commands can you invent for each situation?

1. EVELIA: No me gusta tomar clases por la mañana. Siempre estoy muy cansada durante esas clases y además a esa hora tengo hambre. Pienso constantemente en el almuerzo… y no puedo concentrarme en las explicaciones.
2. FABIÁN: En mi clase de cálculo, ¡no entiendo nada! No puedo hacer los ejercicios y durante la clase tengo miedo de hacer preguntas, porque no quiero parecer (*seem*) tonto.
3. FAUSTO: Fui (*I went*) a México el verano pasado y me gustó (*I liked it*) mucho. Quiero volver a México este verano. Ahora que lo conozco mejor, quiero ir en mi coche y no en autobús como el verano pasado. Desgraciadamente (*Unfortunately*) no tengo dinero para hacer el viaje.

Videoteca

Minidramas

In this **Minidramas** dialogue, Manolo Durán and his wife Lola Benítez are in a restaurant. Pay close attention to the kinds of foods mentioned. What item is mentioned that you know by a different name?

El camarero viene con el vino y el agua. Sirve el vino y pone la botella[a] de agua en la mesa.

> CAMARERO: ¿Ya saben lo que desean de comer los señores?
>
> MANOLO: Creo que sí, pero, ¿qué recomienda Ud.?
>
> CAMARERO: Hoy tenemos un plato especial: gambas[b] al limón con arroz, un plato ligero y delicioso. Y también tenemos un salmón buenísimo[c] que acaba de llegar esta tarde.
>
> LOLA: ¡Qué rico![d] Yo quiero las gambas, por favor.
>
> MANOLO: Eh, para mí, el bistec estilo argentino, poco asado. Y una ensalada mixta para dos.
>
> CAMARERO: ¿Y para empezar? Tenemos una sopa de ajo[e] muy rica.
>
> LOLA: Para mí, una sopa, por favor.
>
> MANOLO: Y para mí, también. Y le dice al chef que por favor le ponga[f] un poco de atún a la ensalada.
>
> CAMARERO: Muy bien, señor.

[a]*bottle* [b]*shrimp* [c]*very good* [d]¡Qué... *How tasty!* [e]*garlic* [f]*le dice... will you tell the chef to please put*

Con un compañero / una compañera

Using the **Minidramas** dialogue as a model, take turns with a partner asking and answering the following questions, playing the role of both customer and waiter/waitress. Try to answer each question in several different ways.

> MODELO: ¿Qué desea Ud. de postre? →
> Para mí, la fruta.
> ¿Me trae un helado, por favor?
> Favor de traerme un helado.
> ¿Todavía hay flan?
> No deseo nada, gracias.

1. ¿Desean Uds. algo para empezar?
2. ¿Va a tomar sopa?
3. ¿Qué desea Ud. de plato principal?
4. ¿Y para beber?

Un poco más sobre... Lola Benítez Guzmán

Lola Benítez Guzmán, una profesora sevillana que enseña inglés a estudiantes norteamericanos, es también esposa y madre. Forma parte de una familia numerosa y tiene recuerdos muy agradables de la niñez[a] que pasó con ellos.

[a]*recuerdos... very pleasant memories of the childhood*

To read more about the characters from this video, visit the *Puntos de partida* Website at www.mhhe.com/puntos

5. ¿Qué quiere de postre?
6. ¿Prefiere Ud. té o café?

En contexto

In this video segment, Mariela shops for produce. As you watch the segment, pay particular attention to the information Mariela gives about the meal she's planning. What does the vendor tell her about the produce?

COSTA RICA

A. Lluvia de ideas

- ¿A Ud. le gusta cocinar? ¿Qué sabe preparar? ¿Cuál es su especialidad?
- Cuando hay una ocasión especial, ¿le gusta celebrar en un restaurante o prefiere cocinar algo en casa? ¿Tiene algunas recetas para días importantes?
- ¿Hace Ud. la compra con frecuencia? Por lo general, ¿a qué tiendas va a comprar comida? ¿Compra muchos alimentos pre-cocinados (*pre-cooked foods*)?

B. Dictado

Aquí está una parte del diálogo entre Mariela y el vendedor, que aparece en la sección de vídeo de este capítulo. Complete el diálogo con las palabras o frases que faltan.

SR. VALDERRAMA: Hola, Srta. Castillo. ¿Qué le doy[a] hoy?

MARIELA: _____ _____ _____ una cena deliciosa, Sr. Valderrama... Es la primera vez que _____ _____ de _____ _____ vienen a cenar. ¡Pienso causar una gran _____!

SR. VALDERRAMA: ¿Qué va a preparar? ¿Tal vez[b] un buen _____ frito con _____?

MARIELA: No, a mi novio no le gusta el pescado frito.

SR. VALDERRAMA: ¿Le gustan _____ _____ a su novio?

MARIELA: Sí, le gustan muchísimo.[c]

SR. VALDERRAMA: Entonces, de _____ _____, prepare un ceviche de camarones.

[a]le... *can I give you* [b]Tal... *Perhaps* [c]*very much*

C. Un diálogo original

Paso 1. Con un compañero / una compañera dramaticen el diálogo entre Mariela y el Sr. Valderrama.

Paso 2. Imagine que Ud. y su compañero/a desean preparar una comida especial para celebrar la visita de sus padres. Hagan un menú y una lista de la comida que deben comprar para hacer la cena.

A. ¿Qué hace Roberto los martes?

Paso 1. Describa la rutina de Roberto, haciendo oraciones según las indicaciones.

1. martes / Roberto / nunca / salir / apartamento / antes de / doce
2. esperar / su amigo Samuel / en / parada (*bus stop*) del autobús
3. (ellos) llegar / universidad / a / una
4. (ellos) buscar / su amiga Ceci / en / cafetería
5. ella / acabar / empezar / estudios / allí
6. (ella) no / conocer / mucha gente (*people*) / todavía
7. a veces / (ellos) ver / profesora de historia en / cafetería / y / hablar / un poco / con ella
8. (ella) ser / persona / muy interesante / que / saber / mucho / de / ese / materia
9. a / dos / todos / tener / clase / de / sicología
10. siempre / (ellos) oír / conferencias (*lectures*) / interesante / y / hacer / alguno / pregunta
11. a veces / tener / oportunidad de / conocer / conferenciante (*m., lecturer*)
12. a / cinco / Samuel y Roberto / volver / esperar / autobús
13. Roberto / preparar / cena / y / luego / mirar / televisión

Paso 2. ¿Quién habla? Base su respuesta en la información del **Paso 1**.

1. Quiero conocer a más gente. ¡Casi no conozco a nadie todavía!
2. Algunos estudiantes hacen buenas preguntas.
3. ¿Dónde está Roberto? Va a llegar tarde otra vez…
4. ¡Ay! ¡Ya son las doce! ¡Tengo que salir!

Paso 3. Ahora vuelva a contar la historia desde el punto de vista de Roberto, usando **yo** o **nosotros** como sujeto donde sea apropiado.

B. La forma de comer.

Complete the following paragraphs with the correct form of the words in parentheses, as suggested by the context. When two possibilities are given, select the correct word.

La forma de comer diferencia a las personas. Aquí habla Pilar Fuentes, una española que (vivir[1]) en California con dos estudiantes (norteamericano[2]).

«Yo creo que las costumbres[a] de mis compañeros son un poco (extraño[3]). Generalmente, (por/para[4]) la mañana, mi compañero Peter (desayunar[5]) dos huevos fritos, y un vaso[b] de leche (frío[6]). También él (preparar[7]) pan tostado sin mantequilla. A la una (almorzar[8]) en la universidad. (Comprar[9]) comida china en uno de (ese[10]) restaurantes pequeños que hay en el *campus*. Por (el/la[11]) tarde, (comer[12]) su cena típica: (un/una[13]) pizza grande y un plato de helado de pistacho con chocolate.

Carol, la otra compañera, es muy diferente. Siempre (ser/estar[14]) a dieta. Además cree que su manera de comer (es/estar[15]) muy natural. (*Ella:* Desayunar[16]) café negro. Para el almuerzo, ella (preparar[17]) un sándwich de pan integral[c] y también (unos/unas[18]) zanahorias y una naranja. Su cena (ser[19]) sencilla:[d] arroz integral y verduras. Parece que ella quiere compensar[e] las calorías de los dulces que (*ella:* comer[20]) para la merienda[f]…»

[a]*customs* [b]*glass* [c]*whole grain* [d]*simple* [e]*make up for* [f]*snack*

Comprensión: ¿Probable o improbable?

1. Pilar cree que la forma de comer de sus compañeros es muy normal.
2. Peter sabe cocinar muy bien.
3. Carol nunca tiene ganas de comer un bistec.
4. Carol es vegetariana.

P A N O R A M A
cultural

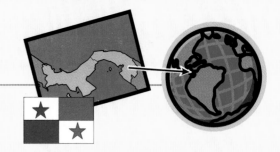

Panamá

Datos esenciales

Nombre oficial: República de Panamá
Capital: Ciudad de Panamá
Población: 2.778.526 de habitantes
Moneda: el balboa (también se usa el dólar
estadounidense)
Idioma oficial: el español

¡Fíjese!

- **Panamá** es una palabra indígena que significa
  «tierra de muchos peces[a]».

- La Carretera[b] Panamericana, el sistema de
  carreteras que va de Alaska al Canadá,
  termina[c] por un tiempo en la densa e[d]
  impenetrable selva[e] panameña de Darién. Para
  llegar a Sudamérica es necesario tomar un
  barco[f] hasta Colombia, donde continúa la
  carretera.

- La Sra. Mireya Moscoso ganó[g] las elecciones
  presidenciales de 1998. La viuda[h] de otro
  presidente, doña Mireya es la primera mujer
  panameña en asumir el cargo.[i]

[a]*fish* [b]*Highway* [c]*ends* [d]*y* [e]*jungle* [f]*boat* [g]*won* [h]*widow*
[i]*post*

Conozca... el Canal de Panamá

El Canal de Panamá, construido a través del[a]
istmo entre los dos continentes americanos,
comunica los océanos Atlántico y Pacífico. Mide[b]
aproximadamente 80 kilómetros (50 millas) de
largo, 12,5 metros (41 pies[c]) de ancho[d] y 200
metros (más de 63 pies) de profundidad. Su
construcción facilita la comunicación marítima
entre las costas este y oeste de los continentes.
Antes de la existencia del canal, los barcos tenían

[a]*construido... built across the* [b]*It measures* [c]*feet* [d]*de... in width*

que darle la vuelta a[e] América del Sur para ir de
una costa a otra. Hoy, el viaje por el Canal de
Panamá toma aproximadamente ocho horas, pues[f]
es necesario pasar por un número de esclusas.[g]

La idea de construir un canal a través del
istmo data de 1534, cuando el emperador
español Carlos V (Quinto) la propone. Más tarde,
en 1881, el ingeniero francés Fernando de
Lesseps también va a sugerir un proyecto similar.
Pero el canal no se construye hasta el siglo XX,
por los Estados Unidos. Esto ocasiona[h] la
presencia de los Estados Unidos en la vida de
Panamá. Como resultado, hay un uso extendido
del inglés en el país, se usa el dólar y ha habido[i]
una gran intervención en la política del país.

El canal se inaugura en 1914 y es administrado
por los Estados Unidos hasta 1999. Desde el
primero de enero del año 2000, la República de
Panamá está a cargo de[j] su gran canal.

[e]*tenían... had to go around* [f]*because* [g]*canal locks* [h]*brings about*
[i]*ha... there has been* [j]*a... in control of*

Una esclusa del Canal de Panamá.

 Capítulo 6 of the video to accompany
Puntos de partida contains cultural
footage of Panama.

 Visit the *Puntos de partida* Website at
www.mhhe.com/puntos.

▼▼▼ Vocabulario

Los verbos

acabar de + *inf.*	to have just (*done something*)
ayudar	to help
cenar	to have (eat) dinner
cocinar	to cook
conocer	to know, be acquainted with
desayunar	to have (eat) breakfast
esperar	to wait (for); to expect
invitar	to invite
llamar	to call
preguntar	to ask a question
preparar	to prepare
saber (*irreg.*)	to know;
saber + *inf.*	to know how to (*do something*)

Repaso: almorzar (ue)

La comida

el arroz	rice
las arvejas	peas
el atún	tuna
el bistec	steak
los camarones	shrimp
la carne	meat
los cereales	cereal
el champiñón	mushroom
la chuleta (de cerdo)	(pork) chop
los dulces	sweets; candy
los espárragos	asparagus
el flan	(baked) custard
los frijoles	beans
la galleta	cookie
el helado	ice cream
el huevo	egg
el jamón	ham
la langosta	lobster
la lechuga	lettuce
la mantequilla	butter
la manzana	apple
los mariscos	shellfish

la naranja	orange
el pan	bread
el pan tostado	toast
el pastel	cake; pie
la patata (frita)	(French fried) potato
el pavo	turkey
el pescado	fish
el pollo (asado)	(roast) chicken
el postre	dessert
el queso	cheese
la salchicha	sausage; hot dog
la sopa	soup
las verduras	vegetables
la zanahoria	carrot

Las bebidas

el agua (mineral)	(mineral) water
el jugo (de fruta)	(fruit) juice
la leche	milk
el refresco	soft drink
el té	tea
el vino (blanco, tinto)	(white, red) wine

Repaso: el café, la cerveza

Los cognados

la banana, la ensalada, la fruta, la hamburguesa, el salmón, el sándwich, el tomate, el yogur

Las comidas

el almuerzo	lunch
la cena	dinner, supper

Repaso: el desayuno

En un restaurante

el/la camarero/a	waiter/waitress
la cuenta	check, bill

el menú	menu
el plato	dish; course

Otros sustantivos

el consejo	(piece of) advice
el detalle	detail
el/la dueño/a	owner
la tarjeta de crédito	credit card

Los adjetivos

fresco/a	fresh
frito/a	fried
fuerte	heavy (*meal, food*); strong
ligero/a	light, not heavy
rápido/a	fast

Palabras indefinidas y negativas

alguien	someone, anyone
algún (alguno/a/os/as)	some, any
jamás	never
nada	nothing, not anything
nadie	no one, nobody, not anybody
ningún (ninguno/a)	no, none, not any
tampoco	neither, not either

Repaso: algo, nunca, siempre, también

Palabras adicionales

tener (*irreg.*) (**mucha**) hambre	to be (very) hungry
tener (*irreg.*) (**mucha**) sed	to be (very) thirsty

Un paso más 6

LECTURA

Estrategia: Words with Multiple Meanings

It is easy to get off track while reading if you assign the wrong meaning to a word that has multiple English equivalents. The word **como** can cause confusion because it can mean *how, like, the way that, as, since,* and *I eat,* depending on the context. Other common words with multiple meanings include **que** (*what, that, who*), **clase** (*class meeting, course, kind,* or *type*), and **esperar** (*to wait for, to hope, to expect*).

You must rely on the context to determine which meaning is appropriate. Practice by telling what **como** means in each of the following sentences.

1. En España, como en Francia, se come mucho pescado.
2. No me gusta cómo habla el profesor; debe hablar más despacio.
3. Como tú no quieres estudiar, ¿por qué no tomamos una cerveza?

▶ **Sobre la lectura...** The readings in previous **Lectura** sections were writ-
▶ ten especially for students like you, or they were simplified versions of au-
▶ thentic materials written for native speakers of Spanish. The following is the
▶ first truly authentic, unsimplified reading you have seen in *Puntos de partida.*
▶ You should be able to get the gist of the reading easily, even though you will
▶ not understand every word. It is a good idea to scan the activities in the **Com-**
▶ **prensión** section first, to get a sense for what is important in the article.

Tapas[a] y vinos, placer español por Virginia Godoy

Las tapas no sustitu-
yen una comida
formal pero son
ideales para una fiesta a la
española o para disfrutar
los deliciosos manjares[b]
de esa tierra.

   Irse de tapas es una
divertida costumbre es-
pañola que llegó a Estados
Unidos durante la década

Calamares en su tinta,[c] una tapa española típica que sirve el restaurante Barcelona Paradis en Nueva York

[a]*Appetizers* [b]*delicacies* [c]*Calamares... Squid cooked in their ink*

de los ochenta. En las ciudades españolas, los mesones,[d] tascas,[e] cervecerías, bares, xampanyeries (<u>champañerías catalanas</u>), restaurantes y bodegones[f] se convierten en <u>centro de reunión</u> donde estudiantes, banqueros y parroquianos[g] en general socializan, hablan del próximo examen universitario, de negocios o simplemente se relajan tomando tapas acompañadas de un buen vino o cerveza.

Aunque las tapas no sustituyen una comida formal, son ideales para <u>una fiesta a la española</u> a base de tapas y vinos. Se debe elegir una variación de tapas fritas, asadas u horneadas en el último minuto, otras con salsa, algunas frías o marinadas y otras servidas con pan o envueltas con masa.

Usualmente, las tapas con salsa como las angulas[h] de Aguinaga, los champiñones al ajillo o los callos a la madrileña se sirven en cazuelitas de barro.[i] En cambio las ensaladas, arroces, pinchos, banderillas, queso y morcilla[j] se colocan en platos pequeños.

Una de las tapas más fáciles de preparar son las aceitunas[k] a la sevillana o las almendras[l] peladas y sofritas en aceite puro de oliva. Este tipo de tapas, junto con las de queso manchego (queso blanco duro español) y el jamón de Jabugo (similar al prosciutto de Parma) son ideales con una copa de jerez,[m] un scotch o cualquier otra bebida.

Existen tantas tapas como tipos de comida en las diferentes <u>provincias españolas</u>. Así por ejemplo los «pescaítos»[n] fritos son típicos de Andalucía, los arroces de Valencia y las combinaciones de mariscos son de Galicia. Otras tapas como los riñones[o] al Jerez o los chorizos al cava reflejan la riqueza vinícola española en la cocina. ●

[d]*tavernas* [e]*bars* [f]*cheap restaurants* [g]*clientes* [h]*eels*
[i]*cazuelitas… clay bowls* [j]*blood sausage* [k]*olives* [l]*almonds*
[m]*sherry* [n]*pescados pequeños* [o]*kidneys*

Comprensión

A. ¿Qué significa? Las siguientes palabras <u>subrayadas</u> tienen doble o triple significado. ¿Entiende Ud. bien su significado?

1. «las tapas con salsa <u>como</u> las angulas de Aguinaga»
   El significado apropiado de **como** es:
   ☐ *I eat*
   ☐ *like*
   ☐ *as it were*
2. «los champiñones al ajillo o los <u>callos</u> a la madrileña»
   El significado apropiado de **callos** es:
   ☐ *calluses*
   ☐ *tripe*
3. «las ensaladas, arroces, pinchos, <u>banderillas</u>, queso»
   El significado apropiado de **banderillas** es:
   ☐ *barbed dart used in bullfighting*
   ☐ *hors d'oeuvres on a toothpick*
   ☐ *a small flag*

B. ¿Cierto o falso? Conteste según la lectura.

1. La costumbre (*custom*) de las tapas viene de España.
2. En general, ir de tapas es una costumbre de la clase alta.
3. Hay gran variedad de tapas, aunque todas se sirven frías.
4. Muchas provincias tienen sus propias (*own*) especialidades.
5. Las tapas son ideales porque reemplazan (*replace*) a la comida formal.
6. Las tapas son todas muy difíciles de preparar.
7. La costumbre europea de tomar vino con las comidas no existe en España.
8. Las tapas se comen solamente en los restaurantes más formales.

C. ¿Qué sirven? En el artículo se menciona que las tapas se sirven en muchos lugares, como por ejemplo en las cervecerías y las champañerías. ¿Puede Ud. deducir el nombre de la bebida que se sirve en estos lugares?

En una cervecería sirven _____.
En una champañeria sirven _____.

E S C R I T U R A

A. También en este país se sirven tapas

Paso 1. Las tapas son parte de la cultura culinaria española, pero también en este país se sirven aperitivos en las fiestas y en los bares. Haga una lista de tres tapas norteamericanas típicas y de los ingredientes necesarios para prepararlas.

Paso 2. Ahora escoja su tapa favorita del **Paso 1.** Va a escribir un breve párrafo (*paragraph*) sobre ella. Aquí hay algunas ideas que puede considerar.

los ingredientes
la apariencia o el modo de servir esta tapa (por ejemplo, se sirve con salsa de tomate)
dónde se sirve (en las fiestas, en casa, en los restaurantes, etcétera)
la bebida ideal para tomar con esta tapa
la historia o el origen de la tapa, si Ud. tiene esa información

Aquí tiene la primera oración de su composición: _____ **es/son una de mis tapas norteamericanas favoritas.**

B. Entre familia. Write a brief paragraph about your eating preferences or those of your family. Use the following questions as a guide in developing your paragraph.

1. ¿Cuántas veces come(n) al día? ¿A qué hora?
2. ¿Comen juntos, a la misma (*same*) hora y en la misma mesa? ¿Come Ud. solo/a?
3. ¿Quién(es) prepara(n) la comida?
4. ¿Qué prepara(n) con frecuencia? ¿Es excelente la comida? ¿buena? ¿mala? ¿regular?
5. ¿Conversa(n) mientras (*while*) comen? ¿Quién habla más? ¿menos? ¿Mira(n) la televisión mientras comen?
6. ¿Qué comida prefiere(n) cuando va(n) a un restaurante? ¿comida china? ¿mexicana? ¿italiana? ¿comida rápida? ¿En qué restaurantes comen?
7. ¿Come(n) allí con frecuencia? ¿Cuántas veces al año? ¿Cuándo va(n) a volver?

De vacaciones

El Museo Guggenheim, en Bilbao (España), abrió sus puertas en octubre del 1997. Con el nuevo museo, diseñado por Frank O. Gehry, Bilbao se convierte en (*becomes*) uno de los centros artísticos más importantes del mundo.

¿Qué opina Ud.?

Conteste cierto o falso, según su propia vida. Diga por qué. ¿Cree Ud. que una persona de otro país diría algo similar? Visite el sitio Web de *Puntos de partida* para leer los comentarios de una persona de Honduras.

Para mis vacaciones, **me gustaría**...

1. **viajar** lejos de aquí.
2. **hacer** *camping* en **las montañas**.
3. ir a una ciudad histórica con muchos lugares de importancia cultural.
4. ir a una **playa** bonita.
5. viajar en **autobús** por todo el país.

En este capítulo...

- In this chapter, you will focus on vocabulary related to vacations and modes of travel.
- You will begin to use indirect object pronouns to express *to whom* or *for whom*. (Grammar 21)
- Do you like to travel? You already know how to express that idea in Spanish. Now you will learn more about using **gustar** to talk about your likes and dislikes. (Grammar 22)
- You'll also be able to talk about actions in the past. (Grammar 23)
- The **Panorama cultural** section will focus on El Salvador and Honduras.

P U N T O S   I N T E R A C T I V O

Videoteca

◀ Minidramas
Elisa va a una agencia de viajes (*travel agency*) porque quiere planear una visita a unas islas famosas. ¿Conoce Ud. alguna isla? ¿Cuál?

En contexto ▶
Juan Carlos compra un billete de tren (*train ticket*) para ir a un pueblo cercano (*nearby town*). ¿Viaja Ud. en tren de vez en cuando (*sometimes*)?

CD-ROM

Además de completar el vocabulario y las actividades de gramática, Ud. va a tener la oportunidad de «hablar» con una agente de viajes (*travel agent*) «virtual» sobre un viaje.

Internet

En la sección del Capítulo 7 en el sitio Web de *Puntos de partida* aparecen enlaces que Ud. puede usar para conseguir información en español sobre los viajes y las vacaciones. Use la dirección **www.mhhe.com/puntos** para llegar al sitio Web.

Vocabulario: Preparación

¡Buen viaje!°   Buen… *Have a good trip!*

Ir en avión

el aeropuerto	airport
el/la asistente de vuelo	flight attendant
la sala de espera	waiting room
la sección de (no) fumar	(non)smoking section
el vuelo	flight

Ir en tren/autobús/barco

el barco	boat, ship
la cabina	cabin (*in a ship*)
la estación	station
de autobuses	bus
del tren	train
el maletero	porter
el puerto	port

De viaje

la agencia de viajes	travel agency
el/la agente de viajes	travel agent
el asiento	seat
el billete/el boleto/ el pasaje*	ticket
de ida	one way
de ida y vuelta	round-trip
la demora	delay
el equipaje	baggage, luggage
la llegada	arrival
el/la pasajero/a	passenger
la salida	departure
bajar (de)	to get down (from, off of)
estar atrasado/a	to be late
facturar el equipaje	to check one's bags
guardar (un puesto)	to save (a place)

hacer (*irreg.*) cola	to stand in line
hacer (*irreg.*) escalas/paradas	to make stops
hacer (*irreg.*) la(s) maleta(s)	to pack one's suitcase(s)
hacer (*irreg.*) un viaje	to take a trip
ir (*irreg.*) / estar (*irreg.*) de vacaciones	to go/be on vacation
sacar fotos	to take photos
subir (a)	to go up; to get on (*a vehicle*)
viajar	to travel

De vacaciones

hacer (*irreg.*) *camping*	to go camping
nadar	to swim
tomar el sol	to sunbathe
la camioneta	station wagon
el *camping*	campground
el mar	sea
las montañas	mountains
el océano	ocean
la playa	beach
la tienda (de campaña)	tent

---

*Throughout Spanish America, **el boleto** is the word used for a *ticket for travel*. **El billete** is commonly used in Spain. **El pasaje** is used throughout the Spanish-speaking world. The words **la entrada** and **la localidad** are used to refer to tickets for movies, plays, or similar functions.

Se venden billetes aquí.	Tickets are sold here.
Aquí no se fuma.	You don't (One doesn't) smoke here. Smoking is forbidden here.

Be alert to this use of **se** when you see it, because it will occur with some frequency in readings and in direction lines in *Puntos de partida*. The activities in this text will not require you to use this grammar point on your own, however.

Nueva York

E. **¿Dónde se hace esto?** Indique el lugar (o los lugares) donde se hacen las siguientes actividades.

Lugares: en casa, en la agencia de viajes, en el aeropuerto, en el avión, en la playa

1. Se factura el equipaje.
2. Se hacen las maletas.
3. Se compran los pasajes.
4. Se hace una reservación.
5. Se espera en la sala de espera.
6. Se pide un cóctel.
7. Se mira una película.
8. Se nada y se toma el sol.

F. **Prueba** (*Quiz*) **cultural.** ¿Cierto o falso? Corrija (*Correct*) las oraciones falsas.

1. Se habla español en el Brasil.
2. Se comen tacos en México.
3. Se puede esquiar en Chile en junio.
4. En España a veces se cena a las diez de la noche.
5. La paella se prepara con lechuga.
6. Se dice «chau» en la Argentina.
7. Se habla español en Miami.
8. En este país se puede votar a los dieciocho años.

Pronunciación: g, gu, and j

- In Spanish, the letter **g** followed by **e** or **i** has the same sound as the letter **j** followed by any vowel: [x]. It is similar to the English **h**, although in some dialects it is pronounced with a harder sound.

general	jamón, jota, jugo
gigante	jersey
	jirafa

- As you know, the letter **g** has another pronunciation, similar to **g** in the English word *go*: [g]. The Spanish letter **g** is pronounced [g] when it is followed directly by **a, o,** or **u** or by the combinations **ue** and **ui.**

    galante   gorila   gusto   guerrilla   siguiente

- The [g] pronunciation actually has two forms, a harder [g] and a fricative [g̶] that sounds softer. The [g] pronunciation is used at the beginning of a phrase (that is, after a pause) or after the letter **n.**

    mango   tango   ángulo

- In any other position, the softer, fricative [g̶] is used.

    el gato   el gorila   el gusto

A. [x]   jamón   Juan   Jesús   joya   rojo
        geranio   genio   gimnasio   gitano   germinal
        Jijona   Jorge   jipijapa

B. [g]   gato galleta gas tengo algodón ganga

C. [g/g̶]   un gato/el gato   un grupo/el grupo
            gracias/las gracias   guapos niños/niños guapos

D. [x/g]   gigante jugoso jugar jugamos juguete

Minidiálogos y gramática

21 Expressing *to whom or for whom* •
Indirect Object Pronouns; *Dar* and *decir*

Prueba: ¿Cómo son sus relaciones con otros?

¿Con qué frecuencia hace Ud. las siguientes cosas, con mucha frecuencia, a veces o nunca?

1. *Les* escribo cartas a mis amigos.
2. *Les* escribo cartas a mis padres (hijos).
3. *Les* doy (*I give*) consejos a mis amigos.
4. *Les* doy consejos a mis padres (hijos).
5. *Les* digo (*I tell*) la verdad a mis amigos.
6. *Les* digo la verdad a mis padres (hijos).
7. *Les* pido dinero a mis amigos.
8. *Les* pido dinero a mis padres (hijos).

La siguiente parte de la prueba le va a mostrar (*show*) si hay reciprocidad en sus relaciones con sus amigos y con sus padres (hijos). Conteste con: **con mucha frecuencia, a veces** o **nunca.**

1. Mis amigos me escriben cartas.
2. Mis padres (hijos) me escriben cartas.
3. Mis amigos me dan consejos.
4. Mis padres (hijos) me dan consejos.
5. Mis amigos me dicen sus problemas.
6. Mis padres (hijos) me dicen sus problemas.
7. Mis amigos me piden dinero.
8. Mis padres (hijos) me piden dinero.

¿Qué le dicen a Ud. sus respuestas? ¿Cómo son sus relaciones con otros?

Indirect Object Pronouns

me	to/for me	**nos**	to/for us
te	to/for you (*fam. sing.*)	**os**	to/for you (*fam. pl.*)
le	to/for you (*form. sing.*), him, her, it	**les**	to/for you (*form. pl.*), them

Note that indirect object pronouns have the same form as direct object pronouns, except in the third person: **le, les.**

A. Indirect object nouns and pronouns are the second recipient of the action of the verb. They usually answer the questions *to whom?* or *for whom?* in relation to the verb. The word *to* is frequently omitted in English.

Indicate the direct and indirect objects in the following sentences.

1. I'm giving her the present tomorrow.
2. Could you tell me the answer now?
3. El profesor nos va a hacer algunas preguntas.
4. ¿No me compras una revista ahora?

B. Like direct object pronouns, *indirect object pronouns* (**los pronombres del complemento indirecto**) are placed immediately before a conjugated verb. They may also be attached to an infinitive or a present participle.

No, no **te** presto el coche.
No, I won't lend you the car.

Voy a guardar**te** el asiento.
Te voy a guardar el asiento.
I'll save your seat for you.

Le estoy escribiendo una carta **a Marisol**.
Estoy escribiéndo**le** una carta **a Marisol**.
I'm writing Marisol a letter.

C. Since **le** and **les** have several different equivalents, their meaning is often clarified or emphasized with the preposition **a** followed by a pronoun (object of a preposition).

Voy a mandar**le** un telegrama **a Ud.** (**a él, a ella**).
I'm going to send you (him, her) a telegram.

Les hago una comida **a Uds.** (**a ellos, a ellas**).
I'm making you (them) a meal.

D. It is common for a Spanish sentence to contain both the indirect object noun and the indirect object pronoun, especially with third person forms.

Vamos a decir**le** la verdad **a Juan**.
Let's tell Juan the truth.

¿**Les** guardo los asientos **a Jorge y Marta**?
Shall I save the seats for Jorge and Marta?

E. As with direct object pronouns, indirect object pronouns are attached to the affirmative command form and precede the negative command form.

Sírva**nos** un café, por favor.
Serve us some coffee, please.

No me dé su número de teléfono ahora.
Don't give me your phone number now.

F. Here are some verbs frequently used with indirect objects.

dar (*irreg.*)	to give	**pedir (i, i)**	to ask for
decir (*irreg.*)	to say; to tell	**preguntar**	to ask (*a question*)
escribir	to write		
explicar	to explain	**prestar**	to lend
hablar	to speak	**prometer**	to promise
mandar	to send	**recomendar (ie)**	to recommend
ofrecer (ofrezco)	to offer	**regalar**	to give (*as a gift*)
		servir (i, i)	to serve

Dar and *decir*

dar		decir	
(to give)		**(to say; to tell)**	
doy	damos	digo	decimos
das	dais	dices	decís
da	dan	dice	dicen

- **Dar** and **decir** are almost always used with indirect object pronouns in Spanish.

¿Cuándo **me das** el dinero?
When will you give me the money?

¿Por qué no **le dice** Ud. la verdad, señor?
Why don't you tell him/her the truth, sir?

OJO

In Spanish it is necessary to distinguish between the verbs **dar** (*to give*) and **regalar** (*to give as a gift*). Also, do not confuse **decir** (*to say* or *to tell*) with **hablar** (*to speak*).

- **Dar** and **decir** also have irregular formal command forms. There is a written accent on **dé** to distinguish it from the preposition **de**.

Formal commands of **dar** and **decir**:

dar → dé, den

decir → diga, digan

Práctica

A. De vuelta a Honduras

Paso 1. Your friends the Padillas, from Honduras, need help arranging for and getting on their flight back home. Explain how you will help them, using the cues as a guide.

MODELO: confirmar el vuelo → Les confirmo el vuelo.

1. llamar un taxi
2. bajar (*to carry down*) las maletas
3. guardar el equipaje
4. facturar el equipaje
5. guardar el puesto en la cola
6. guardar el asiento en la sala de espera
7. comprar una revista
8. por fin decir adiós

Paso 2. Now explain the same sequence of actions as if you were talking about your friend Guillermo: *Le* **confirmo el vuelo.**

Paso 3. Finally, tell your friend Marisol how you will help her: *Te* **confirmo el vuelo.**

B. ¿Qué hacen estas personas? Complete las siguientes oraciones con un verbo lógico y un pronombre de complemento indirecto.

MODELO: El vicepresidente *le ofrece* consejos al presidente.

Verbos posibles: dar, ofrecer, prestar, prometer, servir

1. Romeo _____ flores a Julieta.
2. Snoopy _____ besos (*kisses*) a Lucy… ¡Y a ella no le gusta!
3. Eva _____ una manzana a Adán.
4. Ann Landers _____ consejos a sus lectores (*readers*).
5. Los bancos _____ dinero a las personas que quieren comprar una casa.
6. Los asistentes de vuelo _____ bebidas a los pasajeros.
7. George Washington _____ a su padre decir la verdad.

C. ¿Qué va a pasar? Dé varias respuestas.

Palabras útiles: medicinas, Santa Claus, tarjetas navideñas (*Christmas cards*), flores, juguetes (*toys*)

1. Su amiga Elena está en el hospital con un ataque de apendicitis. Todos le mandan… Le escriben… Las enfermeras (*nurses*) le dan… De comer, le sirven…
2. Es Navidad. Los niños les prometen a sus padres… Les piden… También le escriben… Le piden… Los padres les mandan… a sus amigos. Les regalan…

3. Hay una demora y el avión no despega (*takes off*) a tiempo. Un asistente de vuelo nos sirve... Otra asistente de vuelo nos ofrece... El piloto nos dice...

4. Mi coche no funciona hoy. Mi amigo me presta... Mis padres me preguntan... Luego me dan...

5. Es la última (*last*) semana de clases y hay exámenes finales la próxima semana. En la clase de computación, todos le preguntan al profesor... El profesor les explica a los estudiantes...

D. En un restaurante. Imagine that your four-year-old cousin Benjamín has never eaten in a restaurant before. Explain to him what will happen, filling in the blanks with the appropriate indirect object pronoun.

Primero el camarero _____¹ indica una mesa desocupadaª. Luego tú _____² pides el menú al camarero. También _____³ haces preguntas sobre los platos y las especialidades de la casa y _____⁴ dices tus preferencias. El camarero _____⁵ trae la comida. Por fin tu papá _____⁶ pide la cuenta al camarero. Si tú quieres pagar, _____⁷ pides dinero a tu papá y _____⁸ das el dinero al camarero.

ª*vacant*

Conversación

▲▲▲▲▲▲▲▲

Entrevista: ¿Quién... ? Read through the following items and think about people whom you associate with the indicated action. Then, working with a partner, ask and answer questions to find out information about each topic.

MODELO: darle consejos →
  E1: ¿A quién le das consejos?
  E2: Con frecuencia le doy consejos a mi compañero de cuarto. ¡Él los necesita!
  E1: ¿Quién te da consejos a ti?
  E2: Mis abuelos me dan muchos consejos.

1. darle consejos
2. pedirle ayuda con los estudios
3. prestarle la ropa
4. mandarle flores
5. decirle secretos
6. hacerle favores
7. escribirle tarjetas postales (*postcards*)
8. ofrecerle bebidas

Destinosª hispánicos

Como sabe Ud., no es necesario salir de los Estados Unidos para encontrarᵇ y disfrutar deᶜ la cultura hispánica. Aquí se mencionan tres de los muchos lugares de influencia hispánica que se pueden visitar en este país.

- En el pueblo de **San Juan Bautista, California**, se encuentra una famosa misión, construida por **los frailesᵈ franciscanos** en 1797. Desde 1980, San Juan Bautista es la sedeᵉ

La misión en San Juan Bautista

del **Teatro Campesino**,ᶠ la compañía teatral chicana más antigua del país. El Teatro Campesino, fundado por **Luis Valdez** durante la «Great Delano Grape Strike,» presenta obrasᵍ de teatro en español y también en inglés. Muchas de las obras presentadas son clásicas, pero también hay obras escritasʰ especialmente para el Teatro.
- **Santa Fe, Nuevo México**, está situada en el valle del Río Grande al pieⁱ de las montañas

Sangreʲ de Cristo. Cada verano se celebra allí el **Mercado Tradicional Español**, donde se venden **artesanías** típicas y hechasᵏ con métodos antiguos. Allí se pueden encontrar artículos como santos de bulto (imágenes de santos talladasˡ), retablos (imágenes de santos pintadas), alfombras, muebles y otros objetos de adorno.

- ¿Quiere bailar o escuchar música? Pues, vaya a

Miami, donde se celebra la feria hispánica más grande del país, **el festival de la calleᵐ Ocho**. Cada verano, más de un millón de personas llegan a la calle principal de **la Pequeña Habana**, centro de **la comunidad cubana** en el sur de Florida. Allí se sirve comida hispánica, se escucha música latina y se baila. Y aunqueⁿ predomina la música tropical y caribeña, también hay conjuntos musicales de toda Latinoamérica que ofrecen música de todos los estilos.

ª*Destinations* ᵇ*find* ᶜ*disfrutar... enjoy* ᵈ*priests* ᵉ*headquarters* ᶠTeatro... *Country (Peasant) Theater* ᵍ*works* ʰ*written* ⁱ*foot* ʲ*Blood* ᵏ*made* ˡ*carved* ᵐ*street* ⁿ*although*

¿Recuerda Ud.?

You have already used forms of **gustar** to express your likes and dislikes (**Ante todo**). Review what you know by answering the following questions. Then, changing their form as needed, use them to interview your instructor.

1. ¿Te gusta el café (el vino, el té, ...)?
2. ¿Te gusta jugar al béisbol (al golf, al vólibol, al...)?
3. ¿Te gusta viajar en avión (fumar, viajar en tren, ...)?
4. ¿Qué te gusta más, estudiar o ir a fiestas (trabajar o descansar, cocinar o comer)?

Los chilenos viajeros

Según el anuncio, a muchos chilenos les gusta viajar a otros países. Lea el anuncio y luego indique si las oraciones son ciertas o falsas.

1. A los chilenos les gusta viajar sólo en este hemisferio
2. A los chilenos les gustan mucho las playas.
3. Sólo les gusta viajar en países de habla española.
4. No les gustaría el precio del viaje.

MEDIO MILLON DE CHILENOS
DE VACACIONES 2003 AL EXTRANJERO

Y USTED... NO SE QUEDE SIN VIAJAR
¡ RESERVE AHORA MISMO !

El próximo verano '03, con el bajo valor del dólar, muchas personas desearán viajar, los cupos disponibles se agotarán rapidamente. ¡Asegure sus vacaciones! Elija ahora cualquiera de nuestros fantásticos programas.

MIAMI - ORLANDO - BAHAMAS - MÉXICO - CANCÚN
ACAPULCO - IXTAPA - COSTA RICA - RIO - SALVADOR
PLAYA TAMBOR - PUNTA CANA - LA HABANA
VARADERO - GUATEMALA - SUDÁFRICA

Infórmese sobre nuestro **SUPER CRÉDITO PREFERENCIAL** **Economy Tour**
Santa Magdalena 94, Providencia
☎2334429 - 2331774 - 2314252
2328294 - 2318608 - 2334862
Fax: 2334428

Y a Ud., ¿le gusta viajar? ¿Le gustan los viajes en avión? ¿Cuál de estos lugares le gustaría visitar?

Constructions with *gustar*

Spanish	Literal Equivalent	English Phrasing
Me gusta la playa.	The beach is pleasing to me.	*I like the beach.*
No le gustan sus cursos.	His courses are not pleasing to him.	*He doesn't like his courses.*
Nos gusta leer.	Reading is pleasing to us.	*We like to read.*

You have been using the verb **gustar** since the beginning of *Puntos de partida* to express likes and dislikes. However, **gustar** does not literally mean *to like*, but rather *to be pleasing*.

Me gusta viajar.
Traveling is pleasing to me. (I like traveling.)

A. **Gustar** is always used with an indirect object pronoun: Someone or something is pleasing *to* someone else. The verb must agree with the subject of the sentence—that is, the person or thing that is pleasing.

Me **gusta** la comida mexicana.
Mexican food is pleasing to me. (I like Mexican food.)

Me **gustan** los viajes aventureros.
Adventurous trips are pleasing to me. (I like adventurous trips.)

B. A phrase with **a** + a *noun* or *pronoun* is often used for clarification or emphasis. This prepositional phrase usually appears before the indirect object pronoun, but it can also appear after the verb.

Note that an infinitive is viewed as a singular subject in Spanish.

The indirect object pronoun *must* be used with **gustar** even when the prepositional phrase **a** + *noun* or *pronoun* is used.

CLARIFICATION

¿Le gusta **a Ud.** viajar?
Do you like to travel?

A David no le gustan los aviones.
David doesn't like airplanes.

EMPHASIS

A mí me gusta viajar en avión, pero **a mi esposo** le gusta viajar en coche.
I like to travel by plane, but my husband likes to travel by car.

Would Like/Wouldn't Like

What one *would* or *would not* like to do is expressed with the form **gustaría*** + *infinitive* and the appropriate indirect objects.

A mí me gustaría viajar a Colombia.
I would like to travel to Colombia.

Nos gustaría hacer *camping* este verano.
We would like to go camping this summer.

Práctica

▲▲▲▲▲

A. Gustos y preferencias

Paso 1. Using the models as a guide, tell whether or not you like the following.

MODELOS. ¿el café? → (No) Me gusta el café.
¿los pasteles? → (No) Me gustan los pasteles.

1. ¿el vino?
2. ¿los niños pequeños?
3. ¿la música clásica?
4. ¿Ricky Martin?
5. ¿el invierno?
6. ¿hacer cola?
7. ¿el chocolate?
8. ¿las películas de terror?
9. ¿las clases que empiezan a las ocho de la mañana?
10. ¿cocinar?
11. ¿la gramática?
12. ¿las clases de este semestre/trimestre?
13. ¿los vuelos con muchas escalas?
14. ¿bailar en las discotecas?

Paso 2. Now share your reactions with a classmate. He or she will respond with one of the following reactions. How do your likes and dislikes compare? Keep track of them.

REACCIONES

A mí también.   *So do I.*
A mí tampoco.   *I don't either. (Neither do I.)*
Pues a mí, sí.   *Well, I do.*
Pues a mí, no.   *Well, I don't.*

---

*This is one of the forms of the conditional of **gustar**. You will study all of the forms of the conditional in Grammar Section 50.

B. ¿Adónde vamos este verano?

Paso 1. The members of the Soto family all prefer different vacation activities and, of course, would like to go to different places this summer. Imagine that you are one of the Sotos and describe the family's various preferences, following the model.

> MODELO: padre/nadar: ir a la playa →
> A mi padre le gusta nadar. Le gustaría ir a la playa.

1. padre/el océano: ir a la playa
2. hermanos pequeños/nadar también: ir a la playa
3. hermano Ernesto/hacer *camping*: ir a las montañas
4. abuelos/descansar: quedarse en casa
5. madre/la tranquilidad: visitar un pueblecito (*small town*) en la costa
6. hermana Elena/discotecas: pasar las vacaciones en una ciudad grande
7. mí/¿ ?

Paso 2. Now, remembering what you have learned about the vacation preferences of your imaginary family, answer the following questions.

1. ¿A quién le gustaría ir a Nueva York?
2. ¿A quién le gustaría viajar a Acapulco?
3. ¿Quién no quiere salir de casa?
4. ¿A quién le gustaría ir a Cabo San Lucas?
5. ¿Quién quiere ir a Colorado?

Conversación

▲▲▲▲▲▲▲▲

A. ¿Conoce bien as sus compañeros de clase?

Paso 1. Piense en una persona de la clase de español que Ud. conoce un poco. En su opinión, ¿a esa persona le gustan o no las siguientes cosas?

	SÍ, LE GUSTA(N)	NO, NO LE GUSTA(N)
1. la música clásica	☐	☒
2. el color negro	☒	☐
3. las canciones de los años 70	☒	☐
4. viajar en coche	☒	☐
5. la comida mexicana	☒	☐
6. tener clases por la mañana	☐	☒
7. estudiar otras lenguas	☒	☐
8. el arte surrealista	☐	☒
9. las películas trágicas	☒	☐
10. las casas viejas	☐	☒

Paso 2. Ahora entreviste a su compañero/a para verificar sus respuestas. ¿Cuántas respuestas correctas tiene Ud.? ¿Conoce bien a su compañero/a?

> MODELO: ¿Te gusta la música clásica?

B. En casa, con los señores Castillo. ¿Qué les gusta hacer a los señores Castillo? Conteste según el dibujo. ¿Puede Ud. inventar otros detalles sobre su vida? Por ejemplo, ¿cuántos años tienen? ¿Tienen niños? ¿Dónde viven? ¿Qué cosas *no* les gusta hacer?

Nota comunicativa

More About Expressing Likes and Dislikes

Here are some ways to express intense likes and dislikes.

Me gusta mucho/muchísimo.	*I like it a lot/a whole lot.*
No me gusta (para) nada.	*I don't like it at all.*

To express *love* and *hate* in reference to likes and dislikes, you can use **encantar** and **odiar**.

- **Encantar** is used just like **gustar**.

Me encanta el chocolate.	*I love chocolate.*
Les encanta viajar, ¿verdad?	*You love traveling, right?*

- **Odiar**, on the other hand, functions like a transitive verb (one that can take a direct object).

Odio el apio.	*I hate celery.*
Mi madre **odia** viajar sola.	*My mother hates traveling alone.*

To express interest in something, use **interesar**. This verb is also used like **gustar** and **encantar**.

Me interesa la comida salvadoreña.	*I'm interested in Salvadorian food.*

C. ¿Qué te gusta? ¿Qué odias? Almost every situation has aspects that one likes or dislikes, even hates. Pick at least two of the following situations and tell what you like or don't like about them. Add as many details as you can, using **me gustaría** when possible.

MODELO. en la playa →
Me gusta mucho el agua, pero no me gusta el sol. Por eso no me gusta pasar todo el día en la playa. Me encanta nadar pero odio la arena. Por eso me gustaría más ir a nadar en una piscina.

Situaciones: en un avión, en el coche, en un autobús, en un tren, en una discoteca, en una fiesta, en la biblioteca, en clase, en casa con mis padres/hijos, en casa con mis amigos, en una cafetería, en un almacén grande, en un parque, en la playa

23 ▶ Talking About the Past (1) • Preterite of Regular Verbs and of *dar*, *hacer*, *ir*, and *ser*

Elisa habla de su viaje a Puerto Rico

«Recientemente *fui* a Puerto Rico para escribir un artículo sobre ese país. *Hice* el viaje en avión. El vuelo *fue* largo, pues el avión *hizo* escala en Miami. *Pasé* una semana entera en la isla. *Hablé* con muchas personas de la industria turística y *visité* los lugares más interesantes de Puerto Rico. También *comí* mucha comida típica de la isla. Además, *tomé* el sol en las preciosas playas puertorriqueñas y *nadé* en el mar Caribe. Me *divertí* mucho. ¡Mi viaje *fue* casi como unas vacaciones!»

Comprensión: ¿Cierto o falso?

1. Elisa fue a Puerto Rico para pasar sus vacaciones.
2. El avión hizo escala en los Estados Unidos.
3. Elisa no visitó ningún lugar importante de Puerto Rico.
4. Elisa también pasó tiempo cerca del océano.

In previous chapters of *Puntos de partida*, you have talked about a number of your activities, but always in the present tense. In this section, you will begin to work with the forms of the preterite, one of the tenses that will allow you to talk about the past. To talk about all aspects of the past in Spanish, you need to know how to use two *simple tenses* (tenses formed without an auxiliary or "helping" verb): the preterite and the imperfect. In this chapter,

---

Elisa talks about her trip to Puerto Rico. Recently I went to Puerto Rico to write an article about that country. I made the trip by plane. The flight was long because the plane made a stop in Miami. I spent a whole week on the island. I spoke with many people in the tourist industry and I visited the most interesting places in Puerto Rico. I also ate lots of typical food from the island. Furthermore, I sunbathed on the beautiful Puerto Rican beaches and swam in the Caribbean Sea. I had lots of fun. My trip was almost like a vacation!

you will learn the regular forms of the preterite and those of four irregular verbs: **dar, hacer, ir,** and **ser.** In this chapter and in **Capítulos 8, 9, 10,** and **11,** you will learn more about preterite forms and their uses as well as about the imperfect and the ways in which it is used alone and with the preterite.

The *preterite* (**el pretérito**) has several equivalents in English. For example, **hablé** can mean *I spoke* or *I did speak.* The preterite is used to report finished, completed actions or states of being in the past. If the action or state of being is viewed as completed—no matter how long it lasted or took to complete—it will be expressed with the preterite.

Preterite of Regular Verbs

hablar		comer		vivir	
hablé	*I spoke (did speak)*	comí	*I ate (did eat)*	viví	*I lived (did live)*
hablaste	*you spoke*	comiste	*you ate*	viviste	*you lived*
habló	*you/he/she spoke*	comió	*you/he/she ate*	vivió	*you/he/she lived*
hablamos	*we spoke*	comimos	*we ate*	vivimos	*we lived*
hablasteis	*you spoke*	comisteis	*you ate*	vivisteis	*you lived*
hablaron	*you/they spoke*	comieron	*you/they ate*	vivieron	*you/they lived*

- Note that the **nosotros** forms of regular preterites are the same as the present tense forms for **-ar** and **-ir** verbs. Context usually helps determine meaning.

  Hoy **hablamos** con la profesora Benítez.
  Today we're speaking with Professor Benítez.

  Ayer **hablamos** con el director de la facultad.
  Yesterday we spoke with the head of the department.

- Note the accent marks on the first and third person singular of the preterite tense. These accent marks are dropped in the conjugation of **ver: vi, vio.**

  ver: vi, viste, **vio,** vimos, visteis, vieron

- Verbs that end in **-car, -gar,** and **-zar** show a spelling change in the first person singular **(yo)** of the preterite. (This is the same change you have already learned to make in present subjunctive forms.)

  -car → qu   buscar: bus**qu**é, buscaste, ...
  -gar → gu   pagar: pa**gu**é, pagaste, ...
  -zar → c   empezar: empe**c**é, empezaste, ...

- **-Ar** and **-er** stem-changing verbs show no stem change in the preterite.
  -Ir stem-changing verbs do show a change.*

  despertar (ie): **desperté, despertaste,** ...
  volver (ue): **volví, volviste,** ...

- An unstressed **-i-** between two vowels becomes **-y-.**

  creer: cre**y**ó, cre**y**eron   leer: le**y**ó, le**y**eron

*You will practice the preterite of most stem-changing verbs in **Capítulo 8.**

dar		hacer		ir/ser	
di	dimos	hice	hicimos	fui	fuimos
diste	disteis	hiciste	hicisteis	fuiste	fuisteis
dio	dieron	hizo	hicieron	fue	fueron

- The preterite endings for **dar** are the same as those used for regular **-er/-ir** verbs in the preterite, except that the accent marks are dropped.

- **Hizo** is spelled with a **z** to keep the [s] sound of the infinitive.

  hic- + **-o** → **hizo**

- **Ir** and **ser** have identical forms in the preterite. Context will make the meaning clear.

  Fui a la playa el verano pasado.
  I went to the beach last summer.

  Fui agente de viajes.
  I was a travel agent.

Práctica

A. ¿Qué hizo Ud. el verano pasado? Indique las oraciones que son ciertas para Ud., contestando con **sí** o **no.**

El verano pasado...

1. tomé una clase en la universidad
2. asistí a un concierto
3. trabajé mucho
4. hice *camping* con algunos amigos / mi familia
5. viví con mis padres / mis hijos
6. me quedé en este pueblo / esta ciudad
7. fui a una playa
8. hice una excursión a otro país
9. fui a muchas fiestas
10. no hice nada especial

B. El día de tres compañeras

Paso 1. Teresa, Evangelina y Liliana comparten (*share*) un apartamento en un edificio viejo. Ayer Teresa y Evangelina fueron a la universidad mientras Liliana se quedó en casa. Describa lo que (*what*) hicieron, según la perspectiva de cada una.

1. (nosotras) salir / de / apartamento / a / nueve
2. llegar / biblioteca / a / diez
3. estudiar / toda la mañana / para / examen
4. escribir / muchos ejercicios
5. almorzar / con / amigos / en / cafetería
6. ir / a / laboratorio / a / una
7. hacer / todos los experimentos / de / manual (*m.*)
8. tomar / examen / a / cuatro
9. ¡examen / ser / horrible!
10. regresar / a casa / después de / examen
11. ayudar / Liliana / a / preparar / cena
12. cenar / todas juntas / a / siete

LILIANA

1. (yo) quedarse / en casa / todo el día
2. ver / televisión / por / mañana
3. llamar / mi / padres / a / once
4. tomar / café / con / vecinos (*neighbors*)
5. estudiar / para / examen / de / historia / y / escribir / composición / para / clase / sociología
6. ir / a / garaje / para / dejar / muebles / viejo / allí
7. ir / a / supermercado / y / comprar / comida
8. empezar / a / preparar / cena / a / cinco

Paso 2.   ¿Quién lo dijo (*said*), Evangelina o Liliana?

1. Mis compañeras no pasaron mucho tiempo en casa hoy.
2. ¡El examen fue desastroso!
3. Estudié mucho hoy.
4. Me gustó mucho el programa de «Oprah» hoy.
5. ¿Saben? Hablé con mis padres hoy y...

Paso 3.   Ahora vuelva a contar (*tell*) cómo fue el día de Liliana, pero desde el punto de vista de sus compañeras de cuarto. Luego diga cómo fue el día de Teresa y Evangelina según Liliana.

C. Un semestre en México. Cuente la siguiente historia desde el punto de vista de la persona indicada, usando el pretérito de los verbos.

1. (yo) pasar un semestre an México
2. mis padres: pagarme el vuelo...
3. ...pero (yo) trabajar para ganar el dinero para la matrícula y los otros gastos (*expenses*)
4. vivir con una familia mexicana encantadora (*enchanting*)
5. aprender mucho sobre la vida y la cultura mexicanas
6. visitar muchos sitios de interés turístico e histórico
7. mis amigos: escribirme muchas cartas
8. (yo) mandarles muchas tarjetas postales
9. comprarles recuerdos (*souvenirs*) a todos
10. volver a los Estados Unidos al final de agosto

Nota comunicativa

Putting Events in Sequence

When telling about what you did, you often want to emphasize the sequence in which events took place. Use the following phrases to put events into a simple sequence in Spanish. You will learn additional words and phrases of this kind as you learn more about the past tenses.

Primero...	First . . .
Luego... y...	Then . . . and . . .
Después... y...	Afterward . . . and . . .
Finalmente (Por fin)...	Finally . . .

A. El sábado por la tarde... The following drawings depict what Julián did last Saturday night. Match the phrases with the individual drawings in the sequence. Then narrate what Julián did, using verbs in the preterite. Use as many of the words and phrases from the preceding **Nota comunicativa** as possible.

a. ___8___ hacer cola para comprar las entradas (*tickets*)
b. ___12___ regresar tarde a casa
c. ___1___ volver a casa después de trabajar

d. __11__ ir a un café a tomar algo
e. __7__ llegar al cine al mismo tiempo
f. __2__ llamar a un amigo
g. __10__ no gustarles la película
h. __5__ comer rápidamente
i. __4__ ducharse y afeitarse
j. __9__ entrar en el cine
k. __6__ ir al cine en autobús
l. __3__ decidir encontrarse (*to meet up*) en el cine

B. Preguntas

1. ¿Qué le(s) dio Ud. a su mejor amigo/a (su esposo/a, su novio/a, sus hijos) para su cumpleaños el año pasado? ¿Qué le regaló a Ud. esa persona para su cumpleaños? ¿Alguien le mandó a Ud. flores el año pasado? ¿Le mandó Ud. flores a alguien? ¿Le gusta a Ud. que le traigan chocolates? ¿otras cosas?

2. ¿Dónde y a qué hora comió Ud. ayer? ¿Con quién(es) comió? ¿Le gustaron todos los platos que comió? Si comió fuera, ¿quién pagó?

3. ¿Cuándo decidió Ud. estudiar español? ¿Cuándo lo empezó a estudiar? ¿Va a seguir con el español el semestre/trimestre que viene?

4. ¿Qué hizo Ud. ayer? ¿Adónde fue? ¿Con quién(es)? ¿Ayudó a alguien a hacer algo? ¿Lo/La llamó alguien? ¿Llamó Ud. a alguien? ¿Lo/La invitaron a hacer algo especial algunos amigos?

Videoteca

ECUADOR

Minidramas

In this **Minidramas** dialogue, which takes place in Quito, Ecuador, Elisa Velasco books a trip from Martín Gómez, her travel agent. Pay close attention to the details about Elisa's upcoming trip. Where is she going? How will she travel? How long will she be staying?

FUNCTION

purchasing tickets for a trip

Elisa Velasco va a escribir un artículo sobre las Islas Galápagos. Está en una agencia de viajes para arreglar^a un viaje a las islas. Habla con Martín Gómez, su agente de viajes.

SR. GÓMEZ: ¿Cuánto tiempo piensa quedarse en las islas?

ELISA: Me gustaría pasar una semana allí. Quiero viajar en avión desde Quito. ¿Cuánto cuesta un boleto de ida y vuelta?

SR. GÓMEZ: Cuesta 615.000 sucres si Ud. viaja el sábado en la mañana.

ELISA: Está bien.

SR. GÓMEZ: ¿Desea que le haga una reservación de hotel también?

ELISA: Sí, por favor.

SR. GÓMEZ: Entonces, le hago las siguientes reservaciones: el avión sale de Quito a las islas el sábado 13 y seis noches de reservación en el hotel de la isla Santa Cruz.

ELISA: Perfecto. Muchas gracias.

SR. GÓMEZ: No hay por qué. ¿Cómo le gustaría pagar? ¿Lo de siempre?^b

ELISA: Sí, con tarjeta de crédito... ¡la^c del periódico, por supuesto!

^a*arrange* ^b*¿Lo... The usual?* ^c*la tarjeta*

Con un compañero / una compañera

How would you go about getting the following information? Prepare a series of short statements and questions that will help you get all the information you need. Your instructor will play the role of ticket seller, travel agent, or flight attendant.

MODELO: You need to buy two first-class tickets on Tuesday's 10:50 A.M. train for Guanajuato. →
Dos boletos para Guanajuato, por favor. Para el martes, el tren de las once menos diez. De primera clase, por favor.

1. You need to buy two second-class (**segunda clase**) train tickets for today's 2:50 P.M. train for Barcelona.
2. You are at the train station and need to find out how to get to the university—which you understand is quite some distance away—by 10:00 A.M.
3. The flight you are on is arriving late, and you will probably miss your connecting flight to Mexico City. You want to explain your situation to the flight attendant and find out how you can get to Mexico City by 7:00 this evening.
4. You are talking to a travel agent and want to fly from Santiago, Chile, to Quito, Ecuador. You are traveling with two friends who prefer to travel first class, and you need to arrive in Quito by Saturday afternoon.

En contexto

In this video segment, Juan Carlos is talking to a ticket agent about purchasing a train ticket. As you watch the segment, pay particular attention to the words they use to talk about train schedules and about the arrangements that Juan Carlos makes for travel. What is the problem with the train schedule? What finally happens?

Un poco más sobre... Elisa Velazco

Elisa Velasco es una escritora de Quito, Ecuador, que se especializa en artículos sobre los viajes y el turismo. Por esa razón, es una «pasajera frecuente» a lugares sobre los cuales^a escribe. Cuando está en casa, le dedica mucho tiempo a su hijo José Miguel, que es estudiante de primer año en la universidad.

^a*sobre... about which*

To read more about the characters from this video, visit the *Puntos de partida* Website at **www.mhhe.com/puntos**

PERÚ

A. Lluvia de ideas

- Donde Ud. vive, ¿cuál es el medio de transporte más práctico para viajar de una ciudad a otra? En otras áreas del país, ¿se viaja del mismo (*same*) modo? ¿Cómo viajan las personas que no tienen coche?
- ¿Hay una estación de tren en su pueblo o ciudad? ¿Viaja Ud. en tren con frecuencia? ¿Cuándo fue la última vez (*time*)?

B. Dictado

A continuación está la primera parte del diálogo entre Juan Carlos y la agente de billetes. Complétela con las palabras o frases que faltan (*are missing*).

JUAN CARLOS: Buenas tardes. Un billete de ____ ____ ____ para Tarma, por favor. Sale a las ____ ____ ____, ¿verdad?

VENDEDORA DE BILLETES: Lo siento,[a] pero ese tren ____ ____ hoy. No sale hasta las ____ y ____.

JUAN CARLOS: ¿____ ____? ¿Qué pasa?

VENDEDORA DE BILLETES: No estoy segura, pero parece[b] que hay un ____ ____.

JUAN CARLOS: ¡Pero sólo son las dos y cuarto! ¡Faltan todavía ____ ____!

VENDEDORA DE BILLETES: De veras, lo siento. Pero no hay remedio.[c]

[a]Lo... *I'm sorry* [b]*it seems* [c]*no... it can't be helped*

C. Un diálogo original

Paso 1. Con un compañero/una compañera, dramaticen el diálogo entre Juan Carlos y la agente de billetes.

Paso 2. Un viaje a Nueva York o a San Francisco

ESTUDIANTE 1 Ud. habla con un(a) agente de viajes porque desea ir a Nueva York o a San Francisco. Tiene diez días de vacaciones. No quiere pagar demasiado dinero.

ESTUDIANTE 2 Ud. es el/la agente de viajes. Debe ofrecer más de una opción.

A. Preguntas: La última vez. Conteste las siguientes preguntas. Añada (*Add*) más información si puede.

MODELO: La última vez que Ud. fue a una fiesta, ¿le llevó un regalo al anfitrión (*host*)? →
Sí, le llevé flores / una botella de vino. (No, no le llevé nada.)

La última vez que Ud...

1. hizo un viaje, ¿le mandó una tarjeta postal a un amigo / a una amiga?
2. tomó el autobús / el metro, ¿le ofreció su asiento a una persona mayor?
3. vio a su profesor(a) de español en público, ¿le habló en español?
4. comió en un restaurante, ¿le recomendó un plato a su compañero/a?
5. entró en un edificio, ¿le abrió la puerta a otra persona?

B. Recomendaciones para las vacaciones. Complete the following vacation suggestion with the correct form of the words in parentheses, as suggested by the context. When two possibilities are given in parentheses, select the correct word.

(Les/Los[1]) quiero decir (algo/nada[2]) sobre (el/la[3]) ciudad de Machu Picchu. ¿Ya (lo/la[4]) (saber/conocer[5]) Uds.? (Ser/Estar[6]) situada en los Andes, a unos ochenta kilómetros[a] de la ciudad de Cuzco, Perú. Machu Picchu es conocida[b] como (el/la[7]) ciudad escondida[c] de los incas. Se dice que (ser/estar[8]) una de las manifestaciones (más/tan[9]) importantes de la arquitectura incaica. Era[d] refugio y a la vez[e] ciudad de vacaciones de los reyes[f] (incaico[10]).

Uds. deben (visitarlo/visitarla[11]). (Le/Les[12]) gustaría porque (ser/estar[13]) un sitio inolvidable.[g] Es mejor (ir/van[14]) a Machu Picchu en primavera o verano —son las (mejor[15]) estaciones para visitar este lugar. Pero es necesario (comprar/compran[16]) los boletos con anticipación,[h] porque (mucho[17]) turistas de todos los (país[18]) del mundo visitan este sitio extraordinario. ¡(*Yo:* Saber/Conocer[19]) que a Uds. (los/les[20]) va a gustar el viaje!

[a]ochenta... 50 millas [b]*known* [c]*hidden* [d]*It was* [e]a... *at the same time* [f]*kings* [g]*unforgettable* [h]con... *ahead of time*

Comprensión: ¿Cierto o falso? Conteste según la descripción.

1. Machu Picchu está en Chile.
2. Fue un lugar importante en el pasado.
3. Todavía es una atracción turística de gran interés.
4. Sólo los turistas latinoamericanos conocen Machu Picchu.

PANORAMA *cultural*

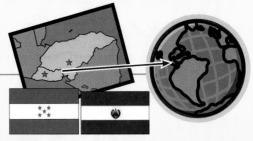

Honduras   El Salvador

Honduras y El Salvador

Datos esenciales

Honduras
- Nombre oficial: República de Honduras
- Capital: Tegucigalpa
- Población: 6.000.000 de habitantes
- Moneda: el lempira
- Idioma oficial: el español

El Salvador
- Nombre oficial: República de El Salvador
- Capital: San Salvador
- Población: 6.000.000 de habitantes
- Moneda: el colón
- Idioma oficial: el español

¡Fíjese!

- El centro ceremonial maya de Copán, en Honduras, es hoy un parque nacional que contiene una colección de ruinas mayas superadas[a] sólo por las ruinas de Tikal en Guatemala.

- La moneda de Honduras, el lempira, lleva el nombre de un cacique[b] indígena que luchó contra[c] los españoles.

- El nombre indígena de la capital de Honduras, Tegucigalpa, significa «cerros de plata».[d] Honduras recibió su nombre español por la profundidad[e] de sus aguas costeras.[f] El nombre indígena de El Salvador era[g] Cuzcatlán, que significa «tierra de joyas[h] y cosas preciosas».

- Las erupciones del Volcán de Izalco en El Salvador fueron constantes entre los años 1770 y 1966, por casi dos siglos.[i] Este volcán se conoce con el nombre de «el faro[j] del Pacífico», porque estuvo encendido[k] por muchos años y sirvió de[l] guía a los navegantes.

[a]*exceeded (in quality)*   [b]*chief*   [c]*luchó... fought against*   [d]*cerros... silver hills*   [e]*depth*   [f]*coastal*   [g]*was*   [h]*jewels*   [i]*centuries*   [j]*lighthouse*   [k]*estuvo... it was lit up*   [l]*sirvió de... served as a*

El Volcán de Izalco, El Salvador

Conozca... al Arzobispo[a] Óscar Arnulfo Romero

El 24 de marzo de 1980 un héroe de El Salvador fue asesinado mientras oficiaba una misa.[b] En vida,[c] el arzobispo Óscar Arnulfo Romero (1917–1980) fue la conciencia de su país. Criticó a los líderes por su violencia e injusticia, y trabajó para mejorar[d] las condiciones económicas y sociales del país. Por eso, fue nominado para el premio Nóbel de la Paz[e] en el 1979 la gran labor del arzobispo.

[a]*Archbishop*   [b]*oficiaba... he was celebrating a Mass*   [c]*life* [d]*improve*   [e]*premio... Nobel Peace Prize*

Capítulo 7 of the video to accompany *Puntos de partida* contains cultural footage about Honduras and El Salvador.

Visit the *Puntos de partida* Website at www.mhhe.com/puntos.

Vocabulario

Los verbos

anunciar	to announce
bajar (de)	to get down (from); to get off (of)
contar (ue)	to tell
dar (*irreg.*)	to give
decir (*irreg.*)	to say; to tell
encantar	to like very much, love
explicar	to explain
facturar	to check (*baggage*)
fumar	to smoke
guardar	to save (*a place*)
gustar	to be pleasing
mandar	to send
mostrar (ue)	to show
nadar	to swim
odiar	to hate
ofrecer	to offer
prestar	to lend
prometer	to promise
recomendar (ie)	to recommend
regalar	to give (*as a gift*)
sacar	to take (*photos*)
subir (a)	to go up; to get on (*a vehicle*)
viajar	to travel

¡Buen viaje!

el aeropuerto	airport
la agencia de viajes	travel agency
el/la agente de viajes	travel agent
el asiento	seat
el/la asistente de vuelo	flight attendant
el autobús	bus
el avión	airplane
el barco	boat, ship
el billete/boleto	ticket
de ida	one-way
de ida y vuelta	round-trip
la cabina	cabin (*in a ship*)
la camioneta	station wagon
el *camping*	campground

la clase turística	tourist class
la demora	delay
el equipaje	baggage, luggage
la estación	station
de autobuses	bus
del tren	train
la foto(grafía)	photo(graph)
la llegada	arrival
el maletero	porter
el mar	sea
la montaña	mountain
el océano	ocean
el pasaje	passage, ticket
el/la pasajero/a	passenger
la primera clase	first class
el puerto	port
el puesto	place (*in line, etc.*)
la sala de espera	waiting room
la salida	departure
la sección de (no) fumar	(non)smoking section
la tarjeta (postal)	(post)card
la tienda (de campaña)	tent
el tren	train
el vuelo	flight
estar (*irreg.*) de vacaciones	to be on vacation
hacer (*irreg.*) *camping*	to go camping
hacer (*irreg.*) cola	to stand in line
hacer (*irreg.*) escalas/paradas	to make stops
hacer (*irreg.*) la(s) maleta(s)	to pack one's suitcase(s)
ir (*irreg.*) de vacaciones	to go on vacation
tomar el sol	to sunbathe

Repaso: hacer (*irreg.*) un viaje, la playa

Otros sustantivos

la flor	flower
el mundo	world
el/la niño/a	child; boy (girl)

Los adjetivos

atrasado/a (*with* **estar**) late
solo/a alone
último/a last

Palabras adicionales

a tiempo on time
de viaje on a trip
lo que what, that which
me gustaría... I would (really) like...

Un paso más 7

LECTURA

Estrategia: Identifying the Source of a Passage

If you pick up the *New England Journal of Medicine*, what sort of articles do you expect to find? For whom are they written and for what purpose? Would you anticipate similar articles in *Popular Science* magazine?

You can often make useful predictions about an article—its narrative style, its target audience, the author's purpose, and so forth—if you know something about the magazine or journal from which it comes. The article you are about to read was adapted from *GeoMundo*, a Spanish-language magazine not unlike *National Geographic*. Knowing this, which of the following topics do you think might be treated in a given issue of this magazine?

1. the Incas and Machu Picchu
2. how to remove coffee stains from silk
3. the search for a great white shark
4. Montreal by night

All but number two might appear in *GeoMundo*. Keeping in mind the source of a reading will often help you to predict its content.

► **Sobre la lectura...** *GeoMundo* is for the reader who is interested in world
► travel, different cultures and customs, the environment, and similar issues.
► The following article was adapted from a travel section called «**Geo-**
► **turismo**». This particular section deals with Mexico.

México es mucho más que playas

Además de[a] los populares centros de vacaciones en las costas como Acapulco y Cancún, México tiene otros lugares donde se puede <u>descubrir</u> algo de la historia y la cultura del país. Uno de ellos es la península de Yucatán, donde floreció[b] la gran civilización maya. Allí se puede visitar Palenque, con su <u>imponente pirámide</u> en una exuberante <u>selva</u> tropical. También se puede visitar Uxmal, una clásica ciudad maya, y Chichén Itzá, centro cultural de la región entre los siglos X al XIII. Todos están cerca de excelentes hoteles y restaurantes.

Otra alternativa son las ciudades coloniales de México, cuya[c] elegante arquitectura del siglo XVI <u>refleja</u> su génesis española. Explore estas ciudades:

- San Miguel de Allende, una bulliciosa[d] ciudad donde se han refugiado[e] artistas de todo el mundo

- Guanajuato, sede[f] del prestigioso Festival <u>Cervantino</u> de teatro, con sus serpenteantes calles adoquinadas[g]

- Zacatecas, con sus edificios <u>construidos</u> de <u>granito</u> rosa

[a]Además... *In addition to* [b]*flourished* [c]*whose* [d]*lively* [e]*se... have taken refuge* [f]*site* [g]serpenteantes... *winding cobblestoned streets*

- Guadalajara, ciudad donde nació[h] el mariachi

En ninguna de ellas hay dificultad en encontrar[i] un buen lugar para quedarse, pues hay hoteles y pensiones para todos los gustos y bolsillos.[j] ●

[h]*was born* [i]*finding* [j]*wallets* (fig., lit. *pockets*)

Guanajuato, México

Comprensión

A. El título. Lea otra vez el título del artículo. ¿Por qué se llama así esta lectura? Es decir, ¿qué significa?

1. México tiene más playas que otros países de Latinoamérica.
2. Cuando se habla de las vacaciones en México, muchas personas piensan solamente en las playas mexicanas.
3. Nadie va a las playas mexicanas para pasar sus vacaciones.

B. ¿Adónde les gustaría ir? A base del (*Based on the*) artículo, identifique un lugar de interés para los siguientes turistas.

1. el profesor Underwood, arqueólogo dedicado al estudio de las culturas indígenas
2. Ana Carbón, guitarrista que tiene interés en la música mexicana
3. Pedro Pérez, pintor y escultor

ESCRITURA

De vacaciones en México. Prepare un reportaje sobre una de las ciudades mencionadas en el artículo. Puede ir a la biblioteca para hacer su investigación. Antes de escribir, haga lo siguiente.

Paso 1. Escoja la ciudad que va a ser el enfoque (*focus*) de su investigación.

Paso 2. Piense en el tipo de información que quiere incluir. Haga una lista de por lo menos (*at least*) tres de los temas que va a investigar (como, por ejemplo, festividades regionales, geografía, platos típicos del lugar, etcétera).

Paso 3. Vaya a la biblioteca o consulte libros de referencia o revistas para hacer su reportaje.

Paso 4. Escriba una breve composición sobre ese lugar.

Los días festivos

Los tres reyes magos (*Magii*), Melchor, Gaspar y Baltasar, entretienen a esta niña mexicana.

¿Qué opina Ud.?

Conteste según su propia vida. ¿Cree Ud. que una persona de otro país diría algo similar? Visite el sitio Web de *Puntos de partida* para leer las respuestas a estas preguntas que da una persona de Cuba.

1. ¿Pasa Ud. **los días festivos** con su familia, con sus amigos o solo/a?
2. ¿Cuál es su día festivo favorito? ¿Cuál es el día festivo que menos le gusta?
3. ¿Hace Ud. algo especial el día de su **cumpleaños**? ¿Qué hace?
4. **¿Se celebra** en su casa algún día festivo de otro país? ¿Cuál es? ¿Cómo se celebra?
5. ¿Conoce Ud. algún festival de otra cultura? ¿Qué le gusta de ese día? ¿En qué se parece (*How is it similar*) a los festivales que Ud. celebra?

En este capítulo...

- In this chapter, you will study vocabulary related to celebrations and feelings. You already know the words **quince** and **años**. What do you think a **fiesta** called **una quinceañera** might celebrate?
- In the previous chapter, you began to use the preterite to talk about events in the past. In this chapter, you will learn more about the preterite. (Grammar 24 and 25)
- Up to now, you have been using the direct and the indirect object pronouns separately. But what happens when you want to say something like *You give it to him,* which uses both kinds of object pronouns? In this chapter, you will learn how to do that. (Grammar 26)
- The **Panorama cultural** section of this chapter will focus on Cuba.

P U N T O S   I N T E R A C T I V O

Videoteca

◀ **Minidramas**
La familia Durán-Benítez celebra la primera comunión de su hija Marta. ¿Qué hace su familia para celebrar los días festivos? ¿Dónde los celebra?

En contexto ▶
Roberto va a una tienda de música a devolver (*return*) un disco compacto. ¿Compra Ud. muchos discos compactos? ¿Regala Ud. discos con frecuencia?

CD-ROM

Además de completar el vocabulario y las actividades de gramática, Ud. va a tener la oportunidad de «hablarle» a un empleado de una tienda de música sobre un disco compacto que Ud. quiere cambiar (*exchange*) por otro.

Internet

En la sección del Capítulo 8 en el sitio Web de *Puntos de partida* aparecen enlaces que Ud. puede usar para conseguir información en español sobre las fiestas y las celebraciones. Use la dirección **www.mhhe.com/puntos** para llegar al sitio Web.

Los días festivos y las fiestas

Feliz Navidad

Porque eres una persona bondadosa y llena de amor, espero que esta Navidad sea para ti la mejor.

Un Próspero Año Nuevo

los entremeses	hors d'œuvres	**gastar dinero**	to spend money
los refrescos	refreshments	**pasarlo bien/mal**	to have a good/bad time
la sorpresa	surprise		
		regalar	to give (*as a gift*)
¡felicitaciones!	congratulations!	**reunirse (me reúno) (con)**	to get together (with)
celebrar	to celebrate	**ser** (*irreg.*) + **en** + *place*	to take place at (*place*)
cumplir años	to have a birthday		
dar (*irreg.*)/**hacer** (*irreg.*) **una fiesta**	to give/have a party	—¿**Dónde es** la fiesta?	*Where is the party?*
divertirse (ie, i)	to have a good time	—(**Es**) **En** casa de Julio.	(*It's*) *At Julio's house.*
faltar	to be absent, lacking		

Vocabulario útil*

el Día de Año Nuevo	New Year's Day
el Día de los Reyes Magos	Day of the Magi (Three Kings)
el Día de San Valentín (de los Enamorados)	Valentine's Day
el Día de San Patricio	Saint Patrick's Day
la Pascua (de los hebreos)	Passover
la Pascua (Florida)	Easter
las vacaciones de primavera	spring break
el Cinco de Mayo	Cinco de Mayo (*Mexican awareness celebration in some parts of the U.S.*)
el Día del Canadá	Canada Day (July 1)
el Cuatro de Julio (el Día de la Independencia (estadounidense)	Independence Day (*U.S.*)
el Día de la Raza	Columbus Day (*Hispanic awareness day in some parts of the U.S.*)
el Día de todos los Santos	All Saints' Day (November 1)
el Día de los Muertos	Day of the Dead (November 2)
el Día de Acción de Gracias	Thanksgiving
la Fiesta de las Luces	Hanukkah
la Nochebuena	Christmas Eve
la Navidad	Christmas
la Noche Vieja	New Year's Eve
el cumpleaños	birthday
el día del santo	saint's day (*the saint for whom one is named*)
la quinceañera	young woman's fifteenth birthday party

Conversación

▲▲▲▲▲▲▲▲

A. **Definiciones.** ¿Qué palabra o frase corresponde a estas definiciones?

1. el día en que se celebra el nacimiento (*birth*) de Jesús
2. algo que alguien no sabe o no espera
3. algo de comer y algo de beber que se sirve en las fiestas (dos respuestas)
4. el día en que algunos hispanos visitan el cementerio para honrar la memoria de los difuntos (*deceased*)
5. la fiesta en que se celebra el hecho (*fact*) de que una muchacha cumple quince años
6. el día en que todo el mundo (*everybody*) debe llevar ropa verde
7. la noche en que se celebra el final del año
8. palabra que se dice para mostrar una reacción muy favorable, por ejemplo, cuando un amigo cumple años

---

*All of the items on this list are not considered active vocabulary for this chapter. Just learn the holidays and celebrations that are relevent to you.

Nota cultural

Celebraciones

En la vida de uno hay muchas ocasiones para dar fiestas. Claro que todos los años hay que celebrar **el cumpleaños**. Pero en partes del mundo hispánico se celebra también **el día del santo**. En el calendario religioso católico cada día corresponde al nombre de un santo. Si Ud. se llama Juan, por ejemplo, su santo es San Juan Bautista y el día de su santo es el 24 de junio. Este día se celebra igual que el día de su cumpleaños.

Para las señoritas, la fiesta de los quince años, **la quinceañera**, es una de las más importantes, porque desde esa edad a la muchacha se le considera ya (*already*) mujer. Para los muchachos, la fiesta de los dieciocho o veintiún años representa la llegada a la mayoría de edad (*coming of age*).

Una quinceañera mexicana

B. Hablando de fiestas

Paso 1. ¿Cuál es su opinión de las siguientes fiestas, positiva, negativa o neutra?

1. el Cuatro de Julio
2. el Día de Acción de Gracias
3. el Día de San Patricio
4. la Noche Vieja
5. el Día de la Raza
6. el Día de los Enamorados

Paso 2. Ahora compare sus respuestas con las (*those*) de sus compañeros de clase. ¿Coinciden todos en su opinión de algunas fiestas?

Paso 3. Ahora piense en su fiesta favorita. Puede ser una de la lista del **Paso 1** o una del **Vocabulario útil** de la página 255. Piense en cómo celebra Ud. esa fiesta, para explicárselo (*explain it*) luego a un compañero / una compañera de clase. Debe pensar en lo siguiente:

* los preparativos que Ud. hace de antemano (*beforehand*)
* la ropa especial que lleva
* las comidas o bebidas especiales que compra o prepara
* el lugar donde se celebra
* los adornos especiales que hay

Vocabulario útil

el árbol	tree	**la fiesta del barrio**	neighborhood (block) party
el corazón	heart		
la corona	wreath	**los fuegos artificiales**	fireworks
el desfile	parade	**el globo**	balloon

David está contento.
Se ríe.

David **llora** porque **se siente triste.**

David **se pone feliz** otra vez y **sonríe.**

discutir (sobre) (con)	to argue (about) (with)	**portarse bien/mal**	to behave well/poorly
enfermar(se)	to get sick	**quejarse (de)**	to complain (about)
enojar(se) (con)	to get mad (at)	**recordar (ue)**	to remember
llorar	to cry	**reír(se) (i, i) (de)**	to laugh (about)
olvidar(se) de	to forget about	**sentir(se) (ie, i)**	to feel
ponerse + *adj.*	to become, get + *adjective*	**sonreír(se) (i, i)**	to smile

Nota comunicativa

Being Emphatic

To emphasize the quality described by an adjective or an adverb, speakers of Spanish often add **-ísimo/a/os/as** to it, adding the idea *extremely (exceptionally; very, very; super)* to the quality. You have already used one emphatic form of this type: **Me gusta muchísimo.**

Estos entremeses son **dificilísimos** de preparar.

These hors d'œuvres are very hard to prepare.

Durante la época navideña, los niños son **buenísimos.**

At Christmastime, the kids are extremely good.

- If the adjective ends in a consonant, **-ísimo** is added to the singular form: **difícil** → **dificilísimo** (and any accents on the word stem are dropped).
- If the adjective ends in a vowel, the final vowel is dropped before adding **-ísimo: bueno** → **buenísimo**.
- Spelling changes occur when the final consonant of an adjective is **c, g,** or **z: riquísimo, larguísimo, felicísimo.**

Conversación

▲▲▲▲▲▲▲▲

A. Reacciones. ¿Cómo reacciona o cómo se pone Ud. en estas situaciones? Use estos adjetivos o cualquier otro, y también los verbos que describen las reacciones emocionales. No se olvide de usar las formas enfáticas cuando sea (*whenever it is*) apropiado.

serio/a	feliz/triste	avergonzado/a (*embarrassed*)
nervioso/a	furioso/a	contento/a

1. Es Navidad y alguien le hace a Ud. un regalo carísimo.
2. Es su cumpleaños y sus padres/hijos no le regalaron nada.
3. Ud. da una fiesta en su casa pero los invitados no se divierten. Nadie ríe ni sonríe.
4. Hay un examen importante hoy, pero Ud. no estudió anoche.
5. Ud. acaba de terminar un examen difícil/fácil y cree que lo hizo bien/mal.
6. En un examen de química, Ud. no puede recordar una fórmula muy importante.

B. ¿Son buenos todos los días festivos? Los días festivos pueden ser difíciles para muchas personas. Para Ud., ¿son ciertas o falsas las siguientes oraciones? Cambie las oraciones falsas para que sean (*so that they are*) ciertas. Luego compare sus respuestas con las de sus compañeros de clase.

EN LAS FIESTAS DE FAMILIA

1. Toda o casi toda mi familia, incluyendo a mis tíos, primos, abuelos, etcétera, se reúne por lo menos (*at least*) una vez al año.
2. Las fiestas de familia me gustan muchísimo.
3. Hay un pariente que siempre se queja de algo.
4. Uno de mis parientes siempre me hace preguntas indiscretas.
5. Alguien siempre bebe/come demasiado y luego se enferma.
6. A todos les gustan los regalos que reciben.
7. Todos lo pasan bien en las fiestas de familia.

LOS DÍAS FESTIVOS EN GENERAL

8. La Navidad / La Fiesta de las Luces es esencialmente una excusa para gastar dinero.
9. La época de fiestas en noviembre y diciembre es triste y deprimente (*depressing*) para mí.
10. Sólo las personas que practican una religión deben tener vacaciones en los días de fiestas religiosas.
11. Las vacaciones de primavera son para divertirse muchísimo. De hecho (*In fact*), son las mejores vacaciones del año.
12. Debería haber (*There should be*) más días festivos… por lo menos uno al mes.

Minidiálogos y gramática

24

Talking About the Past (2) • Irregular Preterites

La fiesta de la Noche Vieja

Conteste las siguientes preguntas sobre esta fiesta.

1. ¿Quién *estuvo* hablando por teléfono?
2. ¿Quién *dio* la fiesta?
3. ¿Quién no *pudo* ir a la fiesta?
4. ¿Quién *puso* su copa de champán en el televisor?
5. ¿Quién *hizo* mucho ruido?
6. ¿Quiénes *tuvieron* que salir temprano?
7. ¿Quiénes no *quisieron* beber más?
8. ¿Quiénes *vinieron* con sus niñas?
9. ¿Quiénes le *trajeron* un regalo al anfitrión (*host*)?

Y Ud., ¿*estuvo* alguna vez en una fiesta como esta? ¿*Tuvo* que salir temprano o se quedó hasta después de la medianoche (*midnight*)? ¿Le *trajo* algo al anfitrión / a la anfitriona?

• You have already learned the irregular preterite forms of **dar, hacer, ir,** and **ser.** The following verbs are also irregular in the preterite. Note that the first and third person singular endings, which are the only irregular ones, are unstressed, in contrast to the stressed endings of regular preterite forms.

estar	
estuve	estuvimos
estuviste	estuvisteis
estuvo	estuvieron

estar:	**estuv-**	**-e**
poder:	**pud-**	-iste
poner:	**pus-**	**-o**
querer:	**quis-**	-imos
saber:	**sup-**	-isteis
tener:	**tuv-**	-ieron
venir:	**vin-**	

- When the preterite verb stem ends in **-j-**, the **-i-** of the third person plural ending is omitted: **dijeron, trajeron**.

decir: **dij-**
traer: **traj-** } -e, -iste, -o, -imos, -isteis, **-eron**

- The preterite of **hay (haber)** is **hubo** (*there was/were*).

Hubo un accidente ayer en el centro.
There was an accident yesterday downtown.

- Several of the following Spanish verbs have an English equivalent in the preterite tense that is different from that of the infinitive.

	Infinitive Meaning	Preterite Meaning
saber	to know (*facts, information*)	to find out
	Ya lo sé. *I already know it.*	Lo **supe** ayer. *I found it out (learned it) yesterday.*
conocer	to know (*be familiar with*) people, places	to meet (*for the first time*)
	Ya la conozco. *I already know her.*	La **conocí** ayer. *I met her yesterday.*
querer	to want	to try
	Quiero hacerlo hoy. *I want to do it today.*	**Quise** hacerlo ayer. *I tried to do it yesterday.*
no querer	not to want	to refuse
	No quiero hacerlo hoy. *I don't want to do it today.*	**No quise** hacerlo anteayer. *I refused to do it the day before yesterday.*
poder	to be able	to succeed (*in doing something*)
	Puedo leerlo *I can (am able to) read it.*	**Pude** leerlo ayer. *I could (and did) read it yesterday.*
no poder	not to be able, capable	to fail (*in doing something*)
	No puedo leerlo. *I can't (am not able to) read it.*	**No pude** leerlo anteayer. *I couldn't (did not) read it the day before yesterday.*

Práctica

A. La última Noche Vieja. Piense en lo que Ud. hizo la Noche Vieja del año pasado e indique si las siguientes oraciones son ciertas o falsas para Ud.

1. Fui a una fiesta en casa de un amigo / una amiga.
2. Di una fiesta en mi casa.
3. No estuve con mis amigos, sino (*but rather*) con la familia.
4. Quise ir a una fiesta, pero no pude.

5. Les dije «¡Feliz Año Nuevo!» a muchas personas.
6. No le dije «¡Feliz Año Nuevo!» a nadie.
7. Conocí a algunas personas nuevas.
8. Todos eran mis amigos.
9. Tuve que preparar la comida de esa noche.
10. Me puse ropa elegante esa noche.
11. Pude quedarme despierto/a (*awake*) hasta la medianoche.
12. No quise bailar. Me sentía mal.

B. Una Nochebuena en casa de los Ramírez

Paso 1. Describa lo que pasó en casa de los Ramírez, haciendo el papel (*playing the role*) de uno de los hijos. Haga oraciones en el pretérito según las indicaciones, usando el sujeto pronominal cuando sea necesario.

1. todos / estar / en casa / abuelos / antes de / nueve
2. (nosotros) poner / mucho / regalos / debajo / árbol
3. tíos y primos / venir / con / comida y bebidas
4. yo / tener / que / ayudar / a / preparar / comida
5. haber / cena / especial / para / todos
6. más tarde / alguno / amigos / venir / a / cantar / villancicos (*carols*)
7. niños / ir / a / alcoba / a / diez y / acostarse
8. niños / querer / dormir / pero / no / poder
9. a / medianoche / todos / decir / «¡Feliz Navidad!»
10. al día siguiente / todos / decir / que / fiesta / estar / estupendo

Paso 2. ¿Cierto, falso o no se sabe? Corrija las oraciones falsas.

1. Hubo muy poca gente (*people*) en la fiesta.
2. Sólo vinieron miembros de la familia.
3. Todos comieron bien… ¡y mucho!
4. Los niños abrieron sus regalos antes de las doce.

C. Hechos históricos.
Describa Ud. algunos hechos históricos, usando una palabra o frase de cada grupo. Use el pretérito de los verbos.

en 1957 los rusos	traer	en Valley Forge con sus soldados
en 1969 los estadounidenses	saber	un hombre en la luna
	conocer	un satélite en el espacio por
Adán y Eva	decir	primera vez
George Washington	estar	«que coman (*let them eat*)
los europeos	poner	pasteles»
los aztecas		el significado (*meaning*) de un
Stanley		árbol especial
María Antonieta		a Livingston en África
		el caballo (*horse*) al Nuevo Mundo
		a Hernán Cortés en Tenochtitlán

Conversación

A. ¡Un viaje de sueños (*dream*)!

Paso 1.   Conteste las siguientes preguntas sobre un viaje de sueños. Debe inventar una historia muy extraordinaria o fantástica. Puede ser de un viaje que a Ud. le gustaría hacer, de un viaje hecho (*taken*) por un amigo o de un viaje totalmente imaginario. ¡Sea creativo/a!

1. ¿Adónde fue de viaje? ¿Con quién(es) fue?
2. ¿Cuánto tiempo estuvo allí? ¿Dónde se alojó (*did you stay*)?
3. ¿A qué persona famosa o interesante conoció allí? ¿Qué le dijo a esa persona cuando la conoció? ¿Supo algo interesante de esa persona?
4. ¿Qué cosa divertida (*enjoyable*) hizo durante el viaje? ¿Qué no pudo hacer?
5. ¿Qué recuerdos (*souvenirs*) trajo a casa?

Paso 2.   Ahora cuénteles su historia a sus compañeros de clase. ¿Quién inventó la mejor historia?

Nota comunicativa

Thanking Someone

You can use the preposition **por** to thank someone for something.

gracias por + *noun*	**gracias por** + *infinitive*
Gracias por el regalo.	**Gracias por** llamarme.
Gracias por la invitación.	**Gracias por** invitarnos.

B. Preguntas

1. ¿En qué mes conoció Ud. al profesor / a la profesora de español? ¿A quién(es) más conoció ese mismo (*same*) día? ¿Tuvo Ud. que hablar español el primer día de clase? ¿Qué les dijo a sus amigos después de esa primera clase? ¿Qué les va a decir hoy?
2. El año pasado, ¿dónde pasó Ud. la Nochebuena? ¿el Día de Acción de Gracias? ¿Dónde estuvo durante las vacaciones de primavera? ¿Dónde piensa Ud. estar este año en estas ocasiones?
3. ¿Alguien le dio a Ud. una fiesta de cumpleaños este año? (¿O le dio Ud. una fiesta a alguien?) ¿Fue una fiesta sorpresa? ¿Dónde fue? ¿Qué le trajeron sus amigos? ¿Qué le regalaron sus parientes? ¿Alguien le hizo un pastel? ¿Qué le dijeron todos? ¿Y qué les dijo Ud.? ¿Quiere Ud. que le den otra fiesta para su próximo cumpleaños?

25

Talking About the Past (3) • Preterite of Stem-Changing Verbs

La quinceañera de Lupe Carrasco

Imagine los detalles de la fiesta de Lupe cuando cumplió quince años.

1. Lupe *se vistió* con
   ☐ un vestido blanco muy elegante.
   ☐ una camiseta y unos *jeans*.
   ☐ el vestido de novia[a] de su abuela.

2. Cortando el pastel de cumpleaños, Lupe
   ☐ *empezó* a llorar.
   ☐ *rió* mucho.
   ☐ *sonrió* para una foto.

3. Lupe *pidió* un deseo[b] al cortar el pastel. Ella
   ☐ les dijo a todos su deseo.
   ☐ *prefirió* guardarlo en secreto.

4. En la fiesta *sirvieron*
   ☐ champán y otras bebidas alcohólicas.
   ☐ refrescos.
   ☐ sólo té y café.

5. Todos *se divirtieron* mucho en la fiesta. Los invitados *se despidieron*[c] a la(s)_____.

[a]vestido... *wedding gown* [b]*wish* [c]se... *said good-bye*

Y Ud., ¿recuerda qué hizo cuando cumplió quince años? ¿Pidió muchos regalos? ¿Se divirtió? ¿Cómo se sintió?

A. As you learned in **Capítulo 7**, the **-ar** and **-er** stem-changing verbs have no stem change in the preterite (or in the present participle).

recordar (ue): recordé, recordaste, recordó, recordamos, recordasteis, recordaron; recordando

perder (ie): perdí, perdiste, perdió, perdimos, perdisteis, perdieron; perdiendo

B. The **-ir** stem-changing verbs do have a stem change in the preterite, but only in the third person singular and plural, where the stem vowels **e** and **o** change to **i** and **u,** respectively. This is the same change that occurs in the present participle of **-ir** stem-changing verbs.

pedir (i, i)		dormir (ue, u)	
pedí	pedimos	dormí	dormimos
pediste	pedisteis	dormiste	dormisteis
pidió	pidieron	durmió	durmieron
	pidiendo		durmiendo

C. Here are some **-ir** stem-changing verbs. You already know or have seen many of them. The reflexive meaning, if different from the non-reflexive meaning, is in parentheses.

O J O

Note the simplification:
ri-ió → **rió; ri-ieron** → **rieron**
son-ri-ió → **sonrió**
son-ri-ieron → **sonrieron**

conseguir (i, i)	to get, obtain
conseguir + *inf.*	to succeed in (*doing something*)
despedirse (i, i) (de)	to say good-bye (to), take leave (of)
divertir(se) (ie, i)	to entertain (to have a good time)
dormir(se) (ue, u)	to sleep (to fall asleep)
morir(se) (ue, u)	to die
pedir (i, i)	to ask for; to order
preferir (ie, i)	to prefer
reír(se) (i, i)	to laugh
sentir(se) (ie, i)	to feel
servir (i, i)	to serve
sonreír(se) (i, i)	to smile
sugerir (ie, i)	to suggest
vestir(se) (ie, i)	to dress (to get dressed)

Práctica

▲▲▲▲▲▲

A. **¿Quién lo hizo?** ¿Ocurrieron algunas de estas cosas en clase la semana pasada? Conteste con el nombre de la persona apropiada. Si nadie lo hizo, conteste con **Nadie...**

1. _____ se vistió de una manera muy elegante.
2. _____ se vistió de una manera rara (*strange*).
3. _____ se durmió en clase.
4. _____ le pidió al profesor / a la profesora más tarea.
5. _____ se sintió muy contento/a.
6. _____ se divirtió muchísimo, riendo y sonriendo.
7. _____ no sonrió ni siquiera (*not even*) una vez.
8. _____ sugirió tener la clase afuera.
9. _____ prefirió no contestar ninguna pregunta.

B. **Historias breves.** Cuente las siguientes historias breves en el pretérito. Luego continúelas, si puede.

1. **En un restaurante:** Juan (sentarse) a la mesa. Cuando (venir) el camarero, le (pedir) una cerveza. El camarero no (recordar) lo que Juan (pedir) y le (servir) una Coca-Cola. Juan no (querer) beber la Coca-Cola. Le (decir) al camarero: «Perdón, señor. Le (pedir: *yo*) una cerveza.» El camarero le (contestar): «_____.»
2. **Un día típico:** Rosa (acostarse) temprano y (dormirse) en seguida. (Dormir) bien y (despertarse) temprano. (Vestirse) y (salir) para la universidad. En el autobús (ver) a su amigo José y los dos (sonreír). A las nueve _____.

3. **Dos noches diferentes:** Yo (vestirse), (ir) a una fiesta, (divertirse) mucho y (volver) tarde a casa. Mi compañero de cuarto (decidir) quedarse en casa y (ver) la televisión toda la noche. No (divertirse) nada. (Perder) una fiesta excelente y lo (sentir) mucho. Yo _____.

C. **Las historias que todos conocemos.** Cuente algunos detalles de unas historias tradicionales, usando una palabra o frase de cada grupo y el pretérito de los verbos.

la Bella Durmiente	conseguir	en un baile
(*Sleeping Beauty*)	perder	encontrar (*to find*) a la mujer
el lobo (*wolf*)	divertirse	misteriosa
Rip Van Winkle	preferir	(por) muchos años
Romeo	morirse	entrar en la chimenea de los Tres
la Cenicienta	sentir	Cochinitos (*Little Pigs*)
(*Cinderella*)	vestirse	por el amor de Julieta
el Príncipe	dormir	hasta que el príncipe la besó (*kissed*)
las hermanastras		de (*as a*) abuela
de la Cenicienta		un zapato
		la envidia (*envy*) de su hermanastra

Conversación

▲▲▲▲▲▲▲▲

A. Una entrevista indiscreta

Paso 1. Lea las siguientes preguntas y piense en cómo va a contestarlas. Debe contestar algunas preguntas con información verdadera. Para otras, debe inventar una respuesta.

1. ¿A qué hora se durmió anoche?
2. En alguna ocasión, ¿perdió Ud. mucho dinero?
3. ¿Cuánto dejó de propina (*tip*) la última vez que comió en un restaurante?
4. Alguna vez, ¿se despidió Ud. de alguien tardísimo?
5. ¿Se rió alguna vez al oír una noticia (*piece of news*) trágica?
6. ¿Con qué programa de televisión se divirtió mucho el año pasado / la semana pasada... pero se avergüenza (*you're ashamed*) de admitirlo?

Paso 2. Ahora use las preguntas para entrevistar a un compañero / una compañera de clase. Luego Ud. va a decirles a todos algunas de las respuestas de su compañero/a. La clase va a decidir si la información es cierta o falsa.

MODELO: E1: ¿A qué hora te dormiste anoche?
          E2: Me dormí a las tres de la mañana... y me levanté a las siete.
          E1: Alicia se durmió a las tres... y se levantó a las siete.
       CLASE: No es cierto.
          E2: ¡Sí, es cierto! (Tienes razón. / No es cierto.)

B. La fiesta de disfraz (*Costume party*).

Paso 1. Use the following sentences as a guide for telling about a childhood or more recent costume party, if appropriate.

Palabras útiles: la bruja (*witch*), el esqueleto, el monstruo

1. ¿De qué se vistió?
2. ¿Cómo se sintió?
3. ¿Fue de casa en casa?
4. ¿Qué les dijo y qué les pidió a los vecinos (*neighbors*)?
5. ¿Qué le dieron?
6. ¿Se rieron los vecinos cuando lo/la vieron?
7. ¿Consiguió muchos dulces?
8. ¿También asistió a una fiesta?
9. ¿Qué sirvieron en la fiesta?
10. ¿Se divirtió mucho?

Paso 2. De todos los miembros de la clase, ¿quién llevó el disfraz más cómico? ¿el más espantoso (*frightening*)? ¿el más original?

En los Estados Unidos y el Canadá...

Celebraciones hispánicas

Cada grupo hispánico de los Estados Unidos celebra sus propios[a] **días festivos**. Aquí hay algunos ejemplos.

- **El Cinco de Mayo** es una de las celebraciones de **los mexicoamericanos**. Conmemora la victoria de un ejército[b] mexicano sobre invasores franceses en la Batalla de Puebla en 1862. Es una fecha patriótica en México, pero en los Estados Unidos, este día festivo es una oportunidad para celebrar la cultura, música, comida y solidaridad de la comunidad mexicoamericana.
- Cada 6 de enero, **los puertorriqueños** suelen[c] celebrar **la Fiesta de los Reyes Magos (la Epifanía)**. Se conmemora la visita al niño Jesús por los Reyes Magos. En Nueva York, es conmemorado con un desfile[d] de niños, organizado por **el Museo del Barrio**, institución que fomenta[e] la cultura puertorriqueña.

Estos mexicoamericanos celebran el Cinco de Mayo en San Francisco, California.

- **El carnaval** es un día festivo **panlatino** que se celebra en casi todas las ciudades donde hay una población latina grande. En los países católicos se celebra el carnaval durante los tres o cuatro días anteriores al **Miércoles de Ceniza**,[f] es decir el principio de la **Cuaresma**.[g] En ciudades como San Francisco, Miami y Nueva York, el carnaval se celebra con música, bailes y desfiles en los que los participantes se visten de un modo extravagante.
- Otro día festivo panlatino es **el Día de la Raza**, el 12 de octubre. Se conmemora el día en que Cristóbal Colón puso pie[h] por primera vez en tierra[i] del hemisferio occidental. Para muchos hispanos es, además, el día para celebrar su hispanidad y la cultura que comparten[j] con todos los hispanos del mundo.

[a]*own*   [b]*army*   [c]*typically*   [d]*parade*   [e]*promotes, encourages*
[f]*Ash*   [g]*Lent*   [h]*puso... landed*   [i]*land*   [j]*they share*

26

Expressing Direct and Indirect Objects Together • Double Object Pronouns

[a]*Pedestrian!*

Susanita es una amiga de Mafalda. A veces se porta muy mal y es un poco egocéntrica. ¿Conoce Ud. a personas como Susanita? ¿Le han pasado (*have happened*) las siguientes cosas a Ud.?

	SÍ	NO
1. Una vez le presté un libro a alguien y no me lo devolvió (*returned*).	☐	☐
2. Le pedí una bebida al camarero en un restaurante y no me la trajo.	☐	☐
3. Pedí algunos regalos específicos para mi cumpleaños, pero nadie me los regaló.	☐	☐
4. Les mostré fotos a unas personas, y las doblaron (*they bent.*)	☐	☐

Order of Pronouns

When both an indirect and a direct object pronoun are used in a sentence, the indirect object pronoun (**I**) precedes the direct (**D**): **ID**. Note that nothing comes between the two pronouns. The position of double object pronouns with respect to the verb is the same as that of single object pronouns.

—¿Tienes el trofeo?
Do you have the trophy?

—Sí, acaban de dár**melo**.
Yes, they just gave it to me.

—Mamá, ¿está listo el almuerzo?
Mom, is lunch ready?

—**Te lo** preparo ahora mismo.
I'll get it ready for you right now.

Le(s) → se

A. When both the indirect and the direct object pronouns begin with the letter **l**, the indirect object pronoun always changes to **se**. The direct object pronoun does not change.

Le compra unos zapatos. — *He's buying her some shoes.*
Se los compra. — *He's buying them for her.*

Les mandamos la blusa. — *We'll send you the blouse.*
Se la mandamos. — *We'll send it to you.*

B. Since **se** can stand for **le** (*to/for you* [sing.], *him, her*) or **les** (*to/for you* [pl.], *them*), it is often necessary to clarify its meaning by using **a** plus the pronoun objects of prepositions.

Se lo escribo (**a Uds., a ellos, a ellas...**). *I'll write it to (you, them...).*

Se las doy (**a Ud., a él, a ella...**). *I'll give them to (you, him, her...).*

Práctica

▲▲▲▲▲▲

A. Lo que se oye en casa. ¿A qué se refieren las siguientes oraciones? Fíjese en (*Note*) los pronombres y en el sentido (*meaning*) de la oración.

> unas fotos
> la sal
> unos billetes de avión para Guadalajara
> la fiesta
> el televisor
> los discos compactos de Luis Miguel

1. No **lo** prendan (*switch on*). Es mejor que los niños lean o que jueguen.
2. ¿Me **la** pasas? Gracias.
3. Tengo muchas ganas de comprárme**los** todos. Me encanta esa música.
4. ¿Por qué no se **las** mandas a los abuelos? Les van a gustar muchísimo.
5. Tengo que reservárte**los** hoy mismo, porque se va a terminar (*expire*) la oferta especial de Aeroméxico.
6. Yo se **la** organicé a Lupe para su cumpleaños. Antonio y Diego le hicieron un pastel.

B. En la mesa. Imagine que Ud. acaba de comer pero todavía tiene hambre. Pida más comida, según el modelo. Fíjese en el uso del tiempo presente como sustituto para el mandato.

MODELO: ensalada → ¿Hay más *ensalada*? ¿Me *la* pasas, por favor?

1. pan 2. tortillas 3. tomates 4. fruta 5. vino 6. jamón

C. En el aeropuerto. Cambie los sustantivos a pronombres para evitar (*avoid*) la repetición.

1. ¿La hora de la salida? Acaban de decirnos la hora de la salida.
2. ¿El horario? Sí, léeme el horario, por favor.
3. ¿Los boletos? No, no tiene que darle los boletos aquí.
4. ¿El equipaje? Claro que le guardo el equipaje.
5. ¿Los pasajes? Acabo de comprarte los pasajes.
6. ¿El puesto? No te preocupes. Te puedo guardar el puesto.
7. ¿La clase turística? Sí, les recomiendo la clase turística, señores.
8. ¿La cena? La asistente de vuelo nos va a servir la cena en el avión.

Conversación

▲▲▲▲▲▲▲

A. Regalos especiales

Paso 1. The drawings in **Grupo A** show the presents that a number of people have just received. They were sent by the people in **Grupo B**. Can you match the presents with the sender? Make as many logical guesses as you can.

GRUPO A

GRUPO B

Paso 2. Now compare your matches with those of a partner.

MODELO: ¿Quién le regaló (mandó) a Maritere _____?
¿Quién les regaló (mandó) a Carlos y Juanita _____?
Se lo/la/los/las regaló (mandó) _____.

B. ¿Quién le regaló eso?

Paso 1. Haga una lista de los cinco mejores regalos que Ud. ha recibido (*have received*) en su vida. Si no sabe cómo decir algo, pregúnteselo a su profesor(a).

Paso 2. Ahora déle a un compañero / una compañera su lista. Él/Ella le va a preguntar: **¿Quién te regaló _____?** Use pronombres en su respuesta. ¡**OJO**! Fíjese en (*Note*) estas formas plurales (**ellos**): **regalaron, dieron, mandaron**.

MODELO: E1: ¿Quién te regaló los aretes?
E2: Mis padres me los regalaron.

▼▲▼▲▼▲▼▲ **Videoteca**   ESPAÑA

Minidramas

In this **Minidramas** dialogue, members of Manolo Durán's family are saying good-bye to each other after a family celebration. Pay close attention to the **vosotros** forms that appear in the dialogue. How would the dialogue be different if it were spoken in Mexico? Argentina?

Jaime, Elena y sus hijos se despiden de los otros miembros[a] de la familia.

JAIME: Bueno, hasta otro,[b] hermano.
MANOLO: ¡Y que sea pronto![c]
ELENA: Hasta luego. Nos divertimos mucho, ¿eh?
ANA: Que tengáis buen viaje.[d]
PEDRO: Nos mandaréis[e] copias de las fotos, ¿no?
JAIME: Por supuesto que sí. Ha sido[f] maravilloso veros. ¡Que haya suerte![g]

[a]*members* [b]*otro día* [c]*¡Y... Let's hope it's soon!* [d]*Que... Have a good trip.* [e]*you will send* [f]*Ha... It's been* [g]*¡Que... Good luck with everything!*

FUNCTION

leave-takings

Un poco más sobre... Marta Durán Benítez

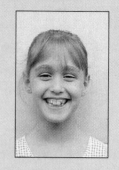

Esta jovencita tan bonita es, por ahora, la única hija de Manolo Durán García y Lola Benítez Guzmán. Acaba de hacer su Primera Comunión y de celebrarla después con sus padres y sus parientes en una fiesta muy deliciosa en un parque sevillano.

To read more about the characters from this video, visit the *Puntos de partida* Website at **www.mhhe.com/puntos**

Con un compañero / una compañera

How do people normally take leave of one another? Are the good-byes long? short? Does it depend on the situation? With a classmate or two, practice taking leave of others in the following situations.

1. Ud. acaba de dar una fiesta de cumpleaños y algunos de sus invitados van a salir. Ellos le regalaron algo que a Ud. le gusta muchísimo.
2. Ud. va a salir de una fiesta de Noche Vieja. La fiesta no estuvo muy buena, pero no quiere ser descortés (*impolite*) con los anfitriones.
3. Algunos parientes que viven lejos (tíos, abuelos, primos, etcétera) han pasado (*have spent*) el fin de semana en la casa de Ud., pero ahora tienen que regresar a su pueblo/ciudad. No se ven (*You don't see each other*) con frecuencia, y la despedida es un poco triste.

En contexto

In this video segment, Roberto talks to a store employee about returning a CD. As you watch the segment, pay attention to the way that Roberto talks about events in the past. Listen, too, to the way he and the employee use direct and indirect objects when they speak.

MÉXICO

A. Lluvia de ideas

- ¿Cuáles son los regalos de cumpleaños que a Ud. más le gustan? Antes de comprarle un regalo a Ud., ¿le preguntan sus parientes y sus amigos qué es lo que desea? ¿Cree Ud. que es buena idea preguntarle a alguien lo que desea de regalo o es mejor darle una sorpresa?
- ¿Qué hace Ud. cuando alguien le regala un libro o un disco que ya (*already*) tiene?

B. Dictado

A continuación está la primera parte del diálogo entre Roberto y el dependiente de la tienda de música. Complétela con las palabras o frases que faltan.

ROBERTO: Quisiera[a] devolver _____ _____ _____.

DEPENDIENTE: Muy bien, _____ _____… ¿Por qué quieres _____?

ROBERTO: Ya _____ _____.

DEPENDIENTE: ¿Tienes el recibo?

ROBERTO: No, no tengo el recibo. _____ _____ el disco para mi cumpleaños.

DEPENDIENTE: Lo siento[b], pero en este caso _____ _____ _____ reembolsar[c] el dinero. Necesitas _____ _____ para un reembolso.

[a]*I would like*   [b]*Lo… I'm sorry*   [c]*refund*

C. Un diálogo original

Con un compañero / una compañera, dramaticen la escena entre Roberto y el dependiente en la tienda de música.

ESTUDIANTE 1   Es su cumpleaños y un buen amigo / una buena amiga le da un regalo (por ejemplo, un libro de Isabel Allende, una camiseta de la universidad, unas entradas [*tickets*] para un concierto). Pero otra persona ya le hizo el mismo (*same*) regalo.

ESTUDIANTE 2   Ud. le hizo un regalo a su buen amigo / buena amiga sin saber (*without knowing*) que su amigo/a ya tiene otro igual. Trate de (*Try to*) resolver el problema.

Un poco de todo

A. Más días festivos. Complete the following paragraphs with the correct form of the words in parentheses, as suggested by the context. When two possibilities are given in parentheses, select the correct word. Use the preterite of the infinitives in italics.

La fiesta de la Virgen de Guadalupe

En (alguno[1]) países hispánicos los días de (varios[2]) santos (ser/estar[3]) fiestas nacionales. El día 12 (de/del[4]) diciembre se (*conmemorar*[5]) a la santa patrona de México, la Virgen de Guadalupe. (Mucho[6]) mexicoamericanos celebran (este[7]) fiesta también. Se cree que la Virgen María se le (*aparecer*[8]) (a/de[9]) Juan, (un/una[10]) humilde pastor,[a] en el pueblo (a/de[11]) Guadalupe. La Virgen (*dejar*[12])[b] su imagen en un rebozo[c] que todavía se puede (*ver*[13]) en su Basílica en la Ciudad de México.

[a]*shepherd* [b]*to leave* [c]*shawl*

La fiesta de San Fermín

No (todo[14]) las fiestas hispánicas (ser/estar[15]) religiosas. Esta fiesta de Pamplona (España) lleva (el/la[16]) nombre de un santo y (ser/estar[17]) de origen religioso, pero es esencialmente secular. Durante diez días —entre (el/la[18]) 7 y (el/la[19]) 17 de julio— se interrumpe la rutina diaria (del / de la[20]) ciudad. (Llegar[21]) personas de todas partes de España e inclusive de (otro[22]) países para beber, cantar, bailar... y (pasarlo[23]) bien. Todas las mañanas algunos toros[a] (correr[24]) sueltos[b] por (el/la[25]) calle de la Estafeta, en dirección (al / a la[26]) plaza de toros.[c] (Alguno[27]) personas atrevidas[d] (correr[28]) delante de ellos. No (haber[29]) duda[e] de que (este[30]) demostración de valor[f] (ser/estar[31]) bastante peligrosa.[g] Luego por (el/la[32]) tarde se celebra una corrida[h] en la famosa plaza de toros que (*describir*[33]) Ernest Hemingway en (su[34]) novela *The Sun Also Rises*. En Pamplona todavía (ser/estar[35]) posible (hablar[36]) con personas que (saber/conocer[37]) a este famoso escritor estadounidense.

[a]*bulls* [b]*free* [c]*plaza... bullring* [d]*daring* [e]*doubt* [f]*courage* [g]bastante... *quite dangerous* [h]*bullfight*

Comprensión: ¿Cierto o falso?   Corrija las oraciones falsas.

1. Todas las fiestas hispánicas son religiosas.
2. Sólo los mexicanos celebran la fiesta de la Virgen de Guadalupe.
3. La fiesta de San Fermín es esencialmente para los niños.
4. Algunos españoles todavía recuerdan a Hemingway.

B. Un día en la vida de...

Paso 1.   Antonio Sifuentes, el compañero de casa de Diego González, es estudiante posgraduado en la UNAM. Los siguientes verbos sirven de base para hacer una descripción de un día típico de la vida de Antonio. Úselos para describir lo que él hizo ayer.

POR LA MAÑANA

despertarse a las siete
levantarse en seguida
ducharse
afeitarse
vestirse
peinarse
desayunar
tomar sólo un café con
    leche
ir a la universidad
asistir a clases toda la
    mañana

POR LA TARDE

almorzar con unos amigos en la cafetería
divertirse hablando con ellos
despedirse de ellos
ir a la biblioteca
quedarse allí estudiando hasta las cuatro y media
volver a casa después
ayudar a Diego a preparar la cena

POR LA NOCHE

cenar con Diego y Lupe
querer estudiar por una hora
no poder (estudiar)
mirar la televisión con sus amigos
darles las buenas noches (a sus amigos)
salir a reunirse con otros amigos en un bar
volver a casa a las dos de la mañana
quitarse la ropa
acostarse
leer por cinco minutos para poder dormirse
dormirse

Paso 2. Use los verbos del **Paso 1** para describir lo que Ud. hizo ayer.
Cambie los detalles necesarios para dar la información correcta. Añada (*Add*)
verbos si es necesario.

C. Situaciones y reacciones

Paso 1.   Imagine que ocurrieron las siguientes situaciones en algún
momento en el pasado. ¿Cómo reaccionó Ud.? ¿Sonrió? ¿Lloró? ¿Rió? ¿Se
enojó? ¿Se puso triste, contento/a, furioso/a? ¿Qué hizo?

MODELO: Su compañero de cuarto hizo mucho ruido a las cuatro de la
mañana. ¿Cómo reaccionó Ud.? →
Me enojé.
(Me puse furiosísimo/a.)
(Salí de casa y fui a dormir en casa de un amigo.)
(Hablé con él.)

SITUACIONES

1. El profesor le dijo que no va a haber clase mañana.
2. Ud. rompió el reloj que era de su abuelo.
3. Su hermano perdió el disco compacto que a Ud. más le gusta.
4. Su mejor amigo lo/la llamó a las seis de la mañana el día de su
   cumpleaños.
5. Nevó muchísimo y Ud. tuvo que hacer un viaje en auto.
6. Ud. recibió el aumento de sueldo (*raise*) más grande de la
   oficina.

Paso 2.   Ahora pregúntele a un compañero / una compañera si se le
ocurrieron algunas de esas cosas y cuáles fueron sus reacciones.

PANORAMA *cultural*

Cuba

Datos esenciales

Nombre oficial: República de Cuba
Capital: La Habana
Población: 11.000.000 de habitantes
Moneda: el peso cubano
Idioma oficial: el español

¡Fíjese!

- Cuba obtuvo[a] su independencia de España en 1898, tras[b] la guerra de Cuba.[c] Los Estados Unidos ayudó a Cuba en esta guerra.

- Hay una distancia de 145 kilómetros (90 millas) entre Florida y Cuba.

- Después de la revolución socialista cubana en 1959, hubo un éxodo de cubanos a los Estados Unidos. La mayor parte de ellos se estableció en Florida, con la esperanza[d] de volver muy pronto a su isla. Pero empezó el milenio y todavía[e] Fidel Castro, el primer líder de la revolución, gobierna a Cuba.

- El régimen de Castro ha reducido[f] el analfabetismo[g] a menos de 5 por ciento y ha reformado el sistema educativo con resultados admirables. Pero la situación económica del país es difícil. Con la caída[h] de la Unión Soviética, Cuba perdió fondos de apoyo[i] indispensables. El embargo económico de los Estados Unidos también sigue afectando las condiciones de vida[j] de los cubanos.

[a]*obtained* [b]*after* [c]*guerra… Spanish-American War* [d]*hope* [e]*still* [f]*ha… has reduced* [g]*illiteracy* [h]*fall* [i]*fondos… economic assistance* [j]*condiciones… living conditions*

Conozca… a Nicolás Guillén

Nicolás Guillén (1902–1989), poeta cubano de origen africano y europeo, es quizás[a] el poeta que mejor refleja la influencia africana en la cultura hispana. El lenguaje, los mitos[b] y las leyendas afro-cubanos aparecen en su obra. Sus temas incluyen la injusticia social y una crítica al colonialismo. El siguiente fragmento de un poema de Guillén es representativo de su obra. Después de leerlo, piense: ¿Quiénes son los hombres del poema? ¿Cuál es su condición de vida? ¿Por qué es la sangre[c] «un mar inmenso»?

[a]*perhaps* [b]*myths* [c]*blood*

Poema con niños

La sangre es un mar inmenso
que baña todas las playas…
sobre sangre van los hombres
navegando[a] en sus barcazas:[b]
reman, que reman,[c] que reman
¡nunca de remar descansan!
Al negro[d] de negra piel
la sangre el cuerpo le baña;
la misma sangre, corriendo,[e]
hierve[f] bajo carne[g] blanca.

[a]*sailing* [b]*boats* [c]*reman… rowing and rowing* [d]*persona negra* [e]*flowing* [f]*boils* [g]*flesh*

Capítulo 8 of the video to accompany *Puntos de partida* contains cultural footage about Cuba.

Visit the *Puntos de partida* Website at www.mhhe.com/puntos.

Vocabulario

Los verbos

conseguir (i, i)	to get, obtain
conseguir + *inf.*	to succeed in (*doing something*)
despedirse (i, i) (de)	to say good-bye (to), take leave (of)
discutir (sobre) (con)	to argue (about) (with)
encontrar (ue)	to find
enfermarse	to get sick
enojarse (con)	to get angry (at)
gastar	to spend (*money*)
llorar	to cry
morir(se) (ue, u)	to die
olvidarse (de)	to forget (about)
ponerse (*irreg.*) + *adj.*	to become, get + *adjective*
portarse	to behave
quejarse (de)	to complain (about)
reaccionar	to react
recordar (ue)	to remember
reír(se) (i, i)	to laugh
sentirse (ie, i)	to feel
sonreír(se) (i, i)	to smile
sugerir (ie, i)	to suggest

Los días festivos y las fiestas

el anfitrión / la anfitriona	host, hostess
el chiste	joke
el deseo	wish
los entremeses	hors d'œuvres
el/la invitado/a	guest
el pastel de cumpleaños	birthday cake
los refrescos	refreshments
la sorpresa	surprise
cumplir años	to have a birthday

dar (*irreg.*) / hacer (*irreg.*) una fiesta	to give/have a party
faltar	to be absent, lacking
pasarlo bien/mal	to have a good/bad time
reunirse (me reúno) (con)	to get together (with)

Repaso: celebrar, el cumpleaños, el dinero, divertirse (ie, i), regalar

Los sustantivos

la emoción	emotion
el hecho	event
la medianoche	midnight
la noticia	piece of news

Los adjetivos

avergonzado/a	embarrassed
feliz (*pl.* felices)	happy
raro/a	strange

Palabras adicionales

¡felicitaciones!	congratulations!
ser (*irreg*) en + *place*	to take place in/at (*place*)
ya	already

Algunos días festivos

la Navidad, la Nochebuena, la Noche Vieja, la Pascua (Florida)

Un paso más 8

LECTURA

Repaso de estrategias: Using What You know

In previous chapters of *Puntos de partida*, you learned that you can use a variety of prereading strategies to help you understand the meaning of a passage in Spanish. Some of these strategies include:

- guessing meaning from context
- learning to recognize cognates and cognate patterns
- using visual aids
- getting a general idea about content

Using a combination of some or all of these strategies will help you to become a more efficient, successful reader in Spanish.

▶ **Sobre la lectura...** La lectura en la siguiente página es de una publica-
▶ ción de la embajada (*embassy*) española en Washington, D.C. Contiene va-
▶ rios artículos de interés, además de (*in addition to*) juegos y rompecabezas
▶ (*puzzles*).

Comprensión

¿Qué se hace y dónde se hace? Empareje (*Match*) cada lugar con la tradición apropiada.

1. _____ Australia
2. _____ Bolivia
3. _____ España
4. _____ Francia

5. _____ Grecia
6. _____ Hungría

7. _____ Irlanda
8. _____ Italia

9. _____ Londres
10. _____ Nápoles
11. _____ Rusia

a. tomar doce uvas
b. escuchar el himno nacional
c. hacer una gran barbacoa
d. reunirse alrededor del árbol de Navidad
e. romper una granada en la puerta
f. escuchar las campanadas de una iglesia (*church*) importante
g. salir a la calle con una maleta
h. poner una moneda (*coin*) en el corcho de una botella de champán
i. tirar muebles viejos
j. comer trece frutos secos
k. ponerse ropa interior de color rojo

12 MANERAS DE RECIBIR EL AÑO NUEVO

Superstición y costumbre[a] *se unen para atraer*[b] *la buena suerte en el año entrante.*[c]

1. En España, lo más tradicional es tomar doce uvas mientras suenan[d] las doce campanadas.[e] Una uva por cada campanada.
2. En Francia suelen comer[f] trece frutos secos.
3. Los londinenses introducen un penique[g] en el corcho[h] de la primera botella de cava[i] que se toma en el año y entierran[j] el corcho en una maceta.[k]
4. En Irlanda, todos se fían de[l] las campanadas del reloj de Christ Church.
5. Los italianos toman un plato de lentejas[m] y usan ropa interior de color rojo.
6. En Grecia suelen romper en la puerta de sus casas una granada madura.[n]
7. En Rusia, Pedro el Grande importó de Occidente[o] el árbol de Navidad, y se reúnen en torno a él.[p]
8. En Hungría, poco antes de dar[q] las doce, apagan[r] las luces y se ponen firmes[s] para escuchar el himno nacional.
9. Los australianos celebran la Noche Vieja, que coincide con el verano, con una barbacoa en la playa.
10. Igual sucede en Argentina, donde los niños se extrañan de la nieve del belén.[t]
11. En Bolivia se cree que salir con una maleta a la calle, después de las doce, ayuda a viajar durante el año.
12. En Nápoles[u] es costumbre tirar[v] los muebles y electrodomésticos[w] viejos.

[a]*custom* / [b]*attract*
[c]*que viene*

[d]*ring*
[e]*chimes (of a bell)*
[f]*suelen… they usually eat*
[g]*penny* / [h]*cork*
[i]*champagne* / [j]*they bury*
[k]*flowerpot*
[l]*se… trust (to tell them the exact time)*
[m]*lentils*

[n]*granada… ripe pomegranate*
[o]*de… del oeste*
[p]*en… around it*
[q]*sonar* / [r]*they turn off*
[s]*se… they stand at attention*

[t]*se… are surprised at the snow decorating the nativity scene*

[u]*Naples (Italy)* / [v]*to throw out*
[w]*electrical appliances*

ESCRITURA

Seguro que habrá (*There certainly must be*) algún día festivo que a Ud. le gusta más que cualquier (*any*) otro. ¿Cómo es ese día festivo? Escriba una breve composición en la que explica cuál es su día favorito y cómo lo celebra.

Paso 1. Complete la siguiente oración.

Mi día festivo favorito es _____.

Paso 2. Ahora conteste las siguientes preguntas.

1. ¿Con quién(es) celebra Ud. ese día festivo?
2. ¿Cuáles son las costumbres y tradiciones de ese día?
3. Ud. y sus parientes, ¿tienen alguna tradición especial que acostumbran seguir (*you always carry out*)?
4. ¿Qué comidas y bebidas se sirven en ese día?
5. ¿Se lleva alguna ropa especial?

Paso 3. Por fin, utilice la información de arriba para escribir su composición.

9

El tiempo libre

Estos españoles esquían en la Sierra Nevada.

WEB

¿Qué opina Ud.?

Conteste según su propia vida. ¿Cree Ud. que una persona de otro país diría algo similar? Visite el sitio Web de *Puntos de partida* para leer las respuestas a estas preguntas que da una persona de Colombia.

1. ¿Cómo pasa Ud. su **tiempo libre**? (Mencione por lo menos dos actividades.)
2. En su opinión, ¿cuál es **el aparato doméstico** más importante?
3. En su casa, apartamento o residencia, ¿quién hace **las tareas domésticas**?
4. ¿Qué opina Ud. de los deportes? ¿Cree Ud. que son **divertidos**? ¿**Le aburren**?
5. ¿Cuál es **el deporte** más popular país? ¿Lo **juega** Ud.? ¿Va a los juegos profesionales?

En este capítulo...

- In this chapter, you will study vocabulary related to leisure time activities, such as pastimes and domestic chores. You will talk about **sus planes para visitar un museo, hacer un *picnic* o ir al teatro**... and much more.

- In past chapters, you started to use the preterite to talk about events that began and ended in the past. In this chapter, you will learn how to talk about things you always did in the past, using the *imperfect tense*. (Grammar 27)

- In this chapter, you will also learn how to express superlatives (**¡Este capítulo es el más divertido de todos!**). (Grammar 28)

- You have been using words like **¿qué?** and **¿cuándo?** to ask questions since the beginning of your experience with Spanish. Now you will learn more about interrogative words. (Grammar 29)

- This chapter's **Panorama cultural** section will focus on Colombia.

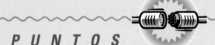

PUNTOS INTERACTIVO

Videoteca

◀ **Minidramas**
En este episodio, Lupe prepara una fiesta sorpresa para el cumpleaños de Diego. ¿Cómo celebró Ud. su último cumpleaños? ¿Le dio alguien una fiesta sorpresa?

En contexto ▶
En este episodio, Mariela y su amiga Amalia hacen planes para el fin de semana. ¿Tiene Ud. planes para el fin de semana? ¿Con quién? ¿Qué piensan hacer?

CD-ROM

Además de completar el vocabulario y las actividades de gramática, Ud. va a tener la oportunidad de «hablarle» a Amalia y de hacer planes virtuales con ella para un fin de semana interesante.

Internet

En la sección del Capítulo 9 en el sitio Web de *Puntos de partida* aparecen enlaces que Ud. puede usar para conseguir información en español sobre algunas actividades de tiempo libre. Use la dirección **www.mhhe.com/puntos** para llegar al sitio Web.

Vocabulario: Preparación

Pasatiempos, diversiones y aficiones°

Pasatiempos… *Pastimes, fun activities, and hobbies*

correr

tomar el sol

pasear en bicicleta

montar a caballo

hacer un *picnic*

patinar en línea

Los pasatiempos

los ratos libres	spare (free) time
dar (*irreg.*) / **hacer** (*irreg.*) **una fiesta**	to give a party
dar (*irreg.*) **un paseo**	to take a walk
hacer (*irreg.*) **camping**	to go camping
hacer (*irreg.*) **planes para** + *inf.*	to make plans to (*do something*)
ir (*irreg.*)…	to go…
al cine / a ver una película	to the movies/to see a movie
a una discoteca / a un bar	to a disco/to a bar
al teatro / a un concierto	to the theater/ to a concert
jugar (ue) a las cartas / al ajedrez	to play cards/chess
visitar un museo	to visit a museum
aburrirse	to get bored

ser (*irreg.*) **divertido/a, aburrido/a**	to be fun, boring

Los deportes

el ciclismo	bicycling
esquiar (esquío)	to ski
el fútbol	soccer
el fútbol americano	football
nadar	to swim
la natación	swimming
patinar	to skate

Otros deportes: el basquetbol, el béisbol, el golf, el hockey, el tenis, el vólibol

entrenar	to practice, train
ganar	to win
jugar (ue) al + *sport*	to play (*a sport*)
perder (ie)	to lose
practicar	to participate (*in a sport*)
ser aficionado/a (a)	to be a fan (of)

Conversación

▲▲▲▲▲▲▲

A. ¿Cómo pasan estas personas su tiempo libre?

Paso 1. ¿Qué cree Ud. que hacen las siguientes personas para divertirse en un sábado típico? Use su imaginación pero manténgase (*keep yourself*) entre los límites de lo posible.

1. una persona rica que vive en Nueva York
2. un grupo de buenos amigos que trabajan en una fábrica (*factory*) de Detroit
3. un matrimonio joven con poco dinero y dos niños pequeños

Paso 2. ¿Cómo se divierten los jóvenes españoles?

TIEMPO QUE DEDICAN A SUS AFICIONES	
(Media de minutos diarios)	
Ver la televisión	**120**
Tomar copas	**60**
Pasear	**22**
Leer libros	**15**
Escuchar música	**15**
Oír la radio	**8**
Hacer deporte	**9**
Practicar *hobbies*	**8**
Leer la prensa	**6**
«Juegos»	**4**

Este recorte (*clipping*) de una revista española indica el tiempo medio (*average*) que los jóvenes españoles dedican a sus aficiones. ¿Puede explicar en español lo que significan los términos **Tomar copas** y **prensa**? ¿A qué tipos de «juegos» cree Ud. que se refiere el recorte?

Paso 3. Indique el número de minutos que Ud. les dedica a estas aficiones cada día. ¿Qué diferencia hay entre Ud. y los jóvenes españoles?

B. ¿Cierto o falso? Corrija (*Correct*) las oraciones falsas según su opinión.

1. Ver una película en vídeo es más aburrido que ir al cine.
2. Lo paso mejor con mi familia que con mis amigos.
3. Las actividades educativas me gustan más que las deportivas.
4. Odio el béisbol tanto como el fútbol.

Nota cultural

El fútbol

Sin duda,[a] el deporte más popular en el mundo hispánico es **el fútbol**. Los niños hispánicos aprenden a jugar al fútbol casi desde que[b] empiezan a caminar. Muchas veces, estos niños son **aficionados** a los equipos que a sus padres les gustan.

Generalmente, hay muchos **campos de fútbol** en todas las ciudades donde los niños (y también los mayores) juegan siempre que pueden.[c] En realidad, ¡cualquier[d] espacio abierto se puede convertir en un campo[e] de fútbol si se tiene una pelota![f]

[a]*doubt* [b]desde... *from the time that* [c]siempre... *whenever they can* [d]*any* [e]*field* [f]*ball*

Un partido de la Copa Mundial entre el Brasil y Honduras

En cada país hispánico hay **ligas profesionales** de fútbol
con varias divisiones, como ocurre en este país con los
deportes profesionales. Los buenos **jugadores** de fútbol
ganan muchísimo dinero. Algunos de los mejores jugadores
de fútbol del mundo son de países hispánicos. Es necesario
mencionar aquí **los nombres sobresalientes[g] del pasado:** el
brasileño Pelé y el argentino Diego Maradona. Hoy muchos
piensan que el mejor jugador es otro brasileño, el
impresionante Rivaldo.

El fútbol femenino empieza a ser tan popular en América
Latina y España como en este país. Muchos equipos
hispánicos participaron en el primer Torneo Copa de Oro
2000 Femenil.[h]

[g]*outstanding* [h]Torneo... *Women's Gold Cup Competition*

Trabajando en casa

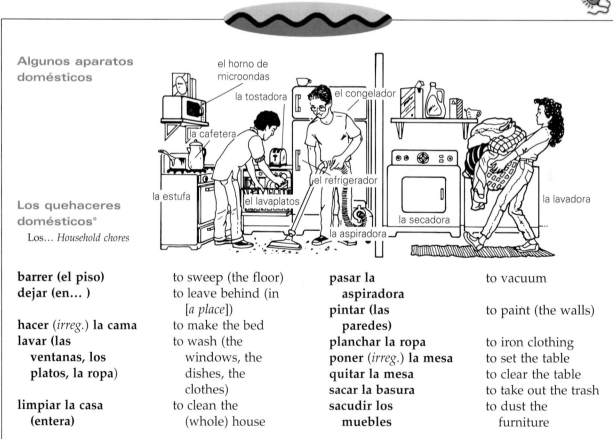

Algunos aparatos domésticos

el horno de microondas

la tostadora

el congelador

la cafetera

el refrigerador

la estufa

el lavaplatos

la aspiradora

la secadora

la lavadora

Los quehaceres domésticos°

Los... *Household chores*

barrer (el piso)	to sweep (the floor)	**pasar la aspiradora**	to vacuum
dejar (en...)	to leave behind (in [*a place*])	**pintar (las paredes)**	to paint (the walls)
hacer (*irreg.*) **la cama**	to make the bed	**planchar la ropa**	to iron clothing
lavar (las ventanas, los platos, la ropa)	to wash (the windows, the dishes, the clothes)	**poner** (*irreg.*) **la mesa**	to set the table
		quitar la mesa	to clear the table
		sacar la basura	to take out the trash
limpiar la casa (entera)	to clean the (whole) house	**sacudir los muebles**	to dust the furniture

Vocabulario útil

Here are some alternative phrases related to household chores and appliances that are used in some parts of the Spanish-speaking world. This vocabulary is for your information only and will not be actively practiced in *Puntos de partida*.

hacer la cama → tender (ie) la cama
lavar los platos → fregar los platos
sacar la basura → tirar la basura
sacudir los muebles → quitar el polvo
    (literally, *to remove the dust*)

el congelador → la nevera
la estufa → la cocina (el horno is
    generally used for *oven*)
el refrigerador → el frigorífico, la
    refrigeradora

Conversación

▲▲▲▲▲▲▲

A. Los quehaceres. ¿En qué cuarto o parte de la casa se hacen las siguientes actividades? Hay más de una respuesta en muchos casos.

1. Se hace la cama en ___ *las alcobas*
2. Se saca la basura de ___ *la cocina* y se deja en ___ *el garaje*
3. Se sacude los muebles de ___ *la sala*
4. Uno se baña en ___. Pero es mejor que uno bañe al perro en ___.
5. Se barre el suelo de ___.
6. Se pasa la aspiradora en ___ *la casa entera*
7. Se lava y se seca la ropa en ___. La ropa se plancha en ___.
8. Se usa la cafetera en ___ *la cocina*

B. ¡Manos a la obra! (*Let's get to work!*)

Paso 1. De los siguientes quehaceres, ¿cuáles le gustan más? Póngalos en orden de mayor (1) a menor (10) preferencia para Ud.

___ barrer el suelo
___ hacer la cama
___ lavar los platos
___ pasar la aspiradora

___ lavar la ropa
___ planchar la ropa
___ limpiar el garaje
___ sacar la basura

___ sacudir los muebles
___ pintar las paredes de un cuarto

Paso 2. ¿Tiene un quehacer favorito entre todos? ¿Hay un quehacer que no le guste a la mayoría de los estudiantes? ¿Hay alguna diferencia entre las preferencias de los hombres y las de las mujeres?

C. Las marcas (*Brand names*). ¿Para qué se usan los siguientes productos? Explíqueselo a su amigo Arturo, que acaba de llegar de la Argentina y no conoce las marcas estadounidenses.

1. Windex
2. Mr. Coffee
3. Endust
4. Glad Bags

5. Joy
6. Cascade
7. Tide
8. Lysol

D. ¿En qué consiste un fin de semana? El concepto del «fin de semana» es diferente para cada individuo según su horario personal... y también según dónde vive y la vida que lleva.

Paso 1. Piense en las siguientes preguntas y organice sus respuestas.

1. Para Ud., ¿cuándo comienza «oficialmente» el fin de semana? (día y hora)
2. ¿Qué hace Ud. para celebrar la llegada del fin de semana?
3. ¿Cuándo termina su fin de semana? (día y hora)
4. ¿Qué hace, generalmente, los días de su fin de semana?

Paso 2. Ahora use las mismas preguntas para entrevistar a un compañero / una compañera para saber algo sobre su fin de semana.

Paso 3. Compare las respuestas de todos los compañeros de clase. ¿Son muy variadas sus respuestas?

Nota comunicativa

Talking About Obligation

You already know several ways to express the obligation to carry out particular activities.

Tengo que			*I have to*	
Necesito	}	barrer el suelo.	*I need to*	} *sweep the floor.*
Debo			*I should*	

Of the three alternatives, **tener que** + *infinitive* expresses the strongest sense of obligation.

The concept *to be someone's turn or responsibility* (to do something) is expressed in Spanish with the verb **tocar** plus an indirect object.

–¿**A quién le toca** lavar los platos esta noche?	*Whose turn is it to wash the dishes tonight?*
–**A mí me toca** solamente sacar la basura. Creo que **a papá le toca** lavar los platos.	*I only have to take out the garbage. I think it's dad's turn to wash the dishes.*

Minidiálogos y gramática

27

Descriptions and Habitual Actions in the Past • Imperfect of Regular and Irregular Verbs

Diego habla de los aztecas

«Los aztecas construyeron grandes pirámides para sus dioses. En lo alto de cada pirámide *había* un templo donde *tenían* lugar las ceremonias y *se ofrecían* los sacrificios. Las pirámides *tenían* muchísimos escalones, y *era* necesario subirlos todos para llegar a los templos.

Cerca de muchas pirámides *había* un terreno como el de una cancha de basquetbol. Allí *se celebraban* partidos que *eran* parte de una ceremonia. Los participantes *jugaban* con una pelota de goma dura, que sólo *podían* mover con las caderas y las rodillas… »

Comprensión: ¿Cierto o falso?
1. Los aztecas creían en un solo dios.
2. Las pirámides aztecas tenían una función religiosa.
3. Los aztecas practicaban un deporte similar al basquetbol.

You have already learned to use the *preterite* (**el pretérito**) to express events in the past. The *imperfect* (**el imperfecto**) is the second simple past tense in Spanish. In contrast to the preterite, which is used when you view actions or states of being as finished or completed, the imperfect tense is used when you view past actions or states of being as habitual or as "in progress." The imperfect is also used for describing the past.

The imperfect has several English equivalents. For example, **hablaba**, the first person singular of **hablar**, can mean *I spoke, I was speaking, I used to speak,* or *I would speak* (when *would* implies a repeated action). Most of these English equivalents indicate that the action was still in progress or was habitual, except for *I spoke,* which can correspond to either the preterite or the imperfect.

Diego talks about the Aztecs. "The Aztecs constructed large pyramids for their gods. At the top of each pyramid there was a temple where ceremonies took place and sacrifices were offered. The pyramids had many, many steps, and it was necessary to climb them all in order to get to the temples.

"Close to many pyramids there was an area of land like that of a basketball court. Ceremonial matches were celebrated there. The participants played with a ball made of hard rubber that they could only move with their hips and knees . . ."

hablar		comer		vivir	
hablaba	hablábamos	comía	comíamos	vivía	vivíamos
hablabas	hablabais	comías	comíais	vivías	vivíais
hablaba	hablaban	comía	comían	vivía	vivían

- Stem-changing verbs do not show a change in the imperfect. The imperfect of **hay** is **había** (*there was, there were, there used to be*).

Pronunciation Hint: Remember that the pronunciation of a **b** between vowels, such as in the imperfect ending **-aba**, is pronounced as a fricative [ß] sound.

  In the other imperfect forms, it is important not to pronounce the ending **-ía** as a diphthong, but to pronounce the **i** and the **a** in separate syllables (the accent mark over the **í** helps remind you of this).

Imperfect of stem-changing verbs = no change

almorzar (ue) → almorzaba
perder (ie) → perdía
pedir (i, i) → pedía

Imperfect of **hay** = **había**

- Only three verbs are irregular in the imperfect: **ir, ser,** and **ver.**

ir		ser		ver	
iba	íbamos	era	éramos	veía	veíamos
ibas	ibais	eras	erais	veías	veíais
iba	iban	era	eran	veía	veían

Uses of the Imperfect

Note the following uses of the imperfect. If you have a clear sense of when and where the imperfect is used, understanding where the preterite is used will be easier. When talking about the past, the preterite *is* used when the imperfect *isn't*. That is an oversimplification of the uses of these two past tenses, but at the same time it is a general rule of thumb that will help you out at first.

The imperfect has the following uses.

- To describe *repeated habitual actions* in the past

Siempre **nos quedábamos** en aquel hotel.
We always stayed (used to stay, would stay) at that hotel.

Todos los veranos **iban** a la costa.
Every summer they went (used to go, would go) to the coast.

- To describe an *action that was in progress* (*when something else happened*)

  Pedía la cena.
  She was ordering dinner.

  Buscaba el coche.
  He was looking for the car.

- To describe two *simultaneous past actions in progress*, with **mientras**

  Tú **leías mientras** Juan **escribía** la carta.
  You were reading while Juan was writing the letter.

- To describe ongoing *physical, mental, or emotional states* in the past

  Estaban muy distraídos.
  They were very distracted.

  La **quería** muchísimo.
  He loved her a lot.

- To tell *time* in the past and to *express age* with **tener**

  | O J O | Just as in the present, the singular form of the verb **ser** is used with one o'clock, the plural form from two o'clock on. |

  Era la una.
  It was one o'clock.

  Eran las dos.
  It was two o'clock.

  Tenía 18 años.
  She was 18 years old.

- To form a *past progressive:* imperfect of **estar** + *present participle**

  Estábamos cenando a las diez.
  We were having dinner at ten.

  ¿No **estabas estudiando**?
  Weren't you studying?

Note that the simple imperfect—**cenábamos, estudiabas**—could also be used in the example sentences to express the ongoing actions. The use of the progressive emphasizes that the action was actually in progress.

Práctica

▲▲▲▲▲▲

A. Mi niñez (*childhood*)

Paso 1. Indique si las siguientes oraciones eran ciertas o falsas para Ud. cuando tenía 10 años.

	C	F
1. Estaba en cuarto (*fourth*) grado.	☐	☐
2. Me acostaba a las nueve todas las noches.	☐	☐
3. Los sábados me levantaba temprano para mirar los dibujos animados.	☐	☐
4. Mis padres me pagaban por los quehaceres que hacía: cortar el césped (*cutting the grass*), lavar los platos…	☐	☐

---

*A progressive tense can also be formed with the preterite of **estar**: *Estuvieron* **cenando hasta las doce**. The use of the progressive with the preterite of **estar**, however, is relatively infrequent, and it will not be practiced in *Puntos de partida*.

5. Me gustaba acompañar a mi madre/padre al supermercado ☐ ☐

6. Le pegaba (*I hit*) a mi hermano/a con frecuencia. ☐ ☐

7. Tocaba un instrumento musical en la orquesta de la escuela. ☐ ☐

8. Mis héroes eran personajes de las tiras cómicas (*comic strip characters*) como Superman y Wonder Woman. ☐ ☐

Paso 2. Ahora corrija las oraciones que son falsas para Ud.

MODELO: 2. Es falso. Me acostaba a las diez, no a las nueve.

B. Cuando Tina era niña... Describa la vida de Tina cuando era muy joven, haciendo oraciones según las indicaciones.

La vida de Tina era muy diferente cuando tenía 6 años.

1. todos los días / asistir / a / escuela primaria
2. por / mañana / aprender / a / leer / y / escribir / en / pizarra
3. a / diez / beber / leche / y / dormir / un poco
4. ir / a / casa / para / almorzar / y / regresar / a / escuela
5. estudiar / geografía / y / hacer / dibujos
6. jugar / con / compañeros / en / patio / de / escuela
7. camino de (*on the way*) casa / comprar / dulces / y / se los / comer
8. frecuentemente / pasar / por / casa / de / abuelos
9. cenar / con / padres / y / ayudar / a / lavar / platos
10. mirar / tele / un rato / y / acostarse / a / ocho

C. El trabajo de niñera (*baby-sitter*)

Paso 1. El trabajo de niñera puede ser muy pesado (*difficult*), pero cuando los niños son traviesos (*mischievous*), también puede ser peligroso (*dangerous*). ¿Qué estaba pasando cuando la niñera perdió por fin la paciencia? Describa todas las acciones que pueda, usando **estaba(n) + -ndo.**

Palabras útiles: ladrar (*to bark*), pelear (*to fight*), sonar (ue)* (*to ring; to sound*)

Paso 2. De joven, ¿trabajaba Ud. de niñero/a? ¿Tuvo alguna vez una mala experiencia? Complete la siguiente oración, si puede, usando un verbo en el pretérito.

MODELO: Una vez, cuando yo estaba (leyendo, mirando la tele, hablando con un amigo / una amiga, ...), el niño / la niña...

---

*Although **sonar** is a stem-changing verb (**o → ue**), remember that the stem of present participles does not change with these verbs (**sonando**).

Conversación

▲▲▲▲▲▲▲

A. ¡Qué cambio! Una entrevista. Hágale las siguientes preguntas a un compañero / una compañera de clase. Él/Ella va a pensar en las costumbres que tenía a los 14 años, es decir, cuando estaba en el noveno (*ninth*) o décimo (*tenth*) grado.

1. ¿Qué te gustaba comer? ¿Y ahora?
2. ¿Qué programa de televisión no te perdías (*missed*) nunca? ¿Y ahora?
3. ¿Qué te gustaba leer? ¿Y ahora?
4. ¿Qué hacías los sábados por la noche? ¿Y ahora?
5. ¿Qué deportes te gustaba practicar? ¿Y ahora?
6. ¿Con quién discutías mucho? ¿Y ahora?
7. ¿A quién te gustaba molestar (*annoy*)? ¿Y ahora?

B. Los tiempos cambian. Muchas cosas y costumbres actuales (*present-day*) son diferentes de las del pasado (*past*). Las siguientes oraciones describen algunos aspectos de la vida de hoy. Con un compañero / una compañera, háganse turnos para describir cómo son las cosas ahora y cómo eran las cosas antes, en otra época.

Ayer

> MODELO: E1: Ahora casi todos los bebés nacen (*are born*) en el hospital.
> E2: Antes casi todos los bebés nacían en casa.

1. Ahora muchas personas viven en apartamentos.
2. Se come con frecuencia en los restaurantes.
3. Muchísimas mujeres trabajan fuera de casa.
4. Muchas personas van al cine y miran la televisión.
5. Ahora las mujeres —no sólo los hombres— llevan pantalones.
6. Ahora hay enfermeros (*male nurses*) y maestros (*male teachers*) —no sólo enfermeras y maestras.
7. Ahora tenemos coches pequeños que gastan (*use*) poca gasolina.
8. Ahora usamos más máquinas y por eso hacemos menos trabajo físico.
9. Ahora las familias son más pequeñas.
10. Muchas parejas viven juntas sin casarse (*getting married*).

Hoy

¿Recuerda Ud.?

Before you move on to the next Grammar Section, review comparisons, which were introduced in **Capítulo 5.** How would you say the following in Spanish?

1. I work as much as you do.
2. I work more/less than you do.
3. Bill Gates has more money than I have.
4. My housemate has fewer things than me.
5. I have as many friends as you do.
6. My computer is worse/better than this one.

Minidiálogos y gramática   Doscientos ochenta y nueve   **289**

28 Expressing Extremes • Superlatives

¡El número uno!

Jennifer López

Enrique Iglesias

Ricky Martin

¿Está Ud. de acuerdo con las opiniones expresadas en estas oraciones?

1. Jennifer López es la mujer más bella (*beautiful*) del mundo.
2. Enrique Iglesias es el mejor cantante (*singer*) de su familia.
3. Ricky Martin es el puertorriqueño más conocido (*well-known*) de hoy.

Ahora le toca a Ud. formular su propia (*own*) opinión.

1. El/La cantante (*singer*) hispánico/a más popular del momento es _____.
2. La mejor actriz (*actress*) del momento es _____.
3. La música popular más interesante es _____.

The *superlative* (**el superlativo**) is formed in English by adding *-est* to adjectives or by using expressions such as *the most* and *the least* with the adjective. In Spanish, this concept is expressed in the same way as the comparative but is always accompanied by the definite article. In this construction **mejor** and **peor** tend to precede the noun; other adjectives follow. *In* or *at* is expressed with **de**.

The superlative forms **-ísimo/a/os/as** cannot be used with this type of superlative construction.

article + *noun* + **más/menos** + *adjective* + **de**

David es **el estudiante más inteligente de** la clase.
David is the most intelligent student in the class.

article + **mejor/peor** + *noun* + **de**

Son **los mejores doctores de** aquel hospital.
They are the best doctors at that hospital.

Práctica

A. ¿Está Ud. de acuerdo o no?

Paso 1. Indique si Ud. está de acuerdo o no con las siguientes oraciones.

	SÍ	NO
1. El descubrimiento (*discovery*) científico más importante del siglo XX fue la vacuna (*vaccine*) contra la poliomielitis.	☐	☐

2. La persona más influyente (*influential*) del mundo es el presidente de los Estados Unidos. ☐ ☐

3. El problema más serio del mundo es la deforestación de la región del Amazonas. ☐ ☐

4. El día festivo más divertido del año es la Noche Vieja. ☐ ☐

5. La mejor novela del mundo es *Don Quijote de la Mancha*. ☐ ☐

6. El animal menos inteligente de todos es el avestruz (*ostrich*). ☐ ☐

7. El peor mes del año es enero. ☐ ☐

8. La ciudad más contaminada de los Estados Unidos es Los Ángeles. ☐ ☐

Paso 2. Para cada oración que no refleja su opinión, invente otra oración.

MODELO: 4. No estoy de acuerdo. Creo que el día festivo más divertido del año es el Cuatro de Julio.

B. Superlativos. Expand the information in these sentences according to the model. Then, if you can, restate each sentence with true information at the beginning.

MODELO: Es una estudiante muy *trabajadora*. (la clase) →
Es la estudiante *más trabajadora de la clase*. →
Carlota es la estudiante más trabajadora de la clase.

1. Es un día festivo muy divertido. (el año)
2. Es una clase muy interesante. (todas mis clases)
3. Es una persona muy inteligente. (todos mis amigos)
4. Es una ciudad muy grande. (los Estados Unidos / el Canadá)
5. Es un estado muy pequeño. (los Estados Unidos / el Canadá)
6. Es un metro muy rápido. (el mundo)
7. Es una residencia muy ruidosa (*noisy*). (la universidad)
8. Es una montaña muy alta. (el mundo)

Conversación

▲▲▲▲▲▲▲▲

Entrevista. With another student, ask and answer questions based on the following phrases. Then report your opinions to the class. Report any disagreements as well.

1. la persona más guapa del mundo
2. la noticia más seria de esta semana
3. un libro interesantísimo y otro pesadísimo (*very boring*)
4. el mejor restaurante de la ciudad y el peor
5. el cuarto más importante de la casa y el menos importante
6. un plato riquísimo y otro malísimo
7. un programa de televisión interesantísimo y otro pesadísimo
8. un lugar tranquilísimo, otro animadísimo y otro peligrosísimo
9. la canción (*song*) más bonita del año y la más fea
10. la mejor película del año y la peor

d a n z a

◆ **Ballet de San Juan**- 28 de octubre a las 7:30 PM en el Teatro del Colegio Universitario Tecnológico de Arecibo.

◆ **Taller de baile experimental con Viveca Vázquez**- 30 de octubre y 6, 13 y 20 de noviembre de 1:00 a 3:00 PM en el centro Dharma, al lado de la USC. Se invita a toda la comunidad a participar en estos talleres. Para más información llamar al 720-1793.

◆ **JFK**- 29 de octubre a las 10:30 AM y 6:00 PM en el Salón Buhomagia del Edificio de Letras del Colegio Universitario de Humacao.

◆ **El amante de Lady Chatterly**-24 de noviembre a las 10:30 AM y 6:00 PM en Buhomagia del CUH.

◆ **Festival Internacional de Cine de Puerto Rico**-del 11 al 22 de noviembre en el Cinema Emperador de Ponce.

Estos recortes son de un periódico universitario puertorriqueño. Léalos y conteste las siguientes preguntas.

1. *¿Cuándo* dan la película *JFK?*
2. *¿Quién* fue JFK?
3. *¿Dónde* es el taller (*workshop*) de baile?

    (**¡OJO!** Recuerde: **ser en** + *place* = *to take place*)

¿Cuántas preguntas más puede Ud. hacer sobre las funciones de cine y ballet en estos anuncios?

¿Cómo?	How?	**¿Dónde?**	Where?
¿Cuándo?	When?	**¿De dónde?**	From where?
¿A qué hora?	At what time?	**¿Adónde?**	Where (to)?
¿Qué?	What? Which?	**¿Cuánto/a?**	How much?
¿Cuál(es)?	What? Which one(s)?	**¿Cuántos/as?**	How many?
¿Por qué?	Why?	**¿Quién(es)?**	Who?
		¿De quién(es)?	Whose?

You have been using interrogative words to ask questions and get information since the beginning of *Puntos de partida*. The preceding chart shows all of the interrogatives you have learned so far. Be sure that you know what they mean and how they are used. If you are not certain, the index and end-of-book vocabularies will help you find where they are first introduced. Only the specific uses of **¿qué?** and **¿cuál?** represent new information.

Using ¿qué? and ¿cuál?

• **¿Qué?** asks for a definition or an explanation.	**¿Qué** es esto? *What is this?* **¿Qué** quieres? *What do you want?* **¿Qué** tocas? *What (instrument) do you play?*
• **¿Qué?** can be directly followed by a noun.	**¿Qué traje** necesitas? *What (Which) suit do you need?* **¿Qué playa** te gusta más? *What (Which) beach do you like most?* **¿Qué instrumento** musical tocas? *What (Which) musical instrument do you play?*
• **¿Cuál(es)?** expresses *what?* or *which?* in all other cases. O J O The **¿cuál(es)?** + *noun* structure is not used by most speakers of Spanish: **¿Cuál de los dos libros quieres?** (*Which of the two books do you want?*) BUT **¿Qué libro quieres?** (*Which [What] book do you want?*)	**¿Cuál** es la clase más grande? *What (Which) is the biggest class?* **¿Cuáles** son tus actrices favoritas? *What (Which) are your favorite actresses?* **¿Cuál** es la capital del Uruguay? *What is the capital of Uruguay?* **¿Cuál** es tu teléfono? *What is your phone number?*

Práctica
▲▲▲▲▲▲

A. ¿Qué o cuál(es)?

1. ¿_____ es esto? —Un lavaplatos.
2. ¿_____ son los Juegos Olímpicos? —Son un conjunto de competiciones deportivas.
3. ¿_____ es el quehacer que más te gusta? —Lavar los platos.
4. ¿_____ bicicleta vas a usar? —La de mi hermana.
5. ¿_____ son los cines más modernos? —Los del centro.
6. ¿_____ vídeo debo sacar? —El nuevo de Robert Rodríguez.
7. ¿_____ es una cafetera? —Es un aparato que se usa para preparar el café.
8. ¿_____ es Rivaldo? —En la foto, es el hombre a la izquierda de la pelota.

B. Datos (*Information*) **personales.** Forme preguntas para averiguar datos (*find out facts*) de un compañero / una compañera de clase. Se puede usar más de una palabra interrogativa para conseguir la información. (Debe usar las formas de **tú.**)

MODELO: su dirección → ¿Cuál es tu dirección? (¿Dónde vives?)

1. su teléfono
2. su dirección
3. su cumpleaños
4. la ciudad en que nació (*you were born*)
5. su número de seguro (*security*) social
6. la persona en que más confía (*you trust*)
7. su tienda favorita
8. la fecha de su próximo examen

Conversación

▲▲▲▲▲▲▲▲

Una encuesta

Paso 1. ¿Cuáles son las preferencias de su compañero/a con respecto a las siguientes categorías? Hágale preguntas, empezándolas con **¿Qué… ?**

MODELO: estaciones del año →
¿Qué estación del año prefieres (entre todas)?

1. tipos de música
2. pasatiempos o deportes
3. programas de televisión
4. materias este semestre/trimestre
5. colores
6. tipos de comida

Paso 2. Ahora use las mismas frases para hacerle preguntas a su compañero/a sobre lo que prefería de niño/a. También trate de (*try to*) sacarle algunos detalles a su compañero/a.

MODELO: estaciones del año →
E1: ¿Qué estación preferías (entre todas) de niño/a?
E2: Prefería el invierno.
E1: ¿Por qué?
E2: Porque me gustaba jugar en la nieve.

En los Estados Unidos y el Canadá...

La música hispánica en el Canadá

Si Ud. vive en el Canadá y tiene un poco de tiempo libre, se puede aprovechar de[a] los ritmos de varios **músicos hispánicos de calidad.** Uno de estos es **Jorge (Papo) Ross.** Ross nació en la República Dominicana y allí fundó[b] su primer **conjunto** a los 18 años. En 1990 se mudó al Canadá y formó otros grupos, entre ellos la **Orquesta Pambiche,**

Papo Ross y miembros de la Orquesta Pambiche

que hoy es uno de los **conjuntos latino-canadienses** más famosos. Papo Ross y Pambiche ganaron un Juno, el prestigioso premio[c] nacional para músicos en el Canadá. A menudo dan **espectáculos explosivos** a través del[d] país, inclusive en el famoso festival de jazz de Montreal.

[a]se... *you can avail yourself of* [b]*started* [c]*prize* [d]a... *across the*

Para gozar aún más de[e] la música hispánica del Canadá, Ud. puede ir a la capital, Ottawa, donde la argentina **Alicia Borisonik** y su **conjunto Folklore Venezuela** tocan **música estilo tango-jazz.** Antes de mudarse al Canadá en 1994, Borisonik experimentó mucho éxito[f] en la esfera músical de otra capital, Buenos Aires, y su nuevo grupo tiene cada vez más[g] fama en su nueva patria. Además de presentar **conciertos** en la Galería Nacional y en el Museo Nacional de la Civilización, y de participar en muchos **festivales de verano,** Borisonik ayudó a formar un **conjunto de música latina para niños.**

[e]gozar… *enjoy even more*   [f]experimentó… *had great success*
[g]cada… *increasing*

Videoteca

MÉXICO

Minidramas

In this **Minidramas** dialogue, Lupe Carrasco invites some friends to a party. What kind of party is it? Who is it for? Who will probably be able to go and who will not be able to?

Lupe entra en la casa de Diego, Antonio y Juan.

ANTONIO: ¡Hola, Lupe!

LUPE: Hola, Antonio. Oye, ¿está aquí Diego?

ANTONIO: No, no está. ¿Por qué?

LUPE: Ah, muy bien. Pues, el próximo fin de semana le quiero dar una fiesta sorpresa a Diego. Es su cumpleaños. Quiero invitar a todos Uds. a la fiesta.

ANTONIO: ¡Qué padre[a]! ¿Y cuándo es la fiesta? ¿El viernes? ¿El sábado?

LUPE: El sábado. Rocío, ¿te gustaría venir?

ROCÍO: Ay, Lupe, me gustaría mucho, pero no puedo. Ya tengo planes para el sábado. Mis padres vienen al D.F. a visitarme, y vamos a ir al Ballet Folklórico esa noche.

JUAN: ¡Qué pena![b] Pero yo sí voy.

ANTONIO: Y yo también. Gracias por la invitación. ¿Puedo invitar a Mónica y a José Luis también?

LUPE: ¡Claro que sí! ¡Muy bien! Entonces, ¿por qué no vienen a mi casa a las siete? Y por favor, no le vayan a decir nada a Diego.

JUAN: No te preocupes.[c] Él va a estar muy sorprendido.

[a]¡Qué… *Cool!*   [b]¡Qué… *What a shame!*   [c]No… *Don't worry.*

Con un compañero / una compañera

Con un compañero / una compañera, inventen conversaciones sobre los siguientes temas, siguiendo el modelo del diálogo anterior.

- invitar a un amigo / una amiga a pasar la tarde en la playa
- invitar a varios amigos a una fiesta; uno/a de ellos no puede venir porque tiene obligaciones previas
- aceptar la invitación a una fiesta de una persona que Ud. no conoce muy bien

En contexto

COSTA RICA

In this video segment, Mariela and Amalia are trying to make plans for the weekend. As you watch the segment, pay particular attention to the friends' use of language variants that are common in Costa Rica, words such as **tenés, salís, vos,** and **sos.** Can you tell what the traditional Spanish meanings of these words are?

A. Lluvia de ideas

- ¿Qué tipo de actividades prefiere Ud. hacer los fines de semana? ¿Con quién las hace? ¿Hay alguna actividad que Ud. haga todos los fines de semana, sin falta (*without fail*)?
- ¿Cómo se entera (*do you find out*) de los eventos en que puede participar? ¿Consulta Ud. algún periódico en particular?

B. Dictado

A continuación está la primera parte del diálogo entre Mariela y Amalia. Complétela con las palabras o frases que faltan.

AMALIA: ¡Hola, Mariela! ¿Cómo _____?

MARIELA: Pura vida,[a] ¿y _____?

AMALIA: Gracias, igual. ¿Qué _____?

MARIELA: Quiero hacer _____ _____ este fin de semana. ¿Vos _____ _____ tenés planes?

AMALIA: No, no tengo planes. Soy _____ _____; nunca salgo de mi casa. ¿_____ _____? ¿Querés hacer _____ juntas?

MARIELA: Me encantaría. ¿Qué _____ hacer?

[a]Pura... *Great*

Diego, el estudiante graduado que asiste a la UNAM, vivía con su tía Matilde cuando primero llegó al Distrito Federal, pero más tarde se mudó a un apartamento con un amigo. Es un estudiante típico: le gustan la pizza y la cerveza y se pasa los fines de semana con sus amigos.

To read more about the characters from this video, visit the *Puntos de partida* Website at **www.mhhe.com/puntos**

C. Un diálogo original

Paso 1. Con un compañero / una compañera, dramaticen la escena entre Amalia y Mariela.

Paso 2. Planes para este fin de semana. Dos amigos/as hacen planes para este domingo.

ESTUDIANTE 1 Ud. desea salir el domingo, porque el sábado por la noche le toca trabajar y no va a poder hacer nada interesante. Afortunadamente (*Luckily*), tiene la mañana del lunes libre (*free*) para estudiar o descansar.

ESTUDIANTE 2 Ud. tiene ganas de salir el domingo. El único obstáculo es que tiene bastante tarea y su primera clase es a las 8 de la mañana el lunes.

Un poco de todo

A. El día que Ricardo tuvo ayer

Paso 1. The following drawings depict what Ricardo did yesterday. Match the phrases (page 298) with individual drawings in the sequence. Then narrate what Ricardo did, using verbs in the preterite. **¡OJO!** Some drawings can be associated with more than one phrase.

Frases útiles: primero... , luego... y... , después... , y... , finalmente (por fin)...

a. _____ llegar tarde a su primera clase
b. _____ almorzar en la cafetería con algunos amigos
c. _____ quedarse en cama mucho tiempo
d. _____ mirar la televisión un rato
e. _____ regresar a casa
f. _____ ir al gimnasio
g. _____ ducharse y vestirse rápidamente

h. _____ acostarse
i. _____ estudiar un poco
j. _____ jugar un partido de basquetbol
k. _____ despertarse temprano
l. _____ preparar la cena
m. _____ sonar el teléfono

Paso 2. Ahora haga oraciones para dar más detalles sobre el día que Ricardo tuvo ayer. Use el imperfecto de los verbos. Los números concuerdan con (*correspond to*) los números de los dibujos.

1. ser / seis y media / mañana
2. Ricardo / tener prisa
3. estudiantes / escuchar / la profesora
4. Ricardo / tener / mucho / hambre
5. haber / mucho / personas / gimnasio
6. ser / temprano / todavía
7. no / querer / hablar / teléfono
8. Ricardo / pensar / en / examen / mañana

B. Los fines de semana. Complete the following paragraphs with the correct form of the words in parentheses, as suggested by the context. When two possibilities are given in parentheses, select the correct word. *P* and *I* stand for preterite and imperfect, respectively, and indicate that you should use the preterite or imperfect of the infinitives provided.

Los fines de semana son como las burbujas[a] de oxígeno del calendario. Para muchos, son (los/las[1]) días más especiales. Casi todos los niños (esperar[2]) el sábado y el domingo con ansiedad. Quieren ir (a el / al[3]) parque, o a ver una película o mirar los dibujos animados toda la mañana.

También para los mayores los fines de semana son días diferentes. Hay novios que sólo (poder[4]) verse[b] los sábados y los domingos. (Otro[5]) personas tienen (de/que[6]) hacer visitas o las compras o limpiar la casa. Algunas necesitan (dormir[7]) porque no (dormir: *P*[8]) lo suficiente[c] durante la semana. Hay gente que no (querer[9]) hacer (nada/nunca[10]) y gente que espera hacer todo lo que no (hacer: *P*[11]) durante la semana.

En el mundo moderno, parece[d] que (hay/son[12]) cosas que sólo se pueden hacer los fines de semana, porque (*nosotros:* estar/ser[13]) muy ocupados durante la semana y no podemos hacer (ese[14]) cosas.

Pero también hay personas que (trabajar[15]) los fines de semana y descansan otros días de la semana. ¡Y a algunas personas no (le/les[16]) (gustar[17]) los fines de semana y (aburrirse[18])!

¿Qué le (gustar[19]) a Ud. hacer los fines de semana? ¿Qué (preferir: *I*[20]) hacer cuando era más joven?

[a]*bubbles* [b]*see each other* [c]*lo... enough* [d]*it seems*

^a*unplugged*

C. ¿De verdad estudia mucho los fines de semana?

Paso 1. Muchos estudiantes se quejan de tener mucha tarea los fines de semana. Calcule cuántas horas pasó el pasado (*last*) fin de semana con sus libros, con sus amigos… y con su almohada (*pillow*). ¡Diga la verdad!

	LIBROS	AMIGOS	ALMOHADA
el viernes	_____	_____	_____
el sábado	_____	_____	_____
el domingo	_____	_____	_____
TOTAL	_____	_____	_____

Paso 2. Ahora compare sus listas con las de sus compañeros de clase para contestar las siguientes preguntas.

¿Quién es la persona… ?

1. más estudiosa de la clase
2. más parrandera (*party-loving*)
3. más perezosa

PANORAMA *cultural*

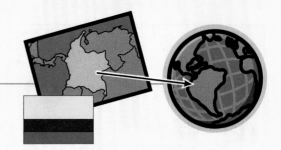

Colombia

Datos esenciales

Nombre oficial: República de Colombia
Capital: Santafé de Bogotá (Bogotá)
Población: 36.000.000 de habitantes
Moneda: el peso
Idioma oficial: el español

¡Fíjese!

* Colombia obtuvo su independencia de España en 1819, bajo la dirección de Simón Bolívar. Bolívar fue declarado el primer presidente de la independiente República de la Gran Colombia.

* Colombia produce más oro que cualquier[a] otro país sudamericano y tiene los yacimientos[b] de platino más grandes del mundo. Las esmeraldas también son un producto minero importante.

* Aunque el café es reconocido[c] como el producto agrícola principal de exportación de Colombia, en los años noventa lo sobrepasó[d] el petróleo como primer producto de exportación.

* Aproximadamente un 14 por ciento de la población colombiana es de origen africano.

* Las misteriosas estatuas de piedra de San Agustin fueron creadas por una cultura indígena de la cual[e] se sabe muy poco. Se cree que las estatuas son del siglo VI antes de Cristo. Una de las estatuas representa un pájaro con una serpiente en el pico,[f] imagen muy similar a la de una leyenda azteca.

[a]any [b]deposits [c]recognized [d]surpassed [f]beak

Estatuas de piedra, de San Agustín

Conozca a... Gabriel García Márquez

El escritor latinoamericano más leído en el mundo entero es el colombiano Gabriel García Márquez, ganador[a] del Premio Nóbel de Literatura en 1982. Su novela *Cien años de soledad* se considera una de las novelas más importantes de este siglo en cualquier lengua. La novela narra la historia de la familia Buendía durante varias generaciones. En ella García Márquez usa una técnica literaria llamada *realismo mágico:* una mezcla[b] de elementos reales y fantásticos en la narración.

Además de ser novelista, García Márquez es un respetado periodista y columnista que escribe para los periódicos más importantes de la lengua castellana.[c]

[a]recipient [b]combination [c]lengua... Castilian (Spanish) language

 Capítulo 9 of the video to accompany *Puntos de partida* contains cultural footage of Colombia.

 Visit the *Puntos de partida* Website at www.mhhe.com/puntos.

Vocabulario

Los verbos

aburrirse	to get bored
dejar (en)	to leave (behind) (in, at)
pegar	to hit
pelear	to fight
sonar (ue)	to ring; to sound

Los pasatiempos, las diversiones y las aficiones

los ratos libres	spare (free) time
dar (*irreg.*) un paseo	to take a walk
hacer (*irreg.*) un picnic	to have a picnic
hacer (*irreg.*) planes para + *inf.*	to make plans to (*do something*)
ir (*irreg.*)…	to go…
al cine / a ver una película	to the movies/ to see a movie
a una discoteca / a un bar	to a disco/to a bar
al teatro / a un concierto	to the theater/to a concert
jugar (ue) a las cartas / al ajedrez	to play cards/chess
ser (*irreg.*) divertido/a	to be fun
visitar un museo	to visit a museum

Repaso: aburrido/a, dar (*irreg.*) / hacer (*irreg.*) una fiesta, hacer *camping*, jugar (ue) (al), pasarlo bien/mal, tomar el sol

Los deportes

el/la aficionado/a (a)	fan (of)
el ciclismo	bicycling
el fútbol	soccer
el fútbol americano	football
el/la jugador(a)	player
la natación	swimming

Otros deportes: el basquetbol, el béisbol, el golf, el hockey, el tenis, el vólibol

correr	to run; to jog
entrenar	to practice, train
esquiar (esquío)	to ski
ganar	to win
montar a caballo	to ride a horse
pasear en bicicleta	to ride a bicycle
patinar	to skate
patinar en línea	to rollerblade
ser aficionado/a (a)	to be a fan (of)

Repaso: nadar, perder (ie), practicar

Algunos aparatos domésticos

la aspiradora	vacuum cleaner
la cafetera	coffeepot
el congelador	freezer
la estufa	stove
el horno de microondas	microwave oven
la lavadora	washing machine
el lavaplatos	dishwasher
el refrigerador	refrigerator
la secadora	clothes dryer
la tostadora	toaster

Algunos quehaceres domésticos

barrer (el piso)	to sweep (the floor)
hacer (*irreg.*) la cama	to make the bed
lavar (las ventanas, los platos, la ropa)	to wash (the windows, the dishes, the clothes)
limpiar la casa (entera)	to clean the (whole) house
pasar la aspiradora	to vacuum
pintar (las paredes)	to paint (the walls)
planchar la ropa	to iron clothing
poner (*irreg.*) la mesa	to set the table
quitar la mesa	to clear the table
sacar la basura	to take out the trash
sacudir los muebles	to dust the furniture

Otros sustantivos

la costumbre	custom, habit
la época	era, time (*period*)
la escuela	school
el grado	grade, year (*in school*)
el/la niñero/a	babysitter
la niñez	childhood

Adjetivos

deportivo/a	sports-loving
pesado/a	boring; difficult

Palabras adicionales

de joven	as a youth
de niño/a	as a child
mientras	while
tocarle a uno	to be someone's turn

Un paso más 9

LECTURA

Estrategia: Recognizing Derivative Adjectives

In previous chapters you learned to recognize cognates, word endings, and new words that are related to familiar words. Another large group of adjectives derived from verbs ends in **-ado** or **-ido**: you can often guess the meaning of these adjectives if you know the related verb. For example: **conocer** (*to know*) → **conocido** (*known, famous*); **preparar** (*to prepare*) → **preparado** (*prepared*). Can you guess the meaning of the following italicized adjectives based on verbs you already know?

1. unas ideas bien *explicadas*
2. una mujer *desconocida*
3. su libro *preferido*

In the following reading there are many **-do** adjectives. Try to guess their meaning from context.

You might also notice past participle forms (**-do**) in conjunction with a verb form you don't recognize, such as **ha comentado** (*has commented*). You will study this form, known as the present perfect, in a later chapter of this text. For now, simply learn to recognize it.

Another adjective form you will see in the reading is derived from nouns and ends in **-oso/a**. Can you guess the meanings of the following adjectives, based on their nouns?

sabor (*taste*) → **sabroso** = ¿ ?
éxito (*success*) → **exitoso** = ¿ ?

▶ **Sobre la lectura...** Esta lectura (de 1995) es otra auténtica, sin cambiar
▶ nada del original. Viene de una revista hispánica que trata de (*deals with*)
▶ temas populares, tales como personajes famosos, el cine, la música popular
▶ y otros de los temas más corrientes (*up-to-date*).

Agua, chocolate y un amor difícil

Entre sabrosos caldos de colitas de res, exquisitas torrejas de nata y unos chiles en nogada para chuparse los dedos,[a] pasa la vida de Tita, la protagonista de *Como agua para chocolate*, una de las películas mexicanas más exitosas de la historia. A caballo entre[b] dos siglos, y teniendo como escenario Texas y Coahuila durante la época revolucionaria, Tita es obligada a <u>renunciar</u> al amor de su vida, Pedro, para cuidar[c] a su madre, Elena. Pedro se casará con[d] la hermana mayor de la heroína para estar cerca de su <u>amada</u>, y esta volcará[e] su pasión en la cocina.

Como agua para chocolate, el sexto largometraje[f] de Alfonso Arau, costó un millón de

[a]caldos... *oxtail stews, exquisite cream puffs, and finger-licking-good chiles in nut and spice sauce* [b]A... *Straddling* [c]*take care of* [d]se... *will marry* [e]*will unleash* [f]sexto... *sixth full-length feature*

Pedro (Marco Leonardi) y Tita (Lumi Cavazos) en la película
Como agua para chocolate

cina y cine sabe, por lo visto,[h] poco. Pero conquistó al público nacional que la siguió fielmente durante cuatro meses de exhibición cinematográfica, antes de comenzar a circular en vídeo.

La cinta[i] se basa en la exitosa primera novela de la esposa del <u>realizador</u>, Laura Esquivel, que ha sido traducida[j] a quince idiomas en veinticinco países.

Esquivel, responsable también del guión,[k] es una educadora especializada en teatro infantil. Ella concibió su libro como «una novela rosa de entregas mensuales con recetas, amores y remedios caseros»,[l] y arranca[m] cada capítulo con una fórmula gastronómica.

<u>Estelarizada</u> por Marco Leonardi, Lumi Cavazos y Regina Torné, la película fue fotografiada por Emmanuel Lubezki y Steve Bernstein, que lograron[n] <u>proyectar</u> el realismo mágico que deseaba el director para <u>emparentar</u> su película con la literatura latinoamericana. •

dólares, <u>recaudó</u> el doble en México y compitió el año pasado por el Óscar. Premiada con diez Arieles, el Óscar mexicano, y con reconocimientos internacionales, *Como agua para chocolate* fue vapuleada[g] por la crítica, que de co-

[g]fue… *was torn apart* [h]por… *it would seem* [i]*film* [j]*ha… has been translated* [k]*script* [l]*novela… romantic novel with monthly offerings of recipes, loves, and homemade remedies* [m]*she starts* [n]*were able to*

Comprensión

A. ¿Quiénes son? El artículo menciona a varias personas, pero no todas son reales. Es decir, algunas son personajes de la película. Para entender bien el pasaje es importante poder distinguir entre las personas ficticias y las reales. A continuación se dan varios nombres y profesiones. Primero, indique si la persona es real (R) o ficticia (F). Después, empareje la persona con su profesión o rol.

1. _____ Alfonso Arau
2. _____ Steve Bernstein
3. _____ Pedro
4. _____ Laura Esquivel
5. _____ Tita

a. director
b. protagonista
c. escritora
d. novio
e. fotógrafo

B. ¿Cierto o falso?

	C	F
1. Laura Esquivel, la autora, había publicado (*had published*) varias novelas antes de escribir *Como agua para chocolate*.	☐	☐
2. Aunque la atacaron muchos críticos, la película recibió la aprobación del público.	☐	☐

	C	F
3. La película cuenta la historia de una pareja y los problemas que se les presentan en los años noventa del siglo XX.	☐	☐

C. Palabras relacionadas. ¿De qué verbos se derivan los siguientes adjetivos?

1. obligada
2. pasado
3. traducida
4. especializada
5. fotografiada

ESCRITURA

A. Una encuesta. El cine es un pasatiempo popular en este país. Imagine que se va a abrir un nuevo cine en su ciudad, cerca de la universidad. El dueño del cine quiere obtener información sobre los gustos de los estudiantes. Conteste las preguntas de su encuesta.

Una encuesta sobre Ud. y el cine

1. Sexo: ☐ Hombre ☐ Mujer
2. Edad: _____ años
3. Profesión: _____
4. Estado civil: ☐ Casado/a ☐ Divorciado/a ☐ Soltero/a
5. Hijos: ☐ Sí (¿Cuántos? _____) ☐ No
6. ¿Cuántas veces a la semana va Ud. al cine? _____
7. ¿Cuántas veces al mes va Ud. al cine? _____
8. ¿Va Ud. al cine… ? ☐ por la tarde ☐ por la noche
9. Ponga Ud. en orden de mayor (1) a menor (13) preferencia los siguientes tipos de películas.

   _____ cómicas   _____ románticas   _____ policíacas
   _____ históricas   _____ documentales   _____ biográficas
   _____ musicales   _____ de misterio   _____ de horror
   _____ de ciencia   _____ de tipo *western*   _____ de aventuras
             ficción
   _____ extranjeras

10. ¿Cuál es su película favorita? _____

B. Mi película favorita. Escriba un breve resumen de su película favorita. Además de escribir sobre el argumento (*plot*) de la película, no se olvide de incluir los nombres de los personajes principales (y, claro, los actores que interpretaron esos papeles) y quién dirigió la película. También diga por qué le gusta tanto esa película.

MODELO: Mi película favorita es… Fue dirigida por (nombre)… Los personajes principales son… Me gusta esta película porque…

La salud

El ejercicio (*exercise*) que hacen estos ciclistas de Marbella, España, es ideal para la salud.

¿Qué opina Ud.?

Conteste cierto o falso, según su propia vida. ¿Cree Ud. que una persona de otro país diría algo similar? Visite el sitio Web de *Puntos de partida* para leer los comentarios de una persona de Venezuela.

1. Yo no fumo. No bebo tampoco.
2. Odio ir al dentista.
3. No hago nada especial para mantener **la salud**.
4. En este país, todos queremos ser delgados. Este énfasis tan exagerado no es bueno para la salud.
5. La cultura de este país estima mucho la experiencia de las personas mayores.

En este capítulo...

- In this chapter, you will study vocabulary related to health and the human body. Have you ever had **un dolor de estómago**? Do you know anyone who has had **un ataque al corazón**? You will be able to use your new vocabulary to talk about these topics.

- In past chapters, you learned to use the preterite and the imperfect to express different kinds of actions in the past. In this chapter, you will practice using both forms when you narrate events. (Grammar 30)

- You have been using **que, quien,** and **lo que** to express *that, who, whom,* and *which.* In this chapter, you will learn more about these relative pronouns. (Grammar 31)

- You'll also learn how to express *each other* in this chapter. (Grammar 32)

- This chapter's **Panorama cultural** section will focus on Venezuela.

PUNTOS INTERACTIVO

Videoteca

◀ **Minidramas**
En este episodio, Lola Benítez lleva a su hija a la oficina de la doctora. De niño/a, ¿iba Ud. al médico a menudo (*often*)? ¿Por qué?

En contexto ▶
En este episodio, Juan Carlos va a la farmacia con una receta (*prescription*) médica. ¿Confía en (*Do you trust*) los consejos de los farmacéuticos?

 CD-ROM

Además de completar el vocabulario y las actividades de gramática, Ud. va a tener la oportunidad de «hablarle» a un farmacéutico sobre una gripe (*flu*) que tiene.

 Internet

En la sección del Capítulo 10 del sitio Web de *Puntos de partida* aparecen enlaces que Ud. puede usar para conseguir información en español sobre la salud y el cuerpo humano. Use la dirección **www.mhhe.com/puntos** para llegar al sitio Web.

Vocabulario: Preparación

La salud y el bienestar°

La... *Health and well-being*

El cuerpo humano

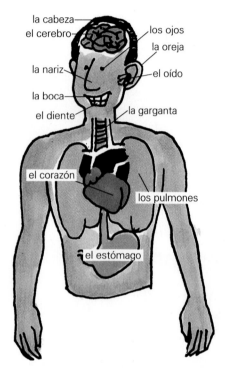

la cabeza
el cerebro
los ojos
la oreja
la nariz
el oído
la boca
el diente
la garganta
el corazón
los pulmones
el estómago

Para cuidar de la salud

caminar	to walk
comer equilibradamente	to eat well-balanced meals
correr	to run; to jog
cuidarse	to take care of oneself
dejar de + *inf.*	to stop (*doing something*)
dormir (ue, u) lo suficiente	to sleep enough
hacer (*irreg.*) **ejercicio**	to exercise; to get exercise
hacer (*irreg.*) **ejercicios aeróbicos**	to do aerobics
llevar gafas / lentes de contacto	to wear glasses / contact lenses
llevar una vida sana/tranquila	to lead a healthy/ calm life
practicar deportes	to practice, play sports

Conversación

A. Asociaciones

Paso 1. ¿Qué partes del cuerpo humano asocia Ud. con las siguientes palabras? A veces hay más de una respuesta posible.

1. un ataque 2. comer 3. cantar 4. las gafas 5. pensar
6. la digestión 7. el amor 8. fumar 9. la música 10. el perfume

Paso 2. ¿Qué palabras asocia Ud. con las siguientes partes del cuerpo?

1. los ojos 2. los dientes 3. la boca 4. el oído 5. el estómago

B. Hablando de la salud. ¿Qué significan, para Ud., las siguientes oraciones?

MODELO: Se debe comer equilibradamente. →
Eso quiere decir (*means*) que es necesario comer muchas verduras, que...

Palabras y frases útiles: Eso quiere decir… , Esto significa que… , También…

1. Se debe dormir lo suficiente todas las noches.
2. Hay que hacer ejercicio.
3. Es necesario llevar una vida tranquila.
4. En general, uno debe cuidarse mucho.

C. ¿Cómo vives? ¿Cómo vivías?

Paso 1. ¿Hace Ud. las siguientes cosas para mantener la salud y el bienestar?

		SÍ	NO
1.	comer una dieta equilibrada	☐	☒
2.	no comer muchos dulces	☐	☒
3.	caminar por lo menos (*at least*) dos millas por día	☐	☒
4.	correr	☒	☐
5.	hacer ejercicios aeróbicos	☒	☐
6.	dormir por lo menos ocho horas por día	☐	☒
7.	tomar bebidas alcohólicas en moderación	☒	☐
8.	no tomar bebidas alcohólicas en absoluto (*at all*)	☐	☒
9.	no fumar ni cigarrillos ni puros (*cigars*)	☒	☐
10.	llevar ropa adecuada (abrigo, suéter, etcétera) cuando hace frío	☒	☐

Paso 2. ¿Lleva una vida sana? Dígale a un compañero / una compañera cómo vive, usando las frases del **Paso 1**.

MODELO: Creo que llevo una vida sana porque como una dieta equilibrada. No como muchos dulces, excepto en los días festivos como Navidad…

Paso 3. Ahora cambie su narración para describir lo que hacía de niño/a. ¿Qué hacía y qué *no* hacía Ud.? Debe organizar las ideas lógicamente.

MODELO: De niño, no llevaba una vida muy sana. Comía muchos dulces. También odiaba las frutas y verduras…

En el consultorio° *doctor's office*

el/la enfermero/a	nurse	**el jarabe**	(cough) syrup
el farmacéutico	pharmacist	**la pastilla**	pill
el/la médico/a	physician	**la receta**	prescription
el/la paciente	patient	**el resfriado**	cold
		la tos	cough
congestionado/a	congested, stuffed-up		
mareado/a	dizzy; nauseated	**doler (ue)**[*]	to hurt, ache
		enfermarse	to get sick
el antibiótico	antibiotic		

---

[*]**Doler** is used like **gustar: Me due***le* **la cabeza. Me due***len* **los ojos.**

guardar cama	to stay in bed
internarse (en)	to check in (to a hospital)
ponerle (irreg.) una inyección	to give (someone) a shot
resfriarse	to get/catch a cold
respirar	to breathe
sacar	to extract
sacar la lengua	to stick out one's tongue
sacar una muela	to extract a tooth
tener (irreg.) dolor (de cabeza, estómago, muela)	to have a (head, stomach, tooth) ache
tener (irreg.) fiebre	to have a fever

— Pero ¿cómo quiere que le opere,[a] si no tiene Ud. nada?
— Mejor, doctor. Así la operación le será[b] más fácil...

[a]cómo... *why do you want me to operate on you*   [b]*will be*

tomar(le) la temperatura	to take someone's temperature
toser	to cough

Conversación

A. Estudio de palabras. Complete las siguientes oraciones con una palabra de la misma (*same*) familia que la palabra en letras cursivas (*italics*).

1. Si me *resfrío*, tengo *el resfriado*
2. La *respiración* ocurre cuando alguien *respira*.
3. Si me _____, estoy *enfermo/a*. Un(a) _____ me toma la temperatura.
4. Cuando alguien *tose*, se oye una _____.
5. Si me *duele* el estómago, tengo un *dolor* de estómago.

Nota cultural

La medicina en los países hispánicos

Como regla general los hispanos tienen como costumbre **consultar** no sólo a los médicos sino[a] a **otros profesionales con sus problemas de salud.** Por ejemplo, ya que[b] muchas drogas se venden sin receta en los países hispánicos, es posible que una persona enferma le explique sus síntomas a un farmacéutico, que puede recomendarle una medicina y aun ponerle inyecciones al paciente. Los farmacéuticos reciben un **entrenamiento** riguroso y están al tanto[c] en **farmacología.** También se puede consultar a un practicante.

[a]*but*   [b]*ya... since*   [c]*al... up-to-date*

Estos tienen tres años de entrenamiento médico y pueden aplicar una serie de tratamientos, incluyendo inyecciones.

Otra característica del sistema médico hispánico es que es fácil y barato conseguir los servicios de una **enfermera particular**[d] que cuide a un enfermo, ya sea[e] en la casa o en el hospital. Las enfermeras no tienen que tener tantos conocimientos teóricos como las de los Estados Unidos, pero tienen mucha experiencia en su campo.[f]

[d]*private* [e]*ya... whether it be* [f]*field*

B. Situaciones. Describa Ud. la situación de estas personas. ¿Dónde y con quiénes están? ¿Qué síntomas tienen? ¿Qué van a hacer?

1.

2.

3.

1. Anamari está muy bien de salud. Nunca le duele(n) _____. Nunca tiene _____. Siempre _____. Más tarde, ella va a _____.
2. Martín tiene _____. Debe _____. El dentista va a _____. Después, Martín va a _____.
3. A Inés le duele(n) _____. Tiene _____. El médico y la enfermera van a _____. Luego, Inés tiene que _____.

Nota comunicativa

The Good News... The Bad News...

To describe general qualities or characteristics of something, use **lo** with the masculine singular form of an adjective.

    lo bueno / lo malo   lo más importante   lo mejor / lo peor   lo mismo

This structure has a number of English equivalents, especially in colloquial speech.

    lo bueno = the good thing / part / news, what's good

C. Ventajas y desventajas (*Advantages and Disadvantages*). Casi todas las cosas tienen un aspecto bueno y otro malo.

Paso 1. ¿Qué es lo bueno y lo malo (o lo peor y lo mejor) de las siguientes situaciones?

1. tener un resfriado
2. ir a una universidad cerca/lejos del hogar familiar (*family home*)
3. tener hijos cuando uno es joven (entre 20 y 25 años)
4. ser muy rico/a

Vocabulario: Preparación

5. ir al consultorio médico
6. ir al consultorio del dentista

Paso 2. Compare sus respuestas con las de sus compañeros. ¿Dijeron algo que Ud. no consideró?

Minidiálogos y gramática

¿Recuerda Ud.?

Throughout the last chapters of *Puntos de partida,* beginning with **Capítulo 7,** you have been using first the preterite and then the imperfect in appropriate contexts. Do you remember which tense you used to do each of the following?

1. to tell what you did yesterday
2. to tell what you used to do when you were in grade school
3. to explain the situation or condition that caused you to do something
4. to tell what someone did as the result of a situation
5. to talk about the way things used to be
6. to describe an action that was in progress

If you understand those uses of the preterite and the imperfect, the following summary of their uses will not contain much that is new information for you.

30 **Narrating in the Past** • Using the Preterite and the Imperfect

En el consultorio de la Dra. Méndez

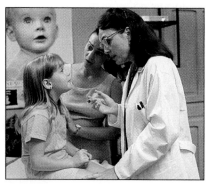

DRA. MÉNDEZ: ¿Cuándo *empezó* a sentirse mal su hija?
LOLA: Ayer por la tarde. *Estaba* congestionada, *tosía* mucho y *se quejaba* de que le *dolían* el cuerpo y la cabeza.
DRA. MÉNDEZ: ¿Y le *notó* algo de fiebre?
LOLA: Sí. Por la noche le *tomé* la temperatura y *tenía* treinta y ocho grados.
DRA. MÉNDEZ: A ver… Tal vez necesito ponerle una inyección…
MARTA: Eh… bueno… ¡Creo que ahora me encuentro un poco mejor!

In Dr. Méndez's office DR. MÉNDEZ: When did your daughter begin to feel bad? LOLA: Yesterday afternoon. She was stuffed up, she coughed a lot, and she complained that her body and head were hurting. DR. MÉNDEZ: And did you note any fever? LOLA: Yes. At night I took her temperature and it was thirty-eight degrees. DR. MÉNDEZ: Let's see. . . Perhaps I'll need to give her a shot. . . MARTA: Um. . . well. . . I think I feel a little bit better now!

In the preceding dialogue, locate all of the verbs that do the following.

 tomé
1. indicate actions (or lack of action)
2. indicate conditions or descriptions
empezó , estaba

98.6 degrees

37.0 grados

When speaking about the past in English, you choose different past tense forms to use, depending on the context: *I wrote letters, I was writing letters, I used to write letters,* and so on. Similarly, you can use either the preterite or the imperfect in many Spanish sentences, depending on the meaning you wish to convey. Often the question is: How do you view the action or state of being?

A. Use the preterite to…

- tell about the beginning or the end of a past action

El sábado pasado, el partido de fútbol **empezó** a la una. **Terminó** a las cuatro.
Last Saturday, the soccer game began at one. It ended at four.

Use the imperfect to…

- talk about the habitual nature of an action (something you always did)

Había un partido todos los sábados. Muchas personas **jugaban** todas las semanas.
There was a game every Saturday. Many people played every week.

B. Use the preterite to…

- express an action that is viewed as completed

El partido **duró** tres horas. **Ganaron** Los Lobos, de Villalegre.
The game lasted three hours. The Lobos of Villalegre won.

Use the imperfect to…

- tell what was happening when another action took place and tell about simultaneous events (with **mientras** = *while*)

Yo no vi el final del partido. **Estaba** en la cocina cuando **terminó**.
I didn't see the end of the game. I was in the kitchen when it ended.

Mientras mi amigo **veía** el vídeo, **hablaba** con su novia.
While my friend was watching the video, he was talking with his girlfriend.

C. Use the preterite to…

- express a series of completed actions

Durante el partido, los jugadores **corrieron, saltaron y gritaron**.
During the game, the players ran, jumped, and shouted.

Use the imperfect to…

- give background details of many kinds: time, location, weather, mood, age, physical and mental characteristics

Llovía un poco durante el partido. Todos los jugadores **eran** jóvenes; **tenían** 17 ó 18 años. ¡Y todos **esperaban** ganar!
It rained a little bit during the game. All the players were young; they were 17 or 18 years old. And all of them hoped to win!

D. Certain words and expressions are frequently associated with the preterite, others with the imperfect.

Some words often associated with the preterite are:
    ayer, anteayer, anoche
    una vez (*once*), dos veces (*twice*), …
    el año pasado, el lunes pasado, …
    de repente (*suddenly*)

Some words often associated with the imperfect are:
    todos los días, todos los lunes, …
    siempre, frecuentemente
    mientras
    de niño/a, de joven

Some English equivalents also associated with the imperfect are:

was _____ *-ing, were* _____ *-ing* (in English)
used to, would (when *would* implies *used to* in English)

OJO

These words do not *automatically* cue either tense, however. The most important consideration is the meaning that the speaker wishes to convey.

Ayer cenamos temprano.
Yesterday we had dinner early.

Ayer cenábamos cuando Juan llamó.
Yesterday we were having dinner when Juan called.

De niño jugaba al fútbol.
He played soccer as a child.

De niño empezó a jugar al fútbol.
He began to play soccer as a child.

E. Remember that, when used in the preterite, **saber, conocer, querer,** and **poder** have English equivalents different from the infinitives (see **Capítulo 8**). The English equivalents of these verbs in the imperfect do not differ from the infinitive meanings.

F. The preterite and the imperfect frequently occur in the same sentence. In the first sentence the imperfect tells what was happening when another action—conveyed by the preterite—broke the continuity of the ongoing activity. In the second sentence, the preterite reports the action that took place because of a condition, described by the imperfect, that was in progress or in existence at that time.

Miguel **estudiaba** cuando **sonó** el teléfono.
Miguel was studying when the phone rang.

Olivia **comió** tanto porque **tenía** mucha hambre.
Olivia ate so much because she was very hungry.

G. The preterite and imperfect are also used together in the presentation of an event. The preterite narrates the action while the imperfect sets the stage, describes the conditions that caused the action, or emphasizes the continuing nature of a particular action.

Práctica

A. En el consultorio. What did your doctor do the last time you had an appointment with him or her? Assume that you had the following conditions and match them with the appropriate procedure.

CONDICIONES: (Yo)...

1. __c__ tenía mucho calor y temblaba.
2. __f__ me dolía la garganta.
3. __g__ tenía un poco de congestión en el pecho (*chest*).
4. __e__ creía que estaba anémico/a.
5. __a__ no sabía lo que tenía.
6. __b__ necesitaba medicinas.
7. __d__ sólo necesitaba un chequeo rutinario.

ACCIONES: El médico...

a. me hizo muchas preguntas.
b. me puso una inyección.
c. me tomó la temperatura.
d. me auscultó (*listened to*) los pulmones y el corazón.
e. me analizó la sangre (*blood*).
f. me hizo sacar la lengua.
g. me hizo toser.

B. Pequeñas historias. Complete the following brief paragraphs with the appropriate phrases from the list. Before you begin, it is a good idea to look at the drawing that accompanies each paragraph and to scan through the complete paragraph to get the gist of it, even though you may not understand everything the first time you read it.

1.

nos quedamos	nos gustó
nos quedábamos	nuestra familia decidió
íbamos	vivíamos

Cuando éramos niños, Jorge y yo _____[1] en la Argentina. Siempre _____[2] a la playa, a Mar del Plata, para pasar la Navidad. Allí casi siempre _____[3] en el Hotel Fénix. Un año, _____[4] quedarse en otro hotel, el Continental. No _____[5] tanto como el Fénix y por eso, al año siguiente, _____[6] en el Fénix otra vez.

2.

estaba leyendo	salí
había	se apagaron[b]
estaban apagadas[a]	me levanté
tenía	

Eran las once de la noche cuando ¡de repente _____[1] todas las luces[c] de la casa! Puse el libro que _____[2] en la mesa y _____[3] para investigar la causa del incidente. La verdad es que _____[4] mucho miedo. _____[5] a la calle y vi que _____[6] las luces de todo el barrio.[d] En ese momento me di cuenta[e] que _____[7] un problema con la electricidad en toda la ciudad.

[a]*out* [b]*se... went out* [c]*lights* [d]*neighborhood* [e]*me... I realized*

3.

examinó	puso
intentaba[a] tomarle	llegó
estaba	dio
esperaba	se sintió

El niño tosía mientras que la enfermera _____[1] la temperatura. La madre del niño _____[2] pacientemente. Por fin _____[3] la médica. Le _____[4] la garganta al niño, le _____[5] una inyección y le _____[6] a su madre una receta para un jarabe. La madre todavía _____[7] muy preocupada, pero inmediatamente después que la médica le habló, _____[8] más tranquila.

[a]*tried to*

C. Rubén y Soledad

Paso 1. Read the following paragraph at least once to familiarize yourself with the sequence of events, and look at the drawing. Then reread the paragraph, giving the proper form of the verbs in parentheses in the preterite or the imperfect, according to the needs of each sentence and the context of the paragraph as a whole.

Rubén (estar[1]) estudiando cuando Soledad (entrar[2]) en el cuarto. Le (preguntar[3]) a Rubén si (querer[4]) ir al cine con ella. Rubén le (decir[5]) que sí porque se (sentir[6]) un poco aburrido con sus estudios. Los dos (salir[7]) en seguida[a] para el cine. (Ver[8]) una película cómica y (reírse[9]) mucho. Luego, como (hacer[10]) frío, (entrar[11]) en su café favorito, El Gato Negro, y (tomar[12]) un chocolate. (Ser[13]) las dos de la mañana cuando por fin (regresar[14]) a casa. Soledad (acostarse[15]) inmediatamente porque (estar[16]) cansada, pero Rubén (empezar[17]) a estudiar otra vez.

[a]*en... right away*

Paso 2.   Now answer the following questions based on the paragraph about Rubén and Soledad. **¡OJO!** A question is not always answered in the same tense as that in which it is asked. Remember this especially when you are asked to explain why something happened.

1. ¿Qué hacía Rubén cuando Soledad entró?
2. ¿Qué le preguntó Soledad a Rubén?
3. ¿Por qué dijo Rubén que sí?
4. ¿Les gustó la película? ¿Por qué?
5. ¿Por qué tomaron un chocolate?
6. ¿Regresaron a casa a las tres?
7. ¿Qué hicieron cuando llegaron a casa?

D. La fiesta de Roberto. Read the following paragraphs once for meaning, and look at the drawing. Then reread the paragraphs, giving the proper form of the verbs in parentheses in the present, preterite, or imperfect.

Durante mi segundo año en la universidad, yo (conocer[1]) a Roberto en una clase. Pronto nos (hacer[2]) muy buenos amigos. Roberto (ser[3]) una persona muy generosa que (organizar[4]) una fiesta en su apartamento todos los viernes. Todos nuestros amigos (venir[5]). (Haber[6]) muchas bebidas y comida, y todos (hablar[7]) y (bailar[8]) hasta muy tarde.

   Una noche algunos de los vecinos[a] de Roberto (llamar[9]) a la policía y (decir[10]) que nosotros (hacer[11]) demasiado ruido. (Venir[12]) un policía al apartamento y le (decir[13]) a Roberto que la fiesta (ser[14]) demasiado ruidosa. Nosotros no (querer[15]) aguar[b] la fiesta, pero ¿qué (poder[16]) hacer? Todos nos (despedir[17]) aunque (ser[18]) solamente las once de la noche.

   Aquella noche Roberto (aprender[19]) algo importantísimo. Ahora cuando (hacer[20]) una fiesta, siempre (invitar[21]) a sus vecinos.

[a]*neighbors*   [b]*to spoil*

Conversación
▲▲▲▲▲▲▲▲

A. El primer día. Dé Ud. sus impresiones del primer día de su primera clase universitaria. Use estas preguntas como guía.

1. ¿Cuál fue la primera clase? ¿A qué hora era la clase y dónde era?
2. ¿Vino a clase con alguien? ¿Ya tenía su libro de texto o lo compró después?
3. ¿Qué hizo Ud. después de entrar en la sala de clase? ¿Qué hacía el profesor / la profesora?
4. ¿A quién conoció Ud. aquel día? ¿Ya conocía a algunos miembros de la clase? ¿A quiénes?
5. ¿Aprendió Ud. mucho durante la clase? ¿Ya sabía algo de esa materia?
6. ¿Le gustó el profesor / la profesora? ¿Por qué sí o por qué no? ¿Cómo era?
7. ¿Cómo se sentía durante la clase? ¿nervioso/a? ¿aburrido/a? ¿cómodo/a?
8. ¿Les dio tarea el profesor / la profesora? ¿Pudo Ud. hacerla fácilmente?
9. ¿Su primera impresión de la clase y del profesor / de la profesora, ¿fue válida o cambió con el tiempo? ¿Por qué?

B. Unas preguntas sobre el pasado

Paso 1. Con un compañero / una compañera, hagan y contesten las siguientes preguntas.

¿Cuántos años tenías cuando... ?

1. aprendiste a pasear en bicicleta
2. hiciste tu primer viaje en avión
3. tuviste tu primera cita
4. empezaste a afeitarte
5. conseguiste tu licencia de manejar (*driver's license*)
6. abriste una cuenta corriente (*checking account*)
7. dejaste de crecer (*grow*)

Paso 2. Con otro compañero / otra compañera, hagan y contesten estas preguntas.

¿Cuántos años tenías cuando tus padres... ?

1. te dejaron cruzar la calle solo/a
2. te permitieron ir de compras a solas
3. te dejaron acostarte después de las nueve
4. te dejaron quedarte en casa sin niñero/a
5. te permitieron usar la estufa
6. te dejaron ver una película «R»
7. te dejaron conseguir un trabajo

Paso 3. Ahora, en grupos de cuatro, comparen sus respuestas. ¿Son muy diferentes las respuestas que dieron? ¿Quién del grupo tiene los padres más estrictos? ¿los menos estrictos?

C. Una historia famosa

Paso 1. La siguiente historia está narrada en el presente. Cámbiela al pasado, poniendo los verbos en el pretérito.

La niña *abre*[1] la puerta y *entra*[2] en la casa. *Ve*[3] tres sillas. *Se sienta*[4] en la primera silla, luego en la segunda, pero no le *gusta*[5] ninguna. Por eso *se sienta*[6] en la tercera. *Ve*[7] tres platos de comida en la mesa y *decide*[8] comer el más pequeño. Luego, *va*[9] a la alcoba para descansar un poco. Después de probar[a] las camas grandes, *se acuesta*[10] en la cama más pequeña y *se queda*[11] dormida.

[a]*trying*

Paso 2. ¿Reconoce Ud. la historia? Es el cuento de Ricitos de Oro y los tres osos (*Goldilocks and the Three Bears*). Pero el cuento está un poco aburrido tal como está (*as it is*). Mejore el cuento con detalles y descripciones. **¡OJO!** Recuerde usar el imperfecto en las descripciones.

MODELO: La niña se llamaba Ricitos de Oro. Abrió la puerta y entró en la casa. La casa estaba muy...

Paso 3. Ahora termine la historia de Ricitos de Oro. ¿Qué pasó al final?

El Dr. Pedro José Greer

En las últimas décadas, un problema sin solución evidente ha surgido[a] en los Estados Unidos: el de **los desamparados**.[b] Aunque muchas personas creen que los desamparados son por lo general drogadictos y alcohólicos del sexo masculino, la realidad es distinta. Pueden ser tanto mujeres, jóvenes y niños como hombres. El problema es especialmente grave en **los centros urbanos**. Pero los desamparados en **Miami, Florida**, tienen un amigo en **el Dr. Pedro José Greer**.

El Dr. Greer estudió en la Universidad de Florida y recibió el título de Doctor en Medicina en la Pontífica Universidad Católica Madre y Maestra en Santo Domingo,

El Dr. Pedro José Greer

República Dominicana. Cuando todavía era estudiante de medicina, el Dr. Greer se ofrecía a trabajar en **Camillus House**, un abrigo[c] para los desamparados en el centro de Miami. Reconociendo la inmensa falta de servicios de salud para los desamparados que hay en esa ciudad, fundó **Camillus Health Concern**, una clínica que ofrece servicios gratuitos[d] a los desamparados. Al principio su consultorio consistía en una sola habitación de Camillus House. Hoy día Camillus Health Concern ofrece sus servicios no sólo en el centro del Miami, sino en todo el condado[e] de Dade.

[a]ha... *has arisen* [b]*homeless people* [c]*shelter* [d]*free* [e]*county*

---

31 ▶ Recognizing *que, quien(es), lo que* •
Relative Pronouns

La salud es *lo que* importa

[a]Malditas... *It wasn't right for me to want to step on it*

¿Sabe Ud. *lo que* debe hacer para ser saludable emocionalmente? ¿Vive Ud. la vida *que* debe vivir? Para estar seguro de *lo que* necesita para la salud física, consulte con un doctor en *quien* confía. Pero para lograr un estado de bienestar mental, hágase estas preguntas:

- ¿Hay personas con *quienes* puedo hablar si es *que* tengo problemas?
- ¿Qué métodos uso para combatir el estrés *que* me causan los problemas diarios?

- ¿Mantengo un balance entre *lo que* es de valor profesional o educativo en mi vida y *lo que* es puramente de diversión personal?
- ¿Tengo un amigo o pariente con *quien* comparto mi vida?

Complete las siguientes oraciones.

1. La persona con quien más hablo cuando tengo problemas es _____.
2. El método que más uso para combatir el estrés es _____.
3. Las actividades que mantienen el balance en mi vida son _____.
4. La persona con quien comparto (*I share*) (o con quien me gustaría compartir) mi vida es _____.

A. There are four principal *relative pronouns* in English: *that, which, who,* and *whom.* They are usually expressed in Spanish by the relative pronouns at the right, all of which you already know.

que: refers to things and people
quien: refers only to people
lo que: refers to a situation

B. Learning to recognize the meaning of these words in context will make reading in Spanish easier for you, especially with authentic materials (written for native speakers of Spanish). See if you can understand the following sentences without looking at the English equivalents.

- **que** = *that, which, who*

  Tuve una cita con el médico **que** duró una hora.
  I had an appointment with the doctor that lasted an hour.

  Es un buen médico **que** sabe mucho.
  He's a good doctor who knows a lot.

- **quien(es)** = *who/whom* after a preposition or as an indirect object

  La mujer con **quien** hablaba era mi hermana.
  The woman with whom I was talking was my sister.

  Ese es el niño a **quien** no le gusta el helado.
  That's the boy who doesn't like ice cream.

- **lo que** = *what, that which*

  No entiendo **lo que** dice.
  I don't understand what he is saying.

  Lo que no me gusta es su actitud hacia los pobres.
  What I don't like is his attitude toward poor people.

C. The antecedent (what it refers to) of **lo que** is always a sentence, a whole situation, or something that hasn't been mentioned yet.

Lo que necesito es estudiar más.

Remember that the relative pronouns **que** and **quien** have an accent mark only in the interrogative or exclamatory form.

—¿Con **quién** hablas?
—*Whom are you talking to?*

—Hablo con la mujer con **quien** doy la fiesta.
—*I'm talking to the woman with whom I'm giving the party.*

—¿**Qué** dices? ¡**Qué** historia tan interesante!
—*What are you saying? What an interesting story!*

—¡Te digo **que** es verdad!
—*I'm telling you (that) it's true!*

Práctica

▲▲▲▲▲

A. Problemas médicos. Complete las oraciones lógicamente, usando **que, quien** o **lo que**.

EN LA SALA DE EMERGENCIAS/URGENCIA

1. ¿Quién fue el hombre _____ la trajo aquí?
2. Desgraciadamente (*Unfortunately*) no podemos localizar a la persona con _____ vive.
3. ¡ _____ necesitamos es más tiempo!
4. Quiero saber el nombre de la medicina _____ Ud. tomaba.
5. ¿Dónde está el ayudante (*assistant*) _____ empezó a trabajar ayer?

EN EL CONSULTORIO DEL MÉDICO

DOCTOR: Pues _____⁶ Ud. tiene es exceso de peso.ª Debe perder por lo menos diez libras.

PACIENTE: Pero, doctor... Es cierto que como mucho, pero... Dígame, ¿a _____⁷ no le gusta comer?

DOCTOR: De ahora en adelante, Ud. puede comer todo _____⁸ le guste... ¡y aquí está la lista de _____⁹ le debe gustar!

ªweight

B. El estrés, la condición humana

Paso 1. Lea la siguiente tira cómica y conteste las preguntas.

ªcansancio... *fatigue, restlessness, worry, nervousness, (emotional) imbalance, and anxiety*

1. Lo que quiere el padre de Libertad (la amiga de Mafalda) es _____.
2. Lo que tiene es _____.
3. Según el médico, lo que tiene su padre es _____.

Paso 2. ¿De cuántas de esas condiciones sufre Ud.? ¿Sufre más de esos problemas durante ciertas épocas del año? ¿Cuáles?

Conversación

▲▲▲▲▲▲▲▲

Problemas y consejos

Paso 1. Déle varios consejos a la persona que tiene los siguientes problemas. Use estas frases como guía: **La persona con quien debes hablar es... , Lo que debes hacer es...**

1. Tengo un resfriado terrible.
2. Necesito descansar, y tengo tres días libres la semana que viene.
3. Tengo ganas de comer comida china esta noche.
4. No sé qué clases debo tomar el semestre/trimestre que viene.
5. ¡Sufro tantas presiones (*I am under so much pressure*) en mi vida privada!
6. Vivo muy lejos de la universidad. Pierdo una hora en ir y venir todos los días.

Paso 2. Ahora invente Ud. problemas similares —o cuente un problema real— y pídales consejos a sus compañeros de clase.

32 **Expressing *each other*** • Reciprocal Actions with Reflexive Pronouns

—¿Tú crees que cada vez que nos encontramos tenemos que *saludarnos dándonos* la mano?[a]

[a]*hand*

1. ¿Dónde *se encuentran* los dos pulpos?
2. ¿Cómo *se saludan* (*do they greet each other*)?
3. ¿*Se conocen*? ¿Cómo se sabe?

▲▲▲▲▲

The plural reflexive pronouns, **nos, os,** and **se,** can be used to express *reciprocal actions* (**las acciones recíprocas**). Reciprocal actions are usually expressed in English with *each other* or *one another.*

Nos queremos.

Nos queremos.   *We love each other.*
¿**Os** ayudáis?   *Do you help one another?*
Se miran.   *They're looking at each other.*

Práctica

▲▲▲▲▲▲

A. **Buenos amigos.** Indique las oraciones que describen lo que hacen Ud. y un buen amigo / una buena amiga para mantener su amistad (*friendship*).

1. ☐ Nos vemos con frecuencia.
2. ☐ Nos conocemos muy bien. No hay secretos entre nosotros.
3. ☐ Nos respetamos mucho.
4. ☐ Nos ayudamos con cualquier (*any*) problema.
5. ☐ Nos escribimos cuando no estamos en la misma ciudad.
6. ☐ Nos hablamos por teléfono con frecuencia.
7. ☐ Nos decimos la verdad siempre, sea esta (*be it*) bonita o fea.
8. ☐ Cuando estamos muy ocupados, no importa si no nos hablamos por mucho tiempo.

B. **¿Qué se hacen?** Describa las siguientes relaciones familiares o sociales, haciendo oraciones completas con una palabra o frase de cada grupo.

los buenos amigos
los parientes
los esposos
los padres y los niños
los amigos que no viven en la misma ciudad
los profesores y los estudiantes
los compañeros de cuarto/casa

(no)

verse con frecuencia
quererse, respetarse
ayudarse (con los quehaceres domésticos, con los problemas económicos, con los problemas personales)
hablarse (todos los días, con frecuencia, sinceramente)
llamarse por teléfono (con frecuencia), escribirse
mirarse (en la clase, con cariño [*affection*])
necesitarse
conocerse bien
saludarse (en la clase, con cariño), darse la mano

Conversación

▲▲▲▲▲▲

Preguntas

1. ¿Con qué frecuencia se ven Ud. y su novio/a (esposo/a, mejor amigo/a)? ¿Cuánto tiempo hace que se conocen? ¿Con qué frecuencia se dan regalos? ¿se escriben? ¿se telefonean? ¿Le gusta a Ud. que se vean tanto (tan poco)?
2. ¿Con qué frecuencia se ven Ud. y sus abuelos/primos? ¿Por qué se ven Uds. tan poco (tanto)? ¿Cómo se mantienen en contacto? En la sociedad norteamericana, ¿los parientes se ven con frecuencia? En su opinión, ¿es esto común entre los hispanos?

Videoteca

Minidramas

In this **Minidramas** dialogue, Lola Benítez and her daughter Marta are in the doctor's office. Pay close attention to the following: Who doesn't feel well? What are her symptoms? How does the doctor treat the illness?

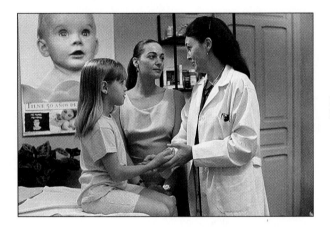

En el consultorio de la Dra. Méndez

DRA. MÉNDEZ: ¿Así que no te sientes bien, Marta? Dime[a] lo que te pasa.

MARTA: Anoche me dolió mucho el estómago. Y también la garganta.

LOLA: Sí, y ayer por la tarde estaba muy congestionada.

DRA. MÉNDEZ: ¿Sí? ¿Y cuándo comenzó a sentir estos síntomas?

LOLA: Fue unos días después de que se reunió con su amiga Carolina, quien ya estaba enferma.

DRA. MÉNDEZ: Ajá. Marta, saca la lengua, por favor. (*La doctora examina la garganta de Marta.*) Di «ahhh.» A ver... (*La doctora escucha el pecho[b] de Marta.*) Respira. Más fuerte. Otra vez.

MARTA: Ahhh...

LOLA: ¿Qué pasa, doctora? ¿Es grave?

DRA. MÉNDEZ: No, no se preocupe.[c] No es nada grave. Lo que tiene es un resfriado. Marta, debes guardar cama durante unos días y tomar muchos líquidos. Señora Durán, voy a darle dos recetas. Las pastillas son para quitarle[d] la congestión. Y el jarabe se lo puede dar cuando ella tosa.

LOLA: Muy bien, doctora.

DRA. MÉNDEZ: Y debe quedarse en casa algunos días.

[a]*Tell me* [b]*chest* [c]*no... don't worry* [d]*getting rid of*

Con un compañero / una compañera

Ahora imagine que es Lola quien no se siente bien. Con un compañero / una compañera, hagan los papeles (*play the roles*) del diálogo. Traten de (*Try to*) variar los detalles del diálogo.

En contexto

In this video segment, Juan Carlos talks to the pharmacist about medication to ease his cold. What cold medications do you prefer? Do you believe that any medication can cure a cold?

PERÚ

A. Lluvia de ideas

- ¿Se enferma Ud. a menudo? ¿De qué se enferma?
- ¿Va Ud. inmediatamente al consultorio médico cuando se siente mal o prefiere esperar a ver si se pone (*you get*) mejor/peor? ¿Por qué hace esto?
- En este episodio, el farmacéutico le dice a Juan Carlos que el sueño (*sleep*) es una de las mejores medicinas. ¿Qué hace Ud. para sentirse mejor?

B. Dictado

A continuación está la primera parte del diálogo entre Juan Carlos y el farmacéutico. Complétela con las palabras o frases que faltan.

FARMACÉUTICO: Buenas tardes, Juan Carlos. ¿_____ _____ hoy? ¿_____?

JUAN CARLOS: Pues, _____ _____ mucho la garganta y estoy bien _____.

FARMACÉUTICO: ¿_____ a ver al _____?

JUAN CARLOS: _____ una consulta esta mañana.

FARMACÉUTICO: ¿Y qué te _____?

JUAN CARLOS: Tengo _____ _____ _____. Me dio una _____ para un antibiótico.

C. Un diálogo original

Paso 1. Con un compañero / una compañera, dramaticen la escena entre Juan Carlos y el farmacéutico.

Paso 2. Consejos de sus padres. Imagine que Ud. y su compañero son miembros de una familia. Tengan la siguiente conversación.

ESTUDIANTE 1 Ud. está bien resfriado/a. Hable con su mamá/papá u otro pariente para preguntarle lo que debe hacer Ud. para curarse. Por ejemplo, Ud. puede decirles que no sabe si debe ir al médico o no.

ESTUDIANTE 2 Ud. es la mamá / el papá u otro pariente de su compañero/a y le dice lo que debe hacer para cuidarse cuando está enfermo/a. No se olvide de preguntarle por todos los síntomas posibles antes de dar sus consejos (*advice*).

A. Lo mejor de estar enfermo

Paso 1. Form complete sentences using the words in the order given. Conjugate the verbs in the preterite or the imperfect and add or change words as needed. Use subject pronouns only when needed.

1. cuando / yo / ser / niño, / pensar / que / lo mejor / de / estar enfermo / ser / guardar cama
2. lo peor / ser / que / con frecuencia / (yo) resfriarse / durante / vacaciones
3. una vez / (yo) ponerme / muy / enfermo / durante / Navidad
4. mi / madre / llamar / a / médico / en / quien / tener / confianza
5. Dr. Matamoros / venir / casa / y / darme / antibiótico / porque / tener / mucho / fiebre
6. ser / cuatro / mañana / cuando / por fin / (yo) empezar / respirar / sin dificultad
7. desgraciadamente (*unfortunately*) / día / de / Navidad / (yo) tener / tomar / jarabe / y / no / gustar / nada / sabor (*taste, m.*)
8. lo bueno / de / este / enfermedad / ser / que / mi / padre / tener / dejar / fumar / mientras / yo / estar / enfermo

Paso 2. Now tell the story again from the point of view of the mother of the sick person. The first sentence is done for you.

MODELO: 1. cuando / yo / ser / niño, / pensar / que / lo mejor / de / estar enfermo / ser / guardar cama → Cuando mi hijo era niño, pensaba que lo mejor de estar enfermo era guardar cama.

B. Un accidente tragicómico.
Complete the following paragraphs with the correct form of the words in parentheses—for verbs, the present, preterite, or imperfect—as suggested by the context. When two possibilities are given in parentheses, select the correct word.

Cuando mi hermana y yo (tener[1]) 9 y 7 años respectivamente, (nuestro[2]) madre (tener[3]) un pequeño accidente. Papá (tener[4]) que pasar unos días fuera a causa del trabajo. (Por/Para[5]) eso, (*nosotras:* ir[6]) a despedirlo al aeropuerto.

Cuando (*nosotras:* salir[7]), vimos un perrito (que/quien[8]) tenía la pata[a] atrapada[b] en una puerta. Las tres (correr[9]) a ayudarlo. Mamá (tomar[10]) al perrito en sus brazos y lo estaba (examinar[11]) mientras (*nosotras:* caminar[12]). Íbamos (tan/tanto[13]) preocupadas por la patita del perro que no (*nosotras:* ver[14]) un escalón.[c] (*Nosotras:* Caerse[15])[d] las tres… bueno, los cuatro. La situación (ser[16]) algo cómica. (*Nosotras:* Levantarse[17]) muertas de risa[e] y un poco avergonzadas.

Por fin (*nosotras:* dejar[18]) al perrito con (su[19]) dueños y (decidir[20]) irnos a casa. Nuestra madre (cojear[21])[f] un poco. Esa misma tarde (*nosotras:* ir[22]) al hospital porque le (doler[23]) mucho todavía la pierna.[g] No (haber[24]) duda.

[a]*paw* [b]*trapped* [c]*step* [d]*To fall down* [e]*muertas… dying of laughter* [f]*to limp* [g]*leg*

(*Ella*: Tener²⁵) el tobillo roto.ʰ Le escayolaronⁱ la pierna y le (*ellos*: dar²⁶) un par de muletas.ʲ Además le (*ellos*: recomendar²⁷) reposo absoluto.

Todavía hoy mi hermana y yo (acordarse²⁸) de lo bien que (*nosotras*: pasarlo²⁹) jugando a ser las enfermeras de mamá. Afortunadamente los abuelos (venir³⁰) a ayudarnos.

ʰel… *a broken ankle* ⁱLe… *They put a cast on* ʲ*crutches*

Comprensión: ¿Quién lo dijo?

1. Tenemos que ir a ayudar a las chicas. No pueden cuidar a Marisa a solas (*alone*).
2. ¿Dónde está el perro? No lo veo en ningún sitio.
3. Siento (*I'm sorry*) decirle, señora, que tiene el tobillo fracturado.
4. ¡Qué torpes (*clumsy*) somos!, ¿verdad?
5. ¿Por qué no te llevamos a la sala de urgencia?

C. Caperucita Roja

Paso 1. Retell this familiar story, based on the drawings, sentences, and cues that accompany each drawing, using the imperfect or preterite of the verbs in parentheses. Add as many details as you can. Using context, try to guess the meaning of words that are glossed with ¿ ?

Vocabulario útil

abalanzarse sobre	to pounce on	**esconderse**	to hide
avisar	to warn	**enterarse de**	to find out about
dispararle	to shoot at someone/ something	**huir (huyó)**	to flee
		saltar	to jump

---

1. Érase una vezᵃ una niña hermosa que (llamarse¹) Caperucita Roja. Todos los animales del bosqueᵇ (ser²) sus amigos y Caperucita Roja los (querer³) mucho.
2. Un día su mamá le (decir⁴): —Lleva en seguida esta jarrita de mielᶜ a casa de tu abuelita. Ten cuidadoᵈ con el loboᵉ feroz.

ᵃ¿ ? ᵇ¿ ? ᶜjarrita… *jar of honey* ᵈTen… *Be careful* ᵉ¿ ?

3. En el bosque, el lobo (salir⁵) a hablar con la niña. Le (preguntar⁶):
   —¿Adónde vas, Caperucita? Esta le (contestar⁷) dulcemente:ᶠ —Voy a casa de mi abuelita.
4. —Pues, si vas por este sendero,ᵍ vas a llegar antes, (decir⁸) el malvadoʰ lobo. Él (irse⁹) por otro camino más corto.

ᶠ*sweetly* ᵍ*path* ʰ¿ ?

Un poco de todo

5. El lobo (llegar[10]) primero a la casa de la abuelita y (entrar[11]) silenciosamente. La abuelita (tener[12]) mucho miedo. (*Ella:* Saltar[13]) de la cama y (correr[14]) a esconderse.

6. Caperucita Roja (llegar[15]) por fin a la casa de la abuelita. (*Ella:* Encontrar[16]) a su «abuelita», que (estar[17]) en la cama. Le (decir[18]): —¡Qué dientes tan largos tienes! —¡Son para comerte mejor!— (decir[19]) su «abuelita».

7. Una ardilla[i] del bosque (enterarse[20]) del peligro. Por eso (avisar[21]) a un cazador.[j]

8. El lobo (saltar[22]) de la cama y (abalanzarse[23]) sobre Caperucita. Ella (salir[24]) de la casa corriendo y pidiendo socorro[k] desesperadamente.

[i]¿ ? [j]¿ ? [k]*help*

9. El cazador (ver[25]) lo que (ocurrir[26]). (*Él:* Dispararle[27]) al lobo y le (hacer[28]) huir.

10. Caperucita (regresar[29]) a la casa de su abuelita. La (abrazar: *ella*[30]) y le (prometer[31]) escuchar siempre los consejos de su mamá.

Paso 2. Hay varias versiones del cuento de Caperucita Roja. La que Ud. acaba de leer termina felizmente, pero otras no. Con otros dos compañeros, vuelvan a contar la historia, empezando por el dibujo número 7. Inventen un diálogo más largo entre Caperucita y el lobo y cambien por completo el final del cuento.

Más vocabulario útil

atacar	to attack	**matar**	to kill
comérselo/la	to eat something up		

PANORAMA *cultural*

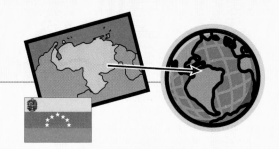

Venezuela

Datos esenciales

Nombre oficial: República de Venezuela
Capital: Caracas
Población: 21.000.000 de habitantes
Moneda: el bolívar
Idiomas: el español (oficial), varios idiomas indígenas

¡Fíjese!

Por su variedad de climas, Venezuela le ofrece al turista atracciones diversas. El clima venezolano varía entre el clima templado de las regiones andinas y el clima tropical de los llanos[a] y la costa. De hecho, el clima es agradable la mayor parte del año. Entre las atracciones turísticas hay lo siguiente:

1. las hermosas[b] playas tropicales de la Isla Margarita y la costa caribeña
2. la famosa catarata[c] Salto Ángel que, siendo dieciséis veces más alta que las cataratas del Niágara, es considerada la más alta del mundo
3. la belleza[d] colonial de Ciudad Bolívar y Coro
4. la progresiva y cosmopolita ciudad de Caracas y las majestuosas montañas andinas

[a]*plains* [b]*beautiful* [c]*waterfall* [d]*beauty*

Conozca a... Simón Bolívar

Simón Bolívar (1783–1830) nació en Caracas. La fecha de su cumpleaños, el 24 de julio, es hoy día una fiesta nacional en Venezuela. Bolívar, llamado «el Libertador», ocupa un puesto[a] importante tanto en la historia de Venezuela

Salto Ángel

como en la historia de Colombia, el Perú, el Ecuador y Bolivia por ser el personaje principal en las luchas[b] por la independencia de estos países. Bolívar, influenciado por las ideas de Jean Jacques Rousseau[c] y por la lucha de las colonias estadounidenses contra Inglaterra en el siglo XVIII, soñaba con[d] una América hispánica unida, sueño que nunca vio realizado.[e]

[a]*position* [b]*struggles* [c]*French writer and philosopher (1712–1778) whose ideas helped spark the French Revolution* [d]soñaba... *dreamt about* [e]*achieved*

 Capítulo 10 of the video to accompany *Puntos de partida* contains cultural footage about Venezuela.

 Visit the *Puntos de partida* Website at www.mhhe.com/puntos.

Vocabulario

Los verbos

encontrarse (ue) (con)	to meet (*someone somewhere*)
saludarse	to greet each other

La salud y el bienestar

caminar	to walk
cuidarse	to take care of oneself
dejar de + *inf.*	to stop (*doing something*)
doler (ue)	to hurt, ache
encontrarse (ue)	to be, feel
examinar	to examine
guardar cama	to stay in bed
hacer (*irreg.*) ejercicios aeróbicos	to do aerobics
internarse (en)	to check in (*to a hospital*)
llevar una vida sana/tranquila	to lead a healthy/calm life
ponerle (*irreg.*) una inyección	to give (someone) a shot, injection
resfriarse	to get/catch a cold
respirar	to breathe
sacar	to extract
sacar la lengua	to stick out one's tongue
sacar una muela	to extract a tooth
tener (*irreg.*) dolor de	to have a pain in
tomarle la temperatura	to take someone's temperature
toser	to cough

Repaso: comer, correr, dormir (ue, u), enfermarse, hacer (*irreg.*) ejercicio, practicar deportes

Algunas partes del cuerpo humano

la boca	mouth
la cabeza	head
el cerebro	brain
el corazón	heart
el diente	tooth
el estómago	stomach
la garganta	throat
la nariz	nose
el oído	inner ear
el ojo	eye
la oreja	outer ear
los pulmones	lungs
la sangre	blood

Las enfermedades y los tratamientos

el antibiótico	antibiotic
el chequeo	check-up
el consultorio	(medical) office
el dolor (de)	pain, ache (in)
la farmacia	pharmacy
la fiebre	fever
las gafas	glasses
el jarabe	(cough) syrup
los lentes de contacto	contact lenses
la medicina	medicine
el/la paciente	patient
la pastilla	pill
la receta	prescription
el resfriado	cold
la sala de emergencias/ urgencia	emergency room
la salud	health
el síntoma	symptom
la temperatura	temperature
la tos	cough

El personal médico

el/la dentista	dentist
el/la enfermero/a	nurse
el/la farmacéutico/a	pharmacist

Repaso: el/la médico/a

Los sustantivos

la desventaja	disadvantage
la ventaja	advantage

Los adjetivos

congestionado/a   congested
mareado/a   dizzy; nauseated
mismo/a   same

Palabras adicionales

de repente   suddenly
dos veces   twice
equilibradamente   in a balanced way

eso quiere decir...   that means...
lo bueno / lo malo   the good thing, news / the bad thing, news

lo suficiente   enough
por lo menos   at least
una vez   once

Repaso: lo que, que, quien

Un paso más 10

LECTURA

Estrategia: Thematic Organization—Cause and Effect

Another strategy that can help your comprehension of a written passage is to identify thematic patterns in the text, or the relationship between different pieces of information. For example, does the author use contrast to get the point across? Is the passage strictly descriptive? Or is the information presented through a cause-and-effect relationship?

In the case of the latter, you should try to identify both the cause and the effect that are presented in the reading. Understanding the argumentative organization of the text can boost your comprehension of both individual sentences and the passage as a whole. In the reading that follows, you will find a series of cause-and-effect relationships, many of which may surprise you. As you read, try to identify these relationships, as you will be asked about them in the **Comprensión** section.

▶ **Sobre la lectura...** Este artículo apareció en una revista para hispanos
▶ en los Estados Unidos para informarles sobre un aspecto de la salud y el
▶ bienestar. La lectura es auténtica; es decir, el lenguaje no ha sido modifi-
▶ cado (*hasn't been modified*).

Las vitaminas y la salud

Las vitaminas son antioxidantes para el cuerpo humano... pero ahora también se sabe que una <u>sobredosis</u> podría perjudicar[a] al organismo más que ayudarlo. Las últimas investigaciones revelan, por ejemplo, que un exceso de vitamina A es responsable de agudos[b] dolores de cabeza, pérdida[c] del pelo, irritación de la piel,[d] deformaciones óseas[e] y defectos en los <u>recién nacidos</u> (en el caso de que la vitamina sea ingerida[f] por las embarazadas[g]). Los médicos recomiendan no ingerir más de 25.000 I.U. (unidades internacionales) de esta vitamina por día.

Vitamina C: una dosis de más de 1.000 miligramos (1 gramo) por día podría ser tóxica, <u>provocando</u> diarrea y otras alteraciones serias.

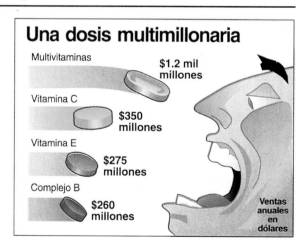

Una dosis multimillonaria

Multivitaminas — $1.2 mil millones
Vitamina C — $350 millones
Vitamina E — $275 millones
Complejo B — $260 millones

Ventas anuales en dólares

Los galenos[h] aconsejan 50 miligramos por día para adultos y 100 miligramos por día para <u>fumadores</u>.

[a]podría... *could damage* [b]*sharp* [c]*loss* [d]*skin* [e]*of or pertaining to bones* [f]*sea... is ingested* [g]*pregnant women* [h]*médicos*

Vitamina E: no ingerir más de 1.600 I.U. por día. El exceso podría causar <u>coágulos</u> en la sangre.[i] El infográfico (página 332) muestra la venta de vitaminas en los Estados Unidos. ●

[i]*blood*

Comprensión

A. ¿Cierto o falso? Conteste según el artículo. Corrija las oraciones falsas.

1. El exceso de vitamina A puede causar problemas gastrointestinales.
2. La vitamina C ayuda a reducir los dolores de cabeza.
3. Una sobredosis de vitamina A puede causar reacciones dermatológicas.
4. El fumar puede afectar la dosis recomendada de algunas vitaminas.

B. Causa y efecto. Identifique por lo menos uno de los efectos que puede causar cada uno de los siguientes. Dé su respuesta en inglés.

1. una sobredosis de vitamina A
2. una sobredosis de vitamina C
3. una sobredosis de vitamina E

ESCRITURA

A. ¿Cómo está de salud?

Paso 1. ¿Lleva Ud. una vida sana o lleva una vida no muy saludable (*healthy*)? Indique las respuestas que se apliquen (*apply*) a Ud.

1. Hago ejercicio...
   □ todos los días
   □ de vez en cuando
   □ Nunca hago ejercicio.
2. Duermo...
   □ ocho horas por día
   □ menos de ocho horas por día
   □ más de ocho horas por día
3. Como frutas y/o verduras...
   □ todos los días
   □ dos o tres veces por semana
   □ Nunca como frutas y/o verduras.

4. Tomo vitaminas...
   - ☐ todos los días
   - ☐ dos o tres veces por semana
   - ☐ sólo cuando me siento mal

5. Voy al consultorio del médico / de la médica...
   - ☐ para recibir un chequeo anual
   - ☐ sólo cuando estoy enfermo/a

6. Me enfermo...
   - ☐ más de cinco veces por año
   - ☐ entre dos y cinco veces por año
   - ☐ menos de dos veces por año

Paso 2. Ahora analice sus respuestas del **Paso 1**. ¿Cómo está Ud. de salud? ¿Está sano/a o necesita mejorar su salud? Escriba un breve reportaje sobre sus respuestas, indicando qué tipo de vida lleva. Al final del reportaje, indique si necesita mejorar sus hábitos o si ya está en buen estado de salud.

B. **Mi última visita al consultorio.** Answer the following questions about your last visit to the doctor, adding as many details as possible. Then, using the words in this **Vocabulario útil** and any others you know, join the sentences together to form three paragraphs that flow smoothly.

Vocabulario útil

además	besides	**pero**	but
así	thus, so	**por ejemplo**	for example
cuando	when	**por eso**	therefore, for that reason
de vez en cuando	from time to time	**por fin**	at last, finally
en cambio	on the other hand	**pues**	well; since
es decir	that is	**sin embargo**	nevertheless
luego	then, next	**también**	also
mientras	while		

PÁRRAFO A

1. ¿Cuándo fue la última vez que Ud. consultó con un médico?
2. ¿Por qué lo hizo? ¿Cuáles eran sus síntomas? ¿O era solamente un chequeo anual?

PÁRRAFO B

1. En el consultorio, ¿tuvo Ud. que esperar mucho tiempo? ¿Esperaban también otros pacientes?
2. Cuando por fin entró en el consultorio, ¿cuánto tiempo duró la consulta? ¿Qué actitud mostró el médico? ¿compasión? ¿humor? ¿preocupación? ¿indiferencia?
3. ¿Le recetó alguna medicina? ¿Qué otras recomendaciones le dio? ¿Las siguió Ud.? ¿Por qué sí o por qué no?

PÁRRAFO C

1. ¿Cuándo se mejoró Ud. por fin? ¿O cuándo va a tener otro chequeo anual?
2. ¿Qué hace ahora para mantenerse en buen estado de salud?

Presiones de la vida moderna

Los estudiantes, como este puertorriqueño, pueden sufrir muchas presiones. ¿Las sufre Ud. también?

¿Qué opina Ud.?

Conteste según su propia vida. ¿Cree Ud. que una persona de otro país diría algo similar? Visite el sitio Web de *Puntos de partida* para leer las respuestas a estas preguntas que da una persona de Puerto Rico.

1. ¿Dónde **sufre** Ud. más **presiones,** en su vida escolar, en su vida social o en su vida familiar?
2. ¿Quiénes lo/la ayudan más en los momentos difíciles de la vida, sus amigos o su familia?
3. ¿Qué institución social lo/la ayuda más en esos momentos? ¿la iglesia? ¿el gobierno? ¿alguna otra institución? ¿o ninguna?
4. ¿Cree Ud. que la gente sufre más presiones hoy en día o que sufría más hace cincuenta años?
5. ¿Prefiere Ud. la vida de hoy, con su ritmo acelerado, o la de antes, que era más tranquila?

En este capítulo...

- In this chapter, you will study vocabulary related to the pressures of student life and to accidents. Can you guess what **estrés** means?
- You have been using the verb **hacer** to mean *to do* or *to make* since Chapter 4. In this chapter, you will learn a different use for **hacer**, which will allow you to express how long ago something happened. (Grammar 33)
- You lost your homework! Do you know how to tell your Spanish teacher how it happened? In this chapter, you will learn to express unexpected events like that one. (Grammar 34)
- You know how to use both **por** and **para** in many contexts. This chapter will review their uses as well as present others. (Grammar 35)
- The **Panorama cultural** section will focus on Puerto Rico.

P U N T O S   I N T E R A C T I V O

Videoteca

◀ **Minidramas**
José Miguel les cuenta a su mamá y a su abuela los accidentes que tuvo durante el día. ¿Tuvo Ud. algún accidente esta semana?

En contexto ▶
Roberto se pierde (*gets lost*) y le pide direcciones a un señor en la calle. ¿Se pierde Ud. con frecuencia? Si se pierde, ¿pide Ud. ayuda?

CD-ROM
Además de completar el vocabulario y las actividades de gramática, Ud. va a tener la oportunidad de «darle direcciones» a una persona virtual que se ha perdido (*has gotten lost*).

Internet
En la sección del Capítulo 11 del sitio Web de *Puntos de partida* aparecen enlaces que Ud. puede usar para conseguir información en español sobre las presiones y los accidentes que sufren los estudiantes. Use la dirección **www.mhhe.com/puntos** para llegar al sitio Web.

Las presiones de la vida estudiantil

Agenda:° del I al 7 de febrero — *Appointment calendar*

1° al 7° de febrero

lunes, 1 de febrero
ir a la biblioteca (sacar libros para historia de arte)
informe oral de sociología

martes, 2 de febrero
examen de química

miércoles, 3 de febrero
recoger[a] nuevo permiso de estacionamiento

jueves, 4 de febrero
fecha límite para entregar informe[b] escrito para
historia del arte

viernes, 5 de febrero
prueba[c] de español

sábado, 6 de febrero
hacer llave para apartamento
fiesta de cumpleaños para Rosa

domingo, 7 de febrero

---

[a]*pick up* [b]*test*

Otros sustantivos

el calendario	calendar
el despertador	alarm clock
la llave	key

acordarse (ue) (de)	to remember
entregar	to turn, hand in
estacionar	to park
llegar a tiempo/tarde	to arrive early/late
pedir (i, i) disculpas	to apologize
Discúlpeme.	Pardon me. / I'm sorry.
¡Lo siento (mucho)!	Pardon me! / I'm (very) sorry!
Perdón.	Pardon me. / I'm sorry.
recoger	to collect; to pick up
sacar	to take out
sacar buenas/malas notas	to get good/bad grades
ser (*irreg.*) **flexible**	to be flexible
sufrir	to suffer
sufrir (muchas) presiones	to be under (a lot of) pressure
la calificación	grade
el estrés	stress
el examen	exam
la (falta de) flexibilidad	(lack of) flexibility
la fecha límite	deadline
el horario	schedule
el informe (oral/ escrito)	(oral/written) report
la prueba	quiz; test
la tarjeta de identificación	identification card
el trabajo	job, work; report, (piece of) work
de tiempo completo/parcial	full/part time

Conversación

▲▲▲▲▲▲▲

A. Asociaciones

Paso 1. ¿Qué palabras asocia Ud. con estos verbos? Pueden ser sustantivos, antónimos o sinónimos.

1. estacionar
2. recoger
3. acordarse
4. entregar
5. sacar

Paso 2. ¿Qué palabras y/o situaciones asocia Ud. con los siguientes sustantivos?

1. el calendario
2. el despertador
3. las calificaciones
4. el estrés
5. la fecha límite
6. el horario
7. los informes
8. la llave
9. la tarjeta de identificación

B. Situaciones.
La primera lista que va a leer consta de (*consists of*) preguntas o comentarios hechos por varias personas. La segunda lista incluye las respuestas de otras personas. Decida qué respuesta corresponde a cada comentario. Luego invente un contexto para cada diálogo. ¿Dónde están las personas que hablan? ¿en casa? ¿en una oficina? ¿en clase?

1. —Anoche no me acordé de poner el despertador.
2. —No puede estacionar el coche aquí. No tiene permiso de estacionamiento para esta zona.
3. —¿Sacaste una buena nota en la prueba?
4. —Ramiro no tiene buen aspecto (*doesn't look right*). Creo que algo le causa mucho estrés.
5. —Aquí tiene mi trabajo escrito sobre el Mercado Común.

a. —Pues estoy cansado de buscar estacionamiento por todo el *campus*. Lo voy a dejar aquí.
b. —¿Lo olvidaste otra vez? ¿A qué hora llegaste a la oficina?
c. —Pero la fecha límite era ayer. Es la última vez que acepto un informe suyo (*of yours*) tarde.
d. —Muy buena, pero no la esperaba. No tuve tiempo de estudiar.
e. —Es porque tiene un trabajo de tiempo completo, y también toma tres cursos este semestre.

C. La educación universitaria

Paso 1. Lea lo que dicen Edward James Olmos y Luis Miguel sobre la vida y la educación.

«*Les digo con todo mi corazón*[g], *con toda mi vida. Yo no tengo talento natural. No soy un genio. Pero mis padres a pesar de*[h] *ser tan humildes*[i] *me dieron educación*».

**Edward James Olmos
actor mexicoamericano**

Ellos han logrado[b] **triunfar. ¡Y cada frase que dicen es una lección gratuita**[c] **para el éxito**[d]**!**

«*El destino es una mezcla*[e] *entre la preparación y la suerte*»[f].

Luis Miguel, cantante mexicano

[a]*winners* [b]*han... have achieved* [c]*free* [d]*success* [e]*mix* [f]*luck* [g]*heart* [h]*a... in spite of* [i]*poor*

¿Cree Ud. que tienen razón estos dos artistas? ¿Qué cree Ud. que sea más importante para tener éxito (*be successful*) en la vida, el talento natural o la preparación? ¿Piensa Ud. que está consiguiendo una educación del tipo que ayudó a Olmos y a Luis Miguel? ¿Va a ser suficiente su educación para obtener un buen trabajo en el futuro?

Paso 2. Los años estudiantiles, ¿una época maravillosa? Con frecuencia se oye a las personas mayores hablar de los años universitarios con nostalgia: años de libertad, sin responsabilidades, sin las tensiones propias de la vida laboral y familiar. ¿Ve Ud. así la época universitaria? Con un compañero / una compañera, comenten este tema. Pueden usar las preguntas siguientes como guía (*guide*).

1. ¿Sufren muchas presiones los estudiantes universitarios? ¿Por qué? ¿Qué les causa estrés?
2. ¿Son más divertidos los años universitarios que los años de la escuela secundaria?

3. ¿Le preocupa a Ud. el costo de la matrícula? Para Ud. o para su familia, ¿es difícil pagarla?
4. ¿Piensa Ud. que la vida va a ser mejor después de graduarse en la universidad? ¿Por qué sí o por qué no?

¡La profesora Martínez se levantó con el pie izquierdo!°

con... *on the wrong side of the bed*

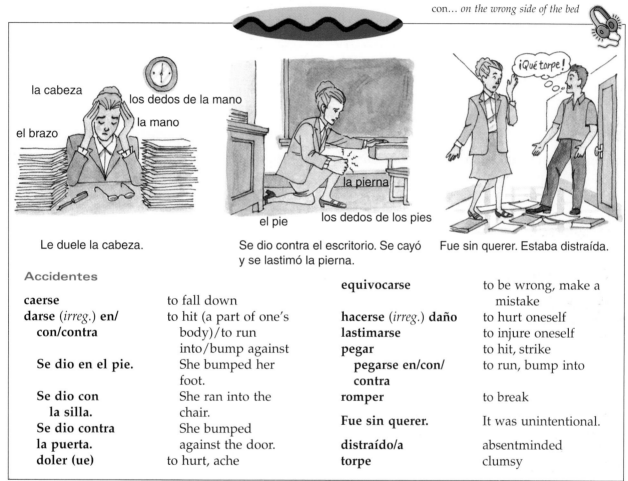

la cabeza
los dedos de la mano
la mano
el brazo

Le duele la cabeza.

la pierna
el pie
los dedos de los pies

Se dio contra el escritorio. Se cayó y se lastimó la pierna.

¡Qué torpe!

Fue sin querer. Estaba distraída.

Accidentes

caerse	to fall down	**equivocarse**	to be wrong, make a mistake
darse (*irreg.*) **en/ con/contra**	to hit (a part of one's body)/to run into/bump against	**hacerse** (*irreg.*) **daño**	to hurt oneself
		lastimarse	to injure oneself
		pegar	to hit, strike
Se dio en el pie.	She bumped her foot.	**pegarse en/con/ contra**	to run, bump into
Se dio con la silla.	She ran into the chair.	**romper**	to break
Se dio contra la puerta.	She bumped against the door.	**Fue sin querer.**	It was unintentional.
doler (ue)	to hurt, ache	**distraído/a**	absentminded
		torpe	clumsy

Conversación

▲▲▲▲▲▲▲▲

A. **Posibilidades.** ¿Qué puede Ud. hacer o decir —o qué le puede pasar— en cada situación?

1. A Ud. le duele mucho la cabeza.
2. Ud. le pega a otra persona sin querer.
3. Ud. se olvida del nombre de otra persona.
4. Ud. está muy distraído/a y no mira por dónde camina.
5. Ud. se lastima la mano (el pie).

B. Accidentes

Un anuncio para un seguro. La palabra **seguro** no sólo significa *sure*. También quiere decir *insurance.* Este es un anuncio de un seguro de accidentes.

SEGURO ESPECIAL ACCIDENTES

Puede ocurrirle esto...

O no ocurrirle nada...

...y suerte que está Asegurado

1. ¿Dónde patina el hombre?
2. ¿Qué le puede ocurrir?
3. ¿Por qué tiene suerte (*good luck*)?
4. ¿Tiene Ud. un seguro de accidentes?

C. Accidentes y tropiezos (*mishaps*)

Paso 1. ¿Le han pasado a Ud. alguna vez las siguientes cosas? Complete las oraciones con información verdadera para Ud. Si nunca le pasó nada de esto, invente una situación que podría haber ocurrido (*could have happened*).

1. Me caí por las escaleras (*stairs*) y _____.
2. No me acordé de hacer la tarea para la clase de _____.
3. Me equivoqué cuando _____.
4. El despertador sonó, pero _____.
5. No pude encontrar _____.
6. Me di con _____ y me lastimé _____.
7. Pasó la fecha límite para entregar un informe y _____.
8. Caminaba un poco distraído/a y _____.

Paso 2. Ahora usando las oraciones del **Paso 1** como guía, pregúntele a un companero / una compañera cómo le fue ayer. También puede preguntarle si le pasaron desastres adicionales.

MODELO: ¿Te caíste por las escaleras ayer? ¿Te hiciste daño?

Nota comunicativa

More on Adverbs

You already know the most common Spanish adverbs: words like **bien/mal, mucho/poco, siempre/nunca...**

    Adverbs that end in *-ly* in English usually end in **-mente** in Spanish. The suffix **-mente** is added to the feminine singular form of adjectives. Note that the accent on the stem word is retained.

Adjective	Adverb	English
rápida	**rápidamente**	*rapidly*
fácil	**fácilmente**	*easily*
paciente	**pacientemente**	*patiently*

D. ¡Seamos (*Let's be*) **lógicos!** Complete estas oraciones lógicamente con adverbios basados en los siguientes adjetivos.

Adjetivos: constante, directo, fácil, inmediato, paciente, posible, puntual, rápido, total, tranquilo

1. La familia está esperando _____ en la cola.
2. Hay examen mañana y tengo que empezar a estudiar _____.
3. ¿Las enchiladas? Se preparan _____.
4. ¿Qué pasa? Estoy _____ confundido/a (*confused*).
5. Cuando mira la tele, mi hermanito cambia el canal _____.
6. Es necesario que las clases empiecen _____.

E. Entrevista. Con un compañero / una compañera, hagan y contesten las siguientes preguntas.

MODELO: E1: ¿Qué haces pacientemente?
        E2: Espero pacientemente a mi esposo cuando se viste para salir. ¡Lo hace muy lentamente (*slowly*)!

1. ¿Qué haces rápidamente?
2. ¿Qué te toca hacer inmediatamente?
3. ¿Qué hiciste (comiste, ...) solamente una vez que te gustó muchísimo (no te gustó nada)?
4. ¿Qué haces tú fácilmente que es difícil para otras personas?
5. ¿Qué hace constantemente tu compañero/a de casa (amigo/a, esposo/a, ...) que te molesta (*bothers*) muchísimo?

Minidiálogos y gramática

33 ▶ Telling How Long Something Has Been Happening or How Long Ago Something Happened • *Hace... que:* Another Use of *hacer*

Las actividades de los Durán

Hace diez años *que* Manolo enseña en la Universidad de Sevilla.

Manolo y Lola se conocieron *hace* quince años.

Hace dos años *que* Marta estudia inglés.

Y Ud., ¿cuánto tiempo hace que estudia español? ¿que asiste a esta universidad? ¿Cuánto tiempo hace que asistió a la escuela secundaria? ¿que conoció a su mejor amigo/a?

- In Spanish, the phrase **hace** + *period of time* + **que** + *present tense* is used to express an action that has been going on over a period of time and is still going on.

  Hace dos horas **que leo**.
  I've been reading for two hours.
  Hace tres años **que vivimos** en esta casa.
  We've been living in this house for three years.

- Use the phrase **¿Cuánto tiempo hace que...?** to ask how long something has been going on. To answer a question posed in this way, it is sufficient to state the period of time.

  —**¿Cuánto tiempo hace que** vives en esta residencia?
  How long have you been living in this dorm?

  —**Dos meses.**
  (For) Two months.

- To say how long *ago* something happened, use the same **hace... que** construction but with the preterite tense instead of the present. Notice also the omission of **que** when the **hace** phrase does not come at the beginning of the sentence.

Hace tres años **que fui** a Bogotá.
I went to Bogotá three years ago.

Fui a Cancún **hace** un mes.
I went to Cancún a month ago.

O
J
O

    The verb form **hace** in this impersonal time construction never varies. However, the verb that accompanies the expression is always conjugated.

Práctica

¿Quién... ?

Paso 1. ¿Quién hace qué? Haga oraciones completas emparejando (*matching*) las personas en la columna A con las acciones correspondientes en la columna B.

MODELO: hace mucho tiempo que / profesor(a) / enseñar español →
Hace mucho tiempo que el profesor / la profesora enseña español.

Hace mucho/poco tiempo que...

A	B
Gloria Estefan	hacen programas para niños
Sammy Sosa	canta en español
Antonio Banderas	habla español
los «Teletubbies»	vive en esta ciudad
John Grisham	escribe novelas
el rector / la rectora (*president*) de la universidad	juega al béisbol
el profesor / la profesora de español	trabaja en esta universidad
un compañero / una compañera de clase	trabaja en Hollywood ¿ ?

Paso 2. ¿Cuánto tiempo hace que pasó lo siguiente? Haga oraciones completas usando las indicaciones que aparecen en la lista. ¿Sabe Ud. todas las respuestas?

MODELO: el primer hombre / llegar a la luna →
Hace casi treinta años que el primer hombre llegó a la luna.

1. Cristóbal Colón / llegar a América
2. la Segunda Guerra Mundial / terminar
3. John Lennon / morirse
4. el presidente actual (el primer ministro) / ser elegido (*to be elected*)
5. el profesor (la profesora) de español / enseñar en esta universidad

Conversación

Entrevista

Paso 1. Find out from a classmate how long he or she has been . . .

1. living in this state
2. attending this university
3. living in his or her house (apartment, dorm, . . .)
4. studying Spanish

Paso 2. Now find out how long ago he or she . . .

1. last visited his or her parents (grandparents, children, . . .)
2. met his or her best friend
3. learned to drive (**manejar**)
4. handed in his or her last major assignment

34 Expressing Unplanned or Unexpected Events • Another Use of *se*

Un día fatal

¡A Diego y a Antonio todo les salió horrible hoy!

A Diego *se le cayó* la taza de café.

También *se le perdió* la cartera.

A Antonio *se le olvidaron* sus libros y su trabajo cuando fue a clase.

También *se le perdieron* las llaves de su apartamento.

¿Le pasaron a Ud. las mismas cosas —o cosas parecidas (*similar*)— esta semana? Conteste, completando las oraciones.

1. Se me perdieron / No se me perdieron las llaves de mi coche/casa.
2. Se me olvidó / No se me olvidó una reunión importante.
3. Se me cayó / No se me cayó una taza de café.
4. Se me rompió / No se me rompió un objeto de mucho valor (*value*) sentimental.

A. Unplanned or unexpected events (*I dropped. . ., We lost. . ., You forgot. . .*) are frequently expressed in Spanish with **se** and a third person form of the verb. In this structure, the occurrence is viewed as happening *to* someone—the unwitting performer of the action. Thus the victim is indicated by an indirect object pronoun, often clarified by **a** + *noun* or *pronoun*. In such sentences, the subject (the thing that is dropped, broken, forgotten, and so on) usually follows the verb.

Se le olvidaron las llaves.
He forgot the keys. (The keys were forgotten by him.)

(*a* + Noun or Pronoun)	*se*	Indirect Object Pronoun	Verb	Subject
(A mí)	Se	me	cayó	la taza de café.
¿(A ti)	Se	te	perdió	la cartera?
A Antonio	se	le	olvidaron	los apuntes.

The verb agrees with the grammatical subject of the Spanish sentence (**la taza, la cartera, los apuntes**), not with the indirect object pronoun. **No** immediately precedes **se**.

A Antonio *no se* le olvidaron los apuntes.
Antonio didn't forget his notes.

B. Here are some verbs frequently used in this construction.

Note: Although all indirect object pronouns can be used in this construction, this section will focus on the singular of first, second, and third persons (**se me... , se te... , se le...**).

acabar	to finish; to run out of
caer	to fall
olvidar	to forget
perder (ie)	to lose
quedar	to remain, be left
romper	to break

Práctica

A. ¡Qué mala memoria! Hortensia sufre muchas presiones en su vida. Por eso cuando se fue de vacaciones al Perú, estaba tan distraída que se le olvidó hacer muchas cosas importantes antes de salir. Empareje (*Match*) los lapsos de Hortensia (esta página) con las consecuencias (en la página 348).

LAPSOS

1. _____ Se le olvidó cerrar la puerta de su casa.
2. _____ Se le olvidó pagar sus cuentas.
3. _____ Se le olvidó pedirle a alguien que cuidara a (*to take care of*) su perro.
4. _____ Se le olvidó cancelar el periódico.
5. _____ Se le olvidó pedirle permiso a su jefa (*boss*).
6. _____ Se le olvidó llevar el pasaporte.
7. _____ Se le olvidó hacer reserva en un hotel.

a. Va a perder el trabajo.
b. No la van a dejar entrar en el Perú.
c. Le van a suspender el servicio de la luz (*electricity*) y de gas… ¡y cancelar sus tarjetas de crédito!
d. Alguien le va a robar el televisor.
e. ¡«King» se va a morir!
f. No va a tener dónde alojarse (*to stay*).
g. Todos van a saber que no está en casa.

B. ¡Desastres por todas partes (*everywhere*)**!**

Paso 1. ¿Es Ud. una persona distraída o torpe? Indique las oraciones que se apliquen (*apply*) a Ud. Puede cambiar algunos de los detalles de las oraciones si es necesario.

1. ☐ Con frecuencia se me caen los libros (los platos, …).
2. ☐ Se me pierden constantemente las llaves (los calcetines, …).
3. ☐ A menudo (*Often*) se me olvida apagar la computadora (la luz, …).
4. ☐ Siempre se me rompen las gafas (las lámparas, …).
5. ☐ De vez en cuando se me quedan los libros (los cuadernos, …) en la clase.
6. ☐ Se me olvida fácilmente mi horario (el teléfono de algún amigo, …).

Paso 2. ¿Es Ud. igual ahora que cuando era más joven? Complete cada oración del **Paso 1** para describir cómo era de niño/a. No se olvide de usar el imperfecto en sus oraciones.

MODELO. De niño/a, (no) se me caían los libros con frecuencia.

Paso 3. Ahora compare sus respuestas con las de un compañero / una compañera. ¿Quién es más distraído/a o torpe ahora? ¿Quién lo era de niño/a?

Conversación

▲▲▲▲▲▲▲

Pablo tuvo un día fatal

Paso 1. Lea la siguiente descripción de lo que le pasó a Pablo ayer. Va a usar los números entre paréntesis en el **Paso 2**.

Pablo no se levantó a las siete, como lo hace generalmente. Se levantó tarde, a las ocho. (1) Se vistió rápidamente y salió de casa descalzo.[a] (2) Entró en el garaje pero no pudo abrir la puerta del coche. (3) Por eso tuvo que llegar a la oficina en autobús, pero cuando quiso pagarle al conductor, no tenía dinero. (4) Por eso tuvo que llegar a pie.

Cuando Pablo por fin entró a la oficina, su jefa se ofendió porque Pablo la trató descortésmente. (5) Su primer cliente se enojó porque Pablo no tenía toda la información necesaria para resolver su caso. (6)

Para las diez de la mañana, Pablo tenía muchísima hambre. (7) Por eso fue a la cafetería a comer algo. Se sentó con el vicepresidente de la compañía. Muy pronto este[b] se levantó furioso de la mesa. (8) Dijo que su chaqueta estaba arruinada. ¡Pablo ya no podía más! También se levantó y regresó a casa.

[a]barefoot [b]the latter

Paso 2. Ahora, con un compañero / una compañera, hagan y contesten preguntas para explicar por qué Pablo lo pasó tan mal ayer. La primera persona debe hacer una pregunta. La segunda persona debe contestar, usando las sugerencias en los dibujos. El número uno está hecho (*done*) para Uds.

MODELO: (1) →
E1: ¿Por qué se levantó tarde Pablo?
E2: Porque se le olvidó poner el despertador.

Frases útiles: Se le olvidó/olvidaron… , Se le perdió/perdieron… , Se le cayó/cayeron… , Se le quedó/quedaron…

En los Estados Unidos y el Canadá...

Ricky Martin

Enrique Martín Morales es el puertorriqueño que todo el mundo[a] conoce como **Ricky Martin**. Nació el día de Nochebuena, 1971, en San Juan, Puerto Rico. Desde niño sabía que quería ser artista. En 1984, cuando tenía solamente 12 años, se presentó a un *casting call* para sustituir a un miembro del famoso grupo juvenil **Menudo**, y ¡ganó el puesto! Se quedó con Menudo hasta 1989, y desde entonces no sólo ha sido[b] cantante sino[c] también actor. Desempeñó un papel[d] en una telenovela en México y otro en el programa norteamericano «**General Hospital**» en 1994.

Ricky Martin

Al talentoso Ricky Martin le gusta todo tipo de música y puede cantar con igual[e] facilidad en inglés como en español. Aunque[f] el español es su lengua materna y siempre cantará[g] en español, le gusta la posibilidad de comunicarse con el público norteamericano también. A finales del siglo[h] XX tuvo tremendo éxito en los Estados Unidos y en el resto del mundo con su álbum «**Livin' La Vida Loca**» y la canción del mismo nombre. Los hispanos no se sorprendieron; ya lo conocían muy bien.

[a]todo... *everybody* [b]ha... *has he been* [c]*but* [d]Desempeñó... *He played a part* [e]*the same* [f]*Although* [g]*he will sing* [h]A... *At the end of the (twentieth) century*

¿Qué se representa?

a.   b.   c.   d.

Empareje cada dibujo con la oración que le corresponde.

1. _____ Le da mil pesetas *para* las revistas.
2. _____ Le da mil pesetas *por* las revistas.
3. _____ Van *por* las montañas.
4. _____ Van *para* las montañas.

You have been using the prepositions **por** and **para** throughout your study of Spanish. Although most of the information in this section will be a review, you will also learn some new uses of **por** and **para**.

Por

The preposition **por** has the following English equivalents.

• *by, by means of*	Vamos **por** avión (tren, barco, …). *We're going by plane (train, ship, . . .).* Nos hablamos **por** teléfono mañana. *We'll talk by (on the) phone tomorrow.*
• *through, along*	Me gusta pasear **por** el parque y **por** la playa. *I like to stroll through the park and along the beach.*
• *during, in* (time of day)	Trabajo **por** la mañana. *I work in the morning.*
• *because of, due to*	Estoy nervioso **por** la entrevista. *I'm nervous because of the interview.*

- *for = in exchange for*

Piden 1.000 dólares **por** el coche.
They're asking $1,000 for the car.

Gracias **por** todo.
Thanks for everything.

- *for = for the sake of, on behalf of*

Lo hago **por** ti.
I'm doing it for you (for your sake).

- *for = duration* (often omitted)

Vivieron allí (**por**) un año.
They lived there for a year.

Por is also used in a number of fixed expressions.

por Dios	for heaven's sake
por ejemplo	for example
por eso	that's why
por favor	please
por fin	finally
por lo general	generally, in general
por lo menos	at least
por primera/ última vez	for the first/ last time
por si acaso	just in case
¡por supuesto!	of course!
por todas partes	everywhere

Para

Although **para** has many English equivalents, including *for*, it always has the underlying purpose of referring to a goal or destination.

- *in order to* + infinitive

Regresaron pronto **para** estudiar.
They returned soon (in order) to study.

Estudian **para** conseguir un buen trabajo.
They're studying (in order) to get a good job.

- *for = destined for, to be given to*

Todo esto es **para** ti.
All this is for you.

Le di un libro **para** su hijo.
I gave her a book for her son.

• *for = by* (deadline, specified future time)	**Para** mañana, estudien **por** y **para**. *For tomorrow, study **por** and **para**.* La composición es **para** el lunes. *The composition is for Monday.*
• *for = toward, in the direction of*	Salió **para** el Ecuador ayer. *She left for Ecuador yesterday.*
• *for = to be used for* **OJO** Compare the example at the right to **un vaso de agua** = *a glass (full) of water.*	El dinero es **para** la matrícula. *The money is for tuition.* Es un vaso **para** agua. *It's a water glass.*
• *for = as compared with others, in relation to others*	**Para** mí, el español es fácil. *For me, Spanish is easy.* **Para** (ser) extranjera, habla muy bien el inglés. *For (being) a foreigner, she speaks English very well.*
• *for = in the employ of*	Trabajan **para** el gobierno. *They work for the government.*

Práctica

▲▲▲▲▲▲

A. **Situaciones.** Escoja una respuesta para cada pregunta o situación. Luego invente un contexto para cada diálogo. ¿Dónde están las personas que hablan? ¿Quiénes son? ¿Por qué dicen lo que dicen?

1. __G__ ¡Huy! Acabo de jugar al basquetbol por dos horas.
2. _____ ¿Por qué quieres que llame a Pili y Adolfo? Nunca están en casa por la noche, sobre todo (*especially*) a estas horas.
3. __E__ ¿No vas a comer nada? ¿Por lo menos un sándwich?
4. _____ ¡Cuánto lo siento, don Javier! Sé que llegué tarde a la cita (*appointment*). No fue mi intención hacerlo esperar.
5. _____ Es imposible que tome el examen hoy, por muchas razones.
6. __D__ ¿No oíste? Juana acaba de tener un accidente horrible.
7. __B__ ¡Pero, papá, quiero ir!
8. __A__ Ay, Mariana, ¿no sabías que hubo un terremoto (*earthquake*)? Murieron más de cien personas.

  a. ¡Por Dios! ¡Qué desgracia!
  b. Te digo que no, por última vez.
  c. No se preocupe. Lo importante es que por fin está aquí.
  d. ¡Por Dios! ¿Qué le pasó?
  e. No, gracias. No tengo mucha hambre y además tengo que salir en seguida.

f. ¿Por ejemplo? Dígame…

g. Ah, por eso tienes tanto calor.

h. Llámalos de todas formas, por si acaso…

B. ¿Por o para? Complete los siguientes diálogos y oraciones con **por** o **para**.

1. Los señores Arana salieron _para_ el Perú ayer. Van _por_ avión, claro, pero luego piensan viajar en coche _por_ todo el país. Van a estar allí _por_ dos meses. Va a ser una experiencia extraordinaria _____ toda la familia.

2. Mi prima Graciela quiere estudiar _para_ (ser) doctora. _Por_ eso trabaja _para_ un médico _por_ la mañana; tiene clases _por_ la tarde.

3. —¿ _por_ qué están Uds. aquí todavía? Yo pensaba que iban a dar un paseo _____ el parque.

   —Íbamos a hacerlo, pero no fuimos _____ la nieve.

4. Este cuadro fue pintado (*was painted*) por Picasso _____ expresar los desastres de la guerra (*war*). _____ muchos críticos de arte, es la obra maestra de este artista.

5. La «Asociación Todo _por_ Ellos» trabaja _____ las personas mayores, _____ ayudarlos cuando lo necesitan. ¿Trabaja Ud. _____ alguna asociación de voluntarios? ¿Qué tuvo que hacer _____ inscribirse (*sign-up*)?

ASOCIACION
TODO
ELLOS
POR

Trabajamos por las personas
mayores que están solas y con
escasos recursos económicos

AYÚDANOS, NO ES POSIBLE SIN TI

Para más información llama al teléfono
907 98 91 15, de 18.00 a 20.00 h.
tardes, martes y viernes

CAJAMADRID, SUC. 1028
C/C 6000854579

TODO POR ELLOS es una asociación
no gubernamental inscrita en el Registro
de Asociaciones del Ministerio del Interior
con el número 160.589

Conversación

▲▲▲▲▲▲▲

Entrevista. Hágale preguntas a su profesor(a) para saber la siguiente información.

1. la tarea para mañana y para la semana que viene
2. lo que hay que estudiar para el próximo examen
3. si para él/ella son interesantes o aburridas las ciencias
4. la opinión que tiene de la pronunciación de Uds., para ser principiantes
5. qué debe hacer Ud. para mejorar su pronunciación del español

▼▼▼▼▼ **Videoteca**

ECUADOR

Minidramas

In this **Minidramas** dialogue, José Miguel encounters a bit of bad luck. Pay close attention to the reactions of Elisa, his mother, and María, his grandmother. Do you think they're angry with him?

F U N C T I O N

apologizing

José Miguel está sentado a la mesa y empieza a pararse.[a]

JOSÉ MIGUEL: Bueno, mamá, aquí están las compras del mercado. (*La bolsa*[b] *se rompe.*)

ELISA: ¡Ay! ¡José Miguel! ¡Se te cayó todo!

JOSÉ MIGUEL: Lo siento, mamá. ¡Fue sin querer!

ELISA: Debes tener más cuidado, hijo.

JOSÉ MIGUEL: Perdóname. Parece que[c] me levanté con el pie izquierdo hoy. ¡Qué lata![d]

ELISA: Ay, no vale la pena molestarte.[e]

MARÍA: Bueno, pero hay algo bueno en todo esto…

ELISA: ¿Qué es?

MARÍA: ¡Que no llevamos una vida aburrida!

[a]*stand up* [b]*paper bag* [c] *Parece… It seems that* [d]¡*Qué… What a drag!*
[e]*no… it's not worth getting upset over*

Un poco más sobre… Elisa Velazco

Elisa Velasco, la escritora de artículos de viaje y de turismo, ya es una figura conocida para Ud. Pero, ¿sabe Ud. de sus otras actividades? Por ejemplo, recientemente se ha interesado[a] en la ecología.

[a]*se… she has become interested*

To read more about the characters from this video, visit the *Puntos de partida* Website at **www.mhhe.com/puntos**

Es cierto que (nuestro[1]) generación (disfrutar[2]) de[a] muchas ventajas comparada con las generaciones (anterior[3]). (Por/Para[4]) ejemplo, la medicina (está/es[5]) muy avanzada: Desde hace[b] muchas décadas (*nosotros: tener[6]*) vacunas[c] (muy/mucho[7]) buenas contra enfermedades que antes (ser[8]) mortales. Además, hoy es más fácil (por/para[9]) los amigos y familiares (ser/estar[10]) en contacto, gracias a los avances tecnológicos.

Sin embargo,[d] nuestra vida es también más complicada (que/de[11]) antes. Ahora (ser[12]) necesario trabajar más. (Por/Para[13]) dar una idea de (este/esto[14]), piense en (todo[15]) las madres que tienen un trabajo de tiempo completo y que también (deber[16]) cuidar a sus niños. O piense en las personas que tienen teléfono en el coche (por/para[17]) hacer negocios en la carretera.[e] Por eso, muchas personas (sufrir[18]) de estrés. Y cuando se sufre de estrés, es mucho más posible (ponerse/ponerte[19]) enfermo y tener accidentes.

¿Es toda (este[20]) actividad necesaria? Quizás[f] todos necesitamos (sentarse/sentarnos[21]) a pensar un poco, y (establecer[22]) un poco de calma en nuestra vida. Los avances científicos deben ser una ayuda (por/para[23]) nosotros, no una fuente[g] de más problemas, ¿verdad?

[a]disfrutar... *to enjoy* [b]Desde... *For* [c]*vaccinations* [d]Sin... *Nevertheless* [e]*highway* [f]*Perhaps* [g]*source*

Comprensión.   Escoja la respuesta más apropiada.

1. Hoy día nuestra vida es (más/menos) complicada que hace un siglo.
2. (Es posible / No es posible) controlar el estrés.
3. Por los avances tecnológicos y científicos, hoy día es posible estar en (más/menos) contacto con nuestra familia.

C. ¡Qué desastre!

Paso 1.   Indique todas las opciones verdaderas para Ud. Haga las modificaciones necesarias de acuerdo con sus experiencias.

Una vez...

1. ☐ se me perdió la tarjeta de identificación de la universidad.
2. ☐ se me cayó un vaso de vino tinto en la ropa.
3. ☐ se me perdieron los lentes de contacto.
4. ☐ se me rompió un objeto caro.
5. ☐ se me quedó en casa un trabajo para la clase.
6. ☐ ¿ ?

Paso 2.   Con un compañero / una compañera, expliquen qué problemas tuvieron Uds. a consecuencia de esos accidentes y cómo los resolvieron (*you solved*).

PANORAMA *cultural*

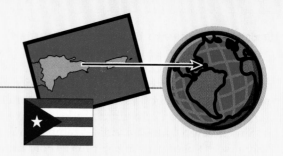

Puerto Rico

Datos esenciales

Nombre oficial: Estado Libre Asociado[a] de
  Puerto Rico
Capital: San Juan
Población: 4.000.000 de habitantes
Moneda: el dólar estadounidense
Idiomas oficiales: el español y el inglés

[a]Estado... *literally, Free Associated State*

Calle en el viejo San Juan

¡Fíjese!

- Puerto Rico ha estado relacionado[a]
  políticamente con los Estados Unidos desde la
  Guerra hispano-norteamericana de 1898, año en
  que España perdió las ultimas colonias de su
  imperio. En 1952, Puerto Rico se convirtió en
  Estado Libre Asociado. Bajo[b] este sistema de
  gobierno, los puertorriqueños son ciudadanos[c]
  estadounidenses. Sin embargo,[d] los que viven
  en la isla no pueden votar por el presidente de
  los Estados Unidos y deben servir en el
  ejército[e] de ese país en caso de guerra.

- Otro nombre de Puerto Rico es Borinquen y
  los puertorriqueños se conocen también

como boricuas. Estas palabras originaron en
el lenguaje de los indios taínos. Los taínos
llegaron a la isla en el siglo[f] XIII pero su
cultura casi desapareció con la llegada de los
españoles en 1493.

- El Parque Nacional del Yunque, ubicado[g] en
  una montaña de 1.065 metros de altura que
  está al noreste de la isla, es pequeño cuando
  se compara a otros bosques[h] nacionales, pero
  es el único bosque tropical del sistema de
  Bosques Nacionales de los Estados Unidos.

[a]ha... *has been associated* [b]*Under* [c]*citizens* [d]Sin... *However*
[e]*army* [f]*century* [g]*located* [h]*forests*

Conozca a... Alonso Ramírez

En 1690 se publica en México la primera novela
del Nuevo Mundo, *Infortunios*[a] *de Alonso Ramírez*. Aunque esta obra[b] se atribuyó al mexicano
Carlos Sigüenza y Góngora, hoy se cree que el
verdadero[c] autor fue el mismo Alonso Ramírez
del título. También se cree que la obra no es ficticia, sino autobiográfica: la vida de un puertorriqueño que se cría[d] en la isla, viaja a México y
tiene aventuras en muchas partes del Mar Pacífico. Sus aventuras incluyen batallas contra piratas, una estadía[e] en una isla desierta y muchos
otros eventos interesantísimos. Es una novela
que vale la pena[f] leer.

[a]*Misfortunes* [b]*work* [c]*real* [d]se... *is brought up* [e]*stay* [f]que...
that is worth the trouble

 Capítulo 11 of the video to accompany
Puntos de partida contains cultural
footage of Puerto Rico.

 Visit the *Puntos de partida* Website at
www.mhhe.com/puntos.

Vocabulario

Los verbos

acabar	to finish; to run out of
acordarse (ue) (de)	to remember
caer (*irreg.*)	to fall
caerse	to fall down
entregar	to turn, hand in
equivocarse	to be wrong, make a mistake
estacionar	to park
quedar	to remain, be left
recoger	to collect; to pick up
romper	to break
sacar	to take out; to get
ser (*irreg.*) flexible	to be flexible
sufrir	to suffer
(muchas) presiones	to be under (a lot of) pressure

Repaso: caminar, doler (ue), llegar a tiempo/tarde olvidarse de

Accidentes

darse (*irreg.*) con	to run, bump into
hacerse (*irreg.*) daño	to hurt oneself
lastimarse	to injure oneself
levantarse con el pie izquierdo	to get up on the wrong side of the bed
pedir (i, i) disculpas	to apologize
pegarse en/contra	to run/bump into
Discúlpeme.	Pardon me. / I'm sorry.
Fue sin querer.	It was unintentional.
¡Lo siento (mucho)!	Pardon me! / I'm (very) sorry!
¡Qué mala suerte!	What bad luck!

Repaso: perdón

Presiones de la vida estudiantil

la calificación	grade
el estrés	stress
la fecha límite	deadline
la (falta de) flexibilidad	(lack of) flexibility
el horario	schedule
el informe (oral/escrito)	(oral/written) report
la nota	grade
la prueba	quiz; test
la tarjeta de identificación	identification card
el trabajo	job, work; report, (piece of) work
de tiempo completo/parcial	full time/part time

Repaso: el examen

Más partes del cuerpo

el brazo	arm
el dedo (de la mano)	finger
el dedo del pie	toe
la pierna	leg

Repaso: la cabeza

Los adjetivos

distraído/a	absentminded
escrito/a	written
flexible	flexible
torpe	clumsy
universitario	(of the) university

Otros sustantivos

el calendario	calendar
el despertador	alarm clock
la llave	key
la luz	light, electricity

Palabras adicionales

hace + *time*	(*time*) ago
hace + *time* + **que...** + *present*	it's been (*time*) since . . .
por Dios	for God's sake
por ejemplo	for example
por lo menos	at least
por primera/ última vez	for the first/last time
por si acaso	just in case
por supuesto	of course
por todas partes	everywhere

Repaso: por eso, por favor, por fin, por lo general, por lo menos

Un paso más 11

LECTURA

Repaso de estrategias: Guessing the Content of a Passage

In previous reading sections, you have learned several different strategies to improve your comprehension of a text. Whenever you can, it's a good idea to utilize as many of these strategies as possible. Of course, this may not always be possible. For example, in the short passages that follow, there is only one visual item that accompanies the text. What else can you rely on to make predictions about the content? One strategy is to identify the source of the passages (see **Sobre la lectura** below). You should also consider the focus of the current chapter. And, of course, the title often reveals a great deal about the content of a passage. Considering all of these sources of information, what do you think these readings will be about?

1. vacation spots in the Spanish-speaking world
2. health-related issues associated with our modern way of life
3. fashion trends in Mexico
4. decorating ideas for your home

If you picked number 2, you were right. The following short passages discuss some of the negative effects that modern life can have on our health.

▶ **Sobre la lectura...** Esta lectura fue recopilada (*compiled*) de varios ejem-
▶ plares (*issues*) de la revista española *GeoMundo*. Como Ud. ya sabe (Capí-
▶ tulo 7), el contenido de esta revista es muy similar al de *National Geographic*.

La vida moderna: ¿Saludable o no?

Pasaje 1

La Organización <u>Mundial</u> de la Salud ha de-terminado[a] que las diez regiones del mundo con mayor <u>incidencia</u> de casos de cáncer en la piel[b] son: Australia, Noruega, Suiza, Dina-marca, Suecia, Escocia, Finlandia, la región francesa de Calvados, Polonia e Italia. En Aus-tralia cerca de 40 de cada 100.000 personas <u>de-sarrollan</u> melanomas malignos, debido[c] prin-cipalmente, afirman los especialistas, al origen

inglés de su población. La piel de los ingleses evolucionó bajo <u>cielos</u> nublados, pero los des-cendientes australianos de los ingleses viven bajo los intensos rayos solares subtropicales.

Actualmente la piel <u>bronceada</u> impresiona a la gente ignorante, y el riesgo de sufrir de cáncer en la piel se ha incrementado[d] por la contaminación y la falta de información. Lo mejor: si es Ud. de piel clara, descanse en la playa debajo de una <u>sombrilla</u>.

[a]ha... *has determined*   [b]*skin*   [c]*due*   [d]se... *has increased*

Pasaje 2

Más del 8% de 15 millones de europeos que trabajan con ordenadores[e] ocho (o seis) horas del día padecen[f] de males <u>oculares</u> por la «fatiga de la pantalla»[g] y los campos[h] magnéticos y electrostáticos producidos por esas <u>máquinas</u>. Han aparecido[i] en París especialistas médicos del «mal[j] del ordenador» que están trabajando rápidamente para encontrar alivio de este mal sufrido por muchos.

Pasaje 3

¿Son los dolores de cabeza, los vahídos[k] y las náuseas los únicos inconvenientes de la inadecuada ventilación en las cabinas de los aviones? Aparentemente no.

Los asistentes de vuelo y muchos viajeros frecuentes se quejan de que a menudo[l] se enferman de gripe[m] después de los vuelos largos. La pobre calidad del aire también puede complicar la bronquitis, el asma, el enfisema y las alergias de los pasajeros. La baja <u>humedad</u> requerida en los aviones <u>agrava</u> estos problemas secando las membranas mucosas y disminuyendo[n] las defensas contra infecciones.

Lo más inquietante[o] es que la pobre ventilación y los asientos estrechamente apiñados[p]

Esta española puede padecer del «mal del ordenador».

pueden conducir a[q] la transmisión de serias enfermedades. ●

[e]computadoras [f]sufren [g]screen [h]fields [i]Han... *Have appeared* [j]*sickness* [k]los... *dizziness* [l]a... *often* [m]*flu* [n]*diminishing* [o]*worrisome* [p]estrechamente... *tightly arranged together* [q]conducir... *lead to*

Comprensión

A. ¿A qué pasaje se refiere? A continuación se presentan tres títulos. En su opinión, ¿qué título mejor le corresponde a cada pasaje de la lectura?

a. _____ Las enfermedades de viaje comienzen en el aire.
b. _____ Los peligros del sol
c. _____ Ojos cansados en el lugar de trabajo

B. Problemas. De los siguientes problemas asociados con el sol, el ordenador y el avión, ¿cuáles *no* se mencionan en la lectura? Indique los problemas no mencionados.

EL SOL

1. el cáncer en la piel
2. los problemas oculares
3. la deshidratación

EL ORDENADOR

1. los problemas con los músculos de las manos
2. los problemas oculares
3. los dolores de cabeza

EL AVIÓN

1. las náuseas
2. los problemas respiratorios
3. el insomnio

ESCRITURA

A. **Resúmenes breves.** Ahora en uno o dos oraciones, resuma (*summarize*) cada uno de los tres pasajes de la lectura. Debe incluir la información más importante de cada uno.

B. **El estrés y los estudiantes.** Aunque las presiones de la vida moderna nos afectan a todos, sin duda (*doubt*) tienen un impacto tremendo en los estudiantes universitarios. Escríbale una carta al editor del periódico local comentando lo que Ud. cree que es la mayor presión para los estudiantes en su universidad. En la carta, debe identificar la causa de la presión, las consecuencias que tiene y algunas soluciones posibles para combatirla.

Puede comenzar su carta así:

Estimado editor: / Estimada editora: ...

CAPÍTULO 12

La calidad de la vida

Este joven de Mirabella, España, hace buen uso de la technología moderna.

¿Qué opina Ud.?

Conteste según su propia vida. ¿Cree Ud. que una persona de otro país diría algo similar? Visite el sitio Web de *Puntos de partida* para leer las respuestas a estas preguntas que da una persona del Perú.

1. ¿Dónde vive Ud.? ¿en una **residencia** estudiantil? ¿en un **apartamento** o una **casa**?
2. ¿Vive Ud. en **el centro** de la ciudad, en **las afueras** o en **el campo**?
3. ¿Dónde vivían sus abuelos de jóvenes?
4. En su opinión, ¿cuál fue la invención más importante de los últimos cien años? ¿el carro? ¿el avión? ¿**el ordenador** o **la red**? ¿**el teléfono**? ¿otra?
5. ¿Qué impacto tiene esa invención en la calidad de la vida de nosotros hoy?

En este capítulo...

- In this chapter, you will study vocabulary related to technology in the home and on the job. You will also be introduced to vocabulary about places to live. Can you guess what **¿Cuál es su dirección?** means?
- You already know how to give formal commands. But how would you warn a younger sibling not to touch your computer? In this chapter, you will learn about both negative and positive informal commands. (Grammar 36)
- This chapter will also introduce the grammatical form that you use to indicate that you want something. (Grammar 37)
- This chapter's **Panorama cultural** section will introduce you to the people and culture of Peru.

P U N T O S   I N T E R A C T I V O

Videoteca

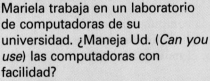

◀ **Minidramas**
José Miguel quiere comprar una computadora. ¿Cuándo compró Ud. su última computadora? ¿Dónde la compró? ¿Cómo hizo las decisiones acerca de la marca (*brand*), la capacidad, etcétera?

En contexto ▶
Mariela trabaja en un laboratorio de computadoras de su universidad. ¿Maneja Ud. (*Can you use*) las computadoras con facilidad?

 CD-ROM

Además de completar el vocabulario y las actividades de gramática, Ud. va a tener la oportunidad de «participar» en la encuesta (*survey*) que hace Mariela sobre el uso de la tecnología.

 Internet

En la sección del Capítulo 12 en el sitio Web de *Puntos de partida* aparecen enlaces que Ud. puede usar para conseguir información en español sobre las nuevas tecnologías. Use la dirección www.mhhe.com/puntos para llegar al sitio Web.

365

Tengo... Necesito... Quiero...

el equipo fotográfico
la cámara

el disco compacto
el equipo estereofónico
la computadora / el ordenador
la cámara de vídeo
la videocasetera
el teléfono celular
la impresora
el walkman
la grabadora
el radio (portátil)
el televisor
la cinta
el control remoto

Los vehículos

la bicicleta (de montaña)	(mountain) bike
el carro / el coche (descapotable)	(convertible) car
el monopatín	skateboard
la moto(cicleta)	motorcycle, moped
los patines	roller skates

La electrónica

el contestador automático	answering machine
el correo electrónico	e-mail
el disco duro	hard drive
la impresora	printer
el ordenador (*Spain*)	computer
el ratón	mouse
la red	net
navegar la red	to surf the net

el teléfono (celular, de coche)	(cellular, car) phone

Cognados

el CD-ROM, la computadora, el disco compacto, el disco de computadora, el fax, la memoria, el módem

Verbos útiles

cambiar (de canal, de cuarto, de ropa...)	to change (channels, rooms, clothing)
conseguir (i, i)	to get, obtain
copiar / hacer copia	to copy
fallar	to "crash" (*a computer*)
funcionar	to work, function (*machines*)
grabar	to record, to tape
guardar	to keep, to save (*documents*)

imprimir	to print	Para poder gastar...	
manejar	to drive; to operate (*a machine*)	el aumento	raise
		el/la jefe/a	boss
obtener (*irreg.*)	to get, obtain	el sueldo	salary
sacar fotos	to take photos		

Conversación

A. Ud. y los aparatos

Paso 1.   ¿Qué se usa en estas situaciones?

1. para mandar copias de documentos no originales que deben llegar inmediatamente
2. para grabar un programa de televisión cuando no podemos verlo a la hora de su emisión
3. para cambiar el programa de la tele sin levantarse del sillón
4. para recibir llamadas telefónicas cuando no estamos en casa
5. para escuchar música mientras hacemos ejercicio

Paso 2.   Con un compañero / una compañera, piensen en cuatro situaciones similares a las del **Paso 1**. La otra persona debe identificar el aparato.

Paso 3.   Para Ud., ¿son ciertas o falsas las siguientes oraciones?

1. Soy una persona que tiene habilidad mecánica. Es decir, entiendo cómo funcionan los aparatos.
2. Aprendí con facilidad a usar la computadora.
3. No me puedo imaginar la vida sin los aparatos electrónicos modernos.
4. Me interesa saber qué vehículo maneja una persona, porque el vehículo es una expresión de la personalidad.
5. Una vez me falló la computadora y perdí unos documentos y archivos (*files*) muy importantes.
6. Uso la videocasetera para ver películas, pero no sé grabar.
7. Me gusta navegar la red porque siempre encuentro lo que busco.

B. ¿Qué vehículos... ?

Paso 1.   ¿Qué vehículo piensa Ud. que deben tener y usar las siguientes personas?

1. una persona joven no convencional y que vive en Sevilla, una ciudad grande en el sur de España
2. una persona joven que vive en Key West, una isla soleada e informal en el sur de Florida
3. una familia con tres hijos
4. un estudiante de una universidad de artes liberales que vive en el *campus*

5. unos chicos que viven en Venice Beach, California, y que pasan gran parte de su tiempo libre en la playa y en el *boardwalk*
6. un matrimonio jubilado (*retired*) que vive en Nueva Inglaterra

Paso 2. ¿Qué vehículo(s) tiene Ud.? ¿Es lo más apropiado para su vida? ¿Por qué? ¿Qué vehículo le gustaría tener?

C. ¿Necesidad o lujo (*luxury*)?

Paso 1. ¿Considera Ud. que las siguientes posesiones son un lujo o una necesidad de la vida moderna? Indique si Ud. tiene este aparato o vehículo.

MODELO: un televisor → Para mí, un televisor es una necesidad. Tengo uno. (No tengo uno ahora.)

1. un contestador automático
2. una videocasetera
3. el equipo estereofónico
4. una computadora
5. un coche
6. una bicicleta
7. un *walkman* (una grabadora)

Paso 2. Ahora dé tres cosas más que Ud. considera necesarias en la vida moderna.

Vocabulario útil

el aviso de llamada, la llamada en espera (*call-waiting*)

la línea de teléfono

el televisor de pantalla (*screen*) **grande**

Paso 3. Para terminar, entreviste a un compañero / una compañera para saber si está de acuerdo con Ud. y si tiene las mismas posesiones.

MODELO: el televisor → E1: ¿El televisor?
E2: Yo lo considero un lujo
y por eso no tengo uno.

La vivienda°

La... *Housing*

La comunidad

el apartamento*	apartment	**el cuarto**	room
el barrio / la vecindad	neighborhood	**el/la dueño/a**	owner; landlord, landlady
la casa	house		

---

*El apartamento is used throughout Latin America and the Caribbean. El departamento is used in Mexico, Peru, and other Latin American countries, but el piso is the word most commonly used in Spain.

el/la inquilino/a	tenant; renter	la dirección	address
el/la portero/a	building manager, doorperson	la planta	floor
		la planta baja	first (ground) floor
la residencia	residence	el piso	floor (of a building)
el/la vecino/a	neighbor	el (primer, segundo) piso	(first, second [*Sp.*: second, third]) floor

El área

las afueras	outskirts, suburbs	la vista	view
la avenida	avenue		
la calle	street	**Los gastos**	
el campo	countryside		
la casa (el bloque) de apartamentos	apartment building	el alquiler	rent
		alquilar	to rent
el centro	(downtown) shopping area	el gas	gas; heat
		la luz (*pl.* luces)	light; electricity

Nota cultural

Los nombres de los pisos de un edificio

En la mayoría de los dialectos del inglés, las frases *ground floor* y *first floor* tienen el mismo significado. En español, hay dos modos de expresar estos conceptos. Aunque ha habido[a] cambios al lenguaje debido a[b] la influencia norteamericana, **la planta baja** es el equivalente más común de *ground floor*, mientras que **el primer piso** se refiere al *second floor* de los anglohablantes.[c] También en español, el segundo piso se refiere al *third floor*, etcétera.

[a]ha... *there have been* [b]debido... *due to* [c]*English speakers*

Conversación

▲▲▲▲▲▲▲

A. A buscar vivienda

Paso 1. Lea los tres anuncios de viviendas en el Perú y conteste las siguientes preguntas.

1. ¿Qué tipo de vivienda se vende en cada anuncio? ¿Son para comprar o alquilar?
2. ¿Cuántos dormitorios tiene cada vivienda?
3. ¿Cree Ud. que estas viviendas son para familias con mucho o poco dinero?

[a]*Partially furnished* [b]sala... *living room; sitting room* [c]*1 ó 2... one- or two-car garage* [d]acabados... *first-class finishing details*

Paso 2. Con un compañero / una compañera, hablen sobre el tipo de vivienda que prefieren.

1. Como estudiante universitario, ¿prefiere vivir en el *campus* o fuera del *campus*? ¿en una residencia o en una casa o apartamento de alquiler con otras personas?
2. ¿Prefiere Ud. vivir en la planta baja o en los pisos más altos?
3. Si Ud. alquila su vivienda, ¿prefiere que el alquiler incluya (*include*) todos los gastos o prefiere pagar la luz y el gas por separado?
4. Si pudiera (*If you could*) escoger, ¿qué le gustaría más, tener un apartamento pequeño en un barrio elegante del centro o una casa grande en las afueras?
5. ¿Qué tipo de vecinos le gusta tener?

B. Definiciones. Dé las definiciones de las siguientes palabras.

MODELO: la residencia →
Es un lugar donde viven muchos estudiantes. Por lo general está situada en el *campus* universitario.

Frases útiles: Es una persona que… Es un lugar donde… Es una cosa que…

1. el inquilino	**3.** el alquiler	**5.** la vecina	**7.** la dirección
2. el centro	**4.** el portero	**6.** la dueña	**8.** las afueras

Minidiálogos y gramática

¿Recuerda Ud.?

In Grammar Section 20 you learned about **Ud.** and **Uds.** commands. Remember that object pronouns (direct, indirect, reflexive) must follow and be attached to affirmative commands; they must precede negative commands.

AFFIRMATIVE:	Háblele Ud.	Duérmase.	Dígaselo Ud.
NEGATIVE:	No le hable Ud.	No se duerma.	No se lo diga Ud.

¿Cómo se dice en español?

1. Bring me the book. (**Uds.**)
2. Don't give it to her. (**Uds.**)
3. Sit here, please. (**Ud.**)
4. Don't sit in that chair! (**Ud.**)
5. Tell them the truth. (**Uds.**)
6. Tell it to them now! (**Uds.**)
7. Never tell it to her. (**Uds.**)
8. Take care of yourself. (**Ud.**)
9. Lead a healthy life. (**Ud.**)
10. Listen to me. (**Ud.**)

Influencing Others • *Tú* Commands

¡Marta, tu cuarto es un desastre!

«¡Marta, qué desordenado está tu cuarto! Por favor, *arréglalo* antes de jugar con tus amigos. *Guarda* la ropa limpia en tu armario, *pon* la ropa sucia en el cesto, *haz* la cama, *recoge* los libros del piso y *ordénalos* en los estantes… Y no *dejes* los zapatos por todas partes… ¡Es muy peligroso!»

¿Quién diría (*would say*) lo siguiente, Marta o Manolo, su padre?

1. No te enojes… Ya voy a arreglarlo todo.
2. Hazlo inmediatamente… ¡antes de salir a jugar!
3. Dime, ¿por qué tengo que hacerlo ahora mismo?
4. La próxima vez, ¡no dejes tu cuarto en tales condiciones!

Informal commands (**los mandatos informales**) are used with persons whom you would address as **tú**.

▲▲▲▲▲

Negative *tú* Commands

-ar verbs		*-er/-ir* verbs	
No hables.	Don't speak.	**No comas.**	Don't eat.
No cantes.	Don't sing.	**No escribas.**	Don't write.
No juegues.	Don't play.	**No pidas.**	Don't order.

A. Like **Ud.** commands (Grammar Section 20), the negative **tú** commands are expressed using the "opposite vowel": **no hable Ud., no hables (tú)**. The pronoun **tú** is used only for emphasis.

No cantes **tú** tan fuerte.
*Don't **you** sing so loudly.*

Marta, your room is a disaster! "Marta, what a messy room you have! Please straighten it up before you go out to play with your friends. Put your clean clothes away in the closet, put your dirty clothes in the hamper, make your bed, pick your books up from the floor and arrange them on the shelves… And don't leave your shoes lying around everywhere… It's very dangerous!"

B. As with negative **Ud.** commands, object pronouns—direct, indirect, and reflexive—precede negative **tú** commands.

No lo mires.
Don't look at him.

No les escribas.
Don't write to them.

No te levantes.
Don't get up.

Affirmative *tú* Commands

-ar verbs		*-er/-ir* verbs	
Habla.	*Speak.*	**Come.**	*Eat.*
Canta.	*Sing.*	**Escribe.**	*Write.*
Juega.	*Play.*	**Pide.**	*Order.*

A. Unlike the other command forms you have learned, most affirmative **tú** commands have the same form as the third person singular of the present indicative.* Some verbs have irregular affirmative **tú** command forms.

decir:	**di**	salir:	**sal**
hacer:	**haz**	ser:	**sé**
ir:	**ve**	tener:	**ten**
poner:	**pon**	venir:	**ven**

Spelling Hint: One-syllable words, like the affirmative **tú** commands of some verbs (**decir, ir, tener, ...**) do not need an accent mark: **di, ve, ten, ...** Exceptions to this rule are those forms that could be mistaken for other words, like the command of **ser** (**sé**), which could be mistaken for the pronoun **se**.

Sé puntual pero **ten** cuidado.
Be there on time, but be careful.

The affirmative **tú** commands for **ir** and **ver** are identical: **ve.** Context will clarify meaning.

¡**Ve** esa película!
See that movie!

Ve a casa ahora mismo.
Go home right now.

---

*As you know, there are two different *moods* in Spanish: the *indicative mood* (the one you have been working with, which is used to state facts and ask questions) and the *subjunctive mood* (which is used to express more subjective actions or states). Beginning with Grammar Section 37, you will learn more about the subjunctive mood.

B. As with affirmative **Ud.** commands, object and reflexive pronouns follow affirmative **tú** commands and are attached to them. Accent marks are necessary except when a single pronoun is added to a one-syllable command.

Dile la verdad.
Tell him the truth.

Léela, por favor.
Read it, please.

Póntelos.
Put them on.

Nota comunicativa

In **Capítulo 1**, you learned about the pronoun **vosotros/vosotras** that is used in Spain as the plural of **tú**. Here is information about forming **vosotros** commands, for recognition only.

- Affirmative **vosotros** commands are formed by substituting **-d** for the final **-r** of the infinitive. There are no irregular affirmative **vosotros** commands.

  hablar → hablad
  comer → comed
  escribir → escribid

- Negative **vosotros** commands are expressed with the present subjunctive. (You will learn more about the present subjunctive in the next and subsequent grammar sections.)

  no habléis
  no comáis
  no escribáis

- Placement of object pronouns is the same as for all other command forms.

  Decídmelo.
  No me lo digáis.

Práctica

▲▲▲▲▲

A. Recuerdos de la niñez

Paso 1. Indique los mandatos afirmativos que Ud. oía con frecuencia cuando era niño/a. Después de leerlos todos, indique los dos que oía más. ¿Hay entre estos algún mandato que Ud. no oyó nunca?

1. _____ Limpia tu cuarto.
2. _____ Cómete el desayuno.
3. _____ Haz la tarea.
4. _____ Cierra la puerta.
5. _____ Bébete la leche.
6. _____ Lávate las manos.
7. _____ Dime la verdad.
8. _____ Quítate el *walkman*.
9. _____ Guarda tu bicicleta en el garaje.

OJO

Note in **Práctica A** the use of the reflexive pronoun with the verbs **comer** and **beber**. This use of the reflexive means *to eat up* and *to drink up*, respectively.

Cómete las zanahorias.
Eat up your carrots.

No **te bebas** la leche tan rápido.
Don't drink up your milk so fast.

Paso 2. Ahora indique los mandatos negativos que escuchaba con frecuencia. Debe indicar también los dos que oía más. ¿Hay alguno que no oyó nunca?

1. _____ No cruces la calle solo/a.
2. _____ No juegues con cerillas (*matches*).
3. _____ No comas dulces antes de cenar.
4. _____ No me digas mentiras (*lies*).
5. _____ No les des tanta comida a los peces.
6. _____ No hables con desconocidos.
7. _____ No dejes el monopatín en el jardín.
8. _____ No cambies los canales tanto.
9. _____ No digas tonterías (*silly things*).

B. Julita, la mal educada

Paso 1. Los señores Villarreal no están contentos con el comportamiento de su hija Julita. Continúe los comentarios de ellos con mandatos informales lógicos según cada situación. Siga los modelos.

MODELOS: *Hablaste* demasiado ayer. → No *hables* tanto hoy, por favor.
Dejaste tu ropa en el suelo anoche. → No la *dejes* allí hoy, por favor.

1. También *dejaste* tus libros en el suelo.
2. ¿Por qué *regresaste* tarde a casa hoy después de las clases?
3. ¿Por qué *vas* al parque todas las tardes?
4. No es bueno que *mires* la televisión constantemente. ¿Y por qué quieres *ver* todos esos programas de detectives?
5. ¿Por qué le *dices* mentiras a tu papá?
6. Siempre *te olvidas* de sacar la basura, que es la única tarea que tienes que hacer.
7. Ay, hija, no te comprendemos. ¡*Eres* tan insolente!

Paso 2. La pobre Julita también escucha muchos mandatos de su maestra en clase. Invente Ud. esos mandatos según las indicaciones.

1. llegar / a / escuela / puntualmente
2. quitarse / abrigo / y / sentarse
3. sacar / libro de matemáticas / y / abrirlo / en / página diez
4. leer / nuevo / palabras / y / aprenderlas / para mañana
5. venir / aquí / a / hablar conmigo / sobre / este / composición

Conversación
▲▲▲▲▲▲▲▲

A. Situaciones.
¿Qué consejos les daría (*would you give*) a las siguientes personas si fueran (*if they were*) sus amigos? Déles a todos consejos en forma de mandatos informales.

1. A Celia le encanta ir al cine, especialmente los viernes por la noche. Pero a su novio no le gusta salir mucho los viernes. Él siempre está muy cansado después de una larga semana de trabajo. Celia, en cambio (*on the other hand*), tiene mucha energía.
2. Nati tiene 19 años. El próximo año quiere vivir en un apartamento con cuatro amigos. Para ella es una situación ideal: un apartamento ecónomico en un barrio estudiantil y unos buenos amigos (dos de

ellos son hombres). Pero los padres de Nati son muy tradicionales y no les va a gustar la situación.

3. Su abuelo va a comprarse su primera computadora y necesita su opinión y experiencia. Tiene muchas preguntas, desde qué tipo debe comprar hasta cómo usarla eficientemente. Él quiere una computadora para conectarse con unos amigos jubilados (*retired*) que ahora viven en otro estado, para navegar la red y para realizar el sueño de su vida: escribir la historia de la llegada de sus padres a este país.

4. Mariana es una *yuppi*. Gana muchísimo dinero pero trabaja demasiado. Nunca tiene tiempo para nada. Duerme poco y bebe muchísimo café para seguir despierta (*awake*). No come bien y jamás hace ejercicio. Acaba de comprarse un teléfono celular para poder trabajar mientras maneja a la oficina.

B. Entre compañeros de casa. En su opinión, ¿cuáles son los cinco mandatos que se oyen con más frecuencia en su casa (apartamento, residencia)? Piense no sólo en los mandatos que Ud. escucha sino (*but*) también en los que Ud. les da a los demás (*others*).

Frases útiles: poner la tele, sacar la basura, apagar la computadora, prestarme dinero, contestar el teléfono, no hacer ruido, lavar los platos, ¿ ?

Frase útil: no seas... impaciente, así, pesado/a (*a pain*), precipitado/a (*hasty*), loco, impulsivo/a, bobo/a (*dumb*)

En los Estados Unidos y el Canadá...

Cristina Saralegui

¿Es posible combinar una carrera exitosa[a] con una vida familiar? **Cristina Saralegui** cree que sí, definitivamente. Saralegui es **anfitriona** de **«Cristina»**, el programa de entrevistas más popular de la televisión en español de los Estados Unidos. También es **jefa de redacción**[b] de *Cristina—La revista*, una revista para mujeres. Y como si eso fuera poco,[c] también tiene un **programa de radio diario**, «Cristina opina». Además de tener una carrera absorbente, Saralegui es **madre y esposa** y lleva una vida familiar llena de amor y cariño.

Cristina Saralegui

¿Cómo lo hace? Ante todo, ella es **una persona muy inteligente, disciplinada y organizada**. Además, tiene en **su esposo** un compañero exitoso en el mundo de los negocios[d] que también **comparte**[e] **con ella todas las obligaciones familiares**, tanto las que tradicionalmente le tocan a la madre como las que le tocan al padre. Ellos han forjado[f] una relación basada en la igualdad, el respeto y el apoyo[g] mutuo. Y ella también pasa mucho tiempo en casa con su familia. Con excepción de la filmación de «Cristina», ¡hace casi todo su trabajo desde allí!

[a]*successful* [b]*jefa... editor-in-chief* [c]*como... as if that weren't enough* [d]*business* [e]*shares* [f]*han... have established* [g]*support*

Una decisión importante

JOSÉ MIGUEL: Quiero comprar una computadora, pero no sé cuál. *No creo que sea* una decisión fácil de tomar.

GUSTAVO: Pues, yo sé bastante de computadoras. Te puedo hacer algunas recomendaciones.

JOSÉ MIGUEL: Bueno, te escucho.

GUSTAVO: Primero, *es buena idea que sepas* para qué quieres una computadora. ¿Quieres navegar por el *Internet*? Entonces, *te sugiero que busques* una computadora con módem y con memoria suficiente para hacerlo. Luego, *quiero que hables* con otras personas que ya manejan computadoras. Y por último, *te aconsejo que vayas* a varias tiendas para comparar precios.

JOSÉ MIGUEL: Bueno, *me alegro de que sepas* tanto de computadoras. ¡Ahora *quiero que vayas* conmigo a las tiendas!

Comprensión: ¿Cierto, falso o no lo dice?

1. José Miguel quiere que Gustavo le compre una computadora.
2. Gustavo le recomienda a José Miguel que aprenda algo sobre computadoras antes de comprarse una.
3. Gustavo no cree que José Miguel tenga suficiente dinero.
4. José Miguel se alegra de que Gustavo esté tan informado sobre computadoras.

Present Subjunctive: An Introduction

A. Except for command forms, all the verb forms you have learned so far in *Puntos de partida* are part of the *indicative mood* (**el modo indicativo**). In both English and Spanish, the indicative is used to state facts and to ask questions; it objectively expresses actions or states of being that are considered true by the speaker.

INDICATIVE:

¿Puedes venir a la fiesta?
Can you come to the party?

Prefiero llegar temprano a casa.
I prefer getting home early.

An important decision JOSÉ MIGUEL: I want to buy a computer, but I don't know which one. I don't think it's an easy decision to make. GUSTAVO: Well, I know quite a bit about computers. I can give you some recommendations. JOSÉ MIGUEL: OK, I'm listening. GUSTAVO: First, it's a good idea for you to know why you want a computer. Do you want to get on the Internet? Then I suggest that you look for a computer with a modem and enough memory to do it. Then I want you to talk with other people who already work with computers. And finally, I suggest you go to various stores to compare prices. JOSÉ MIGUEL: Well, I'm glad you know so much about computers. Now I want you to go to the stores with me!

B. Both English and Spanish have another verb system called the *subjunctive mood* (**el modo subjuntivo**). The subjunctive is used to express more subjective or conceptualized actions or states. These include things that the speaker wants to happen or wants others to do, events to which the speaker reacts emotionally, things that are as yet unknown, and so on.

SUBJUNCTIVE:

Espero que **puedas** venir a la fiesta.
I hope (that) you can come to the party.

Prefiero que **llegues** temprano a casa.
I prefer that you be home early.

C. Sentences in English and Spanish may be simple or complex. A simple sentence is one that contains a single verb.

Complex sentences are comprised of two or more *clauses* (**las cláusulas**). There are two types of clauses: main (independent) clause and subordinate (dependent) clause. *Independent clauses* (**las cláusulas principales**) contain a complete thought and can stand alone. *Dependent clauses* (**las cláusulas subordinadas**) contain an incomplete thought and cannot stand alone. Dependent clauses require an independent clause to form a complete sentence.

Note in the indicative example above that when there is no change of subject in the sentence, the infinitive is used in the subordinate clause.

However, when the two subjects of a complex sentence are different, the subjunctive is often used in the subordinate clause in Spanish. Note that subordinate clauses are linked by the conjunction **que**, which is never optional (as it is in English).

Quiero pan.
I want bread.

INDICATIVE

MAIN CLAUSE	SUBORDINATE CLAUSE
Quiero	comprar pan.
I want	*to buy bread.*

SUBJUNCTIVE

MAIN CLAUSE	SUBORDINATE CLAUSE	
Quiere	**que**	compres pan.
She wants	*(for)*	*you to buy bread.*
Espero	**que**	me visites pronto.
I hope	*(that)*	*you visit me soon.*
¿Dudas	**que**	puedan venir?
Do you doubt	*(that)*	*they can come?*

D. Three of the most common uses of the subjunctive are to express influence, emotion, and doubt or denial. These are signaled in the previous examples by the verb forms **quiere**, **espero**, and **dudas**.

Forms of the Present Subjunctive

You already know that many Spanish command forms are part of the subjunctive. The **Ud./Uds.** command forms are shaded in the box on the following page. What you have already learned about forming **Ud.** and **Uds.** commands will help you learn the forms of the present subjunctive.

	hablar	comer	escribir	volver	decir
Singular	hable	coma	escriba	vuelva	diga
	hables	comas	escribas	vuelvas	digas
	hable	coma	escriba	vuelva	diga
Plural	hablemos	comamos	escribamos	volvamos	digamos
	habléis	comáis	escribáis	volváis	digáis
	hablen	coman	escriban	vuelvan	digan

A. The personal endings of the present subjunctive are added to the first person singular of the present indicative minus its **-o** ending. **-Ar** verbs add endings with **-e**, and **-er/-ir** verbs add endings with **-a**.

-ar ⟶ -e
-er/-ir ⟶ -a

present tense **yo** stem = present subjunctive stem

B. Verbs ending in **-car, -gar,** and **-zar** have a spelling change in all persons of the present subjunctive, in order to preserve the **-c-, -g-,** and **-z-** sounds.

-car: c ⟶ qu
-gar: g ⟶ gu
-zar: z ⟶ c

buscar: bus**que**, bus**que**s, ...
pagar: pa**gue**, pa**gue**s, ...
empezar: empie**ce**, empie**ce**s, ...

C. Verbs with irregular **yo** forms show the irregularity in all persons of the present subjunctive.

conocer:	**conozca,** ...	salir:	**salga,** ...
decir:	**diga,** ...	tener:	**tenga,** ...
hacer:	**haga,** ...	traer:	**traiga,** ...
oír:	**oiga,** ...	venir:	**venga,** ...
poner:	**ponga,** ...	ver:	**vea,** ...

D. A few verbs have irregular present subjunctive forms.

dar:	**dé, des, dé, demos, deis, den**
estar:	**esté,** ...
haber (hay):	**haya**
ir:	**vaya,** ...
saber:	**sepa,** ...
ser:	**sea,** ...

E. **-Ar** and **-er** stem-changing verbs follow the stem-changing pattern of the present indicative.

pensar (ie): **pie**nse, **pie**nses, **pie**nse, pensemos, penséis, **pie**nsen

poder (ue): **pue**da, **pue**das, **pue**da, podamos, podáis, **pue**dan

---

F. **-Ir** stem-changing verbs show a stem change in the four forms that have a change in the present indicative. In addition, however, they show a second stem change in the **nosotros** and **vosotros** forms, similar to the present progressive tense.

-ir stem-changing verbs
(**nosotros** and **vosotros**):
o → u
e → i

dormir (ue, u): **due**rma, **due**rmas, **due**rma, **du**rmamos, **du**rmáis, **due**rman

pedir (i, i): **pi**da, **pi**das, **pi**da, **pi**damos, **pi**dáis, **pi**dan

preferir (ie, i): **prefie**ra, **prefie**ras, **prefie**ra, **prefi**ramos, **prefi**ráis, **prefie**ran

Práctica

A. La vida tecnológica. Indique si está de acuerdo o no con las siguientes oraciones.

1. En la vida actual es absolutamente necesario tener una computadora.
2. Yo quiero comprarme una computadora nueva, pero no creo que pueda comprármela inmediatamente.
3. Hoy día (*These days*) es posible comprar una buena computadora portátil por $1.000.
4. Es horrible que la tecnología cambie tan rápidamente; nadie puede aprender a este ritmo.
5. Prefiero que la gente no dependa tanto de la tecnología.
6. Es ridículo que tantas personas usen un teléfono celular.
7. Dudo que el precio de las llamadas de los teléfonos celulares baje más en los próximos dos años.
8. Espero que mi compañero/a de casa (esposo/a, hijo/a) cambie el mensaje del contestador automático.

B. Su trabajo actual. Use frases de la lista (página 380) para completar las oraciones de modo (*in such a way*) que se refieran a su situación laboral actual. (Siempre hay más de una respuesta posible.) Si Ud. no trabaja ahora, no importa. ¡Invéntese una respuesta!

1. El jefe quiere que _____.
2. También espera que _____.
3. Y duda que _____.
4. Prohíbe (*He forbids*) que _____.
5. En el trabajo, es importante que _____.
6. Yo espero que _____.

a. a veces trabajemos los fines de semana
b. todos lleguemos a tiempo
c. hablemos por teléfono con los amigos
d. me den un aumento de sueldo
e. nos paguen más a todos
f. no usemos el *fax* para asuntos (*matters*) personales
g. me den un trabajo de tiempo completo algún día
h. no perdamos mucho tiempo charlando (*chatting*) con los demás
i. fumemos en la oficina
j. ¿ ?

Conversación

A. ¿Puede Ud. substituir en la ausencia de su profesor(a)? Demuéstrele a su profesor(a) que Ud. lo/la conoce bien, formando oraciones como las que dice él/ella en clase. (Sólo tiene que cambiar el infinitivo.)

Quiero que	(nombre de un[a] estudiante)	estudiar
Espero que	todos Uds.	llegar a tiempo
Prohíbo (*I forbid*) que	nadie	copiar en un examen
Dudo que	alguien de la clase	saber el subjuntivo
Es necesario que	yo	sacar notas mejores
Me alegro de que		entender esto
No creo que		navegar por la red
Recomiendo que		dormirse
		hacer la tarea
		¿ ?

B. Consejos para comprar y usar la tecnología de multimedia

Paso 1. Complete el siguiente párrafo según su opinión y sus conocimientos (*knowledge*). En el primer espacio en blanco, use el subjuntivo del verbo entre paréntesis.

Recomiendo que...

> MODELO: _____ (encontrar) _____ para ayudarlo/la a montar (*set up*) la computadora porque... → *encuentre un experto* para ayudarlo/la a montar la computadora porque *es muy difícil.*

1. _____ (ir) a _____ para comprar la computadora porque...
2. _____ (comprar) _____ [marca y modelo de computadora] porque...
3. _____ (mirar) las revistas especializadas, como _____ [nombre de revista] porque...
4. no _____ (pagar) más de $ _____ porque...
5. no _____ (usar) el *software* _____ [marca o tipo] de *software* porque...
6. _____ (asegurarse [*to make sure*]) de que la computadora tenga _____ porque...
7. _____ (poner) la computadora en _____ [lugar] porque...

Paso 2. Compare sus respuestas con las de algunos compañeros para ver si están de acuerdo. ¿Quién sabe más del tema en la clase?

1.

2.

3.

Escoja la oración que describa cada dibujo.

1. _____

   a. Quiero repasar las formas del subjuntivo.
   b. Quiero que nosotros repasemos juntos las formas del subjuntivo.

2. _____

   a. Insisto en hablar con Jorge.
   b. Insisto en que tú hables con Jorge.

3. _____

   a. Es necesario arreglar esta habitación.
   b. Es necesario que tú arregles esta habitación.

▲▲▲▲▲

A. So far, you have learned to identify the subjunctive by the features listed at the right.

The subjunctive

- appears in a subordinate (dependent) clause.
- has a different subject from the one in the main (independent) clause.
- is preceded by **que**.

B. In addition, the use of the subjunctive is associated with the presence of a number of concepts or conditions that trigger the use of it in the dependent clause. The concept of influence is one trigger for the subjunctive in a dependent clause. When the speaker wants something to happen, he or she tries to influence the behavior of others, as in these sentences.

MAIN (INDEPENDENT) CLAUSE	SUBORDINATE (DEPENDENT) CLAUSE
Yo **quiero**	**que** tú **pagues** la cuenta.
I want	*you to pay the bill.*
La profesora **prefiere**	**que** los estudiantes no **lleguen** tarde.
The professor prefers	*that the students don't arrive late*

The verb in the main clause is, of course, in the indicative, because it is a fact that the subject of the sentence wants something. The subjunctive occurs in the dependent clause.

	STRONG	SOFT
C. **Querer** and **preferir** are not the only verbs that can express the main subject's desire to influence what someone else thinks or does. There are many other verbs of influence, some very strong and direct, some very soft and polite.	insistir en mandar permitir (*to permit*) prohibir (prohíbo)	desear pedir (i, i) recomendar (ie) sugerir (ie, i)
D. An impersonal generalization of influence or volition can also be the main clause that triggers the subjunctive. Some examples of this appear at the right.	Es necesario que… Es urgente que…	Es importante que… Es mejor que…

Práctica

▲▲▲▲▲▲▲

A. **En la tienda de aparatos electrónicos.** Imagine que Ud. y un amigo / una amiga están en una tienda de aparatos electrónicos. Ud. quiere comprarse un estéreo pero no sabe cuál; por eso su amigo/a lo/la acompaña. ¿Quién dice las siguientes oraciones, Ud., su amigo/a o el vendedor (*salesperson*)?

1. Prefiero que busques un estéreo en varias tiendas; así puedes comparar precios.
2. Quiero que el estéreo tenga disco compacto con control remoto.
3. Recomiendo que no le digas cuánto dinero quieres gastar.
4. Insisto en que Ud. vea este modelo. ¡Es lo último!
5. Prefiero que me muestre otro modelo más barato.
6. Es mejor que vaya a buscar en otra tienda. No tengo tanto dinero.
7. Quiero que lo sepa: Este estéreo es el mejor de todos.

B. **Expectativas de la educación**

Paso 1. ¿Qué expectativas de la educación tienen los profesores, los estudiantes y los padres de los estudiantes? Forme oraciones según las indicaciones y añada (*add*) palabras cuando sea necesario.

1. todos / profesores / querer / que / estudiantes / llegar / clase / a tiempo
2. profesor(a) de / español / preferir / que / (nosotros) ir / con frecuencia / laboratorio de lenguas
3. profesores / prohibir / que / estudiantes / traer / comida / y / bebida / clase
4. padres / de / estudiantes / desear / que / hijos / asistir a / clases
5. estudiantes / pedir / que / profesores / no dar / mucho / trabajo
6. también / (ellos) querer / que / haber / más vacaciones
7. padres / insistir en / que / hijos / sacar / buenas / notas

Paso 2. Y Ud., ¿qué quiere que hagan los profesores? Invente tres oraciones más para indicar sus deseos.

C. El día de la mudanza (*moving*). Imagine que Ud., su esposo/a y sus hijos acaban de llegar, con todas sus cosas, a un nuevo apartamento. ¿Dónde quieren Uds. que se pongan los siguientes muebles? Siga el modelo. Luego explique por qué quiere que cada cosa esté en el sitio indicado. Empiece la primera oración con frases como: **Queremos que… , Preferimos que… , Es necesario que… , Es buena idea que…** Use el verbo **gustar** en la segunda oración.

MODELO: LOS MUEBLES   LA EXPLICACIÓN
los trofeos de Julio / la sala   mirarlos todos los días →

Queremos que los trofeos de Julio estén en la sala. ¡Nos gusta mirarlos todos los días!

LOS MUEBLES	LA EXPLICACIÓN
1. el nuevo televisor / la sala	ver la tele todos juntos
2. el televisor portátil / la cocina	ver la tele al cocinar (*while cooking*)
3. el equipo estereofónico / la alcoba de Julio	escuchar música al estudiar
4. el sillón grande / la sala	leer el periódico allí
5. los monopatines de los niños / la patio	jugar allí
6. la computadora / la oficina	hacer las cuentas allí
7. el acuario / la alcoba de Anita	mirar los peces

Conversación

A. Hablan los expertos en tecnología. Imagine que Ud. y sus compañeros de clase son un equipo (*team*) de expertos en problemas relacionados con la tecnología y que juntos (*together*) tienen un programa de radio.

Paso 1. Como miembro del equipo, lea las preguntas que les han mandado (*have sent*) los radioyentes (*radio audience*) por correo electrónico y déles una solución. Es bueno incluir frases como «Le recomiendo/sugiero que…», «Es importante/necesario/urgente que… »

1. Soy una joven de 20 años y soy extremadamente tímida. Por eso no me gusta salir. Prefiero asumir otra personalidad al conectarme en la red. Así estoy feliz por horas. Mi madre dice que esto no es normal y me pide que deje de hacerlo. Ella insiste en que vaya a las discotecas como otros jóvenes de mi edad. ¿Qué piensan Uds.?

2. Mi marido es un hombre muy bueno y trabajador. Tiene un buen trabajo, y es una persona muy respetada en su compañía. El problema es que sólo piensa en *software* y multimedia. Pasa todo su tiempo libre delante de la computadora o leyendo catálogos y revistas sobre computadoras. Yo prefiero que él pase más tiempo conmigo. En realidad (*In fact*), estoy tan aburrida que estoy pensando en dejarlo. ¿Qué recomiendan que haga?

3. Mi jefe quiere que deje de usar mi máquina de escribir (*typewriter*) y empiece a usar una computadora. Pero, no quiero hacerlo: Siempre he hecho bien mi trabajo sin la «caja boba» (*stupid box*). Mi jefe dice que tengo que ponerme al día (*up-to-date*) y me sugiere que tome un curso de computadoras que él promete pagar. Yo no entiendo por qué tengo que cambiar. ¿Me aconsejan (*do you advise*) que hable con un abogado/una abogada (*lawyer*)?

Paso 2. Ahora piense en un problema que se relacione con la tecnología que sea similar a los del **Paso 1**, y escríbalo. El resto de la clase le va a hacer sugerencias de cómo resolverlo.

B. Entrevista

Paso 1. Complete las siguientes oraciones lógicamente... ¡y con sinceridad!

1. Mis padres (hijos, abuelos, ...) insisten en que (yo) _____.
2. Mi mejor amigo/a (esposo/a, novio/a, ...) desea que (yo) _____.
3. Prefiero que mis amigos _____.
4. No quiero que mis amigos _____.
5. Es urgente que (yo) _____.
6. Es necesario que mi mejor amigo/a (esposo/a, novio/a, ...) _____.

Paso 2. Ahora entreviste a un compañero / una compañera para saber cómo él/ella completó las oraciones del **Paso 1**.

MODELO: ¿En qué insisten tus padres?

ECUADOR

Videoteca

Minidramas

In this **Minidramas** dialogue, José Miguel and his friend Gustavo go shopping for a computer in an electronics store in Quito, Ecuador. Pay close attention to the following: Who wants to buy the computer? What are some of the details about the computers they're looking at?

FUNCTION

shopping

José Miguel y Gustavo están en una tienda de aparatos electrónicos.

VENDEDORA:[a] Buenas tardes. ¿En qué les puedo atender?

JOSÉ MIGUEL: Buenas tardes. Leímos su anuncio en el periódico. Quisiéramos[b] ver las computadoras.

VENDEDORA: ¿Qué modelo buscan? Tenemos varios aquí. Este es nuevo. Viene con monitor, ratón ergonómico y un módem interno.

JOSÉ MIGUEL: Pero, no tiene lector[c] de CD-ROM interno, ¿verdad? Prefiero uno que lo tenga.

VENDEDORA: Ese modelo allí tiene lector de CD-ROM interno. Venga. Esta es la mejor de las que tienen CD-ROM.

JOSÉ MIGUEL: ¿Qué te parece, Gustavo?

[a]*Saleswoman* [b]*We would like* [c]*reader*

GUSTAVO: No está mal... ¿Tiene suficiente memoria para navegar por el *Internet*?

VENDEDORA: Sí.

GUSTAVO: ¿Y se puede utilizar también un *browser* de páginas o programas de multimedia?

VENDEDORA: Este modelo es ideal para multimedia. Y lleva incluidos los programas necesarios para navegar la red.

JOSÉ MIGUEL: Ah, muy bien, porque pienso utilizar el *Internet* para ayudarme con mis trabajos en la universidad...

Con un compañero / una compañera

Imagine que Ud. va a comprar una computadora nueva. ¿Para qué va a usar la computadora? ¿Qué programas y capacidades quiere que tenga? Con un compañero / una compañera, hagan los papeles de cliente y vendedor(a). Usen el diálogo anterior como modelo.

En contexto

COSTA RICA

In this video segment, Mariela helps a student in the computer laboratory to use e-mail for sending a document. As you watch the segment, pay particular attention to the use of computer-related vocabulary. What do you think **adjuntar documento** means? And what about **dirección electrónica**?

A. Lluvia de ideas

- ¿A quién le pide ayuda Ud. cuando tiene problemas con los programas informáticos? Otras personas, ¿le piden ayuda a Ud.?
- ¿Dónde prefiere Ud. hacer las tareas universitarias, en casa o en un laboratorio de computadoras? ¿Por qué?

B. Dictado

A continuación están las instrucciones que Mariela le da al estudiante. Complete la explicación con las palabras o frases que faltan.

MARIELA: Vamos a ver. _____ _____...
No, prefiero que Ud. lo _____. Así aprende mejor. Bien. Primero, _____ su cuenta[a] de correo electrónico. No, es mejor que no _____ el documento.

[a]*account*

Un poco más sobre... José Miguel Martín Velazco

A nuestro amigo José Miguel le fascina la tecnología pero todavía no es un perito.[a] Espera que la compra de una nueva computadora sea su puerta al misterioso ciber-mundo. Su amigo Gustavo, como Ud. sabe, ya sí es experto, y para su madre Elisa la computadora es un aparato de uso diario.

[a]*expert*

To read more about the characters from this video, visit the *Puntos de partida* Website at **www.mhhe.com/puntos**

Ahora, le sugiero que _____ primero la _____ electrónica del profesor en ese espacio. Cuidado,[b] un _____ _____ y no _____.

ESTUDIANTE: Ya está...

MARIELA: Ahora, con el _____, _____ «adjuntar documento» del menú... y es necesario que elija[c] el _____ que quiere mandar.

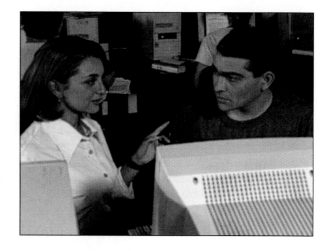

[b]*Careful* [c]*you choose*

C. Un diálogo original

Paso 1. Con un compañero / una compañera, dramaticen la escena entre Mariela y el estudiante.

Paso 2. Ayudando a un compañero / una compañera. Imagine que Ud. y un compañero una compañera tienen una conversación en el laboratorio de computadoras de su universidad.

ESTUDIANTE 1   Ud. es un novato / una novata (*novice*) en eso de computadoras y no sabe llegar al sitio web de su clase de _____ (o no sabe conseguir su correo electrónico). Por eso le pide ayuda a alguien de la clase.

ESTUDIANTE 2   Ud. es «un experto / una experta» en computadoras y ayuda a otro/a estudiante de la clase con los problemas que tiene.

Un poco de todo

A. Dos diablitos (*little devils*)

Paso 1. Alberto y Eduardo Suárez son dos niños que siempre hacen lo que no deben. Para cada par de oraciones, lea el mandato que les da su madre en la primera oración. Luego, complete la segunda oración con el mandato opuesto.

MODELO: Alberto, siéntate en la silla. No _____ (sentarte) en el suelo. →
No *te sientes* en el suelo.

1. Alberto, no escuches la radio ahora. _____ (Escucharme) a mí.
2. Eduardo, haz tu tarea. No _____ (hacer) eso.
3. Eduardo, no juegues con la pelota en casa. _____ (Jugar) afuera.
4. Alberto, no cantes en la mesa. _____ (Cantar) después de cenar.
5. Alberto, dame tu almuerzo a mí. No _____ (dárselo) al perro.
6. Eduardo, pon los pies en el suelo. No _____ (ponerlos) en el sofá.

Paso 2. ¿Qué quiere la Sra. Suárez que hagan los dos niños? ¿Qué prefiere que *no* hagan? Indique sus deseos con oraciones completas.

> MODELO: La Sra. Suárez prefiere que Alberto se siente en la silla. No quiere que se siente en el suelo.

Palabras útiles: querer, desear, esperar, insistir en, preferir, permitir, prohibir

B. ¿Qué quiere o necesita Ud.? Here is a series of answers to that question. Complete them with the correct form of each word in parentheses. When two possibilities are given in parentheses, select the correct word. **¡OJO!** You will use the present indicative, present subjunctive, or preterite of the infinitives. And sometimes, the infinitive itself will be the appropriate form.

PERSONA A: Deseo que (haber[1]) paz[a] en (mí/mi[2]) país. Y quiero que mi familia (estar[3]) bien. También deseo que no (haber[4]) hambre en el mundo y que los niños no (sufrir[5]). Para (mí/mi[6]), (*yo:* pedir[7]) muy poco.

PERSONA B: ¡Yo no (saber[8]) por dónde empezar la lista! Necesitamos una casa (tan/más[9]) grande, camas nuevas para los niños (pocos/pequeños[10]), (un/una[11]) televisor... Pero primero tenemos que (comprar[12]) (un/—[13]) otro coche, porque el que[b] tenemos (dejar[14]) de funcionar la semana pasada. ¡Ay!

PERSONA C: Es necesario que mi jefa me (dar[15]) un aumento de sueldo. Ya trabajo (muchísimo[16]) horas, pero no (*yo:* ganar[17]) lo suficiente. (El/La[18]) cheque que recibo cada dos semanas apenas[c] (cubrir[19])[d] los gastos (al/del[20]) apartamento, como (el/la[21]) alquiler, la luz y el gas. Por lo menos la dueña del apartamento es (mucho/muy[22]) simpática y me (gusta/gustan[23]) mucho el barrio donde vivo.

PERSONA D: ¡Huy! ¡Muchas cosas! Quiero (comprar[24]) (un/una[25]) sofá para la sala, una computadora y equipo estereofónico. Además, me gustaría (comprar[26]) unas pinturas, (un/una[27]) *fax...*

PERSONA E: Yo quiero que mi papá me (llevar[28]) al circo. Mi amigo Enrique (ir[29]) la semana pasada y le (gustar[30]) mucho. También necesito (un/una[31]) bici. Y quiero que el bebé que va (a/de[32]) tener mi mamá (ser[33]) un hermanito. Si es una niña, es un rollo,[e] ¡porque no va a (querer[34]) jugar al basquetbol!

[a]*peace* [b]*el... the one that* [c]*barely* [d]*to cover* [e]*pain*

Comprensión: ¿Cierto o falso?

1. No hay ninguna persona con deseos humanitarios.
2. Es necesario que alguien compre un coche.
3. Una persona quiere que su compañía le pague más.
4. Es completamente necesario que uno de los entrevistados compre unas pinturas y equipo estereofónico.
5. Otro entrevistado quiere que el nuevo bebé de sus padres sea una niña.

C. Una carta al presidente

Paso 1. Divídanse en grupos de tres personas. Cada miembro del grupo va a completar dos de las siguientes oraciones. **¡OJO!** La palabra **presidente** se refiere al presidente de los Estados Unidos. En español, **el rector / la rectora** = *university president.*

Queremos que el presidente (primer ministro) / el rector (la rectora)…

Recomendamos que el presidente (primer ministro) / el rector (la rectora)…

Es importante que el presidente (primer ministro) / el rector (la rectora)…

Sugerimos que el presidente (primer ministro) / el rector (la rectora)…

Paso 2. Ahora los miembros del grupo deben seleccionar las tres mejores oraciones. Una persona de cada grupo las va a escribir en la pizarra.

Paso 3. Lea las oraciones que están en la pizarra y use algunas para escribir una breve carta al presidente de los Estados Unidos, al primer ministro del Canadá o al rector / a la rectora de la universidad. Añada (*Add*) otra información y use **Ud.** en vez de (*instead of*) **el presidente (primer ministro) / el rector (la rectora).**

PANORAMA *cultural*

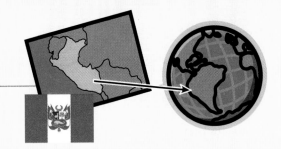

Perú

Datos esenciales

Nombre oficial: República del Perú
Capital: Lima
Población: 24.000.000 de habitantes
Moneda: el nuevo sol
Idiomas oficiales: el español, el quechua, el aimara

¡Fíjese!

- El Lago Titicaca, que queda entre Bolivia y el Perú, es el lago más grande de Sudamérica y es la ruta de transporte principal entre estos dos países.

- Cientos de años antes de la llegada[a] de los españoles, la agricultura de los indígenas del Perú ya era muy sofisticada. Hace más de 2.000 años, los indígenas ya construían[b] terrazas para sembrar en las faldas[c] de los Andes. Muchas de estas terrazas se usan todavía.

- Uno de los cultivos[d] más importantes de los incas es la papa,[e] que originó en la región cerca del Lago Titicaca. La papa es una de las pocas plantas que puede subsistir[f] en altitudes de más de 13.000 pies y en regiones frías y áridas.

[a]*arrival* [b]*ya... were already building* [c]*para... so that they could plant on the slopes* [d]*crops* [e]*potato* [f]*survive*

Conozca... la cultura inca

Cuando los españoles llegaron al Perú en 1532, los incas ya dominaban una gran zona de Sudamérica, desde Colombia hasta Chile, y desde el Pacífico hasta las selvas[a] del este. A partir del siglo[b] XIII, muchos otros pueblos indígenas de la inmensa región vivían bajo[c] el dominio de los incas. La capital del imperio era Cuzco.

La palabra *inca* significa *rey* o *príncipe*[d] en quechua, lengua que todavía se habla en el Perú.

Bajo su inca, el pueblo tenía un gobierno de poder absoluto y un sistema burocrático y social muy complejo.

El imperio inca se destacó[e] por la arquitectura, la ingeniería[f] y las técnicas de cultivo. También estableció un sistema de correo y un censo de la población. Tras la conquista[g] de los incas por los españoles Pizarro y Almagro, el Perú y su capital Lima, fundada por Pizarro en 1535, se convierten en un centro fundamental de las colonias españolas en América.

[a]*jungles* [b]*A... Beginning in the (thirteenth) century* [c]*under* [d]*rey... king or prince* [e]*se... distinguished itself* [f]*engineering* [g]*Tras... After the conquest*

 Capítulo 12 of the video to accompany *Puntos de partida* contains cultural footage of Peru.

 Visit the *Puntos de partida* Website at www.mhhe.com/puntos.

Vocabulario

Los verbos

alegrarse (de)	to be happy (about)
arreglar	to straighten (up); to fix, repair
cambiar (de)	to change
copiar / hacer copia	to copy
dudar	to doubt
esperar	to hope
fallar	to "crash" (*a computer*)
funcionar	to work, function; to run (*machines*)
grabar	to record; to tape
guardar	to keep; to save (*documents*)
haber (*infinitive form of* hay)	(*there is, there are*)
imprimir	to print
mandar	to order
manejar	to drive; to operate (*a machine*)
obtener (*irreg.*)	to get, obtain
permitir	to permit, allow
prohibir	to prohibit, forbid

Repaso: conseguir (i, i), sacar fotos

Vehículos

la bicicleta (de montaña)	(mountain) bike
el carro (descapotable)	(convertible) car
el monopatín	skateboard
la moto(cicleta)	motorcycle, moped
los patines	roller skates

Repaso: el coche

La electrónica

el archivo	(computer) file
el canal	channel
el contestador automático	answering machine

el correo electrónico	e-mail
el disco duro	hard drive
el equipo estereofónico / fotográfico	stereo/photography equipment
la grabadora	tape recorder/player
la impresora	printer
el ordenador (*Sp.*)	computer
el ratón	mouse
la red	net
navegar la red	to surf the net
el teléfono celular / de coche	cellular/car phone
la videocasetera	video cassette recorder (VCR)

Repaso: la cinta, el televisor

Cognados: la cámara (de vídeo), el CD-ROM, la computadora, el control remoto, el disco compacto, el disco de computadora, el fax, la memoria, el módem, el radio (portátil) / la radio,* el *walkman*

Para poder gastar...

el aumento	raise
el/la jefe/a	boss
el sueldo	salary

La vivienda

alquilar	to rent
las afueras	outskirts; suburbs
el alquiler	rent
el área (*but f.*)	area
la avenida	avenue
el barrio	neighborhood
la calle	street
el campo	countryside
el *campus*	(university) campus
la casa (el bloque) de apartamentos	apartment building

***El radio** is the apparatus; **la radio** is the medium.

la comunidad	community
la dirección	address
el/la dueño/a	landlord, landlady
el gas	gas; heat
el/la inquilino/a	tenant; renter
el piso	floor (of a building)
la planta baja	ground floor
el/la portero/a	building manager; doorman
la vecindad	neighborhood
el/la vecino/a	neighbor
la vista	view

Repaso: el apartamento, la casa, el centro, el cuarto, la luz, la residencia

Otros sustantivos

el gasto	expense
el lujo	luxury

Palabras adicionales

los/las demás	others

Un paso más 12

LECTURA

Estrategia: Word Families

Guessing the meaning of a word from context is easier if it has a recognizable root or a relation to another word that you already know. For example, if you know the verb **llover** (*to rain*), you should be able to guess the meaning of **lluvia** (*rain*) and **lluvioso** (*rainy*) quite easily in context. Can you guess the meaning of the following words? Give the English meaning in the first blank, and then in the second blank give a Spanish word that you already know that has the same root form. The first one is done for you.

la locura	En la Edad Media, la locura no era considerada una enfermedad, sino una manifestación en carne y hueso (*flesh and blood; literally, flesh and bone*) del diablo (*devil*).
<u>madness</u>	<u>loco</u>
la pobreza	La pobreza es un problema muy grave en muchas partes de la India y Latinoamérica.
<u>poverty</u>	<u>pobre</u>
la enseñanza	Muchos datos indican que la calidad de la enseñanza actual en los Estado Unidos es inferior a la del año 1960.
<u>education</u>	<u>en señor</u>
la riqueza	El número de personas que llega a Hollywood en busca de fama y riqueza en el cine sigue subiendo.
<u>fortune</u>	<u>rico</u>

Next, check your answers with a classmate or with your instructor.

   The following words are both found in the first paragraph of the reading: **almacenamiento** and **pensadas**. What verbs or nouns do you know that have the same root form as these words? (Hint for **almacenamiento**: In **Capítulo 3** you learned the word **almacén**. Do you recall its meaning?) The word **vendidas** is found in the graph that accompanies the reading. Can you identify the verb that has the same root form? Identifying root forms and knowing their meanings should help you understand some unfamiliar words in the context of this passage.

▷ **Sobre la lectura...** Esta lectura, adaptada de la versión original, viene
▷ de la revista española *Quo,* que publica artículos de interés general para el
▷ público.

Una agenda electrónica

Secretaria de bolsillo[a]

Las agendas electrónicas se presentan como amasijo[b] de chips y circuitos electrónicos que se adapta a las dimensiones de un bolsillo. Después, su <u>potencia</u> se despliega con[c] múltiples funciones, gran capacidad de almacenamiento y conexiones para poder enviar faxes, conectarse al Internet o recibir información por correo electrónico. Hoy en día se han diversificado[d] en distintas familias de productos, pensadas para públicos diferentes con necesidades distintas.

Para uso personal

Se trata de las agendas más sencillas. Cuestan entre 6.000 y 20.000 pesetas y ofrecen poco más que un calendario de citas, una agenda de teléfonos y un pequeño bloc de notas. «Están dirigidas[e] a un público de nivel adquisitivo medio.[f] Son muy ligeras[g] y ofrecen las funciones justas; por sus presentaciones, puede decirse que buscan sustituir a las agendas de papel», asegura Gerard Borrut, jefe de producto de Sistemas Digitales de Sharp.

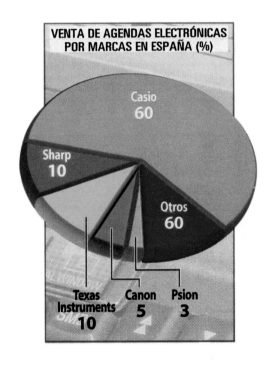

VENTA DE AGENDAS ELECTRÓNICAS POR MARCAS EN ESPAÑA (%)

Casio 60
Sharp 10
Otros 60
Texas Instruments 10
Canon 5
Psion 3

[a]*pocket* [b]*hodgepodge* [c]se... ofrece (*literally, unfolds*) [d]se... *they have diversified* [e]*targeted, directed* [f]nivel... *average purchasing power* [g]*lightweight*

Para usos más profesionales

Las agendas electrónicas de entre 20.000 y 60.000 pesetas son útiles para aquellos profesionales que no necesitan un gran volumen de información portátil ni demasiadas prestaciones,[h] pero a quienes las agendas sencillas se les han quedado pequeñas.[i] Su mejor cualidad reside en que su memoria interna es más <u>amplia</u> y, además de las funciones básicas, incluyen una <u>pantalla</u> más grande, un teclado[j] más accesible y cómodo y capacidad para transferir datos al PC.

La manía[k] por los asistentes de bolsillo en España es evidente en la tabla siguiente, que demuestra la venta de estos entre 1992 y 1998. ●

[h]*features* [i]*se... have become too small* [j]*keyboard* [k]*furor, craze*

Diminutas maravillas

En seis años, el número de asistentes de bolsillo se ha incrementado en España en casi un 70%. En este mercado, Casio sigue siendo el rey.

AGENDAS ELECTRÓNICAS VENDIDAS EN ESPAÑA

Año	Unidades
1992	80.000
1993	85.000
1994	102.000
1995	102.000
1996	120.000
1997	130.000
1998	135.000

Comprensión

A. ¿Cierto o falso? Conteste según el artículo.

1. Las agendas más baratas ofrecen conexión al Internet.
2. Todas las agendas ofrecen la misma capacidad de memoria interna.
3. Una ventaja de la agenda «para uso profesional» es el tamaño de la pantalla.
4. En España se ve un interés creciente (*growing*) por las agendas digitales.

B. Funciones y ventajas. Identifique por lo menos tres ventajas o funciones deseables (*desirable*) de las agendas electrónicas.

ESCRITURA

Un concurso (*contest*). Imagine Ud. que una compañía que fabrica productos electrónicos está montando una campaña de publicidad para una agenda digital nueva. A la persona que mejor pueda explicar cómo una agenda electrónica le facilitaría (*would facilitate*) la vida, la compañía le va a regalar una. Escriba un ensayo en el que Ud. explica y justifica por qué quiere una agenda digital y cómo lo/la va a ayudar esta a organizar su vida. ¡No se olvide de incluir algunos detalles sobre su vida de estudiante!

El arte y la cultura

Los bailarines (*dancers*) del Ballet Folklórico Mexicano incorporan elementos tradicionales e imaginativos en sus interpretaciones.

¿Qué opina Ud.?

Ponga las siguientes actividades en el orden de su interés, del 1 (más interesante) al 10 (menos interesante). ¿Cree Ud. que una persona de otro país las ordenaría (*would put them in order*) de un modo similar? Visite el sitio Web de *Puntos de partida* para averiguar (*find out*) la importancia que tienen estas actividades para una persona de Bolivia.

_____ Ir a un museo
_____ Ir al **cine**
_____ Ir a un concierto de **música** seria
_____ Ver un **ballet** o un recital de **baile**
_____ Leer una novela
_____ Ir al **teatro** a ver un **drama**
_____ **Crear** algo (una **pintura**, una **canción**, etcétera) personalmente
_____ Mirar la televisión
_____ Ver un partido deportivo
_____ Navegar el Internet

En este capítulo...

- In this chapter, you will study vocabulary related to artistic and cultural expression. With the words you acquire now you will be able to talk about **la música y la literatura que le gustan a Ud.**, and express your thoughts about creative activities.
- You were introduced to the subjunctive in the previous chapter. In this chapter, you will learn how to express emotions and doubts using this mood. (Grammar 39 and 40)
- You will also have the opportunity to review the uses of the subjunctive that you already know. (Grammar Section 41)
- This chapter's **Panorama cultural** section will focus on Bolivia and Ecuador.

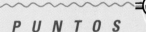

P U N T O S   *I N T E R A C T I V O*

Videoteca

◀ **Minidramas**
Diego y Lupe estudian para un examen de arte. ¿Tiene Ud. algunos artistas favoritos? ¿Qué tipo de arte prefiere?

En contexto ▶
Juan Carlos regatea en una tienda de artesanías peruanas. ¿Le gustan a Ud. los objetos de artesanía? ¿Qué tipo prefiere? ¿Tiene Ud. algunos?

CD-ROM

Además de completar el vocabulario y las actividades de gramática, Ud. va a tener la oportunidad de «regatear» con un vendedor de cerámicas peruano.

Internet

En la sección del Capítulo 13 en el sitio Web de *Puntos de partida* aparecen enlaces que Ud. puede usar para conseguir información en español sobre las artes. Use la dirección **www.mhhe.com/puntos**.

Las artes*

En el teatro

el actor · la directora · la bailarina · el bailarín · el cantante · el guión · el ballet · la cantante · la actriz · el escenario · los músicos

cantar	to sing
crear	to create
dibujar	to draw
escribir	to write
esculpir	to sculpt
pintar	to paint
tejer	to weave

Otras personas

el/la aficionado/a	fan
el/la arquitecto/a	architect
el/la artista	artist
el/la compositor(a)	composer
el/la dramaturgo/a	playwright
el/la escritor(a)	writer
el/la escultor(a)	sculptor
el/la pintora	painter
el/la poeta	poet

La expresión artística

la arquitectura	architecture
el baile / la danza	dance
el cine	film; movies
el drama	drama
la escultura	sculpture
la fotografía	photography
la literatura	literature
la música	music
la ópera	opera
la pintura	painting

La tradición cultural

la artesanía	arts and crafts
la cerámica	pottery, ceramics
las ruinas	ruins
los tejidos	woven goods

Otras palabras útiles

la canción	song
el cuadro / la pintura	painting (*piece of art*) / painting (*piece of art; the art form*)
la obra (de arte)	work (of art)
la obra maestra	masterpiece

---

*The word **arte** is used with masculine articles and adjectives in the singular and with feminine ones when in the plural.

Guillermo es estudiante **del arte moderno**.
Me gustan mucho **las artes gráficas**.

Conversación

A. Obras de arte

Paso 1. ¿Qué tipo de arte representan las siguientes obras?

1. la catedral de Notre Dame y la de Santiago de Compostela
2. los murales de Diego Rivera
3. las estatuas griegas y romanas
4. *El lago de los Cisnes* (*Swan Lake*) y *El amor brujo* (*Love, the Magician*)
5. *El ciudadano Kane* y *El mago* (*Wizard*) *de Oz*
6. *La Bohème* y *La Traviata*
7. las ruinas aztecas y mayas
8. *Don Quijote* y *Como agua para chocolate*

Paso 2. Ahora dé otros ejemplos de obras en cada una de las categorías artísticas que Ud. mencionó en el **Paso 1**.

B. ¿Qué hacen?

Paso 1. Forme oraciones completas, emparejando palabras de cada columna. Hay más de una posibilidad en algunos casos.

la compositora	escribe	novelas y poesía
la actriz	baila	canciones
el director	esculpe	en el ballet
el músico	toca	edificios y casas
el bailarín	interpreta	papeles (*roles*) en la televisión
el dramaturgo	diseña	guiones
la pintora	pinta	con actores
el escritor	mira	obras de teatro
la arquitecta	trabaja	cuadros
	dirige (*directs*)	instrumentos musicales

Paso 2. Ahora, con dos o tres compañeros, den nombres de artistas en cada categoría, ya sean (*whether they be*) hombres o mujeres. ¿Cuántos artistas hispánicos pueden nombrar?

Nota comunicativa

Más sobre los gustos y preferencias

Here are some additional verbs to talk about what you like and don't like.

- The following two verbs are used like **gustar**.

aburrir	**Me aburre** el ballet moderno. *Modern ballet bores me.*
agradar	Pero **me agrada** el ballet folklórico. *But I like folkloric dances.*

- This verb functions as a transitive verb (one that can take a direct object).

apreciar   **Aprecio** mucho la arquitectura precolombina.
I really appreciate pre-Columbian architecture.

C. Preferencias personales

Paso 1. ¿Le gusta el arte? ¿Asiste a funciones culturales de vez en cuando o no asiste a esas funciones nunca? ¡Diga la verdad! (En otras actividades va a hablar de lo que prefiere en general.)

MODELO: asistir a los ballets clásicos →
Me gusta mucho asistir a los ballets clásicos.
(No me agrada para nada asistir a los ballets clásicos. Es aburrido.)
(Me aburre asistir a los ballets clásicos. Prefiero ir a la ópera.)

Palabras útiles: gustar, apreciar, preferir, encantar, aburrir, agradar, interesar

1. ir a los museos de arte moderno
2. asistir a funciones teatrales
3. ver obras maestras en los museos grandes
4. ir a conciertos de música clásica
5. asistir a lecturas de poesía en un café

Paso 2. Ahora entreviste a un compañero / una compañera para saber cuáles son sus preferencias con respecto a este tema.

MODELO: E1: ¿Te gusta ir a los museos de arte moderno?
E2: Sí, me gusta muchísimo. Voy siempre que puedo (*whenever I can*).

Nota cultural

Los toros

El toreo[a] es un espectáculo típicamente hispánico. Viene de una larga tradición histórica. De hecho, no se sabe exactamente cuándo surgió la primera **corrida de toros.**[b]

Para sus aficionados, el toreo es **un arte,** y **el torero** necesita mucho más que valor:[c] necesita destreza[d] técnica, gracia y mucha comprensión de **los toros.** Algunos creen que el toreo *no es* un arte, sino un espectáculo cruel y violento que causa la muerte[e] prematura e innecesaria de un animal bravo.

Sea cual sea la opinión que Ud. tiene[f] de las corridas de toros, las corridas son muy simbólicas para los

[a]El... *Bullfighting* [b]corrida... *bullfight* [c]*bravery* [d]*skill* [e]*death* [f]Sea... *Whatever your opinion may be*

Una corrida de toros en Toledo, España

hispanos. El toro es símbolo de fuerza,[g] coraje, bravura, independencia y belleza.[h] Si Ud. visita un país hispánico y tiene ganas de ver una corrida, es aconsejable que les pregunte a algunas personas nativas cuáles son las corridas que debe ver.

[g]*strength* [h]*beauty*

D. Preguntas

1. ¿Tiene Ud. talento artístico? ¿Para qué? ¿Qué le gusta crear? ¿Cuándo empezó a desarrollar (*develop*) esta actividad? ¿Tiene aspiraciones de dedicarse a esa actividad profesionalmente? ¿Cuáles son las ventajas y las desventajas de esa ocupación?

2. Si Ud. cree que no posee ningún talento artístico en particular, ¿siente alguna atracción por el arte? ¿Qué tipo de arte en particular? ¿Por qué le gusta tanto?

3. ¿Le gusta ir a los mercados de artesanía? ¿Qué compra allí? Cuando va de viaje, ¿le interesa saber cuáles son los trajes y la música tradicionales del lugar que visita? ¿Colecciona Ud. obras de artesanía? ¿Qué colecciona?

Ranking Things: Ordinals

primer(o/a)	first	**cuarto/a**	fourth	**sexto/a**	sixth	**noveno/a**	ninth
segundo/a	second	**quinto/a**	fifth	**séptimo/a**	seventh	**décimo/a**	tenth
tercer(o/a)	third			**octavo/a**	eighth		

- Ordinal numbers are adjectives and must agree in number and gender with the nouns they modify. Ordinals usually precede the noun: **la cuarta lección, el octavo ejercicio.**
- Like **bueno**, the ordinals **primero** and **tercero** shorten to **primer** and **tercer**, respectively, before masculine singular nouns: **el primer niño, el tercer mes.**
- Ordinal numbers are frequently abbreviated with superscript letters that show the adjective ending: **las 1as lecciones, el 1er grado, el 5° estudiante.**

Conversación

A. Mis actividades favoritas

Paso 1. Piense en lo que le gusta hacer en su tiempo libre en cuanto a (*regarding*) actividades culturales. Luego ponga en el orden de su preferencia (del 1 al 10) las siguientes actividades.

_____ ir al cine
_____ ir a ver películas extranjeras o clásicas
_____ ir a museos
_____ asistir a conciertos de música clásica/rock
_____ leer poesía

_____ bailar en una discoteca
_____ ver programas de televisión
_____ ver obras teatrales
_____ leer una novela
_____ ¿ ?

Paso 2. Ahora cuéntele a un compañero / una compañera sus cinco actividades favoritas. Use números ordinales.

MODELO: Mi actividad favorita es ir a ver películas clásicas. Mi segunda actividad favorita es…

B. Preguntas

1. ¿Es Ud. estudiante de cuarto año?
2. ¿Es este su segundo semestre/trimestre de español?
3. ¿A qué hora es su primera clase los lunes? ¿y su segunda clase?
4. ¿Vive Ud. en una casa de apartamentos o en una residencia? ¿En qué piso vive? Si vive en una casa, ¿en qué piso está su alcoba?

Minidiálogos y gramática

39   **Expressing Feelings** • Use of the Subjunctive: Emotion

Diego y Lupe escuchan un grupo de mariachis

México, D.F.

DIEGO: Ay, ¡cómo me encanta esta música!
LUPE: *Me alegro de que te guste.*
DIEGO: Y yo *me alegro de que estemos* aquí. ¿Sabes el origen de la palabra **mariachi**?
LUPE: No… ¿Lo sabes tú?
DIEGO: Sí. Viene del siglo diecinueve, cuando los franceses ocuparon México. Ellos contrataban a grupos de músicos para tocar en las bodas. Y como los mexicanos no podían pronunciar bien la palabra francesa *mariage*, pues acabaron por decir **mariachi**. Y de allí viene el nombre de los grupos.
LUPE: ¡Qué fascinante! *Me sorprende que sepas* tantos datos interesantes de nuestra historia.
DIEGO: Pues, todo buen antropólogo debe saber un poco de historia también, ¿no?

Diego and Lupe are listening to a mariachi group. DIEGO: Oh, how I love this music! LUPE: I'm glad you like it. DIEGO: And I'm glad we're here. Do you know the origin of the word **mariachi**? LUPE: No . . . Do you? DIEGO: Yes. It comes from the nineteenth century, when the French occupied Mexico. They used to hire musical groups to play at weddings. And because the Mexicans couldn't correctly pronounce the French word *mariage*, they ended up saying **mariachi**. And so that's where the name of the groups comes from. LUPE: How fascinating! I'm surprised you know so much interesting information about our history. DIEGO: Well, all good anthropologists should also know a little bit of history, shouldn't they?

1. Lupe se alegra de que _____.
2. Y Diego se alegra de que _____.
3. A Lupe le sorprende que _____.

MAIN (INDEPENDENT) CLAUSE		SUBORDINATE (DEPENDENT) CLAUSE
first subject + *indicative* (expression of emotion)	**que**	second subject + *subjunctive*

A. Expressions of emotion are those in which speakers express their feelings: *I'm glad you're here; It's good that they can come.* Such expressions of emotion are followed by the subjunctive mood in the subordinate (dependent) clause.

Esperamos que Ud. **pueda** asistir.
We hope (that) you'll be able to come.

Tengo miedo de que mi abuelo **esté** muy enfermo.
I'm afraid (that) my grandfather is very ill.

Es una lástima que no **den** aumentos este año.
It's a shame they're not giving raises this year.

B. Some common expressions of emotion are found in the list at the right.

alegrarse de	to be happy about
esperar	to hope
sentir (ie, i)	to regret; to feel sorry
temer	to fear
tener miedo (de)	to be afraid (of)

Some common expressions of emotion used with indirect object pronouns are in the second list at the right.

me (te, le, ...) gusta que	I'm (you're, he's . . . glad that
me (te, le, ...) molesta que	it bothers me (you, him, . . .) that
me (te, le, ...) sorprende que	it surprises me (you, him, . . .) that

C. When a new subject is introduced after a generalization of emotion, it is followed by the subjunctive in the subordinate (dependent) clause. Here are some general expressions of emotion.

es extraño	it's strange
es increíble	it's incredible
es mejor/bueno/malo	it's better/good/bad

es ridículo	it's ridiculous
es terrible	it's terrible
es una lástima	it's a shame
es urgente	it's urgent
¡qué extraño!	how strange!
¡qué lástima!	what a shame!

Práctica

▲▲▲▲▲▲

A. Opiniones sobre el cine

Paso 1. Indique si las siguientes oraciones son ciertas o falsas para Ud.

1. Me molesta que muchas películas sean tan violentas.
2. Es ridículo que algunos actores ganen tanto dinero.
3. Espero que salgan más actores asiáticos e hispánicos en las películas.
4. Temo que muchas actrices no desempeñen (play) papeles inteligentes.
5. Es increíble que gasten millones de dólares en hacer películas.
6. Me sorprende que Julia Roberts sea tan famosa.

Paso 2. Ahora invente oraciones sobre lo que Ud. quiere o no quiere que pase con respecto al cine. Use las oraciones del **Paso 1** como base.

MODELO: **1.** Quiero que las películas sean menos violentas.

B. **Comentarios.** Complete las oraciones con la forma apropiada del verbo entre paréntesis.

1. Dicen en la tienda que esta videocasetera es fácil de usar. Por eso me sorprende que no (funcionar) bien. Temo que (ser) muy complicada. Me sorprende que ni (not even) mi compañera (entenderla).
2. ¡Qué desastre! El profesor dice que nos va a dar un examen. ¡Es increíble que (darnos) otro examen tan pronto! Es terrible que yo (tener) que estudiar este fin de semana. Espero que el profesor (cambiar) de idea.
3. Este año sólo tengo dos semanas de vacaciones. Es ridículo que sólo (tener) dos semanas. No me gusta que las vacaciones (ser) tan breves. Es una lástima que yo no (poder) ir a ningún sitio.

Nota comunicativa

Expressing Wishes with *ojalá*

¡**Ojalá** que yo **gane** la lotería algún día!   *I hope I win the lottery some day!*

The word **ojalá** is invariable in form and means *I wish* or *I hope*. It is used with the subjunctive to express wishes or hopes. The use of **que** with it is optional.

¡**Ojalá (que) haya** paz en el mundo algún día!	*I hope (that) there will be peace in the world some day!*
Ojalá que no **pierdan** tu equipaje.	*I hope (that) they don't lose your luggage.*

Ojalá can also be used alone as an interjection in response to a question.

—¿Te va a ayudar Julio a estudiar para el examen?
—¡**Ojalá**!

C. Una excursión a la ópera. Imagine que Ud. y su amigo/a van a la ópera por primera vez en su vida. Piense en todas las expectativas que Ud. tiene y exprésalas usando **ojalá**.

MODELO: las entradas / no costar mucho →
Ojalá que las entradas no cuesten mucho.

1. el escenario / ser / extravagante
2. haber / subtítulos / en inglés
3. el director (*conductor*) / estar / preparado
4. los cantantes / saber / sus papeles
5. nuestros asientos / no estar / lejos del escenario
6. (nosotros) llegar / a tiempo

Conversación

A. Situaciones. Las siguientes personas están pensando en otra persona o en algo que van a hacer. ¿Qué emociones sienten? ¿Qué temen? Conteste las preguntas según los dibujos.

1. Jorge piensa en su amiga Estela. ¿Por qué piensa en ella? ¿Dónde está? ¿Qué siente Jorge? ¿Qué espera? ¿Qué espera Estela? ¿Espera que la visiten los amigos? ¿que le manden algo?

Minidiálogos y gramática

2. Fausto quiere comer fuera esta noche. ¿Quiere que alguien lo acompañe? ¿Dónde espera que cenen? ¿Qué teme Fausto? ¿Qué le parecen (*seem*) los precios del restaurante?

3. ¿Dónde quiere pasar las vacaciones Mariana? ¿Espera que alguien la acompañe? ¿Dónde espera que pasen los días? ¿Qué teme Mariana? ¿Qué espera?

B. Los valores de nuestra sociedad. Express your feelings about the following situations by restating the situations, beginning with one of the following phrases or any others you can think of: **es bueno/malo que, es extraño/increíble que, es una lástima que**.

1. Muchas personas viven para trabajar. No saben descansar.
2. Somos una sociedad de consumidores.
3. Muchas personas no asisten a las funciones teatrales.
4. Juzgamos (*We judge*) a los otros por las cosas materiales que tienen.
5. Las personas ricas tienen mucho prestigio en esta sociedad.
6. Las mujeres generalmente no ganan tanto como los hombres cuando hacen el mismo trabajo.
7. Los jugadores profesionales de fútbol norteamericano ganan sueldos fenomenales.
8. Para la gente joven, la televisión es más popular que los libros.

C. ¿Qué le molesta más? The following phrases describe aspects of university life. React to them, using phrases such as: **Me gusta que… , Me molesta que… , Es terrible que…**

1. Se pone mucho énfasis en los deportes.
2. Pagamos mucho/poco por la matrícula.
3. Se ofrecen muchos/pocos cursos en mi especialización (*major*).
4. Es necesario estudiar ciencias/lenguas para graduarse.
5. Hay muchos/pocos requisitos (*requirements*) para graduarse.
6. En general, hay muchas/pocas personas en las clases.

D. Tres deseos. Imagine que Ud. tiene tres deseos: uno que se relaciona con Ud. personalmente, otro con algún amigo o miembro de su familia y otro con su país, para el mundo o para la humanidad en general. Exprese sus deseos con **Ojalá (que)…**

Palabras útiles: las elecciones, la gente (*people*) que no tiene hogar (casa), la guerra (*war*), el hambre (*hunger*), el millonario / la millonaria, el partido (*game*), la pobreza (*poverty*), resolver (ue) (*to solve; to resolve*), terminar (*to end*)

40 **Expressing Uncertainty** • **Use of the Subjunctive: Doubt and Denial**

Mire Ud. la siguiente pintura detenidamente (*carefully*) y luego complete las siguientes oraciones de acuerdo con su opinión.

Familia andina, por Héctor Poleo
(venezolano)

Vocabulario útil

la alegría	happiness
la esperanza	hope
el miedo	fear
la tristeza	sadness
los guardias	guardsmen

1. *Es posible que* los miembros de esta familia tengan (miedo/esperanza). Estoy seguro/a de que no tienen (miedo/esperanza).
2. Creo que los colores representan (la alegría / la tristeza). *Dudo que* representen (la alegría / la tristeza).
3. *Es probable que* los guardias estén (enojados/contentos). Estoy seguro/a de que no están (enojados/contentos).

MAIN (INDEPENDENT) CLAUSE		SUBORDINATE (DEPENDENT) CLAUSE
first subject + *indicative* (expression of doubt or denial)	**que**	second subject + *subjunctive*

A. Expressions of doubt and denial are those in which speakers express uncertainty or negation. Such expressions, however strong or weak, are followed by the subjunctive in the dependent clause in Spanish.

No creo que **sean** estudiantes.
I don't believe they're students.

Es imposible que ella **esté** con él.
It's impossible for her to be with him.

B. Some expressions of doubt and denial appear at the right. Not all Spanish expressions of doubt are given here. Remember that any expression of doubt is followed by the subjunctive in the dependent clause.

no creer	*to disbelieve*
dudar	*to doubt*
no estar seguro/a (de)	*to be unsure (of)*
negar (ie)	*to deny*

Creer and **estar seguro/a** are usually followed by the indicative in affirmative statements because they do not express doubt, denial, or negation. Compare these examples.

Estamos seguros de (Creemos) que el examen **es** hoy.
We're sure (We believe) the exam is today.

No estamos seguros de (No creemos) que el examen **sea** hoy.
We're not sure (We don't believe) that the exam is today.

C. When a new subject is introduced after a generalization of doubt, the subjunctive is used in the dependent clause. Some generalizations of doubt and denial are included at the right.

Generalizations that express certainty are not followed by the subjunctive but by the indicative: **Es verdad que cocina bien. No hay duda de que Julio lo paga.**

es posible	it's possible
es imposible	it's impossible
es probable	it's probable (likely)
es improbable	it's improbable (unlikely)
no es cierto	it's not certain
no es seguro	it's not a sure thing
no es verdad	it's not true

Práctica

A. ¿Qué opina Ud.?

Paso 1. Lea las siguientes oraciones e indique lo que opina de cada una.

	ES CIERTO	NO ES CIERTO
1. A la mayoría de la gente le gustan los museos.	☐	☒
2. Todos mis amigos prefieren el teatro al cine.	☐	☒
3. Conozco a muchas personas que son aficionadas a la arquitectura.	☐	☒
4. En esta clase hay mucha gente con talento artístico.	☒	☐
5. La expresión artística más popular entre los jóvenes es la música.	☒	☐
6. Me encanta regalar objetos de cerámica.	☐	☒
7. Voy a conciertos de música clásica con frecuencia.	☐	☒
8. *El cascanueces* (*The Nutcracker*) es un ballet típico del mes de mayo.	☐	☒

Paso 2. Ahora diga las oraciones del **Paso 1**, empezando con **Es cierto que...** o **No es cierto que...** según sus respuestas. ¡OJO! Hay que usar el subjuntivo con **No es cierto que...**

B. Opiniones distintas. Imagine que Ud. y un amigo / una amiga están en un museo arqueológico. En este momento están mirando una figura. Desafortunadamente, no hay ningún letrero (*sign*) cerca de Uds. para indicar lo que representa la figura. Haga oraciones completas según las indicaciones. Añada (*Add*) palabras cuando sea necesario.

Habla Ud.:

1. creo / que / ser / figura / de / civilización / maya
2. es cierto / que / figura / estar / hecho (*made*) / de oro
3. es posible / que / representar / dios (*god*) / importante
4. no estoy seguro/a de / que / figura / estar / feliz / o / enojado

Habla su amigo/a:

5. no creo / que / ser / figura / de / civilización / maya
6. creo / que / ser / de / civilización / tolteca
7. estoy seguro/a de / que / estar / hecho / de bronce
8. creo / que / representar / víctima [*m.*] / de / sacrificio humano

Conversación

▲▲▲▲▲▲▲

A. ¿Una ganga? Imagine que Ud. va a un mercado al aire libre. Encuentra algunos objetos de artesanía muy interesantes que parecen ser de origen azteca… ¡y son baratísimos! ¿Cómo reacciona Ud.?

Empiece sus oraciones con estas frases:

1. ¡Es imposible que… !
2. No creo que…
3. Dudo muchísimo que…
4. Estoy seguro/a de que…
5. Es improbable que…

Vocabulario útil

el calendario	calendar	**auténtico/a**	authentic
el escudo	shield	**falsificado/a**	forged
la joyería	jewelry		
la lanza	spear		
la máscara	mask		

Verbs That Require Prepositions

As you have already learned, when two verbs occur in a series (one right after the other), the second verb is usually the infinitive.

Prefiero *cenar* a las siete.　　　　　*I prefer to eat at seven.*

Some Spanish verbs, however, require that a preposition or other word be placed before the second verb (still the infinitive). You have already used many of the important Spanish verbs that have this feature.

- The following verbs require the preposition **a** before an infinitive.

  Mis padres me **enseñaron**　　　*My parents taught me to dance.*
  　a bailar.

aprender a	enseñar a	venir a
ayudar a	invitar a	volver (ue) a
empezar (ie) a	ir a	

- These verbs or verb phrases require **de** before an infinitive.

  Siempre **tratamos de llegar**　　*We always try to arrive on time.*
  　puntualmente.

acabar de	dejar de	tener ganas de
acordarse (ue) de	olvidarse de	tratar de

- **Insistir** requires **en** before an infinitive.

  Insisten en venir esta noche.　　*They insist on coming over tonight.*

- Two verbs require **que** before an infinitive: **haber que, tener que**.

  Hay que ver el nuevo museo.　　*It's necessary to see the new museum.*

B. ¿Qué piensa Ud. del futuro?

Paso 1. Combine una frase de cada columna para formar oraciones que expresen su opinión sobre lo que le puede ocurrir a Ud. en los próximos cinco años. **¡OJO!** No se olvide de usar el subjuntivo en expresiones de duda o negación.

En los próximos cinco años…

(no) creo que…	ir a	ser famoso/a
(no) dudo que…	aprender a	estar casado/a
es (im)posible que…	empezar a	ganar la lotería
(no) estoy seguro/a de que…　(yo)	dejar de	jugar a la lotería
(no) es cierto que…	tratar de	pintar cuadros
	volver a	fumar
		tener hijos
		terminar mis
		estudios
		esculpir
		¿ ?

Paso 2. Compare sus respuestas con las de uno o dos de sus compañeros. ¿Cuántas respuestas similares hay? ¿Cuántas diferentes?

En los Estados Unidos y el Canadá...

El arte de Pablo Urbanyi

Pablo Urbanyi

El canadiense Pablo Urbanyi ofrece un buen ejemplo del **carácter universal de la literatura**. La familia de este conocido[a] **escritor** emigró de Hungría a la Argentina cuando él tenía sólo 7 años. Fue en su nuevo país donde Urbanyi se educó y donde empezó a escribir cuentos.

Su primera **colección**, *Noche de los revolucionarios*, apareció en 1972 y fue seguida por una **novela policíaca de tono paródico**, *Un revólver para Mack*. Ese mismo año, Urbanyi empezó a trabajar de redactor[b] en un periódico de Buenos Aires, pero en 1977 los acontecimientos[c] políticos de su país lo obligaron a emigrar de nuevo.[d]

En el Canadá, Urbanyi escribió su segunda novela, *En ninguna parte*, que luego **se tradujo** al inglés y al francés. En 1993 fue finalista del prestigioso Premio Planeta Argentino por su tercera novela, *Silver*, la cual se publicó en francés para sus lectores en Quebec y Francia.

Hoy Urbanyi **vive y escribe en la ciudad de Ottawa**. Sus libros más recientes son *Puesta de Sol*[e] y *2058, en la Corte de Eutopía*, una novela que cuenta una historia sobre el futuro y a la vez refleja[f] la sociedad actual. Además de[g] ser escritor de ficción, Urbanyi presenta y **publica artículos críticos** en Hungría, los Estados Unidos, España, la Argentina, Alemania y el Canadá. Es en verdad un autor internacional.

[a]*well-known* [b]*editor* [c]*eventos* [d]*de... again* [e]*Puesta... Sunset* [f]*a... at the same time reflects* [g]*Además... In addition to*

41 Expressing Influence, Emotion, Doubt, and Denial • The Subjunctive: A Summary

Lola Benítez les habla a sus estudiantes norteamericanos

«Y para la próxima semana, *quiero que escriban* una composición sobre el arte de Sevilla. Como Uds. ya saben, Sevilla es una ciudad llena de todo tipo de arte: pintura, escultura, arquitectura, música, baile... ¡y también están los toros, por supuesto! Sí, los aficionados consideran que el toreo es una forma de arte. *Espero que vayan* a ver una corrida durante su estancia en España. Sin embargo, *es muy posible que no les guste* este espectáculo para nada. De todos modos, *ojalá que intenten* asistir a una. Bueno, por lo menos la plaza de toros sí es una gran muestra del arte sevillano... »

La plaza de los toros en Sevilla, España

Lola Benítez is talking to her American students. "And for next week, I want you to write a composition on art in Seville. As you already know, Seville is a city filled with all kinds of art: painting, sculpture, architecture, music, dance. . . and also bulls, of course! Yes, fans consider bullfighting to be an art form. I hope you go to see a bullfight during your stay in Spain. Nevertheless, it's very possible you won't like this spectacle at all. In any case, I hope that you try to attend one. Well, at least the bullring is a good example of Sevillian art. . . "

Minidiálogos y gramática

1. ¿Qué quiere la profesora Benítez que hagan los estudiantes para la próxima semana?
2. ¿Qué tipo de arte se encuentra en Sevilla?
3. ¿Qué forma de arte menciona la profesora Benítez que puede sorprender a los estudiantes?
4. ¿Adónde quiere Lola que vayan los estudiantes?
5. ¿Qué quiere que hagan allí?
6. ¿Está segura ella de que a todos los estudiantes les van a gustar las corridas de toros?
7. ¿Qué dice ella de la plaza de toros de Sevilla?

MAIN (INDEPENDENT) CLAUSE		SUBORDINATE (DEPENDENT) CLAUSE
first subject + *indicative*	**que**	second subject + *subjunctive*
expression of ⎧ influence ⎨ emotion ⎩ doubt, denial		

A. Remember that, in Spanish, the subjunctive occurs primarily in two-clause sentences with a different subject in each clause. If there is no change of subject, an infinitive follows the first verb. Compare the examples at the right.

Quiero ⎫
Es necesario ⎬ sacar una buena nota.

I want ⎫
It's necessary ⎬ *to get a good grade.*

Quiero ⎫ que los estudiantes saquen
Es necesario ⎬ una buena nota.

I want ⎫ *the students to get a good grade.*
It's necessary for ⎬

B. The main clause, in addition to fulfilling the preceding conditions, must contain an expression of influence, emotion, or doubt in order for the subjunctive to occur in the subordinate clause. If there is no such expression, the indicative is used.* Compare the following.

Dicen que maneje Julio.
They say that Julio should drive.

Dicen que Julio **maneja** muy mal; por eso quieren que maneje Carlota.
They say that Julio drives very badly; that's why they want Carlota to drive.

---

*See Grammar Sections 38 through 40 for a more detailed presentation of the uses of the subjunctive in noun clauses.

C. Some expressions of influence are frequently used with indirect object pronouns.

The indirect object indicates the subject of the subordinate clause, as in the sentences at the right: **nos** → **vayamos**.

$$\left.\begin{array}{l} \textbf{Nos } dicen \\ \textbf{Nos } piden \\ \textbf{Nos } recomiendan \end{array}\right\} que\ vayamos.$$

$$\left.\begin{array}{l} \textit{They tell us to} \\ \textit{They ask us to} \\ \textit{They recommend that we} \end{array}\right\} go.$$

D. These uses of the subjunctive fall into the general category of the subjunctive in *noun clauses* (**las cláusulas nominales**). The clause in which the subjunctive appears functions like a noun in the sentence as a whole. That is, it is the subject or the direct object of the verb.

In the first set of sentences at the right, the subordinate clause (**que el mecánico...**) is the direct object of the verb **quiere**.

In the second set of sentences at the right, the subordinate clause (**que los precios...**) is the subject of the verb **gusta**.

¿Qué quiere el dueño del coche?
What does the car's owner want?

Quiere **que el mecánico le arregle el coche**.
He wants the mechanic to fix the car.

¿Qué no les gusta a los clientes?
What don't the clients like?

No les gusta **que los precios sean muy altos**.
They don't like the prices to be very high.

Práctica

A. En el Museo del Prado

Imagine que Ud. vive en Madrid, España, y que va a escribir un informe sobre la vida y el arte del famoso pintor español Diego Velázquez. Va al Museo del Prado para examinar los cuadros de Velázquez de cerca (*up close*). Pero también cree que va a necesitar la ayuda de un guía (*guide*).

Paso 1. ¿Qué quiere Ud. que pase en el museo?

Quiero que el guía...

1. enseñarme los cuadros más famosos de Velázquez
2. explicarme algunos detalles de los cuadros
3. saber mucho sobre la vida del pintor

Paso 2. Claro está que Ud. va a aprender mucho sobre Velázquez. Pero, ¿qué es lo que le sorprende?

Me sorprende que muchos cuadros de Velázquez...

1. tener como tema la vida cotidiana (*everyday*)
2. estar en otros museos fuera de España
3. ser de la familia real (*royal*) de Carlos IV

Las meninas, por Diego Velázquez (español)

Paso 3. Ud. está muy agradecido/a (*grateful*) por la ayuda del guía. Sin embargo (*Nevertheless*), todavía quiere saber más sobre la vida y el arte de Velázquez.

Es posible que el guía...

1. recomendarme algunos libros sobre la vida y el arte del pintor
2. preguntarle a un(a) colega si sabe algo más sobre Velázquez
3. no tener más tiempo para hablar conmigo

B. **¡Qué maravilla de robot!** Imagine que Ud. tiene un robot último modelo que va a hacer todo lo que Ud. le diga, especialmente las cosas que a Ud. no le gusta hacer. ¿Qué le va a mandar al robot que haga?

Le voy a decir que...
Le voy a pedir que...
{
escribirme el informe para la clase de literatura
hacerme una crítica de una película para la clase de composición avanzada
poner la mesa
asistir a todas mis clases en la universidad
pagar mis cuentas
trabajar por mí en la oficina todas las tardes
¿ ?
}

Conversación

▲▲▲▲▲▲▲

Un nuevo lugar para vivir

Paso 1. Piense Ud. en el lugar ideal para vivir. ¿Es una casa o un apartamento? ¿Cómo es? Lea la siguiente lista de factores e indique los que tengan más importancia para Ud. Debe añadir (*add*) también otros factores que no estén en la lista. ¡Sea realista! Debe ser un lugar donde Ud. pueda vivir mientras asiste a la universidad.

_____ cerca de la universidad   __|__ piscina
_____ grande   _____ aire acondicionado
_____ económico/a   _____ compañero(s) de casa
_____ más de dos alcobas   _____ lavaplatos
__|__ buena vista   __|__ lavadora y secadora
_____ ascensor (*elevator*)   _____ ¿ ?
_____ dos o más baños

Paso 2. Ahora describa la casa o el apartamento que Ud. quiere. Puede usar las siguientes oraciones como modelo.

MODELOS: Deseo que la casa / el apartamento...
(No) Me importa que la casa / el apartamento...
Es bueno que tenga/sea...
Espero que (no)...
(No) Es absolutamente necesario que...
Dudo que la casa / el apartamento...

Minidramas

In this **Minidramas** dialogue, Diego and Lupe are chatting at the UNAM campus. Pay close attention to their discussion. Do you recognize any of the names they mention? Whose art does Lupe admire and why?

Diego y Lupe están estudiando y conversando en el campus de la UNAM.

DIEGO: ¿Ya sabes sobre qué vas a escribir tu trabajo para la clase de arte?

LUPE: Creo que sí. Me interesan mucho el arte y la vida de Frida Kahlo, así que voy a escribir algo sobre ella.

DIEGO: Kahlo pintó muchos autorretratos,[a] ¿no?

LUPE: Sí, y sus autorretratos siempre tienen elementos simbólicos que representan sus emociones y su estado de ánimo.[b] Sus cuadros me gustan muchísimo. Su esposo fue Diego Rivera, uno de los muralistas más famosos de México. Mira. Aquí ves uno de sus cuadros.

DIEGO: Conozco varios murales de Rivera. Los vi en el Palacio de Bellas Artes.[c] Pero a mí me impresionan más los murales de José Clemente Orozco.

LUPE: Sí, Orozco fue un muralista excelente. Mira. Aquí ves uno de sus cuadros.

DIEGO: Así que vas a escribir sobre Frida Kahlo. ¿Qué más te interesa sobre ella?

LUPE: Bueno, me interesa mucho su arte, claro. Pero también me interesa porque llevó una vida muy difícil. Sufrió mucho, pero nunca dejó de apreciar la belleza[d] de vivir...

[a]*self-portraits* [b]*estado... state of mind* [c]*Bellas... Fine Arts* [d]*beauty*

Con un compañero / una compañera

Imagine que Ud. y un compañero / una compañera quieren hacer algo divertido este fin de semana, pero tienen gustos muy diferentes. Practiquen las siguientes situaciones. Pueden usar expresiones del diálogo anterior, si quieren.

1. A uno/a de Uds. le gusta el arte moderno, pero al otro / a la otra le gusta el arte clásico.

2. Los dos quieren ir a un concierto, pero uno/a de Uds. quiere ir a uno de rock y el otro / la otra quiere asistir a uno de música clásica.
3. Quieren ir al cine, pero a uno/a de Uds. no le gustan las películas violentas. El otro / La otra prefiere las películas de mucha acción; la violencia no le molesta mucho.

En contexto

PERÚ

A. Lluvia de ideas

- ¿Qué tipo de artesanía se elabora (*is crafted*) en su estado o país? ¿Tiene Ud. algo hecho por artesanos locales?
- ¿Es común regatear en su país? ¿En qué tipo de negocio (*business*) se puede regatear? En su opinión, ¿sabe Ud. regatear bien? Dé un ejemplo.

B. Dictado

A continuación aparece un segmento del diálogo entre Juan Carlos y la vendedora de artesanías. Complete la explicación con las palabras o frases que faltan.

JUAN CARLOS: El original de esta pieza está en el _____ en _____, ¿verdad? Es una buena reproducción.

VENDEDORA: Sí, _____ es. Todas mis artesanías son muy buenas. ¿_____ _____ esa pieza? Le rebajoª un poco el _____, por ser mi _____ venta.

JUAN CARLOS: ¿En cuánto _____ _____ deja?ᵇ Soy un estudiante _____.

VENDEDORA: Ay, otro estudiante pobre. Todos los estudiantes que _____ a mi puestoᶜ son pobres, ¿_____? A ver… _____ _____ _____ en sesenta soles.
[…]

VENDEDORA: Bueno, a Ud., nuestro joven viajero, _____ _____ _____ en un precio especial. Si me compra la _____ y la _____, sólo le pido cien soles en total. _____, ¡qué _____!

JUAN CARLOS: Muy amable… ¿Cien soles me dijo? ¡Qué pena! No tengo _____ dinero. ¿Por qué no _____ en ochenta soles?

ªI'll lower the price ᵇwill you give ᶜstand

C. Un diálogo original

Paso 1. Con un compañero / una compañera, dramaticen el diálogo entre Juan Carlos y la vendedora.

Paso 2. Ayudando a un compañero / una compañera

ESTUDIANTE 1 Ud. es un(a) estudiante de cuarto año, a punto de (*just about to*) graduarse. Como va a mudarse muy pronto, desea vender algunas cosas en una venta (*sale*) de garaje. Entre ellas hay tres cuadros que Ud. pintó en su clase de arte. Póngale un precio a cada uno y haga una lista de las características de sus «obras maestras».

ESTUDIANTE 2 Ud. es un(a) estudiante de primer año y quiere decorar su cuarto en la residencia. Piensa comprar algunas cosas en la venta de garaje de otro estudiante. Se interesa especialmente en uno de los cuadros, pero el precio que tiene no le parece bueno.

Un poco de todo

A. Reacciones

Paso 1. Las siguientes oraciones mencionan temas de vital importancia en el mundo de hoy. ¿Qué cree Ud.? Reaccione Ud. a estas oraciones, empezando con una de estas expresiones.

Dudo que…	Es bueno/malo que…
(No) Es verdad que…	Es una lástima que…
No hay duda que…	Es increíble que…
Es probable que…	(No) Me gusta que…

1. Los niños miran la televisión seis horas al día.
2. Hay mucha pobreza (*poverty*) en el mundo.
3. En este país gastamos mucha energía.
4. Hay mucho sexo y violencia en la televisión y en el cine.
5. Se come poco y mal en muchas partes del mundo.
6. Los temas de la música *rap* son demasiado violentos.
7. Hay mucho interés en la exploración del espacio.
8. El fumar no es malo para la salud.
9. Los deportes para las mujeres no reciben tanto apoyo (*support*) financiero como los de los hombres.
10. No se permite el uso de la marihuana.

Paso 2. Indique Ud. soluciones para algunos de los problemas que se mencionan en el **Paso 1.** Empiece las soluciones con estas frases.

Es urgente que…	Es necesario que…
Es preferible que…	Es importante que…
Quiero que…	Insisto en que…

B. En el Museo de Arte Moderno Reina (*Queen*) **Sofía.** Imagine que Ud. y su amigo/a están en Madrid con un grupo turístico. Ahora están en el Museo de Arte Moderno Reina Sofía y el guía les habla sobre *Guernica*, el famoso cuadro del pintor español Pablo Picasso. Complete el siguiente diálogo con la forma correcta de los verbos entre paréntesis. Cuando se den dos posibilidades, escoja la palabra correcta.

Guernica,
por Pablo Picasso
(español)

GUÍA: (Pasar[1]) Uds. por aquí, por favor. También les pido que (dejar[2]) suficiente espacio para todos. Y bien, aquí estamos (delante/detrás[3]) de *Guernica*, la obra maestra pintada por Picasso. (Ser[4]) obvio que el cuadro (representar[5]) los horrores de la guerra,[a] ¿no? En 1937 Picasso (pintar[6]) este cuadro como reacción al bombardeo[b] (del / de la[7]) ciudad de Guernica durante la Guerra Civil Española. Por razones políticas, (durante / encima de[8]) la dictadura[c] de Franco,[d] el cuadro (fue/estuvo[9]) muchos años en el Museo de Arte Moderno de Nueva York. Pero por deseo expreso del pintor, el cuadro (trasladarse[10])[e] a España después de la muerte de Franco…

UD.: Yo dudo que (este/esto[11]) cuadro (ser[12]) una obra maestra. Creo que no (ser[13]) nada bonito. ¡No hay colores en él!

SU AMIGO/A: Yo no (creer[14]) que todos los cuadros (tener[15]) que (ser[16]) bonitos. Para mí, la falta de color (servir[17]) para expresar el dolor y el desastre… (Por/Para[18]) eso uno (poder[19]) sentir el mensaje de la destrucción de la guerra en la pintura.

[a]*war* [b]*bombing* [c]*dictatorship* [d]Francisco Franco (1892–1975), dictador de España desde 1939 hasta su muerte [e]*to move*

Comprensión. ¿Quién pudo haber dicho (*could have said*) lo siguiente: el guía, Ud. o su amigo/a?

1. Yo prefiero los cuadros en colores.
2. Ahora voy a mostrarles una obra maestra de la pintura española.
3. No me molesta que esta pintura esté pintada en blanco y negro.
4. Quiero que todos me sigan y que se pongan delante del cuadro.

PANORAMA *cultural*

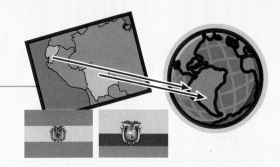

Bolivia y el Ecuador

Datos esenciales

Bolivia

Nombre oficial: República de Bolivia
Capital: La Paz (sede[a] del gobierno), Sucre
   (capital constitucional)
Población: 8.000.000 de habitantes
Moneda: el (peso) boliviano
Idiomas oficiales: el español, el quechua, el
   aimara

El Ecuador

Nombre oficial: República del Ecuador
Capital: Quito
Población: 11.000.000 de habitantes
Moneda: el sucre (el dolar)
Idiomas: el español (oficial), el quechua

[a]*seat*

¡Fíjese!

• Bolivia formó parte del antiguo imperio inca.
  Aproximadamente, el 55 por ciento de la
  población boliviana actual es de origen indígena.

• Bolivia fue nombrada[a] en honor a Simón Bolívar,
  quien luchó por la independencia del país.

• A 12.000 pies de altura, La Paz es la capital
  más alta del mundo.

• Las Islas Galápagos pertenecen[b] al Ecuador y
  son de origen volcánico. Fueron descubiertas[c]
  en 1535, por el español Berlanga. Berlanga las
  llamó las Islas Encantadas[d] porque las fuertes
  corrientes[e] marinas confundían a los navegantes[f] como si fuera por[g] acto de magia. Trescientos años más tarde, el biólogo Charles
  Darwin llegó a las islas a bordo del barco *HMS
  Beagle*. De sus investigaciones de las plantas y
  animales de cuatro de las islas resultaron sus
  ideas sobre la evolución y su famoso libro, *El*

origen de las especies. Darwin teorizó que los
animales y las plantas cambian y se adaptan a
su medio ambiente.[h]

[a]fue... *was named* [b]*belong* [c]*Fueron... They were discovered*
[d]*Enchanted* [e]*currents* [f]*sailors* [g]como... *as if by* [h]*medio...
environment*

Conozca a... Oswaldo Guayasamín

Oswaldo Guayasamín (1919–) es un pintor
ecuatoriano cuyo[a] arte es un testimonio del
sufrimiento[b] humano y de la vida difícil de los
indios y los pobres de su país. Guayasamín se
inspiró en los símbolos y motivos de los pueblos
precolombinos y en el arte colonial del Ecuador.

[a]*whose* [b]*suffering*

Madre y niño, por Oswaldo Guayasamín

 Capítulo 13 of the video to accompany
Puntos de partida contains cultural
footage of Bolivia and Ecuador.

 Visit the *Puntos de partida* Website at
www.mhhe.com/puntos.

Vocabulario

Los verbos

aburrir	to bore
agradar	to please
apreciar	to appreciate
intentar	to try
negar (ie)	to deny
parecer	to seem
representar	to represent
sentir (ie, i)	to regret; to feel sorry
temer	to fear
tratar de + *inf.*	to try to (*do something*)

Repaso: alegrarse de, creer, dudar, esperar, gustar, tener (*irreg.*) miedo de

La expresión artística

la arquitectura	architecture
el arte (*but* las artes *pl.*)	art
el baile	dance
el ballet	ballet
la danza	dance
el drama	drama
la escultura	sculpture
la música	music
la ópera	opera
la pintura	painting (*general*)
el teatro	theater

Repaso: el cine, la fotografía, la literatura

crear	to create
desempeñar	to play, perform (*a part*)
dibujar	to draw
esculpir	to sculpt
tejer	to weave

Repaso: cantar, escribir, pintar

Los artistas

el actor / la actriz	actor, actress
el/la aficionado/a	fan

el/la arquitecto/a	architect
el/la artista	artist
el bailarín/ la bailarina	dancer
el/la cantante	singer
el/la compositor(a)	composer
el/la director(a)	director
el/la dramaturgo/a	playwright
el/la escritor(a)	writer
el/la escultor(a)	sculptor
el/la músico	musician
el/la pintor(a)	painter
el/la poeta	poet

La tradición cultural

la artesanía	arts and crafts
la cerámica	pottery, ceramics
las ruinas	ruins
los tejidos	woven goods

Otros sustantivos

la canción	song
el cuadro / la pintura	painting (*piece of art*) / painting (*piece of art; the art form*)
el escenario	stage
el/la guía	guide
el guión	script
la obra (de arte)	work (of art)
la obra maestra	masterpiece
el papel	role

Repaso: el museo

Los adjetivos

clásico/a	classic(al)
folklórico/a	folkloric
moderno/a	modern

Los números ordinales

primer(o/a), segundo/a, tercer(o/a), cuarto/a,
quinto/a, sexto/a, séptimo/a, octavo/a,
noveno/a, décimo/a

Palabras adicionales

es extraño	it's strange
¡qué extraño!	how strange!
es...	it is . . .
cierto	certain
increíble	incredible
preferible	preferable
seguro	a sure thing
urgente	urgent
es una lástima	it's a shame
¡qué lástima!	what a shame!
hay que + *inf.*	it is necessary to (*do something*)
me (te, le, ...) molesta	it bothers me (you, him, . . .)
me (te, le, ...) sorprende	it surprises me (you, him, . . .)
ojalá (que)	I hope, wish (that)

Un paso más 13

Repaso de estrategias: Guessing the Content of a Passage

Look at the photograph that accompanies the reading. Read the title of the passage also. Based on these clues, what do you think the article is going to be about? How do you know? What important information do the photo and the title provide? Remember to always look for these types of visual clues as a useful strategy to facilitate comprehension when reading in a second language (or even in your first language).

▶ **Sobre la lectura...** Esta lectura es la adaptación de un artículo de la re-
▶ vista GeoMundo. Ud. ya leyó otro artículo de esta revista en el Capítulo 7.
▶ Recuerde que GeoMundo es como la revista National Geographic y que
▶ publica artículos sobre las ciencias, la geografía y otros temas similares.

Museo Virtual de Artes

Aprovechando las ventajas del ciberespacio, se creó el MUVA o Museo Virtual de Artes, sitio dedicado a divulgar el arte uruguayo y latinoamericano. Su directora es la historiadora de arte y curadora Alicia Haber. El sitio es recreativo, educativo y sin fines de lucro.[a]

La idea con que surgió este espacio es la de brindar[b] la sensación de estar en un museo real, pues debido a[c] las limitaciones originadas por la realidad socioeconómica de Uruguay, se ha visto impedida la construcción[d] de un museo nuevo. Cuatro arquitectos diseñaron un edificio con todos los adelantos,[e] la infraestructura técnica y las características edilicias[f] de un museo de primer nivel.[g] Existen innumerables museos en la supercarretera de la información,

pero a diferencia de ellos, el MUVA no está construido como las páginas de un catálogo. Se trata de presentar arte uruguayo en el contexto más realista posible y brindarle al visitante la

Sitio Web del Museo Virtual de las Artes

[a]sin... *not-for-profit* [b]*ofrecer* [c]pues... *because due to* [d]*se... construction has been impossible* [e]*latest advances (in architecture)* [f]*for preservation and inspection (of a public trust)* [g]*class*

sensación de estar en un verdadero museo. Y no en cualquier museo, sino en una obra arquitectónica atractiva, cómoda, moderna y eficiente, con escaleras mecánicas, ascensor, sala de acceso con esculturas, varias salas con instalaciones, pisos encerados[h] y hasta un buen sistema de iluminación.

Este museo ya ha recibido[i] 32 premios internacionales desde que entró en línea el 20 de mayo de 1997. El más importante es *Best of the Web* (Lo Mejor de la Red), pero también se ha hecho acreedor[j] al *Best Virtual Exhibition* (Mejor Exhibición Virtual del Mundo) entre más de 155 museos en línea. Debido a sus peculiares características, ha sido filmado en CNN Internacional, en la televisión brasileña y en muchos otros medios uruguayos e internacionales.

Se puede encontrar el MUVA en la dirección **http://www.diarioelpais.com/muva**. ●

[h]pisos… *waxed floors*   [i]ha… *has received*   [j]se… *it has been deemed worthy of inclusion*

Comprensión

A. Preguntas. Conteste las siguientes preguntas.

1. ¿Qué tipo de museo es el MUVA?
2. ¿En qué país latinoamericano se creó el MUVA?
3. ¿Cuáles son algunos ejemplos del éxito de este museo?
4. ¿Cuál fue el objetivo de los diseñadores del MUVA?

B. Identificación. Identifique las conveniencias que le ofrece el MUVA al visitante, según el artículo.

	SÍ	NO
1. diversas salas con exhibiciones	☐	☐
2. un tour guiado	☐	☐
3. un sistema de iluminación de alta calidad	☐	☐
4. diferentes maneras de navegar por el museo (ascensores, etcétera)	☐	☐
5. conversaciones con los artistas	☐	☐

ESCRITURA

La expresión artística. Muchas personas se expresan mediante el arte en sus varias formas. Es decir, el arte no se limita solamente a la pintura y la escultura. El arte puede tomar varias formas: la música, la escritura, el diseño de ropa o muebles, etcétera. ¿Qué «arte» usa Ud. para expresar su personalidad? Escriba un breve ensayo (*essay*) para explicar cómo Ud. se expresa por medio del arte. Ideas para considerar:

- el medio artístico (la música, etcétera)
- cómo el arte expresa sus emociones y personalidad
- si sus preferencias con respecto a la expresión artística están cambiando o si se mantienen estables

Cuando termine su ensayo, entrégueselo a su profesor(a). El profesor / La profesora lo va a presentar al resto de la clase para ver si puede adivinar quién es el autor / la autora.

El medio ambiente

El coquí dorado (*golden*) fue incluido en la lista de especies en peligro (*danger*) en 1977.

¿Qué opina Ud.?

Conteste sí (si es verdad) o no (si es falso), según su propia opinión. ¿Cree Ud. que una persona de otro país contestaría del mismo modo? Visite el sitio Web de *Puntos de partida* para averiguar (*find out*) cómo contesta una persona de la Argentina.

1. Es absolutamente necesario para mí tener mi propio **coche**.
2. Es importante tener un coche que no **gaste** demasiada **gasolina**.
3. Los daños que se le han hecho (*have been done*) a **la capa de ozono** no afectan mi vida diaria.
4. Tenemos que **explotar** nuestros **recursos naturales** si queremos mantener un buen **nivel** de vida.
5. El **medio ambiente** hay que **protegerlo**.

En este capítulo...

- In this chapter, you will study vocabulary related to the environment and to automobiles. If an ecologist urged you to **conservar los recursos naturales**, what would this person be asking you to do?
- In this chapter, you will learn how to modify a noun using past participles. You know the verb **abrir**, for example. Now you will be able to say **la puerta abierta** when you want to talk about an open door. (Grammar 42)
- In this chapter, you will be introduced to the present perfect. This is a compound form of the indicative that expresses actions and events that are already completed at the present time. (Grammar 43)
- This chapter's **Panorama cultural** section will introduce you to the people and customs of Argentina.

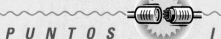

PUNTOS INTERACTIVO

Videoteca

◀ **Minidramas**
Elisa y José Miguel le dan direcciones a una mujer que tiene problemas con su coche. ¿Tiene Ud. coche? ¿Le gusta conducir?

En contexto ▶
El coche de Roberto se le ha averiado (*has broken down*). Y Ud., ¿puede arreglar un coche que no funciona o necesita que alguien se lo repare?

CD-ROM

Además de completar el vocabulario y las actividades de gramática, Ud. va a tener la oportunidad de «hablar» con un mecánico acerca de un coche que no funciona.

Internet

En la sección del Capítulo 14 en el sitio Web de *Puntos de partida* aparecen enlaces que Ud. puede usar para conseguir información en español sobre la ecología. Use la dirección **www.mhhe.com/puntos**.

El medio ambiente°

medio... *environment*

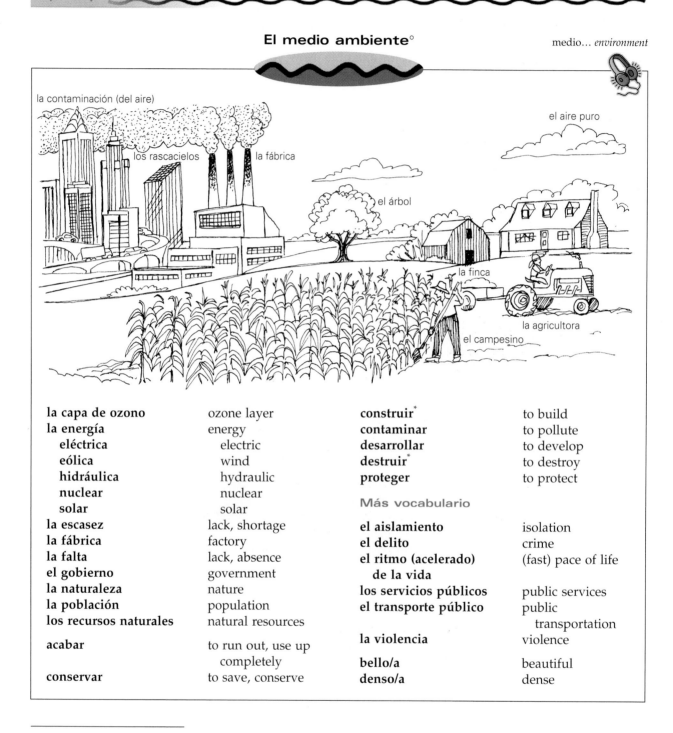

la contaminación (del aire)

el aire puro

los rascacielos   la fábrica

el árbol

la finca

la agricultora

el campesino

la capa de ozono	ozone layer	**construir***	to build
la energía	energy	**contaminar**	to pollute
eléctrica	electric	**desarrollar**	to develop
eólica	wind	**destruir***	to destroy
hidráulica	hydraulic	**proteger**	to protect
nuclear	nuclear		
solar	solar	**Más vocabulario**	
la escasez	lack, shortage	**el aislamiento**	isolation
la fábrica	factory	**el delito**	crime
la falta	lack, absence	**el ritmo (acelerado)**	(fast) pace of life
el gobierno	government	**de la vida**	
la naturaleza	nature	**los servicios públicos**	public services
la población	population	**el transporte público**	public
los recursos naturales	natural resources		transportation
		la violencia	violence
acabar	to run out, use up completely	**bello/a**	beautiful
conservar	to save, conserve	**denso/a**	dense

---

*Note the present indicative conjugation of **construir: construyo, construyes, construye, construímos, construís, construyen. Destruir** is conjugated like **construir.**

A. Un recurso natural importante

Paso 1. Lea este anuncio de una empresa (compañía) colombiana y conteste las preguntas.

En ECOPETROL tenemos conciencia ambiental y social. Nuestra planeación incluye siempre los estudios de localización e impacto ambiental, buscando no perturbar la naturaleza y la vida de las poblaciones vecinas a nuestras futuras operaciones. En esta planeación el trabajo con la comunidad es indispensable.

Nuestro propósito:
Una mejor convivencia

EMPRESA COLOMBIANA
DE PETROLEOS
ECOPETROL

1. ¿Qué tipo de negocio cree Ud. que es Ecopetrol? ¿Qué produce?
2. ¿Qué asuntos (*matters*) son de mayor interés para esta empresa? ¿el tránsito? ¿la deforestación? ¿las poblaciones humanas? ¿otros asuntos?
3. ¿Le parece que la foto que han elegido (*they have chosen*) para el anuncio es buena para la imagen de la empresa? ¿Por qué?
4. El sustantivo **convivencia** se relaciona con el verbo **vivir** y contiene la preposición **con**. ¿Qué cree Ud. que significa **convivencia**?
5. ¿Sabe Ud. cuáles son algunos de los países que producen lo mismo que Ecopetrol?

Paso 2. Hay varias formas de energía. ¿Las conoce Ud. bien? Diga a qué tipo de energía corresponde cada descripción.

1. Es la energía más usada en los hogares (*homes*).
2. Según los expertos, es la forma de energía más limpia; es decir, es la que menos contaminación produce.
3. Puede ser la forma de energía más eficiente, pero también la más peligrosa (*dangerous*).
4. Esta energía viene del viento; por eso sólo se puede desarrollar en lugares específicos.
5. Para producir esta forma de energía son necesarios los ríos y las cataratas.

Vocabulario: Preparación

B. Problemas del mundo en que vivimos

Paso 1. Los siguientes problemas afectan en cierta medida (*in some measure*) a los habitantes de nuestro planeta. ¿Cuáles le afectan más a Ud. en este momento de su vida? Póngalos en orden, del 1 al 10, según la importancia que tienen para Ud. ¡No va a ser fácil!

_____ la contaminación del aire
_____ la destrucción de la capa de ozono
_____ la escasez de petróleo
_____ la deforestación de la selva (jungla) de Amazonas
_____ la falta de viviendas (*housing*) para todos
_____ el ritmo acelerado de la vida moderna
_____ el uso de drogas ilegales
_____ el abuso de los recursos naturales
_____ la sobrepoblación (*overpopulation*) del mundo
_____ el crimen y la violencia en el país

Paso 2. Ahora comente las siguientes opiniones. Puede usar las siguientes expresiones para aclarar (*clarify*) su posición con respecto a cada tema. **¡OJO!** Todas las expresiones requieren el uso del subjuntivo o del infinitivo, porque expresan deseos e influencia

> Es / Me parece (*It seems to me*) fundamental
>   importantísimo
>   ridículo
>   ¿ ?
> Me opongo a que (*I am against*)…
> No creo que…

1. Para conservar energía debemos mantener bajo el termostato en el invierno y elevarlo en el verano.
2. Es mejor calentar las casas con estufas de leña (*wood stoves*) que con gas o electricidad.
3. Se debe crear más parques urbanos, estatales y nacionales.
4. La protección del medio ambiente no debe impedir la explotación de los recursos naturales.
5. Para evitar la contaminación urbana, debemos limitar el uso de los coches y no usarlos algunos días de la semana, como se hace en otros países.
6. El gobierno debe poner multas (*fines*) muy graves a las compañías e individuos que causan la contaminación.
7. El desarrollo de las tecnologías promueve (*promotes*) el ritmo tan acelerado de nuestra vida.
8. Los países desarrollados están destruyendo los recursos naturales de los países más pobres.

C. ¿La ciudad o el campo?

Paso 1. De las siguientes oraciones, ¿cuáles corresponden a la ciudad? ¿al campo?

1. El aire es más puro y hay menos contaminación.
2. La naturaleza es más bella.
3. El ritmo de la vida es más acelerado.
4. Los delitos son más frecuentes.
5. Los servicios financieros y legales son más asequibles (*available*).
6. Hay pocos medios de transporte públicos.
7. La población es menos densa.
8. Hay escasez de viviendas.

D. Definiciones. Dé Ud. una definición de estas palabras.

MODELO: el agricultor → Es el dueño de una finca.

1. la fábrica
2. el campesino
3. el delito
4. la finca
5. la naturaleza
6. la población
7. el aislamiento
8. el rascacielos

Nota cultural

El paisaje de la Argentina

El área continental de la Argentina equivale a un tercio del territorio de los Estados Unidos (la Argentina también tiene islas en el Atlántico y territorios en la zona de Antártida). Es un país de **increíble variedad geográfica**, que va desde la selva del noreste hasta las zonas de intenso frío en la Tierra del Fuego.

Los Andes cruzan la Argentina de norte a sur, y allí se encuentra el lugar de mayor altura del continente americano: el **Aconcagua**, montaña de 6.959 metros (casi 21.000 pies). También hay unas mesetas[a] secas y áridas, llamadas **punas**, de más de 3.000 metros (9.000 pies) de altura.

Un aspecto muy interesante de la geografía argentina es la **Pampa** (palabra de origen quechua que significa campo raso,[b] sin nada). Las pampas son grandes llanos[c] sin árboles ni arbustos,[d] donde el viento es fuerte. Las tierras de la Pampa sirven para criar ganado,[e] y los cuidadores tradicionales de ganado se llaman **gauchos**. Los gauchos son el equivalente del *cowboy* en el folklore argentino: hombres de vida nomádica, de espíritu libre y que viven, con frecuencia, fuera de la ley.[f]

[a]*mesas* [b]*flat* [c]*plains* [d]*árboles... trees and bushes* [e]*criar... raise cattle* [f]*fuera... beyond the law*

Los coches

En la gasolinera Gómez

el taller

¡Aquí recibe Ud. un servicio completo!

el mecánico

la mecánica

Revisamos el aceite.

Limpiamos el parabrisas.

el conductor

Revisamos las llantas.

Llenamos el tanque con gasolina.

la autopista	freeway	**chocar (con)**	to run into, collide (with)
la calle	street		
el camino	street, road	**doblar**	to turn
la carretera	highway	**estacionar**	to park
la circulación, el tránsito	traffic	**gastar (mucha gasolina)**	to use (a lot of gas)
la esquina	(street) corner	**manejar, conducir**	to drive
la licencia de manejar/conducir	driver's license	**obedecer**	to obey
		parar	to stop
el semáforo	traffic light	**seguir (i, i) (todo derecho)**	to keep on going; to go (straight ahead)
arrancar	to start up (*a car*)		
arreglar	to fix, repair		

Conversación

▲▲▲▲▲▲▲▲

A. Definiciones

Paso 1. Busque Ud. la definición de las palabras de la columna de la derecha.

1. _____ Se pone en el tanque.
2. _____ Se llenan de aire.
3. _____ Lubrica el motor.
4. _____ Es necesaria para arrancar el motor.
5. _____ Cuando se llega a una esquina, hay que hacer esto o seguir todo derecho.
6. _____ No contiene aire suficiente y por eso es necesario cambiarla.
7. _____ Es un camino público ancho (*wide*) donde los coches circulan rápidamente.
8. _____ Se usan para parar el coche.
9. _____ El policía nos la pide cuando nos para en el camino.
10. _____ Allí se revisan y se arreglan los coches.

    a. los frenos (*brakes*)
    b. doblar
    c. la carretera
    d. la batería
    e. el taller
    f. una llanta desinflada (*flat*)
    g. la gasolina
    h. las llantas
    i. el aceite
    j. la licencia

Paso 2. Ahora, siguiendo el modelo de las definiciones anteriores, ¿puede Ud. dar una definición de las siguientes palabras?

1. el semáforo
2. la circulación
3. estacionarse
4. gastar gasolina
5. la gasolinera
6. la autopista

B. Entrevista: Un conductor responsable

Paso 1. Entreviste a un compañero / una compañera de clase para determinar con qué frecuencia hace las siguientes cosas.

1. dejar la licencia en casa cuando va a manejar
2. acelerar (*to speed up*) cuando ve a un policía
3. manejar después de tomar bebidas alcohólicas
4. respetar o exceder el límite de velocidad
5. estacionar el coche donde dice «Prohibido estacionarse»
6. revisar el aceite y la batería
7. seguir todo derecho a toda velocidad cuando no sabe llegar a su destino
8. rebasar (*to pass*) tres carros a la vez (*at the same time*)

Paso 2. Ahora, con el mismo compañero / la misma compañera, hagan una lista de diez cosas que hace —o no hace— un conductor responsable. Pueden usar frases del **Paso 1**, si quieren.

Paso 3. Ahora, analice Ud. sus propias (*own*) costumbres y cualidades como conductor(a). ¡Diga la verdad! ¿Es Ud. un conductor / una conductora responsable? ¿Cuál de los dos es el mejor conductor?

Minidiálogos y gramática

42 ▶ Más descripciones • Past Participle Used As an Adjective

Algunos refranes y dichos en español

1. En boca *cerrada* no entran moscas.

2. Estoy tan *aburrido* como una ostra.

3. Cuando está *abierto* el cajón, el más *honrado* es ladrón.

Empareje estas oraciones con el refrán o dicho que explican.

1. Es posible que una persona honrada caiga en la tentación de hacer algo malo si la oportunidad se le presenta.

2. Hay que ser prudente. A veces es mejor no decir nada para evitar (*avoid*) problemas.

3. Las ostras ejemplifican el aburrimiento (*boredom*) porque llevan una vida tranquila… siempre igual.

Forms of the Past Participle

A. The past participle of most English verbs ends in *-ed*: for example, *to walk → walked; to close → closed.* Many English past participles, however, are irregular: *to sing → sung; to write → written.* In Spanish, the *past participle* (**el participio pasado**) is formed by adding **-ado** to the stem of **-ar** verbs, and **-ido** to the stem of **-er** and **-ir** verbs. An accent mark is used on the past participle of **-er/-ir** verbs with stems ending in **-a, -e,** or **-o.**

hablar	comer	vivir
hablado (*spoken*)	comido (*eaten*)	vivido (*lived*)

caer → **caído**	oír → **oído**
creer → **creído**	(son)reír → **(son)reído**
leer → **leído**	traer → **traído**

A few Spanish proverbs and sayings 1. Into a closed mouth no flies enter. 2. I am as bored as an oyster. 3. When the (cash) drawer is open, the most honest person is (can become) a thief.

Pronunciation hint: Remember that the Spanish **d** between vowels, as found in past participle endings, is pronounced as the fricative [đ] (see **Pronunciación** in **Capítulo 6**).

B. The Spanish verbs at the right have irregular past participles.

abrir:	**abierto**	morir:	**muerto**
cubrir:	**cubierto**	poner:	**puesto**
(*to cover*):			
decir:	**dicho**	resolver:	**resuelto**
descubrir:	**descubierto**	romper:	**roto**
escribir:	**escrito**	ver:	**visto**
hacer:	**hecho**	volver:	**vuelto**

The Past Participle Used as an Adjective

A. In both English and Spanish, the past participle can be used as an adjective to modify a noun. Like other Spanish adjectives, the past participle must agree in number and gender with the noun modified.

Tengo una bolsa **hecha** en El Salvador.
I have a purse made in El Salvador.

El español es una de las lenguas **habladas** en los Estados Unidos y en el Canadá.
Spanish is one of the languages spoken in the United States and in Canada.

B. The past participle is frequently used with **estar** to describe conditions that are the result of a previous action.

La puerta **está abierta**.
The door is open.

Todos los lápices **estaban rotos**.
All the pencils were broken.

OJO

English past participles often have the same form as the past tense: *I **closed** the book. The thief stood behind the **closed** door.* The Spanish past participle is never identical in form or use to a past tense. Compare the sentences at the right.

Cerré la puerta. Ahora la puerta está **cerrada**.
*I **closed** the door. Now the door is **closed**.*

Práctica

A. En este momento...

Paso 1. En este momento, ¿son ciertas o falsas las siguientes oraciones con relación a su sala de clase?

Palabras útiles: colgar (ue) (*to hang*), enchufar (*to plug in*), prender (*to turn on* [*lights or an appliance*])

1. La puerta está abierta.
2. Las luces están apagadas.
3. Las ventanas están cerradas.
4. Algunos libros están abiertos.
5. Los estudiantes están sentados.
6. Hay algo escrito en la pizarra.
7. Una silla está rota.
8. Hay carteles y anuncios colgados en la pared.
9. Un aparato está enchufado.
10. Las persianas (*blinds*) están bajadas.

Paso 2. Ahora describa el estado de las siguientes cosas en su casa (cuarto, apartamento).

1. las luces
2. la cama
3. el televisor
4. las ventanas
5. la puerta
6. las cortinas (*curtains*)

B. Situaciones. ¿Cuál es la situación en este momento? Conteste según el modelo.

MODELO: Natalia les tiene que *escribir* una carta a sus abuelos. →
La carta no está *escrita* todavía.

1. Los Sres. García deben *abrir* la tienda más temprano. ¡Ya son las nueve!
2. Pablo tiene que *cerrar* las ventanas; entra un aire frío.
3. Los niños siempre esperan que la tierra se *cubra* de nieve para la Navidad.
4. Delia debe *poner* la mesa. Los invitados llegan a las nueve y ya son las ocho.
5. Claro está que la contaminación va a contribuir a la *destrucción* de la capa de ozono.
6. Es posible que los ingenieros *descubran* el error en la construcción del reactor nuclear.
7. Se debe *resolver* pronto el problema de la escasez de energía.

C. Comentarios sobre el mundo de hoy. Complete cada párrafo con los participios pasados de los verbos apropiados de la lista.

Información sobre el reciclaje: desperdiciar (*to waste*), destruir, hacer, reciclar

Todos los días, Ud. tira en el basurero[a] aproximadamente media libra[b] de papel. Si Ud. trabaja en un banco, en una compañía de seguros[c] o en una agencia del gobierno, el promedio[d] se eleva a tres cuartos de libra al día. Todo ese papel _____[1] constituye un gran número de árboles _____.[2] Esto es un buen motivo para que Ud. comience un proyecto de recuperación de papeles hoy en su oficina. Ud. puede completar el ciclo del reciclaje únicamente si compra productos _____[3] con materiales _____.[4]

[a]*wastebasket* [b]media... *half a pound* [c]*insurance* [d]*average*

La conservación de la energía: acostumbrar, agotar (*to use up*), apagar (*to turn off*), bajar, cerrar, limitar

Las fuentes[a] de energía no están _____[5] todavía. Pero estas fuentes son _____.[6] Desgraciadamente, todavía no estamos _____[7] a conservar energía diariamente. ¿Qué podemos hacer? Cuando nos servimos la comida, la puerta del refrigerador debe estar _____.[8] Cuando miramos la televisión, algunas luces de la casa deben estar _____.[9] El regulador termómetro debe estar _____[10] cuando nos acostamos.

[a]*sources*

Conversación
▲▲▲▲▲▲▲

A. ¡Ojo alerta! Hay por lo menos cinco cosas que difieren (*are different*) entre un dibujo y el otro. ¿Puede Ud. encontrarlas? Use participios pasados como adjetivos cuando pueda.

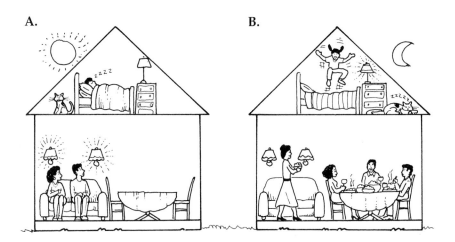

A.   **B.**

B. ¡Rápidamente! Dé Ud. el nombre de…

1. algo contaminado
2. una persona muy/poco organizada
3. un programa de computadora bien diseñado
4. un edificio bien/mal construido
5. algo que puede estar cerrado o abierto
6. un servicio necesitado por muchas personas
7. un tipo de transporte usado a la vez por muchas personas
8. algo deseado por muchas personas

¿Qué has hecho? • Perfect Forms: Present Perfect Indicative and Present Perfect Subjunctive

Una llanta desinflada

MANOLO: ¡Ay, qué mala suerte!

LOLA: ¿Qué pasa?

MANOLO: Parece que el coche tiene una llanta desinflada. Y como no hay ningún taller por aquí, tengo que cambiarla yo mismo.

LOLA: *¿Has cambiado* una llanta alguna vez?

MANOLO: No. Siempre *he llevado* el coche a un taller cuando hay problemas.

LOLA: Pues, yo nunca *he cambiado* una llanta tampoco. Pero te puedo ayudar, si quieres.

MANOLO: Gracias. ¡Espero que la llanta de recambio no esté desinflada también!

¿Y Ud.? ¿Ha... ?

1. cambiado una llanta desinflada
2. revisado el aceite de su coche
3. arreglado otras cosas del coche
4. tenido un accidente con el coche
5. excedido el límite de velocidad en la autopista

Present Perfect Indicative

he hablado	*I have spoken*	**hemos** hablado	*we have spoken*
has hablado	*you have spoken*	**habéis** hablado	*you (pl.) have spoken*
ha hablado	*you have spoken, he/she has spoken*	**han** hablado	*you (pl.) / they have spoken*

A flat tire MANOLO: Aw, what bad luck! LOLA: What's wrong? MANOLO: It seems the car has a flat tire. And, as there aren't any repair shops around here, I have to change it myself. LOLA: Have you ever changed a flat tire before? MANOLO: No. I've always taken the car to a repair shop when there are problems. LOLA: Well, I've never changed a tire either. But I can help you, if you want. MANOLO: Thanks. I hope that the spare tire isn't flat too!

A. In English, the present perfect is a compound tense consisting of the present tense form of the verb *to have* plus the past participle: *I have written, you have spoken,* and so on.

In the Spanish *present perfect* (**el presente perfecto**), the past participle is used with present tense forms of **haber**, the equivalent of English *to have* in this construction.

In general, the use of the Spanish present perfect parallels that of the English present perfect.

No **hemos estado** aquí antes.
We haven't been here before.

Me he divertido mucho.
I've had a very good time.

Ya le **han escrito** la carta.
They've already written her the letter.

 Haber, an auxiliary verb, is not interchangeable with **tener**.

B. The form of the past participle never changes with **haber**, regardless of the gender or number of the subject. The past participle always appears immediately after the appropriate form of **haber** and is never separated from it. Object pronouns and **no** are always placed directly before the form of **haber**.

[Práctica A–B]

Ella **ha cambiado** una llanta desinflada varias veces.
She's changed a flat tire several times.

Todavía **no le** han revisado el aceite al coche.
They still haven't checked the car's oil.

C. The present perfect form of **hay** is **ha habido** (*there has/have been*).

O J O Remember that **acabar** + **de** + *infinitive*—not the present perfect tense—is used to state that something *has just occurred.*

Ha habido un accidente.
There's been an accident.

Acabo de mandar la carta.
I've just mailed the letter.

Present Perfect Subjunctive

The *present perfect subjunctive* (**el perfecto del subjuntivo**) is formed with the present subjunctive of **haber** plus the past participle. It is used to express *I have spoken* (*written,* and so on) when the subjunctive is required. Although its most frequent equivalent is *I have* plus the past participle, its exact equivalent in English depends on the context in which it occurs.

Note in the model sentences at the right that the English equivalent of the present perfect subjunctive can be expressed as a simple or as a compound tense: *did / have done; came / have come; built / have built.*

[Práctica C]

haya hablado	**hayamos** hablado
hayas hablado	**hayáis** hablado
haya hablado	**hayan** hablado

Es posible que lo **haya hecho**.
It's possible (that) he may have done (he did) it.

Me alegro de que **hayas venido**.
I'm glad (that) you have come (you came).

Es bueno que lo **hayan construido**.
It's good (that) they built (have built) it.

Práctica

A. El pasado y el futuro

Paso 1. Indique las actividades que Ud. ha hecho en el pasado.

1. _____ He hecho un viaje a Europa.
2. _____ He montado a camello (*camel*).
3. _____ He tomado una clase de informática.
4. _____ He buceado (*gone scuba diving*).
5. _____ He ido de safari a África.
6. _____ He comprado un coche.
7. _____ He preparado una comida italiana.
8. _____ He ocupado un puesto (*position*) político.
9. _____ He tenido una mascota.
10. _____ He escrito un poema.

Paso 2. Ahora, entre las cosas que Ud. no ha hecho, ¿cuáles le gustaría hacer? Conteste, siguiendo los modelos.

MODELOS: Nunca he montado a camello, pero me gustaría hacerlo.
(Nunca he montado a camello y no me interesa hacerlo.)

B. El coche de Carmina.
Carmina, la hermana menor de Diego González, acaba de comprarse un coche usado. (Claro, su papá es vendedor de autos en Los Ángeles. ¡Así que el coche fue una ganga!) Describa lo que le ha pasado a Carmina, según el modelo.

MODELO: ir a la agencia de su padre → Ha ido a la agencia de su padre.

1. pedirle ayuda a su padre
2. hacer preguntas acerca de (*about*) los diferentes coches
3. ver uno bastante barato
4. revisar las llantas
5. conducirlo como prueba
6. regresar a la agencia
7. decidir comprarlo
8. comprarlo
9. volver a casa
10. llevar a sus amigas al cine esa noche

C. ¡No lo creo!
¿Tienen espíritu aventurero sus compañeros de clase? ¿Llevan una vida interesante? ¿O están tan aburridos como una ostra? ¡A ver!

Paso 1. De cada par de oraciones, indique la que (*the one that*) expresa su opinión acerca de los estudiantes de esta clase.

Vocabulario útil: el paracaidismo (*skydiving*), escalar (*to climb*), hacer *autostop* (*to hitchhike*)

1. ☐ Creo que alguien en esta clase ha visto las pirámides de Egipto.
   ☐ Es dudoso que alguien haya visto las pirámides de Egipto.

2. ☐ Estoy seguro/a de que por lo menos uno de mis compañeros ha escalado una montaña alta.

☐ No creo que nadie haya escalado una montaña alta.

3. ☐ Creo que alguien ha viajado haciendo *autostop*.

☐ Dudo que alguien haya hecho *autostop* en un viaje.

4. ☐ Creo que alguien ha practicado el paracaidismo.

☐ Es improbable que alguien haya practicado el paracaidismo.

5. ☐ Estoy seguro/a de que alguien ha tomado el metro en Nueva York a medianoche (*midnight*).

☐ No creo que nadie haya tomado el metro neoyorquino a medianoche.

Paso 2. Ahora escuche mientras el profesor / la profesora pregunta si alguien ha hecho estas actividades. ¿Tenía Ud. razón en el **Paso 1**?

Conversación
▲▲▲▲▲▲▲▲

A. Entrevista. Con un compañero / una compañera, háganse y contesten preguntas con estos verbos. La persona que contesta debe decir la verdad.

MODELO: visitar México →
E1: ¿Has visitado México?
E2: Sí, he visitado México una vez.
(No, no he visitado México nunca.)
(Sí, he visitado México durante las vacaciones de los últimos años.)

1. comer en un restaurante hispánico
2. estar en Nueva York
3. manejar un Alfa Romeo
4. correr en un maratón
5. abrir hoy tu libro de español
6. escribir un poema
7. actuar en una obra teatral
8. ver un monumento histórico
9. conocer a una persona famosa
10. romperse la pierna alguna vez

B. ¿Verdad o mentira?

Paso 1. Invente Ud. tres oraciones sobre cosas que ha hecho y no ha hecho en su vida. Dos oraciones deben ser verdaderas y una debe ser una mentira.

MODELO: He hecho un viaje a Sudamérica.
Nunca he conocido a mis primos.
He visto muchas películas en español.

Paso 2. Lea sus oraciones a unos compañeros o a la clase entera. Ellos van a tratar de encontrar la mentira.

MODELO: Creo que has hecho un viaje a Sudamérica y que has visto muchas películas en español. Dudo que no hayas conocido a tus primos.

Nota comunicativa

Talking About What You Had Done

Use the past participle with the imperfect form of **haber** (**había, habías, ...**) to talk about what you had—or had not—done before a given time in the past. This form is called the past perfect.

Antes de graduarme en la escuela secundaria, no **había estudiado** español.

Before graduating from high school, I hadn't studied Spanish.

Antes de 1985, siempre **habíamos vivido** en Kansas.

Before 1985, we had always lived in Kansas.

C. Entrevista. Use the following cues to interview a classmate about his or her activities before coming to this campus. Begin your questions with **Dime...**

MODELO: algo / no haber aprendido a hacer antes del año pasado →
E1: Dime algo que no habías aprendido a hacer antes del año pasado.
E2: Pues... no había aprendido a nadar. Aprendí a nadar este año en mi clase de natación.

1. algo / no haber aprendido a hacer antes del año pasado
2. una materia / no haber estudiado antes del año pasado
3. el nombre de un deporte / haber practicado mucho
4. algo sobre un viaje / haber hecho varias veces
5. el nombre de un libro importante / no haber leído
6. una decisión / no haber tomado
7. ¿ ?

En los Estados Unidos y el Canadá...

El Dr. Mario Molina

En 1995 **el Dr. Mario Molina**, junto con Paul Crutzen y el Dr. F. Sherwood Rowland, otros dos **científicos**, compartieron el primer Premio Nóbel por estudios en **las ciencias ambientales**. Los científicos descubrieron el proceso químico a través del cual[a] **los clorofluorocarbonos** (CFC) destruyen **la capa de ozono** que protege a la Tierra de los rayos ultravioletas.

El Dr. Molina, el más joven de los tres, nació en 1943 en **México, D.F.**, y es ahora **ciudadano estadounidense**.

El Dr. Mario Molina

Obtuvo su doctorado en química física en la Universidad de California, Berkeley. Ahora es profesor de la Facultad de Ciencias de la Tierra,[b] la Atmósfera y los Planetas del Massachusetts Institute of Technology.

El Dr. Molina y el Dr. Rowland descubrieron que los CFC depositados en la atmósfera podían subir al nivel[c] de la capa de ozono. También supieron que, gracias a la estabilidad química de los CFC, pueden persistir allí por un siglo, aproximadamente. En 1974

[a] *a... through which*   [b] *Earth*   [c] *level*

publicaron la predicción de que la emisión continuada de los CFC a la atmósfera resultaría[d] en una **reducción catastrófica** de la capa de ozono. Esta predicción causó protestas por parte de las industrias que producían los CFC, y también por algunos científicos que expresaron sus dudas respecto a esos cálculos.

En 1985, Paul Crutzen descubrió **el «agujero»**[e] en la capa de ozono sobre el continente de la Antártida. Para resolver el problema, en 1987 los gobernantes de la Tierra firmaron un acuerdo (el Protocolo de Montreal) para proteger la capa de ozono. Unas enmiendas[f] en 1992 resultaron en la prohibición de la producción de los CFC a partir de[g] 1995. Se ha visto este acuerdo como un ejemplo trascendental de **la cooperación internacional** para solucionar un problema ambiental que afecta a toda la Tierra.

[d]*would result* [e]*hole* [f]*amendments* [g]*a… beginning in*

Videoteca

ECUADOR

Minidramas

In this **Minidramas** dialogue, Elisa Velasco and her son José Miguel meet a woman who is having car trouble. What suggestions do they give her? How do they end up helping her directly?

Elisa y José Miguel están en el campo. Una conductora se acerca a[a] ellos.

CONDUCTORA: Buenos días. Disculpe, señora. ¿Podría[b] decirme a cuánto queda[c] el pueblo más cercano[d]?

ELISA: Bueno, hay un pueblo no muy lejos de aquí, como a unos diez minutos. Pero es muy pequeño. ¿Qué busca?

CONDUCTORA: Es el carro. Temo que tenga algo serio. Ha comenzado a hacer un ruido muy extraño, y quiero que lo revise un mecánico. ¿Sabe Ud. si hay un taller en el pueblo?

> **F U N C T I O N**
>
> *asking for and giving directions*

ELISA: Ay, lo dudo mucho. Pero hay otro pueblo más grande no muy lejos, y es muy posible que haya un taller allí. Siga todo derecho unos cinco kilómetros, y luego doble a la izquierda en la carretera para Quito. ¿Sabe? Se me ocurre algo. Nosotros vamos en esa dirección. La podemos acompañar. No me gusta que se quede sola en este camino con un carro que no arranca.

CONDUCTORA: Eso es muy amable de su parte, pero no se molesten.

JOSÉ MIGUEL: De veras, no es ninguna molestia. Necesitamos encontrar una gasolinera. Tenemos que llenar el tanque.

CONDUCTORA: Muchas gracias. Uds. me han ayudado muchísimo.

ELISA: No hay de qué. ¿Vamos?

[a]*se… approaches* [b]*Could you* [c]*a… how far it is to* [d]*más… closest*

Con un compañero / una compañera

Con un compañero / una compañera practiquen las siguientes situaciones. Pueden usar las expresiones en el diálogo anterior como modelo, si quieren.

1. Ud. está manejando por el desierto en el sur de California cuando de repente se le para el coche. Ud. teme que al coche le falte gasolina, pero no está seguro/a. Después de esperar una hora, otro coche viene y se detiene (*it stops*) para ayudarlo/la.

2. Ud. se pierde mientras maneja por una ciudad extraña. Necesita ir a su hotel, pero no sabe dónde queda. Para su coche y le pide ayuda a un(a) transeúnte (*passerby*).

En contexto

MÉXICO

In this video segment, Roberto talks to Miguel, his car mechanic, about the problems that he has been having with his car. As you watch the segment, pay particular attention to the problems that Roberto imagines his car has, as opposed to the real problem that Miguel discovers. Have you ever diagnosed a car's problems incorrectly and worried unnecessarily, or do you think Roberto is overreacting?

A. Lluvia de ideas

- ¿Tiene Ud. su propio coche? (Si no tiene uno, refiérase al coche de otra persona al contestar las siguientes preguntas.) ¿Cuándo lo compró? ¿De qué año es el modelo de su coche? ¿Está Ud. contento/a con el coche?
- ¿Sabe Ud. arreglar un coche? ¿Sabe Ud. algo de mecánica en general? ¿Cuáles son los problemas más típicos de un coche?

B. Dictado

A continuación aparece un fragmento del diálogo entre Roberto y Miguel, el mecánico. Complete la explicación con las palabras o frases que faltan.

ROBERTO: _____ _____ _____ este carro es ser _____ para convertirlo en lata de aluminio.[a]

MIGUEL: Bueno. No hace falta que lo _____, Roberto. ¿Por qué no me explicas qué _____?

ROBERTO: Muy bien. Tuve un día horrible. Primero _____ _____ tarde y por eso _____ tarde al trabajo. Después del trabajo, _____ _____ perdieron las llaves.

MIGUEL: El carro, Roberto. El carro.

ROBERTO: Ah, sí. Bueno, _____ del trabajo. Metí la _____ e _____ arrancar el motor. Y nada.

MIGUEL: ¿Y se prendieron las _____ dentro del carro?

ROBERTO: Sí, las luces se prendieron. Y no es la _____, Miguel. La batería es nueva.

[a]lata... *tin can*

C. Un diálogo original

Paso 1. Con un compañero / una compañera, dramaticen el diálogo entre Roberto y Miguel.

Paso 2. La compra de un carro. Con un compañero / una compañera, piensen en un carro que Uds. podrían (*could*) comprar. Como no tienen mucho dinero, van a comprar un carro de segunda mano. Hagan una lista de todas las cosas que le deben preguntar al dueño antes de hacer la compra.

Un poco de todo

A. ¿Ya lo has hecho? Con un compañero / una compañera, háganse preguntas y contéstenlas, según el modelo.

MODELO: escribir la carta →
E1: ¿Ya *está escrita* la carta?
E2: No, no la *he escrito.*
E1: ¡Hombre! Es imposible que no la *hayas escrito* todavía.

1. hacer las maletas
2. comprar los boletos
3. preparar la cena
4. facturar el equipaje
5. sacudir los muebles
6. poner la mesa

B. Dos dibujos, un punto de vista. Un español hizo el dibujo de la derecha; un argentino, el de la izquierda. Pero los dos comentan el mismo tema.

Palabras útiles: el arado (*plow*), la deshumanización, la flor, la gente, la mecanización, la mula, el tractor

Paso 1. Conteste estas preguntas sobre el dibujo de la derecha.

1. Describa la ciudad que se ve en el dibujo.
2. ¿Qué ha descubierto la gente? ¿Por qué mira con tanto interés?
3. Para construir esta ciudad, ¿qué han hecho? ¿Qué han destruido?

Paso 2. Conteste estas preguntas sobre el dibujo de la izquierda.

1. ¿Qué se ha comprado el agricultor agricultor? ¿Qué ha vendido?

2. ¿Qué es «más moderno», según el otro agricultor?

3. ¿Qué desventaja tiene el tractor?

Paso 3. Ahora explique su reacción personal a estos dos dibujos. ¿Son chistosos (*funny*)? ¿serios?

C. ¡Qué descuidado (*careless*) eres! Complete the following paragraphs with the correct form of the words in parentheses, as suggested by the context. When two possibilities are given in parentheses, select the correct word. Begin with the present indicative. There are also command forms. Use the preterite or the imperfect of infinitives in italics.

En casa

RIGOBERTO: Me parece que debo (llevar / a llevar[1]) el coche (al / a la[2]) taller. Hace varios días que tiene una lucecita encendida.[a] No sé (qué/que[3]) puede ser.

MARGARITA: (*Tú:* Ser/Estar[4]) muy descuidado con esas cosas. Un día vas a tener una sorpresa desagradable.

RIGOBERTO: Bueno, espero que el mecánico (tener[5]) tiempo (por/para[6]) arreglarlo. Hasta luego.

En el taller

MECÁNICO: Buenos días. ¿(Lo que / Qué[7]) desea?

RIGOBERTO: Pues, (mirar: *Ud.*[8]). ¿Ve Ud. (este[9]) luz roja que está encendida? ¿Qué puede ser?

MECÁNICO: Eso es (el/la[10]) aceite. ¿Hace mucho tiempo que no (lo/la[11]) cambia?

RIGOBERTO: La verdad es que no lo (*yo: recordar*[12]).

MECÁNICO: (Dejarme: *Ud.*[13]) revisarlo todo. (Volver: *Ud.*[14]) dentro de (un/una[15]) par de horas.

Más tarde

MECÁNICO: Ud. no (preocuparse[16]) mucho por el auto, ¿verdad? Todos los niveles (*estar*[17]) muy bajos. También le (*yo: poner*[18]) agua en el depósito del limpiaparabrisas[b] y le (*cambiar*[19]) el filtro del aceite.

RIGOBERTO: ¿Eso (*ser*[20]) todo?

MECÁNICO: El coche casi no (*tener*[21]) aceite. Sinceramente, si Ud. (seguir[22]) manteniendo el auto así, algún día va a quemar[c] el motor.

RIGOBERTO: No me diga... [d]

MECÁNICO: Y otro consejo. (Cambiar: *Ud.*[23]) pronto las llantas. Hace tiempo que (*perder*[24]) el dibujo,[e] y eso (ser/estar[25]) peligroso.

[a]lucecita... *little light turned on*   [b]¿ ?   [c]*burn up*   [d]*No... You don't say . . .*   [e]*tread*

Comprensión: ¿Cierto o falso? Corrija las oraciones falsas.

1. Rigoberto se interesa mucho por su coche.
2. Su esposa sabe más de coches que él.
3. El mecánico trata a Rigoberto muy descortésmente.
4. El coche estaba en muy malas condiciones.
5. Rigoberto va a empezar a cuidar su coche.

PANORAMA *cultural*

Argentina

Datos esenciales

Nombre oficial: República Argentina
Capital: Buenos Aires
Población: 37.000.000 de habitantes
Moneda: el peso
Idioma oficial: el español

¡Fíjese!

- La inmigración de europeos en el siglo XIX ha tenido un papel decisivo en la formación de la población de la Argentina (así como en la del Uruguay). En 1856 la población argentina era de 1.200.000 de habitantes; para 1930, 10.500.000 de extranjeros habían entrado en la Argentina por el puerto de Buenos Aires. La mitad[a] estaba formada por italianos, una tercera parte por españoles, y el resto estaba formado principalmente por alemanes y eslavos. Muchos de los que llegaron fueron trabajadores temporales que, más tarde o más temprano, regresaron a Europa. El resto, sin embargo,[b] se estableció permanentemente, porque el gobierno quería estimular la inmigración para poblar la Pampa. Pero muchos, acostumbrados a la vida urbana, se quedaron en Buenos Aires.

- Buenos Aires es una ciudad con una población de más de 10.000.000 de habitantes, lo cual supone[c] el 30 por ciento de la población del país. Es el centro cultural, comercial, industrial y financiero, así como el puerto principal de la Argentina. A las personas de Buenos Aires se les llama «porteños», derivado de «puerto».

[a]*half* [b]sin... *however* [c]lo... *which constitutes*

La Plaza de Mayo data de 1580, año de la fundación de Buenos Aires

Conozca... el tango

El tango se originó en los barrios pobres de Buenos Aires a finales del siglo XIX. El tango se toca con los instrumentos de los inmigrantes: la guitarra española, el violín italiano y el típico bandoleón, una especie de acordeón alemán.

Los temas del tango muestran una dualidad. Por un lado, representan la agresividad machista,[a] que incluye dramas pasionales y peleas con cuchillos.[b] Por otro, simbolizan la nostalgia, la soledad[c] y el sentimiento de pérdida.[d] El intérprete de tangos más famoso fue el porteño Carlos Gardel (1887–1935).

[a]*male* [b]peleas... *knife fights* [c]*solitude* [d]*loss*

 Capítulo 14 of the video to accompany *Puntos de partida* contains cultural footage of Argentina.

 Visit the *Puntos de partida* Website at www.mhhe.com/puntos.

Vocabulario

El medio ambiente

acabar	to run out, use up completely
conservar	to save, conserve
construir	to build
contaminar	to pollute
cubrir	to cover
desarrollar	to develop
descubrir	to discover
desperdiciar	to waste
destruir	to destroy
evitar	to avoid
proteger	to protect
reciclar	to recycle
resolver (ue)	to solve, resolve

el aire	air
el bosque	forest
la capa de ozono	ozone layer
la energía	energy
eléctrica	electric
eólica	wind
hidráulica	hydraulic
nuclear	nuclear
solar	solar
la escasez	lack, shortage
la fábrica	factory
la falta	lack, absence
el gobierno	government
la naturaleza	nature
la población	population
los recursos naturales	natural resources

Repaso: la contaminación

¿La ciudad o el campo?

el/la agricultor(a)	farmer
el aislamiento	isolation
el árbol	tree
el/la campesino/a	farm worker; peasant
el delito	crime
la finca	farm
el rascacielos	skyscraper

el ritmo	rhythm, pace
el servicio	service
el transporte	(means of) transportation
la vida	life
la violencia	violence
la vivienda	housing

Hablando de coches

arrancar	to start (a car)
gastar	to use, expend
llenar	to fill (up)
revisar	to check

el aceite	oil
la batería	battery
la estación de gasolina	gas station
los frenos	brakes
la gasolina	gasoline
la gasolinera	gas station
la llanta (desinflada)	(flat) tire
el/la mecánico/a	mechanic
el nivel	level
el parabrisas	windshield
el taller	(repair) shop
el tanque	tank

Repaso: arreglar, limpiar

En el camino

chocar (con)	to run into, collide (with)
conducir	to drive
doblar	to turn
estacionar(se)	to park
obedecer	to obey
parar	to stop
seguir (i, i)	to continue

la autopista	freeway
la calle	street
el camino	street, road

la carretera	highway
la circulación	traffic
el/la conductor(a)	driver
la esquina	(street) corner
la licencia de manejar/conducir	driver's license
el límite de velocidad	speed limit
el/la policía	police officer
el semáforo	traffic signal
el tránsito	traffic

todo derecho	straight ahead

Repaso: manejar

Los adjetivos

acelerado/a	fast, accelerated
bello/a	beautiful
denso/a	dense
público/a	public
puro/a	pure

Un paso más 14

LECTURA

Estrategia: Using Background Knowledge

Another useful strategy that you can use to facilitate your reading comprehension is the "activation" of any background knowledge that you might have about the topic. That is, if you think about all that you know about the topic of the passage, you can begin to formulate a hypothesis and make predictions about the content.

The following passage is entitled "La Amazonia pierde cada año un millón y medio de hectáreas". No doubt you already know something about the Amazon, given that it is frequently mentioned in the press and on television. To begin, note three things that you already know about the Amazon.

1.

2.

3.

Think about these things as you read the article. This information might be mentioned in the passage.

▶ **Sobre la lectura...** Este artículo es de un periódico español, *El Diario*, de
▶ Sevilla, y se publicó en el verano de 1999. El tema de la Amazonia sigue
▶ siendo de interés internacional, y recibe la atención del mundo, no sólo de
▶ este país.

La Amazonia pierde cada año un millón y medio de hectáreas[a]

L a Amazonia, espacio vital para el equilibrio del Planeta, pierde cada año 1,5 millones de hectáreas, debido principalmente a la extracción ilegal de madera[b] por parte de las multinacionales de explotación forestal.

Según un informe de Greenpeace, *Plantando cara a[c] la deforestación*, el 80 por ciento de la madera obtenida de la Amazonia se extrae ilegalmente y el 72 por ciento de los treinta y seis

Área deforestada de la Amazonia

[a]*land measurement equivalent to 2.47 acres* [b]*wood*
[c]*Plantando... Confronting*

«puntos críticos» de deforestación de la zona son consecuencia de la actividad maderera.[d]

El documento, que responsabiliza a diecisiete multinacionales de explotación forestal de la destrucción progresiva de este «pulmón del Planeta», resalta[e] que la contribución de la Amazonia a la producción total de madera en Brasil se ha disparado[f] del 14 por ciento al 85 por ciento en sólo dos décadas.

«A la cabeza de la destrucción de los bosques primarios de la Amazonia se encuentra la industria de la madera, que en 1997 causó daños en cerca de 1,5 millones de hectáreas», afirma el documento.

El informe y la denuncia[g] sobre la actual situación de la Amazonia se encuadran[h] en una campaña mundial de Greenpeace para frenar la destrucción acelerada de la Amazonia y la gira[i] por varios países de una delegación amazónica, que estos días se encuentra en España.

Tras destacar[j] que la explotación forestal intensiva aumenta[k] de forma preocupante, los portavoces[l] alertaron de que, en los últimos cuatro años, ocho multinacionales han comprado una extensión de selva amazónica del tamaño de la Comunidad Valenciana[m] –2,3 millones de hectáreas— y ya controlan el 12 por ciento de la capacidad de producción que hay en la zona.

También subrayaron[n] que, en los últimos veinte años, se ha destruido el 15 por ciento de la Amazonia —un territorio equivalente a Francia— y afirmaron que «es posible e imprescindible[o] compatabilizar la vida de los trabajadores indígenas con la conservación de este ecosistema que da equilibrio al Planeta.» ●

[d]*wood-related* [e]*emphasizes* [f]*se... has increased* [g]*accusation* [h]*se... are included* [i]*tour* [j]*Tras... After emphasizing* [k]*is increasing* [l]*spokespersons* [m]*Comunidad... region in Spain* [n]*they underscored* [o]*necesario*

Comprensión

A. Confirmación. Vuelva a la lista que Ud. escribió antes de leer el artículo. ¿Qué información de su lista aparece en el pasaje?

B. Los responsables. Según el artículo, ¿quiénes son los responsables de la deforestación de la Amazonia?

C. Una metáfora. En el artículo, a la Amazonia se le llama el «pulmón del Planeta». Explique esta metáfora en español con sus propias palabras.

E S C R I T U R A

Problemas ecológicos. ¿Qué problema ecológico le preocupa más a Ud.? ¿Ha pensado en las varias maneras (*ways*) en que puede proteger el medio ambiente? Escoja uno de los problemas de la lista a continuación (u otro, si quiere) que le gustaría comentar. Luego escriba una breve composición en la que describe el problema. También comente lo que ha hecho Ud. o lo que piensa hacer para resolver el problema.

Problemas medio ambientales

- La deforestación
- La contaminación de los ríos (*rivers*) y lagos (*lakes*)
- El uso de pesticidas (*m.*) en las verduras y frutas
- La escasez de energía eléctrica
- La falta de recursos naturales
- El desecho (*waste*) de productos de plástico y de papel
- La destrucción de la capa de ozono

La vida social y la vida afectiva

Estos novios españoles, tratan de estudiar. ¿Cree Ud. que lo van a lograr (*manage*)?

¿Qué opina Ud.?

Conteste cierto o falso, según su propia vida. ¿Cree Ud. que una persona de otro país diría algo similar? Visite el sitio Web de *Puntos de partida* para leer las respuestas a estas preguntas que da una persona de Chile.

1. Es necesario **casarse** para tener una vida feliz y completa.
2. Se debe prohibir que la gente (*people*) se case antes de los veinticinco años, ya que inevitablemente **los matrimonios** entre personas muy jóvenes resultan en **el divorcio**.
3. Los padres deben vivir con sus hijos en su **vejez**.
4. Los jóvenes deben empezar a salir con sus **novios** a la edad de 12 años.
5. Lo más importante en la vida es la familia y luego, en orden de importancia, los amigos y el trabajo.

En este capítulo...

- In this chapter, you will study vocabulary related to relationships and marriage, and to the stages of life, such as your **adolescencia** and **juventud.**
- In this chapter, you will start using the subjunctive after clauses that suggest indefinite or nonexistent situations, such as **Busco un compañero / una compañera que me quiera.** (Grammar 44)
- In addition, you will learn how to use the subjunctive to describe situations that hinge upon a prior event, such as going to classes **a menos que haya un huracán o un tornado.** Can you guess what **a menos que** means? (Grammar 45)
- The **Panorama cultural** section will introduce you to the culture and people of Chile.

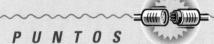

PUNTOS *INTERACTIVO*

Videoteca

◀ **Minidramas**
En este episodio, Lola Benítez y su amiga íntima Eva Díaz hacen planes para el fin de semana. ¿Ve Ud. a sus mejores amigos con frecuencia? ¿En qué se diferencian sus amigos íntimos de sus otras amistades?

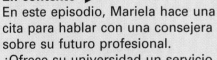

En contexto ▶
En este episodio, Mariela hace una cita para hablar con una consejera sobre su futuro profesional. ¿Ofrece su universidad un servicio semejante (*similar*)?

 CD-ROM

Además de completar el vocabulario y las actividades de gramática, Ud. va a tener la oportunidad de «hablar» con una recepcionista y de «hacer una cita» con una consejera.

 Internet

En la sección del Capítulo 15 en el sitio Web de *Puntos de partida* aparecen enlaces que Ud. puede usar para conseguir información en español sobre las etapas de la vida. Use la dirección **www.mhhe.com/puntos.**

Las relaciones sentimentales

la amistad

la cita

el amor

el noviazgo

la luna de miel

el matrimonio

la boda

el divorcio

Más vocabulario

el/la amigo/a	friend	**amistoso/a**	friendly
la esposa / la mujer	wife	**cariñoso/a**	affectionate
el esposo / el marido	husband	**casado/a**[*]	married
el/la novio/a	boyfriend/girlfriend; fiancé(e); groom/bride	**soltero/a**[*]	single, not married
la pareja	(married) couple; partner	**amar**	to love
		casarse (con)	to marry
		divorciarse (de)	to get divorced (from)
		enamorarse (de)	to fall in love (with)

---

[*]In the activities and exercises of **Capítulo 2**, you began to use **ser casado/a**. A variation of this phrase is **estar casado/a**. **Estar casado/a** means *to be married*; **ser casado/a** means *to be a married person*. **Ser soltero/a** is used exclusively to describe an unmarried person.

llevarse bien/mal (con)	to get along well/poorly (with)	romper (con)	to break up (with)
pasar tiempo (con)	to spend time (with)	salir (con)	to go out (with)
querer (ie)	to love	separarse (de)	to separate (from)

Conversación

A. Definiciones. Empareje las palabras con sus definiciones. Luego, para cada palabra definida, dé un verbo y también el nombre de una persona asociada con esa relación social. Hay más de una respuesta posible en cada caso.

1. _____ el matrimonio *e*
2. _____ el amor *c*
3. _____ el divorcio *b*
4. _____ la boda *d*
5. _____ la amistad *a*

a. Es una relación cariñosa entre dos personas. Se llevan bien y se hablan con frecuencia.

b. Es el posible resultado de un matrimonio, cuando los esposos no se llevan bien.

c. Es una relación sentimental, apasionada, muy especial, entre dos personas. Puede llevar al (*lead to*) matrimonio.

d. Es una ceremonia religiosa o civil en la que (*which*) la novia a veces lleva un vestido blanco.

e. Es una relación legal entre dos personas que viven juntas (*together*) y que a veces tienen hijos.

B. ¡Seamos lógicos! Complete las oraciones lógicamente.

1. Mi abuelo es el _____ de mi abuela.
2. Muchos novios tienen un largo _____ antes de la boda.
3. María y Julio tienen una _____ el viernes para comer en un restaurante. Luego van a bailar.
4. La _____ de Juan y Pati es el domingo a las dos de la tarde, en la iglesia (*church*) de San Martín.
5. En una _____, ¿quién debe pagar o comprar los boletos, el hombre o la mujer?
6. La _____ entre los ex esposos es imposible. No pueden ser amigos.
7. ¡El _____ es ciego (*blind*)!
8. Para algunas personas, el _____ es un concepto anticuado. Prefieren vivir juntos, sin casarse.
9. Algunas parejas modernas no quieren gastar su dinero en _____.
10. Algunas personas creen que es posible _____ a primera vista (*at first sight*).

Nota cultural

Relaciones de la vida social

Dos palabras españolas que no tienen equivalente exacto en inglés son **amigo** y **novio**. En el diagrama se indica cuándo es apropiado usar estas palabras para describir relaciones sociales en muchas culturas hispánicas y en la norteamericana.

friend *girlfriend/boyfriend* *fiancée/fiancé* *bride/groom*

amiga/amigo novia/novio

Como en todas partes del mundo, los enamorados hispanos usan muchos términos de cariño: **mi amor, mi amorcito/a, mi vida, viejo/vieja, querido/querida, cielo, corazón.** Es también frecuente el uso afectuoso de las frases **mi hijo/mi hija** entre esposos y aun[a] entre buenos amigos.

[a]*even*

Etapas de la vida°

Etapas... *Stages of life*

el nacimiento	birth	**nacer**	to be born
la infancia	infancy	**crecer**	to grow
la niñez	childhood	**morir (ue, u)**	to die
la adolescencia	adolescence		
la juventud	youth		
la madurez	middle age		
la vejez	old age		
la muerte	death		

Conversación

▲▲▲▲▲▲▲

A. Etapas de la vida. Relacione las siguientes palabras y frases con las distintas etapas de la vida de una persona. **¡OJO!** Hay más de una posible relación en algunos casos.

1. el amor
2. los nietos
3. los juguetes (*toys*)
4. no poder comer sin ayuda
5. los hijos en la universidad
6. los granos (*pimples*)
7. la universidad
8. la boda

B. Preguntas

1. ¿Son importantes los amigos en su vida? ¿Quién es su mejor amigo/a? ¿Cuánto tiempo hace que lo/la conoce? ¿Crecieron Uds. juntos/as? Es decir, ¿se han conocido desde la niñez? ¿desde la adolescencia? ¿Por qué se lleva bien con esa persona?

2. ¿Quiere Ud. casarse algún día? (¿Ya se casó?) ¿Le gusta la idea de tener una boda grande? (¿Tuvo una boda grande?) ¿Piensa hacer un viaje de luna de miel? (¿Hizo un viaje de luna de miel?) ¿Adónde?

3. ¿Qué es lo bueno de estar casado? ¿y lo malo? ¿Qué es lo bueno de ser soltero? ¿y lo malo?

4. ¿En qué década del siglo (*century*) pasado nació Ud.? ¿Ha visto muchos cambios desde entonces? ¿Cuáles son? ¿Cómo piensa pasar su vejez? (Si Ud. ya es una persona madura, ¿cómo pasa su tiempo?)

5. ¿Ha sido Ud. afectado/a personalmente por la muerte de alguien? ¿Quién murió? ¿Cómo se sintió Ud.? ¿Tiene buenos recuerdos (*memories*) de esa persona? ¿Cuáles son?

C. Una receta para unas buenas relaciones. Piense en su propio (*own*) matrimonio o en el de sus padres / unos amigos. O, si lo prefiere, piense en sus relaciones con su mejor amigo/a o en las de un par de amigos que Ud. tiene. En su opinión, ¿cuáles son los ingredientes necesarios para un buen matrimonio o una buena amistad?

Paso 1. Haga una lista de los cinco ingredientes más esenciales. Los ingredientes pueden expresarse con una palabra o una frase.

Paso 2. Compare su lista con las de otros tres estudiantes. ¿Coinciden en la selección de algunos ingredientes? Hablen de todos los ingredientes y hagan una lista de los cinco más importantes.

Paso 3. Ahora comparen los resultados de todos los grupos. ¿Han contestado todos más o menos de la misma manera?

Minidiálogos y gramática

44 ¿Hay alguien que... ? ¿Hay un lugar donde... ? • Subjunctive after Nonexistent and Indefinite Antecedents

La persona ideal

PALOMA: Dime, José Miguel… ¿Cómo es la novia ideal para ti? ¿Cómo es la persona que buscas?

JOSÉ MIGUEL: Bueno, *busco una persona que sea* cariñosa, *que me comprenda* y *que tenga* mucha paciencia. También *quiero una novia que sea* lista y muy guapa.

PALOMA: No me parecen mal tus requisitos. Pues, yo *tengo un novio que es* muy cariñoso y *que me comprende.* En Gustavo *tengo un amigo especial, que* además *es* muy paciente. Y, claro, ¡es muy inteligente y bastante guapo!

JOSÉ MIGUEL: Sí, sí, yo lo sé… Como no haces más que hablar de él…

Comprensión: ¿Cierto o falso?

1. José Miguel ya tiene novia.
2. José Miguel busca una novia que tenga muchas cualidades deseables.
3. Paloma busca un novio que sea inteligente y guapo.
4. Parece que Paloma ya tiene el novio perfecto.

A. In English and Spanish, statements or questions that give or ask for information about a person, place, or thing often contain two clauses.

Each of the example sentences contains a main clause (*I have a car, Is there a house for sale*). In addition, each sentence also has a subordinate clause (*that gets good mileage; that is closer to the city*) that modifies a noun in the main clause: *car, house.* The noun (or pronoun) modified is called the *antecedent* (**el antecedente**) of the subordinate clause, and the clause itself is called an adjective clause because—like an adjective—it modifies a noun (or pronoun).

I have a **car** *that gets good mileage.*
Is there a **house for sale** *that is closer to the city*?

B. Sometimes the antecedent of an adjective clause is something that, in the speaker's mind, does not exist or whose existence is indefinite or uncertain.

NONEXISTENT ANTECEDENT:

There is *nothing* that you can do.

INDEFINITE ANTECEDENT:

We need *a car* that will last us for years. (We don't have one yet.)

The ideal person PALOMA: Tell me, José Miguel . . . What's your ideal girlfriend like? The person you're looking for, what's she like? JOSÉ MIGUEL: Well, I look for a person who's affectionate, who understands me, and who has lots of patience. I also want a girlfriend who's intelligent and very pretty. PALOMA: Your requirements aren't that bad. Well, I have a boyfriend who's very affectionate and who understands me. In Gustavo I have a special friend who is also very patient. And, of course, he's very intelligent and rather handsome! JOSÉ MIGUEL: Yes, yes, I already know… Since all you do is talk about him…

In these cases, the subjunctive must be used in the adjective (subordinate) clause in Spanish.

Note in the examples that adjective clauses that describe a place can be introduced with **donde...** as well as with **que...**

EXISTENT ANTECEDENT:

Hay algo aquí que me **interesa**.
There is something here that interests me.

NONEXISTENT ANTECEDENT:

No veo nada que me **interese**.
I don't see anything that interests me.

DEFINITE ANTECEDENT:

Hay muchos restaurantes donde **sirven** comida mexicana auténtica.
There are a lot of restaurants where they serve authentic Mexican food.

INDEFINITE ANTECEDENT:

Buscamos un restaurante donde **sirvan** comida salvadoreña auténtica.
We're looking for a restaurant where they serve authentic Salvadoran food.

O J O

The dependent adjective clause structure is often used in questions to find out about someone or something the speaker does not know much about. Note, however, that the indicative is used to answer the question if the antecedent is known to the person who answers.

INDEFINITE ANTECEDENT:

¿Hay algo aquí que te **guste?**
Is there anything here that you like?

DEFINITE ANTECEDENT:

Sí, **hay varias bolsas** que me **gustan**.
Yes, there are several purses that I like.

O J O

The personal **a** is not used with direct object nouns that refer to hypothetical persons.* Compare the use of the indicative and the subjunctive in the sentences at the right.

NONEXISTENT ANTECEDENT:

Busco **un señor** que **sepa francés**.
I'm looking for a man who knows French.

EXISTENT ANTECEDENT:

Busco **al señor** que **sabe francés**.
I'm looking for the man who knows French.

---

*Remember that **alguien** and **nadie** always take the personal **a** when they are used as direct objects: **Busco a alguien que lo sepa. No veo a nadie que sea norteamericano.**

A. Hablando de gente que conocemos. En su familia, ¿hay personas que tengan las siguientes características? Indique la oración apropiada en cada par de oraciones.

TENGO UN PARIENTE…	NO TENGO NINGÚN PARIENTE…
1. ☐ que habla alemán	☐ que hable alemán
2. ☐ que vive en el extranjero	☐ que viva en el extranjero
3. ☐ que es dueño de un restaurante	☐ que sea dueño de un restaurante
4. ☐ que sabe tocar el piano	☐ que sepa tocar el piano
5. ☐ que es médico/a	☐ que sea médico/a
6. ☐ que fuma	☐ que fume
7. ☐ que está divorciado/a	☐ que esté divorciado/a
8. ☐ que trabaja en la televisión	☐ que trabaje en la televisión

B. Las preguntas de Carmen

Paso 1. Carmen acaba de llegar aquí de otro estado. Quiere saber algunas cosas sobre la universidad y la ciudad. Haga las preguntas de Carmen según el modelo.

MODELO: restaurantes / sirven comida latinoamericana →
¿Hay restaurantes que sir**van** (donde se sirv**a**) comida latinoamericana?

1. librerías / venden libros usados
2. tiendas / se puede comprar revistas de Latinoamérica
3. cafés cerca de la universidad / se reúnen muchos estudiantes
4. apartamentos cerca de la universidad / son buenos y baratos
5. cines / pasan (*they show*) películas en español
6. un gimnasio en la universidad / se juega al ráquetbol
7. parques / la gente corre o da paseos
8. museos / hacen exposiciones de arte latinoamericano

Paso 2. ¿Son ciertas o falsas las siguientes declaraciones?

1. A Carmen no le interesa la cultura hispánica.
2. Carmen es deportista.
3. Es posible que sea estudiante.
4. Este año piensa vivir con unos amigos de sus padres.

Paso 3. Ahora conteste las preguntas de Carmen con información verdadera sobre la ciudad donde Ud. vive y su universidad.

Conversación

A. Una encuesta. Las habilidades o características de un grupo de personas pueden ser sorprendentes. ¿Qué sabe Ud. de los compañeros de su clase de español? Pregúnteles a los miembros de la clase si saben hacer lo siguiente o a quién le ocurre lo siguiente. Deben levantar la mano sólo los que puedan contestar afirmativamente. Luego la persona que hizo la pregunta debe hacer un comentario apropiado. Siga el modelo.

MODELO: hablar chino →
En esta clase, ¿hay alguien que hable chino? (*Nadie levanta la mano.*) No hay nadie que hable chino.

1. hablar ruso
2. saber tocar la viola
3. conocer a un actor / una actriz
4. saber preparar comida vietnamita
5. tener el cumpleaños hoy
6. escribir poemas
7. vivir en las afueras
8. ¿ ?

B. Entrevista. With another student, ask and answer the following questions. Then report any interesting details to the class.

1. ¿Hay alguien en tu vida que te quiera locamente?
2. ¿Hay algo que te importe más que los estudios universitarios?
3. ¿Con qué tipo de persona te gusta salir?
4. Para el semestre/trimestre que viene, ¿qué clases buscas? ¿una que empiece a las ocho de la mañana?
5. ¿Tienes algún amigo o alguna amiga de la escuela secundaria que esté casado/a? ¿que tenga hijos? ¿que esté divorciado/a?
6. ¡OJO! Unas preguntas indiscretas: ¿Has conocido recientemente a alguien que te haya gustado mucho? ¿de quien te hayas enamorado? ¿Hay alguna persona de tu familia con quien te lleves muy mal? ¿o muy, muy bien?

En los Estados Unidos y el Canadá...

Isabel Allende

Es posible que la chilena Isabel Allende (1942–) sea **la escritora hispánica más conocida de Norteamérica**. Sobrina del presidente de Chile, Salvador Allende, que fue derrocado[a] violentamente y murió en 1973, Isabel viene de **una familia que tiene un pasado muy interesante.** Este pasado, con su mezcla[b] de lo familiar y lo político, aparece como uno de los elementos más salientes[c] de sus novelas. Estas[d] se caracterizan también por el uso del «realismo mágico», técnica literaria en que elementos fantásticos se entretejen[e] con aspectos de la vida diaria. Su primera novela, *La casa de los espíritus*, apareció en 1982 y fue seguida por otras de igual éxito:[f] entre ellas, *Eva Luna*, *El plan infinito* y *De amor y de sombra*.

La vida de Allende no ha sido fácil. Después de los eventos políticos en que murió su tío, tuvo que **abandonar su país** con sus hijos pequeños. Vivió por un tiempo en Venezuela y hoy reside en los Estados Unidos con su **segundo esposo. Perdió su segunda hija**, Paula, después de una larga y trágica enfermedad, cuando esta tenía 28 años. A ella le dedicó un libro en el que[g] cuenta la historia de la familia a la vez que narra los cambios que sufre la escritora a consecuencia del trauma de la enfermedad de su adorada hija. Pero los contratiempos[h] no parecen detener a la incansable Isabel Allende. Sus libros se consiguen en español y en traducción en los Estados Unidos y el Canadá y son popularísimos.

[a]*overthrown* [b]*mixture* [c]*prominent* [d]*These (novels)* [e]*se... are interwoven* [f]*success* [g]*en... in which* [h]*mishaps, disappointments*

45

Lo hago para que tú... • Subjunctive after
Conjunctions of Contingency and Purpose

Un baile de máscaras

ESTELA: Bueno, María, esta fiesta está muy divertida, ¿no?

MARÍA: Sí, Estela, gracias por invitarme. ¡Y qué disfraces más interesantes! Espero bailar mucho *antes de que nos vayamos.*

ESTELA: Pues, yo no voy *a bailar a menos que toquen* unos ritmos caribeños. Me encanta la salsa.

MARÍA: ¡Qué gracioso! Tú, vestida de princesa medieval, vas a bailar salsa...

ESTELA: No te rías de mí, María. *En caso de que no te hayas fijado,* ¡tú también estás vestida de princesa!

MARÍA: Tienes razón. ¡Qué casualidad!

Según la lectura, ¿son ciertas o falsas estas oraciones?

1. Estela tiene planes de bailar mucho después de salir de la fiesta.
2. Estela es la única (*the only one*) vestida de princesa.
3. A Estela no le gustan los ritmos caribeños.

A. When one action or condition is related to another—X will happen provided that Y occurs; we'll do Z unless A happens—a relationship of *contingency* is said to exist: one thing is contingent, or depends, on another.

The Spanish *conjunctions* (**las conjunciones**) at the right express relationships of contingency or purpose. The subjunctive always occurs in subordinate clauses introduced by these conjunctions.

a menos que	unless
antes (de) que	before
con tal (de) que	provided (that)
en caso de que	in case
para que	so that

B. Note that these conjunctions introduce subordinate clauses in which the events have not yet materialized; the events are conceptualized, not real-world, events.

Voy **con tal de que** ellos me **acompañen**.
I'm going, provided (that) they go with me.

En caso de que llegue Juan, dile que ya salí.
In case Juan arrives, tell him that I already left.

A Costume Ball ESTELA: Well, María, this is a very enjoyable party, isn't it? MARÍA: Yes, thanks for inviting me. And the costumes are so interesting! I expect to dance a lot before I leave. ESTELA: Well, I'm not going to dance unless they play some Caribbean music. I love salsa. MARÍA: That's funny! Here you are dressed like a medieval princess, and dancing salsa... ESTELA: Don't you laugh at me, María. In case you haven't noticed, you're also dressed as a princess! MARÍA: You're right. What a coincidence!

C. When there is no change of subject in the dependent clause, Spanish more frequently uses the prepositions **antes de** and **para**, plus an infinitive, instead of the corresponding conjunctions plus the subjunctive. Compare the sentences at the right.

PREPOSITION: Estoy aquí **para aprender**.
I'm here to (in order to) learn.

CONJUNCTION: Estoy aquí **para que Uds. aprendan**.
I'm here so that you will learn.

PREPOSITION: Voy a comer **antes de salir**.
I'm going to eat before leaving.

CONJUNCTION: Voy a comer **antes de que salgamos**.
I'm going to eat before we leave.

Práctica

A. ¿Es Ud. un buen amigo / una buena amiga? La amistad es una de las relaciones más importantes de la vida. Indique si las siguientes oraciones son ciertas o falsas para Ud. con respecto a sus amigos. ¡OJO! No todas las características son buenas. Hay que leer con cuidado.

	C	F
1. Les hago muchos favores a mis amigos, con tal que ellos después me ayuden a mí.	☐	☐
2. Les ofrezco consejos a mis amigos para que tomen buenas decisiones.	☐	☐
3. Les presto dinero a menos que sepa que no me lo pueden devolver.	☐	☐
4. Les traduzco el menú en los restaurantes mexicanos en caso de que no sepan leer español.	☐	☐
5. Los llevo a casa cuando beben, para que no tengan accidentes de coche.	☐	☐

B. Julio siempre llega tarde. Siempre es buena idea llegar un poco temprano al teatro o al cine. Sin embargo, su amigo Julio, quien va al cine con Ud. esta tarde, no quiere salir con un poco de anticipación. Trate de convencerlo de que Uds. deben salir pronto.

JULIO: No entiendo por qué quieres que lleguemos al teatro tan temprano.
UD.: Pues, para que (nosotros)…

Sugerencias: poder estacionar el coche, no perder el principio de la función, poder comprar los boletos, conseguir buenas butacas (*seats*), no tener que hacer cola, comprar palomitas (*popcorn*) antes de que empiece la película, hablar con los amigos

C. Un fin de semana en las montañas

Paso 1. Hablan Manolo y Lola. Use la conjunción entre paréntesis para unir las oraciones, haciendo todos los cambios necesarios.

1. No voy. Dejamos a la niña con los abuelos. (a menos que)
2. Vamos solos. Pasamos un fin de semana romántico. (para que)
3. Esta vez voy a aprender a esquiar. Tú me enseñas. (con tal de que)
4. Vamos a salir temprano por la mañana. Nos acostamos tarde la noche anterior. (a menos que)
5. Es importante que lleguemos a la estación (*resort*) de esquí. Empieza a nevar. (antes de que)
6. Deja la dirección y el teléfono del hotel. Tus padres nos necesitan. (en caso de que)

Paso 2. ¿Cierto, falso o no lo dice?

1. Manolo y Lola acaban de casarse.
2. Casi siempre van de vacaciones con su hija.
3. Los dos son excelentes esquiadores.
4. Van a dejar a la niña con los abuelos.

Conversación
▲▲▲▲▲▲▲▲

Situaciones. Cualquier acción puede justificarse. Con un compañero / una compañera o con un grupo de estudiantes, den una explicación para las siguientes situaciones. Luego comparen sus explicaciones con las de otro grupo.

1. Los padres trabajan mucho para (que)…
2. Los profesores les dan tarea a los estudiantes para (que)…
3. Los dueños de los equipos deportivos profesionales les pagan mucho a algunos jugadores para (que)…
4. Las películas extranjeras se doblan (*are dubbed*) para (que)…
5. Los padres castigan (*punish*) a los niños para (que)…
6. Las parejas se divorcian para (que)…
7. Los jóvenes forman pandillas (*gangs*) para (que)…

Videoteca

ESPAÑA

Minidramas

In this **Minidramas** dialogue, Lola Benítez and her good friend Eva Díaz talk about their plans for the weekend. What are some of the plans they already have? What do they talk about doing?

F U N C T I O N
making weekend plans

Lola y su amiga Eva Díaz se reúnen el viernes por la tarde.

LOLA: ¡Por fin es viernes! ¡Qué semana más larga! ¿eh?

EVA: ¿Qué vais a hacer este fin de semana?

LOLA: Pues, nos vamos a pasar el día con mi hermano en Cádiz. Es el cumpleaños de mi sobrino. Y el domingo no tenemos planes. Y vosotros, ¿qué hacéis?

EVA: El domingo vamos a una boda aquí en Sevilla. Se casa una prima mía.[a] ¿Tenéis planes para esta noche?

LOLA: Creo que no, a menos que Manolo haya hecho planes.

EVA: ¿Y por qué no salimos todos juntos? ¡Hace tanto tiempo que no lo hacemos!

LOLA: Por mí, encantada. Vamos. Podemos ir a cenar o al cine. Hay dos o tres películas interesantes que a Manolo y a mí nos gustaría ver. También podemos llevar a las niñas. ¡Carolina y Marta ya son como hermanas! Se lo voy a preguntar a Manolo y te llamo después.

EVA: Muy bien. Yo también hablo con Jesús. Hablamos luego y entonces decidimos qué hacer, ¿vale?

LOLA: Estupendo.

[a]*of mine*

Con un compañero / una compañera

Con un compañero / una compañera, inventen un diálogo para por lo menos una de las siguientes situaciones. Pueden usar el **Vocabulario útil** en la página 464.

1. Una persona quiere ir al cine (tomar un café, …), pero la otra rechaza (*declines*) la invitación.
2. Dos personas, un hombre y una mujer, están en un museo. Los dos miran una pintura muy famosa. Él quiere hablar con ella y ella con él. Uno de ellos inicia la conversación y luego invita a la otra persona a tomar café.
3. Un joven de 14 años invita a una chica de 13 años a una fiesta. Los dos están muy nerviosos.
4. Dos personas van a una fiesta. Tienen que arreglar todos los detalles: a qué hora van, qué ropa van a llevar, cómo van, etcétera.

En contexto

ESPAÑA

In this video segment, Mariela makes an appointment to see the university's career counselor. As you watch the segment, pay attention to the exchange between Mariela and the receptionist and how they decide upon a time that suits both Mariela and the counselor. Does your university or college provide a similar service?

A. Lluvia de ideas

- Aparte de (*Aside from*) sus clases, ¿tiene Ud. muchos compromisos sociales y citas? ¿Cómo recuerda Ud. cuándo tiene sus compromisos? ¿Usa una agenda o un calendario?

- ¿Cuándo tiene sus próximas citas? ¿Puede decir con quién las tiene o prefiere que no se sepa?

B. Dictado

A continuación aparece un fragmento del diálogo entre Mariela y la recepcionista de la consejera Valenzuela. Complete la explicación con las palabras o frases que faltan.

RECEPCIONISTA: Buenos días, oficina de la consejera Valenzuela. ¿En qué _____ puedo servir?

MARIELA: _____ buenos días. ¿_____ _____ con la consejera Valenzuela, por favor?

RECEPCIONISTA: Disculpe.[a] ¿De parte de[b] _____? [...] Lo siento pero la consejera está con un _____ en este momento. ¿Quiere dejar un recado?

MARIELA: Bueno, _____ _____ _____ es hacer una cita.

[a]*Excuse me.* [b]*De… On behalf of*

C. Un diálogo original

Opción 1. Con un compañero / una compañera, dramaticen el diálogo entre Mariela y la recepcionista.

Opción 2. Una cita para ir a tomar una lección de baile. Ud. y su amigo/a han decidido tomar juntos unas lecciones de baile (rumba, merengue, tango, flamenco, *square dancing, two-step,* etcétera). Tienen que escoger el día y la hora más convenientes para los dos (hay muchas clases a horas diferentes). Si uno/a de Uds. tiene alguna experiencia en este tipo de baile, no se olvide de darle recomendaciones a la persona que no tenga experiencia (decirle, por ejemplo, qué tipo de ropa y zapatos debe llevar).

Un poco de todo

A. Situaciones de la vida. Con un compañero / una compañera, háganse preguntas y contéstenlas, según el modelo. Deben justificar sus respuestas.

> MODELOS: compañero/a de cuarto // tener coche →
> E1: ¿Buscas un compañero de cuarto que tenga coche?
> E2: No, ya tengo coche.
> (Sí, para que yo no tenga que manejar tanto.)
> (Sí, en caso de que mi coche viejo no funcione.)

1. marido/mujer // ser médico/a
2. amigo/a // no haber roto recientemente con su pareja
3. casa // estar lejos de la ciudad
4. ciudad // haber un buen sistema de transporte público
5. amistad // estar basada en la confianza (*trust*)
6. coche // arrancar inmediatamente, sin problemas

B. La luna de miel. Complete the following dialogues with the correct form of the words in parentheses, as suggested by the context. When two possibilities are given in parentheses, select the correct one. **¡OJO!** You will use indicative, present subjunctive, and command forms. *P* and *I* stand for *preterite* and *imperfect*, respectively. Use the past participle of infinitives in italics.

En el aeropuerto

> MUJER: ¡Por fin hemos (*llegar*[1])! ¡Qué vuelo más largo!
> MARIDO: Sí. (Soy/Estoy[2]) bastante cansado. Quiero (descansar[3]) un rato antes de que (*nosotros:* salir[4]) a ver la ciudad.
> MUJER: Yo (también/tampoco[5]). Vamos a recoger[a] el equipaje. ¡Ojalá que no se nos (ha/haya[6]) perdido!
> MARIDO: No (preocuparte[7]). Todo saldrá bien.[b] Vamos.

[a]*pick up*   [b]saldrá... *will turn out alright*

En el hotel

MARIDO: Ay, ¡qué desgracia! ¿Qué hemos (*hacer*[8]) nosotros para merecer[a] esto?

MUJER: (Calmarte[9]), mi amor. No pasa (nunca/nada[10]). Si sólo[b] se nos (*P:* perder[11]) una maleta. Y la empleada de la aerolínea nos (*P:* prometer[12]) que (lo/la[13]) vamos a tener para mañana.

MARIDO: Sí, tienes razón. Verdad que hasta (este/esto[14]) momento, todo ha (*salir*[15]) muy bien. ¡Qué boda más (bonito[16]) (*P, nosotros:* tener[17])! (*I:* Haber[18]) muchas más personas de lo que (*I, nosotros:* esperar[19]). Pero creo que todos (*P:* divertirse[20]).

MUJER: Creo que sí. En mi opinión, no hay nadie a quien no le (gustar[21]) una fiesta de bodas…

MARIDO: Bueno, descansemos[c] un poco para que (*nosotros:* poder[22]) disfrutar del[d] resto (del / de la[23]) noche. No quiero que una maleta perdida (aguar[e] [24]) la luna de miel.

MUJER: ¡Ni yo (también/tampoco[25])!

[a]*deserve* [b]*Si… Only* [c]*let's rest* [d]*disfrutar… enjoy the* [e]*to spoil*

Comprensión: ¿Cierto, falso o no lo dice?

1. Las dos personas son recién casadas.
2. La fiesta de bodas tuvo lugar en casa de los padres de la mujer.
3. Los esposos perdieron dos maletas.
4. Fueron a Cancún en su luna de miel.
5. La boda fue bonita y muy divertida.

C. ¿Qué prefiere Ud.? ¿Qué espera? Complete las siguientes oraciones con información verdadera.

1. Prefiero comer en restaurantes donde _____.
2. No me gusta que los programas de televisión _____.
3. Voy a graduarme en _____ a menos que _____.
4. Me gusta que los profesores _____.
5. Algún día deseo tener un coche que _____.
6. Este verano voy a _____ a menos que _____.
7. Me gustan las personas que _____.
8. En el futuro, quiero tener _____ hijos, con tal de que _____.

PANORAMA *cultural*

Chile

Datos esenciales

Nombre oficial: República de Chile
Capital: Santiago
Población: 15.000.000 de habitantes
Moneda: el peso
Idiomas: el español (oficial), el mapuche, el quechua

¡Fíjese!

- El nombre de Chile se deriva de la palabra indígena *chilli* que significa «lugar donde termina la tierra».

- A través del largo y estrecho territorio de Chile, la geografía va de selva[a] a desierto, a fértil valle,[b] a zona de nieves perpetuas en el extremo sur.

- Chile tiene una de las economías más fuertes de Sudamérica. Es el mayor productor de cobre[c] del mundo, y tiene una importante industria vinícola.[d]

[a]*jungle* [b]*valley* [c]*copper* [d]*wine*

Un viñedo (*vineyard*) chileno, con los Andes al fondo (*in the background*)

Conozca a... Gabriela Mistral

La primera hispanoamericana en ganar el premio Nóbel de Literatura fue Gabriela Mistral (1889–1957). Maestra de escuela, además de poeta, fue una mujer que vivió tristes momentos en su vida (el abandono de su padre, el suicidio de su prometido[a] y su maternidad frustrada) que se ven reflejados en su poesía. El siguiente poema, es uno de sus más conocidos.

[a]*fiancé*

Riqueza[a]

Tengo la dicha fiel[b]
y la dicha perdida:
la una como una rosa,
la otra como una espina.[c]
De lo que me robaron
no fui desposeída:[d]
tengo la dicha fiel
y la dicha perdida
y estoy rica de púrpura[e]
y de melancolía.
   ¡Ay, qué amada[f]
     es la rosa
y qué amante[g] es la espina!
Como el noble contorno[h]
de las frutas mellizas[i]
tengo la dicha fiel
y la dicha perdida...

[a]*Wealth* [b]*dicha... constant happiness* [c]*thorn* [d]*no... I was not dispossessed* [e]*purple* [f]*qué... how beloved* [g]*qué... how loving* [h]*contour* [i]*twin*

Capítulo 15 of the video to accompany *Puntos de partida* contains cultural footage of Chile.

Visit the *Puntos de partida* Website at www.mhhe.com/puntos.

Vocabulario

Las relaciones sentimentales

amar	to love
casarse (con)	to marry
divorciarse (de)	to get divorced (from)
enamorarse (de)	to fall in love (with)
llevarse bien/mal (con)	to get along well/poorly (with)
pasar tiempo (con)	to spend time (with)
querer (ie)	to love
romper (con)	to break up (with)
salir (salgo) (con)	to go out (with)
separarse (de)	to separate (from)

la amistad	friendship
el amor	love
la boda	wedding (*ceremony*)
la cita	date
el divorcio	divorce
la luna de miel	honeymoon
el marido	husband
el matrimonio	marriage; married couple
la mujer	wife
el noviazgo	engagement
la pareja	(married) couple; partner

Repaso: el/la amigo/a, el/la esposo/a, el/la novio/a

amistoso/a	friendly

Repaso: cariñoso/a, casado/a, soltero/a

Etapas de la vida

la adolescencia	adolescence
la infancia	infancy
la juventud	youth
la madurez	middle age
la muerte	death
el nacimiento	birth
la vejez	old age

Repaso: la niñez

crecer	to grow
nacer	to be born

Repaso: morir (ue, u)

Otras palabras y expresiones útiles

la gente	people
a primera vista	at first sight
bastante	rather, sufficiently; enough
juntos/as	together
propio/a	own

Conjunciones

a menos que	unless
antes (de) que	before
con tal (de) que	provided (that)
en caso de que	in case
para que	so that

Un poco más 15

LECTURA

Estrategia: Using Graphics to Get Information

Reading graphics such as tables and pie charts requires as much concentration as, if not more than, any other reading, since a lot of information is summarized in a compact space. Paying attention to the heading of the section as well as to the categories within the graphic can help you to focus your attention on important parts of the information presented. Moreover, the heading highlights the aspect of the information that the author has found most interesting.

The article on page 470 includes three different sets of information based on numbers. However, the heading suggests that one specific set is more important. As you read, try to decide which one it is and why you think it is presented as more important.

▶ **Sobre la lectura...** La lectura en la siguiente página es otra de la revista
▶ española *Quo*. Como se mencionó en la lectura del Capítulo 3, el uso de grá-
▶ ficos y otros elementos visuales hace que la revista sea muy popular y di-
▶ vertida. Como Ud. va a ver en la lectura, los gráficos también pueden pro-
▶ porcionarle (*provide you with*) información útil y necesaria para la
▶ comprensión del artículo.

Comprensión

Paso 1. Conteste las siguientes preguntas.

1. Según el artículo, ¿cómo prefieren casarse la mayoría de los españoles? ¿Cuál es la opción menos popular?
2. ¿Qué tipo de boda es el más barato?
3. ¿Cuál es el aspecto más caro de todas las bodas?

Paso 2. A continuación hay posibles títulos para el artículo completo. En su opinión, ¿cuál de los títulos cree Ud. que es el verdadero (*the real one*)?

1. ¿Casarse o no?
2. Anillos de oro: Cuánto cuesta casarse
3. Lugares bonitos para las bodas

Un 6% de los españoles prefiere convivir un tiempo antes de casarse

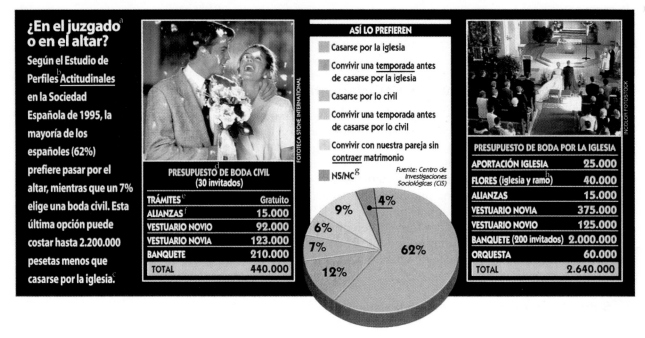

¿En el juzgado[a] o en el altar?

Según el Estudio de Perfiles[b] Actitudinales en la Sociedad Española de 1995, la mayoría de los españoles (62%) prefiere pasar por el altar, mientras que un 7% elige una boda civil. Esta última opción puede costar hasta 2.200.000 pesetas menos que casarse por la iglesia.[c]

PRESUPUESTO DE BODA CIVIL[d]
(30 invitados)

TRÁMITES[e]	Gratuito
ALIANZAS[f]	15.000
VESTUARIO NOVIO	92.000
VESTUARIO NOVIA	123.000
BANQUETE	210.000
TOTAL	440.000

ASÍ LO PREFIEREN

- Casarse por la iglesia
- Convivir una temporada antes de casarse por la iglesia
- Casarse por lo civil
- Convivir una temporada antes de casarse por lo civil
- Convivir con nuestra pareja sin contraer matrimonio
- NS/NC[g]

Fuente: Centro de Investigaciones Sociológicas (CIS)

4%
9%
6%
7%
62%
12%

PRESUPUESTO DE BODA POR LA IGLESIA	
APORTACIÓN IGLESIA	25.000
FLORES (iglesia y ramo)[h]	40.000
ALIANZAS	15.000
VESTUARIO NOVIA	375.000
VESTUARIO NOVIO	125.000
BANQUETE (200 invitados)	2.000.000
ORQUESTA	60.000
TOTAL	2.640.000

[a]court [b]Profiles [c]church [d]Budget [e]Marriage licenses [f]Wedding rings [g]«No está seguro/a» / «No contesta» [h]bouquet

ESCRITURA

Según el artículo, el 6 por ciento de los españoles prefiere convivir antes de casarse por lo civil, y otro 12 por ciento prefiere convivir antes de casarse por la iglesia. Sin duda, en la sociedad contemporánea, es común que algunas parejas convivan antes de contraer matrimonio. Esta decisión puede traer ventajas y desventajas.

Paso 1. Imagine que un amigo suyo / una amiga suya le pide consejos respecto al asunto (*about this question*). ¿Qué le va a recomendar? Haga una lista de tres ventajas y tres desventajas de convivir antes de casarse.

VENTAJAS

1. _____

2. _____

3. _____

DESVENTAJAS

1. _____

2. _____

3. _____

Paso 2.   Ahora, escríbale una carta a su amigo/a, presentándole una de las dos perspectivas. Intente formular un buen argumento para persuadirle a que siga sus consejos. Puede empezar su carta así:

Querido/a _____ ,

    He pensado mucho en tu situacíon y creo que...

¿Trabajar para vivir o vivir para trabajar?

Esta médica mexicana ha dedicado muchos años de preparación a su especialidad.

¿Qué opina Ud.?

Ponga en el orden de importancia para Ud., del 1 (más importante) al 8, las características del trabajo ideal. ¿Cree Ud. que una persona de otro país diría algo similar? Visite el sitio Web de *Puntos de partida* para leer las respuestas a estas preguntas que da una persona de Uruguay.

_____ Pasar mucho tiempo al aire libre

_____ Trabajar independientemente o sin mucha supervisión

_____ Viajar con frecuencia

_____ Leer y escribir mucho

_____ Ganar mucho dinero y **jubilarme** joven

_____ Tener muchas posibilidades de mejorarme y de recibir **aumentos de sueldo**

_____ Hacer mucho trabajo físico

_____ Tomar muchas decisiones

En este capítulo...

- In this chapter, you will study vocabulary related to the world of work and personal finances. You know the word **trabajar**. What do you think **un trabajador / una trabajadora social** does for a living?
- When you wanted to express an event in the future, you have primarily used the form **ir** + **a**. Now you will learn how to express your plans and aspirations in a different way. (Grammar 46)
- Additionally, you will learn how to use time markers with the subjunctive to express ideas about the future, such as *when I graduate . . . , as soon as I finish college . . . ,* and *before I start my career . . .* (Grammar 47)
- This chapter's **Panorama cultural** section will focus on Uruguay and Paraguay.

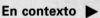

PUNTOS INTERACTIVO

Videoteca

◀ **Minidramas**
En este episodio, Lupe se entrevista para un trabajo en un banco. ¿Ha tenido Ud. estas experiencias alguna vez? ¿Cuál ha sido su mejor (o peor) entrevista?

En contexto ▶
En este episodio, Juan Carlos abre una cuenta (*account*) en el banco. ¿Tiene Ud. una cuenta en algún banco? ¿Tiene mucho dinero en su cuenta?

CD-ROM

Además de completar el vocabulario y las actividades de gramática, Ud. va a tener la oportunidad de «abrir» una cuenta virtual en el ciber-banco del CD-ROM.

Internet

En la sección del **Capítulo 16** en el sitio Web de *Puntos de partida* aparecen enlaces que Ud. puede usar para conseguir información en español sobre los empleos. Use la dirección **www.mhhe.com/puntos**.

Profesiones y oficios° — *trades*

Profesiones

el/la abogado/a	lawyer
el/la bibliotecario/a	librarian
el/la consejero/a	counselor
el/la contador(a)	accountant
el/la enfermero/a	nurse
el hombre / la mujer de negocios	business person
el/la ingeniero/a	engineer
el/la maestro/a	schoolteacher
el/la médico/a	doctor
el/la periodista	journalist
el/la trabajador(a) social	social worker
el/la traductor(a)	translator

Oficios

el/la cajero/a	cashier; teller
el/la cocinero/a	cook; chef
el/la comerciante	merchant, shopkeeper

el/la criado/a	servant
el/la dependiente/a	clerk
el/la obrero/a	worker, laborer
el/la peluquero/a	hairstylist
el/la plomero/a	plumber
el soldado / la mujer soldado	soldier
el/la vendedor(a)	salesperson

Cognados

el/la analista de sistemas, el/la dentista, el/la electricista, el/la fotógrafo/a, el/la mecánico/a, el/la profesor(a), el/la programador(a), el/la secretario/a, el/la sicólogo/a, el/la siquiatra, el/la técnico/a, el/la veterinario/a

In the preceding chapters of *Puntos de partida* you have learned to use a number of the words for professions and trades that are listed here. You will practice all of these words in the following activities. However, you will probably want to learn only those new terms that are particularly important or interesting to you. If the vocabulary needed to describe your career goal is not listed here, look it up in a dictionary or ask your instructor.

Conversación

A. ¿A quién necesita Ud.? ¿A quién debe llamar o con quién debe consultar en estas situaciones? Hay más de una respuesta posible en algunos casos.

1. La tubería (*plumbing*) de la cocina no funciona bien.
2. Ud. acaba de tener un accidente automovilístico; el otro conductor dice que Ud. tuvo la culpa (*blame*).
3. Por las muchas tensiones y presiones de su vida profesional y personal, Ud. tiene serios problemas afectivos (*emotional*).
4. Ud. está en el hospital y quiere que alguien le dé una aspirina.
5. Ud. quiere que alguien lo/la ayude con las tareas domésticas porque no tiene mucho tiempo para hacerlas.
6. Ud. quiere que alguien le construya un muro (*wall*) en el jardín.
7. Ud. conoce todos los detalles de un escándalo en el gobierno de su ciudad y quiere divulgarlos.

B. Asociaciones. ¿Qué profesiones u oficios asocia Ud. con estas frases? Consulte la lista de profesiones y oficios y use las siguientes palabras también. Haga asociaciones rápidas. ¡No lo piense demasiado!

1. creativo/rutinario	actor/actriz	detective
2. muchos/pocos años de preparación	arquitecto/a	niñero/a
3. mucho/poco salario	asistente de vuelo	pintor(a)
4. mucha/poca responsabilidad	*barman*	poeta
5. mucho/poco prestigio	camarero/a	policía/mujer policía
6. flexibilidad/«de nueve a cinco»	carpintero/a	político/a
7. mucho/poco tiempo libre	chófer	presidente/a
8. peligroso (*dangerous*)/seguro	consejero/a	senador(a)
9. en el pasado, sólo para hombres/mujeres	cura/pastor(a)/	
10. todavía, sólo para hombres/mujeres	rabino/a	

C. Qué preparación se necesita para ser... ? Imagine que Ud. es consejero universitario / consejera universitaria. Explíquele a un estudiante qué cursos debe tomar para prepararse para las siguientes carreras. Consulte la lista de cursos académicos del Capítulo 1 y use la siguiente lista. Piense también en el tipo de experiencia que debe obtener.

Vocabulario útil

las comunicaciones	**el *marketing*/mercadeo**
la contabilidad (*accounting*)	**la organización administrativa**
el derecho (*law*)	**la pedagogía/enseñanza**
la gerontología	**la retórica** (*speech*)
la ingeniería	**la sociología**

---

1. traductor(a) en la ONU (Organización de las Naciones Unidas)
2. reportero/a en la televisión, especializado/a en los deportes
3. contador(a) para un grupo de abogados
4. periodista en la redacción (*editorial staff*) de una revista de ecología
5. trabajador(a) social, especializado/a en los problemas de los ancianos
6. maestro/a de primaria, especializado/a en la educación bilingüe

D. Entrevista. Con un compañero / una compañera, háganse preguntas y contéstenlas para averiguar (*find out*) la siguiente información.

1. lo que hacían sus abuelos
2. la profesión u oficio de sus padres
3. si tiene un amigo o pariente que tenga una profesión extraordinaria o interesante y el nombre de esa profesión
4. lo que sus padres (su esposo/a) quiere(n) que Ud. sea (lo que Ud. quiere que sean sus hijos)
5. lo que Ud. quiere ser (lo que sus hijos quieren ser)
6. la carrera para la cual (*which*) se preparan muchos de sus amigos (los hijos de sus amigos)

Nota cultural

Los nombres de las profesiones

En el mundo de habla española hay poco acuerdo sobre las palabras que deben usarse para referirse a las mujeres que ejercen ciertas profesiones. En gran parte, eso se debe al hecho de que, en muchos de estos países, las mujeres acaban de empezar a ejercer esas profesiones; por eso el idioma todavía está cambiando para acomodarse a esa nueva realidad. En la actualidad se emplean, entre otras, las siguientes formas:

- Se usa el artículo **la** con los sustantivos que terminan en **-ista**.

  el dent**ista** ⟶ **la** dent**ista**

- En otros casos se usa una forma femenina.

  el médic**o** ⟶ **la** médic**a**
  el trabajad**or** ⟶ **la** trabajad**ora**

- Se usa la palabra **mujer** con el nombre de la profesión.

  el policía ⟶ **la mujer** policía
  el soldado ⟶ **la mujer** soldado

Escuche lo que dice la persona con quien Ud. habla para saber las formas que él o ella usa. No se trata de[a] formas correctas o incorrectas, sólo de usos y costumbres locales.

[a]No... *It's not a question of*

caerle bien a la entrevistadora

¡renunciar al puesto!

graduarse

llenar las solicitudes

escribir a máquina y contestar el teléfono todo el día

caerle bien/mal a alguien	to make a good/bad impression on someone
dejar	to quit
llenar	to fill out (*a form*)
renunciar (a)	to resign (from)
el/la aspirante	candidate, applicant
el currículum	resumé
la dirección de personal	personnel office, employment office
el/la director(a) de personal	personnel director
la empresa	corporation, business
el puesto	job, position
la solicitud	application (*form*)

Una cuestión de dinero

el banco	bank
el cajero automático	automatic teller machine
el cheque	check (*bank*)
la cuenta / la factura	bill
la cuenta corriente	checking account
la cuenta de ahorros	savings account
el efectivo	cash
el préstamo	loan
el presupuesto	budget
el salario / el sueldo	salary

la tarjeta de crédito	credit card
ahorrar	to save (*money*)
cargar (a la cuenta de uno)	to charge (to someone's account)
depositar/sacar	to deposit/withdraw (*money*)
devolver (ue)	to return (*something*)
economizar	to economize
ganar	to earn
pagar a plazos / con cheque	to pay in installments / by check
pagar en efectivo / al contado	to pay in cash
pedir (i, i) prestado/a	to borrow
prestar	to lend

Conversación

A. En busca de un puesto. Imagine que Ud. solicitó un puesto recientemente. Usando los números del 1 al 14, indique en qué orden ocurrió lo siguiente. El número 1 ya está indicado.

a. _____ Se despidió de Ud. cordialmente, diciendo que lo/la iba a llamar en una semana.

b. _____ Fue a la biblioteca para informarse sobre la empresa: su historia, dónde tiene sucursales (*branches*), etcétera.

c. _____ Ud. llenó la solicitud tan pronto como la recibió y la mandó, con el currículum, a la empresa.

d. _____ Por fin, el secretario le dijo que Ud. se iba a entrevistar con la directora de personal.

e. __1__ En la oficina de empleos de su universidad, Ud. leyó un anuncio para un puesto en su especialización.

f. _____ Le dijo que le iba a mandar una solicitud para que la llenara (*you could fill it out*) y también le pidió que mandara (*you send*) su currículum.

g. _____ Cuando por fin lo/la llamó la directora, ¡fue para ofrecerle el puesto!

h. _____ Mientras esperaba en la dirección de personal, Ud. estaba nerviosísimo/a.

i. _____ La directora le hizo una serie de preguntas: cuándo se iba a graduar, qué cursos había tomado, etcétera.

j. _____ Llamó al teléfono que daba el anuncio y habló con un secretario en la dirección de personal.

k. _____ La mañana de la entrevista, Ud. se levantó temprano, se vistió con cuidado y salió temprano para la empresa para llegar puntualmente.

l. _____ Al entrar en la oficina de la directora, Ud. la saludó con cortesía, tratando de caerle bien desde el principio.

m. _____ También le pidió que hablara (*you speak*) un poco en español, ya que la empresa tiene una sucursal en Santiago, Chile.

n. _____ En una semana lo/la llamaron para arreglar una entrevista.

B. El mes pasado. Piense en sus finanzas personales del mes pasado. ¿Fue un mes típico? ¿Tuvo dificultades al final del mes o todo le salió bien?

Paso 1. Indique las respuestas apropiadas para Ud.

	¡CLARO QUE SÍ!	¡CLARO QUE NO!
1. Hice un presupuesto al principio del mes.	☐	☐
2. Deposité más dinero en el banco del que (*than what*) saqué.	☐	☐
3. Saqué dinero del cajero automático sin apuntar (*writing down*) la cantidad.	☐	☐
4. Pagué todas mis cuentas a tiempo.	☐	☐
5. Saqué un préstamo (Le pedí dinero prestado al banco) para pagar mis cuentas.	☐	☐
6. Tomé el autobús en vez de (*instead of*) usar el coche, para economizar un poco.	☐	☐
7. Gasté mucho dinero en diversiones.	☐	☐
8. Saqué el saldo (*I balanced*) de mi cuenta de cheques (*checkbook*) sin dificultades.	☐	☐
9. Le presté dinero a un amigo.	☐	☐
10. Usé mis tarjetas de crédito sólo en casos de urgencia.	☐	☐

Paso 2. Vuelva a mirar sus respuestas. ¿Fue el mes pasado un mes típico? Pensando todavía en sus respuestas, sugiera tres cosas que Ud. debe hacer para mejorar su situación económica.

MODELO: Debo hacer un presupuesto mensual.

C. Diálogos

Paso 1. Empareje las preguntas de la izquierda con las respuestas de la derecha.

1. _____ ¿Cómo prefiere Ud. pagar?
2. _____ ¿Hay algún problema?
3. _____ Me da su pasaporte, por favor. Necesito verlo para que pueda cobrar (*cash*) su cheque.
4. _____ ¿Quisiera (*Would you like*) usar su tarjeta de crédito?
5. _____ ¿Va a depositar este cheque en su cuenta corriente o en su cuenta de ahorros?
6. _____ ¿Adónde quiere Ud. que mandemos la factura?

a. En la cuenta de ahorros, por favor.
b. Me la manda a la oficina, por favor.
c. No, prefiero pagar al contado.
d. Sí, señorita. Ud. me cobró demasiado por el jarabe.
e. Aquí lo tiene Ud. Me lo va a devolver pronto, ¿verdad?
f. Cárguelo a mi cuenta, por favor.

Paso 2. Ahora invente un contexto posible para cada diálogo. ¿Dónde están las personas que hablan? ¿en un banco? ¿en una tienda? ¿Quiénes son? ¿clientes? ¿cajeros? ¿dependientes?

D. Situaciones. Describa lo que pasa en los siguientes dibujos, contestando por lo menos estas preguntas: ¿Quiénes son estas personas? ¿Dónde están? ¿Qué van a comprar? ¿Cómo van a pagar? ¿Qué van a hacer después?

1.   2.   3.   4.

Minidiálogos y gramática

46

Talking about the Future • Future Verb Forms

Panel 1: BUENO, Y AL FINAL ¿QUÉ DEBERES[a] HAY QUE HACER PARA MAÑANA? / ESPERA A VER...

Panel 2: UNA COMPOSICIÓN SOBRE "EL MUNDO DEL PORVENIR[b]" Y TRAER UNAS ORACIONES CON EL FUTURO DEL VERBO VIVIR

Panel 3: ¿UNAS ORACIONES O UNAS PLEGARIAS[c]?

[a]tareas [b]futuro [c]*prayers*

¿Cómo será su vida dentro de diez años? Conteste sí o no a las primeras cinco oraciones. Complete las últimas dos con información verdadera —¡o por lo menos deseable!

1. Viviré en otra ciudad/otro país.
2. Estaré casado/a.
3. Tendré uno o más hijos (nietos).
4. Seré dueño/a de mi propia casa.
5. Llevaré una vida más tranquila.
6. Trabajaré como _____ (nombre de profesión).
7. Ganaré por lo menos _____ dólares al año.

A. You have already learned to talk about the future in a number of ways. The forms of the present can be used to describe the immediate future, and the **ir** + **a** + *infinitive* construction (Grammar 11) is very common in both spoken and written Spanish. The future can also be expressed, however, with future verb forms.

hablar		comer		vivir	
hablar**é**	hablar**emos**	comer**é**	comer**emos**	vivir**é**	vivir**emos**
hablar**ás**	hablar**éis**	comer**ás**	comer**éis**	vivir**ás**	vivir**éis**
hablar**á**	hablar**án**	comer**á**	comer**án**	vivir**á**	vivir**án**

B. In English, the future is formed with the auxiliary verbs *will* or *shall: I **will/shall** speak.* In Spanish, the *future* (**el futuro**) is a simple verb form (only one word). It is formed by adding future endings to the infinitive. No auxiliary verbs are needed.

Future verb endings:

-e	-emos
-ás	-éis
-á	-án

C. The verbs on the right add the future endings to irregular stems.

decir: diré, dirás, dirá, diremos, diréis, dirán

decir:	**dir-**	
hacer:	**har-**	-é
poder:	**podr-**	-ás
poner:	**pondr-**	-á
querer:	**querr-**	-emos
saber:	**sabr-**	-éis
salir:	**saldr-**	-án
tener:	**tendr-**	
venir:	**vendr-**	

The future of **hay** (**haber**) is **habrá** (*there will be*).*

D. Remember that indicative and subjunctive present tense forms can be used to express the immediate future. Compare the following.

Llegaré a tiempo.
I'll arrive on time.

Llego a las ocho mañana. ¿Vienes a buscarme?
I'll arrive at 8:00 tomorrow. Will you pick me up?

No creo que Pepe **llegue** a tiempo.
I don't think Pepe will arrive on time.

When the English *will* refers not to future time but to the willingness of someone to do something, Spanish uses the verb **querer**, not the future.

¿**Quieres** cerrar la puerta, por favor?
Will you please close the door?

Práctica

A. Mis compañeros de clase. ¿Cree Ud. que conoce bien a sus compañeros de clase? ¿Sabe lo que les va a pasar en el futuro? Vamos a ver.

Paso 1. Indique si las siguientes oraciones serán ciertas para Ud. algún día.

	SÍ	NO
1. Seré profesor(a) de idiomas.	☐	☐
2. Me casaré (Me divorciaré) dentro de tres años.	☐	☐

---

*The future forms of the verb **haber** are used to form the *future perfect tense* (**el futuro perfecto**), which expresses what *will have* occurred at some point in the future.

Para mañana, ya **habré hablado** con Miguel.

By tomorrow, I will have spoken with Miguel.

You will find a more detailed presentation of these forms in Appendix 3, Additional Perfect Forms (Indicative and Subjunctive).

3. Me mudaré (*I will move*) a otro país. ☐ ☐
4. Compraré un coche deportivo. ☐ ☐
5. Tendré una familia muy grande (mucho más grande). ☐ ☐
6. Asistiré a una escuela de estudios graduados (*graduate*). ☐ ☐
7. Visitaré Latinoamérica. ☐ ☐
8. Estaré en bancarrota (*bankruptcy*). ☐ ☐
9. Estaré jubilado/a (*retired*). ☐ ☐
10. No tendré que trabajar porque seré rico/a. ☐ ☐

Paso 2. Ahora, para cada oración del **Paso 1**, indique el nombre de una persona de la clase para quien Ud. cree que la oración es cierta. Puede ser un compañero/una compañera de clase o su profesor(a).

Paso 3. Ahora compare sus predicciones con las respuestas de estas personas. ¿Hizo Ud. predicciones correctas?

B. ¿Qué harán?

Paso 1. Imagine que un grupo de amigos está hablando de cómo será su vida en cinco o seis años. Haga oraciones usando el futuro de las frases de abajo.

1. yo
   - hablar bien el español
   - pasar mucho tiempo en la biblioteca
   - escribir artículos sobre la literatura latinoamericana
   - dar clases en español

2. tú
   - trabajar en una oficina y en la corte
   - ganar mucho dinero
   - tener muchos clientes
   - cobrar por muchas horas de trabajo

3. Felipe
   - ver a muchos pacientes
   - escuchar muchos problemas
   - leer a Freud y a Jung constantemente
   - hacerle un sicoanálisis a un paciente

4. Susana y Juanjo
   - pasar mucho tiempo sentados
   - usar el teclado (*keyboard*) constantemente
   - inventar nuevos programas
   - mandarles mensajes electrónicos a todos los amigos

Paso 2. ¿A qué profesiones se refieren las oraciones anteriores?

C. Mi amigo Gregorio

Paso 1. Describa Ud. las siguientes cosas que hará su compañero Gregorio. Luego indique si Ud. hará lo mismo (**Yo también... Yo tampoco...**) u otra cosa.

MODELO: no / gastar / menos / mes →
Gregorio no gastará menos este mes. Yo tampoco gastaré menos. (Yo sí gastaré menos este mes. ¡Tengo que ahorrar!)

1. pagar / tarde / todo / cuentas
2. tratar / adaptarse a / presupuesto

3. volver / hacer / presupuesto / próximo mes
4. no / depositar / nada / en / cuenta de ahorros
5. quejarse / porque / no / tener / suficiente dinero
6. seguir / usando / tarjetas / crédito
7. pedirles / dinero / a / padres
8. buscar / trabajo / de tiempo parcial

Paso 2. ¿Cuál de las siguientes oraciones describe mejor a su amigo?

1. Gregorio es muy responsable en cuanto a (*regarding*) asuntos de dinero. Es un buen modelo para imitar.
2. Gregorio tiene que aprender a ser más responsable con su dinero.

Conversación

▲▲▲▲▲▲▲▲

A. **Ventajas y desventajas.** What can you do to get extra cash or to save money? Some possibilities are shown in the following drawings. What are the advantages and disadvantages of each suggestion?

MODELO: dejar de tomar tanto café →
Si dejo de tomar tanto café, ahorraré sólo un poco de dinero. Estaré menos nervioso/a, pero creo que será más difícil despertarme por la mañana.

1. pedirles dinero a mis amigos o parientes
2. cometer un robo
3. alquilar unos cuartos de mi casa a otras personas
4. dejar de fumar (beber cerveza, tomar tanto café…)
5. buscar un trabajo de tiempo parcial
6. vender mi disco compacto (coche, televisor…)
7. comprar muchos billetes de lotería

B. **El mundo en el año 2500.** ¿Cómo será el mundo del futuro? Haga una lista de temas o cosas que Ud. cree que van a ser diferentes en el año 2500. Por ejemplo: el transporte, la comida, la vivienda… Piense también en temas globales: la política, los problemas que presenta la capa de ozono…

Ahora, a base de su lista, haga una serie de predicciones para el futuro.

MODELO: La gente comerá (Nosotros comeremos) comidas sintéticas.

Vocabulario útil

la colonización
la energía nuclear/solar
el espacio
los OVNIs (Objetos Volantes No
  Identificados)
el planeta
la pobreza (*poverty*)
el robot
el satélite

el transbordador espacial
la vida artificial

diseñar (*to design*)
eliminar

intergaláctico/a
interplanetario/a
sintético/a

Nota comunicativa

Expressing Conjecture

Estela, en el aeropuerto

Cecilia, en la carretera

¿Dónde **estará** Cecilia?	*I wonder where Cecilia is. (Where can Cecilia be?)*
¿Qué le **pasará**?	*I wonder what's up with her (what can be wrong)?*
Estará en un lío de tráfico.	*She's probably (must be) in a traffic jam. (I bet she's in a traffic jam.)*

The future can also be used in Spanish to express probability or conjecture about what is happening now. This use of the future is called the *future of probability* (**el futuro de probabilidad**). Note in the preceding examples that the English cues for expressing probability (*probably, I bet, must be, I wonder . . . , Where can . . . ,* and so on) are not directly expressed in Spanish. Their sense is conveyed in Spanish by the use of the future form of the verb.

C. Predicciones.
¿Quiénes serán las siguientes personas? ¿Qué estarán haciendo? ¿Dónde estarán? Invente todos los detalles que pueda sobre los siguientes dibujos.

Palabras útiles: el botones (*bellhop*), Cristóbal Colón (*Christopher Columbus*), la propina (*tip*), redondo/a (*round*)

1.

2.

3.

4.

En los Estados Unidos y el Canadá...

Fernando Espuelas

Fernando Espuelas, un uruguayo de treinta y pico[a] años, es **el fundador de StarMedia**, una de las compañías principales del Internet en Latinoamérica. También es el presidente del Consejo de Dirección de la compañía y su director ejecutivo. Fernando Espuelas **llegó a los Estados Unidos** con su madre **cuando tenía 9 años**. Casi no sabía hablar inglés. En 1996, con la ayuda de un viejo amigo y con dinero prestado por la familia, los amigos y las tarjetas de crédito, Espuelas empezó StarMedia; tres años más tarde se había convertido en **una**

Fernando Espuelas

compañía con un valor de 165 millones de dólares. Hoy, StarMedia tiene oficinas en Miami, San Juan, Madrid y casi todas las capitales latinoamericanas, y está representada en la Bolsa[b] de Wall Street.

Antes de la creación de StarMedia, Espuelas había sido **director ejecutivo de comunicaciones de *marketing* de AT&T** para la región del Caribe y Latinoamérica, y ha ocupado varios cargos en agencias de publicidad importantes. Con StarMedia, Espuelas reafirma su visión de **la importancia de tener una comunidad latinoamericana** y del Internet como vehículo de cohesión entre los pueblos hispánicos.

[a]treinta... *thirty-some* [b]*Stock Market*

Antes de la entrevista

SRA. CARRASCO: Hija, ¿estás lista para la entrevista?

LUPE: Sí, mamá.

SRA. CARRASCO: Bien. *Cuando llegues* a la oficina, no te olvides de darle la mano a la directora de personal. También debes sentarte sólo *después de que* ella *se siente*.

LUPE: Sí, mamá…

SRA. CARRASCO: *Y tan pronto como termine* la entrevista, no te olvides de darle las gracias.

LUPE: ¡Ay, mamá! Creo que voy a sufrir un ataque de nervios *en cuanto salga* de casa.

SRA. CARRASCO: No te preocupes, Lupe. No debes sentirte nerviosa…

LUPE: No es por los nervios, mamá, ¡sino por todos estos consejos!

Comprensión: ¿Cierto o falso?

1. La Sra. Carrasco tiene una entrevista hoy.
2. La Sra. Carrasco le da a su hija consejos sobre cómo portarse durante la entrevista con la directora de personal.
3. Lupe cree que va a sufrir un ataque de nervios tan pronto como termine la entrevista.
4. Lupe está nerviosísima por la entrevista.

A. The subjunctive is often used in Spanish in adverbial clauses, which function like adverbs, telling when the action of the main verb takes place. Such adverbial clauses are introduced by conjunctions (see **Capítulo 15**).

Lo veré **mañana**. (adverb)
I'll see him tomorrow.

Lo veré **cuando venga mañana**. (adverbial clause)
I'll see him when he comes tomorrow.

B. Future events are often expressed in Spanish in two-clause sentences that include conjunctions of time such as those on the right.

antes (de) que	before
cuando	when
después (de) que	after

Before the interview SRA. CARRASCO: Dear, are you ready for the interview? LUPE: Yes, Mom. SRA. CARRASCO: Good. When you arrive at the office, don't forget to shake the personnel director's hand. You should also sit down only after she sits down. LUPE: Yes Mom . . . SRA. CARRASCO: And as soon as the interview ends, don't forget to thank her. LUPE: Geez, Mom! I think I'm going to suffer a nervous breakdown as soon as I leave the house. SRA. CARRASCO: Don't worry, Lupe. You shouldn't feel nervous . . . LUPE: It's not nerves, Mom, but rather all your advice!

en cuanto	as soon as
hasta que	until
tan pronto como	as soon as

C. In a subordinate clause after these conjunctions of time, the subjunctive is used to express a future action or state of being—that is, one that is still pending or has not yet occurred from the point of view of the main verb. This use of the subjunctive is very frequent in conversation in phrases such as the example on the right.

The events in the subordinate clause are imagined—not real-world—events. They haven't happened yet.

Cuando sea grande/mayor…
When I'm older . . .

Cuando tenga tiempo…
When I have the time . . .

Cuando me gradúe…
When I graduate . . .

D. When the present subjunctive is used in this way to express pending actions, the main-clause verb is in the present indicative or future.

PENDING ACTION (SUBJUNCTIVE):

Pagaré las cuentas **en cuanto reciba** mi cheque.
I'll pay the bills as soon as I get my check.

Debo depositar el dinero **tan pronto como** lo **reciba**.
I should deposit money as soon as I get it.

E. However, the indicative (not the present subjunctive) is used after conjunctions of time to describe a habitual action or a completed action in the past. Compare the following.

HABITUAL ACTIONS (INDICATIVE):

Siempre **pago** las cuentas **en cuanto recibo** mi cheque.
I always pay bills as soon as I get my check.

Deposito el dinero **tan pronto como** lo **recibo**.
I deposit money as soon as I receive it.

COMPLETED PAST ACTION (INDICATIVE):

El mes pasado **pagué** las cuentas **en cuanto recibí** mi cheque.
Last month I paid my bills as soon as I got my check.

O J O The subjunctive is always used with **antes (de) que.** (See **Capítulo 15.**)

Deposité el dinero **tan pronto como** lo **recibí**.
I deposited the money as soon as I got it.

Práctica

▲▲▲▲▲▲

A. Decisiones económicas

Paso 1. Lea las siguientes oraciones sobre Rigoberto y decida si se trata de una acción habitual o de una acción que no ha pasado todavía. Luego indique la frase que mejor complete la oración.

Minidiálogos y gramática

1. Rigoberto se va a comprar una computadora en cuanto...
   a. el banco le dé el préstamo   **b.** el banco le da el préstamo
2. Siempre usa su tarjeta de crédito cuando...
   a. no tenga efectivo   **b.** no tiene efectivo
3. Cada mes saca el saldo de su cuenta corriente después de que...
   a. reciba el estado de cuentas (*statement*)
   b. recibe el estado de cuentas
4. Piensa abrir una cuenta de ahorros tan pronto como...
   a. consiga un trabajo   **b.** consigue un trabajo
5. No puede pagar sus cuentas este mes hasta que...
   a. su hermano le devuelva el dinero que le prestó
   b. su hermano le devuelve el dinero que le prestó

Paso 2. Ahora describa cómo lleva Ud. sus propios asuntos económicos, completando las siguientes oraciones semejantes.

1. Voy a comprarme _____ en cuanto el banco me dé un préstamo.
2. Cuando no tengo efectivo, siempre uso _____.
3. Después de que el banco me envía el estado de cuentas, yo siempre _____.
4. Tan pronto como consiga un trabajo, voy a _____.
5. No te presto más dinero hasta que tú me _____ el dinero que me debes.
6. Este mes, voy a _____ antes de que se me olvide.

B. Hablando de dinero: Planes para el futuro. Complete las siguientes oraciones con el presente del subjuntivo de los verbos indicados.

1. Voy a ahorrar más en cuanto... (darme [ellos] un aumento de sueldo [*raise*]; dejar [yo] de gastar tanto)
2. Pagaré todas mis cuentas tan pronto como... (tener el dinero para hacerlo; ser absolutamente necesario)
3. El semestre que viene, pagaré la matrícula después de que... (cobrar mi cheque en el banco; mandarme [¿quién?] un cheque)
4. No podré pagar el alquiler hasta que... (sacar dinero de mi cuenta de ahorros; depositar el dinero en mi cuenta corriente)
5. No voy a jubilarme (*retire*) hasta que mis hijos... (terminar sus estudios universitarios; casarse)

C. Algunos momentos en la vida. Las siguientes oraciones describen algunos aspectos de la vida de Mariana en el pasado, en el presente y en el futuro. Lea cada grupo de oraciones para tener una idea general del contexto. Luego dé la forma apropiada de los infinitivos.

1. Hace cuatro años, cuando Mariana (graduarse) en la escuela secundaria, sus padres (darle) un reloj. El año que viene, cuando (graduarse) en la universidad, (darle) un coche.
2. Cuando (ser) niña, Mariana (querer) ser enfermera. Luego, cuando (tener) 18 años, (decidir) que quería estudiar computación. Cuando (terminar) su carrera este año, yo creo que (poder) encontrar un buen trabajo como programadora.
3. Generalmente Mariana no (escribir) cheques hasta que (tener) los

fondos en su cuenta corriente. Este mes tiene muchos gastos, pero no
(ir) a pagar ninguna cuenta hasta que le (llegar) el cheque de su
trabajo de tiempo parcial.

Conversación

A. Descripciones. Describa Ud. los dibujos, completando las oraciones e
inventando un contexto para las escenas. Luego describa su propia vida.

1.   **2.**   **3.**

1. Pablo va a estudiar hasta que _____.

   Esta noche yo voy a estudiar hasta que _____.
   Siempre estudio hasta que _____.
   Anoche estudié hasta que _____.

2. Los señores Castro van a cenar tan pronto como _____.

   Esta noche voy a cenar tan pronto como _____.
   Siempre ceno tan pronto como _____.
   Anoche cené tan pronto como _____.

3. Lupe va a viajar al extranjero en cuanto _____.

   En cuanto gane la lotería, yo voy a _____.
   En cuanto tengo el dinero, siempre _____.
   De niño/a, _____ en cuanto tenía el dinero.

B. Reacciones. ¿Cómo reaccionará o qué hará cuando ocurran los siguientes
acontecimientos? Complete las oraciones con el futuro.

1. Cuando colonicemos otro planeta, _____.
2. Cuando descubran una cura para el cáncer, _____.
3. Cuando haya una mujer presidenta, _____.
4. Cuando me jubile, _____.
5. Cuando yo sea anciano/a, _____.
6. Cuando me gradúe, _____.

Minidiálogos y gramática

Minidramas

In this **Minidramas** dialogue, Lupe Carrasco is on a job interview in Mexico City. What type of job is she applying for? Where will she work? What will she do there?

Lupe solicita el puesto de recepcionista en un banco. Ahora habla con la Sra. Ibáñez, directora de personal del banco.

SRA. IBÁÑEZ: He hablado con varios aspirantes para el puesto de recepcionista, pero Ud. tiene el currículum más interesante. Veo que ha trabajado como recepcionista en la oficina de un abogado. ¿Por qué renunció a ese trabajo?

LUPE: Bueno, soy estudiante en la universidad. Me gustaba mucho el trabajo en la oficina del abogado, pero querían que trabajara[a] la jornada completa.[b] Desafortunadamente, no me era posible.

SRA. IBÁÑEZ: Y cuando trabajaba para el abogado, ¿cuáles eran sus responsabilidades?

LUPE: Contestaba el teléfono, hacía las citas con los clientes, organizaba el archivo… También le llevaba sus cuentas y pagaba los gastos básicos de la oficina. Eran las típicas responsabilidades de una recepcionista.

SRA. IBÁÑEZ: Ajá, entiendo. Srta. Carrasco, buscamos una persona que sea amable, que aprenda rápidamente, que sepa escribir a máquina y utilizar una computadora y que tenga paciencia con los clientes. Parece que Ud. cumple con estos requisitos. ¿Podrá asistir a un entrenamiento[c] de seis horas la semana que viene?

LUPE: Sí, Sra. Ibáñez.

SRA. IBÁÑEZ: ¿Y podrá trabajar de vez en cuando en las otras sucursales del banco?

LUPE: ¡Claro que sí! No hay problema.

SRA. IBÁÑEZ: Muy bien.

[a]querían… *they wanted me to work* [b]la… *full-time* [c]*training session*

Con un compañero / una compañera

Hágale preguntas a un compañero / una compañera de clase que tiene un trabajo (de tiempo completo o de tiempo parcial) para saber la siguiente información. Si su compañero/a no tiene trabajo, hágale preguntas sobre un amigo / una amiga o un miembro de su familia que sí trabaja. También puede entrevistar a su profesor(a).

- el nombre exacto del trabajo que tiene
- la carrera que hizo en la universidad
- el tiempo que tardó en colocarse (*getting a job*)
- la experiencia que tenía en ese campo (*field*) cuando se colocó
- el tiempo que lleva en el empleo

En contexto

In this video segment, Juan Carlos opens an account at the bank. As you watch, pay attention to the vocabulary Juan Carlos and the bank employee use for opening an account. Do you have a bank account? Was your experience similar when you went to open it?

PERÚ

A. Lluvia de ideas

- ¿Es Ud. bueno/a para manejar el dinero? ¿Por qué? ¿Sabe Ud. ahorrar o se le va el dinero como agua en las manos?
- ¿Cuántas cuentas tiene Ud.? ¿De qué tipo son? ¿Cuándo las abrió? ¿Por qué razón eligió ese banco?

B. Dictado

A continuación aparece un fragmento del diálogo entre Juan Carlos y el empleado del banco. Complete el diálogo con las palabras o frases que faltan.

EMPLEADO: ¿Y qué tipo de _____ quiere Ud. abrir?

JUAN CARLOS: Necesito una cuenta _____ y una cuenta de _____. ¿_____ intereses sus cuentas corrientes?

EMPLEADO: Depende del tipo de cuenta corriente. Si Ud. _____ esta cuenta, gana intereses mensualmente, _____ _____ _____ que mantenga un mínimo de 100 soles en la cuenta.

JUAN CARLOS: ¿Qué pasa si el balance de la cuenta _____ de los 100 soles?

EMPLEADO: En ese caso le _____ una multa a su cuenta.

C. Un diálogo original

Opción 1. Con un compañero / una compañera, dramaticen el diálogo entre Juan Carlos y el empleado del banco.

Opción 2. También dramaticen la siguiente situación.

ESTUDIANTE 1   Ud. habla con un amigo / una amiga que entiende mucho de finanzas personales. Ud. necesita algún tipo de cuenta, pero no sabe exactamente cuál.

ESTUDIANTE 2   Ud. actúa de consejero de finanzas. Si su amigo/a no le da suficiente información, hágale preguntas para poder darle consejos mejores.

Un poco de todo

A. Los planes de la familia Alonso

Paso 1. Forme oraciones completas, según las indicaciones. Use el futuro donde sea posible.

1. ser / necesario / que / (nosotros) ahorrar / más
2. yo / no / usar / tanto / tarjetas / crédito
3. mamá / buscar / trabajo / donde / (ellos) pagarle / más
4. (nosotros) pedir / préstamo / en / banco
5. nos / lo / (ellos) dar, / ¿no / creer (tú)?
6. papá / estar / tranquilo / cuando / todos / empezar / economizar
7. (tú) deber / pagar / siempre / al contado
8. no / (nosotros) poder / irse / de vacaciones / este verano

Paso 2. Según los comentarios de las personas en el **Paso 1**, ¿cree Ud. que la familia Alonso está muy bien económicamente o no? Explique.

B. Planes para una boda. Use las conjunciones entre paréntesis para unir cada oración con la frase que la sigue. Haga todos los cambios necesarios. **¡OJO!** No se usa el subjuntivo en todos los casos. Tenga cuidado con las formas verbales.

MODELO: Miguel quiere casarse con Carmen./él: conseguir un trabajo (tan pronto como) → Miguel quiere casarse con Carmen tan pronto como él consiga un trabajo.

1. Carmen quiere esperar. / ella: graduarse en la universidad (hasta que)
2. Miguel se lo va a decir a los padres de Carmen. / ellos: llegar a la ciudad (tan pronto como)
3. Los padres de Carmen siempre quieren ver a Miguel. / él: visitar a su hija (cuando)
4. Los padres se van a alegrar. / (ellos) oír las noticias (en cuanto)
5. Miguel y Carmen van a Acapulco en su luna de miel. / (ellos) tener dinero (cuando)

6. Todos nosotros les vamos a dar una fiesta. / ellos: regresar de su viaje (después de que)

C. ¿Cómo se ganan la vida (*earn a living*) **los estudiantes?** Complete the following paragraphs with the correct form of the words in parentheses, as suggested by the context. When two possibilities are given in parentheses, select the correct word. Use an adverb derived from the adjectives in italics.

La preocupación por el dinero es (algo/alguien[1]) compartido[a] por los estudiantes en todo el mundo. En (el/la[2]) mayor parte de los países de habla española, (el/la[3]) sistema universitario es gratuito.[b] Sin embargo, hay (de/que[4]) tener dinero para los (gastar/gastos[5]) personales y también para (los/las[6]) cines y otras diversiones.

Aquí, algunos estudiantes hispánicos contestan la pregunta: ¿Cómo (te/se[7]) ganaba Ud. la vida cuando era estudiante?

Una joven de México: A los trece años, (*yo:* empezar[8]) a trabajar en una oficina. Así (*yo:* poder[9]) pagar la colegiatura[c] de mis estudios. (*Yo:* Trabajar[10]) de día y (estudiar[11]) de noche.

Un joven uruguayo: Cuando (*yo:* ser/estar[12]) estudiante, me (ganar[13]) la vida como fotógrafo. (*Yo:* Sacar[14]) fotos de bodas, bautismos, fiestas de cumpleaños. (*Yo:* Trabajar[15]) en cualquier ocasión y en cualquier sitio.

Una mujer española: (*Yo:* Ayudar[16]) a enseñar a párvulos.[d]

Algunos estudiantes (ofrecer[17]) los siguientes comentarios adicionales.

Una joven chilena: Los padres (*normal*[18]) mantienen a sus hijos (*económico*[19]). Pero muchos chicos (trabajar[20]) de todas maneras. Las chicas (cuidar[21]) niños o (ayudar[22]) en casa y los chicos (trabajar[23]) en talleres. Si los padres tienen dinero, es raro que los hijos (trabajar[24]) hasta que no (terminar[25]) su carrera.[e]

Un joven argentino: En la Argentina, la enseñanza universitaria (ser/estar[26]) gratuita. De todos modos, los estudiantes siempre (necesitar[27]) tener más de un trabajo y los padres los ayudan con (que / lo que[28]) pueden. Muchos estudiantes no (irse[29]) a otras ciudades a (estudiar[30]). (*Ellos:* Vivir[31]) con (su[32]) padres y estudian en (el/la[33]) universidad más cercana.

[a]*shared* [b]*free* [c]*fees* [d]*tots* [e]*studies*

Comprensión: ¿Cierto o falso? Corrija las oraciones falsas.

1. El sistema universitario es gratuito en muchos países hispánicos.
2. Los estudiantes hispánicos nunca tienen que trabajar.
3. Generalmente los padres mantienen a sus hijos mientras estos son estudiantes.

PANORAMA *cultural*

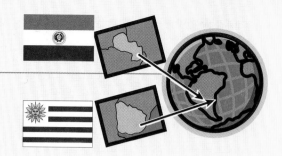

Uruguay y Paraguay

Datos esenciales

Uruguay

Nombre oficial: República Oriental del Uruguay
Capital: Montevideo
Población: 3.000.000 de habitantes
Moneda: el peso uruguayo
Idioma oficial: el español

Paraguay

Nombre oficial: República del Paraguay
Capital: Asunción
Población: 5.000.000 de habitantes
Moneda: el guaraní
Idiomas oficiales: el español y el guaraní

¡Fíjese!

- Aproximadamente el 45 por ciento de la población uruguaya vive en Montevideo.

- Para los uruguayos, la educación primaria, secundaria y universitaria es gratuita.[a] La tasa de alfabetización[b] es de un 96 por ciento, una de las más altas de Latinoamérica.

- El Paraguay es uno de los dos países latinoamericanos sin costa marítima (el otro es Bolivia). Por eso, sus numerosos ríos navegables tienen gran importancia económica para el país.

- La ciudad de Asunción, en el Paraguay, la primera ciudad permanente en la región del Río de la Plata, fue fundada por los españoles en 1537.

- La represa[c] hidroeléctrica de Itaipú, terminada en 1982, es la más grande y potente del

[a]*free*   [b]*tasa... rate of literacy*   [c]*dam*

mundo. Fue construida en la frontera entre el Paraguay y la Argentina y el Brasil. con la ayuda financiera del Brasil, país que recibe la energía eléctrica de la represa.

Conozca... el guaraní

El Paraguay es el único país latinoamericano que tiene dos lenguas oficiales, una de ellas indígena. El 90 por ciento de la población paraguaya habla guaraní (sólo el 75 por ciento habla español). Hoy hay literatura, música y hasta páginas Web en guaraní.

Guaraní significa *guerrero*[a] en esa lengua, nombre que recuerda las disputas de las diversas etnias guaraníes contra los poderosos incas.

[a]*warrior*

Asunción, Paraguay

 Capítulo 16 of the video to accompany *Puntos de partida* contains cultural footage about Uruguay and Paraguay.

 Visit the *Puntos de partida* Website at www.mhhe.com/puntos.

Vocabulario

Los verbos

jubilarse	to retire
mudarse	to move (*residence*)

Profesiones y oficios

el/la abogado/a	lawyer
el/la cajero/a	cashier; teller
el/la cocinero/a	cook; chef
el/la comerciante	merchant, shopkeeper
el/la contador(a)	accountant
el/la criado/a	servant
el hombre / la mujer de negocios	business person
el/la ingeniero/a	engineer
el/la maestro/a	schoolteacher
el/la obrero/a	worker, laborer
el/la peluquero/a	hairstylist
el/la periodista	journalist
el/la plomero/a	plumber
el soldado / la mujer soldado	soldier
el/la trabajador(a) social	social worker
el/la traductor(a)	translator
el/la vendedor(a)	salesperson

Cognados: el/la analista de sistemas, el/la electricista, el/la fotógrafo/a, el/la programador(a), el/la sicólogo/a, el/la siquiatra, el/la técnico/a, el/la veterinario/a

Repaso: el/la bibliotecario/a, el/la consejero/a, el/la dentista, el/la dependiente/a, el/la enfermero/a, el/la mecánico/a, el/la médico/a, el/la profesor(a), el/la secretario/a

En busca de un puesto

el/la aspirante	candidate; applicant
el currículum	resumé
la dirección de personal	personnel office, employment office
el/la director(a) de personal	personnel director
la empresa	corporation; business
el/la entrevistador(a)	interviewer
la solicitud	application (*form*)
la sucursal	branch (*office*)

Repaso: el teléfono

caerle bien/ mal a alguien	to make a good/bad impression on someone
dejar	to quit
entrevistar	to interview
escribir a máquina	to type
graduarse (en)	to graduate (from)
llenar	to fill out (*a form*)
renunciar (a)	to resign (from)

Repaso: contestar

Una cuestión de dinero

el aumento de sueldo	raise
el banco	bank
el cajero automático	automatic teller machine
el cheque	check
la cuenta corriente	checking account
la cuenta de ahorros	savings account
el efectivo	cash
la factura	bill
el préstamo	loan
el presupuesto	budget
el salario	salary

Repaso: la cuenta, el sueldo, la tarjeta de crédito

ahorrar	to save (*money*)
cargar	to charge (*to an account*)
cobrar	to cash (*a check*); to charge (*someone for an item or service*)
depositar	to deposit
devolver (ue)	to return (*something*)
economizar	to economize
pedir (i, i) prestado/a	to borrow
sacar	to withdraw, take out
sacar el saldo	to balance a checkbook

Repaso: ganar, pagar, prestar

a plazos	in installments
al contado / en efectivo	in cash
con cheque	by check

Conjunciones

después (de) que	after
en cuanto	as soon as
hasta que	until

tan pronto como	as soon as

Repaso: antes (de) que, cuando

Palabras adicionales

al principio de	at the beginning of
en vez de	instead of

Un paso más 16

LECTURA

Note: The readings in the final three chapters of *Puntos de partida*, beginning with this chapter, are poems from the Spanish-speaking world. Although your professor may have already introduced you to some of the great works of Spanish and Latin American literature, this is your first encounter with literary works in Spanish in this textbook. Reading poetry will present new challenges for you, but your developing language proficiency will provide you a solid foundation with which to approach the task. As you read, remember to utilize the various reading strategies that have been introduced in previous chapters, as some of these will be applicable to the reading of literature as well.

Estrategia: Using Language Cues to Understand Poetry (1)

Much of the information you get in a poem is conveyed through its adjectives. Classifying the adjectives can often help you understand the poet's project or the poem's deeper "message." It can also help you to focus your attention on the important aspects of the poem.

You can classify the adjectives in the following poem as negative and positive. As you read, decide which adjectives describe the noun in favorable terms and which describe the noun in unfavorable terms. How is the central figure of the poem described? Why do you think the poet may have chosen this strategy?

▶ **Sobre la autora...** Juana Fernández de Ibarbourou (1895–1970) nació en
▶ Melo, Uruguay, donde pasó una niñez feliz. Demostró su interés en poesía
▶ a una temprana edad y publicó sus primeros versos en un periódico local
▶ a los 8 años. Después de su matrimonio a los 20 años, ella y su esposo se
▶ fueron a vivir a Montevideo.
▶   La poesía de Ibarbourou refleja la satisfacción de ser esposa, madre y
▶ poeta. A menudo (*Often*) escribía sobre la naturaleza y la reencarnación, dos
▶ de sus temas favoritos. En el siguiente poema, Ibarbourou crea la fuerte
▶ imagen de un elemento «feo» dentro de un medio ambiente muy bello y
▶ nos hace pensar en lo que constituye la belleza verdadera.

La higuera[a]

Porque es áspera[b] y fea;
Porque todas sus ramas[c] son grises,
Yo le tengo piedad[d] a la higuera.

En mi quinta[e] hay cien árboles bellos:
   Ciruelos redondos,[f]
   Limoneros rectos[g]
Y naranjos de brotes[h] lustrosos

   En las primaveras,
Todos ellos se cubren de flores
   En torno a[i] la higuera.

Y la pobre parece tan triste
Con sus gajos torcidos[j] que nunca
De apretados capullos[k] se visten...

   Por eso,
Cada vez que yo paso a su lado
Digo, procurando[l]
Hacer dulce y alegre mi acento:
—Es la higuera el más bello
De los árboles todos del huerto.[m]

   Si ella escucha,
Si comprende el idioma en que hablo,
¡Qué dulzura tan honda hará nido[n]
En su alma sensible[o] de árbol!

   Y tal vez, a la noche,
Cuando el viento abanique su copa,[p]
Embriagada de gozo[q] le cuente:
—Hoy a mí me dijeron hermosa.[r] ●

[a]*fig tree* [b]*rough* [c]*branches* [d]*pity* [e]*casa de campo* [f]Ciruelos... *Round plum trees* [g]*Straight lemon trees* [h]*shoots* [i]En... *Around* [j]gajos... *twisted branches* [k]apretados... *tight buds* [l]*striving* [m]*orchard* [n]¡Qué... *How deep the sweetness that will nest* [o]alma...*sensitive soul* [p]Cuando... *When the wind fans its upper branches* [q]Embriagada... *Drunk with joy* [r]*beautiful*

Una higuera

Comprensión

A. Descripción. Escriba una lista de adjetivos y frases que usa la autora para describir a la higuera.

B. Interpretación. ¿Por qué cree Ud. que la autora siente piedad por la higuera?

E S C R I T U R A

Imagine que Ud. es la higuera en el huerto de la autora. ¿Cómo se siente, rodeada (*surrounded*) de tantos árboles tan bonitos? ¿Qué opina Ud. sobre el cariño (*affection*) que le muestra la autora a la higuera? Escriba un breve ensayo en la que expresa sus emociones y perspectiva. El título de su ensayo puede ser «Yo soy la higuera».

En la actualidad

Esta reportera de Caracas, Venezuela, mantiene al día (*up to date*) al público.

¿Qué opina Ud.?

Ponga los siguientes tipos de noticias en orden, según sus preferencias, del 1 (el tipo que más le gusta) al 8. ¿Cree Ud. que una persona de otro país diría algo similar? Visite el sitio Web de *Puntos de partida* para leer cómo ordena estas noticias una persona de la República Dominicana.

_____ **noticias** mundiales
_____ noticias sobre su pueblo o ciudad
_____ noticias sobre su vecindad
_____ noticias sobre **desastres** o tragedias
_____ noticias sobre **eventos** inspirativos que le hayan ocurrido a algún individuo
_____ noticias sobre los deportes
_____ noticias sobre los negocios
_____ noticias sociales o culturales

En este capítulo...

- In this chapter, you will study vocabulary related to news and to government. Among other topics, you will be able to talk about **los desastres que se comentan en los medios de comunicación** and about **los reporteros,** people who announce the news.
- In this chapter, you will learn how to express actions or states in the past form of the subjunctive. For example, you will be able to say that your parents always insisted that you read the newspaper. (Grammar 48)
- In addition, you will learn some new ways of expressing possession. You know how to say *This is my book* in Spanish. Now you will learn to say *This book is mine.* (Grammar 49)
- The **Panorama cultural** section will focus on the Dominican Republic.

PUNTOS INTERACTIVO

Videoteca

◀ **Minidramas**
En este episodio, Manolo comenta la política del día con dos buenos amigos. ¿Le interesa a Ud. la política? ¿Con quién le gusta hablar del tema?

En contexto ▶
En este episodio, Roberto compra periódicos en su quiosco favorito. ¿Lee Ud. la prensa (*press*) habitualmente? ¿Qué periódicos o revistas le gustan más?

 CD-ROM

Además de completar el vocabulario y las actividades de gramática, Ud. va a tener la oportunidad de «comprar» un periódico en un quiosco virtual y de «hablar» con la dueña.

Internet

 En la sección del Capítulo 17 en el sitio Web de *Puntos de partida* aparecen enlaces que Ud. puede usar para conseguir información en español sobre los medios de comunicación. Use la dirección **www.mhhe.com/puntos.**

Vocabulario: Preparación

Las noticias

Y ahora, el canal 45 les ofrece a Uds. el NOTICIERO 45 con los últimos eventos del mundo...

Asesinato de un dictador

Huelga de obreros en Alemania

Guerra en el Oriente Medio

Erupción de un volcán en Centroamérica

Choque de trenes

Bombas en un avión

el acontecimiento	event	**la esperanza**	hope
el medio de comunicación	means of communication	**la paz**	peace
la prensa	press; news media	**comunicarse (con)**	to communicate (with)
el/la reportero/a	reporter	**enterarse (de)**	to find out, learn (about)
el/la testigo	witness		
el choque	collision	**informar**	to inform
el desastre	disaster	**ofrecer**	to offer

Conversación

A. ¿Cómo se entera Ud.? El público utiliza diferentes medios para enterarse de los acontecimientos locales, nacionales e internacionales. ¿Cómo se entera Ud. de las noticias?

Paso 1. Indique con qué frecuencia utiliza los siguientes medios.

	TODOS LOS DÍAS	DE 3 A 5 VECES POR SEMANA	CASI NUNCA
1. Leo un periódico local.	☐	☒	☐
2. Leo un periódico nacional.	☐	☐	☒
3. Leo una revista.	☐	☐	☒
4. Leo las noticias en el Internet.	☐	☒	☐
5. Miro el telediario (*newscast*) local.	☒	☐	☐
6. Miro el telediario nacional.	☒	☐	☐
7. Miro CNN.	☒	☐	☐
8. Escucho la radio.	☐	☒	☐

Paso 2. Compare sus respuestas con las de sus compañeros. ¿Cuál es el medio preferido por la mayoría de Uds. para informarse?

B. Definiciones. ¿Qué palabra se asocia con cada definición?

1. __A__ un programa que nos informa de lo que pasa en nuestro mundo
2. __f__ la persona que está presente durante un acontecimiento y lo ve todo
3. __i__ un medio importantísimo de comunicación
4. __g__ la persona que nos informa de las novedades
5. __d__ la persona que gobierna un país de una forma absoluta
6. __c__ la persona que emplea la violencia para cambiar el mundo según sus deseos
7. __h__ cuando los obreros se niegan a (*refuse*) trabajar
8. __e__ la frecuencia en que se transmiten y se reciben los programas de televisión
9. __B__ la confrontación armada entre dos o más países

a. el noticiero
b. la guerra
c. el/la terrorista
d. el/la dictador(a)
e. el canal
f. el/la testigo
g. el/la reportero/a
h. la huelga
i. la prensa

C. Ud. y la televisión. Diga si está de acuerdo con las siguientes opiniones. Si no está de acuerdo, haga los cambios necesarios para expresar su opinión. En cualquier caso, intente dar un ejemplo que justifique su punto de vista.

1. Los reporteros de la televisión nos informan imparcialmente de los acontecimientos.
2. Por lo general ofrecen los programas más interesantes en el canal de televisión pública.
3. En este país la prensa es irresponsable. Nos da sólo los detalles que apoyan (*support*) sus ideas políticas.
4. Las telenovelas (*soap operas*) reflejan la vida tal (*just*) como es.
5. Los anuncios son sumamente (*extremely*) informativos y más interesantes que muchos programas.
6. Me gusta que los reporteros y meteorólogos cuenten chistes durante el noticiero.

[a]un… *not at all*   [b]¡Justo… *That's all I'd need!*

el/la ciudadano/a	citizen	la ley	law
el deber	responsibility, obligation	la política	politics
		el/la político/a	politician
los/las demás	others, other people	el rey / la reina	king/queen
el derecho	right	el servicio militar	military service
la (des)igualdad	(in)equality		
la dictadura	dictatorship	durar	to last
la discriminación	discrimination	obedecer	to obey
el ejército	army	votar	to vote

Nota cultural

La tertulia

Una costumbre muy común en muchas partes del mundo hispánico es **la tertulia**, que consiste en un grupo de amigos a quienes les gusta pasar el rato **conversando**. Los participantes se reúnen periódicamente, por ejemplo, a la misma hora de la tarde todos los días. Generalmente la tertulia se celebra en **un bar** o **café** donde se puede tomar vino o cerveza y hablar. Las conversaciones pueden abarcar[a] muchos temas, pero sin duda dos de los más comunes son **los deportes** y **la política**. Ya que la gente hispánica se muda con menos frecuencia que la de este país, muchos de estos grupos duran años y años, con los mismos amigos que se reúnen en el mismo sitio y a la misma hora.

[a]*cover*

Conversación

A. Asociaciones. ¿Qué cosas, personas o ideas asocia Ud. con las siguientes palabras?

1. el deber
2. el ejército
3. la política
4. la ley
5. la monarquía
6. la dictadura

B. ¡Peligro! (*Jeopardy!*) ¿Cuánto sabe Ud. de la historia y la política? Conteste rápidamente con la información necesaria y en forma de pregunta.

1. Fue un dictador argentino que tenía una esposa famosa. *Juan Perón*
2. Se llama Elizabeth y vive en Buckingham Palace. *la reina Elizabeth*
3. Es una famosa película de Orson Welles, y su protagonista se llama Kane. *El ciudadano Kane*
4. Fue un presidente estadounidense que se opuso a (*opposed*) la esclavitud de los negros.
5. En algunos países, es un deber de los hombres de cierta edad. Generalmente, tienen que entrar en el ejército por dos años, más o menos.
6. Es la forma de gobierno que existe en España. *la monarquía*
7. Existe cuando muchas personas no tienen los mismos derechos que los demás.
8. Es un deber de los ciudadanos en una democracia.

C. Opiniones. ¿Qué piensa Ud. de las siguientes ideas? Dé su opinión, empezando con una de estas expresiones.

Dudo que… *I doubt that*	(No) Creo que…
Es probable que…	Es bueno/malo que…
Es una lástima que… *shame*	Es increíble que…
Me parece terrible/buena idea que… *it seems too much*	

1. En este país consumimos demasiada energía.
2. La paz mundial completa es (im)posible.
3. En este país, la igualdad de todos los ciudadanos es una realidad, no sólo una esperanza.
4. Los policías, los bomberos (*firefighters*) y los médicos no tienen derecho a declararse en huelga.
5. El servicio militar obligatorio es necesario para formar un ejército.
6. El mundo de la política está lleno de gente (des)honesta.
7. La edad permitida para tomar bebidas alcohólicas debe ser la misma que la edad para votar.
8. Hay muchos países que tienen dictadores.

Minidiálogos y gramática

¿Recuerda Ud.?

In Grammar Section 48, you will learn about and begin to use the forms of the past subjunctive. As you learn this new tense, you will be continually using the past tense forms you have already learned along with the new material, so this section presents many opportunities for review. The following brief exercises will help you get started.

A. To learn the forms of the past subjunctive, you will need to know the forms of the preterite well, especially the third person plural. Regular **-ar** verbs end in **-aron** and regular **-er/-ir** verbs in **-ieron** in the third person plural of the preterite. Stem-changing **-ir** verbs show the second change in the third person: **servir (i, i)** → **sirvieron; dormir (ue, u)** → **durmieron**. Verbs with a stem ending in a vowel change the **i** to **y**: **leyeron, cayeron, construyeron**. Many common verbs have irregular stems in the preterite: **quisieron, hicieron, dijeron**, and so on. Four common verbs are totally irregular in this tense: **ser/ir** → **fueron, dar** → **dieron, ver** → **vieron**.

Give the third person plural of the preterite for these infinitives.

1. hablar	6. dormir	11. destruir	16. vestirse
2. comer	7. reír	12. mantener	17. decir
3. vivir	8. leer	13. traer	18. creer
4. jugar	9. estar	14. dar	19. ir
5. perder	10. tener	15. saber	20. poder

B. The forms of the imperfect are relatively regular. Only three verbs have irregular imperfect forms: **ir, ser,** and **ver**. Give their first person singular and plural forms.

48 ¡No queríamos que fuera así! • Past Subjunctive

¡Qué pena que no nos lleváramos bien!

MARÍA: ¿No recuerdas? ¡Qué mala memoria!

ELISA: Pero, mamá, ¿tú permitías que yo *hablara* así? ¡Qué falta de respeto hacia ti!

MARÍA: Eras muy cabezuda. No había nadie que *pudiera* contigo. ¡Cómo discutíamos! Tú creías que siempre tenías razón. Era imposible que *te equivocaras*. Tampoco querías que te *dijeran* lo que debías hacer.

ELISA: Bueno, por lo menos ahora no soy así. Digo, no tanto…

MARÍA: Sí, pero de todos modos, es necesario que una buena periodista sea un poco terca.

ELISA: Estoy de acuerdo. Es probable que, sin esa cualidad mía, yo no hubiera obtenido ese puesto.

It's a shame we didn't get along! MARÍA: You don't remember? What a bad memory! ELISA: But Mom, did you allow me to speak in that way? What a lack of respect towards you! MARÍA: You were very stubborn. No one could change your mind. How we used to argue! You thought you were always right. It was impossible that you could ever make a mistake. Nor did you want anyone to tell you what to do. ELISA: Well, at least I'm not like that now. I mean, not as much… MARÍA: Yes, but, in any case, it's necessary for a good journalist to be a little bit stubborn. ELISA: I agree. It's probable that, without that quality of mine, I wouldn't have gotten that job.

Hace diez años…

1. ¿era difícil que Ud. hablara con sus padres sobre algún tema? ¿Cuál?
2. ¿con quién era imposible que Ud. se pusiera de acuerdo?
3. ¿con quién era imposible que Ud. se comunicara?
4. ¿contra qué orden de sus padres era común que Ud. protestara?

Cuando Ud. era niño/a…

5. ¿era probable que discutiera con alguien en la escuela primaria o en el barrio? ¿Con quién?
6. ¿dónde le prohibían sus padres que jugara?
7. ¿qué era obligatorio que comiera o bebiera?
8. ¿de qué temía que sus padres se enteraran?

Although Spanish has two simple indicative past tenses (preterite and imperfect), it has only one simple subjunctive past tense, the *past subjunctive* (**el imperfecto del subjuntivo**). Generally speaking, this tense is used in the same situations as the present subjunctive but, of course, when talking about past events. The exact English equivalent depends on the context in which it is used.

Forms of the Past Subjunctive

Past Subjunctive of Regular Verbs*

hablar: hablarøⱥ		comer: comierøⱥ		vivir: vivierøⱥ	
hablara	habláramos	comiera	comiéramos	viviera	viviéramos
hablaras	hablarais	comieras	comierais	vivieras	vivierais
hablara	hablaran	comiera	comieran	viviera	vivieran

A. The past subjunctive endings **-a, -as, -a, -amos, -ais, -an** are identical for **-ar, -er,** and **-ir** verbs. These endings are added to the third person plural of the preterite indicative, minus its **-on** ending. For this reason, the forms of the past subjunctive reflect the irregularities of the preterite.

PAST SUBJUNCTIVE ENDINGS

-ar → -ara
-er, -ir → -iera

B. Stem-changing verbs

-Ar and **-er** verbs: no change

-Ir verbs: all persons of the past subjunctive reflect the vowel change in the third person plural of the preterite.

empezar (ie): empezarøⱥ → **empezara, empezaras, …**
volver (ue): volvierøⱥ → **volviera, volvieras, …**
dormir (ue, u): durmierøⱥ → **durmiera, durmieras, …**
pedir (i, i): pidierøⱥ → **pidiera, pidieras, …**

---

*An alternative form of the past subjunctive (used primarily in Spain) ends in **-se: hablase, hablases, hablase, hablásemos, hablaseis, hablasen.** This form will not be practiced in *Puntos de partida.*

C. Spelling changes

All persons of the past subjunctive reflect the change from **i** to **y** between two vowels.

i → y (caer, construir, creer, destruir, leer, oír)
creer: creyer~~on~~ → **creyera, creyeras, creyera, creyéramos, creyerais, creyeran**

D. Verbs with irregular preterites

dar: dier~~on~~ → **diera, dieras, diera, diéramos, dierais, dieran**

decir:	dijer~~on~~ → **dijera**	poner:	pusier~~on~~ → **pusiera**
estar:	estuvier~~on~~ → **estuviera**	querer:	quisier~~on~~ → **quisiera**
haber:	hubier~~on~~ → **hubiera**	saber:	supier~~on~~ → **supiera**
hacer:	hicier~~on~~ → **hiciera**	ser:	fuer~~on~~ → **fuera**
ir:	fuer~~on~~ → **fuera**	tener:	tuvier~~on~~ → **tuviera**
poder:	pudier~~on~~ → **pudiera**	venir:	vinier~~on~~ → **viniera**

Uses of the Past Subjunctive

A. The past subjunctive usually has the same applications as the present subjunctive, but it is used for past events. Compare these pairs of sentences.

Quiero que **jueguen** esta tarde.
I want them to play this afternoon.

Quería que **jugaran** por la tarde.
I wanted them to play in the afternoon.

Siente que no **estén** allí esta noche.
He's sorry (that) they aren't there tonight.

Sintió que no **estuvieran** allí anoche.
He was sorry (that) they weren't there last night.

Dudamos que se **equivoquen**.
We doubt that they will make a mistake.

Dudábamos que se **equivocaran**.
We doubted that they would make a mistake.

B. Remember that the subjunctive is used after
(1) expressions of *influence, emotion,* and *doubt;*
(2) *nonexistent* and *indefinite antecedents;* and
(3) *conjunctions* of *contingency and purpose,* as well as those of *time.*

(1) ¿**Era necesario** que **regatearas**?
Was it necessary for you to bargain?

(1) **Sentí** que no **tuvieran** tiempo para ver Granada.
I was sorry that they didn't have time to see Granada.

(2) **No había nadie** que **pudiera** resolverlo.
There wasn't anyone who could (might have been able to) solve it.

(3) Los padres **trabajaron para que** sus hijos **asistieran** a la universidad.
The parents worked so that their children could (might) go to the university.

(3) Anoche, **íbamos** a salir **en cuanto llegara** Felipe.
Last night, we were going to leave as soon as Felipe arrived.

C. The past subjunctive of the verb **querer** is often used to make a request sound more polite.

Quisiéramos hablar con Ud. en seguida.
We would like to speak with you immediately.

Quisiera un café, por favor.
I would like a cup of coffee, please.

Práctica

A. Si pudiera regresar... ¿Le gusta la idea de volver a la escuela secundaria? ¿O prefiere la vida de la universidad?

Paso 1. Lea las siguientes oraciones e indique las que son verdaderas para Ud. Cambie las oraciones falsas para que expresen su propia experiencia.

En la escuela secundaria…

1. ☐ era obligatorio que yo asistiera a todas mis clases
2. ☐ mis padres insistían en que yo estudiara mucho
3. ☐ era necesario que yo trabajara para que pudiera asistir a la universidad algún día
4. ☐ no había ninguna clase que me interesara
5. ☐ tenía que sacar buenas notas para que mis padres me dieran dinero
6. ☐ era necesario que volviera a casa a una hora determinada, aun en los fines de semana
7. ☐ mis padres me exigían que limpiara mi cuarto cada semana
8. ☐ mis padres no permitían que saliera con alguna persona o con los miembros de ciertos grupos

Paso 2. Ahora considere sus respuestas. ¿Realmente era mejor la vida en la escuela secundaria? ¿Le gustaría regresar a esa época? ¿Por qué sí o por qué no?

B. Y ahora, la niñez. ¿Qué quería Ud. de la vida cuando era niño/a? ¿Y qué querían los demás que Ud. hiciera? Conteste, haciendo oraciones con una frase de cada grupo.

1. Mis padres (no) querían que yo…
2. Mis maestros me pedían que…
3. Yo buscaba amigos que…
4. Me gustaba mucho que nosotros…

ir a la iglesia / al templo con ellos
portarse bien, ser bueno/a
estudiar mucho, hacer la tarea todas las noches, sacar buenas notas
ponerse ropa vieja para jugar, jugar en la calle, pelear con mis amigos
mirar mucho la televisión, leer muchas tiras cómicas, comer muchos dulces
vivir en nuestro barrio, asistir a la misma escuela, tener muchos juguetes, ser aventureros
ir de vacaciones en verano, pasar todos juntos los días feriados, tener un árbol de Navidad muy alto

C. El noticiero de las seis. En las noticias los reporteros nos informan de los acontecimientos del día, pero a veces también ofrecen sus propias opiniones.

Paso 1. Lea las siguientes oraciones y cámbielas al pasado. Debe usar el imperfecto del primer verbo en cada oración y luego el imperfecto del subjuntivo en la segunda parte.

1. «Los obreros quieren que les den un aumento de sueldo.»
2. «Es posible que los trabajadores sigan en huelga hasta el verano.»
3. «Es necesario que las víctimas reciban atención médica en la Clínica del Sagrado Corazón.»
4. «Es una lástima que no haya espacio para todos allí.»
5. «Los terroristas piden que los oficiales no los persigan.»
6. «Parece imposible que el gobierno acepte sus demandas.»
7. «Es necesario que el gobierno informe a todos los ciudadanos del desastre.»
8. «Dudo que la paz mundial esté fuera de nuestro alcance (*reach*).»
9. «El presidente y los directores prefieren que la nueva fábrica se construya en México.»
10. «Temo que el número de votantes sea muy bajo en las próximas elecciones.»

Paso 2. Ahora indique si las oraciones representan un hecho o si son una opinión del reportero o de la persona citada (*quoted*).

Conversación

A. Preguntas

1. ¿A qué le tenía miedo Ud. cuando era pequeño/a? ¿Era probable que ocurrieran las cosas que Ud. temía? ¿Temía a veces que sus padres

lo/la castigaran (*punish*)? ¿Lo merecía a veces? ¿Era necesario que Ud. siempre los obedeciera? ¿Qué le prohibían a Ud. que hiciera?

2. ¿Qué tipo de clases buscaba Ud. para este semestre/trimestre? ¿clases que fueran fáciles? ¿interesantes? ¿Las encontró? ¿Han sido las clases tal como Ud. las esperaba? ¿Qué tipo de clases va a buscar para el semestre/trimestre que viene?

3. ¿Qué buscaban los primeros inmigrantes que vinieron a los Estados Unidos? ¿Buscaban un lugar donde pudieran practicar su religión? ¿un lugar donde hubiera abundancia de recursos naturales? ¿menos restricciones? ¿más libertad política y personal? ¿más respeto por los derechos humanos? ¿menos gente? ¿más espacio?

B. Situaciones. El niño del dibujo sabe que está molestando a sus padres cuando los despierta pidiendo ahora un vaso de agua que no quiere pero que podría querer más tarde. Por eso les habla de una forma muy cortés: «quisiera un vaso de agua... quisiera saber... ». ¿Cómo podría Ud. pedir de una forma muy cortés lo que necesita en las siguientes situaciones? ¿Qué diría para conseguirlo?

1. Ud. quiere tener el número de teléfono de un chico/una chica que acaba de conocer. Habla con un amigo de él/una amiga de ella.

2. En un restaurante, el camarero no lo/la atiende como debe. Ud. no quiere perder la paciencia con él, pero quiere la taza de café que le pidió hace diez minutos... y la cuenta.

3. Uds. quieren saber cuándo es el examen final en esta clase y qué va a incluir.

—Verás, quisiera un vaso de agua. Pero no te molestes, porque ya no tengo sed. Sólo quisiera saber si, en el caso de que tuviese otra vez sed, podría (*I could*) venir a pedirte un vaso de agua.

Nota comunicativa

I wish I could . . . I wish they would . . .

There are many ways to express wishes in Spanish. As you know, one of the most common is **ojalá (que)** with the subjunctive. The past subjunctive following **ojalá** is one of the most frequent uses of those verb forms.

Ojalá (que) pudiera acompañarlos, pero no es posible.	*I wish I could go with you, but it's not possible.*
Ojalá inventaran una máquina que hiciera todas las tareas domésticas.	*I wish they would invent a machine that would do all the household chores.*

C. ¡Ojalá! Complete las oraciones lógicamente.

1. Ojalá que (yo) tuviera _____.
2. Ojalá que pudiera _____.
3. Ojalá inventaran una máquina que _____.
4. Ojalá solucionaran el problema de _____.
5. Ojalá que en esta universidad fuera posible _____.

Minidiálogos y gramática

Rubén Salazar

El 29 de agosto de 1970, día del **Moratorio Chicano,*** murió **Rubén Salazar, jefe de información** de la estación KMEX-TV, de Los Ángeles, y **columnista** del periódico *Los Angeles Times*. Después de filmar el moratorio y los disturbios subsecuentes, Salazar y su equipo habían entrado en el Silver Dollar café del Bulevar Whittier. Un escuadrón de agentes de policía del Departamento del Sheriff del condado de Los Ángeles, reaccionando a la información de que había dentro un hombre armado, cercó[a] el café y dispararon[b] varias bombas de gases lacrimógenos[c] hacia el interior. Uno de los proyectiles golpeó a Salazar en la cabeza, matándolo inmediatamente.

Rubén Salazar

Al momento de su muerte, Rubén Salazar era **el periodista mexicoamericano más conocido** del país. Salazar nació en Juárez, México, en 1928 y se crió en El Paso, Texas. En 1956 se mudó a California. De 1959 a 1965, fue reportero del *Los Angeles Times*, y comunicaba las noticias de la comunidad chicana de Los Ángeles. Cómo **corresponsal en el extranjero** del *Times*, reportó sobre la intervención estadounidense en la República Dominicana en 1965 y la guerra en Vietnám. En 1966, llegó a ser[d] jefe de la agencia del *Times* en la Ciudad de México. En 1970 dejó su puesto de reportero en el *Times* para aceptar el de jefe de información de la estación KMEX-TV, que emitía en español. Según él, había escrito tantos artículos en inglés acerca de los hispanos que ahora quería comunicarse con este mismo público en su propio lenguaje.

Asimismo[e] comenzó a escribir una columna semanal en el *Times* sobre **asuntos[f] chicanos** en Los Ángeles. En ella denunció el racismo y varias injusticias serias sufridas por la comunidad chicana. Escribió sobre temas que todavía tienen gran importancia: la inmigración, la discriminación racial, la educación bilingüe y bicultural y la Acción Afirmativa. Sus columnas y reportajes le ganaron la enemistad de las agencias de la policía de Los Ángeles. Varias autoridades llegaron a sugerir a la dirección del *Times* que despidieran[g] a Salazar o que dejaran de publicar su columna.

Aunque la encuesta judicial sobre las causas de la muerte de Rubén Salazar absolvió a los diputados[h] de las acusaciones de conspirar para asesinarlo, eso no consiguió disipar todas esas sospechas, algunas de las cuales persisten todavía.

[a]*surrounded* [b]*fired* [c]*tear-causing* [d]*llegó... he became* [e]*Likewise* [f]*matters* [g]*they fire* [h]*deputies*

¿Recuerda Ud.?

Review the forms and uses of possessive adjectives (Grammar Section 6) before beginning Grammar Section 49.

When the possessive adjectives modify a singular noun, use the following.

> **mi tu su nuestro/a vuestro/a su**

When the possessive adjectives modify a plural noun, use the following.

> **mis tus sus nuestros/as vuestros/as sus**

---

*El **Moratorio Chicano** fue una manifestación (*demonstration*) contra la guerra en Vietnám. Los participantes del Moratorio protestaron contra la participación chicana en la guerra.

Exprese lo siguiente con adjetivos posesivos.

1. el país de él
2. los derechos (que tienes tú)
3. la obligación de nosotros
4. la prensa de nosotros
5. el gobierno de Uds.
6. el crimen de ellos

49 More About Expressing Possession • Stressed Possessives

Algún día, hijo mío, todo esto va a ser tuyo.

1. ¿Quién es el dueño del mundo en esta visión del futuro?
2. ¿A quién le va a dar todo el padre robot?
3. ¿A qué se refieren las palabras «todo esto»?
4. ¿Quisiera Ud. heredar «todo esto» algún día?
5. Imagine que Ud. le dice a su hijo/a que «todo esto va a ser tuyo». ¿A qué se refiere Ud. con estas palabras? Es decir, ¿qué quiere dejarle para el futuro?

- When in English you would emphasize the possessive with your voice, or when you want to express English *of mine* (*of yours, of his,* and so on), you will use the *stressed forms* (**las formas tónicas**) of the possessive in Spanish. As the term implies, they are more emphatic than the *unstressed forms* (**las formas átonas**).

Forms of the stressed possessive adjectives

mío/a/os/as	my, (of) mine	**nuestro/a/os/as**	our, (of) ours
tuyo/a/os/as	your, (of) yours	**vuestro/a/os/as**	your, (of) yours
suyo/a/os/as	your, (of) yours; his, (of) his; her, (of) hers; its	**suyo/a/os/as**	your, (of) yours; their, (of) theirs

- The stressed forms of the possessive adjective follow the noun, which must be preceded by a definite or indefinite article or by a demonstrative adjective. The stressed forms agree with the noun modified in number and gender.

Es **mi** amigo. — He's *my friend.*

Es **un** amigo **mío.** {
  He's **my friend.**
  He's a friend of mine.
}

Es **su** perro. — It's her dog.

Es **un** perro **suyo.**
Es **suyo.** {
  It's **her** dog.
  It's a dog of hers.
  It's hers.
}

- The stressed possessives are often used as nouns.

la maleta suya → la suya
el pasaporte tuyo → el tuyo.*

---

*For more information, see Appendix 2, Using Adjectives as Nouns.

Práctica

A. En el hotel. Complete el siguiente diálogo con las formas apropiadas del posesivo.

—Perdone, señorita, pero esta maleta que Uds. me han dado no es (mío[1]).

—¿No es (suyo[2])? ¿No es Ud. el doctor Méndez?

—Sí, soy yo, pero esta maleta no es (mío[3]). Ud. todavía tiene la (mío[4]). Está allí a la derecha.

—Ah, nos equivocamos. Esta es la de los señores Palma. Aquí tengo la (suyo[5]). ¡Cuánto lo siento!

B. En el departamento de objetos perdidos. ¿Son suyos los objetos que le ofrecen? Con un compañero/una compañera, háganse preguntas y contéstenlas según los modelos.

MODELO: de Ud. →
E1: Esta maleta, ¿es *de Ud.*?
E2: No, no es *mía.*

1. de Juan
2. de Uds.
3. de Alicia
4. mía
5. tuya

MODELO: libro →
E1: ¿Y este *libro*?
E2: No, no es *mío. El mío* es más pequeño.

6. despertador
7. zapatos
8. llave
9. televisor
10. pastillas
11. periódico

Conversación

A. Comparaciones: En general... Compare the following aspects of your life with what is generally the case. Complete only those sentences that have meaning for you personally.

1. Las clases en esta universidad son fáciles/regulares/difíciles. Pienso que las mías...
2. Las clases aquí son grandes/pequeñas. Pienso que la nuestra...
3. En esta ciudad, los alquileres son altos. Creo que el mío...
4. Dicen que el perro es el mejor amigo del hombre. Sin duda, el mío...
5. La familia es un apoyo (*support*) cuando uno tiene problemas. En general, la mía...
6. Los coches modernos son más pequeños que los de la década de los cincuenta. El mío...

B. Entrevista. Use the cues on the following page to interview a classmate about the following aspects of his or her life. Find out as much as you can about the topic. Then state the results of your interview, using stressed possessives when possible.

Las clases: ¿cuántas clases en total?, ¿a qué hora empiezan?, ¿muchos cursos de ciencias?, ¿de humanidades?

De los dos, ¿quién... ?

1. tiene el horario más exigente (*demanding*)
2. tiene el horario que empieza más temprano
3. tiene el horario más interesante

MODELO: El horario de Burt es más exigente que el mío.
(Burt tiene clases muy difíciles, pero mi horario es más exigente que el suyo.)

La vivienda: ¿el tamaño (*size*) del apartamento/casa?, ¿un alquiler alto?, ¿un barrio elegante?

De los dos, ¿quién... ?

4. tiene el apartamento más grande
5. tiene el alquiler más barato
6. vive en el barrio más elegante

Videoteca

ESPAÑA

Minidramas

In this **Minidramas** dialogue, Manolo Durán and some colleagues take part in a **tertulia**, an informal gathering at which participants chat about current topics (see **Nota cultural**, this chapter). Pay close attention to what Manolo and his friends are talking about. Also note their reactions to what the others say. Do you think they are angry with each other?

F U N C T I O N
expressing disagreement

Manolo llega al bar. Se sienta a la mesa con sus amigos.

MANOLO: Muy bien, ¿de qué hablamos hoy?
MARICARMEN: Hablamos del partido político de Paco. Y este, como siempre, cree que los líderes políticos de su partido tienen el derecho de dictar cómo viven los demás. Y yo, claro, no estoy de acuerdo.

PACO: Maricarmen, te equivocas. Es todo lo contrario. Mira. Mi partido ofrece soluciones razonables a los problemas más graves de hoy.

MANOLO: Hasta cierto punto, estoy de acuerdo con Maricarmen. ¿Viste las noticias del Canal 2 anoche? Paco, tu querido partido quería votar cuanto antes[a] la nueva legislación, para que nadie más pudiera protestar.

PACO: ¡No, señor! No es así. ¿Siempre crees todo lo que dicen la prensa y la televisión? ¡Ojalá el asunto[b] fuera tan sencillo!

MARICARMEN: Pero, Paco, no me parecen razonables las soluciones propuestas por tu partido. Es verdad que necesitamos nuevas leyes laborales, pero estas no resuelven nada.

PACO: ¡Al contrario! Maricarmen, el anterior presidente no había hecho nada en los últimos años. Mira las noticias. Hay huelgas, desempleo, desastres económicos…

MANOLO: ¡Paco! ¿Tú siempre crees todo lo que dicen la prensa y la televisión?

PACO: Pues, ¡parece que lo único en que estamos de acuerdo es en que *no* estamos de acuerdo!

[a]cuanto… *as soon as possible*   [b]*matter*

Con un compañero / una compañera

Exprese dos opiniones distintas sobre cada uno de los siguientes temas en diálogos de cinco o seis oraciones. **¡OJO!** *No* es necesario que los diálogos expresen sus opiniones personales. Sólo deben presentar dos puntos de vista opuestos.

- la pena de muerte: ¿castigo (*punishment*) inhumano o freno necesario para el crimen?
- la censura (*censorship*) del Internet: ¿tema «de moda» o medida necesaria para proteger a la juventud?
- la legalización de la marihuana: ¿amenaza (*threat*) a la juventud o compromiso inteligente?

En contexto

A. Lluvia de ideas

MÉXICO

- En su opinión, ¿qué medios de información debe leer una persona que quiere estar bien informada de lo que pasa en el país o en el mundo? ¿Se considera Ud. una persona bien informada? ¿Por qué?
- ¿Está Ud. suscrito/a a alguna revista o algún periódico? ¿Cuáles? Si Ud. compra alguna revista o algún periódico, ¿dónde los compra? ¿Los compra a menudo (*often*)? ¿Qué calidades o valores espera encontrar en una revista o un periódico?
- ¿Sabía Ud. que en los países hispánicos no es tan común como en este país estar suscrito a los periódicos y a las revistas? ¿Qué prefiere Ud., suscribirse a una publicación o comprarla en un quiosco (o puesto de periódicos)? ¿Por qué?

Un poco más sobre… Manolo Durán García

Aunque Ud. ya conocía bien a don Manolo y a su familia —su esposa Lola y su hija Marta—, hasta ahora no sabía mucho de la vida del señor fuera de la esfera doméstica. Como sabe, enseña literatura en Sevilla. Pero también tiene una vida social muy activa.

To read more about the characters from this video, visit the *Puntos de partida* Website at **www.mhhe.com/puntos**

B. Dictado

A continuación aparece un fragmento del diálogo entre Juan Carlos y la vendedora de periódicos. Complete el diálogo con las palabras o frases que faltan.

ROBERTO: ¿Cuánto _____ _____, doña Beatriz?

VENDEDORA: Son _____ pesos.

ROBERTO: ¿Me puede _____ un billete de _____ pesos?

VENDEDORA: No, Roberto. Es muy _____. ¿No tienes uno _____ _____?

ROBERTO: Sí, un billete de _____ pesos. ¿Está _____?

VENDEDORA: Sí, perfecto. A ver. _____ _____ _____ pesos... Aquí los tienes.

ROBERTO: Gracias, doña Beatriz. _____ _____ mañana, ¿no?

VENDEDORA: Claro, hijo. Y no me _____ a dar otro susto. ¡Si yo _____ tu madre...!

C. Un diálogo original

Opción 1. Con un compañero / una compañera, dramaticen el diálogo entre Roberto y doña Beatriz.

Opción 2. ¡Qué desesperación! En esta dramatización uno/a de Uds. hace el papel de una persona que está desesperada por comprar un periódico del extranjero. El otro / La otra es el dueño / la dueña de un quiosco de periódicos.

ESTUDIANTE 1   Ud. tiene un buen amigo que está en un país del Oriente Medio, en un área donde ha estallado (*has broken out*) una guerra. Quiere un periódico de ese país para averiguar (*find out*) más acerca de los acontecimientos. Pero el periódico tiene que ser en inglés o en español, ya que Ud. no sabe leer ni árabe ni hebreo.

ESTUDIANTE 2   Aunque Ud. vende periódicos del extranjero, ninguno de los periódicos del Oriente Medio que tiene es en inglés o en español. Pero Ud. conoce a una reportera árabe en su ciudad que está enterada sobre la guerra. Ud. ofrece comunicarse con ella para que su cliente se pueda informar sobre su amigo.

Un poco de todo

A. ¡No es justo (*fair*)!

Paso 1. Complete las siguientes oraciones, según las indicaciones, para enterarse de lo que le pasó a Pepe Ramírez ayer. Añada otras palabras cuando sea necesario. **¡OJO!** Va a usar el imperfecto del subjuntivo en algunos casos.

1. ayer / (yo) ver / mi / nota /en / último / examen
2. no / poder / creer / que / nota / ser / tan / bajo
3. no / ser / posible / que / yo / hacer / examen / tan / mal
4. por eso / (yo) hablar / con / profesor / para que / (él) explicarme / causa / de / nota
5. (él) decirme / que / haber / errores / importante / pero / que / haber /partes / bueno / también

6. (él) pedirme / que / leer / examen / otro / vez
7. ser / verdad / que / haber / errores / en / examen
8. pero / ¡no / ser / justo / que / profesor / darme / nota / tan / bajo!

Paso 2. Con un compañero / una compañera, háganse las siguientes preguntas y contéstenlas.

1. ¿Te ha ocurrido algo similar?
2. ¿Qué hiciste? ¿Te cambió la nota tu profesor(a) o no?
3. ¿Piensas que muchos profesores son injustos? ¿Por qué?

B. Escenas históricas

Paso 1. La gente emigra por varias razones. Complete las siguientes oraciones con la forma correcta del infinitivo. Luego, si puede, nombre un grupo que emigró por la razón citada.

1. Las leyes de su país de origen no permitían que este grupo (practicar) libremente su religión.
2. Algunas personas esperaban que (haber) oro y plata en América.
3. El rey no quería que estos criminales (seguir) viviendo en su país.
4. Estos inmigrantes buscaban un país donde (haber) paz y esperanza y seguridad (*safety*) personal.
5. Los miembros de este grupo buscaban un país donde no (tener) que pasar hambre.

Paso 2. Dé una breve descripción del pasado histórico de los Estados Unidos, haciendo oraciones según las indicaciones. Empiece en el pasado. Desde el número 8, las oraciones se refieren al presente.

1. indios / temer / que / colonos / quitarles / toda la tierra
2. colonos / no / gustar / que / ser necesario / pagarle / impuestos / rey
3. parecía imposible / que / joven república / tener éxito (*success*)
4. los del sur / no / gustar / que / gobernarlos / los del norte
5. abolicionistas / no / gustar / que / algunos / no / tener / mismo / libertades
6. era necesario / que / declararse / en huelga / obreros / para / obtener / alguno / derechos
7. era terrible / que / haber / dos / guerra / mundial
8. para que / nosotros / vivir / en paz / es cuestión de / aprender / comunicarse
9. también / es necesario / que / haber / leyes / que / garantizar / derechos

C. ¿Qué lees?
Complete the following dialogue with the correct form of the words in parentheses, as suggested by the context. When two possibilities are given in parentheses, select the correct word.

EDUARDO: ¿De quién (ser/estar[1]) esta revista?
LINDA: Es (mío[2]). Te (lo/la[3]) puedo prestar, si quieres.
EDUARDO: Pues me gustaría que me la (dejar[4]). La he (hojear[a] [5]) y me ha gustado.

[a]*to look over*

LINDA: Para (yo/mí[6]) también ha sido una sorpresa. No pensaba que (ser/estar[7]) (tan/tanto[8]) buena. Tiene un poco de todo. Aunque yo temía que (resultar[b] [9]) superficial, no es así.

EDUARDO: (*Yo:* Ser/Estar[10]) de acuerdo. Trae artículos de política internacional (muy/mucho[11]) interesantes. Quiero terminar de (leer[12]) ese artículo sobre la situación de las antiguas[c] repúblicas soviéticas.

LINDA: (Leer: *Tú*[13]) también el reportaje sobre África. Hace un análisis muy interesante sobre (el/la[14]) relación entre el hambre, la guerra y (el/la[15]) desertización. Pero también habla de la política nacional, de ciencia…

EDUARDO: Sí, y ya (ver: *yo*[16]) que además trae (un/una[17]) reportaje sobre mi actor favorito.

LINDA: (Es/Está[18]) cierto. Trae bastantes comentarios sobre el cine. También puedes (enterarse[19]) de las últimas novedades, tanto sobre libros (que/como[20]) sobre música.

EDUARDO: Y también me imagino[d] (que/lo que[21]) tiene secciones sobre viajes, salud, deportes…

LINDA: Tienes (suerte/razón[22]). Es una buena forma de enterarse de todo lo actual.

[b]*to turn out* [c]*former* [d]*me… I imagine*

Comprensión: ¿Cierto o falso?

1. A Linda le gusta leer más que a Eduardo.
2. La revista de que hablan se publica una vez al año.
3. Es posible que tenga también una sección sobre viajes.

PANORAMA *cultural*

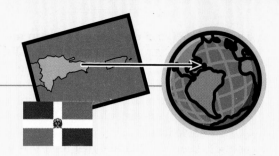

República Dominicana

Datos esenciales

Nombre oficial: República Dominicana
Capital: Santo Domingo
Población: 8.000.000 de habitantes
Moneda: el peso
Idiomas: el español (oficial), el francés criollo

¡Fíjese!

- Santo Domingo fue fundada en 1496 por Bartólome Colón, hermano de Cristóbal Colón. Esta población en lo que entonces se llamaba la isla de La Española fue la primera colonia europea en el Nuevo Mundo.

- En el siglo XV, bucaneros franceses, que en realidad no eran más que piratas, fundaron la colonia de Sant Domingue en el oeste de la isla. Dentro de poco tiempo, se estableció un sistema de plantaciones basado en la labor de esclavos africanos.

- España le cedió[a] a Francia, en 1697, el tercio occidental[b] de La Española. Por esta razón, este territorio, el actual país de Haití, tiene una cultura y un idioma diferentes a los de la República Dominicana.

- Muchos atletas dominicanos han tenido gran éxito[c] en las Grandes Ligas de los Estados Unidos. Entre los que se han destacado[d] recientemente han sido Sammy Sosa, Juan Marichal y Roberto y Sandy Alomar.

[a]*ceded*   [b]*tercio… western third*   [c]*success*   [d]*se… have stood out*

Conozca a... Julia Álvarez

Julia Álvarez

Aunque la novelista Julia Álvarez (1950–) nació en la ciudad de Nueva York y ahora es profesora de inglés en Middlebury College en Vermont, pasó su niñez en la República Dominicana. Cuando tenía apenas[a] 10 años, su padre tuvo que exiliarse con la familia después de tratar de derrotar[b] el régimen del dictador Trujillo. Al llegar a la madurez, se destacó como[c] poeta y ganó su primer premio de importancia en 1974, el mismo año en que publicó su primer libro de poesía, *Homecoming*. Pero cuando, en 1991, publicó su primera novela *How the García Girls Lost their Accents* —en verdad, una serie de cuentos entrelazados[d]— recibió atención crítica y pública del mundo entero. Esta obra, como las que la han seguido, refleja su múltiple existencia como mujer, como latina y como americana.

[a]*barely*   [b]*defeat*   [c]*se… she distinguished herself as a*   [d]*linked*

 Capítulo 17 of the video to accompany *Puntos de partida* contains cultural footage of the Dominican Republic.

 Visit the *Puntos de partida* Website at www.mhhe.com/puntos.

Vocabulario

Los verbos

apoyar	to support
castigar	to punish
comunicarse (con)	to communicate (with)
durar	to last
enterarse (de)	to find out (about)
gobernar (ie)	to govern, rule
informar	to inform
votar	to vote

Repaso: obedecer, ofrecer

Las últimas novedades

el acontecimiento	event, happening
el asesinato	assassination
el choque	collision
el desastre	disaster
el evento	event
el ejército	army
la esperanza	hope, wish
la guerra	war
la huelga	strike (*labor*)
la libertad	liberty, freedom
el medio de comunicación	means of communication
el noticiero	newscast
la paz (*pl.* paces)	peace

la prensa	press; news media
el/la reportero/a	reporter
el/la terrorista	terrorist
el/la testigo	witness

Repaso: el canal, el/la obrero/a

El gobierno y la responsabilidad cívica

el/la ciudadano/a	citizen
el deber	responsibility, obligation
el derecho	right
la (des)igualdad	(in)equality
el/la dictador(a)	dictator
la dictadura	dictatorship
la discriminación	discrimination
la ley	law
la política	politics
el/la político/a	politician
el rey / la reina	king/queen
el servicio militar	military service

Repaso: los/las demás

Las formas posesivas

mío/a(s), tuyo/a(s), suyo/a(s), nuestro/a(s), vuestro/a(s)

Un paso más 17

LECTURA

Estrategia: Using Language Cues to Understand Poetry (2)

In **Capítulo 16,** you examined a poet's use of adjectives to better understand a poem. You can also consider how the particular grammatical forms in a poem convey information or contribute to its unique mood. For example, a poem written primarily in the imperfect may convey a sense of timelessness or of things recurring in the poet's personal history. The use of the preterite may give you the feeling that the moment was fleeting, perhaps all too fleeting.

As you read the following poem, note the instances of the past subjunctive that you have learned in this chapter. Why do you think the poet chose this form? What or how does it make you feel? Do you think the poem would be different if the poet had chosen a different grammatical form?

▶ **Sobre el autor...** Gustavo Pérez Firmat (1949–) nació en La Habana,
▶ Cuba, y se crió en Miami, Florida. Su poesía tiene una variedad de temas,
▶ entre los que se incluyen las relaciones de familia y la experiencia cubano-
▶ americana en los Estados Unidos. Pérez Firmat recibió un doctorado de la
▶ Universidad de Michigan y ahora enseña en la Universidad de Columbia.
▶ El poema que aquí se presenta, «Cubanita descubanizada», es de una colec-
▶ ción que se titula *Bilingual Blues.*

Cubanita descubanizada

Cubanita descubanizada
quién te pudiera recubanizar.
Quién supiera devolverte
el ron[a] y la palma,[b]
el alma y el son.[c]

Cubanita descubanizada,
tú que pronuncias todas las eses*
y dices ómnibus[d] y autobús
quién te pudiera
quién te supiera
si te quisieras recubanizar.

[a]*rum* [b]*palm tree* [c]*el... the soul and the sound (the* **son** *is also a popular Cuban dance)* [d]*synonym for* **autobús** *(the author is referring to the rich lexical variety that exists in Cuban Spanish, but that in this case signals a departure from its local, rural roots).*

---

*In general, Cuban Spanish is characterized by a lack of pronunciation of the letter *s* when found in certain positions within a word.

Comprensión

A. Definiciones. El autor toma libertades poéticas en su poema e inventa palabras que sirven para expresar sus ideas. Con un compañero / una compañera, traten de definir las siguientes palabras inventadas por Pérez Firmat. Comparen sus definiciones con las de otra persona en la clase.

- descubanizada
- recubanizar

B. Interpretación. ¿Cuál cree Ud. que es el punto de vista del narrador del poema? ¿Tiene una actitud positiva hacia la vida en el extranjero? ¿Qué mensaje intenta expresar? ¿Qué elementos de la poesía comunican este mensaje?

ESCRITURA

El tema de la inmigración es uno que provoca mucha reacción en este país. A continuación hay dos puntos de vista contrarios. Escoja una de estas posturas y escriba un breve informe en el que presenta y apoya su opinión.

- El bilingüismo y el biculturalismo enriquecen la vida de este país.
- Los inmigrantes a este país deben asimilarse por completo a la lengua, la vida y la cultura.

En el extranjero

Sin un buen libro de guía o un mapa, es muy fácil perderse en una ciudad que no se conoce.

¿Qué opina Ud.?

Conteste según su propia vida. ¿Cree Ud. que una persona de otro país contestaría del mismo modo? Visite el sitio Web de *Puntos de partida* para averiguar cómo contesta una persona de España.

1. ¿Ha viajado Ud. al **extranjero**? ¿A qué países?
2. ¿Le gustaría seguir viajando? ¿A qué país iría primero?
3. ¿Le gustaría pasar un año en el extranjero? ¿Por qué sí o por qué no?
4. Si pudiera, ¿le gustaría vivir para siempre en el extranjero? ¿Por qué sí o por qué no?
5. ¿En qué país le gustaría vivir? ¿Por qué? ¿Hay algún país en el que nunca podría vivir? ¿Por qué no?

En este capítulo...

- In this chapter, you will study vocabulary related to travel abroad. Many of the words you will study are terms for items you might need to purchase if you were a tourist. Can you guess what you would be buying if you asked for **champú** or **pasta dental**?
- In this chapter, you will learn how to talk about what you and others would do in hypothetical situations. You might wonder, for example, **¿Qué diría mi profesor?** if you were to skip a week of class. (Grammar 50)
- Many hypothetical situations in English are signaled by the word *if*. In this chapter, you will learn to use the word **si**, the Spanish equivalent. Soon you will be able to say: **Si yo fuera rico/a, me quedaría en los mejores hoteles de Buenos Aires.** (Grammar 51)
- This chapter's **Panorama cultural** section will focus on Spain.

PUNTOS INTERACTIVO

Videoteca

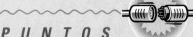

◀ **Minidramas**
En este capítulo, Lupe y Diego van a una agencia de viajes porque quieren hacer un viaje. ¿Cómo hace Ud. sus planes de viaje? ¿con un agente de viajes? ¿en el Web?

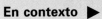

En contexto ▶
Mariela va a la oficina de correos (*post office*) para mandar un paquete. ¿Usa Ud. el servicio postal con frecuencia? ¿Cree Ud. que la nueva tecnología ha disminuido por completo la necesidad del correo tradicional?

CD-ROM
Además de completar el vocabulario y las actividades de gramática, Ud. va a tener la oportunidad de «hablar» con un empleado de correos.

Internet
En la sección del Capítulo 18 en el sitio Web de *Puntos de partida* aparecen enlaces que Ud. puede usar para conseguir información en español sobre el turismo español. Use la dirección www.mhhe.com/puntos.

Vocabulario: Preparación

Lugares y cosas en el extranjero° en… *abroad*

- la oficina de correos
- el café
- el estanco
- la farmacia
- la pastelería
- la papelería
- la estación del metro
- el quiosco
- el sello
- el fósforo
- la tarjeta postal
- la parada del autobús

Más cosas

el champú	shampoo	**la revista**	magazine
el jabon	soap	**el sobre**	envelope
la pasta dental	toothpaste	**el batido**	*drink similar to a milkshake*
el correo	mail		
el papel para cartas	stationery	**una copa / un trago**	(*alcoholic*) drink
el paquete	package	**el pastelito**	small pastry

Nota cultural

De compras en el extranjero

Aunque los nombres de muchos lugares y tiendas del mundo hispánico se parecen a los de este país, no siempre son iguales los productos que en ellos se venden. Tomen en cuenta sobre todo las siguientes diferencias.

- En **las farmacias** no venden la variedad de cosas — dulces, tarjetas postales, etcétera— que se venden en las farmacias de los EE.UU.* y el Canadá. Por lo general, sólo se venden medicinas y productos para **la higiene personal** como jabón, pasta dental, champú…
- En **los estancos**, además de productos tabacaleros, se venden **sellos**, así que[a] uno no tiene que ir a una oficina de correos para comprarlos. También se venden **sobres** y **tarjetas postales** en los estancos.
- En **los quioscos** se vende una **gran variedad** de cosas: periódicos, revistas, libros, etcétera, pero también lápices, papel para cartas…

[a]así… *so*

Madrid, España

Conversación

▲▲▲▲▲▲▲▲

A. En el extranjero. Conteste con oraciones completas.

1. ¿Dónde se compra el champú? ¿el jabón?
2. ¿Cuál es la diferencia entre una farmacia de este país y una farmacia en el extranjero?
3. ¿Dónde se puede comprar sellos? (dos lugares)
4. Si se necesitan cigarrillos o fósforos, ¿adónde se va?
5. ¿Qué es un quiosco? ¿Qué cosas se venden allí?
6. ¿Qué venden en una papelería?

B. ¿Cierto o falso? Corrija las oraciones falsas.

1. Se puede comprar batidos y pastelitos en una pastelería.
2. Si yo quisiera tomar una copa, iría (*I would go*) a un quiosco.
3. Se va a un quiosco para mandar paquetes.
4. Es más rápido ir a pie que tomar el metro.
5. Se va a un café a comprar champú.
6. Si yo necesitara pasta dental, iría a la oficina de correos.
7. Se puede comprar fósforos en un estanco.
8. Un batido se hace con vino.

*****EE.UU.** is one way to abbreviate **Estados Unidos**. **E.U.** and **USA** are also used.

En un viaje al extranjero

CRUZAR LA FRONTERA

el viajero
DECLARAR LAS COMPRAS

la inspectora (de aduanas)
REGISTRAR LAS MALETAS

PAGAR LOS DERECHOS / UNA MULTA

viajar al/en el extranjero	to travel abroad
la aduana	customs
los derechos de aduana	customs duty
la multa	fine, penalty
la nacionalidad	nationality
el pasaporte	passport

El alojamiento° — El... *Lodging*

alojarse/quedarse	to stay (*in a place*)
hacer (*irreg.*)/confirmar las reservas/ reservaciones*	to make / to confirm reservations
la criada	maid

la habitación individual/doble con/sin baño/ducha	room (*in a hotel*) single/double with/without bath/shower
el hotel (de lujo)	(luxury) hotel
el/la huésped(a)	(*hotel*) guest
el mozo/botones	bellhop
la pensión pensión completa media pensión	boardinghouse room and full board room with breakfast and one other meal
la propina	tip (*to an employee*)
la recepción	front desk
completo/a	full, no vacancy
con anticipación	ahead of time
desocupado/a	vacant, unoccupied

Conversación

▲▲▲▲▲▲▲▲

A. En la aduana. ¿Ha viajado Ud. al extranjero? ¿Sabe Ud. cómo portarse al pasar por la aduana? Aunque no lo haya hecho, va a poder contestar las preguntas de esta actividad, pues se trata de (*it's a question of*) utilizar el sentido común.

De las siguientes acciones, ¿cuáles pueden causar problemas en la aduana?

1. ser cortés con el inspector
2. escribir información falsa en el formulario de inmigración
3. no tener el pasaporte (o el visado necesario)
4. declarar todas sus compras
5. llevar gafas oscuras y parecer que está nervioso/a
6. esconder (*hiding*) artículos de contrabando en su equipaje, con la esperanza (*hope*) que el inspector no los encuentre
7. pagar los derechos (o la multa) sin quejarse

---

*La reserva is used in Spain for a reservation (for accommodations). La reservación is widely used in other parts of the Spanish-speaking world.

8. intentar cruzar la frontera con un pasaporte falsificado
9. traficar en drogas
10. tratar de distraer al inspector mientras este (*he*) registra sus maletas

B. ¿Quiénes son? Empareje las personas con la descripción apropiada.

1. el huésped B
2. el recepcionista f
3. el botones A
4. la turista c
5. la inspectora de aduanas e
6. el viajero D

a. la persona que nos ayuda con el equipaje en un hotel
b. la persona que se aloja en un hotel o una pensión
c. una persona que va de un lugar a otro
d. alguien que viaja para ver otros lugares
e. la persona que nos registra las maletas y toma la declaración en la aduana
f. la persona que nos atiende en la recepción de un hotel

C. Cuando Ud. viaja...

Paso 1. A continuación hay una lista de acciones que son típicas de los viajeros. ¿Hace Ud. lo mismo cuando viaja? Indique las acciones que son verdaderas para Ud.

1. ☒ Hago una reserva en un hotel (motel) o en una pensión con un mes de anticipación.
2. ☒ Confirmo la reserva antes de salir de viaje.
3. ☒ Voy al banco a conseguir cheques de viajero.
4. ☒ Alquilo un coche.
5. ☐ Me alojo en un hotel de lujo.
6. ☐ Pido que el mozo me suba las maletas.
7. ☐ Llamo al servicio de cuartos en vez de comer en el restaurante.
8. ☒ Le dejo una propina a la criada el último día de mi estancia (*stay*) en la habitación.

Paso 2. Ahora piense en su último viaje. ¿Hizo Ud. las cosas de la lista del **Paso 1**? Conteste según el modelo y cambie los detalles de esas oraciones por los que en realidad ocurrieron en su viaje.

MODELO: La última vez que hice un viaje... →
Hice una reserva en un hotel de lujo, pero con sólo dos días de anticipación.

D. Situaciones. Con un compañero / una compañera, hagan los papeles de un viajero / una viajera y del / de la recepcionista de un hotel.

Paso 1. El/La recepcionista le pregunta al viajero / a la viajera, que acaba de llegar:

- si tiene una reserva
- cuánto tiempo piensa quedarse
- el tipo de habitación reservada (o deseada)
- la forma de pago

Paso 2. El huésped / La huéspeda pide los siguientes servicios:

- el desayuno en su cuarto
- más toallas (*towels*) / jabón
- información sobre lugares turísticos de interés

Paso 3. Por fin, el huésped / la huéspeda pasa por la recepción para pagar la cuenta. Encuentra los siguientes errores en su cuenta.

- Le cobraron (*they charged*) por un desayuno que no tomó.
- Le cobraron por cuatro noches en vez de tres.
- Le cobraron por una llamada a larga distancia que nunca hizo.

Minidiálogos y gramática

50 Expressing What You Would Do •
Conditional Verb Forms

La fantasía de la maestra de Mafalda

«¡Ya no aguanto este puesto! Creo que me *gustaría* ser abogada… *Pasaría* todo el día con tipos interesantes… *Ganaría* mucho dinero… *Viajaría* mucho, pues *tendría* clientes en todas partes del país… Me *llamarían* actores, actrices, políticos, hombres y mujeres de negocios para consultar conmigo… También *haría* viajes internacionales para investigar casos en el extranjero… Todo el mundo me *respetaría* y me *escucharía*… »

Y Ud., siendo la maestra / el maestro de Mafalda, ¿cómo sería? Use **no** cuando sea necesario.

The fantasy of Mafalda's teacher   I can't bear this job anymore! I think I would like to be a lawyer . . . I would spend all day with interesting people . . . I would earn a lot of money . . . I would travel a lot, since I would have clients all over the country . . . Actors, actresses, politicians, businesspeople would call me to consult with me . . . I would also travel internationally to investigate cases abroad . . . Everyone would respect me and listen to me . . .

- estar contento/a → *Estaría* contento/a.
- ser un tipo / una tipa coherente
- desorientar a los estudiantes
- mirarlos con ojos furiosos
- hacerlos morir de miedo (¡OJO! **har-**)
- ponerles cara de poco sueldo (¡OJO! **pondr-**)
- hacer a los estudiantes llorar de lástima

You have been using the phrase **me gustaría...** for some time to express what you *would like* (to do, say, and so on). **Gustaría** is a conditional verb form, part of a system that will allow you to talk about what you and others would do (say, buy, and so on) in a given situation.

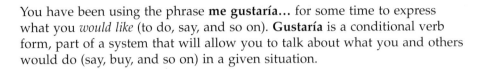

hablar		comer		vivir	
hablaría	hablaríamos	comería	comeríamos	viviría	viviríamos
hablarías	hablaríais	comerías	comeríais	vivirías	viviríais
hablaría	hablarían	comería	comerían	viviría	vivirían

A. Like the English future, the English conditional is formed with an auxiliary verb: *I would speak, I would write.* The Spanish *conditional* (**el condicional**), like the Spanish future, is a simple verb form (only one word). It is formed by adding conditional endings to the infinitive. No auxiliary verbs are needed.

CONDITIONAL ENDINGS

-ía, -ías, -ía, -íamos, íais, -ían

B. Verbs that form the future on an irregular stem use the same stem to form the conditional.

The conditional of **hay (haber)** is **habría** (*there would be*).*

decir: diría, dirías, diría, diríamos, diríais, dirían

decir:	**dir-**	
hacer:	**har-**	-ía
poder:	**podr-**	-ías
poner:	**pondr-**	-ía
querer:	**querr-**	-íamos
saber:	**sabr-**	-íais
salir:	**saldr-**	-ían
tener:	**tendr-**	
venir:	**vendr-**	

---

*The conditional forms of the verb **haber** are used to form the *conditional perfect tense* (**el condicional perfecto**), which expresses what *would have* occurred at some point in the past.

  Habríamos tenido que buscarla   *We would have had to pick her up*
    en el aeropuerto.   *at the airport.*

You will find a more detailed presentation of these forms in Appendix 3, Additional Perfect Forms (Indicative and Subjunctive).

C. The conditional expresses what you would do in a particular situation, given a particular set of circumstances.

—¿**Hablarías** español en el Brasil?
Would you speak Spanish in Brazil?

—No. **Hablaría** portugués.
No. I would speak Portuguese.

O J O: When *would* implies *used to* in English, Spanish uses the imperfect.

Íbamos a la playa todos los veranos.
We would go (used to go) to the beach every summer.

Práctica

A. ¿Qué haría Ud.?

Paso 1. Imagine que hace un viaje a España. Complete las siguientes oraciones de manera que corresponda a la realidad y a lo que a Ud. le gustaría hacer. ¡Es una gran oportunidad de demostrarles a sus compañeros y a su profesor(a) su conocimiento (*knowledge*) sobre la vida y la cultura españolas!

1. Hablaría *español*.
2. Comería ____ y bebería ____.
3. Iría a ____ y allí vería ____.
4. No podría irme sin antes visitar ____.
5. Me compraría ____.
6. Me divertiría mucho ____ (¡**OJO**! Se necesita un gerundio: **-iendo** o **-ando**).

Paso 2. Claro que durante un viaje no sólo se hacen actividades culturales. Las oraciones a continuación muestran actividades típicas durante un viaje, pero Ud. debe completarlas con algunos detalles.

1. Yo haría el viaje a España con ____.
2. Tendría que sacar muchas fotos para mostrárselas a ____.
3. Le(s) mandaría tarjetas postales a ____.
4. Querría ____ durante el viaje, pero probablemente no lo haría.
5. Conocería a ____.

Paso 3. Ahora con un compañero / una compañera, hagan una lista similar a las del Paso 1 y el Paso 2, pero sobre otro país hispánico.

B. ¿Es posible escapar?

Cuente Ud. la fantasía de esta trabajadora social, dando la forma condicional de los verbos.

Necesito salir de todo esto... Creo que me (gustar[1]) ir a Puerto Rico o a algún otro lugar exótico del Caribe... No (trabajar[2])... (Poder[3]) nadar todos los días... (Tomar[4]) el sol en la playa... (Comer[5]) platos exóticos... (Ver[6]) bellos lugares naturales... El viaje (ser[7]) ideal...

Pero… , tarde o temprano, (tener[8]) que volver a lo de siempre… a los rascacielos de la ciudad… al tráfico… al medio ambiente contaminado… al mundo del trabajo… (Poder[9]) usar mi tarjeta de crédito, como dice el anuncio —pero ¡(tener[10]) que pagar después!

Comprensión: ¿Cierto, falso o no lo dice? Corrija las oraciones falsas.

1. Esta persona trabaja en una ciudad grande.
2. No le interesan los deportes acuáticos.
3. Puede pagar este viaje de sueños (*dreams*) al contado.
4. Tiene un novio con quien quisiera hacer el viaje.

C. ¿Qué harías si pudieras?

Paso 1. Con un compañero / una compañera, háganse preguntas y contéstenlas según el modelo. Pueden cambiar los detalles, si quieren.

MODELO: estudiar árabe/japonés →
E1: ¿Estudiarías árabe?
E2: No. Estudiaría japonés.

1. estudiar italiano / chino
2. renunciar un puesto sin avisar / con dos semanas de anticipación
3. hacer un viaje a España / la Argentina
4. salir de casa sin apagar el estéreo / las luces
5. seguir un presupuesto rígido / flexible
6. gastar menos en ropa / libros
7. poner el aire acondicionado en invierno / verano
8. alquilar un coche de lujo / económico

Paso 2. Ahora sigan con el mismo modelo, pero inventen las respuestas.

1. dejar de estudiar /¿ ?
2. vivir en otra ciudad /¿ ?
3. ser presidente/a de los Estados Unidos / primer ministro (primera ministra) del Canadá /¿ ?
4. gustarle conocer a una persona famosa /¿ ?

Conversación

▲▲▲▲▲▲▲

Entrevista. ¿Cómo será su futuro? ¿Qué hará? ¿Qué haría? Con otro/a estudiante, háganse las siguientes preguntas y contéstenlas.

MODELO: E1: ¿Dejarás de fumar algún día? →
E2: No. No dejaré de fumar nunca. No puedo.
(Creo que sí. Dejaré de fumar algún día.)

PREGUNTAS CON EL FUTURO

1. ¿Te graduarás en esta universidad (o en otra)?
2. ¿Vivirás en esta ciudad después de graduarte?
3. ¿Buscarás un puesto aquí?
4. ¿Te casarás (¿Te divorciarás) después de graduarte?
5. ¿Cuántos niños (nietos) crees que tendrás algún día?
6. ¿Serás famoso/a algún día?

1. ¿Te casarías con una persona de otro país?
2. ¿Podrías estar contento/a sin la televisión?
3. ¿Serías capaz de (*capable of*) ahorrar el 10 por ciento de tu salario?
4. ¿Te gustaría ayudar a colonizar otro planeta?
5. ¿Podrías vivir sin las tarjetas de crédito?
6. ¿Renunciarías tu trabajo para viajar por el mundo?

En los Estados Unidos y el Canadá...

Manjares[a] hispano-canadienses

Los que han viajado por la Península Ibérica ya conocen **los sabores[b] de los platos españoles y portugueses**. En la capital canadiense, Ottawa, tanto los turistas como los nativos disfrutan de[c] estos mismos platos en dos restaurantes que sirven **auténticas recetas de los países ibéricos**. **El Mesón**, que se encuentra en una casa al estilo victoriano, provee una cocina para satisfacer al cliente más exigente.[d] Desde 1987 José Alves ofrece un **menú de platos típicos regionales** de España y de Portugal que incluye calamares al ajillo, mejillones marineros, vieia a la gallega[e] y tres variedades de paella, el sabroso[f] plato a base de arroz y azafrán. También se ofrece un menú especial para vegetarianos. Para complementar sus platos, El Mesón tiene una impresionante lista de vinos españoles y una selección de los famosos «vinhos verdes»[*] de Portugal.

Lejos de la vecindad de El Mesón y más cerca del centro de la capital, Ud. puede encontrar un ambiente acogedor[g] y relajado en donde hablar y tomar una copa

Una paella tipo español

de vino tinto mientras Alfonso Pérez, del restaurante **Don Alfonso**, le prepara uno de sus famosos platos. Nativo de Galicia, el Sr. Pérez vivió en Venezuela antes de emigrar al Canadá adonde vino primero con el propósito de aprender inglés. Hace más de veinticinco años que los ciudadanos de Ottawa y sus muchos turistas del extranjero disfrutan de los mariscos y los sabrosos platos a la plancha[h] preparados por don Alfonso. Entre muchos, se ofrecen escalopines[i] Tío Pepe, una zarzuela de mariscos y gazpacho andaluz.[j]

A pesar de la autenticidad de sus platos, las horas de comer en El Mesón y en Don Alfonso son típicamente norteamericanas. Se puede almorzar entre las once y media y las dos y media, y la cena se sirve a partir de las cinco. Bienvenidos y que aproveche.[k]

[a]*Delicacies* [b]*flavors* [c]*disfrutan… enjoy* [d]*demanding* [e]*calamares… squid in garlic sauce, mussels cooked sailor-style, scallops Galician-style* [f]*tasty* [g]*welcoming* [h]*a… grilled* [i]*breaded cutlet* [j]*zarzuela… seafood stew, and a cold vegetable soup from Andalucía* [k]*Bienvenidos… Welcome and enjoy your meal.*

[*]**Vinho verde** (*Young wine*) is produced in the Minho region of northwest Portugal. Slightly sparkling, it can be either red or white.

Los deseos de los amigos hispánicos

JOSÉ MIGUEL: Si *tuviera* el dinero, me *compraría* una computadora.

DIEGO: Si *pudiera, me quedaría* otro año estudiando en el D.F.

LOLA Y MANOLO: Si la universidad nos *diera* un aumento de sueldo, *viajaríamos* por Italia.

¿Y Ud.? Exprese algunos de sus deseos, completando las siguientes oraciones.

1. Si yo tuviera dinero suficiente, iría a _____.
2. Si pudiera conocer a alguna persona famosa, me gustaría conocer a _____.
3. Si consiguiera una beca (*scholarship*), estudiaría en _____.
4. Si ganara la lotería, me compraría _____.
5. Si visitara Latinoamérica, me quedaría en _____.

A. Both English and Spanish use clauses with *if* (**si**) to speculate or hypothesize about situations that are possible. In Spanish, when the **si** clause is in the present tense, the indicative (present or future) is used.

Si **tiene** tiempo, **va/irá** a las montañas.
If he has time, he goes/will go to the mountains.

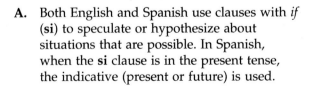

The wishes of our Hispanic friends JOSÉ MIGUEL: If I had the money, I would buy myself a computer. DIEGO: If I could, I would stay in Mexico City studying for another year. LOLA AND MANOLO: If the university gave us a raise, we would travel throughout Italy.

B. To express a contrary-to-fact situation, the **si** in the first clause is followed by the past subjunctive. The conditional is used in the other clause.

Si **tuviera** tiempo, **iría** a las montañas.
If he had time, he would go to the mountains.*

Si yo **fuera** tú, no **haría** eso.
If I were you, I wouldn't do that.*

Si **estudiara** más, **podría** hacerse médica.
If she studied more, she could become a doctor.*

C. When the verb in the **si** clause is in the past tense and the event is not contrary to fact, the indicative is used in both clauses. This is especially true when habitual actions or situations are expressed.

Si **tenía** tiempo, **iba** a las montañas.
If (When) he had time, he would go (used to go) to the mountains.

Práctica

▲▲▲▲▲▲

A. ¿Qué haría Ud.? Complete las oraciones lógicamente.

1. Si yo quisiera comprar comida, iría a _____.
2. Si necesitara comprar un libro, iría a _____.
3. Si necesitara usar un libro, iría a _____.
4. Si tuviera sed en este momento, tomaría _____.
5. Si tuviera que emigrar, iría a _____.
6. Si quisiera ir a _____, viajaría en avión.
7. Si no funcionara(n) _____, compraría un coche nuevo.
8. Si me gustara(n) _____, iría a ver un concierto de Pearl Jam.

B. Si viajara a otro país... ¿Qué haría Ud. si viajara a la Argentina? Forme oraciones según el modelo.

MODELO: si / viajar / otro / país, / ir / la Argentina →
Si viajara a otro país, iría a la Argentina.

1. si / ir / la Argentina, / quedarme / en / Buenos Aires
2. si / tener / interés / en / población / italiano, / visitar / barrio italiano La Boca
3. si / querer / mandar / tarjeta postal, / comprarla / en / quiosco
4. si / tener ganas / de / comprar / libros, / pedir / direcciones / barrio San Telmo
5. si / querer / ver / obra de teatro, / ir / Teatro Colón
6. si / interesarme / visitar / sitios / turístico, / ver / obelisco / y / réplica / de / Big Ben

---

*The contrary-to-fact situations in these sentences express speculations about the present. The perfect forms of the conditional and the past subjunctive are used to speculate about the past: what *would have* happened if a particular event *had* or *had not* occurred.

Si **hubiera tenido** el dinero, **habría hecho** el viaje.
If I had had the money, I would have made the trip.

You will find a more detailed presentation of this structure in Appendix 3, Additional Perfect Forms (Indicative and Subjunctive).

7. si / querer / probar (*to try*) / comida / auténtico, / comer / carne / argentino

8. si / querer / escuchar / música / típico, / escuchar / tango

C. Situaciones

Paso 1. Empareje cada oración con su dibujo.

1.

2.

3.

4.

5.

a. __5__ Los Martínez quieren usar su coche.
b. __1__ A Mariana le encanta ese vestido.
c. __4__ Simón quiere encender (*to turn on*) la luz.
d. _____ Julia no tiene ganas de levantarse.   *feel like*
e. __2__ La Sra. Blanco tiene miedo de viajar en avión.

Paso 2. Ahora haga una oración con **si** para cada situación. Use su imaginación para añadir detalles.

MODELO: Mariana se compraría ese vestido si...

Conversación
▲▲▲▲▲▲▲

A. El horario de todos los días. ¿Tiene Ud. un horario bastante fijo y rutinario? A ver si puede contestar las siguientes preguntas.

¿Dónde estaría Ud. ... ?

1. si fuera miércoles a las tres de la tarde
2. si fuera jueves a las diez de la mañana
3. si fuera viernes a las nueve de la noche
4. si fuera domingo a las nueve de la mañana
5. si fuera lunes a la una de la tarde

B. Entrevista: ¿Bajo (*Under*) qué circunstancias... ? Entreviste a otro/a estudiante según el modelo.

MODELO: comprar un coche nuevo →
   E1: ¿En qué circunstancias comprarías un coche nuevo?
   E2: Compraría un coche nuevo si tuviera más dinero.

1. dejar de estudiar en esta universidad
2. emigrar a otro país
3. estudiar otro idioma
4. no obedecer a sus padres / a su jefe/a
5. votar por _____ para presidente/a / primer ministro (primera ministra)
6. ser candidato/a para presidente/a / primer ministro (primera ministra)
7. casarse / divorciarse
8. no decirle la verdad a un amigo / una amiga

Minidramas

In this **Minidramas** dialogue, Diego and Lupe are planning a trip. Pay close attention to the details of their trip. Where are they going? How will they get there? Where will they stay?

Diego y Lupe están en una agencia de viajes. Quieren hacer un viaje a Mérida.

AGENTE: ¿Ya tienen alojamiento en Mérida?

LUPE: No, todavía no. Buscamos un hotel que sea decente, pero que tampoco sea muy caro. No tenemos el dinero para pagar un hotel de lujo.

AGENTE: Entiendo. Muy pocos estudiantes tienen mucho dinero. Bueno, les puedo ofrecer habitaciones en varios hoteles a precios muy razonables. A ver... ¿Cuándo piensan hacer el viaje?

DIEGO: La última semana de mayo.

F U N C T I O N

booking a hotel room

AGENTE: Ajá... Eso va a estar un poco difícil. Casi todos los hoteles estarán completamente ocupados durante esa semana. Si viajaran una semana más tarde, encontrarían más habitaciones desocupadas.

LUPE: Bueno, está bien. Entonces, la primera semana de junio.

AGENTE: Excelente. Les puedo ofrecer dos habitaciones individuales con baño privado en el hotel Estrella del Mar. No es un hotel de lujo, pero es bueno y muy lindo. El precio por cada habitación es de 150 pesos por noche.

LUPE: Perfecto.

AGENTE: Y, ¿cuántos días piensan quedarse?

DIEGO: Unos cuatro o cinco días, nada más. Yo soy de California, y debo regresar pronto.

AGENTE: Muy bien. Tienen habitaciones reservadas para la primera semana de junio. ¿Sus nombres, por favor?

DIEGO: Sí, cómo no. Yo me llamo Diego González y la señorita es Guadalupe Carrasco.

AGENTE: Muy bien.

DIEGO: Gracias.

Con un compañero / una compañera

Hagan los papeles de un(a) recepcionista de un hotel y de un huésped / una huéspeda. El huésped / La huéspeda acaba de llegar a la ciudad y todavía no tiene reservada una habitación. También quiere visitar algunos lugares de interés turístico durante su estancia. A continuación se dan algunas preguntas sugeridas para el diálogo.

Vocabulario útil: Si yo fuera Ud., ... (*If I were you, . . .*); Yo en su lugar, ... (*If I were in your position, . . .*)

1. ¿Qué tipo de habitación se necesita?
2. ¿Cuánto cuesta por noche?
3. ¿Por cuántos días piensa quedarse?
4. ¿Qué lujos tiene el hotel?
5. ¿Cómo quiere pagar?
6. ¿Qué lugares debo visitar?

En contexto

A. Lluvia de ideas

- ¿Para qué tipo de cartas o paquetes usa Ud. el correo? ¿Con cuánta frecuencia?
- ¿Cuánto cuesta actualmente en este país mandar una carta por correo doméstico? ¿y una tarjeta postal al extranjero?

COSTA RICA

B. Dictado

A continuación aparece un fragmento del diálogo entre Mariela y el empleado de la oficina de correos. Complete el diálogo con las palabras o frases que faltan.

MARIELA: Buenos días, _____. Necesito estampillas para _____ _____.

DEPENDIENTE: ¿Son _____ para correo _____ o correo _____?

MARIELA: Esta _____ es para correo _____. Esta tarjeta va al _____ y esta a los _____ _____.

DEPENDIENTE: Las estampillas para correo doméstico cuestan _____ colones... Para correo internacional, _____ colones. Muy bien. ¿Hay _____ _____?

MARIELA: Sí, _____ _____ este paquete a Francia. ¿_____ _____?

DEPENDIENTE: Eso depende de cómo _____ mandarlo, señorita. Por correo aéreo cuesta _____ colones, pero llega en dos _____. Si _____ mandarlo por _____, sólo le cuesta solamente _____ colones.

C. Un diálogo original

Opción 1. Con un compañero / una compañera, dramaticen el diálogo entre Mariela y el empleado de la oficina de correos.

Opción 2. ¿Vale la pena? (*Is it worthwhile?*) Dos amigos han comprado un regalo de cumpleaños para otro amigo que vive en otro estado. El problema es que el libro que mandan es grande y pesado (*heavy*), y el correo resulta más caro que el libro mismo. Por otro lado, el cumpleaños es pasado mañana (*the day after tomorrow*) y tendrían que mandar el regalo por correo urgente para que llegara a tiempo.

Con un compañero / una compañera, representen el papel de los amigos y solucionen el problema de cómo mandar el regalo.

Un poco más sobre... Diego González

Aunque hace menos de un año que está en el D. F., Diego se siente muy a gusto[a] en el país de sus abuelos. Ahora le gustaría viajar un poco más por el resto de México. Por ejemplo, le gustaría visitar la ciudad universitaria de Guanajuato, en el centro del país, y también quiere ver los grandes centros arqueológicos mayas en la Península de Yucatán.

[a]a... *at home*

To read more about the characters from this video, visit the *Puntos de partida* Website at **www.mhhe.com/puntos**

A. ¡Entendiste mal! Con un compañero / una compañera, háganse preguntas y contéstenlas según el modelo.

MODELO: llegar el trece de junio / tres →
E1: Llegaré el trece de junio.
E2: ¿No dijiste que llegarías el tres?
E1: ¡Que no! Te dije que llegaría el trece. Entendiste mal.

1. estar en el café a las dos / doce
2. estudiar con Juan / Juana
3. ir de vacaciones en julio / junio
4. verte en casa / en clase
5. comprar la blusa rosada / roja

B. Si el mundo fuera diferente... Adaptarse a un nuevo país o a nuevas circunstancias es difícil, pero también es una aventura interesante. ¿Qué ocurriría si el mundo fuera diferente?

MODELO: Si yo fuera la última persona en el mundo... →
• tendría que aprender a hacer muchas cosas.
• sería la persona más importante —y más ignorante— del mundo.
• me adaptaría fácilmente/difícilmente.
• los animales y yo nos haríamos buenos amigos.

1. Si yo pudiera tener solamente un amigo / una amiga, _____.
2. Si yo tuviera que pasar un año en una isla desierta, _____.
3. Si yo fuera (otro persona), _____.
4. Si el presidente fuera presidenta, _____.
5. Si yo viviera en Puerto Rico, _____.

C. En busca de alojamiento. Complete the following dialogue with the correct form of the words in parentheses, as suggested by the context. When two possibilities are given in parentheses, select the correct word.

ALFONSO: Yo no (saber/conocer[1]) cómo vamos a encontrar alojamiento. No tenemos (mucho/muy[2]) dinero, y ya (ser/estar[3]) un poco tarde.

ELENA: Y (el/la[4]) equipaje pesa[a] mucho. No podemos (ir[5]) muy lejos.

ALFONSO: (Mirar: *Tú*[6]), en esa oficina parece que dan información sobre alojamientos. Vamos.

EMPLEADO: ¿Qué (desear: *Uds.*[7])?

ALFONSO: Pues quisiéramos una habitación (por/para[8]) los dos. Sólo (por/para[9]) esta noche, pues solamente estamos (hacer[10]) escala aquí y mañana (*nosotros:* seguir[11]) con nuestro viaje.

[a]*weighs*

ELENA: (Por/Para[12]) favor, no queremos que (ser/estar[13]) muy cara. Hemos (cambiar[14]) muy poca moneda. Tampoco queremos que (ser/estar[15]) muy lejos.

EMPLEADO: Bien, (esperar: *Uds.*[16]) un momento. Voy a llamar a una pensión (mucho/muy[17]) agradable que no (ser/estar[18]) muy lejos de la estación.

Pocos minutos después...

EMPLEADO: Sí, me dicen que (haber[19]) una habitación doble disponible[b] todavía.

ALFONSO: ¡Qué bien! ¿Pagamos ahora?

EMPLEADO: No (ser/estar[20]) necesario. Aquí tienen los datos. (Este/Esta[21]) papel sirve como reserva. También (los/les[22]) he anotado el precio. Pero no tarden mucho en (llegar[23]).

ELENA: Muy bien. ¿Podría Ud. indicarnos cómo llegar allí?

EMPLEADO: (Mirar: *Uds.*[24]). Estamos aquí y la pensión (ser/estar[25]) en esta plaza. Se lo marco en (el/la[26]) mapa. Caminando, puede tomarles unos quince o veinte minutos. Si (tomar[27]) el metro, sólo son dos estaciones.

ELENA: ¡Ah! ¿Sabe si (ser/estar[28]) incluido el desayuno en el precio?

EMPLEADO: Sí, lo que Uds. (llamar[29]) desayuno continental.

ALFONSO: Y otra cosa. ¿(Ser/Estar[30]) posible dejar parte de nuestro equipaje en la estación? Mañana tenemos (de/que[31]) volver a la estación.

EMPLEADO: Sí. Cuando salgan de la oficina, a mano derecha (*Uds.:* ver[32]) la consigna.[c] Pueden dejar(lo/la[33]) allí.

ALFONSO: Adiós y gracias (por/para[34]) todo.

---

[b]*available* [c]*baggage check*

Comprensión: ¿Quién lo dice?

1. Sí, todavía tenemos una habitación para esta noche.
2. ¡Qué suerte hemos tenido! Una habitación barata y cerca de la estación.
3. A ver qué quieren estos dos jóvenes.
4. Sí, señor. El empleado de la estación nos dio este papel como reserva para una habitación.

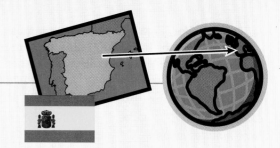

PANORAMA *cultural*

España

Datos esenciales

Nombre oficial: Reino de España
Capital: Madrid
Población: 39.000.000 de habitantes
Moneda: la peseta
Idiomas: el español, el catalán, el gallego y el vasco*

¡Fíjese!

- España es una país donde muchas culturas se han encontrado a través de[a] la historia. Sin embargo fueron los romanos los que marcaron el principio de la historia de la España que hoy conocemos, pues ellos introdujeron el latín a la península durante su dominio (desde el año 200 a.C.[b] hasta la invasión de los visigodos, un pueblo germánico, en el 419 d.C.[c]).

- El latín es la lengua madre del español y también del catalán, el gallego y el portugués. La otra lengua que se habla en la península, el vasco, es una lengua ancestral de origen desconocido: ni siquiera es[d] una lengua indoeuropea.

- España no fue siempre un solo país. De hecho,[e] España se unificó en el siglo XV cuando los Reyes Católicos, Isabel y Fernando, monarcas de dos reinos[f] independientes, se casaron. Su campaña[g] de unificación terminó en 1492 con la conquista del reino musulmán[h] de Granada.

- Los árabes vivieron en España durante ocho siglos, hasta su expulsión, junto con los judíos, en el año 1492.

[a]a... *throughout* [b]a.C.... *antes de Cristo* [c]d.C.... *después de Cristo* [d]ni... *it is not even* [e]De... *In fact* [f]*kingdoms* [g]*campaign* [h]*Moslem*

El escudo (*shield*) de Fernando e Isabel

Conozca a... Pedro Almodóvar

Las películas del cineasta[a] Pedro Almodóvar (1951–) han tenido y siguen teniendo un éxito enorme dentro y fuera de España, y Almodóvar es el director de cine español más conocido de las últimas décadas. Con temas que satirizan actitudes tradicionales respecto a la familia, la religión, el machismo y la moralidad convencional, sus películas presentan una sociedad española moderna y cambiante.[b]

Muchas de sus películas se pueden conseguir en las bibliotecas públicas y universitarias, así como en los videoclubs de este país: *Mujeres al borde de un ataque de nervios*, *La ley del deseo*, *¿Qué he hecho yo para merecer esto?*, *¡Átame!*,[c] *Kika*, *La flor de mi secreto* y *Todo sobre mi madre*, esta última de 1999 y ganadora del Óscar para la mejor película extranjera.

[a]director de cine [b]*changing* [c]*Tie Me Up! Tie Me Down!*

  Capítulo 18 of the video to accompany *Puntos de partida* contains cultural footage of Spain.

  Visit the *Puntos de partida* Website at www.mhhe.com/puntos.

---

*El español es el lenguaje oficial de todo el país; el catalán, el gallego y el vasco también son lenguas oficiales en Cataluña, Galicia y el País Vasco, respectivamente.

Vocabulario

Cosas y lugares en el extranjero

el batido	drink similar to a milkshake
el café	café
el champú	shampoo
una copa / un trago	(alcoholic) drink
el correo	mail
la oficina de correos	post office
la estación del metro	subway stop
el estanco	tobacco stand/shop
los fósforos	matches
el jabón	soap
el papel para cartas	stationery
la papelería	stationery store
el paquete	package
la parada del autobús	bus stop
la pasta dental	toothpaste
la pastelería	pastry shop
el pastelito	small pastry
el quiosco	kiosk
el sello	stamp
el sobre	envelope

Repaso: la farmacia, la revista, la tarjeta postal

Ir al extranjero

cruzar	to cross
declarar	to declare
registrar	to search, examine

Repaso: pagar, viajar

la aduana	customs
el cheque de viajero	traveler's check
los derechos (de aduana)	(customs) duty
el extranjero	abroad

el formulario	form (to fill out)
la frontera	border
la inmigración	immigration
el/la inspector(a) (de aduanas)	(customs) inspector
la multa	fine, penalty
el pasaporte	passport
el/la viajero/a	traveler

Repaso: las compras, la maleta, la nacionalidad

El alojamiento

alojarse	to stay (in a place)
confirmar	to confirm
el botones/mozo	bellhop
la criada	maid
la estancia	stay (in a hotel)
la habitación	room (in a hotel)
individual/doble	single/double
con/sin baño/ducha	with(out) bath/shower
el hotel (de lujo)	(luxury) hotel
el/la huésped(a)	(hotel) guest
la pensión	boardinghouse
pensión completa	room and full board
media pensión	room with breakfast and one other meal
la propina	tip (to an employee)
las reservaciones / las reservas	reservations
recepción	front desk

Repaso: quedarse

completo/a	full, no vacancy
con anticipación	ahead of time
desocupado/a	vacant, unoccupied

Vocabulario

Un paso más 18

LECTURA

Estrategia: Using Language Cues to Understand Poetry (3)

One of the things that distinguishes poetry from prose is its use of repetition. Sometimes this repetition is straightforward: a word appears in the same form more than once in the course of the poem, although it does not necessarily have the same meaning each time it appears. But there are other forms of repetition. Variants of the word or synonyms may appear. Sometimes you will find several words with the same root. Finding these words will help you further understand the poem and its meaning.

In the following poem, you will find repetitions of this sort. Why do you think the poet chose to repeat the same word so often in such a short poem? What kind of repetition can you find? Do you think this usage of language makes the poem stronger or more interesting? Why or why not?

▶ **Sobre el autor:** Antonio Machado (1875–1939) nació en Sevilla, España,
▶ de padres liberales y progresistas. Su padre fue por un tiempo abogado en
▶ Puerto Rico, pero al morir este (*the latter*) Machado volvió a Sevilla a cursar
▶ estudios de Filosofia y Letras. A los 24 años viajó a Paris, donde conoció a
▶ muchos de los grandes autores europeos. En esa capital escribió muchos de
▶ los poemas de su primera colección, *Soledades* (*Solitudes*). A principios del
▶ nuevo siglo, con su hermano Manuel, forma parte de un famoso movimiento
▶ literario que vino a llamarse la «Generación del 98», ya que muchos de sus
▶ miembros habían empezado a publicar sus primeras obras (*works*) en ese
▶ año. La poesía de Machado es seria y dramática y tiene como su tema el am-
▶ biente de la región de Castilla, en España. Machado tuvo que salir de su
▶ amada patria (*beloved homeland*) durante la Guerra Civil española y murió en
▶ Colliure, Francia, después de haber cruzado a pie las montañas que dividen
▶ los dos países. El siguiente poema es de su colección *Proverbios y cantares*.

XXIX

Caminante,[a] son tus huellas[b]
el camino, y nada más;
caminante, no hay camino:
se hace camino al andar.[c]
Al andar se hace el camino,
y al volver la vista atrás[d]
se ve la senda[e] que nunca
se ha de volver a pisar.[f]
Caminante, no hay camino,
sino estelas[g] en la mar.

[a]*Traveler (person who walks)* [b]*footprints; traces* [c]*al... as you walk* [d]*al... when you look back* [e]*path*
[f]*nunca... will never be tread upon again* [g]*wakes (of boats)*

Comprensión

Paso 1.   Conteste las siguientes preguntas.

1. ¿A quién se dirige el poeta?
2. ¿Por qué dice el autor que «no hay camino»?
3. ¿Hay algún momento en que sí hay camino?
4. ¿Qué se ve al mirar atrás? ¿Por qué?

Paso 2.   Interpretación. Con un compañero / una compañera, contesten las siguientes preguntas.

1. ¿Creen Uds. que el caminante del poema es verdaderamente una persona que va de paseo? Si no lo es, ¿qué clase de camino sigue esta persona?
2. En este poema, ¿se trata de un camino por un lugar sin carreteras? Y si no, ¿qué experiencia es la que se describe aquí?
3. En el contexto de este poema, ¿qué son las estelas del mar?

E S C R I T U R A

La «Generación del 98» a la que perteneció Machado (*to which Machado belonged*) fue uno de los movimientos literarios españoles más importantes del último milenio. Use los recursos del Internet y de la biblioteca para investigar este movimiento. Escoja uno de los siguientes temas y escriba un breve informe.

1. Los poetas y novelistas de la «Generación del 98» y sus ideas sobre la literatura
2. Un poeta de este grupo y su obra
3. Un poema o un grupo de poemas (puede describir un poema o comparar las ideas de dos o más poemas)

Appendix 1

Glossary of Grammatical Terms

ADJECTIVE A word that describes a noun or pronoun.

una casa **grande**
a *big* house

Ella es **inteligente.**
She is ***smart.***

Demonstrative adjective An adjective that points out a particular noun.

este chico, **esos** libros, **aquellas** personas
this *boy,* ***those*** *books,* ***those*** *people (over there)*

Interrogative adjective An adjective used to form questions.

¿Qué cuaderno?
Which *notebook?*

¿Cuáles son los carteles que buscas?
What *(****Which****) posters are you looking for?*

Possessive adjective (unstressed) An adjective that indicates possession or a special relationship.

sus coches
their *cars*

mi hermana
my *sister*

Possessive adjective (stressed) An adjective that more emphatically describes possession.

Es **una** amiga **mía.**
She's ***my*** *friend / She's a friend* ***of mine.***

Es **un** coche **suyo.**
It's ***her*** *car / It's a car* ***of hers.***

ADVERB A word that describes an adjective, a verb, or another adverb.

Él es **muy** alto.
He is ***very*** *tall.*

Ella escribe **bien.**
She writes ***well.***

Van **demasiado** rápido.
They are going ***too*** *quickly.*

ARTICLE A determiner that sets off a noun.
Definite article An article that indicates a specific noun.

el país
the country

la silla
the chair

las mujeres
the women

Indefinite article An article that indicates an unspecified noun.

un chico
a boy

una ciudad
a city

unas zanahorias
(some) carrots

CLAUSE   A construction that contains a subject and a verb.

Main (Independent) clause   A clause that can stand on its own because it expresses a complete thought.

Busco una muchacha.
I'm looking for a girl.

Si yo fuera rica, **me compraría una casa.**
*If I were rich, **I would buy a house.***

Subordinate (Dependent) clause   A clause that cannot stand on its own because it does not express a complete thought.

Busco a la muchacha **que juega al tenis.**
*I'm looking for the girl **who plays tennis.***

Si yo fuera rico, me compraría una casa.
***If I were rich,** I would buy a house.*

COMPARATIVE   The form of adjectives and adverbs used to compare two nouns or actions.

Luis es **menos hablador** que Julián.
*Luis is **less talkative** than Julián.*

Él corre **más rápido** que Julián.
*He runs **faster** than Julián.*

CONJUGATION   The different forms of a verb for a particular tense or mood. A present indicative conjugation:

(yo) hablo	(nosotros/as) hablamos
(tú) hablas	(vosotros/as) habláis
(Ud., él/ella) habla	(Uds., ellos/as) hablan

I speak — *we speak*
you (fam. sing.) speak — *you (fam. pl.) speak*
you (form. sing.) speak — *you (pl. fam. & form.) speak*

he/she speaks — *they speak*

CONJUNCTION   An expression that connects words, phrases, or clauses.

Cristóbal **y** Diana
*Cristóbal **and** Diana*

Hace frío, **pero** hace buen tiempo.
*It's cold, **but** it's nice out.*

DIRECT OBJECT   The noun or pronoun that receives the action of a verb.

Veo **la caja.**
*I see **the box.***

La veo.
*I see **it.***

GENDER   A grammatical category of words. In Spanish there are two genders: masculine and feminine. Here are a few examples.

	MASCULINE	FEMININE
ARTICLES AND NOUNS:	**el** disco compacto	**la** cinta
PRONOUNS:	**él**	**ella**
ADJECTIVES:	bonit**o**, list**o**	bonit**a**, list**a**
PAST PARTICIPLES:	El informe está **escrito.**	La composición está **escrita.**

IMPERATIVE   *See* Mood.

IMPERFECT (*IMPERFECTO*)   In Spanish a verb tense that expresses a past action with no specific beginning or ending.

Nadábamos con frecuencia.
*We **used to swim** often.*

548

Appendix 1

IMPERSONAL CONSTRUCTION One that contains a third-person singular verb but no specific subject in Spanish. The subject of English impersonal constructions is generally *it*.

Es importante que...
It is important that . . .

Es necesario que...
It is necessary that . . .

INDICATIVE *See* Mood.

INDIRECT OBJECT The noun or pronoun that indicates for whom or to whom an action is performed. In Spanish, the indirect object pronoun must always be included. The noun that the pronoun stands for may be included for emphasis or clarification.

Marcos **le** da el suéter a **Raquel**. / Marcos **le** da el suéter.
*Marcos gives the sweater **to Raquel**. / Marcos gives **her** the sweater.*

INFINITIVE The form of a verb introduced in English by *to*: *to play, to sell, to come*. In Spanish dictionaries, the infinitive form of the verb appears as the main entry.

Luisa va a **comprar** un periódico.
*Luisa is going **to buy** a newspaper.*

MOOD A set of categories for verbs indicating the attitude of the speaker towards what he or she is saying.

Imperative mood A verb form expressing a command.

¡**Ten** cuidado!
Be careful!

Indicative mood A verb form denoting actions or states considered facts.

Voy a la biblioteca.
I am going to the library.

Subjunctive mood A verb form, uncommon in English, used primarily in subordinate clauses after expressions of desire, doubt, or emotion. Spanish constructions with the subjunctive have many possible English equivalents.

Quiero que **vayas** inmediatamente.
I want you to go immediately.

NOUN A word that denotes a person, place, thing, or idea. Proper nouns are capitalized names.

abogado, ciudad, periódico, libertad, Luisa
lawyer, city, newspaper, freedom, Luisa

NUMBER

Cardinal number A number that expresses an amount.

una silla, **tres** estudiantes
one chair, three students

Ordinal number A number that indicates position in a series.

la **primera** silla, el **tercer** estudiante
*the **first** chair, the **third** student*

PAST PARTICIPLE The form of a verb used in compound tenses (*see* Perfect Tenses). Used with forms of *to have* or *to be* in English and with **ser, estar** or **haber** in Spanish.

comido, terminado, perdido
eaten, finished, lost

PERFECT TENSES Compound tenses that combine the auxiliary verb **haber** with a past participle.

Present perfect indicative This form uses a present indicative form of **haber**. The use of the Spanish present perfect generally parallels that of the English present perfect.

No **he viajado** nunca a México.
*I've never **traveled** to Mexico.*

Past perfect indicative This form uses **haber** in the imperfect tense to talk about something that had or had not been done before a given time in the past.

Antes de 1997, **no había estudiado** español.
*Before 1997, I **hadn't studied** Spanish.*

Present perfect subjunctive This form uses the present subjunctive of **haber** to express a present perfect action when the subjunctive is required.

¡Ojalá que Marisa **haya llegado** a su destino!
*I hope Marisa **has arrived** at her destination!*

PERSON The form of a pronoun or verb that indicates the person involved in an action.

	SINGULAR	PLURAL
FIRST PERSON	*I* / yo	*we* / nosotros/as
SECOND PERSON	*you* / tú, Ud.	*you* / vosotros/as, Uds.
THIRD PERSON	*he, she* / él, ella	*they* / ellos, ellas

PREPOSITION A word or phrase that specifies the relationship of one word (usually a noun or pronoun) to another. The relationship is usually spatial or temporal.

a la escuela
to school

cerca de la biblioteca
near the library

con él
with him

antes de la medianoche
before midnight

PRETERITE (*PRETÉRITO*) In Spanish, a verb tense that expresses a past action with a specific beginning and ending.

Salí para Roma el jueves.
I left for Rome on Thursday.

PRONOUN A word that refers to a person (I, you) or that is used in place of one or more nouns.

Demonstrative pronoun A pronoun that singles out a particular person or thing.

Aquí están dos libros. **Este** es interesante, pero **ese** es aburrido.
*Here are two books. **This one** is interesting, but **that one** is boring.*

Interrogative pronoun A pronoun used to ask a question.

¿Quién es él?
Who is he?

¿Qué prefieres?
What do you prefer?

Object pronoun A pronoun that replaces a direct object noun or an indirect object noun. Both direct and indirect object pronouns can be used together in the same sentence. However, when the pronoun **le** is used with **lo** or **la**, it changes to **se**.

Veo a **Alejandro. Lo** veo.
*I see **Alejandro**. I see **him**.*

Le doy el libro (**a Juana**).
*I give the book **to Juana**.*

Se lo doy (**a ella**).
*I give **it** to **her**.*

Reflexive pronoun A pronoun that represents the same person as the subject of the verb.

Me miro en el espejo.
*I look at **myself** in the mirror.*

Relative pronoun A pronoun that introduces a dependent clause and denotes a noun already mentioned.

El hombre con **quien** hablaba era mi vecino.
*The man with **whom** I was talking was my neighbor.*

Aquí está el bolígrafo **que** buscas.
*Here is the pen (**that**) you are looking for.*

Subject pronoun A pronoun representing the person or thing performing the action of a verb.

Lucas y Julia juegan al tenis.
Lucas and Julia are playing tennis.

Ellos juegan al tenis.
They are playing tennis.

SUBJECT The word(s) denoting the person, place, or thing performing an action or existing in a state.	**Sara** trabaja aquí. *Sara works here.* ¡**Buenos Aires** es una ciudad magnífica! *Buenos Aires is a great city!* Mis **libros** y mi **computadora** están allí. *My books and my computer are over there.*
SUBJUNCTIVE *See* Mood.	
SUPERLATIVE The form of adjectives or adverbs used to compare three or more nouns or actions. In English, the superlative is marked by *most, least,* or *-est.*	Escogí el vestido **más caro.** *I chose **the most expensive** dress.* Ana es la persona **menos habladora** que conozco. *Ana is **the least talkative** person I know.*
TENSE The form of a verb indicating time: present, past, or future.	Raúl **era, es** y siempre **será** mi mejor amigo. *Raúl **was, is,** and always **will be** my best friend.*
VERB A word that reports an action or state.	Ella **llegó.** *She **arrived.*** Ella **estaba** cansada. *She **was** tired.*
Auxiliary verb A verb in conjuction with a participle to convey distinctions of tense and mood. In Spanish, this auxiliary verb is **haber.**	**Han** viajado por todas partes del mundo. *They **have** traveled everywhere in the world.*
Reflexive verb A verb whose subject and object are the same.	Él **se corta** la cara cuando **se afeita.** *He **cuts himself** when he **shaves** (**himself**).*

Appendix 2

Using Adjectives as Nouns

Nominalization means using an adjective as a noun. In Spanish, adjectives can be nominalized in a number of ways, all of which involve dropping the noun that accompanies the adjective, then using the adjective in combination with an article or other word. One kind of adjective, the demonstrative, can simply be used alone. In most cases, these usages parallel those of English, although the English equivalent may be phrased differently from the Spanish.

Article + Adjective

Simply omit the noun from an *article + noun + adjective* phrase.

> el **libro** azul → **el azul** (*the blue one*)
> la **hermana** casada → **la casada** (*the married one*)

el **señor** mexicano → **el mexicano** (*the Mexican one*)
los **pantalones** baratos → **los baratos** (*the inexpensive ones*)

You can also drop the first noun in an *article + noun + **de** + noun* phrase.

> la **casa** de Julio → **la de Julio** (*Julio's*)
> los **coches** del Sr. Martínez → **los del Sr. Martínez** (*Mr. Martínez's*)

In both cases, the construction is used to refer to a noun that has already been mentioned. The English equivalent uses *one* or *ones,* or a possessive without the noun.

—Do you need the big book?
—No. I need the small one.

—¿Usamos el coche de Ernesto?
—No. Usemos **el de Ana.**
—*Shall we use Ernesto's car?*
—*No. Let's use Ana's.*

Note that in the preceding examples the noun is mentioned in the first part of the exchange (**libro, coche**) but not in the response or rejoinder.

Note also that a demonstrative can be used to nominalize an adjective: **este rojo** (*this red one*), **esos azules** (*those blue ones*).

Lo + Adjective

As seen in **Capítulo 10, lo** combines with the masculine singular form of an adjective to describe general qualities or characteristics. The English equivalent is expressed with words like *part* or *thing*.

lo mejor	*the best thing (part), what's best*
lo mismo	*the same thing*
lo cómico	*the funny thing (part), what's funny*

Article + Stressed Possessive Adjective

The stressed possessive adjectives—but not the unstressed possessives—can be used as possessive pronouns: **la maleta suya → la suya.** The article and the possessive form agree in gender and number with the noun to which they refer.

—¿Necesitas el libro grande?
—No. Necesito **el pequeño.**

Este es mi **banco.** ¿Dónde está **el suyo**?
This is my bank. Where is yours?

Sus **bebidas** están preparadas; **las nuestras,** no.
Their drinks are ready; ours aren't.

No es la **maleta** de Juan; es **la mía.**
It isn't Juan's suitcase; it's mine.

Note that the definite article is frequently omitted after forms of **ser: ¿Esa maleta? Es suya.**

Demonstrative Pronouns

The demonstrative adjective can be used alone, without a noun. An accent mark can be added to the demonstrative pronoun to distinguish it from the demonstrative adjectives (**este, ese, aquel**).

Necesito este diccionario y **ese** (**ése**).
I need this dictionary and that one.

Estas señoras y **aquellas** (**aquéllas**) son las hermanas de Sara, ¿no?
These women and those (over there) are Sara's sisters, aren't they?

It is acceptable in modern Spanish, per the **Real Academia Española,** to omit the accent on demonstrative pronouns when context makes the meaning clear and no ambiguity is possible.

Appendix 3

Additional Perfect Forms (Indicative and Subjunctive)

Some indicative verb tenses have corresponding perfect forms in the indicative and subjunctive moods. Here is the present tense system.

el presente:	yo hablo, como, pongo
el presente perfecto:	yo he hablado, comido, puesto
el presente perfecto de subjuntivo:	yo haya hablado, comido, puesto

Other indicative forms that you have learned also have corresponding perfect indicative and subjunctive forms.

Here are the most important ones, along with examples of their use. In each case, the tense or mood is formed with the appropriate form of **haber.**

El pluscuamperfecto del subjuntivo

yo:	hubiera hablado, comido, vivido, *etc.*
tú:	hubieras hablado, comido, vivido, *etc.*
Ud./él/ella:	hubiera hablado, comido, vivido, *etc.*
nosotros:	hubiéramos hablado, comido, vivido, *etc.*

| vosotros: | hubierais hablado, comido, vivido, *etc.* |
| Uds./ellos/ellas: | hubieran hablado, comido, vivido, *etc.* |

These forms correspond to **el presente perfecto de indicativo (Capítulo 14)**. These forms are most frequently used in **si** clause sentences, along with the conditional perfect. See examples below.

El futuro perfecto

yo:	habré hablado, comido, vivido, *etc.*
tú:	habrás hablado, comido, vivido, *etc.*
Ud./él/ella:	habrá hablado, comido, vivido, *etc.*
nosotros:	habremos hablado, comido, vivido, *etc.*
vosotros:	habréis hablado, comido, vivido, *etc.*
Uds./ellos/ellas:	habrán hablado, comido, vivido, *etc.*

These forms correspond to **el futuro (Capítulo 16)** and are most frequently used to tell what *will have already happened* at some point in the future. (In contrast, the future is used to tell what *will happen*.)

Mañana **hablaré** con Miguel.
I'll speak with Miguel tomorrow.

Para las tres, ya **habré hablado** con Miguel.
By 3:00, I'll already have spoken to Miguel.

El año que viene **visitaremos** a los nietos.
We'll visit our grandchildren next year.

Para las Navidades, ya **habremos visitado** a los nietos.
We'll already have visited our grandchildren by Christmas.

El condicional perfecto

yo:	habría hablado, comido, vivido, *etc.*
tú:	habrías hablado, comido, vivido, *etc.*
Ud./él/ella:	habría hablado, comido, vivido, *etc.*
nosotros:	habríamos hablado, comido, vivido, *etc.*
vosotros:	habríais hablado, comido, vivido, *etc.*
Uds./ellos/ellas:	habrían hablado, comido, vivido, *etc.*

These forms correspond to **el condicional (Capítulo 18)**. These forms are frequently used to tell what *would have happened* at some point in the past. (In contrast, the conditional tells what one *would do*.)

Yo **hablaría** con Miguel.
I would speak with Miguel (if I were you, at some point in the future).

Yo **habría hablado** con Miguel.
I would have spoken with Miguel (if I had been you, at some point in the past).

Si Clause: Sentences About the Past

You have learned (**Capítulo 18**) to use the past subjunctive and conditional to speculate about the present in **si** clause sentences: what *would happen* if a particular event *were* (or *were not*) to occur.

Si **tuviera** el tiempo, **aprendería** francés.
If I had the time, I would learn French (in the present or at some point in the future).

The perfect forms of the past subjunctive and the conditional are used to speculate about the past: what *would have happened* if a particular event *had* (or *had not*) occurred.

En la escuela superior, si **hubiera tenido** el tiempo, **habría aprendido** francés.
In high school, if I had had the time, I would have learned French.

Appendix 4

Verbs

A. Regular Verbs: Simple Tenses

Infinitive / Present Participle / Past Participle	INDICATIVE					SUBJUNCTIVE		IMPERATIVE
	Present	Imperfect	Preterite	Future	Conditional	Present	Imperfect	
hablar hablando hablado	hablo hablas habla hablamos habláis hablan	hablaba hablabas hablaba hablábamos hablabais hablaban	hablé hablaste habló hablamos hablasteis hablaron	hablaré hablarás hablará hablaremos hablaréis hablarán	hablaría hablarías hablaría hablaríamos hablaríais hablarían	hable hables hable hablemos habléis hablen	hablara hablaras hablara habláramos hablarais hablaran	habla tú, no hables hable Ud. hablemos hablen
comer comiendo comido	como comes come comemos coméis comen	comía comías comía comíamos comíais comían	comí comiste comió comimos comisteis comieron	comeré comerás comerá comeremos comeréis comerán	comería comerías comería comeríamos comeríais comerían	coma comas coma comamos comáis coman	comiera comieras comiera comiéramos comierais comieran	come tú, no comas coma Ud. comamos coman
vivir viviendo vivido	vivo vives vive vivimos vivís viven	vivía vivías vivía vivíamos vivíais vivían	viví viviste vivió vivimos vivisteis vivieron	viviré vivirás vivirá viviremos viviréis vivirán	viviría vivirías viviría viviríamos viviríais vivirían	viva vivas viva vivamos viváis vivan	viviera vivieras viviera viviéramos vivierais vivieran	vive tú, no vivas viva Ud. vivamos vivan

B. Regular Verbs: Perfect Tenses

INDICATIVE														
Present Perfect		Past Perfect		Preterite Perfect		Future Perfect		Conditional Perfect						
he has ha hemos habéis han	hablado comido vivido	había habías había habíamos habíais habían	hablado comido vivido	hube hubiste hubo hubimos hubisteis hubieron	hablado comido vivido	habré habrás habrá habremos habréis habrán	hablado comido vivido	habría habrías habría habríamos habríais habrían	hablado comido vivido					

SUBJUNCTIVE			
Present Perfect		Past Perfect	
haya hayas haya hayamos hayáis hayan	hablado comido vivido	hubiera hubieras hubiera hubiéramos hubierais hubieran	hablado comido vivido

C. Irregular Verbs

Infinitive / Present Participle / Past Participle	INDICATIVE Present	Imperfect	Preterite	Future	Conditional	SUBJUNCTIVE Present	Imperfect	IMPERATIVE
andar / andando / andado	ando / andas / anda / andamos / andáis / andan	andaba / andabas / andaba / andábamos / andabais / andaban	anduve / anduviste / anduvo / anduvimos / anduvisteis / anduvieron	andaré / andarás / andará / andaremos / andaréis / andarán	andaría / andarías / andaría / andaríamos / andaríais / andarían	ande / andes / ande / andemos / andéis / anden	anduviera / anduvieras / anduviera / anduviéramos / anduvierais / anduvieran	anda tú, no andes / ande Ud. / andemos / anden
caer / cayendo / caído	caigo / caes / cae / caemos / caéis / caen	caía / caías / caía / caíamos / caíais / caían	caí / caíste / cayó / caímos / caísteis / cayeron	caeré / caerás / caerá / caeremos / caeréis / caerán	caería / caerías / caería / caeríamos / caeríais / caerían	caiga / caigas / caiga / caigamos / caigáis / caigan	cayera / cayeras / cayera / cayéramos / cayerais / cayeran	cae tú, no caigas / caiga Ud. / caigamos / caigan
dar / dando / dado	doy / das / da / damos / dais / dan	daba / dabas / daba / dábamos / dabais / daban	di / diste / dio / dimos / disteis / dieron	daré / darás / dará / daremos / daréis / darán	daría / darías / daría / daríamos / daríais / darían	dé / des / dé / demos / deis / den	diera / dieras / diera / diéramos / dierais / dieran	da tú, no des / dé Ud. / demos / den
decir / diciendo / dicho	digo / dices / dice / decimos / decís / dicen	decía / decías / decía / decíamos / decíais / decían	dije / dijiste / dijo / dijimos / dijisteis / dijeron	diré / dirás / dirá / diremos / diréis / dirán	diría / dirías / diría / diríamos / diríais / dirían	diga / digas / diga / digamos / digáis / digan	dijera / dijeras / dijera / dijéramos / dijerais / dijeran	di tú, no digas / diga Ud. / digamos / digan
estar / estando / estado	estoy / estás / está / estamos / estáis / están	estaba / estabas / estaba / estábamos / estabais / estaban	estuve / estuviste / estuvo / estuvimos / estuvisteis / estuvieron	estaré / estarás / estará / estaremos / estaréis / estarán	estaría / estarías / estaría / estaríamos / estaríais / estarían	esté / estés / esté / estemos / estéis / estén	estuviera / estuvieras / estuviera / estuviéramos / estuvierais / estuviera	está tú, no estés / esté Ud. / estemos / estén
haber / habiendo / habido	he / has / ha / hemos / habéis / han	había / habías / había / habíamos / habíais / habían	hube / hubiste / hubo / hubimos / hubisteis / hubieron	habré / habrás / habrá / habremos / habréis / habrán	habría / habrías / habría / habríamos / habríais / habrían	haya / hayas / haya / hayamos / hayáis / hayan	hubiera / hubieras / hubiera / hubiéramos / hubierais / hubieran	
hacer / haciendo / hecho	hago / haces / hace / hacemos / hacéis / hacen	hacía / hacías / hacía / hacíamos / hacíais / hacían	hice / hiciste / hizo / hicimos / hicisteis / hicieron	haré / harás / hará / haremos / haréis / harán	haría / harías / haría / haríamos / haríais / harían	haga / hagas / haga / hagamos / hagáis / hagan	hiciera / hicieras / hiciera / hiciéramos / hicierais / hicieran	haz tú, no hagas / haga Ud. / hagamos / hagan

C. Irregular Verbs (continued)

Infinitive Present Participle Past Participle	INDICATIVE						SUBJUNCTIVE		IMPERATIVE
	Present	Imperfect	Preterite	Future	Conditional		Present	Imperfect	
ir yendo ido	voy vas va vamos vais van	iba ibas iba íbamos ibais iban	fui fuiste fue fuimos fuisteis fueron	iré irás irá iremos iréis irán	iría irías iría iríamos iríais irían		vaya vayas vaya vayamos vayáis vayan	fuera fueras fuera fuéramos fuerais fueran	ve tú, no vayas vaya Ud. vayamos vayan
oír oyendo oído	oigo oyes oye oímos oís oyen	oía oías oía oíamos oíais oían	oí oíste oyó oímos oísteis oyeron	oiré oirás oirá oiremos oiréis oirán	oiría oirías oiría oiríamos oiríais oirían		oiga oigas oiga oigamos oigáis oigan	oyera oyeras oyera oyéramos oyerais oyeran	oye tú, no oigas oiga Ud. oigamos oigan
poder pudiendo podido	puedo puedes puede podemos podéis pueden	podía podías podía podíamos podíais podían	pude pudiste pudo pudimos pudisteis pudieron	podré podrás podrá podremos podréis podrán	podría podrías podría podríamos podríais podrían		pueda puedas pueda podamos podáis puedan	pudiera pudieras pudiera pudiéramos pudierais pudieran	
poner poniendo puesto	pongo pones pone ponemos ponéis ponen	ponía ponías ponía poníamos poníais ponían	puse pusiste puso pusimos pusisteis pusieron	pondré pondrás pondrá pondremos pondréis pondrán	pondría pondrías pondría pondríamos pondríais pondrían		ponga pongas ponga pongamos pongáis pongan	pusiera pusieras pusiera pusiéramos pusierais pusieran	pon tú, no pongas ponga Ud. pongamos pongan
querer queriendo querido	quiero quieres quiere queremos queréis quieren	quería querías quería queríamos queríais querían	quise quisiste quiso quisimos quisisteis quisieron	querré querrás querrá querremos querréis querrán	querría querrías querría querríamos querríais querrían		quiera quieras quiera queramos queráis quieran	quisiera quisieras quisiera quisiéramos quisierais quisieran	quiere tú, no quieras quiera Ud. queramos quieran
saber sabiendo sabido	sé sabes sabe sabemos sabéis saben	sabía sabías sabía sabíamos sabíais sabían	supe supiste supo supimos supisteis supieron	sabré sabrás sabrá sabremos sabréis sabrán	sabría sabrías sabría sabríamos sabríais sabrían		sepa sepas sepa sepamos sepáis sepan	supiera supieras supiera supiéramos supierais supieran	sabe tú, no sepas sepa Ud. sepamos sepan
salir saliendo salido	salgo sales sale salimos salís salen	salía salías salía salíamos salíais salían	salí saliste salió salimos salisteis salieron	saldré saldrás saldrá saldremos saldréis saldrán	saldría saldrías saldría saldríamos saldríais saldrían		salga salgas salga salgamos salgáis salgan	saliera salieras saliera saliéramos salierais salieran	sal tú, no salgas salga Ud. salgamos salgan
ser siendo sido	soy eres es somos sois son	era eras era éramos erais eran	fui fuiste fue fuimos fuisteis fueron	seré serás será seremos seréis serán	sería serías sería seríamos seríais serían		sea seas sea seamos seáis sean	fuera fueras fuera fuéramos fuerais fueran	sé tú, no seas sea Ud. seamos sean

C. Irregular Verbs (continued)

Infinitive Present Participle Past Participle	INDICATIVE					SUBJUNCTIVE		IMPERATIVE
	Present	Imperfect	Preterite	Future	Conditional	Present	Imperfect	
tener teniendo tenido	tengo tienes tiene tenemos tenéis tienen	tenía tenías tenía teníamos teníais tenían	tuve tuviste tuvo tuvimos tuvisteis tuvieron	tendré tendrás tendrá tendremos tendréis tendrán	tendría tendrías tendría tendríamos tendríais tendrían	tenga tengas tenga tengamos tengáis tengan	tuviera tuvieras tuviera tuviéramos tuvierais tuvieran	ten tú, no tengas tenga Ud. tengamos tengan
traer trayendo traído	traigo traes trae traemos traéis traen	traía traías traía traíamos traíais traían	traje trajiste trajo trajimos trajisteis trajeron	traeré traerás traerá traeremos traeréis traerán	traería traerías traería traeríamos traeríais traerían	traiga traigas traiga traigamos traigáis traigan	trajera trajeras trajera trajéramos trajerais trajeran	trae tú, no traigas traiga Ud. traigamos traigan
venir viniendo venido	vengo vienes viene venimos venís vienen	venía venías venía veníamos veníais venían	vine viniste vino vinimos vinisteis vinieron	vendré vendrás vendrá vendremos vendréis vendrán	vendría vendrías vendría vendríamos vendríais vendrían	venga vengas venga vengamos vengáis vengan	viniera vinieras viniera viniéramos vinierais vinieran	ven tú, no vengas venga Ud. vengamos vengan
ver viendo visto	veo ves ve vemos veis ven	veía veías veía veíamos veíais veían	vi viste vio vimos visteis vieron	veré verás verá veremos veréis verán	vería verías vería veríamos veríais verían	vea veas vea veamos veáis vean	viera vieras viera viéramos vierais vieran	ve tú, no veas vea Ud. veamos vean

D. Stem-Changing and Spelling Change Verbs

Infinitive Present Participle Past Participle	INDICATIVE					SUBJUNCTIVE		IMPERATIVE
	Present	Imperfect	Preterite	Future	Conditional	Present	Imperfect	
pensar (ie) pensando pensado	pienso piensas piensa pensamos pensáis piensan	pensaba pensabas pensaba pensábamos pensabais pensaban	pensé pensaste pensó pensamos pensasteis pensaron	pensaré pensarás pensará pensaremos pensaréis pensarán	pensaría pensarías pensaría pensaríamos pensaríais pensarían	piense pienses piense pensemos penséis piensen	pensara pensaras pensara pensáramos pensarais pensaran	piensa tú, no pienses piense Ud. pensemos piensen
volver (ue) volviendo vuelto	vuelvo vuelves vuelve volvemos volvéis vuelven	volvía volvías volvía volvíamos volvíais volvían	volví volviste volvió volvimos volvisteis volvieron	volveré volverás volverá volveremos volveréis volverán	volvería volverías volvería volveríamos volveríais volverían	vuelva vuelvas vuelva volvamos volváis vuelvan	volviera volvieras volviera volviéramos volvierais volvieran	vuelve tú, no vuelvas vuelva Ud. volvamos vuelvan

D. Stem-Changing and Spelling Change Verbs (continued)

Infinitive Present Participle Past Participle	INDICATIVE					SUBJUNCTIVE		IMPERATIVE
	Present	Imperfect	Preterite	Future	Conditional	Present	Imperfect	
dormir (ue, u) durmiendo dormido	duermo duermes duerme dormimos dormís duermen	dormía dormías dormía dormíamos dormíais dormían	dormí dormiste durmió dormimos dormisteis durmieron	dormiré dormirás dormirá dormiremos dormiréis dormirán	dormiría dormirías dormiría dormiríamos dormiríais dormirían	duerma duermas duerma durmamos durmáis duerman	durmiera durmieras durmiera durmiéramos durmierais durmieran	duerme tú, no duermas duerma Ud. durmamos duerman
sentir (ie, i) sintiendo sentido	siento sientes siente sentimos sentís sienten	sentía sentías sentía sentíamos sentíais sentían	sentí sentiste sintió sentimos sentisteis sintieron	sentiré sentirás sentirá sentiremos sentiréis sentirán	sentiría sentirías sentiría sentiríamos sentiríais sentirían	sienta sientas sienta sintamos sintáis sientan	sintiera sintieras sintiera sintiéramos sintierais sintieran	siente tú, no sientas sienta Ud. sintamos sientan
pedir (i, i) pidiendo pedido	pido pides pide pedimos pedís piden	pedía pedías pedía pedíamos pedíais pedían	pedí pediste pidió pedimos pedisteis pidieron	pediré pedirás pedirá pediremos pediréis pedirán	pediría pedirías pediría pediríamos pediríais pedirían	pida pidas pida pidamos pidáis pidan	pidiera pidieras pidiera pidiéramos pidierais pidieran	pide tú, no pidas pida Ud. pidamos pidan
reír (i, i) riendo reído	río ríes ríe reímos reís ríen	reía reías reía reíamos reíais reían	reí reíste rió reímos reísteis rieron	reiré reirás reirá reiremos reiréis reirán	reiría reirías reiría reiríamos reiríais reirían	ría rías ría riamos riáis rían	riera rieras riera riéramos rierais rieran	ríe tú, no rías ría Ud. riamos rían
seguir (i, i) (g) siguiendo seguido	sigo sigues sigue seguimos seguís siguen	seguía seguías seguía seguíamos seguíais seguían	seguí seguiste siguió seguimos seguisteis siguieron	seguiré seguirás seguirá seguiremos seguiréis seguirán	seguiría seguirías seguiría seguiríamos seguiríais seguirían	siga sigas siga sigamos sigáis sigan	siguiera siguieras siguiera siguiéramos siguierais siguieran	sigue tú, no sigas siga Ud. sigamos sigan
construir (y) construyendo construido	construyo construyes construye construimos construís construyen	construía construías construía construíamos construíais construían	construí construiste construyó construimos construisteis construyeron	construiré construirás construirá construiremos construiréis construirán	construiría construirías construiría construiríamos construiríais construirían	construya construyas construya construyamos construyáis construyan	construyera construyeras construyera construyéramos construyerais construyeran	construye tú, no construyas construya Ud. construyamos construyan
producir (zc) produciendo producido	produzco produces produce producimos producís producen	producía producías producía producíamos producíais producían	produje produjiste produjo produjimos produjisteis produjeron	produciré producirás producirá produciremos produciréis producirán	produciría producirías produciría produciríamos produciríais producirían	produzca produzcas produzca produzcamos produzcáis produzcan	produjera produjeras produjera produjéramos produjerais produjeran	produce tú, no produzcas produzca Ud. produzcamos produzcan

Appendix 5

Answers to *¿Recuerda Ud.?* Exercises

CAPÍTULO 2
GRAMMAR SECTION 5 1. Soy estudiante. 2. Sí, (No, no) soy una persona sentimental. 3. Es (Son) la(s)… (La clase de español) Es a la(s)… 4. Es un edificio.

CAPÍTULO 4
GRAMMAR SECTION 12 quiero, quieres, quiere, quieren; puedo, puedes, puede, pueden

CAPÍTULO 5
GRAMMAR SECTION 16 *¿Cómo está Ud.? Asks how someone is feeling at a particular moment. ¿Cómo es Ud.? Asks about someone's nature, that is, what he or she is like as a person.*

CAPÍTULO 7
GRAMMAR SECTION 22 *Use this model for all answers and questions:* Sí, me gusta… (No, no me gusta…) ¿Le gusta?

CAPÍTULO 9
GRAMMAR SECTION 28 1. Trabajo tanto como tú (Ud.). 2. Yo trabajo más/menos que tú (Ud.). 3. Bill Gates tiene más dinero que yo. 4. Mi com-

pañero/a de casa tiene menos cosas que yo. 5. Tengo tantos amigos como tú (Ud.). 6. Mi computadora es peor/mejor que ésta.

CAPÍTULO 10
GRAMMAR SECTION 30 1. *preterite* 2. *imperfect* 3. *imperfect* 4. *preterite* 5. *imperfect* 6. *imperfect*

CAPÍTULO 12
GRAMMAR SECTION 36 1. Tráiganme el libro. 2. No se lo den (a ella). 3. Siéntese aquí, por favor. 4. ¡No se siente en esa silla! 5. Díganles la verdad. 6. ¡Dígansela ahora! 7. No se la digan nunca. 8. ¡Cuídese! 9. ¡Lleve (Ud.) una vida sana! 10. Escúcheme.

CAPÍTULO 17
GRAMMAR SECTION 48 1. hablaron 2. comieron 3. vivieron 4. jugaron 5. perdieron 6. durmieron 7. rieron 8. leyeron 9. estuvieron 10. tuvieron 11. destruyeron 12. mantuvieron 13. trajeron 14. dieron 15. supieron 16. se vistieron 17. dijeron 18. creyeron 19. fueron 20. pudieron

GRAMMAR SECTION 49 1. su país 2. tus derechos 3. nuestra obligación 4. nuestra prensa 5. su gobierno 6. su crimen

---

Appendix 6

Answers to Exercises

CAPÍTULO PRELIMINAR:
ANTE TODO
PRIMERA PARTE
SALUDOS Y EXPRESIONES DE CORTESÍA: Conversación A 1. Muy buenas. (Buenas tardes.) (Muy buenas tardes.) 2. Hasta luego. (Adiós.) (Hasta mañana.) 3. Bien (Muy bien) (Regular), gracias. ¿y tú? 4. Hola. (¿Qué tal?) 5. Bien (Muy bien), gracias, ¿y usted? 6. Buenas noches. (Muy buenas.) (Adiós.) (Hasta mañana.) 7. De nada. (No hay de qué.) 8. Hasta mañana. (Hasta luego.) (Adiós.) 9. (Me llamo _____.) 10. Encantado/a. (Igualmente.)
Conversación C 1. Con permiso. (Perdón.) 2. Perdón. 3. Perdón. 4. Con permiso. (Por favor.) 5. Perdón. 6. Perdón.
EL ALFABETO ESPAÑOL: Práctica A 1. c 2. e 3. i 4. a 5. f 6. h 7. b 8. g 9. d
SEGUNDA PARTE
MÁS COGNADOS: Práctica A Lugares: *Places;* Cosas: *Things;* Bebidas: *Drinks;* Deportes: *Sports*
Práctica B 1. Es una cosa. 2. Es un animal. 3. Es una comida. 4. Es un deporte. 5. Es una nación. 6. Es una persona. 7. Es un lugar. 8. Es una bebida. 9. Es un animal. 10. Es una cosa. 11. Es un lugar. 12. Es un concepto. 13. Es una persona. 14. Es un instrumento musical. 15. Es un concepto.
Conversación 1. ¿Qué es un saxofón? —Es un instrumento musical. 2. ¿Qué es un autobús? —Es una cosa. 3. ¿Qué es un rancho? —Es un lugar. 4. ¿Qué es un doctor? —Es una persona. 5. ¿Qué es Bolivia? —Es una

nación (un lugar). 6. ¿Qué es una Coca-Cola? —Es una bebida. 7. ¿Qué es una enchilada? —Es una comida. 8. ¿Qué es una jirafa? —Es un animal. 9. ¿Qué es una turista? —Es una persona.
LOS NÚMEROS 0–30; hay: Práctica A 1. Hay cuatro señoras. 2. Hay doce pianos. 3. Hay un café. 4. Hay veintiún (veinte y un) cafés. 5. Hay catorce días. 6. Hay una clase. 7. Hay veintiuna (veinte y una) ideas. 8. Hay once personas. 9. Hay quince estudiantes. 10. Hay trece teléfonos. 11. Hay veintiocho (veinte y ocho) naciones. 12. Hay cinco guitarras. 13. Hay un león. 14. Hay treinta señores. 15. Hay veinte oficinas.
Práctica B 1. Dos y cuatro son seis. 2. Ocho y diecisiete (diez y siete) son veinticinco (veinte y cinco). 3. Once y uno son doce. 4. Tres y dieciocho (diez y ocho) son veintiuno (veinte y uno). 5. Nueve y seis son quince. 6. Cinco y cuatro son nueve. 7. Uno y trece son catorce. 8. Quince menos dos son trece. 9. Nueve menos nueve es cero. 10. Trece menos ocho son cinco. 11. Catorce y doce son veintiséis (veinte y seis). 12. Veintitrés (Veinte y tres) menos trece son diez.
TERCERA PARTE
¿QUÉ HORA ES?: Práctica A 1. Las doce menos veinte de la noche. 2. Las dos menos un minuto de la tarde. 3. Las diez y veintitrés (veinte y tres) de la noche. 4. Las dos y diecinueve (diez y nueve) de la mañana. 5. Las cinco y cuarto (quince) de la tarde. 6. Las nueve y media de la mañana. 7. La una y siete de la noche (de la mañana). 8. Las seis y dieciséis (diez y seis) de la mañana.

Práctica B 1. Es la una. 2. Son las seis. 3. Son las once. 4. Es la una y media. 5. Son las tres y cuarto (quince). 6. Son las siete menos cuarto (quince). 7. Son las cuatro y cuarto (quince). 8. Son las doce menos cuarto (quince) en punto. 9. Son las nueve y diez en punto. 10. Son las diez menos diez en punto.
Conversación A *Paso 1* 1. ¿A qué hora es la clase de francés? —A las dos menos cuarto (quince) de la tarde… ¡en punto! 2. ¿A qué hora es la sesión de laboratorio? —A las tres y diez de la tarde… ¡en punto! 3. ¿A qué hora es la excursión? —A las nueve menos cuarto (quince) de la mañana… ¡en punto! 4. ¿A qué hora es el concierto? —A las siete y media de la tarde (noche)… ¡en punto!
LAS PALABRAS INTERROGATIVAS: Práctica *Paso 1* 1. ¿A qué hora… ? 2. ¿Dónde… ? 3. ¿Qué… ? 4. ¿Cómo… ? 5. ¿Cómo… ? 6. ¿Cuántos… ? 7. ¿Cuánto… ? 8. ¿Cuál… ? 9. ¿Qué… ? 10. ¿Cuándo… ? 11. ¿Qué hora… ? 12. ¿Quién… ?
Paso 2 Possible answers: 1. ¿A qué hora es la clase? 2. ¿Dónde está Madrid? 3. ¿Qué es usted? 4. ¿Cómo está(s)? 5. ¿Cómo es (él/ella)? 6. ¿Cuántos habitantes hay? 7. ¿Cuánto es? 8. ¿Cuál es la capital de Venezuela? 9. ¿Qué es un saxofón? 10. ¿Cuándo es la fiesta? 11. ¿Qué hora es? 12. ¿Quién es usted (eres tú)?

CAPÍTULO 1
VOCABULARIO: PREPARACIÓN
EN LA CLASE: Conversación A **1. en la clase:** 1. la profesora 2. la estudiante 3. el papel 4. la silla 5. el escritorio (la mesa) 6. el bolígrafo 7. el lápiz 8. la calculadora 9. la pizarra **2. la biblioteca:** 1. el estudiante 2. la estudiante 3. el bibliotecario 4. el libro de texto 5. el diccionario 6. el cuaderno 7. la mesa 8. la silla 9. la ventana **3. la librería:** 1. la estudiante 2. el lápiz 3. el libro de texto 4. el bolígrafo 5. la mochila 6. el dinero 7. la estudiante **4. la oficina (la universidad):** 1. el estudiante 2. la consejera 3. la mesa 4. la estudiante 5. el profesor
Conversación B 1. Es hombre. 2. Es mujer. 3. Es hombre. 4. Es hombre. 5. Es mujer. 6. Es hombre.
LAS MATERIAS: Conversación A 1. las ciencias, la química 2. la sicología 3. las comunicaciones 4. la filosofía 5. la literatura, el inglés 6. el arte 7. la computación 8. la física
GRAMMAR SECTION 1
Práctica A 1. el 2. la 3. el 4. la 5. el 6. el 7. la 8. el 9. la 10. la 11. el 12. la; 1. un 2. una 3. un 4. un 5. una 6. una 7. un 8. una 9. un
Práctica B: *Paso 1* 1. Hay un consejero en la oficina. 2. Hay una profesora en la clase. 3. Hay un lápiz en la mesa. 4. Hay un cuaderno en el escritorio. 5. Hay una silla en la mochila. 6. Hay un bolígrafo en la silla. 7. Hay una palabra en el papel. 8. Hay una oficina en la residencia. 9. Hay un compañero en la biblioteca.
Conversación A 1. ¿El/La cliente? —Es una persona. 2. ¿El bolígrafo? —Es una cosa. 3. ¿La residencia? —Es un edificio. 4. ¿El/La dependiente/a? —Es una persona. 5. ¿El hotel? —Es un edificio. 6. ¿La calculadora? —Es una cosa. 7. ¿La computación? —Es una materia. 8. ¿El inglés? —Es una materia (lengua).
Conversación B *Possible answers:* 1. el libro, la mesa; el/la estudiante, el/la bibliotecario/a 2. el libro (de texto), el cuaderno; el/la cliente, el/la dependiente/a 3. el escritorio, el papel; el/la consejero/a, el/la profesor(a) 4. la puerta, la ventana; el/la estudiante, el/la compañero/a de cuarto
GRAMMAR SECTION 2
Práctica A 1. las mesas 2. los papeles 3. los amigos 4. las oficinas 5. unos cuadernos 6. unos lápices 7. unas universidades 8. unos bolígrafos 9. unos edificios.
Práctica B 1. el profesor 2. la calculadora 3. la bibliotecaria 4. el estudiante 5. un hombre 6. una residencia 7. una silla 8. un escritorio
GRAMMAR SECTION 3
Práctica A: *Paso 2* 1. ¿Necesitas… ? 2. ¿Trabajas… ? 3. ¿Tomas… ? 4. En clase, ¿cantas… ? 5. ¿Deseas practicar… ? 6. ¿Tomas… ? 7. ¿Enseñas… ? 8. ¿Hablas… ?
Práctica B 1. cantan 2. bailan 3. toca 4. escuchan 5. busca 6. habla 7. desea 8. bailar 9. baila 10. necesitan
Comprensión 1. falso 2. falso 3. cierto 4. cierto
GRAMMAR SECTION 4
Práctica 1. ¿Eres norteamericano? 2. ¿Estudias con frecuencia? 3. ¿Tocas el piano? 4. ¿Deseas trabajar más horas? 5. ¿Hablas francés? 6. ¿Eres reservado?
Conversación *Pasos 1* 1. ¿Estudias… ? 2. ¿Practicas… ? 3. ¿Tomas… ? 4. ¿Bailas… ? 5. ¿Tocas… ? 6. ¿Regresas…?
UN POCO DE TODO
Ejercicio A: *Pasos 1 y 2* (*Questions and answers are combined.*) 1. — 2. ¿Buscas un libro de español? No, busco una mochila. 3. — 4. ¿No trabaja Paco

aquí en la cafetería? No, él trabaja en la biblioteca. 3. — 3. ¿Qué más necesitan Uds. en la clase de cálculo? Necesitamos una calculadora y un cuaderno. 4. — 5. ¿Dónde está Juanita? Ella trabaja en la residencia por las tardes. 5. — 1. ¿No deseas estudiar unos minutos más? No, necesito regresar a casa.
Ejercicio B 1. es 2. toma 3. Estudiamos 4. me 5. Compro 6. estudio 7. la 8. una 9. practicamos 10. la 11. canta 12. baila 13. trabajamos 14. por 15. la 16. es 17. dependienta 18. estamos 19. el
Comprensión 1. cierto 2. falso; Le gusta la clase. 3. falso; Ángela estudia mucho. 4. falso; Luisa habla español.

CAPÍTULO 2
VOCABULARIO: PREPARACIÓN
LA FAMILIA Y LOS PARIENTES: Conversación A 1. falso; Es el primo de Marta. 2. cierto 3. cierto 4. falso; Son hermanos. 5. falso; Es la hermana de Manolo. 6. falso; Es el padre de José Jaime. 7. cierto 8. cierto
Conversación B: *Paso 1* 1. abuela 2. primo 3. tía 4. abuelo
Paso 2 1. Es la hija de mi tío/a. 2. Es el hijo de mi hermano/a. 3. Es el hermano de mi madre/padre. 4. Es el padre de mi madre/padre.
ADJETIVOS: Conversación A 1. Es tonto. 2. Es perezoso. 3. Es alto. 4. Es malo, antipático y feo. 5. Es soltero y joven. 6. Es nuevo y largo.
LOS NÚMEROS 31–100: Conversación A 1. Treinta y cincuenta son ochenta. 2. Cuarenta y cinco y cuarenta y cinco son noventa. 3. Treinta y dos y cincuenta y ocho son noventa. 4. Setenta y siete y veintitrés (veinte y tres) son cien. 5. Cien menos cuarenta y uno son sesenta. 6. Noventa y nueve menos treinta y nueve son sesenta. 7. Ochenta y cuatro menos treinta y cuatro son cincuenta. 8. Setenta y ocho menos treinta y seis son cuarenta y dos. 9. Ochenta y ocho menos veintiocho (veinte y ocho) son sesenta.
PRONUNCIACIÓN
Ejercicio B 1. mo-chi̱-la 2. me̱-nos 3. re-gu-la̱r 4. i-gual-me̱nt-e 5. E-cua-do̱r 6. e-le-ga̱n-te 7. li-be-ra̱l 8. hu-ma-ni-da̱d
GRAMMAR SECTION 5
Práctica A 1. falso; Somos esposos. 2. falso; Es la tía de Patricia. 3. cierto 4. cierto 5. cierto. 6. falso; Es abuelo (el abuelo de Marta, José Jamie y Patricia). 7. cierto
Práctica B: *Paso 1* 1. John Doe es de los Estados Unidos. 2. Karl Lotze es de Alemania. 3. Graziana Lazzarino es de Italia. 4. María Gómez es de México. 5. Claudette Moreau es de Francia. 6. Timothy Windsor es de Inglaterra.
Práctica C: *Paso 1* 1. Carlos Miguel es médico. Es de Cuba. Ahora trabaja en Milwaukee. 2. Maripili es profesora. Es de Burgos. Ahora trabaja en Miami. 3. Mariela es dependienta. Es de Buenos Aires. Ahora trabaja en Nueva York. 4. Juan es dentista. Es de Lima. Ahora trabaja en Los Ángeles.
Práctica D 1. ¿De quién es la casa en Beverly Hills? —Es de la actriz. 2. ¿De quién es la casa en Viena? —Es de los señores Schmidt. 3. ¿De quién es la camioneta? —Es de la familia con diez hijos. 4. ¿De quién es el perro? —Es del niño. 5. ¿De quién son las fotos de la Argentina? —Son del estudiante extranjero. 6. ¿De quién son las mochilas con todos los libros? —Son de los estudiantes.
Conversación A 1. La calculadora es para Raulito, el primo. Le gustan las matemáticas. Por eso necesita la calculadora. 2. Los libros de literatura clásica son para Joey, el hermano. Le gustan mucho las historias viejas. Por eso necesita los libros. 3. Los discos compactos de Andrés Segovia son para Julián y María, los abuelos. Les gusta mucho la música de guitarra clásica. Por eso necesitan los discos compactos. 4. El televisor es para Carmen, la madre. Le gusta mirar programas cómicos. Por eso necesita la televisión. 5. El radio es para José, el padre. Le gusta escuchar las noticias. Por eso necesita el radio. 6. El dinero es para Carmina, la hermana. Ella desea estudiar en otro estado. Por eso necesita el dinero.
GRAMMAR SECTION 6
Práctica A 1. problema, dinero, familia 2. hijos, profesoras 3. ventana, cuarto, coche, abuela 4. animales, materias 5. materias, sobrinas 6. (*none*)
Práctica B 1. Su hijo pequeño es guapo. 2. Su esposa es fea. 3. Su retrato es bueno. 4. Sus hijas son solteras. 5. Su familia es importante y rica.
GRAMMAR SECTION 7
Práctica A 1. trabajador, alto, grande, amable 2. inteligentes, viejos, religiosos 3. elegante, sentimental, simpática 4. solteras, morenas
Práctica D Dolores es una buena estudiante. Es lista y trabajadora y estudia mucho. Es norteamericana de origen mexicano, y por eso habla español. Desea ser profesora de antropología. Dolores es morena, guapa y atlética. Le gustan las fiestas grandes y tiene buenos amigos en la universidad. Tiene parientes norteamericanos y mexicanos.
Práctica E 1. …es francesa y vive en Francia. 2. …es español y vive en España. 3. …son alemanes y viven en Alemania. 4. …es portugués y vive en

Portugal. 5. ...son italianas y viven en Italia. 6. ...es inglés y vive en Inglaterra. 7. ...son chinos y viven en la China.

GRAMMAR SECTION 8

Práctica A: *Paso 2* 1. ¿Debes... 2. ¿Lees... 3. ¿Comprendes... 4. ¿Asistes... 5. ¿Deben Uds... 6. ¿Escriben Uds... 7. ¿Aprenden Uds... 8. ¿Venden Uds...

Práctica B 1. vende 2. aprendemos 3. deben 4. asistir 5. cree 6. leer 7. leemos 8. escribimos 9. creo 10. comprende

Práctica C 1. Yo leo el periódico. 2. Mi hija, Marta, mira la televisión. 3. También escribe una composición. 4. Mi esposa, Lola, abre y lee unas cartas. 5. ¡Hoy recibimos una carta del tío Ricardo! 6. Es de España pero ahora vive en México. 7. ¡Ay! Son las dos de la tarde. 8. ¡Debemos comer ahora!

UN POCO DE TODO

Ejercicio A: *Paso 1* 1. Yo soy la abuela panameña. 2. El nuevo nieto es de los Estados Unidos. 3. Juan José es el padre del nieto. 4. Juan José también es el hijo del abuelo panameño. 5. Una de las tías del nieto es médica. 6. La otra tía es una profesora famosa. 7. La madre del niño es norteamericana. 8. La hermana del niño se llama Concepción.
Paso 2 1. Son de Panamá. 2. Es de los Estados Unidos. 3. Se llama Juan José.

Ejercicio B 1. creen 2. todas 3. hispánicas 4. grandes 5. es 6. grandes 7. Es 8. típica 9. todas 10. trabajan 11. necesario 12. urbanos 13. son 14. muchos 15. industrializada 16. trabajan 17. pagan 18. hablar 19. hispánica 20. norteamericana

Comprensión 1. falso; Todas las familias hispánicas no son iguales. 2. cierto 3. cierto 4. cierto

CAPÍTULO 3

VOCABULARIO: PREPARACIÓN

DE COMPRAS: LA ROPA: Conversación A 1. El Sr. Rivera lleva un traje, unos zapatos, unos calcetines, un sombrero, una corbata, una camisa y un cinturón. 2. La Srta. Alonso lleva unos pantalones, una chaqueta, unas botas y unos calcetines. El perro lleva un suéter. 3. Sara lleva una falda, una blusa, unas medias y unos zapatos. 4. Alfredo lleva una camiseta, una chaqueta, unos *bluejeans* y unos zapatos de tenis. Necesita comprar ropa nueva. (*Different answers are possible.*) *Possible answers:* El Sr. Rivera trabaja hoy. Sara se prepara para una fiesta. Alfredo (La Srta. Alonso, Sara) no trabaja en este momento.

Conversación B 1. almacén 2. regatear 3. venden, rebajas 4. centros comerciales 5. centro 6. *Possible answers:* faldas, blusas, vestidos. 7. *Possible answers:* camisetas, pantalones, camisas, chaquetas, cinturones, calcetines, zapatos, botas, suéteres, abrigos 8. seda 9. algodón

Conversación D 1. En un almacén hay precios fijos, ¿no? (¿verdad?) 2. Regateamos mucho en los Estados Unidos, ¿no? (¿verdad?) 3. No hay muchos mercados en esta ciudad, ¿no? (¿verdad?) 4. Los *bluejeans* Gap son muy baratos, ¿no? (¿verdad?) 5. Es necesario llevar traje y corbata a clase, ¿no? (¿verdad?) 6. Eres una persona muy independiente, ¿no? (¿verdad?) 7. Tienes una familia muy grande, ¿no? (¿verdad?) 8. No hay examen mañana, ¿verdad?

¿DE QUÉ COLOR ES?: Conversación A 1. En el dibujo A hay un traje azul, pero en el dibujo B hay un traje azul de cuadros. 2. En el dibujo A hay dos sandalias, pero en el dibujo B hay una. 3. En el dibujo A hay un sombrero, pero en el dibujo B hay dos sombreros. 4. En el dibujo A hay un sombrero verde, pero en el dibujo B los sombreros son rojos. 5. En el dibujo A hay un precio de 50 pesos, pero en el dibujo B hay un precio de 40 dólares. 6. En el dibujo A hay un suéter morado, pero en el dibujo B hay un suéter azul. 7. En el dibujo A hay una bolsa parda, pero en el dibujo B hay una bolsa gris. 8. En el dibujo A hay un vestido con cinturón, pero en el dibujo B hay una blusa y una falda sin cinturón.

LOS NÚMEROS MÁS ALLÁ DEL NÚMERO 100: Conversación A: *Paso 1* el elefante: cinco mil kilos, el rinoceronte indio: cuatro mil kilos, el hipopótamo: dos mil kilos, el bisonte: mil kilos, la jirafa: mil doscientos kilos, el oso Grizzly: setecientos ochenta kilos, el dromedario: seiscientos kilos, el alce: quinientos noventa y cinco kilos, el tigre: trescientos kilos, el gorila: doscientos veinte kilos

Conversación B 1. siete mil trescientas cuarenta y cinco pesetas 2. cien dólares 3. cinco mil setecientos diez quetzales 4. seiscientos setenta bolívares 5. un millón de dólares 6. quinientos veintiocho (veinte y ocho) nuevos pesos 7. ochocientos treinta y seis bolívares 8. ciento una pesetas 9. cuatro millones de dólares 10. seis millones de quetzales

PRONUNCIACIÓN

Ejercicio B 1. exámenes (written accent mark) 2. lápiz (written accent mark) 3. necesitar (ends in consonant) 4. perezoso (ends in vowel) 5. acti-

tud (ends in consonant) 6. acciones (ends in -s) 7. dólares (written accent mark) 8. francés (written accent mark) 9. están (written accent mark) 10. hombre (ends in vowel) 11. peso (ends in vowel) 12. mujer (ends in consonant) 13. plástico (written accent mark) 14. María (written accent mark) 15. Rodríguez (written accent mark) 16. Patricia (ends in diphthong)

GRAMMAR SECTION 9

Práctica A: *Paso 1* 1. Esa falda también es muy pequeña. 2. Esos pantalones también son muy largos. 3. Ese libro también es muy bueno. 4. Esas corbatas también son muy feas.
Paso 2 1. Aquella falda también es muy pequeña. 2. Aquellos pantalones también son muy largos. 3. Aquel libro también es muy bueno. 4. Aquellas corbatas también son muy feas.

Práctica B *Possible answers:* 1. ¡Esto es fantástico! 2. ¡Esto es horrible! 3. ¡Eso es muy bueno! 4. ¡Eso es terrible! 4. ¡Esto es magnífico!

GRAMMAR SECTION 10

Práctica A: *Paso 1* 1. Sara tiene muchos exámenes. 2. Viene a la universidad todos los días. 3. Hoy trabaja hasta las nueve de la noche. 4. Prefiere estudiar en la biblioteca. 5. Quiere leer más pero no puede. 6. Por eso regresa a casa. 7. Tiene ganas de leer más. 8. Pero unos amigos vienen a mirar la televisión. 9. Sara decide mirar la televisión con ellos.
Paso 2 1. Yo tengo muchos exámenes. 2. Vengo a la universidad todos los días. 3. Hoy trabajo hasta las nueve de la noche. 4. Prefiero estudiar en la biblioteca. 5. Quiero leer más pero no puedo. 6. Por eso regreso a casa. 7. Tengo ganas de leer más. 8. Pero unos amigos vienen a mirar la televisión. 9. Decido mirar la televisión con ellos.
1. Nosotros/as tenemos muchos exámenes. 2. Venimos a la universidad todos los días. 3. Hoy trabajamos hasta las nueve de la noche. 4. Preferimos estudiar en la biblioteca. 5. Queremos leer más pero no podemos. 6. Por eso regresamos a casa. 7. Tenemos ganas de leer más. 8. Pero unos amigos vienen a mirar la televisión. 9. Decidimos mirar la televisión con ellos.

Práctica B 1. ... tengo _____ años. 2. ... tengo miedo. 3. ... tengo sueño. 4. ... no tienes razón. 5. ... tengo prisa. 6. ... tienen (tenemos) miedo. 7. ... tengo que estudiar (tengo miedo). 8. ... tienes razón.

GRAMMAR SECTION 11

Práctica A 1. Ud. va a una *boutique*. 2. Francisco va al almacén Goya. 3. Jorge y Carlos van al centro comercial. 4. Tú vas a un mercado. 5. Nosotros vamos a una tienda pequeña. 6. Yo voy...

Práctica B 1. Vamos a llegar al centro a las diez de la mañana. 2. La niña va a querer comer algo. 3. Voy a comprar unos chocolates para Marta. 4. Manolo va a buscar una blusa de seda. 5. No vas a comprar esta blusa de rayas, ¿verdad? 6. Vamos a buscar algo más barato. 7. ¿Vas a ir de compras mañana también?

UN POCO DE TODO

Ejercicio B 1. las. 2. gran 3. ir 4. elegantes 5. los 6. fijos 7. pequeñas 8. formar 9. cree 10. otros 11. va 12. puede 13. debe 14. los 15. tiene 16. que 17. informal 18. grandes 19. debe 20. a

Comprensión 1. falso; Hay una gran variedad de tiendas. 2. falso; Los precios son fijos en los almacenes. 3. falso; Es posible comprar papel. 4. falso; El precio es alto al principio.

CAPÍTULO 4

VOCABULARIO: PREPARACIÓN

¿QUÉ DÍA ES HOY?: Conversación A 1. Hoy es _____. Mañana es _____. Si hoy es sábado, mañana es domingo. Si hoy es jueves, mañana es viernes. Ayer fue _____. 2. Tenemos clase los _____. No tenemos clases los _____. 3. Sí, (No, no) estudio mucho durante el fin de semana. Sí, (No, no) estudio mucho los domingos por la noche. 4. Los viernes por la tarde me gusta _____. Sí, (No, no) me gusta salir con los amigos los sábados por la noche.

LOS MUEBLES, LOS CUARTOS Y OTRAS PARTES DE LA CASA: Conversación A *Possible answers:* 1. Es el garaje. En el garaje hay un coche. 2. Es la sala. En la sala hay un sillón, un televisor, una mesa y una lámpara. 3. Es la alcoba. En la alcoba hay una cama. 4. Es el cuarto de baño. En el cuarto de baño hay un lavabo. 5. Es la cocina. En la cocina hay platos. 6. Es el comedor. En el comedor hay dos sillas y una mesa. 7. Es el patio. En el patio no hay piscina. Solamente hay plantas.

Conversación B: *Paso 1* *Possible answers:* 1. el escritorio, la mesa, la silla, la lámpara, la alcoba 2. el sofá, la cama, la alcoba, la sala 3. el sofá, el televisor, la sala, el comedor, la cocina 4. el comedor, la mesa, las sillas, la cocina 5. el patio, la piscina 6. la sala, el sofá, el sillón, la alcoba

¿CUÁNDO? PREPOSICIONES: Conversación A 1. después de 2. después de 3. antes de 4. antes de 5. después de (antes de) 6. antes de

GRAMMAR SECTION 12

Conversación A *Possible answers:* 1. ... hago un viaje a Colorado. 2. ...

traigo el libro a clase. 3. ... salgo para la biblioteca. 4. ... pongo el televisor. 5. ... oigo al profesor. 6. ... salgo para la residencia. 7. ... pongo el estéreo. 8. ... hago una pregunta.

GRAMMAR SECTION 13
Práctica A 1. Está en la cocina (el comedor). 2. Está en la sala. 3. Están en el comedor (la cocina). 4. Están en la sala. 5. Está en la alcoba (el baño). 6. Está en el garaje. 7. Está en la alcoba (la sala). 8. Está en la sala (la alcoba). **Práctica C: *Paso 1*** 1. La familia de Ismael tiene ganas de comer paella. 2. Vuelven a su restaurante favorito. 3. Piensan que la paella del restaurante es estupenda. 4. Piden paella para seis personas. 5. Pero hoy sólo sirven un menú mexicano. 6. Por eso piden tacos y guacamole. 7. Almuerzan mucho y ahora quieren dormir la siesta. 8. Pero también quieren estar más tiempo juntos. 9. Por eso juegan al dominó en el parque. *Paso 2* 1. Nuestra familia tiene ganas de comer paella. 2. Volvemos a nuestro restaurante favorito. 3. Pensamos que la paella del restaurante es estupenda. 4. Pedimos paella para seis personas. 5. Pero hoy sólo sirven un menú mexicano. 6. Por eso pedimos tacos y guacamole. 7. Almorzamos mucho y ahora queremos dormir la siesta. 8. Pero también queremos estar más tiempo juntos. 9. Por eso jugamos al dominó en el parque.

GRAMMAR SECTION 14
Práctica B: *Paso 1* 1. Me levanto a las siete. 2. Mi esposa Lola se levanta más tarde. 3. Nos duchamos por la mañana. 4. Por costumbre, nuestra hija Marta se baña por la noche. 5. Lola se viste después de tomar un café. 6. Lola se viste después de tomar un café. 7. Por la noche, Marta se acuesta muy temprano. 8. Yo me acuesto más tarde, a las once. 9. Por lo general, Lola se acuesta más tarde que yo. *Paso 2* 1. Manolo 2. Marta 3. Marta 4. Manolo
Práctica C: *Paso 1* *Possible answers:* 1. despertarme 2. me ducho; me afeito 3. después de afeitarme 4. tomar el desayuno 5. vestirme; tomar un café 6. me acuesto 7. después de bañarme; me duermo

UN POCO DE TODO
Ejercicio A *Possible answers:* 1. empiezo; es 2. empiezan 3. hablan (entienden) 4. almuerzo; almorzamos; pedimos 5. vuelvo; empiezo; duermo 6. cierra; vuelvo (voy)
Ejercicio B 1. Me 2. compras 3. ganas 4. Este 5. buscar 6. del 7. trabaja 8. Mis 9. son 10. están 11. políticas 12. viene 13. nuestra 14. celebran 15. eso 16. ir 17. de 18. es 19. asiste 20. Quiero 21. rayas 22. trece 23. empieza 24. vestirse 25. Sus 26. llevan 27. voy 28. se divierten 29. estás 30. haces 31. Leo 32. inglesa 33. vamos 34. muchas 35. estos 36. Encantada 37. ponerme 38. salgo
Comprensión 1. la persona que narra la historia 2. Margarita 3. los niños de los Suárez 4. la madre de la persona que narra la historia 5. Ana Suárez 6. Margarita 7. uno de los hijos de los Sres. Suárez

CAPÍTULO 5
VOCABULARIO: PREPARACIÓN
¿QUÉ TIEMPO HACE HOY?: Conversación A 1. Hace calor (sol). 2. Hace fresco. 3. Hace frío (fresco). 4. Llueve. 5. Hace (mucho) frío.
Conversación B *Possible answers:* 1. Joaquín, no debes vivir en Seattle porque allí llueve mucho. 2. No debes vivir en Los Ángeles porque allí hay mucha contaminación. 3. No debes vivir en Phoenix porque allí hace mucho calor y nunca llueve. 4. No debes vivir en Nueva Orleans porque allí hace mucho calor y llueve mucho. 5. No debes vivir en Buffalo porque allí hace mucho frío y nieva mucho.
Conversación D *Possible answers:* 1. Nieva. El hombre tiene mucho frío. 2. Hace mucho sol y calor. El hombre tiene mucho calor. 3. Hace mucho viento. Las personas tienen frío. 4. Llueve mucho. Las personas tienen frío. 5. Hay mucha contaminación. Las personas no están bien. 6. Hace buen tiempo. Las personas están muy bien. 7. Hace fresco por la noche. Las personas están bien.
LOS MESES Y LAS ESTACIONES DEL AÑO: Conversación A 1. El doce es viernes. 2. El primero es lunes. 3. El veinte es sábado. 4. El dieciséis (diez y seis) es martes. 5. El once es jueves. 6. El cuatro es jueves. 7. El veintinueve (veinte y nueve) es lunes.
Conversación B: *Paso 1* 1. el siete de marzo, invierno 2. el veinticuatro (veinte y cuatro) de agosto, verano 3. el primero de diciembre, otoño (invierno) 4. el cinco de junio, primavera 5. el diecinueve (diez y nueve) de septiembre de mil novecientos noventa y siete, verano 6. el treinta de mayo de mil ochocientos cuarenta y dos, primavera 7. el treinta y uno de enero de mil seiscientos sesenta, invierno 8. el cuatro de julio de mil setecientos setenta y seis, verano
Paso 2 1. el 12 de octubre 2. el 1° de enero 3. el 14 de febrero 4. el 4 de julio 5. el 1° de abril 6. el 25 de diciembre 7. ¿ ?

¿DÓNDE ESTÁ? LAS PREPOSICIONES: Conversación A *Paso 3* Brasilia es la capital del Brasil. Buenos Aires es la capital de la Argentina. Bogotá es la capital de Colombia. La Paz es la capital de Bolivia. Santiago es la capital de Chile. Asunción es la capital del Paraguay. Quito es la capital del Ecuador. Caracas es la capital de Venezuela. Montevideo es la capital del Uruguay. Lima es la capital del Perú.

GRAMMAR SECTION 15
Práctica B 1. ... está hablando con su tío Ricardo. 2. ... están tomando un café en la universidad. 3. ... está jugando con Ricardo. 4. ... están comiendo a las tres. 5. ... está leyendo el periódico con su tío. 6. ... no está escribiendo la tarea a las ocho. 7. ... están viendo un vídeo. 8. ... están bebiendo champán.
Práctica C: *Paso 1* 1. A 2. C 3. B 4. C 5. A 6. A 7. B 8. B 9. B 10. C
Paso 2 *Possible answers:* Dibujo A: Son las seis de la mañana. Los gemelos están durmiendo. El padre está duchándose. La hija está levantándose. La madre está leyendo el periódico. Dibujo B: Son las ocho de la mañana. Los gemelos están comiendo (tomando el desayuno). El padre está trabajando. La madre está vistiéndose. La hija está saliendo para la escuela. Dibujo C: Son las siete y media de la tarde. El padre está preparando la cena. Los gemelos están jugando con el perro. La hija está escribiendo cartas. La madre está quitándose la ropa después de trabajar.

GRAMMAR SECTION 16
Conversación a. 5 b. 9 c. 4 d. 1 e. 8 f. 6 g. 11 h. 3 i. 2 j. 10 k. 7
Práctica A 1. está 2. es 3. es 4. es 5. está 6. es 7. es 8. es 9. es 10. es
Práctica B 1. son 2. son 3. están 4. están 5. son 6. están 7. están
Práctica C 1. son 2. están 3. están 4. son 5. son 6. es 7. es 8. son
Comprensión 1. sí 2. no 3. no 4. no
Práctica D: *Paso 1* 1. mal tiempo 2. mal 3. sucio 4. nervioso 5. abierto 6. aburridos 7. triste 8. desordenada

GRAMMAR SECTION 17
Práctica C *Possible answers:* Alfredo tiene más cuartos que Gloria. Alfredo tiene más baños que Gloria. Alfredo tiene tantas alcobas como Gloria. Gloria tiene más camas que Alfredo. Alfredo tiene más coches que Gloria. Gloria tiene menos dinero en el banco que Alfredo.

UN POCO DE TODO
Ejercicio B 1. muchas 2. es 3. es 4. salgo 5. llevar 6. los 7. puede 8. a 9. cortos 10. durante 11. hace 12. nieva 13. gran 14. mucho 15. ese 16. toman 17. va 18. hacer 19. es 20. llevan
Comprensión 1. improbable 2. probable 3. improbable

CAPÍTULO 6
VOCABULARIO: PREPARACIÓN
LA COMIDA: Conversación A 1. una cena elegante 2. un desayuno estilo norteamericano 3. un menú ligero para una dieta 4. una comida rápida
Conversación B 1. la ensalada 2. el vino 3. la sopa 4. la zanahoria 5. el bistec 6. el arroz 7. la patata 9. la manzana 10. la banana
¿QUÉ SABE UD: Y A QUIÉN CONOCE? *SABER* AND *CONOCER*; **PERSONAL *A*: Conversación A: *Paso 1*** 1. Gloria Estefan sabe cantar en español. Mikhail Baryshnikov sabe bailar. José Canseco sabe jugar al béisbol. Lance Armstrong sabe montar en bicicleta. Michael Crichton sabe escribir novelas. Arantxa Sánchez Vicario sabe jugar al tenis. Julia Child sabe cocinar bien.
Paso 2 Adán conoce a Eva. Napoleón conoce a Josefina. Romeo conoce a Julieta. Rhett Butler conoce a Scarlett O'Hara. Marco Antonio conoce a Cleopatra. George Washington conoce a Martha.
Conversación 1. Sabes 2. sé 3. Conoces 4. sé 5. conoce 6. Sabes 7. sé 8. Sabes 9. sabe

GRAMMAR SECTION 18
Práctica A: *Paso 1* 1. Las va a comer. 2. Lo va a comer. 3. No las va a comer. 4. No los va a comer. 5. La va a comer. 6. La va a comer. 7. No los va a comer. 8. Lo va a comer. 9. Los va a comer. 10. La va a comer.
Práctica B 1. El camarero trae una botella de vino tinto y la pone en la mesa. 2. El camarero trae las copas de vino y las pone delante de Lola y Manolo. 3. Lola quiere la especialidad de la casa y la va a pedir (a pedirla). 4. Manolo prefiere el pescado fresco y lo pide. 5. Lola quiere una ensalada también y por eso la pide. 6. El camarero trae la comida y la sirve. 7. Manolo necesita otra servilleta y la pide. 8. «¿La cuenta? El dueño está preparándola (la está preparando) para Uds.» 9. Manolo quiere pagar con tarjeta de crédito pero no la trae. 10. Por fin Lola toma la cuenta y la paga.
Práctica C *Possible answers:* 1. el despertador 2. el camarero 3. el barbero 4. la doctora 5. los buenos amigos 6. los buenos amigos 7. Su padre, Su padre 8. los profesores, los estudiantes

Práctica D *Possible answers:* 1. Acabo de escribirlas. (Las acabo de escribir.) 2. Acabo de comprarlo. (Lo acabo de comprar.) 3. Acabo de pagarlos. (Los acabo de pagar.) 4. Acabo de prepararla. (La acabo de preparar.) 5. Acabo de pedirla. (La acabo de pedir.) 6. Acabo de comerlos. (Los acabo de comer.)

GRAMMAR SECTION 19
Práctica A 1. No hay nada interesante en el menú. 2. No tienen ningún plato típico. 3. El profesor no cena allí tampoco. 4. Mis amigos no almuerzan allí nunca. 5. No preparan nada especial para grupos grandes. 6. No hacen nunca platos nuevos. 7. Y no sirven paella, mi plato favorito, tampoco.
Práctica B: Paso 1 1. Pues, no hay ninguna clase interesante en el departamento. 2. No me gusta tomar café con mis estudiantes nunca. (Nunca me gusta tomar café con mis estudiantes.) 3. No hay ninguna persona buena en la administración. 4. No hay un / ningún candidato bueno para el puesto de director de la facultad tampoco. (Tampoco hay un candidato bueno para el puesto de director de la facultad.) 5. No hay ninguna persona inteligente en la universidad. 6. No me gustan las conferencias que están planeada para este mes.
Paso 2 1. ¿Hay algo interesante en la tele esta noche? 2. ¿Hay alguien cómico en el programa? 3. ¿Hay algunas películas buenas en el cine esta semana? 4. ¿Siempre comes en la facultad? 5. ¿Y almuerzas entre tus clases también?
Práctica C 1. falso 2. falso 3. cierto 4. cierto 5. cierto 6. falso 7. falso

GRAMMAR SECTION 20
Práctica A a. 3 b. 7 c. 4 d. 1 e. 8 f. 5 g. 2 h. 6
Práctica B 1. Lleguen a tiempo. 2. Lean la lección. 3. Escriban una composición. 4. Abran los libros. 5. Estén en clase mañana. 6. Traigan los libros a clase. 7. Estudien los verbos nuevos.
Práctica C: Paso 2 No trabaje tanto. No sea tan impaciente. No critique a los otros. No sea tan impulsivo. No fume tanto. No beba bebidas alcohólicas. No almuerce y no cene tan fuerte. Desayune. No salga tanto con los amigos. No vuelva a casa tarde.
Práctica D *Possible answers:* 1. No lo beba. 2. Cómalas. 3. No lo coma. 4. No los coma. 5. No la beba. 6. No las coma. 7. Cómalas. 8. Bébalos. 9. Cómalo. 10. No la coma. 11. No la coma. 12. Bébalo.
Práctica E 1. Despiértese más temprano. 2. Levántese más temprano. 3. Báñese más. 4. Quítese esa ropa sucia. 5. Póngase ropa limpia. 6. Vístase mejor. 7. Estudie más. 8. No se divierta tanto con los amigos. 9. Vaya más a la biblioteca. 10. No se acueste tan tarde. 11. Ayude con los quehaceres.

UN POCO DE TODO
Ejercicio A: Paso 1 1. Los martes Roberto nunca sale del apartamento antes de las doce. 2. Espera a su amigo Samuel en la parada del autobús. 3. Llegan a la universidad a la una. 4. Buscan a su amiga Ceci en la cafetería. 5. Ella acaba de empezar sus estudios allí. 6. No conoce a mucha gente todavía. 7. A veces, ven a la profesora de historia en la cafetería y hablan un poco con ella. 8. Es una persona muy interesante que sabe mucho de esa materia. 9. A las dos todos tienen clase de sicología. 10. Siempre oyen conferencias interesantes y hacen algunas preguntas. 11. A veces tienen oportunidad de conocer a los conferenciantes. 12. A las cinco, Samuel y Roberto vuelven a esperar el autobús. 13. Roberto prepara la cena y luego mira la televisión.
Paso 2 1. Ceci 2. el profesor de la clase de sicología 3. Samuel 4. Roberto
Paso 3 1. Los martes yo nunca salgo del apartamento antes de las doce. 2. Espero a mi amigo Samuel en la parada del autobús. 3. Llegamos a la universidad a la una. 4. Buscamos a nuestra amiga Ceci en la cafetería. 5. Ella acaba de empezar sus estudios allí. 6. No conoce a mucha gente todavía. 7. A veces, vemos a la profesora de historia en la cafetería y hablamos un poco con ella. 8. Es una persona muy interesante que sabe mucho de esa materia. 9. A las dos todos tenemos clase de sicología. 10. Siempre oímos conferencias interesantes y hacemos algunas preguntas. 11. A veces tenemos oportunidad de conocer a los conferenciantes. 12. A las cinco, Samuel y yo volvemos a esperar el autobús. 13. Preparo la cena y luego miro la televisión.
Ejercicio B 1. vive 2. norteamericanos 3. extraña 4. por 5. desayuna 6. fría 7. prepara 8. almuerza 9. come 10. las 11. la 12. come 13. una 14. está 15. es 16. Desayuna 17. prepara 18. unas 19. es 20. come
Comprensión 1. improbable 2. improbable 3. probable 4. probable

CAPÍTULO 7
VOCABULARIO: PREPARACIÓN
¡BUEN VIAJE! Conversación A a. 8 b. 5 c. 3 d. 2 e. 7 f. 1 g. 9 h. 4 i. 6
Conversación B 1. a 2. a 3. c 4. b

Conversación E 1. en el aeropuerto 2. en casa 3. en la agencia de viajes 4. en la agencia de viajes 5. en el aeropuerto 6. en el avión 7. en el avión 8. en la playa
Conversación F 1. falso; Se habla portugués en el Brasil. 2. cierto 3. cierto 4. cierto 5. falso; La paella se prepara con arroz, mariscos y pollo. 6. cierto 7. cierto 8. cierto

GRAMMAR SECTION 21
Práctica A: Paso 1 1. Les llamo un taxi. 2. Les bajo las maletas. 3. Les guardo el equipaje. 4. Les facturo el equipaje. 5. Les guardo el puesto en la cola. 6. Les guardo el asiento en la sala de espera. 7. Les compro una revista. 8. Por fin les digo adiós.
Paso 2 1. Le llamo un taxi. 2. Le bajo las maletas. 3. Le guardo el equipaje. 4. Le facturo el equipaje. 5. Le guardo el puesto en la cola. 6. Le guardo el asiento en la sala de espera. 7. Le compro una revista. 8. Por fin le digo adiós.
Paso 3 1. Te llamo un taxi. 2. Te bajo las maletas. 3. Te guardo el equipaje. 4. Te facturo el equipaje. 5. Te guardo el puesto en la cola. 6. Te guardo el asiento en la sala de espera. 7. Te compro una revista. 8. Por fin te digo adiós.
Práctica B 1. le da 2. le da 3. le da 4. les da 5. les prestan 6. les ofrecen 7. le dice
Práctica C *Possible answers:* 1. Todos le mandan flores. Le escriben cartas. Las enfermeras le dan medicinas. De comer, le sirven sopa. 2. Les prometen a sus padres ser buenos. Les piden muchos regalos. También le escriben cartas a Santa Claus. Le piden muchos regalos. Los padres les mandan tarjetas navideñas a sus amigos. Les regalan flores y frutas. 3. Un asistente de vuelo nos sirve bebidas. Otra asistente de vuelo nos ofrece comida. El piloto nos dice que todo está bien. 4. Mi amigo me presta su coche. Mis padres me preguntan si necesito un coche nuevo. Luego me dan dinero. 5. Todos le preguntan al profesor qué debemos estudiar. El profesor les explica a los estudiantes la materia difícil.
Práctica D 1. te 2. le 3. le 4. le 5. te 6. le 7. le 8. le

GRAMMAR SECTION 22
Práctica A 1. (No) Me gusta el vino. 2. (No) Me gustan los niños pequeños. 3. (No) Me gusta la música clásica. 4. (No) Me gusta Ricky Martin. 5. (No) Me gusta el invierno. 6. (No) Me gusta hacer cola. 7. (No) Me gusta el chocolate. 8. (No) Me gustan las películas de terror. 9. (No) Me gustan las clases que empiezan a las ocho de la mañana. 10. (No) Me gusta cocinar. 11. (No) Me gusta la gramática. 12. (No) Me gustan las clases de este semestre / trimestre. 13. (No) Me gustan los vuelos con muchas escalas. 14. (No) Me gusta bailar en las discotecas.
Práctica B: Paso 1 1. A mi padre le gusta el océano. Le gustaría ir a la playa. 2. A mis hermanos pequeños les gusta nadar también. Les gustaría ir a la playa. 3. A mi hermano Ernesto le gusta hacer *camping*. Le gustaría ir a las montañas. 4. A mis abuelos les gusta descansar. Les gustaría quedarse en casa. 5. A mi madre le gusta la tranquilidad. Le gustaría visitar un pueblecito en la costa. 6. A mi hermana Elena le gustan las discotecas. Le gustaría pasar las vacaciones en una ciudad grande. 7. A mí me gusta(n)… me gustaría…
Paso 2 1. A Elena. 2. Al padre y a los hermanos pequeños. 3. Los abuelos. 4. A la madre. 5. Ernesto.

GRAMMAR SECTION 23
Práctica B: Paso 1 TERESA Y EVANGELINA 1. Salimos del apartamento a las nueve. 2. Llegamos a la biblioteca a las diez. 3. Estudiamos toda la mañana para el examen. 4. Escribimos muchos ejercicios. 5. Almorzamos con amigos en la cafetería. 6. Fuimos al laboratorio a la una. 7. Hicimos todos los experimentos del manual. 8. Tomamos el examen a las cuatro. 9. ¡El examen fue horrible! 10. Regresamos a casa después del examen. 11. Ayudamos a Liliana a preparar la cena. 12. Cenamos todas juntas a las siete. LILIANA: 1. Yo me quedé en casa todo el día. 2. Vi la televisión por la mañana. 3. Llamé a mis padres a las once. 4. Tomé café con los vecinos. 5. Estudié para el examen de historia y escribí una composición para la clase de sociología. 6. Fui al garaje para dejar unos muebles viejos allí. 7. Fui al supermercado y compré comida. 8. Empecé a preparar la cena a las cinco.
Paso 2 1. Liliana 2. Evangelina 3. Evangelina 4. Liliana 5. Liliana
Paso 3 1. Liliana se quedó en casa todo el día. 2. Vio la televisión por la mañana. 3. Llamó a sus padres a las once. 4. Tomó café con los vecinos. 5. Estudió para el examen de historia y escribió una composición para la clase de sociología. 6. Fue al garaje para dejar unos muebles viejos allí. 7. Fue al supermercado y compró comida. 8. Empezó a preparar la cena a las cinco. 1. Teresa y Evangelina salieron del apartamento a las nueve. 2. Llegaron a la biblioteca a las diez. 3. Estudiaron toda la mañana para el examen. 4. Escribieron muchos ejercicios. 5. Almorzaron con amigos en la cafetería. 6. Fueron al laboratorio a la una. 7. Hicieron todos los experi-

mentos del manual. 8. Tomaron el examen a las cuatro. 9. ¡El examen fue horrible! 10. Regresaron a casa después del examen. 11. Me ayudaron a preparar la cena. 12. Cenamos todas juntas a las siete.

Práctica C 1. Pasé un semestre en México. 2. Mis padres me pagaron el vuelo… 3. … pero trabajé para ganar el dinero para la matrícula y los otros gastos. 4. Viví con una familia mexicana encantadora. 5. Aprendí mucho sobre la vida y la cultura mexicanas. 6. Visité muchos sitios de interés turístico e histórico. 7. Mis amigos me escribieron muchas cartas. 8. Les mandé muchas tarjetas postales. 9. Les compré muchos recuerdos a todos. 10. Volví a los Estados Unidos al final de agosto.

Conversación A a. 8 b. 12 c. 1 d. 11 e. 7 f. 2 g. 10 h. 5 i. 4 j. 9 k. 6 l. 3

Possible answers: Julián volvió a casa después de trabajar. Llamó a un amigo y decidieron encontrarse en el cine. Luego se duchó y se afeitó, y después comió rápidamente. Fue al cine en autobús. Los dos amigos llegaron al cine al mismo tiempo. Hicieron cola para comprar las entradas y entraron en el cine. No les gustó nada la película. Después fueron a un café a tomar algo. Finalmente Julián regresó a casa tarde.

UN POCO DE TODO

Ejercicio B 1. Les 2. algo 3. la 4. la 5. conocen 6. Está 7. la 8. es 9. más 10. incaicos 11. visitarla 12. Les 13. es 14. ir 15. mejores 16. comprar 17. muchos 18. países 19. Sé 20. les

Comprensión 1. falso 2. cierto 3. cierto 4. falso

CAPÍTULO 8

VOCABULARIO: PREPARACIÓN

LOS DÍAS FESTIVOS Y LAS FIESTAS: Conversación A 1. la Navidad 2. una sorpresa 3. los refrescos y los entremeses 4. el Día de los Muertos 5. la quinceañera 6. el día de San Patricio 7. la Nochevieja 8. ¡Felicitaciones!

EMOCIONES Y CONDICIONES: Conversación A *Possible answers:* 1. Me pongo felicísimo/a (contentísimo/a). Le doy las gracias. 2. Me pongo tristísimo/a (furiosísimo/a). Lloro. 3. Me pongo nerviosísimo/a. Les ofrezco más refrescos y entremeses. Cambio la música. 4. Me pongo muy nervioso/a y avergonzado/a. 5. Me pongo muy contento/a (triste). Me río. (Lloro.) 6. Me pongo muy triste.

GRAMMAR SECTION 24

Práctica B 1. Todos estuvimos en casa de los abuelos antes de las nueve. 2. Pusimos muchos regalos debajo del árbol. 3. Mis tíos y mis primos vinieron con comida y bebidas. 4. Yo tuve que ayudar a preparar la comida. 5. Hubo una cena especial para todos. 6. Más tarde algunos de mis amigos vinieron a cantar villancicos. 7. Los niños fueron a la alcoba a las diez y se acostaron. 8. Los niños quisieron dormir pero no pudieron. 9. A medianoche todos dijimos «¡Feliz Navidad!». 10. Al día siguiente todos dijimos que la fiesta estuvo estupenda.

Paso 2 1. falso (Hubo mucha gente.) 2. falso (También vinieron amigos a cantar villancicos.) 3. cierto 4. falso (Los niños no abrieron sus regalos por la noche.)

Práctica C En 1957 los rusos pusieron un satélite en el espacio por primera vez. En 1969 los estadounidenses pusieron a un hombre en la Luna. Adán y Eva supieron el significado de un árbol especial. George Washington estuvo en Valley Forge con sus soldados. Los europeos trajeron el caballo al Nuevo Mundo. Los aztecas conocieron a Hernán Cortés en Tenochtitlán. Stanley conoció a Livingston en África. María Antonieta dijo: «Que coman pasteles».

GRAMMAR SECTION 25

Práctica B 1. se sentó, vino, pidió, recordó, pidió, sirvió, quiso, dijo, pedí, contestó 2. se acostó, se durmió, Durmió, se despertó, Se vistió, salió, vio, sonrieron. 3. me vestí, fui, me divertí, volví, decidió, vio, se divirtió, Perdió, sintió

Práctica C *Possible answers:* La Bella Durmiente durmió hasta que el príncipe la besó. El lobo consiguió entrar en la chimenea de los Tres Cochinitos (se vistió de abuela). Rip van Winkle durmió muchos años. Romeo murió por el amor de Julieta. La Cenicienta se divirtió en un baile (perdió un zapato). El Príncipe encontró a la mujer misteriosa. Las hermanastras de la Cenicienta sintieron envidia de su hermanastra.

GRAMMAR SECTION 26

Práctica A 1. el televisor 2. la sal 3. los discos compactos de Luis Miguel 4. unas fotos 5. unos billetes de avión para Guadalajara 6. la fiesta

Práctica B 1. ¿Hay más pan? ¿Me lo pasas, por favor? 2. ¿Hay más tortillas? ¿Me las pasas, por favor? 3. ¿Hay más tomates? ¿Me los pasas, por favor? 4. ¿Hay más fruta? ¿Me la pasas, por favor? 5. ¿Hay más vino? ¿Me lo pasas, por favor? 6. ¿Hay más jamón? ¿Me lo pasas, por favor?

Práctica C 1. Acaban de decírnosla. (Nos la acaban de decir.) 2. Léemelo, por favor. 3. No, no tiene que dárselos (se los tiene que dar) aquí. 4. Claro

que se lo guardo. 5. Acabo de comprártelo. (Te lo acabo de comprar.) 6. Te lo puedo guardar. (Puedo guardártelo.) 7. Sí, se lo recomiendo. 8. La asistente de vuelo nos la va a servir (va a servírnosla) en el avión.

UN POCO DE TODO

Ejercicio A 1. algunos 2. varios 3. son 4. de 5. conmemora 6. Muchos 7. esta 8. apareció 9. a 10. en 11. de 12. dejó 13. ver 14. todas 15. son 16. el 17. es 18. el 19. el 20. de la 21. Llegan 22. otros 23. pasarlo 24. corren 25. la 26. a 27. Algunas 28. corren 29. hay 30. esta 31. es 32. la 33. describió 34. su 35. es 36. hablar 37. conocieron

Comprensión 1. falso (No todas las fiestas hispánicas son religiosas.) 2. falso (Algunos mexicoamericanos también celebran esa fiesta.) 3. falso (La fiesta de San Fermín es esencialmente para los adultos.) 4. cierto

Ejercicio B: Paso 1 *Possible answers:* Ayer por la mañana Antonio se despertó a las ocho y se levantó en seguida. Se duchó, se afeitó, se peinó y desayunó: sólo tomó (tomó sólo) un café con leche. Entonces fue a la universidad; asistió a clases toda la mañana. Por la tarde almorzó con unos amigos en la cafetería estudiantil. Se divirtió hablando con ellos. Después se despidió de ellos y fue a la biblioteca. Se quedó allí estudiando hasta las 4:30 y después volvió a casa a las ocho. Entonces ayudó a Diego a preparar la cena. Por la noche cenó con Diego y Lupe. Entonces quiso estudiar por una hora pero no pudo. Miró la televisión con sus amigos. Después les dijo buenas noches y salió a reunirse con otros amigos en un bar. Volvió a casa a las dos. Se quitó la ropa y se acostó. Leyó por cinco minutos para poder dormirse y se durmió.

CAPÍTULO 9

VOCABULARIO: PREPARACIÓN

PASATIEMPOS, DIVERSIONES Y AFICIONES: Conversación A *Possible answers:* 1. visita museos 2. hacen (dan) fiestas 3. hace *camping*

TRABAJANDO EN CASA: Conversación A *Possible answers:* 1. la alcoba 2. la cocina, el garaje (el patio) 3. la sala 4. el baño, el patio (el garaje) 5. la cocina 6. la sala (el comedor, las alcobas) 7. la cocina, la cocina 8. la cocina

Conversación C 1. Se usa para limpiar las ventanas. 2. Se usa para hacer café. 3. Se usa para sacudir los muebles. 4. Se usa para poner (sacar) la basura. 5. Se usa para lavar los platos. 6. Se usa para el lavaplatos. 7. Se usa para lavar la ropa. 8. Se usa para limpiar el cuarto de baño.

GRAMMAR SECTION 27

Práctica B 1. Todos los días asistía a la escuela primaria. 2. Por la mañana aprendía a leer y escribía en la pizarra. 3. A las diez bebía leche y dormía un poco. 4. Iba a casa para almorzar y regresaba a la escuela. 5. Estudiaba geografía y hacía dibujos. 6. Jugaba con sus compañeros en el patio de la escuela. 7. Camino de casa compraba dulces y se los comía. 8. Frecuentemente pasaba por la casa de los abuelos. 9. Cenaba con sus padres y los ayudaba a lavar los platos. 10. Miraba la tele un rato y se acostaba a las ocho.

Práctica C: Paso 1 *Possible answers:* El bebé estaba llorando. El perro y el gato estaban peleando. Un niño pequeño estaba peleando con su hermana pequeña. El teléfono estaba sonando. Un vendedor estaba llamando a la puerta. Unos jóvenes adolescentes estaban discutiendo. El radio estaba sonando muy fuerte. El televisor estaba funcionando también.

GRAMMAR SECTION 28

Práctica B 1. _____ es el día festivo más divertido del año. 2. _____ es la clase más interesante de todas mis clases. 3. _____ es la persona más inteligente de todos mis amigos. 4. Nueva York es la ciudad más grande de los Estados Unidos. 5. Rhode Island es el estado más pequeño de los Estados Unidos. 6. _____ es el metro más rápido del mundo, creo. 7. _____ es la residencia más ruidosa de la universidad. 8. Everest es la montaña más alta del mundo.

GRAMMAR SECTION 29

Práctica A 1. Qué 2. Qué 3. Cuál 4. Cuál 5. Cuáles 6. Qué 7. Qué 8. Cuál

Práctica B *Possible answers:* 1. ¿Cuál es tu teléfono? 2. ¿Cuál es tu dirección? 3. ¿Cuándo es tu cumpleaños? 4. ¿En qué ciudad naciste? ¿Dónde naciste? 5. ¿Cuál es tu número de seguro social? 6. ¿Quién es la persona en que más confías? ¿Cuál es la persona en que más confías? 7. ¿Cuál es tu tienda favorita para ir de compras? ¿Dónde prefieres ir de compras? 8. ¿Cuál es la fecha de tu próximo examen? ¿Cuándo es tu próximo examen?

UN POCO DE TODO

Ejercicio A: Paso 1 1. Primero, Ricardo se despertó temprano, pero se quedó en cama mucho tiempo. 2. Luego se duchó y se vistió rápidamente. 3. Llegó tarde a su primera clase. 4. Almorzó en la cafetería con algunos amigos. 5. Después fue al gimnasio y jugó un partido de basquetbol. 6. Regresó a casa. Luego preparó la cena y estudió un poco. 7. Después miró la televisión un rato hasta que sonó el teléfono. 8. Finalmente se acostó.

Paso 2 1. Eran las seis y media de la mañana. 2. Ricardo tenía prisa. 3. Los estudiantes escuchaban a la profesora. 4. Ricardo tenía mucha hambre. 5. Había muchas personas en el gimnasio. 6. Era temprano todavía. 7. No quería hablar por teléfono. 8. Ricardo pensaba en el examen de mañana.
Ejercicio B 1. los 2. esperan 3. al 4. pueden 5. Otras 6. que 7. dormir 8. durmieron 9. quieren 10. nada 11. hicieron 12. hay 13. estamos 14. esas 15. trabajan 16. les 17. gusta 18. se aburren 19. gusta 20. prefería

CAPÍTULO 10
VOCABULARIO: PREPARACIÓN
LA SALUD Y EL BIENESTAR: Conversación A: Paso 1 *Possible answers:* 1. el corazón 2. la boca; los dientes; el estómago 3. la boca; la garganta 4. los ojos 5. el cerebro; la cabeza 6. el estómago 7. el corazón 8. los pulmones; la boca 9. los oídos; las orejas 10. la nariz
Paso 2 *Possible answers:* 1. ver; mirar; leer 2. comer; la boca 3. comer; hablar; los dientes 4. oír; escuchar; la oreja 5. comer; tener hambre; la digestión
Conversación B *Possible answers:* 1. Eso quiere decir que es necesario dormir ocho horas todas las noches. 2. Eso quiere decir que es necesario hacer media hora de ejercicio todos los días. 3. Eso quiere decir que no se debe ir a fiestas todas las noches y dormir poco. 4. Eso quiere decir que es necesario comer bien, dormir lo suficiente y hacer ejercicio diariamente.
EN EL CONSULTORIO: Conversación A 1. un resfriado 2. respira 3. enfermo, enfermero/a 4. tos 5. dolor
Conversación B *Possible answers:* 1. Anamari está muy bien de salud. Nunca le duele la cabeza (le duelen los pies). Nunca tiene fiebre. Siempre hace ejercicio. 2. Martín tiene un dolor de muela. Debe tomar una aspirina. El dentista va a examinarlo. Después, Martín va a guardar cama. 3. A Inés le duele el estómago. Tiene apendicitis. El médico y la enfermera van a examinarla. Luego, Inés tiene que tener una operación.
GRAMMAR SECTION 30
Práctica A 1. c 2. f 3. g 4. e 5. a 6. b 7. d
Práctica B 1. vivíamos 2. íbamos 3. nos quedábamos 4. nuestra familia decidió 5. nos gustó 6. nos quedamos 1. se apagaron 2. estaba leyendo 3. me levanté 4. tenía 5. Salí 6. estaban apagadas 7. había 1. intentaba tomarle 2. esperaba 3. llegó 4. examinó 5. puso 6. dio 7. estaba 8. se sintió
Práctica C: Paso 1 1. estaba 2. entró 3. preguntó 4. quería 5. dijo 6. sentía 7. salieron 8. Vieron 9. se rieron 10. hacía 11. entraron 12. tomaron 13. Eran 14. regresaron 15. se acostó 16. estaba 17. empezó
Paso 2 1. Estudiaba. 2. Le preguntó si quería ir al cine con ella. 3. Porque se sentía un poco aburrido. 4. Sí, porque se rieron mucho. 5. Porque hacía frío. 6. No regresaron a casa a las dos. 7. Soledad se acostó, pero Rubén, empezó a estudiar otra vez.
Práctica D 1. conocí 2. hicimos 3. era 4. organizaba 5. venían 6. Había 7. hablaba 8. bailaba 9. llamaron 10. dijeron 11. hacíamos 12. Vino 13. dijo 14. era 15. queríamos 16. podíamos 17. despedimos 18. eran 19. aprendió 20. hace 21. invita
Conversación C: Paso 1 abrió; entró; vio; se sentó; gustó; se sentó; vio; decidió; fue; se acostó; se quedó
GRAMMAR SECTION 31
Práctica A 1. que 2. quien 3. Lo que 4. que 5. que 6. lo que 7. quién 8. lo que 9. lo que
Práctica B: Paso 1 1. algo contra su cansancio, intranquilidad, preocupación, nerviosismo, desequilibrio y ansiedad 2. estrés 3. la normalidad
UN POCO DE TODO
Ejercicio A: Paso 1 1. Cuando yo era niño, pensaba que lo mejor de estar enfermo era guardar cama. 2. Lo peor era que con frecuencia yo me resfriaba durante las vacaciones. 3. Una vez yo me puse muy enfermo durante la Navidad. 4. Mi madre llamó al médico con quien tenía confianza. 5. El Dr. Matamoros vino a casa y me dio un antibiótico porque tenía mucha fiebre. 6. Eran las cuatro de la mañana cuando por fin yo empecé a respirar sin dificultad. 7. Desgraciadamente, el día de Navidad yo tuve que tomar jarabe y no me gustaba nada el sabor. 8. Lo bueno de esta enfermedad era que mi padre tuvo que dejar de fumar mientras yo estaba (estuve) enfermo.
Paso 2 1. Cuando mi hijo era niño, pensaba que lo mejor de estar enfermo era guardar cama. 2. Lo peor era que con frecuencia se resfriaba durante las vacaciones. 3. Una vez se puso muy enfermo durante la Navidad. 4. Llamé al médico con quien tenía confianza. 5. El Dr. Matamoros vino a casa y le dio un antibiótico porque tenía mucha fiebre. 6. Eran las cuatro de la mañana cuando por fin mi hijo empezó a respirar sin dificultad. 7. Desgraciadamente, el día de Navidad tuvo que tomar jarabe y no le gus-

taba nada el sabor. 8. Lo bueno de esta enfermedad era que mi esposo tuvo que dejar de fumar mientras mi hijo estaba (estuvo) enfermo.
Ejercicio B 1. teníamos 2. nuestra 3. tuvo 4. tenía 5. Por 6. fuimos 7. salimos 8. que 9. corrimos 10. tomó 11. examinando 12. caminábamos 13. tan 14. vimos 15. Nos caímos 16. fue (era) 17. Nos levantamos 18. dejamos 19. sus 20. decidimos 21. cojeaba 22. fuimos 23. dolía 24. había 25. Tenía 26. dieron 27. recomendaron 28. nos acordamos 29. lo pasamos 30. vinieron
Comprensión B 1. los abuelos 2. los dueños del perro. 3. el médico 4. la mamá y las hijas 5. las hijas
Ejercicio C: Paso 1 1. se llamaba 2. eran 3. quería 4. dijo 5. salió 6. preguntó 7. contestó 8. dijo 9. se fue 10. llegó 11. entró 12. tenía 13. Saltó 14. corrió 15. llegó 16. Encontró 17. estaba 18. dijo 19. dijo 20. se enteró 21. avisó 22. saltó 23. se abalanzó 24. salió 25. vio 26. ocurría 27. Le disparó 28. hizo 29. regresó 30. abrazó 31. prometió

CAPÍTULO 11
VOCABULARIO: PREPARACIÓN
LAS PRESIONES DE LA VIDA ESTUDIANTIL: Conversación B 1. b 2. a 3. d 4. e 5. c
¡LA PROFESORA MARTÍNEZ SE LEVANTÓ CON EL PIE IZQUIERDO!: Conversación A *Possible answers:* 1. Tomo una aspirina. 2. Digo «fue sin querer». 3. Me pongo avergonzado/a. 4. Me doy con una silla y me caigo. 5. Me duele.
MORE ON ADVERBS: Conversación D 1. pacientemente 2. inmediatamente 3. fácilmente 4. totalmente 5. constantemente 6. puntualmente
GRAMMAR SECTION 33
Práctica: Paso 1 Hace mucho tiempo que Gloria Estefan canta en español. Hace mucho tiempo que Sammy Sosa juega al béisbol. Hace mucho tiempo que Antonio Banderas trabaja en Hollywood. Hace poco tiempo que los «Teletubbies» hacen programas para niños en la televisión. Hace mucho tiempo que John Grisham escribe novelas. Hace mucho/poco tiempo que el rector / la rectora trabaja (vive) en esta universidad. Hace mucho tiempo que el profesor / la profesora de español habla español (trabaja [vive] en esta universidad). Hace mucho/poco tiempo que un compañero / una compañera de clase vive en esta ciudad (habla español).
Paso 2 1. Hace más de quinientos años que Cristóbal Colón llegó a América. 2. Hace unos cincuenta años que la Segunda Guerra Mundial terminó. 3. Hace casi veinte años que John Lennon se murió. 4. Hace casi cuatro años que el presidente actual fue elegido. 5. Hace _____ años (meses) que el profesor (la profesora) de español enseñó en esta universidad.
Conversación: Paso 1 *Possible answers:* 1. ¿Cuánto tiempo hace que vives en este estado? 2. ¿Cuánto tiempo hace que asistes a esta universidad? 3. ¿Cuánto tiempo hace que vives en tu casa (apartamento, residencia, …)? 4. ¿Cuánto tiempo hace que estudias español?
Paso 2 *Possible answers:* 1. ¿Cuánto tiempo hace que visitaste a tus padres (abuelos, hijos, …)? 2. ¿Cuánto tiempo hace que conociste a tu mejor amigo/a? 3. ¿Cuánto tiempo hace que aprendiste a manejar? 4. ¿Cuánto tiempo hace que entregaste tu última tarea?
GRAMMAR SECTION 34
Práctica A 1. d 2. c 3. e 4. g 5. a 6. b 7. f
Conversación: Paso 2 *Possible answers:* 2. ¿Por qué salió descalzo de su casa? —Porque se le olvidó ponerse los zapatos. 3. ¿Por qué no pudo abrir la puerta del coche? —Porque se le quedó la llave del coche en casa. 4. ¿Por qué no pudo pagar el autobús? —Porque se le olvidó la cartera. 5. ¿Por qué trató descortésmente a su jefa? —Porque no la saludó. 6. ¿Por qué no tenía toda la información? —Porque se le perdieron los papeles. 7. ¿Por qué tenía hambre a las diez de la mañana? —Porque se le olvidó desayunar en casa. 8. ¿Por qué dijo el vicepresidente que su chaqueta estaba arruinada? —Porque a Pablo se le cayó el café.
GRAMMAR SECTION 35
Práctica A 1. g 2. h 3. e 4. c 5. f 6. d 7. b 8. a
Práctica B 1. para, por, por, por, para 2. para, por, para, por 3. Por, por, por 4. para, Para 5. para, para, para, para, para
UN POCO DE TODO
Ejercicio A: Paso 1 1. Anoche la Sra. Ortega puso trajes de baño y toallas en su bolsa. 2. Cuando era pequeña, Cecilia se acostaba tarde todas las noches. 3. Esta mañana a Lorenzo se le perdieron las llaves y se le cayó la taza de café. 4. Esta noche los estudiantes de la clase de historia no van a dormir mucho. 5. Ahora Amalia está contenta.
Paso 2 1. Anoche la Sra. Ortega puso trajes de baño y toallas en su bolsa porque su familia empieza la clase de natación hoy. 2. Cuando era pequeña, Cecilia se acostaba tarde todas las noches porque veía la tele hasta muy tarde todas las noches. 3. Esta mañana a Lorenzo se le perdieron las llaves y se le cayó la taza de café porque estaba distraído. 4. Esta noche los

estudiantes de la clase de historia no van a dormir mucho porque tienen un examen final mañana. 5. Ahora Amalia está contenta porque hay una fiesta grande en casa de la profesora.

Ejercicio B 1. nuestra 2. disfruta 3. anteriores 4. Por 5. está 6. tenemos 7. muy 8. eran 9. para 10. estar 11. que 12. es 13. Para 14. esto 15. todas 16. deben 17. para 18. sufren 19. ponerse 20. esta 21. sentarnos 22. establecer 23. para

Comprensión 1. más 2. Es posible 3. más

CAPÍTULO 12

VOCABULARIO: PREPARACIÓN

TENGO... NECESITO... QUIERO... : Conversación A: Paso 1 1. Le mando el documento por *fax*. 2. Lo grabo con la videocasetera. 3. Uso el control remoto. 4. Uso el contestador automático. 5. Escucho el *walkman*. **Conversación B: Paso 1** 1. Debe comprarse una motocicleta. 2. Debe comprarse un coche descapotable. 3. Debe comprarse una camioneta. 4. Debe comprarse una bicicleta. 5. Debe comprarse un monopatín. 6. Debe comprarse un carro nuevo.

LA VIVIENDA: Conversación B 1. Es una persona que paga dinero para vivir en un apartamento o una casa. 2. Es un lugar donde hay muchos edificios y tiendas. 3. Es el dinero que se paga cada mes. Los inquilinos tienen que pagarles el alquiler a los dueños. 4. Es una persona que trabaja en una casa de apartamentos. 5. Es una persona que vive cerca en la vecindad, la residencia o la casa de apartamentos. 6. Es una persona que tiene un apartamento o una casa (de apartamentos) que se alquila. 7. Es una cosa que indica dónde vive alguien. 8. Es el área que está fuera de una ciudad.

GRAMMAR SECTION 36

Práctica B: *Paso 1* 1. No los dejes allí, por favor. 2. No regreses a casa tan tarde, por favor. 3. No vayas al parque todas las tardes, por favor. 4. No mires la televisión constantemente y no veas programas de detectives, por favor. 5. No le digas mentiras, por favor. 6. No te olvides de sacar la basura, por favor. 7. No seas tan insolente, por favor.

Paso 2 1. Llega a la escuela puntualmente. 2. Quítate el abrigo y siéntate. 3. Saca el libro de matemáticas y ábrelo en la página diez. 4. Lee las nuevas palabras y apréndelas para mañana. 5. Ven aquí a hablar conmigo sobre esta composición.

GRAMMAR SECTION 37

Práctica B *Possible answers:* 1. b (a) 2. a (b) 3. f (b) 4. c (i) 5. h 6. g (e, d)

GRAMMAR SECTION 38

Práctica A 1. su amigo 2. Ud. 3. su amigo 4. el vendedor 5. Ud. 6. Ud. 7. el vendedor

Práctica B: *Paso 1* 1. Todos los profesores quieren que los estudiantes lleguen a clase a tiempo. 2. El/La profesor(a) de español prefiere que vayamos con frecuencia al laboratorio de lenguas. 3. Los profesores prohíben que los estudiantes traigan comida y bebida a clase. 4. Los padres de los estudiantes desean que sus hijos asistan a sus clases. 5. Los estudiantes piden que los profesores no den mucho trabajo. 6. También quieren que haya más vacaciones. 7. Los padres insisten en que sus hijos saquen buenas notas.

Práctica C *Possible answers:* 1. Queremos que el nuevo televisor esté en la sala. Nos gusta ver la tele todos juntos. 2. Preferimos que el televisor portátil esté en la cocina. A mamá le gusta ver la tele al cocinar. 3. Es necesario que el equipo estereofónico esté en la alcoba de Julio. A él le gusta escuchar música al estudiar. 4. Es buena idea que el sillón grande esté en la sala. A papá le gusta leer el periódico allí. 5. Queremos que los monopatines de los niños estén en el patio. A ellos les gusta jugar allí. 6. Es buena idea que la computadora esté en la oficina. Nos gusta hacer las cuentas allí. 7. Queremos que el acuario esté en la alcoba de Anita. A ella le gusta mirar los peces.

UN POCO DE TODO

Ejercicio A: *Paso 1* 1. Escúchame 2. hagas 3. Juega 4. Canta 5. se lo des 6. los pongas

Ejercicio B 1. haya 2. mi 3. esté 4. haya 5. sufran 6. mí 7. pido 8. sé 9. más 10. pequeños 11. un 12. comprar 13. — 14. dejó 15. dé 16. muchísimas 17. gano 18. El 19. cubre 20. del 21. el 22. muy 23. gusta 24. comprar 25. en 26. comprar 27. un 28. lleve 29. fue 30. gustó 31. una 32. a 33. sea 34. querer

Comprensión 1. falso 2. cierto 3. cierto 4. falso 5. falso

CAPÍTULO 13

VOCABULARIO: PREPARACIÓN

LAS ARTES: Conversación A: Paso 1 1. la arquitectura 2. la pintura 3. la escultura 4. el ballet (el baile / la danza) 5. el cine 6. la ópera 7. las ruinas (la arquitectura) 8. la literatura

GRAMMAR SECTION 39

Práctica B 1. funcione, sea, la entienda 2. nos dé, tenga, cambie 3. tenga, sean, pueda

Práctica C 1. Ojalá que el escenario sea extravagante. 2. Ojalá que haya subtítulos en inglés. 3. Ojalá que el conductor esté preparado. 4. Ojalá que los cantantes sepan sus papeles. 5. Ojalá que nuestros asientos no estén lejos del escenario. 6. Ojalá que lleguemos a tiempo.

GRAMMAR SECTION 40

Práctica B 1. Creo que es una figura de la civilización maya. 2. Es cierto que la figura está hecha de oro. 3. Es posible que represente un dios importante. 4. No estoy seguro/a de que la figura se sienta feliz o enojada. 5. No creo que sea una figura de la civilización maya. 6. Creo que es de la civilización tolteca. 7. Estoy seguro/a de que está hecha de bronce. 8. Creo que representa una víctima de sacrificio humano.

GRAMMAR SECTION 41

Práctica A: *Paso 1* 1. ... me enseñe los cuadros más famosos de Velázquez. 2. ... me explique algunos detalles de los cuadros. 3. ... sepa mucho sobre la vida del pintor.

Paso 2 1. ... muestren la vida cotidiana. 2. ... estén en otros museos fuera de España. 3. ... sean de la familia real de Carlos IV.

Paso 3 1. ... me recomiende algunos libros sobre la vida y el arte del pintor. 2. ... le pregunte a un(a) colega si sabe algo más sobre Velázquez. 3. ... no tenga más tiempo para hablar conmigo.

Práctica B *Possible answers:* Le voy a decir que / Le voy a pedir que ... me escriba el informe para la clase de literatura: me haga una crítica de una película para la clase de composición avanzada; ponga la mesa; asista a todas mis clases en la universidad; pague mis cuentas; trabaje por mí en la oficina todas las tardes.

UN POCO DE TODO

Ejercicio B 1. Pasen 2. dejen 3. delante 4. Es 5. representa 6. pintó 7. de la 8. durante 9. estuvo 10. se trasladó 11. este 12. sea 13. es 14. creo 15. tengan 16. ser 17. sirve 18. Por 19. puede

Comprensión 1. Ud. 2. el guía 3. su amigo 4. el guía

CAPÍTULO 14

VOCABULARIO: PREPARACIÓN

EL MEDIO AMBIENTE: Conversación C *Possible answers:* 1. el campo 2. el campo 3. la ciudad 4. la ciudad 5. la ciudad 6. el campo 7. el campo 8. la ciudad

Conversación D *Possible answers:* 1. Es un lugar donde se hacen cosas. 2. Es una persona que trabaja en el campo. 3. Es un acto ilegal. 4. Es un lugar donde hay muchos animales domésticos y plantas. 5. Los árboles, los animales, la vegetación son parte de la naturaleza. 6. Son todas las personas que viven en un lugar. 7. Es la condición de estar solo/a. 8. Es un edificio muy alto con muchos pisos. Está generalmente en una gran ciudad.

LOS COCHES: Conversación A: Paso 1 1. g 2. h 3. i 4. d 5. b 6. f 7. c 8. a 9. j 10. e

Paso 2 *Possible answers:* 1. Son las luces que controlan la circulación. Son de color rojo, amarillo y verde. 2. Son los vehículos que se ven en la carretera o en la calle. 3. Es poner el coche en un lugar para dejarlo allí. 4. Es lo que hace el coche para poder funcionar. 5. Es el lugar donde se compra gasolina para el coche. 6. Es una carretera grande sin semáforos y donde los coches pueden circular a gran velocidad.

GRAMMAR SECTION 42

Práctica B 1. La tienda no está abierta todavía. 2. Las ventanas no están cerradas todavía. 3. La tierra no está cubierta de nieve todavía. 4. La mesa no está puesta todavía. 5. El medio ambiente no está destruido todavía. 6. El error no está descubierto todavía. 7. El problema no está resuelto todavía.

Práctica C 1. desperdiciado 2. destruidos 3. hechos 4. reciclados 5. agotadas 6. limitadas 7. acostumbrados 8. cerrada 9. apagadas 10. bajado

GRAMMAR SECTION 43

Práctica B 1. Le ha pedido ayuda a su padre. 2. Ha hecho preguntas acerca de los diferentes coches. 3. Ha visto uno bastante barato. 4. Ha revisado las llantas. 5. Lo ha conducido como prueba. 6. Ha regresado a la agencia. 7. Ha decidido comprarlo. 8. Lo ha comprado. 9. Ha vuelto a casa. 10. Ha llevado a sus amigas al cine esa noche.

UN POCO DE TODO

Ejercicio C 1. llevar 2. al 3. qué 4. Eres 5. tenga 6. para 7. Qué 8. mire 9. esta 10. el 11. lo 12. recuerdo 13. Déjeme 14. Vuelva 15. un 16. se preocupa 17. estaban 18. puse 19. cambié 20. es (era) 21. tenía 22. sigue 23. Cambie 24. perdieron 25. es

Comprensión 1. falso (Rigoberto no se interesa nada por su coche.) 2. cierto 3. falso (El mecánico no trata a Rigoberto descortesmente.) 4. cierto 5. cierto (Es posible.)

CAPÍTULO 15
VOCABULARIO: PREPARACIÓN
LAS RELACIONES SENTIMENTALES: Conversación A *Possible answers:* 1. e, casarse, el esposo / la esposa 2. c, enamorarse, querer, el novio / la novia 3. b, divorciarse, el ex esposo / la ex esposa 4. d, casarse, el novio / la novia 5. a, hablarse, el amigo / la amiga

Conversación B 1. esposo 2. noviazgo 3. cita 4. boda 5. pareja 6. amistad 7. amor 8. matrimonio 9. una boda 10. el amor

ETAPAS DE LA VIDA: Conversación A *Possible answers:* 1. la adolescencia; la juventud 2. la vejez 3. la niñez 4. la infancia; la vejez 5. la madurez 6. la adolescencia; la juventud 7. la juventud 8. la juventud; la madurez

GRAMMAR SECTION 44
Práctica B: *Paso 1* 1. ¿Hay librerías que (donde) vendan libros usados? 2. ¿Hay tiendas donde se pueda comprar revistas de Latinoamérica? 3. ¿Hay cafés cerca de la universidad donde se reúnan muchos estudiantes? 4. ¿Hay apartamentos cerca de la universidad que sean buenos y baratos? 5. ¿Hay cines donde pasen películas en español? 6. ¿Hay un gimnasio en la universidad donde se juegue al ráquetbol? 7. ¿Hay parques donde la gente corra o dé paseos? 8. ¿Hay museos donde hagan exposiciones de arte latinoamericano?
Paso 2 1. falso 2. cierto 3. cierto 4. falso

GRAMMAR SECTION 45
Práctica B Pues, para que podamos estacionar el coche, no perdamos el principio de la función, podamos comprar los boletos, consigamos buenas butacas, no tengamos que hacer cola, compremos palomitas de maíz antes de que empiece la película, hablemos con los amigos.
Práctica C: *Paso 1* 1. No voy a menos que dejemos a la niña con los abuelos. 2. Vamos solos para que pasemos un fin de semana romántico. 3. Esta vez voy a aprender a esquiar con tal que tú me enseñes. 4. Vamos a salir temprano por la mañana a menos que nos acostemos tarde la noche anterior. 5. Es importante que lleguemos a la estación de esquí antes de que empiece a nevar. 6. Deja la dirección y el teléfono del hotel en caso de que tus padres nos necesiten.
Paso 2 1. falso (no lo dice) 2. no lo dice 3. falso 4. cierto

UN POCO DE TODO
Ejercicio B: *Paso 1* 1. llegado 2. Estoy 3. descansar 4. salgamos 5. también 6. haya 7. te preocupes 8. hecho 9. Cálmate 10. nada 11. perdió 12. prometió 13. la 14. este 15. salido 16. bonita 17. tuvimos 18. Había 19. esperábamos 20. se divirtieron 21. guste 22. podamos 23. de la 24. agüe 25. tampoco
Comprensión 1. cierto 2. no lo dice 3. falso 4. no lo dice 5. cierto

CAPÍTULO 16
VOCABULARIO: PREPARACIÓN
PROFESIONES Y OFICIOS: Conversación A *Possible answers:* 1. el plomero / la plomera 2. el abogado / la abogada 3. el/la siquiatra 4. el enfermero / la enfermera 5. el criado / la criada 6. el obrero / la obrera 7. el/la periodista
EL MUNDO DEL TRABAJO: Conversación A a. 13 b. 2 c. 5 d. 7 e. 1 f. 4 g. 14 h. 9 i. 11 j. 3 k. 8 l. 10 m. 12 n. 6
Conversación C: *Paso 1* 1. f. 2. d 3. e 4. c 5. a 6. b

GRAMMAR SECTION 46
Práctica B: *Paso 1* 1. Yo hablaré bien el español. Pasaré mucho tiempo en la biblioteca. Escribiré artículos sobre la literatura latinoamericana. Daré clases en español. 2. Tú trabajarás en una oficina y en la corte. Ganarás mucho dinero. Tendrás muchos clientes. Cobrarás por muchas horas de trabajo. 3. Felipe verá a muchos pacientes. Escuchará muchos problemas. Leerá a Freud y a Jung constantemente. Le hará un sicoanálisis a un paciente. 4. Susana y Juanjo pasarán mucho tiempo sentados. Usarán el teclado constantemente. Inventarán nuevos programas. Les mandarán mensajes electrónicos a todos los amigos.
Paso 2 1. profesor(a) 2. abogado(a) 3. siquiatra 4. programador(a)
Práctica C: *Paso 1* 1. Gregorio pagará tarde todas las cuentas. 2. Tratará de adaptarse a un presupuesto. 3. Volverá a hacer un presupuesto el próximo mes. 4. No depositará nada en la cuenta de ahorros. 5. Se quejará porque no tendrá suficiente dinero. 6. Seguirá usando tarjetas de crédito. 7. Les pedirá dinero a sus padres. 8. Buscará un trabajo de tiempo parcial.

Paso 2 2. Gregorio tiene que aprender a ser más responsable con su dinero.
GRAMMAR SECTION 47
Práctica A: *Paso 1* 1. No ha pasado todavía. a 2. Acción habitual. b 3. Acción habitual. b 4. No ha pasado todavía. a 5. No ha pasado todavía. a
Práctica B 1. … me den un aumento de sueldo, deje de gastar tanto. 2. … tenga el dinero para hacerlo, sea absolutamente necesario. 3. … cobre mi cheque en el banco, me mande _____ un cheque. 4. … saque dinero de mi cuenta de ahorros, deposite el dinero en mi cuenta corriente. 5. … terminen sus estudios universitarios, se casen.
Práctica C 1. se graduó, le dieron, se gradúe, le darán 2. era, quería, tenía, decidió, termine, podrá 3. escribe, tiene, va, llegue

UN POCO DE TODO
Ejercicio A: *Paso 1* 1. Es necesario que ahorremos más. 2. Yo no usaré tantas tarjetas de crédito. 3. Mamá buscará un trabajo donde le paguen más. 4. Pediremos un préstamo en el banco. 5. Nos lo darán, ¿no crees? 6. Papá estará tranquilo cuando todos empecemos a economizar. 7. Deberás pagar siempre al contado. 8. No podremos irnos de vacaciones este verano.
Paso 2 No, tiene problemas económicos.
Ejercicio B 1. Carmen quiere esperar hasta que se gradúe en la universidad. 2. Miguel se lo va a decir a los padres de Carmen tan pronto como ellos lleguen a la ciudad. 3. Los padres de Carmen siempre quieren ver a Miguel cuando visitan a su hija. 4. Los padres se van a alegrar en cuanto oigan las noticias. 5. Miguel y Carmen van a Acapulco en su luna de miel cuando tengan dinero. 6. Todos nosotros les vamos a dar una fiesta después de que ellos regresen de su viaje.
Ejercicio C 1. algo 2. la 3. el 4. que 5. gastos 6. los 7. se 8. empecé 9. pude 10. Trabajaba 11. estudiaba 12. era 13. ganaba 14. Sacaba 15. Trabajaba 16. Ayudaba 17. ofrecieron 18. normalmente 19. económicamente 20. trabajan 21. cuidan 22. ayudan 23. trabajan 24. trabajen 25. termine 26. es 27. necesitan 28. lo que 29. se van 30. estudiar 31. Viven 32. sus 33. la
Comprensión 1. cierto 2. falso (Muchos estudiantes hispánicos trabajan.) 3. cierto

CAPÍTULO 17
VOCABULARIO: PREPARACIÓN
LAS NOTICIAS: Conversación B 1. a 2. f 3. i 4. g 5. d 6. c 7. h 8. a 9. b
EL GOBIERNO Y LA RESPONSABILIDAD CÍVICA: Conversación A: *Possible answers:* 1. el/la ciudadano/a; los demás; votar 2. el servicio militar; la guerra 3. el/la político/a; la ley 4. el/la ciudadano/a; votar; el deber 5. el rey / la reina; el gobierno 6. obedecer; el ejército
Conversación B 1. Juan Perón 2. la reina Elizabeth de Inglaterra 3. *El ciudadano Kane* 4. Abraham Lincoln 5. el servicio militar 6. la monarquía 7. la discriminación 8. votar

GRAMMAR SECTION 48
Práctica C: *Paso 1* 1. Los obreros querían que les dieran un aumento de sueldo. 2. Era posible que los trabajadores siguieran en huelga hasta el verano. 3. Era necesario que las víctimas recibieran atención médica en la Clínica del Sagrado Corazón. 4. Era una lástima que no hubiera espacio para todos allí. 5. Los terroristas pidieron que los oficiales no los persiguieran. 6. Parecía imposible que el gobierno aceptara sus demandas. 7. Era necesario que el gobierno informara a todos los ciudadanos del desastre. 8. Dudaba que la paz mundial estuviera fuera de nuestro alcance. 9. El presidente y los directores preferían que la nueva fábrica se construyera en México. 10. Temía que el número de votantes fuera muy bajo en las próximas elecciones.
Paso 2 1. hecho 2. opinión 3. opinión 4. opinión 5. hecho 6. opinión 7. opinión 8. opinión 9. hecho 10. opinión

GRAMMAR SECTION 49
Práctica A 1. mía 2. suya 3. mía 4. mía 5. suya
Práctica C 1. Esta maleta, ¿es de Juan? —No, no es suya. 2. Esta maleta, ¿es de Uds.? —No, no es nuestra. 3. Esta maleta, ¿es de Alicia? —No, no es suya. 4. Esta maleta, ¿es mía? —No, no es tuya. 5. Esta maleta, ¿es tuya? —No, no es mía. 6. ¿Y este despertador? —No, no es mío. El mío es más pequeño. 7. ¿Y estos zapatos? —No, no son míos. Los míos son más pequeños. 8. ¿Y esta llave? —No, no es mía. La mía es más pequeña. 9. ¿Y este televisor? —No, no es mío. El mío es más pequeño. 10. ¿Y estas pastillas? —No, no son mías. Las mías son más pequeñas. 11. ¿Y este periódico? —No, no es mío. El mío es más pequeño.

UN POCO DE TODO
Ejercicio A: *Paso 1* 1. Ayer vi mi nota en el último examen. 2. No podía creer que la nota fuera tan baja. 3. No era posible que yo hiciera un exa-

men tan mal. 4. Por eso hablé con el profesor para que me explicara la causa de la nota. 5. Me dijo que había errores importantes, pero que había partes buenas también. 6. Me pidió que leyera el examen otra vez. 7. Era verdad que había errores en el examen. 8. Pero, ¡no era justo que el profesor me diera una nota tan baja!

Ejercicio B: *Paso 1* *Possible answers:* 1. Las leyes de su país de origen no permitían que este grupo practicara su religión libremente. (los puritanos) 2. Algunas personas esperaban que hubiera oro y plata en América. (los españoles) 3. El rey no quería que estos criminales siguieran viviendo en su país. (los ingleses que llegaron a Australia) 4. Estos inmigrantes buscaban un país donde hubiera paz y esperanza y seguridad personal. (los judíos) 5. Los miembros de este grupo buscaban un país donde no tuvieran que pasar hambre. (los irlandeses)
Paso 2 1. Los indios temían que los colonos les quitaran toda la tierra. 2. A los colonos no les gustaba que fuera necesario pagarle impuestos al rey. 3. Parecía imposible que la joven república tuviera éxito. 4. A los del sur no les gustaba que los gobernaran los del norte. 5. A los abolicionistas no les gustaba que algunos no tuvieran las mismas libertades. 6. Era necesario que se declararan en huelga los obreros para obtener algunos derechos. 7. Era terrible que hubiera dos guerras mundiales. 8. Para que nosotros vivamos en paz, es cuestión de aprender a comunicarnos. 9. También es necesario que haya leyes que garanticen los derechos.
Ejercicio C 1. es 2. mía 3. la 4. dejaras 5. hojeado 6. mí 7. fuera 8. tan 9. resultara 10. Estoy 11. muy 12. leer 13. Lee 14. la 15. la 16. veo 17. un 18. Es 19. enterarte 20. como 21. que 22. razón
Comprensión 1. falso 2. no se sabe 3. cierto

CAPÍTULO 18
VOCABULARIO: PREPARACIÓN
LUGARES Y COSAS EN EL EXTRANJERO: Conversación A *Possible answers:* 1. Se compran en la farmacia. 2. En una farmacia en el extranjero no se venden tantas cosas como en los Estados Unidos. 3. En el correo o en un estanco. 4. Se va al estanco. 5. Es un lugar donde se venden periódicos y revistas, lápices y libros, papel para cartas, etcétera. 6. Venden libros, cuadernos, lápices, papel para cartas, etcétera.
Conversación B 1. cierto 2. falso (Iría a un bar.) 3. falso (Para mandar paquetes se va al correo.) 4. falso (El metro es más rápido.) 5. falso (Se va a una farmacia.) 6. falso (Deberías ir a una farmacia.) 7. cierto 8. falso (Un batido se hace con leche.)
EN UN VIAJE AL EXTRANJERO: Conversación A 2, 3, 5, 6, 8, 9, 10
Conversación B 1. b 2. f 3. a 4. d 5. e 6. c
GRAMMAR SECTION 50
Práctica B: *Paso 1* 1. gustaría 2. trabajaría 3. Podría 4. Tomaría 5. Comería 6. Vería 7. sería 8. tendría 9. Podría 10. tendría
Paso 2 1. cierto 2. falso (Le gustaría nadar todos los días.) 3. falso (Tendría que usar su tarjeta de crédito.) 4. No lo dice.
Práctica C: *Paso 1* 1. ¿Estudiarías italiano? —No, estudiaría chino. 2. ¿Renunciarías a un puesto sin avisar? —No, avisaría con dos semanas de anticipación. 3. ¿Harías un viaje a España? —No, haría un viaje a la Argentina. 4. ¿Saldrías de casa sin apagar el estéreo? No, saldría sin apagar las luces. 5. ¿Seguirías un presupuesto rígido? —No, seguiría uno flexible. 6. ¿Gastarías menos en ropa? —No, gastaría menos en libros. 7. ¿Pondrías el aire acondicionado en invierno? —No, lo pondría en verano. 8. ¿Alquilarías un coche de lujo? —No, alquilaría uno económico.
GRAMMAR SECTION 51
Práctica B 1. Si fuera a la Argentina, me quedaría en Buenos Aires. 2. Si tuviera interés en la población italiana, visitaría el barrio italiano La Boca. 3. Si quisiera mandar una tarjeta postal, la compraría en un quiosco. 4. Si tuviera ganas de comprar libros, pediría direcciones al barrio San Telmo. 5. Si quisiera ver una obra de teatro, iría al Teatro Colón. 6. Si me interesara visitar unos sitios turísticos, vería el obelisco y la réplica de Big Ben. 7. Si quisiera probar comida auténtica, comería carne argentina. 8. Si quisiera escuchar música típica, escucharía el tango.
Práctica C: *Paso 1* a. 5 b. 1 c. 4 d. 3 e. 2
UN POCO DE TODO
Ejercicio C 1. sé 2. mucho 3. es 4. el 5. ir 6. Mira 7. desean 8. para 9. para 10. haciendo 11. seguimos 12. Por 13. sea 14. cambiado 15. esté 16. esperen 17. muy 18. está 19. hay 20. es 21. Este 22. les 23. llegar 24. Miren 25. está 26. el 27. toman 28. está 29. llaman 30. Es 31. que 32. verán 33. lo 34. por
Comprensión 1. la pensión 2. Elena y Alfonso 3. el empleado 4. Elena y Alfonso

Vocabularies

This **Spanish-English Vocabulary** contains all the words that appear in the text, with the following exceptions: (1) most close or identical cognates that do not appear in the chapter vocabulary lists; (2) most conjugated verb forms; (3) diminutives ending in **-ito/a**; (4) absolute superlatives in **-ísimo/a**; and (5) most adverbs in **-mente**. Active vocabulary is indicated by the number of the chapter in which a word or given meaning is first listed (**AT-Ante todo**); vocabulary that is glossed in the text is not considered to be active vocabulary and is not numbered. Only meanings that are used in the text are given. The **English-Spanish Vocabulary** is based on the chapter lists of active vocabulary.

The gender of nouns is indicated, except for masculine nouns ending in **-o** and feminine nouns ending in **-a**. Stem changes and spelling changes are indicated for verbs: **dormir (ue, u); llegar (gu)**. Because **ch** and **ll** are no longer considered separate letters, words beginning with **ch** and **ll** are found as they would be found in English. The letter **ñ** follows the letter **n: añadir** follows **anuncio,** for example. The following abbreviations are used:

adj.	adjective	*interj.*	interjection	*pl.*	plural
adv.	adverb	*inv.*	invariable form	*poss.*	possessive
conj.	conjunction	*i.o.*	indirect object	*p.p.*	past participle
d.o.	direct object	*irreg.*	irregular	*prep.*	preposition
f.	feminine	*L.A.*	Latin America	*pron.*	pronoun
fam.	familiar	*m.*	masculine	*refl. pron.*	reflexive pronoun
form.	formal	*Mex.*	Mexico	*s.*	singular
gram.	grammatical term	*n.*	noun	*Sp.*	Spain
inf.	infinitive	*obj. (of prep.)*	object (of a preposition)	*sub. pron.*	subject pronoun

Spanish–English Vocabulary

A

a to; at (*with time*) (AT); **a causa de** because of, on account of; **a dieta** on a diet; **a la(s)...** at . . . (hour) (AT); **a la derecha (izquierda) de** to the right (left) of (5); **a menos que** *conj.* unless (15); **a plazos** in installments (16); **a primera vista** at first sight (15); **¿a qué hora... ?** (at) what time . . . ? (AT); **a tiempo** on time (7); **a veces** at times, sometimes (2)

abajo below, underneath

abalanzarse (c) to pounce

abandonar to abandon; to leave

abierto/a *p.p.* open(ed) (5)

abogado/a lawyer (16)

abrazar (c) to embrace, hug

abrigo overcoat (3)

abril *m.* April (5)

abrir (*p.p.* **abierto/a**) to open (2)

absoluto/a absolute

absolver (ue) to absolve, acquit

absorbente absorbing

abuelo/a grandfather / grandmother (2)

abuelos *m. pl.* grandparents (2)

abundancia abundance

aburrido/a bored (5); **ser** (*irreg.*) **aburrido/a** to be boring (9)

aburrimiento boredom

aburrir to bore (13); **aburrirse** to get bored (9)

abuso abuse

acabar to finish (11); **acabarse** to run out of (11); to use up completely (14); **acabar de** (+ *inf.*) to have just (*done something*) (6)

academia: Real Academia Española Royal Spanish Academy

académico/a *adj.* academic

acaso: por si acaso just in case (11)

accesible accessible

acceso access

accidente *m.* accident (11)

acción *f.* action; **Día** (*m.*) **de Acción de Gracias** Thanksgiving (8)

aceite *m.* oil (14)

aceituna olive

acelerado/a accelerated, fast (14)

acento accent (14)

acentuado/a accented

aceptar to accept

acerca de *prep.* about, concerning

aclarar to clarify

acogedor(a) welcoming

acomodarse (a) to adapt oneself (to)

acompañar to accompany; to go with

aconsejable advisable

aconsejar to advise

acontecimiento event, happening (17)

acordarse (ue) (de) to remember (11)

acordeón *m.* accordion

acostarse (ue) to go to bed (4)

acostumbrarse a to become accustomed to, get used to

actitud *f.* attitude

activación *f.* activation

actividad *f.* activity
activo/a active
actor *m.* actor (13)
actriz *f.* (*pl.* **actrices**) actress (13)
actual *adj.* current, up to date
actualidad *f.* present time
actualmente currently
actuar (actúo) to act
acuario aquarium
acuático/a: deportes (*m. pl.*) **acuáticos** water sports
acueducto aqueduct
acuerdo agreement; **de acuerdo** agreed; **(no) estoy de acuerdo** I (don't) agree (2); **ponerse** (*irreg.*) **de acuerdo** to reach an agreement
acusación *f.* accusation, charge
adaptación *f.* adaptation
adaptado/a adapted; adjusted
adaptarse (a) to adapt oneself (to)
adecuado/a appropriate
adelantarse (a) to get ahead (of); to beat, surpass
adelante: de ahora en adelante from now on
adelgazar (c) to lose weight
además *adv.* moreover; **además de** *prep.* besides
adicional additional (AT)
adiós good-bye (AT)
adjetivo adjective (2)
adjuntar to enclose, attach
administración (*f.*) **de empresas** business administration (1)
admirar to admire
admitir to admit; to accept
adolescencia adolescence (15)
¿adónde? where (to)? (3)
adoquinado/a cobblestoned
adorar to adore
adorno decoration
adquisitivo/a acquisitive
aduana *s.* customs (18); **derechos** (*m. pl.*) **(de aduana)** (customs) duty (18); **inspector(a) (de aduanas)** (customs) inspector (18)
adulto/a adult (9)
adverbio adverb
advertencia warning
aeróbico/a aerobic (10); **hacer** (*irreg.*) **ejercicios aeróbicos** to do aerobic exercise (10)
aerolínea airline
aeropuerto airport (7)
afectar to affect
afectivo/a affective, emotional
afectuoso/a affectionate
afeitarse to shave oneself (4)
afición *f.* hobby (9)
aficionado/a *n.* fan (9); **ser** (*irreg.*) **aficionado/a (a)** to be a fan (of) (9)
afirmación *f.* statement
afirmar to affirm
afirmativo/a *adj.* affirmative
africano/a *n., adj.* African
afuera *adv.* outdoors (5)

afueras *n. pl.* suburbs, outskirts (12)
agencia de viajes travel agency (7)
agenda agenda; date book; **agenda digital/electrónica** digital/electronic datebook
agente *m., f.* agent; **agente de billetes** ticket agent; **agente de inmobiliaria** real estate agent; **agente de viajes** travel agent (7)
agosto August (5)
agotar to deplete
agradable pleasant, nice
agradar to please (13)
agradecer (zc) to thank
agresividad *f.* aggressiveness
agresivo/a aggressive
agrícola *adj. m., f* agricultural
agricultor(a) farmer (14)
agricultura agriculture
agua *f.* (*but* **el agua**) water; **agua mineral** mineral water (6); **cama de agua** waterbed (4)
aguacate *m.* avocado
aguar (gü) to spoil (*a party*)
agudo/a sharp; acute
agujero hole
ahí there
ahora now (1); **ahora mismo** right now; at once
ahorrar to save (*money*) (16)
ahorros *m. pl.* savings; **cuenta de ahorros** savings account (16)
aire *m.* air (14); **aire acondicionado** air conditioning; **al aire libre** outdoors (9)
aislamiento isolation (14)
ajedrez *m.* chess (4); **jugar (ue) (gu) al ajedrez** to play chess (4)
ají *m.* bell pepper
ajillo: al ajillo *adj.* in garlic sauce
ajo garlic; **diente** (*m.*) **de ajo** garlic clove
al (*contraction of* **a** + **el**) to the (3); **al** + *inf.* upon, while, when + *verb form*; **al aire libre** outdoors (9); **al contado** in cash (16); **al lado de** next to (5); **al principio (de)** at the beginning (of) (16)
álbum *m.* album
alcance *m.* reach
alcoba bedroom (4)
alcohol *m.* alcohol
alcohólico/a *adj.* alcoholic
alegrarse (de) to be happy (about) (12)
alegre happy (5)
alegría happiness
alemán *m.* German (*language*) (1)
alemán, alemana *n., adj.* German (2)
Alemania Germany
alergia allergy; **tener** (*irreg.*) **alergia (a)** to be allergic (to)
alérgico/a: ser (*irreg.*) **alérgico/a (a)** to be allergic (to)
alerta: ojo alerta be alert, watch out
alfabetizado/a alphabetized
alfabetizar (c) to alphabetize
alfabeto alphabet
alfombra rug (4)

alfombrado/a carpeted
algo something, anything (3)
algodón *m.* cotton (3); **es de algodón** it's made of cotton (3)
alguien someone, anyone (6)
algún, alguno/a some; any (6); **algún día** some day; **alguna vez** once; ever
alimento food
aliviar to ease, lessen
alivio relief
allá over there (4)
allí (over) there (3)
alma *f.* (*but* **el alma**) soul
almacén *m.* department store (3)
almacenamiento storing; storage
almendra almond
almohada pillow
almorzar (ue) (c) to have lunch (4)
almuerzo lunch (6)
alojamiento lodging (18)
alojarse to remain, stay (*as a guest*) (18)
alquilar to rent (12)
alquiler *m.* rent (12)
alrededor de *prep.* around
alteración *f.* irregularity
alternativa alternative; choice
alto/a tall (2); high; **en voz alta** out loud
altura height, altitude
aluminio aluminum
ama *f.* (*but* **el ama**) **de casa** housekeeper; homemaker
amable kind; nice (2)
amante *m., f.* lover
amar to love (15)
amarillo/a yellow (3)
amasijo hodgepodge
Amazonas *m. s.* Amazon
ambiental environmental
ambiente *m.* environment, atmosphere; **medio ambiente** environment (14)
ambos/as *pl.* both
amenazador(a) threatening
amenazar (c) to threaten
americano/a *n., adj.* American; **fútbol** (*m.*) **americano** football (9)
amigo/a friend (1)
amistad *f.* friendship (15)
amistoso/a friendly (15)
amor *m.* love (15)
amoroso/a loving
amplio/a large, spacious
analfabetismo illiteracy
análisis *m. s., pl.* analysis
analista (*m., f.*) **de sistemas** systems analyst (16)
analizar (c) to analyze
anaranjado/a *adj.* orange (*color*) (3)
ancho/a wide
anciano/a *n.* old person (9); *adj.* old
andar (*irreg.*) **en bicicleta** to ride a bicycle
andino/a Andean
anémico/a anemic
anfitrión, anfitriona host(ess) (8)
anglosajón, anglosajona *n., adj.* Anglo-Saxon

angula eel
anillo ring
animado/a animated; full of life; **dibujos animados** cartoons
animal *m.* animal
ánimo: estado de ánimo state of mind
anoche *adv.* last night
anotar to write down
ansiedad *f.* anxiety
antártico/a *adj.* Antarctic
Antártida Antarctica
ante before; **ante todo** first of all
anteayer the day before yesterday
antecedente *m. gram.* antecedent (*of a pronoun*)
antemano: de antemano beforehand
anterior previous, preceding
antes *adv.* before; **antes de** (*prep.*) before (4); **antes (de) que** *conj.* before (15)
antibiótico antibiotic (10)
anticipación *f.*: **con anticipación** ahead of time (7)
anticuado/a antiquated, old-fashioned
antigüedad *n. f.* antique
antiguo/a old; ancient
antipático/a unpleasant (2)
antropología anthropology
antropólogo/a anthropologist
anual annual, yearly
anunciar to announce (7)
anuncio advertisement; announcement
añadir to add
año year (5); **cumplir años** to have a birthday (8); **Día** (*m.*) **de Año Nuevo** New Year's Day (8); **el año pasado** last year; **Feliz Año Nuevo** Happy New Year; **tener** (*irreg.*) **... años** to be . . . years old (2)
apagado/a out; turned off (*light*)
apagar (gu) to turn off (*light*)
aparato appliance (9); **aparato doméstico** home appliance (9); **aparato electrónico** electronic device
aparcar (qu) to park
aparecer (zc) to appear
apartamento apartment (1); **casa (bloque** *m.*) **de apartamentos** apartment house (12)
aparte *adv.* apart
apasionado/a passionate
apellido last name, surname
apenas hardly any
apendicitis *f. s.* appendicitis
aperitivo appetizer; aperitif
apiñado/a crammed or packed together
apio celery
aplicación *f.* application
aplicar (qu) to apply
apoderarse (de) to gain control (of)
aportación *f.* contribution
aporte *m.* contribution
apoyar to support (17)
apoyo *n.* support
apreciado/a appreciated
apreciar to appreciate (13)
aprender to learn (2)

apretado/a tight
apretar (ie) to press; to squeeze
aprobación *f.* approval
apropiado/a appropriate
aprovechar to make use of, take advantage of; **que aproveche** enjoy your meal
aproximadamente approximately
apuntar to note down
apuntes *m. pl.* notes
aquel, aquella *adj.* that (*over there*) (3); *pron.* that one (*over there*) (3)
aquello that; that thing (4)
aquellos/as *adj.* those (*over there*) (3); *pron.* those ones (*over there*) (3)
aquí here (1)
árabe *n. m.* Arab; *adj.* Arabic
árbol *m.* tree (14)
arbusto bush
archivo computer file (12)
ardilla squirrel
área *f.* (*but* **el área**) area (12)
arena sand
arete *m.* earring (3)
argentino/a *n., adj.* Argentinian
argumento argument; plot (*of a play, film*)
árido/a dry, arid
armado/a armed
armario closet (4)
arqueológico/a archaeological
arqueólogo/a archaeologist
arquitecto/a architect (13)
arquitectura architecture (13)
arrancar (qu) to start (*a motor*) (14)
arreglar to fix, repair (12); to straighten (up) (12)
arriba *adv.* above; up
arrogante arrogant; brave
arroz *m.* rice (6)
arruinado/a ruined
arte *f.* (*but* **el arte**) art (1); **obra de arte** work of art (13)
artesanía arts and crafts (13)
artesano/a craftsperson
artículo article (1)
artista *m., f.* artist (13)
artístico/a artistic (13)
arveja green pea (6)
arzobispo archbishop
asado/a roasted (6)
ascendencia ancestry
ascensor *m.* elevator
asco: me da asco it makes me sick
asegurarse to make sure
asentarse (ie) to settle
asequible available
asesinado/a assassinated
asesinar to murder, assassinate
asesinato assassination (17)
así thus, so; **así como** as well as; **así que** therefore, consequently
asiático/a *n., adj.* Asian
asiento seat (7)
asimilarse to assimilate
asimismo likewise

asistente (*m., f.*) **de vuelo** flight attendant (7)
asistir (a) to attend, go (to) (*a function*) (2)
asma *f.* (*but* **el asma**) asthma
asociación *f.* association
asociado/a: estado libre asociado free associated state
asociar to associate; to combine
aspecto aspect; appearance
áspero/a rough; harsh
aspiración *f.* aspiration; hope
aspiradora vacuum cleaner (9); **pasar la aspiradora** to vacuum (9)
aspirante *m., f.* candidate; applicant (16)
aspirina aspirin
astronomía astronomy
asumir to assume
asunto subject, topic, issue
atacar (qu) to attack
ataque *m.* attack
atención *f.* attention; **prestar atención** to pay attention
atender (ie) to attend to; to serve
atlántico/a: Océano Atlántico Atlantic Ocean
atleta *m., f.* athlete
atlético/a athletic
atmósfera atmosphere
atómico/a: bomba atómica atom bomb
atracción *f.* attraction; *pl.* amusements
atractivo/a attractive
atraer (*like* **traer**) to attract
atrapado/a trapped
atrás: para atrás backward
atrasado/a: estar (*irreg.*) **atrasado/a** to be late (7)
atravesar (ie) to cross
atrevido/a daring
atún *m.* tuna (6)
audaz (*pl.* **audaces**) adventurous
aumento raise (12); **aumento de sueldo** raise in salary (16)
aun *adv.* even
aún *adv.* still, yet
aunque although
auscultar to listen (*medical*)
ausencia absence
ausente absent
australiano/a *n., adj.* Australian
autenticidad *f.* authenticity
auténtico/a authentic
auto car
autobiográfico/a autobiographical
autobús *m.* bus (7); **estación** (*f.*) **de autobuses** bus stop (7); **parada del autobús** bus stop (18)
autoestima self-confidence
autoexilio self-exile
automático/a automatic; **cajero automático** automatic teller machine (16); **contestador** (*m.*) **automático** answering machine (12)
automovilístico/a *adj.* automobile
autónomo/a autonomous
autopista freeway (14)

autor(a) author
autoridad *f.* authority
autorretrato self-portrait
autoservicio self-service
autostop *m.*: **hacer** (*irreg.*) **autostop** to hitchhike
autosuficiencia self-sufficiency
avance *m.* advance
avanzar (c) to advance
avenida avenue (12)
aventura adventure
aventurero/a adventurous
avergonzado/a embarrassed (8)
avergonzar (ue) (c) to shame
averiguar (gü) to find out
avestruz *m.* (*pl.* **avestruces**) ostrich
avión *m.* airplane (7)
avisar to warn
ayer yesterday (4)
ayudante *m., f.* assistant
ayudar to help (6)
azteca *m., f.* Aztec
azúcar *m.* sugar
azul blue (3)

B

bailar to dance (1)
bailarín, bailarina dancer (13)
baile *m.* dance (8)
bajado/a lowered
bajar (de) to get off (of) (7); to get down (from) (7)
bajo *prep.* under
bajo/a short (*in height*) (2); low; **planta baja** ground floor (12)
balance *m.* balance
balancear to balance (*an account*)
ballet *m.* ballet (13)
banana banana (6)
bancarrota bankruptcy
banco bank (16)
banderilla *Sp.* appetizer
bando faction; flock
bandoneón *m.* large concertina
banquero/a banker
banquete *m.* banquet
bañarse to take a bath (4)
bañera bathtub (4)
baño bathroom (4); **habitación** (*f.*) **con/sin baño** room with(out) bath (18); **traje** (*m.*) **de baño** bathing suit (3)
bar *m.* bar (9)
barato/a inexpensive, cheap (3)
barbacoa barbecue
barbería barbershop
barco ship, boat (7)
barrer (el piso) to sweep (the floor) (9)
barrera barrier
barrio neighborhood (12)
barro mud; clay
basar to base, support
base *f.* base, foundation; **a base de** by, based on
básico/a basic
basquetbol *m.* basketball (9)

bastante *adv.* rather; sufficiently, enough (15)
basura garbage; **sacar (qu) la basura** to take out the trash (9)
basurero trash can
bata robe, housecoat
batalla battle
batería battery (14)
batido *drink similar to a milkshake* (18)
bautismo baptism
bebé *m., f.* baby
beber to drink (2)
bebida drink, beverage (6)
beca scholarship
béisbol *m.* baseball (9)
belleza beauty
bello/a beautiful (14)
beso kiss
biblioteca library (1)
bibliotecario/a librarian (1)
bicicleta (de montaña) (mountain) bicycle (12); **pasear (montar) en bicicleta** to ride a bicycle (9)
bien *adv.* well (AT); **caerle** (*irreg.*) **bien a alguien** to make a good impression on someone (16); **estar** (*irreg.*) **bien** to be comfortable (*temperature*) (5); **llevarse bien (con)** to get along well (with) (15); **muy bien** very well, fine (AT); **pasarlo bien** to have a good time (8)
bienestar *m.* well-being (10)
bienvenido/a welcome
bilingüe bilingual (11)
bilingüismo bilingualism
billete *m.* ticket (7); **billete de ida** one-way ticket (7); **billete de ida y vuelta** round-trip ticket (7)
biodiversidad *f.* biodiversity
biográfico/a biographical
biología biology (2)
biológico/a biological
biólogo/a biologist
bistec *m.* steak (6)
blanco/a white (3); **vino blanco** white wine (6)
bloc *m.* writing pad
bloque (*m.*) **de apartamentos** apartment building (12)
blusa blouse (3)
bobo/a dumb
boca mouth (10)
boda wedding (15)
bodegón *m.* inexpensive restaurant, tavern
boicot *m.* boycott
boleto ticket (7); **boleto de ida** one-way ticket (7); **boleto de ida y vuelta** round-trip ticket (7)
bolígrafo ballpoint pen (1)
bolsa purse (3)
bolsillo pocket
bomba atómica atomic bomb
bombardeo bombing
bombero/a firefighter
bonito/a pretty (2)
borde *m.*: **al borde de** on the brink of

bosque *m.* forest (14)
bota boot (3)
botella bottle
botones *m. s., pl.* bellhop (18)
brasileño/a *n., adj.* Brazilian
bravo/a fierce; brave
bravura fierceness; bravery
brazo arm (11)
bregar (gu) to deal with
breve *adj.* brief
brindar to drink a toast
bronce *m.* bronze
bronceado/a tanned
bronquitis *f. s.* bronchitis
brote *m.* bud, shoot
bruja witch
brujo magician
bucear to snorkle (8)
buen, bueno/a *adj.* good (2); **buenas noches** good night (AT); **buenas tardes** good afternoon/evening (AT); **buenos días** good morning (AT); **hace buen tiempo** it's good weather (5); **lo bueno** the good thing, news (10); **muy buenas** good afternoon/evening (AT)
bueno... *interj.* well . . . (2)
bulevar *m.* boulevard
bullicioso/a lively
bulto package
burbuja bubble
burocracia bureaucracy
burocrático/a bureaucratic
burro burro, donkey
busca: en busca de in search of (16)
buscar (qu) to look for (1)
butaca seat (*in a theater*)

C

caballo horse; **montar a caballo** to ride horseback (9)
cabeza head (10); **dolor** (*m.*) **de cabeza** headache
cabezudo/a obstinate; stubborn
cabina cabin (*on a ship*) (7)
cacique *m.* Indian chieftain
cada *inv.* each, every (4); **cada uno/a** each one; **cada vez** each time
cadera hip (*anatomy*)
caer (*irreg.*) to fall (11); **caerle bien/mal a alguien** to make a good/bad impression on someone (16); **caerse** to fall down (11)
café *m.* coffee (1); café (18)
cafeína caffeine
cafetera coffee pot (9)
cafetería cafeteria (1)
caída fall
caja box
cajero/a cashier, teller (16); **cajero automático** automatic teller machine (16)
cajón *m.* drawer
calamar *m.* squid
calcetín, calcetines *m.* sock(s) (3)
calculadora calculator (1)
cálculo calculation; computation

calendario calendar (11)
calentar (ie) to heat
calidad *f.* quality
cálido/a hot
caliente hot
calificación *f.* grade (11)
calle *f.* street (12)
callos (*m. pl.*) **a la madrileña** *tripe specialty of Madrid*
calma calm, composure
calor *m.* heat (5); **hace calor** it's hot (*weather*) (5); **tener** (*irreg.*) **calor** to be (feel) warm, hot (5)
caloría calorie
cama (de agua) (water) bed (4); **guardar cama** to stay in bed (10); **hacer** (*irreg.*) **la cama** to make the bed (9)
cámara camera (12)
camarero/a waiter/waitress (6)
camarón *m.* shrimp (6)
cambiar (de) to change (12)
cambio change; (rate of) exchange (*currency*); **en cambio** on the other hand
camello camel
caminar to walk (10)
camino road, street (14); **en camino** en route
camioneta station wagon (7)
camisa shirt (3)
camiseta T-shirt (3)
campanada chime of bell
campaña campaign; **tienda de campaña** tent (7)
campeonato championship
campesino/a farm worker; peasant (14)
camping *m.* campground (7); **hacer** (*irreg.*) *camping* to go camping (7)
campo countryside (12)
campus *m. s.* university campus (12)
canal *m.* channel (12); canal
cancelar to cancel; **cancelar una reserva** to cancel a reservation (10)
cáncer *m.* cancer
cancha field (for football, baseball); court (for tennis)
canción *f.* song (13)
candidato/a candidate
cansado/a tired (5); **estar** (*irreg.*) **cansado/a** to be tired (6)
cansancio fatigue; weariness
cansarse to get tired
cantante *m., f.* singer (13)
cantar to sing (1)
cantidad *f.* quantity
capa de ozono ozone layer (14)
capacidad *f.* capacity
capaz (*pl.* **capaces**) capable
capital *f.* capital city (5)
capitán *m.* captain
Capricornio Capricorn
cara face
carácter *m.* character, personality
característico/a *adj.* characteristic
caracterizar (c) to characterize

cardinal: puntos (*m. pl.*) **cardinales** cardinal directions (5)
cargar (gu) to charge (*to an account*) (16)
cargo post; **a cargo de** in charge of
Caribe *n. m.* Caribbean
caribeño/a *adj.* Caribbean
cariño affection
cariñoso/a affectionate (5)
carnaval *m.* carnival
carne *f.* meat (6)
caro/a expensive (3)
carpintero/a carpenter
carrera major (*academic*); career (2)
carretera highway (14)
carro (descapotable) (convertible) car (12)
carta letter (2); **jugar (ue) (gu) a las cartas** to play cards (9); **papel** (*m.*) **para cartas** stationery (18)
cartera wallet (3)
casa house, home (2); **casa de apartamentos** apartment building (12); **casa particular** private/single-family house; **en casa** at home (1); **limpiar la casa (entera)** to clean the (whole) house (9)
casado/a married (2)
casarse (con) to marry (15)
cascanueces *m. s.* nutcracker
casi almost; **casi nunca** almost never; hardly ever (5)
caso case; **en caso de que** *conj.* in case (15)
castellano/a Castillian
castigar (gu) to punish (17)
castigo punishment
catálogo catalogue
catastrófico/a catastrophic
catedral *f.* cathedral
categoría category; class
catolicismo Catholicism
católico/a *n., adj.* Catholic
catorce fourteen (AT)
causa *n.* cause; **a causa de** because of
causar to cause
cava wine cellar; **al cava** with wine
cazador(a) hunter
cazuelita de barro clay bowl
CD-ROM *m.* CD-ROM (12)
cebiche *m. raw fish marinated in lemon juice*
ceder to cede, hand over
celebración *f.* celebration
celebrar to celebrate (5)
celular: teléfono celular cellular telephone (12)
cementerio cemetery
cena dinner, supper (6)
cenar to have (eat) dinner (6)
Cenicienta Cinderella
ceniza ash
censo census
censura censorship
centavo cent
central: América Central Central America

centro downtown (3); **centro comercial** shopping mall (3)
cepillarse los dientes to brush one's teeth (4)
cerámica ceramics, pottery (13)
cerca de *prep.* close to (5)
cercanía closeness
cercano/a near, close
cerdo pork; **chuleta de cerdo** pork chop (6)
cereales *m. pl.* cereal (6)
cerebro brain (10)
ceremonia ceremony
cerilla match (*for lighting things*)
cero zero (AT)
cerrado/a closed (5)
cerrar (ie) to close (4)
cervecería beer hall
cerveza beer (1)
césped m. lawn, grass
cesto basket
champán *m.* champagne
champanería champagne bar
champiñón *m.* mushroom (6)
champú *m.* shampoo (18)
chaperón, chaperona chaperone
chaqueta jacket (3)
charlar to chat
cheque *m.* (bank) check (16); **cheque de viajero** traveler's check (18); **con cheque** by check (16); **talonario de cheques** checkbook
chequeo check-up (10)
¡chévere! *colloquialism* cool! great! (*Caribbean*)
chicano/a *n., adj.* Chicano, Mexican-American
chico/a *n.* young man/young woman; *adj.* small
chileno/a *n., adj.* Chilean
chimenea fireplace
chimpancé *m.* chimpanzee
chino/a *n., adj.* Chinese
chiste *m.* joke (8)
chistoso/a amusing
chocar (qu) (con) to run into, collide (with) (14)
chocolate *m.* chocolate
chofer *m., f.* driver
choque *m.* collision (17)
chorizo sausage
chuleta (de cerdo) (pork) chop (6)
ciberespacio cyberspace
ciclismo bicycling (9)
ciclo cycle
ciego/a blind
cien, ciento one hundred (2)
ciencia science (1); **ciencia ficción** science fiction; **ciencias** (*f. pl.*) **políticas** political science
científico/a scientist
cierto/a certain (13); true
cigarrillo cigarette
cilantro cilantro, fresh coriander
cinco five (AT); **Cinco de Mayo** Cinco de Mayo

cincuenta fifty (2)
cine *m.* movie theater (4); movie (4); ir (*irreg.*) al cine to go to the movies (9)
cinematográfico/a *adj.* film
cinta tape (3)
cinturón *m.* belt (3)
circo circus
circuito circuit
circulación *f.* traffic (14)
circunstancia circumstance
ciruelo cherry tree
cisne *m.* swan
cita date, appointment (15)
citado/a booked up; cited
ciudad *f.* city (2)
ciudadano/a citizen (17)
cívico/a civic (17)
civil: guerra civil civil war
civilización *f.* civilization
clarinete *m.* clarinet
claro/a clear; light
clase *f.* class (1); clase turística tourist class (7); compañero/a de clase classmate (1); primera clase first class (7)
clásico/a classical (13)
clasificado/a classified
clave *f.* key (*to a code*)
cliente *m., f.* client (1)
clima *m.* climate (5)
climatología climatology
clínica *n.* clinic
coágulo clot
coalición *f.* coalition
cobrar to charge (*someone for an item or service*) (16); to cash (*a check*) (16)
cobre *m.* copper
coche *m.* car (2); coche deportivo sports car; teléfono de coche car telephone (12)
cocina kitchen (4); cooking
cocinar to cook (6)
cocinero/a cook; chef (16)
coctel *m.* cocktail
cognado *gram.* cognate (6)
coherente coherent
cohesión *f.* cohesion
coincidir to coincide; to agree
cola line (*of people*); hacer (*irreg.*) cola to stand in line (7)
colección *f.* collection
colega *m., f.* colleague
colegio elementary or secondary school
colgar (ue) (gu) to hang
colocar (qu) to place
colombiano/a *n., adj.* Colombian
colonia colony; camp
colonialismo *f.* colonization
colonizar (c) to colonize, settle
color *m.* color (3)
columna column
columnista *m., f.* columnist
combatir to fight (against)
combinación *f.* combination
combinar to combine
comedor *m.* dining room (4)
comentar to comment on; to discuss

comentario comment, commentary
comenzar (ie) (c) to begin
comer to eat (2)
comercial: centro comercial shopping mall (3)
comerciante *m., f.* merchant, shopkeeper (16)
comercio business
cometer to commit
cómico/a funny, comical; tira cómica comic strip
comida food (6); meal (6)
comienzo *n.* beginning
como like; as ; tan... como as . . . as (5); tan pronto como as soon as (16); tanto/a... como *conj.* as much/many as (5)
¿cómo? how? what? (AT); ¿cómo es usted? what are you like? (AT); ¿cómo está(s)? how are you? (1); ¿cómo te llamas? / ¿cómo se llama usted? what's your name? (AT)
cómoda dresser, bureau (4)
comodidades *f. pl.* amenities, comforts
cómodo/a comfortable (4)
compacto/a: disco compacto compact disc (12)
compadres *m. pl.* godparents
compañero/a companion; compañero/a de clase classmate (1); compañero/a de cuarto roommate (1)
compañía company
comparación *f.* comparison (5)
comparar to compare
comparativo *gram.* comparative
compartir to share
compasión *f.* compassion
compensar to compensate, make up for
competencia skill
competición *f.* competition
complejo/a complex
complementar to complement
complemento complement
completar to complete
completo/a full, no vacancy (18); pensión (*f.*) completa room and full board (all meals) (18); trabajo de tiempo completo full-time job (12)
complicado/a complicated
complicar (qu) to complicate
comportamiento behavior
composición *f.* composition
compositor(a) composer (13)
comprar to buy (1)
compras: ir de compras to go shopping (3)
comprender to understand (2)
comprensión *f.* comprehension
comprensivo/a comprehensive; capable of understanding
compromiso compromise; commitment
computación *f.* computer science (1)
computadora computer (12); computadora portátil laptop computer (12)
común common, usual, ordinary

comunicación *f.* communication (1); medio de comunicación means of communication (17)
comunicar (qu) to communicate; comunicarse (con) to communicate (with) (17)
comunicativo/a communicative
comunidad *f.* community
comunismo communism
con with (1); con anticipación ahead of time (7); con cheque by (with a) check (16); con frecuencia frequently (1); con permiso pardon me, excuse me (AT); con tal (de) que *conj.* provided (that) (15)
concentración *f.* concentration
concentrar to concentrate; to focus
concepción *f.* conception; idea
concepto concept, idea
conciencia conscience
concierto concert (9); ir (*irreg.*) a un concierto to go to a concert (9)
concluir (y) to conclude
conclusión *f.* conclusion
concurso contest; game show
condado county
condenar to condemn
condición *f.* condition
condicional conditional
conducir (*irreg.*) to drive (*a vehicle*) (14)
conductor(a) driver (14)
conectar to connect
conexión *f.* connection
conferencia conference; lecture
conferenciante *m., f.* lecturer; speaker
confesarse (ie) to confess
confianza confidence
confiar (confío) (en) to confide (in); to trust (in)
confirmar to confirm (18)
confrontación *f.* confrontation
confundido/a confused
congelado/a frozen (5); very cold (5)
congelador *m.* freezer (9)
congestión *f.* congestion
congestionado/a congested (10)
congreso congress
conjugar (gu) *gram.* to conjugate
conjunción *f. gram.* conjunction (15)
conjunto collection, group
conmemorar to commemorate, remember
conmigo with me
conocer (zc) to know, be acquainted with (6); to meet
conocimiento awareness; *pl.* knowledge
conquista conquest
consecuencia consequence
conseguir (i, i) (g) to get, obtain (8); conseguir + *inf.* to succeed in (*doing something*) (8)
consejero/a advisor (1)
consejo (piece of) advice (6)
conservación *f.* preservation
conservador(a) *adj.* conservative
conservar to save, conserve (14)

considerar to consider, think
consistir en to consist of
conspirar to conspire, plot
constante *adj.* constant
constar de to consist of
constituir (y) to constitute; to be
construcción *f.* construction
construir (y) to build (14)
consultar to consult
consultorio (medical) office (10)
consumidor(a) consumer
consumir to eat; to use up
contabilidad *f.* accounting
contacto contact; **lentes** (*m. pl.*) **de contacto** contact lenses (10)
contado: pagar (gu) al contado to pay in cash (16)
contador(a) accountant (16)
contaminación *f.* pollution (5)
contaminado/a polluted
contaminar to pollute (14)
contar (ue) to count; to tell (17); **contar con** to count on
contener (*like* **tener**) to contain
contenido content(s)
contento/a happy, content (5)
contestador (*m.*) **automático** answering machine (12)
contestar to answer (4)
contexto context
contigo *fam. s.* with you
continente *m.* continent
continuación *f.*: **a continuación** following, below
continuar (continúo) to continue
contorno contour, outline
contra against; **en contra** opposed
contrabando contraband
contraer (*like* **traer**): **contraer matrimonio** to get married
contrario contrary, opposite; **al contrario** on the contrary; **lo contrario** the opposite
contratar to hire
contratiempo mishap, disappointment
contrato contract
contribución *f.* contribution
contribuir (y) to contribute
control (*m.*) **remoto** remote control (12)
controlar to control
convencer (z) to convince
convencional conventional
conveniencia convenience
conveniente convenient
conversación *f.* conversation
conversar to converse, talk
convertir (ie, i) to change; **convertirse (en)** to turn into
convivencia living together, cohabitation
convivir to live together
cooperación *f.* cooperation
cooperativo/a *adj.* cooperative
copa (*alcoholic*) drink (18); **Copa Mundial** World Cup
copia copy (12)
copiar to copy (12)

coraje *m.* courage
corazón *m.* heart (10)
corbata (neck) tie (3)
corcho cork
cordialmente cordially, warmly
cordillera mountain range
corona wreath
correcto/a correct
corregir (i, i) (j) to correct
correo mail (18); post office; **correo electrónico** electronic mail, e-mail (12); **oficina de correos** post office (18)
correr to run (9); to jog (9)
corresponder to correspond
correspondiente *adj.* corresponding
corresponsal *m., f.* correspondent, reporter
corrida bullfight
corrido ballad
corriente *adj.* current, present; **cuenta corriente** checking account (16)
cortar to cut
cortés *m., f.* courteous, polite
cortesía courtesy (AT); **saludos y expresiones de cortesía** greetings and expressions of courtesy (AT)
cortina curtain
corto/a short (*in length*) (2); **pantalones** (*m. pl.*) **cortos** shorts
cosa thing (2)
cosechar to harvest
cosmopolita *adj. m., f.* cosmopolitan
costa coast
costar (ue) to cost
costarricense *n., adj.* Costa Rican
costo cost
costumbre *f.* custom, habit (9)
cotidiano/a *adj.* daily
cráter *m.* crater
creación *f.* creation
crear to create (13)
creatividad *f.* creativity
creativo/a creative
crecer (zc) to grow (15)
creciente *adj.* growing
crédito credit; **tarjeta de crédito** credit card (6)
creer (y) (en) to think, believe (in) (2)
criado/a servant (16); **criada** maid (18)
criar(se) (me crío) to grow up, be raised
crimen *m.* crime (14)
criminal *m., f.* criminal
criollo/a Creole
cristiano/a Christian
crítica criticism
criticar (qu) to criticize
crítico/a *n.* critic
crónico/a *adj.* chronic
cronológico/a chronological
crudo/a raw
cruzar (c) to cross (18)
cuaderno notebook (1)
cuadro painting (13); **de cuadros** plaid (3)
¿cuál(es)? what? which? (AT); **¿cuál es la fecha de hoy?** what's today's date? (5)
cualidad *f.* quality

cualquier(a) any
cuando when
¿cuándo? when? (AT)
¿cuánto/a? how much? (AT); **¿cuánto cuesta?** how much does it cost? (3); **¿cuánto es?** how much is it? (3)
cuanto: en cuanto *conj.* as soon as (16); **en cuanto a** *prep.* regarding
¿cuántos/as? how many? (AT)
cuarenta forty (2)
cuaresma Lent
cuarto quarter (of an hour); room (1); **compañero/a de cuarto** roommate (1); **son/a (las tres) menos cuarto** it's/at a quarter to (three) (AT); **y cuarto** quarter past (*with time*) (AT)
cuarto/a *adj.* fourth (13)
cuatro four (AT); **Cuatro de Julio** Independence Day (8)
cuatrocientos/as four hundred (3)
cubano/a *n., adj.* Cuban
cubierto/a *p.p.* covered
cubrir (*p.p.* **cubierto/a**) to cover (14)
cuchara spoon
cuchillo knife
cuenta bill, check (6); account (16); **cargar (gu) (a la cuenta de uno)** to charge (to someone's account); **cuenta corriente** checking account (16); **cuenta de ahorros** savings account (16)
cuento short story
cuero leather
cuerpo body (10)
cuesta: ¿cuánto cuesta? how much does it cost? (3)
cuestión *f.* question (16)
cuidado care; **con cuidado** carefully; **tener** (*irreg.*) **cuidado** to be careful
cuidador(a) careful, cautious
cuidarse to take care of oneself (10)
culinario/a culinary
cultivar to cultivate
cultivo cultivation, raising (*crops*)
cultura culture
cumpleaños *m. s., pl.* birthday (5); **pastel** (*m.*) **de cumpleaños** birthday cake (8)
cumplir (con) to fulfill, carry out; **cumplir años** to have a birthday (8)
cuñado/a brother-in-law / sister-in-law
cupo quota, share
cura *m.* priest
curador(a) *m., f.* caretaker; curator; *adj.* curing, healing
curarse to cure oneself; **curarse de** to be cured of
currículum *m.* résumé (16)
cursar to frequent; to study (*in a university*)
cursivo/a: letras (*f. pl.*) **cursivas** italics
curso course
cuyo/a whose

D

danza dance (13)
daño damage; **hacerse** (*irreg.*) **daño** to hurt oneself (11)

dar (*irreg.*) to give (7); **dar un paseo** to take a walk (9); **dar una fiesta** to give a party (8); **darse con** to run, bump into (11); **me da asco** it makes me sick

datos *m. pl.* data, facts

de *prep.* of; from (AT); **de compras** shopping (3); **de cuadros** plaid (3); **¿de dónde es Ud.?** where are you from? (2); **de hecho** in fact (9); **de ida** one-way (ticket) (7); **de joven** as a youth (9); **de ida y vuelta** round trip (ticket) (7); **de la mañana/tarde** in the morning/afternoon (AT); **de la noche** in the evening, at night (AT); **de lujo** deluxe (18); **de lunares** polka-dotted (3); **de nada** you're welcome (AT); **de niño/a** as a child (9); **de rayas** striped (3); **de repente** suddenly (10); **de todo** everything (3); **de última moda** the latest style (3); **de viaje** on a trip (7)

debajo de *prep.* below (5)

deber (+ *inf.*) ought to, must, should (*do something*) (2)

deber *m.* responsibility, obligation (17)

debido a due to

débil weak

debilitamiento weakness

década decade

decente decent, suitable

decidir to decide

décimo/a *adj.* tenth (13)

decir (*irreg.*) to say (7); to tell (7); **es decir** that is to say (7)

decisión *f.* decision

decisivo/a decisive

declaración *f.* declaration; statement

declarar to declare (18)

decoración *f.* decoration; decor

decorar to decorate, adorn

dedicarse (**qu**) (**a**) to dedicate (oneself) (to)

dedo (de la mano) finger (11); **dedo del pie** toe (11)

deducir (*irreg.*) to deduct; to infer

defecto defect

defensa defense

definición *f.* definition

definir to define

deforestación *f.* deforestation

deformación *f.* deformation

dejar (en) to leave (behind) (in, at) (9); to quit (16); **dejar de** + *inf.* to stop (*doing something*) (10)

del (*contraction of* **de** + **el**) of the, from the (2)

delante de *prep.* in front of (5)

delegación *f.* delegation

delgado/a thin, slender (2)

delicado/a delicate

delicioso/a delicious

delito crime (14)

demanda demand

demás *adj.* other, rest of; **los/las demás** the others, the rest (12)

demasiado *adv.* too, too much (9)

demasiado/a *adj.* too much; *pl.* too many

democracia democracy

demonio devil, demon

demora delay (7)

demostración *f.* demonstration

demostrar (**ue**) to demonstrate

demostrativo/a *gram.* demonstrative (3)

denso/a dense (14)

dental: pasta dental toothpaste (18)

dentista *m., f.* dentist (10)

dentro *adv.* in, within, inside; **dentro de** *prep.* inside of

denunciar to denounce

departamento department; apartment

depender de to depend on

dependiente/a clerk (1)

deporte *m.* sport (9); **practicar** (**qu**) **deportes** to participate in sports (9)

deportista *m., f.* sports player (8)

deportivo/a *adj.* sports-loving (9)

depositar to deposit (16)

depósito deposit

deprimente *adj.* depressing

derecha *n.* right; **a la derecha (de)** to the right (of) (5)

derecho *n.* right (*legal*) (17); *adv.* straight ahead; **derechos** (*m. pl.*) (**de aduana**) (customs) duty (18); **seguir** (**i, i**) (**g**) **derecho** to continue straight ahead; **todo derecho** straight ahead (14)

derechos (*m. pl.*) **humanos** human rights

derivar to derive

dermatológico/a dermatologic, skin

derrocar (**qu**) to overthrow

derrotar to defeat

desafortunadamente unfortunately

desagradable unpleasant

desamparados *m. pl.* homeless people

desaparecer (**zc**) to disappear

desarrollar to develop (14)

desarrollo development

desastre *m.* disaster (17)

desastroso/a disastrous

desayunar to have (eat) breakfast (6)

desayuno breakfast (4)

descafeinado/a decaffeinated

descalzo/a barefooted

descansar to rest (4)

descapotable convertible (*car*) (12)

descendiente *m., f.* descendant

desconocido/a unknown

descortés *m., f.* impolite

describir (*p.p.* **descrito/a**) to describe

descripción *f.* description

descubierto/a *p.p.* discovered

descubrimiento discovery

descubrir (*p.p.* **descubierto/a**) to discover (14)

descuidado/a careless

desde *prep.* from; since; **desde que** *conj.* since

deseable desirable (12)

desear to want (1)

desempeñar to play, perform (*a part*) (13)

desempleo unemployment

desenchufado/a unplugged (*appliances*)

deseo wish (8)

desequilibrio unbalance, imbalance

desértico/a *adj.* desert-like; deserted

desertización *f.* process of turning into a desert

desesperación *f.* desperation

desesperadamente desperately

desfile *m.* parade

desgracia misfortune; **¡qué desgracia!** what a shame!

deshidratación *f.* dehydration

desierto/a deserted; **desierto** desert

desigualdad *f.* inequality (17)

desinflado/a flat (*tire*) (14)

desocupado/a vacant, unoccupied (18)

desordenado/a messy (5)

desorientado/a disoriented

despacio *adv.* slowly

despedida good-bye, farewell

despedirse (**i, i**) (**de**) to say good-bye (to), take leave (of) (8)

despegar (**gu**) to take off (*airplane*)

desperdiciar to waste (14)

despertador *m.* alarm clock (11)

despertarse (**ie**) to wake up (4)

desplegar (**ie**) (**gu**) to unfold

desposeído/a dispossessed

después *adv.* afterwards; **después de** *prep.* after (4); **después (de) que** *conj.* after (16)

destacado/a outstanding

destacar (**qu**) to stand out

destinación *f.* destination

destinado/a (**a**) destined (for)

destino destination

destreza skill

destrucción *f.* destruction

destruir (**y**) to destroy (14)

desventaja disadvantage (10)

detalle *m.* detail (6)

detective *m.* detective

detener (*like* **tener**) to stop, detain

detenidamente carefully, in detail

determinar to determine

detestar to detest

detrás de *prep.* behind (5)

devolver (**ue**) (*p.p.* **devuelto/a**) to return (*something*) (16)

día *m.* day (1); **buenos días** good morning (AT); **Día de Acción de Gracias** Thanksgiving; **Día de Año Nuevo** New Year's Day; **Día de la Independencia** Independence Day; **Día de la Raza** Columbus Day; **Día de los Enamorados (de San Valentín)** St. Valentine's Day; **Día de los Muertos** Day of the Dead; **Día de los Reyes Magos** Day of the Magi; **Día de San Patricio** St. Patrick's Day; **Día de Todos los Santos** All Saints' Day; **día del santo** saint's day; **día festivo** holiday (8); **hoy (en) día** nowadays; **todos los días** every day (1)

diablo devil

diálogo dialogue

diamante *m.* diamond

diario/a *adj.* daily; **rutina diaria** daily routine (4)
dibujar to draw (13)
dibujo drawing; **dibujos** (*m. pl.*) **animados** cartoons
diccionario dictionary (1)
dicho *n.* saying
dicho/a *p.p.* said
diciembre *m.* December (5)
dictador(a) dictator (17)
dictadura dictatorship (17)
dictar to dictate
diecinueve nineteen (AT)
dieciocho eighteen (AT)
dieciséis sixteen (AT)
diecisiete seventeen (AT)
diente *m.* tooth (10); **cepillarse los dientes** to brush one's teeth (4)
dieta diet; **a dieta** on a diet
dietético/a *adj.* diet, dietetic
diez ten (AT)
diferencia difference; **a diferencia de** unlike
diferente different
difícil difficult, hard (5)
dificultad *f.* difficulty
difunto/a deceased
dignidad *f.* dignity
dimensión *f.* dimension
Dinamarca Denmark
dinero money (1)
Dios *s. m.* God; **por Dios** for God's sake (11)
diplomático/a diplomatic, tactful; *n.* diplomat
diptongo *gram.* diphthong
diputado/a deputy, representative
dirección *f.* address (12); **dirección de personal** personnel office, employment office (16)
directo/a direct; straight
director(a) director (13); **director(a) de personal** personnel director (16)
dirigir (j) to direct
disciplinado/a disciplined, trained
disco compacto compact disc (12); **disco de computadora** computer disk (12); **disco duro** hard drive (12)
discoteca discotheque (9)
discriminación *f.* discrimination (17)
disculpa excuse, apology; **pedir (i, i) disculpas** to apologize (11)
disculparse to excuse oneself, apologize; **discúlpeme** pardon me, I'm sorry (11)
discutir (sobre) (con) to argue (about) (with) (8)
diseñador(a) designer
diseñar to draw; to design
diseño design
disfraz *m.* (*pl.* **disfraces**) costume, disguise
disfrutar to enjoy
disipar to dissipate
disminuir (y) to lower (*temperature*); to reduce, diminish
disparar to fire, shoot

disponible available
disputa dispute, argument
distancia distance
distante distant
distinto/a different
distraer (*like* **traer**) to distract
distraído/a absentminded (11)
distrito district
disturbio disturbance
diversificado/a diversified
diversión *f.* entertainment, amusement (9)
diverso/a diverse; various
divertido/a fun; **ser** (*irreg.*) **divertido/a** to be fun (9)
divertirse (ie, i) to enjoy oneself, have a good time (4)
divorciarse (de) to get divorced (from) (15)
divorcio divorce (15)
divulgar (gu) to divulge, disclose
doblar to bend; to turn (14)
doble *adj.* double (18); **habitación** (*f.*) **doble** double room (18)
doce twelve (AT)
docena dozen
doctor(a) doctor
doctorado doctorate
documental *m.* documentary
documentar to document
documento document
dólar *m.* dollar
doler (ue) to hurt, ache (10); **me/te duele(n)...** my/your . . . hurt(s)
dolor *m.* pain, ache (10); **dolor de cabeza** headache; **tener** (*irreg.*) **dolor (de)** to have a pain (in) (10)
doméstico/a domestic; **aparato doméstico** home appliance (9); **quehacer** (*m.*) **doméstico** household chore (9)
domingo Sunday (4)
dominicano/a *n., adj.* of the Dominican Republic
dominio power; control
don *m. title of respect used with a man's first name*
donde where
¿dónde? where? (AT); **¿adónde?** where (to)?; **¿de dónde es Ud.?** Where are you from? (2)
dondequiera *adv.* wherever, anywhere
doña *title of respect used with a woman's first name*
dormir (ue, u) to sleep (4); **dormir la siesta** to take a nap (4); **dormirse** to fall asleep (4)
dormitorio bedroom
dos two (AT); **dos veces** twice (10)
doscientos/as two hundred (3)
dosis *f. s.* dose
drama *m.* drama (13)
dramatización *f.* dramatization
dramatizar (c) to dramatize
dramaturgo/a playwright (13)
droga drug

drogadicto/a drug addict
dualidad *f.* duality
ducha shower (18); **habitación** (*f.*) **con/sin ducha** room with(out) a shower (18)
ducharse to take a shower (4)
duda doubt; **no hay duda** there's no doubt; **sin duda** without a doubt
dudar to doubt (17)
dueño/a owner (6); landlord, landlady (12)
dulces *m. pl.* sweets (6); candy (6)
dulzura sweetness
durante during (4)
durar to last (17)
durmiente: Bella Durmiente Sleeping Beauty
duro/a hard; firm; **disco duro** hard drive (12)

E

e and (*used instead of* **y** *before words beginning with stressed* **i** *or* **hi**)
ecología ecology
ecológico/a ecological
economía economy (1)
económico/a economic
economizar (c) to economize (16)
ecosistema *m.* ecosystem
ecoturismo ecoturism
ecuador *m.* equator
ecuatoriano/a *n., adj.* Ecuadorean
edad *f.* age
edificio building (1)
editar to edit
educación *f.* education
educado/a educated; polite; **mal educado/a** rude, bad-mannered
educativo/a educational
efectivo cash; **en efectivo** in cash (16)
efecto effect
eficiencia efficiency
Egipto Egypt
ejecutivo/a executive
ejemplar *m.* issue (*of a magazine*)
ejemplificar (qu) to exemplify; illustrate
ejemplo example; **por ejemplo** for example
ejercicio exercise (3); **hacer** (*irreg.*) **ejercicios** to do exercise (4); **hacer** (*irreg.*) **ejercicio aeróbico** to do aerobics (10)
ejército army (17)
el the (*definite article m.*)
él *sub. pron.* he (1); *obj.* (*of prep.*) him
elección *f.* election
electricidad *f.* electricity
electricista *m., f.* electrician (16)
eléctrico/a electric (14)
electrodoméstico electric appliance
electrónica *f. s.* electronics (12)
electrónico/a *adj.* electronic; **agenda electrónica** electronic calendar; **aparato electrónico** electronic device; **correo electrónico** electronic mail, e-mail (12)

electrostático/a electrostatic
elefante *m.* elephant
elegancia elegance
elegante elegant
elegir (i, i) (j) to choose, select
elemento element
elevar to raise, lift; to rise, increase
eliminar to get rid of, "drop"
ella *sub. pron.* she (1); *obj. (of prep.)* her
ellos/as *sub. pron. f.* they (1); *obj. (of prep.)* them
embajada embassy
embarazada pregnant
embarcar (qu) to set off (for a destination)
embargo: sin embargo however, nevertheless
embotellamiento traffic jam
emergencia emergency; **sala de emergencias** emergency room (10)
emigrar to emigrate
emisión *f.* broadcast
emoción *f.* emotion (8)
emocional emotional
emocionante moving, touching
empapelado/a wallpapered
emparejar to match
emperador *m.* emperor
empezar (ie) (c) to begin (4); **empezar a** + *inf.* to begin to (*do something*)
empleado/a employee
empleo job
empresa corporation, business (16); **administración** (*f.*) **de empresa** business administration (1)
en in; on; at (AT); **en casa** at home (1); **en caso de que** *conj.* in case (15); **en cuanto** as soon as (16); **en efectivo** in cash (16); **en punto** exactly, on the dot (*time*) (AT); **en vez de** instead of (16)
enamorado/a (de) *adj.* in love (with); **Día** (*m.*) **de los Enamorados (de San Valentín)** St. Valentine's Day (8)
enamorarse (de) to fall in love (with) (15)
encabezar (c) to lead, head
encaje *m.* lace
encantado/a delighted; pleased to meet you (AT)
encantador(a) *adj.* delightful, charming
encantar to like very much, love (7)
encargarse (gu) de to be in charge of
encender (ie) to turn on, light
encendido/a lit up
enchufar to plug in
encima de *prep.* on top of (5)
encontrar (ue) to find (8); **encontrarse** to be, feel (10); **encontrarse (con)** to meet (*someone somewhere*) (10)
encuesta survey
enemistad *f.* animosity
energía energy (14)
enero January (5)
énfasis *m. s.* emphasis
enfático/a emphatic
enfermarse to get sick (8)

enfermedad *f.* sickness (10)
enfermero/a *n.* nurse (10)
enfermo/a *adj.* sick (5)
enfisema *m.* emphysema
enfoque *m.* focus
enfrente *adv.* in front; **enfrente de** *prep.* in front of
enhorabuena congratulations
enlace *m.* link
enojarse (con) to get angry (at) (8)
enorme enormous
enriquecer (zc) to enrich
ensalada salad (6)
ensayista *m., f.* essayist
ensayo essay
enseñanza teaching
enseñar to teach (1)
entender (ie) to understand (4)
enterarse (de) to find out (about) (17)
entero/a whole, entire (9); **limpiar la casa entera** to clean the whole house (9)
enterrar (ie) to bury
entonces then
entrada entrance; ticket
entrar to enter
entre *prep.* between, among (5)
entregar (gu) to hand in, turn in (11)
entrelazado/a intertwined
entremeses *m. pl.* hors d'oeuvres (8)
entrenamiento training
entrenar to train, practice (9)
entretejerse to interweave
entrevista interview
entrevistado/a interviewee
entrevistador(a) interviewer (16)
entrevistar to interview (16)
enviar (envío) to send
envidia envy
envuelto/a *p.p.* wrapped
eólico/a *adj.* wind (14)
epifanía Epiphany
episodio episode
época era, time (*period*) (9)
equilibradamente in a balanced way (10)
equilibrado/a well-balanced
equilibrio balance
equipado/a equipped
equipaje *m.* baggage, luggage (7); **facturar el equipaje** to check one's bags (7)
equipo team; equipment; **equipo estereofónico** stereo equipment (12)
equivalente *n. m.* equivalence; *adj.* equivalent
equivocarse (qu) to be wrong, make a mistake (11)
eres you (*fam.*) are (AT)
ergonómico/a ergonomic
error *m.* error, mistake
erupción *f.* eruption
es he/she/it is (AT); **¿cómo es usted?** what are you like?; **¿cuánto es?** how much is it? (3); **es cierto** it's certain

(13); **es de algodón** it is made of cotton (3); **es de lana** it is made of wool (3); **es de seda** it is made of silk (3); **es extraño** it's strange (13); **es increíble** it's incredible (13); **es la (una)** it's (one) o'clock (AT); **es lástima** it is a shame (13); **es preferible** it's preferable (13); **es seguro** it's a sure thing (5); **es urgente** it's urgent (13) **¿qué hora es?** what time is it? (AT)
escala: hacer (*irreg.*) **escalas** to make stops (7)
escalar to climb
escalera stairs; ladder
escalón *m.* stair, step
escalopines *m. pl.* breaded cutlets
escándalo scandal
escapar (de) to escape (from)
escaparate *m.* store (display) window
escasez *f.* (*pl.* **escaseces**) lack, shortage (14)
escaso/a scarce
escayolar to put a cast on
escena scene
escenario stage (13)
esclavitud *f.* slavery
esclavo/a slave
Escocia Scotland
escoger (j) to choose
escolar of or pertaining to school
esconder(se) to hide
Escorpio Scorpio
escribir (*p.p.* **escrito/a**) to write (2); **escribir a máquina** to type (16)
escrito/a *p.p.* written (11)
escritor(a) writer (13)
escritorio desk (1)
escritura writing
escuadrón *m.* squadron
escuchar to listen (to) (1)
escudo shield
escuela school (9)
esculpir to sculpt (13)
escultor(a) sculptor (13)
escultura sculpture (13)
ese, esa *adj.* that (3); *pron.* that one (3)
esencial essential
esfera sphere
esfuerzo effort
eso that (3); **eso quiere decir...** that means . . . (10); **por eso** therefore (1)
esos/as *adj.* those (3); *pron.* those (ones) (3)
espacial *adj.* space
espacio *n.* space
espacioso/a spacious
espantoso/a frightening
español *m.* Spanish (*language*) (1)
español(a) *n., adj.* Spanish (1)
espárragos *m. pl.* asparagus (6)
especial special
especialidad *f.* specialty
especialista *m., f.* specialist
especie *f. s.* species
específico/a specific
espectáculo spectacle, sight

espeleología spelunking
espera: sala de espera waiting room (7)
esperanza *n.* hope, wish (17)
esperar to wait (for) (6); to expect (6); to hope (12)
espina thorn
espíritu *m.* spirit
esposo/a husband/wife (2)
esqueleto skeleton
esquí *m.* skiing
esquiar (esquío) to ski (9)
esquina (street) corner (14)
está he/she/it is (AT); **¿cómo está?** how are you? (AT); **está nublado** it is cloudy (5)
esta noche tonight (5)
estabilidad *f.* stability
establecer (zc) to establish
estación *f.* season (5); station (7); **estación de autobuses** bus station (7); **estación de gasolina** gas station (14); **estación del metro** subway station (18); **estación del tren** train station (7)
estacionamiento parking lot
estacionar to park (11)
estadía *n.* stay
estado state; condition (2); **Estados Unidos** *m. pl.* United States
estadounidense *n., adj. m., f.* American (from the United States)
estallar to break out (*epidemic, war*)
estampilla stamp
estancia *n.* stay (*in a hotel*) (18)
estanco tobacco stand/shop (18)
estante *m.* bookshelf (4)
estar (*irreg.*) to be (1); **¿cómo está(s)?** how are you? (AT); **está nublado** it's cloudy (5); **estar a dieta** to be on a diet; **estar atrasado/a** to be late (7); **estar bien** to be comfortable (*temperature*) (5); **estar cansado/a** to be tired; **estar de acuerdo** to agree (2); **estar de vacaciones** to be on vacation (7); **estar distraído/a** to be absentminded; **estar enfermo/a** to be sick; **(no) estoy de acuerdo** I (don't) agree (2)
estatal *adj.* state
estatua statue
este *m.* east (5)
este/a *adj.* this (2); *pron.* this one (2)
estéreo stereo
estereofónico/a: equipo estereofónico stereo equipment (12)
estereotipo stereotype
estilo style
estimar to estimate; to value
estimulante stimulating
estimular to stimulate; to encourage
esto *pron.* this (3)
estómago stomach (10)
estos/as *adj.* these (2); *pron.* these (ones) (2)
estoy de acuerdo I agree (2); **no estoy de acuerdo** I don't agree (2)
estrategia strategy

estratégico/a strategic
estrecho/a close
estrella star
estrés *m.* stress (11)
estricto/a strict
estructura structure
estudiante *m., f.* student (1)
estudiantil *adj.* student (11)
estudiar to study (1)
estudio study; *pl.* studies, schooling
estudioso/a studious
estufa stove (9)
estupendo/a stupendous
etapa step; stage (15)
étnico/a ethnic
europeo/a *n., adj.* European
evaluar (evalúo) to evaluate
evento chance event
evidente evident
evitar to avoid (14)
evolución *f.* evolution
exacto/a exact
exagerado/a exaggerated
examen *m.* test, exam (3)
examinar to examine (10)
excedente excessive, superfluous
exceder to exceed
excelente excellent
excepción *f.* exception
excepto *prep.* except
exceso excess
exclusivo/a exclusive
excursión *f.* excursion
excusa excuse
exhibición *f.* exhibition
exigente *adj.* demanding
exigir (j) to demand
exilarse to be exiled
existencia existence
existir to exist
éxito success; **tener** (*irreg.*) **éxito** to be successful
exitoso/a successful
éxodo exodus, emigration
exótico/a exotic; strange
expectativa expectation
experiencia experience
experimento experiment
experto/a *n., adj.* expert
explicación *f.* explanation
explicar (qu) to explain (7)
exploración *f.* exploration
explosión *f.* explosion
explosivo/a explosive
explotación *f.* exploitation, development
explotar to exploit
exportación *f.* exportation
exposición *f.* show, exhibition
expresar to express
expresión *f.* expression; **saludos y expresiones de cortesía** greetings and expressions of courtesy (AT)
expuesto/a *p.p.* exposed; on display
expulsar to expel
expulsión *f.* expulsion
extender (ie) to extend

extensión *f.* extension
extenso/a extensive, vast
extinguido/a extinguished
extraer (*like* **traer**) to extract
extranjero/a *n.* foreigner (1); *m.* abroad (18); *adj.* foreign; **lenguas** (*f. pl.*) **extranjeras** foreign languages (1)
extrañar to miss
extraño/a strange (13); **¡qué extraño!** how strange! (13)
extraordinario/a extraordinary
extravagante extravagant
extremo end, tip
extroversión *f.* extroversion
extrovertido/a extrovert
exuberancia exuberance
exuberante exuberant

F

fábrica factory (14)
fabricar (qu) to make, manufacture
fabuloso/a fabulous
fachada facade
fácil easy (5)
facilidad *f.* facility; ease; ability
facilitar to facilitate
factible feasible, workable
factor *m.* factor, cause
factura bill, invoice (16)
facturar (el equipaje) to check (one's bags) (7)
facultad *f.* faculty; campus; department (*of a university*)
falda skirt (3)
fallar to "crash" (*computer*) (12)
falsificado/a falsified
falso/a false
falta lack (11); absence (14)
faltar to be absent, lacking (8)
familia family (2)
familiar *n. m.* relation, member of the family; *adj.* pertaining to a family
famoso/a famous
fantasía fantasy
fantástico/a fantastic
farmacéutico/a pharmacist (10)
farmacia pharmacy (10)
farmacología pharmacology
faro lighthouse
fascinante *adj.* fascinating
fatiga fatigue
favor *m.* favor; **por favor** please (AT)
favorable favorable
favorecer (zc) to favor; to support
favorito/a favorite
fax *m.* fax (12)
febrero February (5)
fecha date (*calendar*) (5); **¿cuál es la fecha de hoy?** what is the date today? (5); **fecha límite** deadline (11)
felicitaciones *f. pl.* congratulations (8)
feliz (*pl.* **felices**) happy (8); **Feliz Año Nuevo** Happy New Year; **feliz cumpleaños** happy birthday; **Feliz Navidad** Merry Christmas; **ser** (*irreg.*) **feliz** to be happy

femenino/a feminine
feminidad *f.* femininity
fenicio/a Phoenician
fenomenal great
fenómeno phenomenon
feo/a ugly (2)
feria holiday
feriado/a: día (*m.*) **feriado** holiday
feroz (*pl.* **feroces**) ferocious
festival *m.* festival
festividad *f.* festivity
festivo/a: día (*m.*) **festivo** holiday (8)
ficción *f.*: **ciencia ficción** science fiction
ficticio/a fictional
fiebre *f.* fever (10); **tener** (*irreg.*) **fiebre** to have a fever
fiel faithful (2)
fiesta party (1); **dar** (*irreg.*)/**hacer** (*irreg.*) **una fiesta** to give/have a party (8)
figura figure
fijar to imagine; **fijarse en** to take note of
fijo/a fixed; **precio fijo** fixed price (3)
filmación *f.* shooting, filming
filmar to film
filosofía philosophy (1)
fin *m.* end; **en fin** in short; **fin de semana** weekend (1); **por fin** finally, at last (4)
final *n. m.* end; **al final de** at the end of; *adj.* final
financiamiento *n.* financing
financiar to finance
financiero/a financial
finanzas *f. pl.* finances
finca farm (14)
firmar to sign
firme firm, steady: **ponerse** (*irreg.*) **firme** to stand at attention
física physics (1)
físico/a physical (6)
flan *m.* baked custard (6)
flexibilidad *f.* flexibility (11)
flexible flexible (11)
flor *f.* flower (7)
florecer (**zc**) to flourish
folklore *m.* folklore (15)
folklórico/a folkloric (13)
fomentar to promote; to encourage
fondo fund; **al fondo** background
forjar to forge
forma form (3); shape
formación *f.* background
formar to form
fórmula formula; prescription
formular to formulate
formulario form (*to fill out*) (18)
fósforo match (*for lighting things*) (18)
foto(grafía) photo(graph) (7); **sacar** (**qu**) **fotos** to take photos (7)
fotografiado/a photographed
fotográfico/a photographic
fotógrafo/a photographer (16)
fotos (*f. pl.*): **sacar** (**qu**) **fotos** to take pictures
fracturado/a fractured, broken

frágil fragile
fragmento excerpt
fraile *m.* friar, monk, priest
francés *n. m.* French (*language*) (1)
francés, francesa *n., adj.* French (2)
franciscano/a Franciscan
frase *f.* sentence, phrase
frecuencia: con frecuencia frequently (1)
frecuente frequent
fregar (**ie**) (**gu**) to scrub, scour
frenar to brake
frenos *m. pl.* brakes (14)
fresco/a fresh (6); cool; **hace fresco** it's cool (*weather*) (5)
frialdad *f.* coldness
frigidez *f.* frigidity
frigorífico *Sp.* refrigerator
frijol *m.* bean (6)
frío *n.* cold(ness) (5); **hace frío** it's cold (*weather*) (5); **tener** (*irreg.*) **frío** to be cold (5)
frío/a *adj.* cold;
frito/a fried (6); **patata/papa frita** French-fried potato (6)
frontera border (16)
frustrado/a frustrated
fruta fruit (6); **jugo de fruta** fruit juice (6)
fruto fruit
fue sin querer it was unintentional (11)
fuego fire; **fuegos artificiales** fireworks
fuente *f.* source; fountain
fuera de *prep.* outside (of)
fuerte strong (6); heavy (*meal, food*) (6)
fuerza strength; **fuerzas armadas** *pl.* armed forces
fumador(a) smoker
fumar to smoke (7); **sección** (*f.*) **de (no) fumar** (non)smoking section (7)
función *f.* function; performance
funcionar to work, function (12); to run (*machines*) (12)
fundación *f.* founding, foundation
fundador(a) founder
fundar to found
furioso/a furious, angry (5)
fútbol *m.* soccer (9); **fútbol americano** football (9)
futuro *n.* future (12)

G

gafas *f. pl.* (eye)glasses (10)
galería gallery
galleta cookie (6)
gallinero henhouse
gamba shrimp, prawn
ganado cattle
ganador(a) winner
ganar to win (9); to earn (12)
ganas *f. pl.* desire, wish; **tener** (*irreg.*) **ganas de** + *inf.* to feel like (*doing something*) (3)
ganga bargain (3)
garaje *m.* garage (4)
garantizar (**c**) to guarantee
garganta throat (10)

gas *m.s.* gas (12); heat (12)
gasolina gasoline (14)
gasolinera gas station (14)
gastar to spend (*money*) (8); to use, expend (14)
gasto expense (12)
gastronómico/a gastronomic
gato/a cat (2)
gazpacho *Sp.* cold soup prepared with oil, vinegar, tomatoes, garlic, and onions
gemelo/a twin
Géminis Gemini
generación *f.* generation
general *adj.* general; **en general** in general; **por lo general** generally
género gender; type
generoso/a generous
génesis *m. s.* beginning(s)
genio genius
gente *f. s.* people (15)
geografía geography
geográfico/a geographical
germánico/a Germanic
gerontología gerontology
gerundio *gram.* present participle
gigante *adj.* giant, huge
gimnasio gymnasium
glaciación *f.* glaciation
globo balloon
gobernador(a) governor
gobernante *m.* ruler, leader
gobernar (**ie**) to govern, rule (17)
gobierno government (14)
golf *m.* golf (9)
gordo/a fat (2)
gorra cap
gozar (**c**) **de** to enjoy
grabadora tape recorder/player (12)
grabar to record (12); to tape (12)
gracias thank you (AT); **Día** (*m.*) **de Acción de Gracias** Thanksgiving (8); **gracias por** thanks for (8); **muchas gracias** thank you very much (AT)
grado grade, year (*in school*) (9)
graduado/a *adj.* graduate
graduarse (**me gradúo**) (**en**) to graduate (from) (16)
gráfico/a *adj.* graphic
gramática grammar
gran, grande big, large (2); great (2)
granada pomegranate
grandeza majesty; grandeur; greatness
grasa *n.* fat; grease
gratis *adv. inv.* free (of charge)
gratuito/a *adj.* free (of charge)
grave serious; important
Grecia Greece
griego/a *n., adj.* Greek
gripe *f.* flu
gris gray (3)
gritar to yell, shout
grotesco/a grotesque
grupo group
guapo/a handsome; good-looking (2)
guaraní *m.* Guarani (*L.A. Indian language*)

guardar to watch over; to keep (12); to save (*a place*) (7); to save (*documents*) (12); **guardar cama** to stay in bed (10)

guardia *m.* guard, guardsman

guerra war (17)

guerrero/a *adj.* war; warlike

guía *m., f.* guide (13); **guía** (*f.*) **telefónica** telephone book

guiar (guío) to guide

guión *m.* script (13)

guitarra guitar

guitarrista *m., f.* guitarist

gustar to be pleasing (7); **¿le gusta... ?** do you (*form.*) like . . . ? (AT); **(no) me gusta(n)...** I (don't) like . . . (AT); **(no) te gusta(n)...** you (*fam.*) (don't) like . . . (AT); **me gustaría...** I would like . . . (7)

gusto like, preference (AT); **a su gusto** to your taste; **buen gusto** good taste; **mucho gusto** pleased to meet you (AT)

H

haber (*irreg.*) (*inf. form of* **hay**) (there is/are) (12)

habilidad *f.* ability; skill

habitación *f.* room (*in a hotel*) (18); **habitación individual/doble** single/double room (18); **habitación con/sin baño/ducha** room with(out) bath/shower (18)

habitante *m., f.* inhabitant

hábito habit

hablar to speak (1); to talk (1); **hablar por teléfono** to talk on the phone (1)

hace + *time* ago (11); **hace** + *period of time* + **que** + *present tense* to have been (*doing something*) for (*a period of time*) (11)

hacer (*irreg.*) to make; to do (4); **hace** + *time* (*time*) ago (11); **hace** + *time* + **que...** + *present tense* it's been (*time*) since . . . (11); **hace buen/mal tiempo** it's good/bad weather (5); **hace fresco** it's cool (5); **hace frío/calor** it's cold/hot (5); **hace sol** it's sunny (5); **hace viento** it's windy (5); **hacer** *camping* to go camping (7); **hacer cola** to stand in line (7); **hacer copia** to copy (12); **hacer ejercicios (aeróbicos)** to do (aerobic) exercise (4); **hacer escalas/paradas** to make stops (7); **hacer la cama** to make the bed (9); **hacer la(s) maleta(s)** to pack one's suitcase(s) (7); **hacer planes para** + *inf.* to make plans to (*do something*) (9); **hacer un** *picnic* to have a picnic (9); **hacer un viaje** to take a trip (4); **hacer una fiesta** to give/have a party (8); **hacer una pregunta** to ask a question (4); **hacerse daño** to hurt oneself (11)

hacia toward

hambre *f.* (*but* **el hambre**) hunger (6); **tener** (*irreg.*) **(mucha) hambre** to be (very) hungry (6)

hamburguesa hamburger (6)

hasta *prep.* until (4); **hasta luego** see you later (AT); **hasta mañana** see you tomorrow (AT); **hasta que** *conj.* until (16)

hay: (no) hay there is (not), there are (not) (AT); **hay (mucha) contaminación** there's (lots of) pollution (5); **hay que** + *inf.* it is necessary to (*do something*) (13); **no hay de qué** you're welcome (AT)

hebreo Hebrew (*language*) (15)

hecho *n.* event, fact (8); **de hecho** in fact (9)

hecho/a *p.p.* made, done

hectárea *land measure equal to 2.5 acres*

helado ice cream (6)

hemisferio hemisphere

heredar to inherit

herencia heritage

hermanastro/a stepbrother/stepsister

hermano/a brother/sister (2); **medio hermano/media hermana** half-brother/half-sister

hermoso/a beautiful

héroe *m.* hero

hidráulico/a hydraulic (14)

hidroeléctrico/a hydroelectric

higiene *f.* hygiene

higiénico/a hygienic

higuera fig tree

hijastro/a stepson/stepdaughter

hijo/a son/daughter (2); *m. pl.* children (2)

himno hymn

hipopótamo hippopotamus

hipoteca mortgage

hipótesis *f. s.* hypothesis

hispánico/a *n., adj.* Hispanic

hispanidad *f.* community of Spanish-speaking cultures

hispano/a *n., adj.* Hispanic

hispanoamericano/a Latin American

historia history (1)

historiador(a) historian

histórico/a historical

hockey *m.* hockey (9)

hogar *m.* home

hola hello (AT)

hombre *m.* man (1); **hombre de negocios** businessperson (16)

honesto/a honest, sincere (15)

honrado/a *p.p.* honored

hora hour; **¿a qué hora?** (at) what time? (AT); **¿qué hora es?** what time is it? (AT)

horario schedule (11)

hornear to bake

horno de microondas microwave oven (9)

horóscopo horoscope

hospicio hospice

hospital *m.* hospital

hotel *m.* **(de lujo)** (luxury) hotel (18)

hoy today (AT); **¿cuál es la fecha de hoy?** what's today's date? (5); **hoy (en) día** nowadays

huelga *n.* strike (*labor*) (17)

huerto orchard

hueso: carne (*f.*) **y hueso** flesh and blood

huésped(a) (hotel) guest (18)

huevo egg (6)

huir (y) to flee

humanidad *f.* humanity; *pl.* humanities (1)

humanitario/a humanitarian

humano/a *n., adj.* human (10)

humedad *f.* humidity

humilde humble

humor *m.* humor; mood; **estar** (*irreg.*) **de mal humor** to be in a bad mood; **sentido del humor** sense of humor

Hungría Hungary

huracán *m.* hurricane

I

ibérico/a Iberian

ida: boleto de ida one-way ticket (7); **boleto de ida y vuelta** round-trip ticket (7)

idéntico/a identical

identificación *f.* identification

identificarse (qu) to identify

idioma *m.* language

iglesia church

ignorante ignorant

igual equal

igualdad *f.* equality (17)

igualmente likewise, same here (AT)

ilegal illegal

iluminación *f.* illumination

imagen *f.* image

imaginación *f.* imagination

imaginar to imagine

imaginario/a imaginary

imitar to imitate

impaciente impatient

impacto impact

impar odd (*with numbers*)

imperfecto/a imperfect

imperio empire

impermeable *m.* raincoat (3)

importancia importance

importante important

importar to matter, be important; **(no) importar(le)** to (not) matter (to someone)

importe *m.* amount, cost, value

imposible impossible

imprescindible indispensable

impresión *f.* impression

impresionante impressive

impresionar to impress

impresora printer (12)

imprimir to print (12)

impulsivo/a impulsive

inadecuado/a inadequate

inaugurar to inaugurate

inca *m.* Inca

incaico/a *adj.* Inca, Incan

incidencia incidence

incidente *m.* incident

incluir (y) to include

inclusive *adj.* including
incomodar to inconvenience, bother
inconcebible inconceivable
inconveniente *m.* drawback, difficulty
incorrecto/a incorrect
increíble unbelievable (13)
incrementar to increase, augment
incursión *f.* incursion
indefinido/a indefinite (6)
independencia independence; **Día** (*m.*) **de la Independencia** Independence Day (8)
independiente independent
indicación *f.* instruction; direction
indicado/a indicated
indicar (qu) to indicate
indicativo *gram.* indicative
índice *m.* index
indígena *adj. m., f.* indigenous
indio/a *n.* Indian
indirecto/a indirect
indiscreto/a indiscreet
indispensable essential
individual: habitación (*f.*) **individual** single room (18)
individuo person; individual
industria industry
inevitablemente inevitably
infancia infancy (15)
infantil *adj.* infant
infección *f.* infection
inferior inferior; lower
infinito/a infinite
infinitivo *gram.* infinitive
influencia influence
influyente influential
información *f.* information
informar to inform (17)
informativo/a informative
informe *m.* report (11)
infortunio misfortune
infraestructura infrastructure
ingeniería engineering
ingeniero/a engineer (16)
ingenuo/a innocent, naive
ingerir (ie, i) to eat, drink, ingest
Inglaterra England
inglés *m.* English (*language*) (1)
inglés, inglesa *n.* English person; *adj.* English (2)
ingrediente *m.* ingredient
inhumano/a inhuman, cruel
iniciar to initiate
injusticia injustice
injusto/a unfair
inmediato/a immediate
inmenso/a immense
inmigración *f.* immigration (18)
inmigrante *n. m., f.; adj.* immigrant
inmobiliaria real estate; **agente** (*m., f.*) **de inmobiliaria** real estate agent
innecesario/a unnecessary
inocente innocent
inolvidable unforgettable
inquietante worrisome
inquilino/a tenant, renter (12)

inquisición *f.* inquisition
inscribirse (*p.p.* **inscrito/a**) to register
insistir to insist; **insistir en** + *inf.* to insist on (*doing something*)
insolente insolent
insomnio insomnia
inspector(a) (de aduanas) (customs) inspector (18)
inspiración *f.* inspiration
inspirar to inspire
inspirativo/a inspiring
instalación *f.* installation
institución *f.* institution
instrucción *f.* instruction
instrumento instrument
intacto/a intact
integral: arroz (*m.*) **integral** whole grain rice; **pan** (*m.*) **integral** whole wheat bread
integridad *f.* integrity
intelectual *adj.* intellectual
inteligente intelligent (2)
intención *f.* intention
intenso/a intense, acute
intentar to try (13)
intercambio *n.* exchange
interés *m.* interest
interesante interesting
interesar to interest, be interesting; **interesar(le)** to be interesting (*to someone*)
interior *n. m.; adj.* interior; inside; **ropa interior** underwear (3)
internacional international
internarse en to check into (*a hospital*) (10)
interno/a *n.* intern; *adj.* internal
interpretación *f.* interpretation
interpretar to interpret, explain
interrogativo/a *gram.* interrogative (AT)
interrumpir to interrupt
intervención *f.* intervention
íntimamente intimately
íntimo/a intimate
intranquilidad *f.* uneasiness, restlessness
intricado/a intricate
introducción *f.* introduction
introducir (*irreg.*) to introduce
intromisión *f.*: **sin intromisiones** without intrusions
introversión *f.* abstraction
introvertido/a introverted
invasión *f.* invasion
invasor(a) invader
invención *f.* invention
inventar to invent, discover
investigación *f.* research
investigar (gu) to investigate
invierno winter (5)
invitación *f.* invitation
invitado/a *n.* guest (8)
invitar to invite (6)
inyección *f.* shot, injection (10); **poner(le)** (*irreg.*) **una inyección** to give (someone) a shot, injection (10)
ir (*irreg.*) to go (3); **ir a** + *inf.* to be going to (*do something*) (3); **ir a pie** to go on

foot (walk) (10); **ir de compras** to go shopping (3); **ir de vacaciones** to go on vacation (7); **ir de viaje** to go on a trip (10); **ir en (autobús/avión/barco/ tren)** to go by (bus/airplane/boat/ train) (7); **irse** to go away, leave
Irlanda Ireland
irresponsable irresponsible, unreliable
irreverente irreverent
isla island (5)
Italia Italy
italiano *m.* Italian (*language*) (1)
italiano/a *n., adj.* Italian (2)
izquierda *n.* left-hand side; **a la izquierda** (**de**) to the left (of) (5)
izquierdo/a left (*direction*); **levantarse con el pie izquierdo** to get up on the wrong side of the bed (11)

J

jabón *m.* soap (18)
jamás never, not ever (6)
jamón *m.* ham (6)
Japón *m.* Japan
japonés, japonesa *n., adj.* Japanese (1)
jarabe *m.* (cough) syrup (10)
jardín *m.* garden (4)
jeans *m. pl.* jeans (3)
jefe/a boss, chief (11)
jerez *m.* (*pl.* **jereces**) sherry
jeroglífico/a hieroglyphical
jirafa giraffe
jornada (de tiempo completo/parcial) (full-time/part-time) workday (12)
joven *n. m., f.* youth (2); *adj.* young (2); **de joven** as a youth (9)
joya jewel, jewelry
joyería jewelry store
jubilado/a retired (*from work*)
jubilarse to retire (*from work*) (16)
judío/a *n.* Jew; *adj.* Jewish
juego game
jueves *m. s., pl.* Thursday (4)
jugador(a) player (9)
jugar (ue) (gu) (al) to play (*a game, sport*) (4); **jugar al ajedrez** to play chess (4); **jugar a las cartas** to play cards (9)
jugo (de fruta) (fruit) juice (6)
juguete *m.* toy
julio July (5)
jungla jungle
junio June (5)
juntos/as together (15)
justicia justice
justificar (qu) to justify
justo/a fair
juvenil youthful
juventud *f.* youth (15)
juzgar (gu) to judge

L

la *definite article f. s.* the; *d.o. f. s.* you (*form.*), her it; **a la una** at one o'clock (AT)
labor *f.* work

laboral *adj. pertaining to work or labor*
laboratorio lab, laboratory (2)
lado *n.* side; **al lado** *adv.* beside; alongside; **al lado (de)** *prep.* beside (5)
ladrar to bark
ladrón, ladrona thief
lagarto lizard
lago lake
lámpara lamp (4)
lana wool (3); **es de lana** it is made of wool (3)
langosta lobster (6)
lanza *n.* spear
lápiz *m.* (*pl.* **lápices**) pencil (1)
largo/a long (2)
las *definite article f. pl.* the; *d.o. f. pl.* you (*form.*), them; **a las dos** at two o'clock (AT); **las demás** others (12)
lástima shame (13); **¡qué lástima!** what a shame! (13)
lastimarse to injure oneself (11)
lata (tin) can; **es una lata** it's a pain, drag
Latinoamérica Latin America
latinoamericano/a *n., adj.* Latin American
lavabo (bathroom) sink (4)
lavadora washing machine (9)
lavaplatos *m. s., pl.* dishwasher (9)
lavar to wash (9); **lavar (las ventanas, los platos, la ropa)** to wash (the windows, the dishes, clothes) (9); **lavar(se)** to wash (oneself)
le *i.o. s.* to/for you (*form.*), him, her, it; **¿le gusta... ?** do you like . . . ? (AT)
lección *f.* lesson
leche *f.* milk (6)
lechuga lettuce (6)
lector(a) reader (13)
lectura *n.* reading
leer (y) to read (2)
legalización *f.* legalization
legislación *f.* legislation
lejos *adv.* far away; **lejos de** *prep.* far from (5)
lengua tongue; language; **lenguas extranjeras** foreign languages (1); **sacar (qu) la lengua** to stick out one's tongue (10)
lenguaje *m.* speech, idiom
lenteja lentil
lentes (*m. pl.*) **de contacto** contact lenses (10)
lento/a slow
leña (fire)wood; **estufa de leña** wood stove
letra letter (*of the alphabet*); *pl.* arts, letters (2); **letras cursivas** italics
letrero sign
levantar to lift, raise up; **levantarse** to get up (4); to stand up (4); **levantarse con el pie izquierdo** to get up on the wrong side of the bed (11)
ley *f.* law (17)
leyenda legend
libertad *f.* liberty, freedom (17)

libertador(a) liberator
libra pound
libre free; **al aire libre** outdoors (9); **ratos** (*m. pl.*) **libres** spare time (9); **tiempo libre** free time
librería bookstore (1)
libro (de texto) (text)book (1)
licencia license (14)
líder *m.* leader
liga league
ligero/a light, not heavy (6)
limitación *f.* limitation
limitar to limit
límite *m.* limit (14); **fecha límite** deadline (11); **límite de velocidad** speed limit (14)
limón *m.* lemon (5)
limonada lemonade
limonero lemon tree
limpiaparabrisas *m. s. pl.* windshield wiper
limpiar to clean (9); **limpiar la casa (entera)** to clean the (whole) house (9)
limpio/a clean (5)
línea line; **patinar en línea** to rollerblade (9)
lingüístico/a linguistic
lío mess; **lío de tráfico** traffic jam
líquido/a liquid
lista list
listo/a smart; clever (2)
literario/a literary
literatura literature (1)
litro liter
llamada *n.* (telephone) call
llamar to call (6); **llamarse** to be called, named (4); **¿cómo se llama usted?** *form.* what's your name? (AT); **¿cómo te llamas?** *fam.* what's your name? (AT); **me llamo...** my name is . . . (AT)
llano *n.* level ground, plain
llanta tire (14)
llanura plain; flatness
llave *f.* key (11)
llegada arrival (7)
llegar (gu) to arrive (2); **llegar a tiempo/tarde** to arrive on time/late (11)
llenar to fill (up) (14); to fill out (*a form*) (16)
lleno/a full
llevar to take (3); to carry (3); to wear (*clothing*) (3); **llevar una vida sana/tranquila** to lead a healthy/calm life (10); **llevarse bien/mal (con)** to get along well/poorly (with) (15)
llorar to cry (8)
llover (ue) to rain (5); **llueve** it's raining (5)
lluvia rain; **lluvia de ideas** brainstorm
lluvioso/a rainy
lo *d.o. m. s.* you (*form.*), him, it; **lo bueno / lo malo** the good/bad news (10); **lo siento (mucho)** I'm (very) sorry (11); **lo suficiente** enough (10)
lobo wolf

localidad *f.* ticket (*theater, etc.*)
localización *f.* location
localizar (c) to find, locate
loco/a crazy (5)
locura madness, craziness
lógico/a logical
lograr to achieve, attain
los *definite article m. pl.* the; *d.o. m. pl.* you (*form.*), them; **los demás** the rest (12)
lotería lottery
lubricar (qu) to lubricate
lucha fight
luchar to fight
luego *adv.* then; **hasta luego** see you later (AT); **luego de** *prep.* after
lugar *m.* place (1)
lujo luxury (12); **hotel** (*m.*) **de lujo** luxury hotel (18)
luna moon; **luna de miel** honeymoon (15)
lunar *m.*: **de lunares** polka-dotted (3)
lunes *m. s., pl.* Monday (4)
lustroso/a lustrous, shiny
luz *f.* (*pl.* **luces**) light (11); electricity (11)

M

maceta flowerpot
machista *adj. m., f.* he-man, chauvinistic
macho *n.* male
madera wood
maderero/a *adj. of or pertaining to wood*
madrastra stepmother
madre *f.* mother (2)
madrileño/a from Madrid; **callos** (*m. pl.*) **a la madrileña** *tripe specialty of Madrid*
madurez *f.* middle age (15)
maduro/a ripe, mature (5)
maestro/a schoolteacher (16)
maestro/a: obra maestra masterpiece (13)
mágico/a *adj.* magic
magnético/a magnetic
magnífico/a magnificent; great
magos *m. pl.*: **Día** (*m.*) **de los Reyes Magos** Day of the Magi (8)
maíz *m.* corn (5)
majestuoso/a majestic
mal *adv.* poorly (1); **caerle** (*irreg.*) **mal a alguien** to make a bad impression on someone (16); **llevarse mal (con)** to get along badly (with) (15); **pasarlo mal** to have a bad time (8)
mal, malo/a *adj.* bad (2); **hace mal tiempo** it's bad weather (5); **lo malo** the bad thing, news (10)
maleducado/a ill-mannered, rude; poorly brought up
maleta suitcase (7); **hacer** (*irreg.*) **las maletas** to pack one's suitcases (7)
maletero porter (7)
maligno/a malignant
malvado/a evil, wicked
mamá mom, mother (2)
mancha stain

mandar to send (7); to order (12)
mandato command
manejar to drive (12); to operate (*a machine*) (12)
manera manner, way
manía furor, craze
manifestación *f.* demonstration
manjares *m. pl.* delicacies
mano *f.* hand (11)
mantener (*like* tener) to maintain
mantequilla butter (6)
manzana apple (6)
mañana *n.* morning (AT); *adv.* tomorrow (AT); **de la mañana** in the morning (AT); **hasta mañana** until tomorrow (AT); **pasado mañana** day after tomorrow (4); **por la mañana** during the morning (1)
mapa *m.* map
máquina machine; **escribir a máquina** to type (16)
mar *m.* sea (7)
maratón *m.* marathon
maravilloso/a marvelous
marca brand
marcar (qu) to dial; to mark
mareado/a dizzy, nauseated (10)
marido husband (15)
marihuana marijuana
marinero sailor
marisco shellfish (6)
marítimo/a *adj.* maritime; nautical
martes *m. s., pl.* Tuesday (4)
marzo March (5)
más *adv.* more (1); **más... que** more . . . than (5)
masa mass
máscara mask
mascota pet (2)
masculino/a masculine
matar to kill
matemáticas *f. pl.* mathematics (1)
materia subject (*school*) (1)
material *n. m.* material (3)
maternidad *f.* maternity
materno/a maternal
matrícula tuition (1)
matrimonio marriage; married couple (15)
máximo/a *adj.* maximum
maya *n., adj. m., f.* Maya(n)
mayo May (5); **Cinco de Mayo** Cinco de Mayo (8)
mayor older (5); greater
mayoría majority (14)
me *d.o.* me; *i.o.* to/for me; *refl. pron.* myself; **me gustaría...** I would like . . . (7); **me llamo...** my name is . . . (AT); **no, no me gusta...** no, I don't like . . . (AT); **sí, me gusta...** yes, I like . . . (AT)
mecánico/a mechanic (14)
media: (las tres) y media (three) thirty, half past (three) (*with time*) (AT)
medianoche *f.* midnight (8)
medias *f. pl.* stockings (3)
medicina medicine (10)

médico/a (medical) doctor (2); *adj.* medical (10)
medida *s.* means, measure; measurement
medio *n. s.* means, middle; *pl.* media; **medio ambiente** environment (14); **medio de comunicación** means of communication (17)
medio/a *adj.* half; middle; **media pensión** (*f.*) room with breakfast and one other meal (18); **medio hermano / media hermana** half-brother/half-sister
mediodía *m.* noon, midday; **a mediodía** at noon
mediterráneo/a Mediterranean
mejillón *m.* mussel
mejor better (5); best (5); **mejor que** better than (5)
mejora improvement
mejorar to improve
melancólico/a melancholic
mellizo/a twin
melodrama *m.* melodrama
membrana mucosa mucose membrane
memoria memory (12)
mencionar to mention
menor younger (5); least
menos less (5); minus; least; **a menos que** *conj.* unless (15); **(las tres) menos cuarto (quince)** a quarter to (three) (AT); **menos... que** less . . . than (5); **por lo menos** at least (10)
mensaje *m.* message
mensual monthly
mensualidad *f.* monthly installment
mentira lie
menú *m.* menu (6)
menudo: a menudo frequently, often
mercadeo marketing
mercado market(place) (3)
merecer (zc) to deserve
merengue *m.* merengue (*Latin dance*)
merienda (afternoon) snack
mes *m.* month (5)
mesa table (1); **poner** (*irreg.*) **la mesa** to set the table (9); **quitar la mesa** to clear the table (9)
meseta plain (*geographic*)
mesita end table (4)
mesón *m.* inn; tavern
mestizo/a mixed-race (*person*)
metáfora metaphor
meteorólogo/a meteorologist
método method
metro meter; metro (subway); **estación** (*f.*) **del metro** metro (subway) stop (18)
metrópolis *f.* city, metropolis
mexicano/a *n., adj.* Mexican (2)
mexicoamericano/a *n., adj.* Mexican American
mezcla mixture
mezclar to mix; to blend
mi(s) *poss.* my (2)
mí *obj. of prep.* me (5)
microondas *f. pl.*: **horno de microondas**

microwave oven (9)
miedo fear (3); **tener** (*irreg.*) **miedo (de)** to be afraid (of) (11)
miel *f.* honey; **luna de miel** honeymoon (15)
miembro/a member
mientras *conj.* while (9)
miércoles *m. s., pl.* Wednesday (4)
migrante *adj.* migrant
mil *m.* thousand, one thousand (3)
milenio millennium
miligramo milligram
militar *adj.* military; **servicio militar** military service (17)
milla mile
millón *m.* million (3)
millonario/a millionaire
mineral: agua (*f. but* el agua) **mineral** mineral water (6)
minero/a *adj.* mining
minidiálogo minidialogue
minidrama *m.* minidrama
minifalda miniskirt
ministerio ministry
minucioso/a meticulous, thorough
minúsculo/a minuscule
minuto *n.* minute (*time*)
mío/a(s) *poss.* my, (of) mine (17)
mirar to look at, watch (2); **mirar la televisión** to watch television (2)
mismo/a self; same (10); **ahora mismo** right now; **lo mismo** the same thing
misquito *indigenous language spoken in Nicaragua*
misterio mystery
misterioso/a mysterious
mitad *f.* half
mito myth
mitología mythology
mixto/a mixed
mochila backpack (1)
moda fashion; **de última moda** the latest style (3)
modales *m. pl.* manners, behavior
modelo model
módem *m.* modem (12)
moderación *f.* moderation
moderado/a moderate
moderno/a modern (13)
modificación *f.* modification
modificar (qu) to modify
modo way, manner; **de todos modos** anyway
molestar to bother (13); **me (te, le,...) molesta** it bothers me (you, him, . . .) (13)
molestia *n.* bother
momento moment, instant
monarca *m.* monarch, king
monarquía monarchy
moneda currency; coin
monólogo monologue
monopatín *m.* skateboard (12)
monstruo monster
monstruoso/a monstrous, outrageous
montaña mountain (7)

montañismo mountaineering
montañoso/a mountainous
montar to ride (9); to set up; **montar a caballo** to ride horseback (9)
monumento monument (10)
morado/a purple (3)
moralidad f. morality
moratorio moratorium
morcilla blood sausage
moreno/a n., adj. brunet(te) (2)
morir(se) (ue, u) (p.p. **muerto/a**) to die
mosaico/a adj. mosaic
mosca fly
mostrar (ue) to show (7)
motivo motive, reason
moto(cicleta) motorcycle, moped (12)
moverse (ue) to move (around)
movimiento movement
mozo bellhop (18)
muchacho/a boy/girl (4)
mucho adv. much, a lot (1); **lo siento mucho** I'm very sorry (11)
mucho/a(s) adj. a lot (of) (2); pl. many (2); **muchas gracias** thank you very much, many thanks (AT); **mucho gusto** pleased to meet you (AT)
mudanza moving (from one residence to another)
mudarse to move (residence) (16)
muebles m. pl. furniture (4); **sacudir los muebles** to dust the furniture (9)
muela: sacar (qu) una muela to extract a tooth (10)
muerte f. death (15)
muerto/a p.p. dead; **Día** (m.) **de los Muertos** Day of the Dead (8)
mujer f. woman (1); wife (15); **mujer de negocios** businessperson (16); **mujer soldado** female soldier (16)
muleta crutch
multa fine, penalty (18)
multicentro multicenter
multimillonario/a multimillionaire
multinacional adj. multinational
múltiple multiple
mundial adj. worldwide
mundo world (7)
muralista m., f. muralist
músculo muscle
museo museum (9); **visitar un museo** to visit a museum (9)
música music (13)
músico/a musician (13)
musulmán, musulmana n., adj. Moslem
mutuo/a mutual
muy very (1); **muy bien** very well (AT); **muy buenas** good afternoon/evening (AT)

N

nacer (zc) to be born (15)
nacido/a: recién nacido/a newborn
nacimiento birth (15)
nación f. nation
nacional national
nacionalidad f. nationality (2)

nacionalista m., f. nationalist; adj. nationalistic
nada nothing, not anything (6); **de nada** you're welcome (AT)
nadar to swim (7)
nadie nobody, not anybody, no one (6)
naranja orange (fruit) (6)
nariz f. (pl. **narices**) nose (10)
narración f. narration
narrador(a) narrator
narrar to narrate
natación f. swimming (9)
natal adj. native (country)
nativo/a native, indigenous
natural: recursos (m. pl.) **naturales** natural resources (14)
naturaleza nature (14)
náuseas f. pl. nausea
navegable navigable
navegante m., f. navigator; adj. navigating, sailing
navegar (gu) la red to surf the net (12)
Navidad f. Christmas (8)
navideño/a adj. pertaining to Christmas
necesario/a necessary (2)
necesidad f. necessity
necesitar to need (1)
negación f. negation
negar (ie) (gu) to deny (13)
negativo/a negative (6)
negocio business; **hombre** (m.)/**mujer** (f.) **de negocios** businessperson (16)
negro/a black (3)
nervio nerve
nervioso/a nervous (5)
neutro/a neutral
nevar (ie) to snow (5); **nieva** it's snowing (5)
nevera refrigerator
ni neither; nor; **ni siquiera** not even
nicaragüense n., adj. m., f. Nicaraguan
nido nest
nieto/a grandson/granddaughter; m. pl. grandchildren (2)
nieva it's snowing (5)
ningún, ninguno/a no, none, not any (6)
niñero/a baby-sitter (9)
niñez f. childhood (9)
niño/a child; boy/girl (2); **de niño/a** as a child (9)
nivel m. level (14)
no no, not (AT); **¿no?** right? (3)
noche f. night; **buenas noches** good evening/night (AT); **de la noche** in the evening/at night (AT); **esta noche** tonight (5); **Noche Vieja** New Year's Eve (8); **por la noche** in the night (1)
Noche Vieja New Year's Eve (8)
Nochebuena Christmas Eve (8)
nomádico/a nomadic
nombrar to name
nombre m. (first) name
nominar to nominate
noreste m. northeast
norma norm; rule
normalidad f. normalcy

noroeste m. northwest
norte m. north (5)
Norteamérica North America
norteamericano/a n., adj. North American (2)
Noruega Norway
nos d.o. us; i.o. to/for us; refl. pron. ourselves; **nos vemos** see you around (AT)
nosotros/as sub. pron. we (1); obj. of prep. us
nostalgia nostalgia
nota note; grade (in a class) (11)
notable outstanding
noticia piece of news (8); pl. news (17)
noticiero newscast (17)
novato/a novice
novecientos/as nine hundred (3)
novedades f. pl. news (17)
novela novel (3)
novelista m., f. novelist
noveno/a adj. ninth (13)
noventa ninety (2)
noviazgo engagement (15)
noviembre m. November (5)
novio/a boyfriend/girlfriend (5); fiancé(e); groom/bride (15)
nublado/a cloudy; **está (muy) nublado** it's (very) cloudy, overcast (5)
nuclear nuclear (14)
núcleo nucleus, core
nuera daughter-in-law
nuestro/a poss. our (2); ours, of ours (17)
nueve nine (AT)
nuevo/a new (2); **Día** (m.) **de Año Nuevo** New Year's Day (8)
número number (AT)
numeroso/a numerous
nunca never (2); **casi nunca** almost never (2)

O

o or (AT)
obedecer (zc) to obey (14)
objetivo objective
objeto object
obligación f. obligation
obligado/a obliged, compelled
obligar (gu) to obligate
obligatorio/a required
obra (de arte) work (of art) (13); **obra maestra** masterpiece (13)
obrero/a worker, laborer (16)
observación f. observation
observar to observe, watch
obstáculo obstacle
obtener (like **tener**) to get, obtain (12)
obvio/a obvious
ocasión f. occasion
occidental occidental, western
occidente m. west
océano ocean (7)
ochenta eighty (2)
ocho eight (AT)
ochocientos/as eight hundred (3)
octavo/a adj. eighth (13)

octubre *m.* October (5)
ocular *adj. of the eye*, ocular
ocupado/a busy (5)
ocupar to occupy
ocurrir to occur, happen
odiar to hate (7)
odioso/a hateful, odious
oeste *m.* west (5)
ofender to offend, insult
oferta offer (12)
oficial official
oficiar to officiate
oficina office (1); **oficina de correos** post office (18)
oficio trade (16)
ofrecer (zc) to offer (7)
oído inner ear (10)
oír *(irreg.)* to hear (4)
ojalá (que) I hope, wish (that) (13)
ojear to look over
ojo eye (10); **¡OJO!** watch out, be careful
olímpicos: juegos *(m. pl.)* **olímpicos** Olympic Games
oliva: aceite *(m.)* **de oliva** olive oil
olvidadizo/a forgetful
olvidarse (de) to forget (about) (8)
ombligo navel
ómnibus *m.* bus
once eleven (AT)
opción *f.* option
ópera opera (13)
operación *f.* operation
opinar to think, believe
opinión *f.* opinion
oportunidad *(f.)* **de avanzar** opportunity for advancement (12)
optimista *n. m., f.* optimist; *adj.* optimistic
opuesto/a opposite
oración *f.* sentence
oral oral (11)
orden *m.* order *(chronological)*; *f.* order, command; **en orden** in order, orderly
ordenado/a neat (5)
ordenador *m. (Sp.)* computer (12); **ordenador portátil** laptop computer (12)
ordenar to arrange, put in order; to order, command
oreja outer ear (10)
organismo organism
organización *f.* organization
organizar (c) to organize
orgulloso/a proud
orientación *f.* orientation, direction
Oriente *(m.)* **Medio** Middle East
origen *m.* origin
originar to originate
orilla riverbank
oro gold
orquesta orchestra
ortográfico/a orthographical; spelling
os *Sp. d.o.* you *(fam.)*; *i.o. pl.* to/for you *(fam.)*; *refl. pron. pl.* yourselves *(fam.)*
oscuro/a dark
óseo/a bony
ostra oyster

otoño fall, autumn (5)
otorgar (gu) to grant, give
otro/a other, another (2)
oxígeno oxygen
ozono: capa de ozono ozone layer (14)

P

paciencia patience
paciente *n., adj. m., f.* patient (10)
pacífico/a peaceful
padecer (zc) to suffer, feel deeply
padrastro stepfather
padre *m.* father; *pl.* parents (2)
padrinos godparents (3)
paella paella *(dish made with rice, shellfish, and often chicken, and flavored with saffron)*
pagar (gu) to pay (1); **pagar a plazos** to pay in installments (16); **pagar al contado** to pay cash (16); **pagar en efectivo** to pay cash (16)
página page
país *m.* country (2)
paisaje *m.* countryside
pájaro bird (2)
palabra word (1)
palacio palace
palma palm tree
paloma dove
palomitas *f. pl.* popcorn
palpitante palpitating, beating
pampa pampa, prairie
pan *m.* bread (6); **pan tostado** toast (6)
panameño/a *n., adj.* Panamanian
panamericano/a Panamerican
panda panda
pandilla group of friends
panorama *m.* panorama
pantalla screen
pantalón, pantalones *(m.)* pants (3); **pantalones cortos** shorts
papa potato *(L.A.)* (5); *m.* pope; **papa frita** *(L.A.)* French-fried potato
papá *m.* dad, father (2)
papel *m.* paper (1); role (13); **papel para cartas** stationery (18)
papelería stationery store (18)
paquete *m.* package (18)
par *m.* pair (3)
para *prep.* (intended) for; in order to (2); **para + inf.** in order to *(do something)* (9); **para que** *conj.* so that (15)
parabrisas *m. s.* windshield (14)
paracaidismo parachute jumping
parada stop; **hacer** *(irreg.)* **paradas** to make stops; **parada de autobús** bus stop (18)
paraguas *m. s., pl.* umbrella
parar to stop (14)
parcial partial; **trabajo de tiempo parcial** part-time job (12)
pardo/a brown (3)
parecer (zc) to seem (13)
pared *f.* wall (4)
pareja (married) couple; partner (15)

paréntesis *m. s., pl.* parenthesis
pariente *m., f.* relative (2)
paródico/a parodical
parque *m.* park (5)
párrafo paragraph
parrandero/a party-loving
parrilla: a la parrilla grilled
parroquiano/a customer, client
parte *(f.)* part (4); **por todas partes** everywhere (11)
participante *m., f.* participant
participar to participate
particular particular; private
partida departure; **punto de partida** starting point
partido game
partir: a partir de starting from
pasado/a *adj.* past; **el año pasado** last year; **pasado mañana** day after tomorrow (4)
pasaje *m.* passage, ticket (7)
pasajero/a *n.* passenger (7); *adj.* passing, fleeting (10)
pasaporte *m.* passport (18)
pasar to spend *(time)* (5); to happen (5); **pasar la aspiradora** to vacuum (9); **pasar tiempo (con)** to spend time (with) (15); **pasarlo bien/mal** to have a good/bad time (8)
pasatiempo pastime, hobby (9)
Pascua (Florida) Easter (8); **Pascua de los hebreos** Passover (8)
pasear en bicicleta to ride a bicycle (9)
paseo stroll; **dar** *(irreg.)* **un paseo** to take a walk (9)
pasión *f.* passion
pasivo/a passive
paso step
pasta dental toothpaste (18)
pastel *m.* cake (6); pie (6); **pastel de cumpleaños** birthday cake (8)
pastelería pastry shop (18)
pastelito small pastry (18)
pastilla pill (10)
pastor(a) pastor; shepherd; **pastor** *(m.)* **alemán** German shepherd *(dog)*
pata *paw, foot of an animal*
patata *(Sp.)* **(frita)** (French-fried) potato (6)
patinar to skate (9); **patinar en línea** to rollerblade (9)
patines *m. pl.* roller skates (12)
patio yard, patio (4)
patriótico/a patriotic
patrona: santa patrona patron saint
pavo turkey (6)
paz *f. (pl.* **paces)** peace (17)
peatón, peatona pedestrian
pecho chest
pedagogía pedagogy; education
pedir (i, i) to ask for; to order (4); **pedir disculpas** to apologize (11); **pedir prestado/a** to borrow (16)
pegar (gu) to hit (9); **pegarse en / contra** to run/bump into (11)
peinarse to comb one's hair (4)

pelado/a peeled
pelear to fight (9)
película movie (4)
peligro danger
peligroso/a dangerous
pelo hair
pelota ball (9)
peluquero(a) hairstylist (16)
pena penalty; sorrow; **¡qué pena!** what a shame; **vale la pena** it's worth the trouble
península peninsula
pensar (ie) to think (4); to intend (4)
pensión *f.* boarding house (18); **media pensión** room with breakfast and one other meal (18); **pensión completa** room and full board (18)
peor worse (5); worst
pequeño/a small (2)
percibido/a perceived
perder (ie) to lose (9); to miss (*a function, bus, plane, etc.*) (4)
pérdida loss (13)
perdón pardon me, excuse me (AT)
perezoso/a lazy (2)
perfecto/a perfect
perfil *m.* profile
perfume *m.* perfume
periódicamente periodically
periódico newspaper (2)
periodista *m., f.* journalist (16)
período period
perjudicar (qu) to harm
permiso permission; **(con) permiso** pardon me, excuse me (AT)
permitir to allow, permit (12)
pero *conj.* but (AT)
perpetuo/a perpetual
perro/a dog (2)
perseguir (i, i) (g) to pursue, chase
persiana Venetian blind
persistir to persist, continue
persona person (1)
personaje *m.* character (*fictional*)
personal *n. m.* personnel (10); **dirección** (*f.*) **de personal** personnel office (16); **director(a) de personal** personnel director (16)
personalidad *f.* personality
perspectiva perspective
persuadir to persuade
pertenecer (zc) to belong
pertinencia relevance
perturbar to disturb
peruano/a *n., adj.* Peruvian
pesado/a heavy
pesar to weigh; **a pesar de** (*prep.*) in spite of, despite
pesas *f. pl.*: **levantar pesas** to lift weights
pescado fish (*cooked*) (6)
peseta *unit of currency in Spain*
pesimista *n. m., f.* pessimist; *adj.* pessimistic
peso weight; *unit of currency in Mexico and several other Latin American countries*
pesticida *m.* pesticide

petróleo *m.* petroleum, oil
pez *m.* (*pl.* **peces**) fish (*live*)
picnic *m.*: **hacer** (*irreg.*) **un** *picnic* to have a picnic (9)
pie *m.* foot (11); **levantarse con el pie izquierdo** to get up on the wrong side of the bed (11)
piedad *f.* piety
piedra stone
piel *f.* skin
pierna leg (11)
pieza piece
píldora pill
pincho *tidbits broiled and served on skewers*
pingüino penguin
pintar (las paredes) to paint (the walls) (9)
pintor(a) painter (13)
pintura *n.* painting (13)
pirámide *f.* pyramid
pirata *m., f.* pirate
piscina swimming pool (4)
piso floor (*of building*) (12); **barrer el piso** to sweep the floor (9)
pito: no me importa un pito I don't care a bit
pizarra chalkboard (1)
placer *m.* pleasure
plan *m.*: **hacer** (*irreg.*) **planes para** + *inf.* to make plans to (*do something*) (9)
planchar la ropa to iron clothing (9)
planeación *f.* planning, designing
planear to plan
planeta *m.* planet
planta plant; floor (*of a building*); **planta baja** ground floor (12)
plantación *f.* plantation
plantar to plant
plástico *n.* plastic
plata silver (*metal*)
plato dish, plate (4); (*prepared*) dish (4); course (*of a meal*) (6)
playa beach (5)
plaza town square; **plaza de toros** bullring
plazo period, time; **pagar (gu) a plazos** to pay in installments (16)
plomero/a plumber (16)
pluralismo pluralism
población *f.* population (14)
pobre poor (2)
pobreza poverty
poco *adv.* little (1); **un poco** a little bit (1)
poco/a *adj.* little, few (3)
poder *v.* (*irreg.*) to be able, can (3)
poder *n. m.* power
poderoso/a powerful
poema *m.* poem
poesía poetry
poeta *m., f.* poet (13)
poético/a poetic
policía *m., f.* police officer (14); *f.* police force
policíaco/a *pertaining to the police*
política *s.* politics (17)

político/a politician (17); *adj.* political; **ciencias** (*f. pl.*) **políticas** political science
pollo chicken (6)
polvo dust
poner (*irreg.*) to put; to place (4); to turn on (*machines*) (11); **poner la mesa** to set the table (9); **poner(le) una inyección** to give (*someone*) a shot, injection (10); **ponerse** to put on (*clothing*) (4); **ponerse** + *adj.* to become, get + *adj.* (8)
por *prep.* in (*the morning, evening, etc.*) (1); by, through, during, for (4); **por ciento** percent (11); **por Dios** for God's sake (11); **por ejemplo** for example (11); **por eso** therefore (1); **por favor** please (AT); **por fin** finally (4); **por la noche/mañana/tarde** in the evening/morning/afternoon (1); **por lo general** generally (4); **por lo menos** at least (10); **por primera/última vez** for the first/last time (11); **¿por qué?** why? (2); **por si acaso** just in case (11); **por supuesto** of course (11); **por todas partes** (*f. pl.*) everywhere (11); **por último**
¿por qué? why? (2)
porque because (2)
portarse to behave (8)
portátil *adj.* portable; **computadora portátil** laptop computer (12); **ordenador** (*m.*) **portátil** laptop computer (12)
portavoz *m.* (*pl.* **portavoces**) spokesperson
porteño/a from Buenos Aires
portero/a building manager; doorman (12)
portugués *m.* Portuguese (*language*)
porvenir *m.* future
posesión *f.* possession
posesivo/a *gram.* possessive (2)
posgraduado/a *adj.* graduate; postgraduate
posibilidad *f.* possibility
posible possible (2)
posición *f.* position
positivo/a positive
postal: tarjeta postal postcard (7)
postre *m.* dessert (6)
potente potent, strong
práctica practice
practicante *m., f.* apprentice
practicar (qu) to practice (1); to participate (*in a sport*) (9)
práctico/a practical (2)
precio price (3); **precio fijo** fixed price (3)
precioso/a precious; lovely
precipitado/a hasty
precocinado/a pre-cooked
precolombino/a pre-Columbian (before Columbus)
predicción *f.* prediction
predominar to dominate

preferencia preference (AT)
preferible preferable (13)
preferir (ie, i) to prefer (3)
pregunta *n.* question; **hacer** *(irreg.)* **una pregunta** to ask a question (4)
preguntar to ask a question (6)
prematuro/a premature
premio prize
prender to switch on *(an appliance)*
prensa press; news media (17)
prenupcial prenuptial
preocupación *f.* worry, care, concern
preocupado/a worried (5)
preocuparse (por) to worry (about)
preparación *f.* preparation
preparar to prepare (6)
preposición *f. gram.* preposition
presencia presence; appearance
presentación *f.* presentation
presentar to present; to introduce
presente *n. m.; adj.* present
preservación *f.* preservation
presidente/a president
presión *f.* pressure (11); **sufrir presiones** to be under pressure (11)
prestación *f.* lending, loan
prestado/a: pedir (i, i) prestado/a to borrow (16)
préstamo loan (16)
prestar to lend (7)
prestigio prestige
prestigioso/a prestigious
presupuesto budget (16)
previo/a previous
primario/a primary
primavera spring (5)
primer, primero/a *adj.* first (4); **a primera vista** at first sight (15); **el primero de** first of *(month)* (5); **primera clase** first class (7)
primo/a cousin (2)
princesa princess
principal main, principal
príncipe *m.* prince
principiante *m., f.* beginner
principio beginning; **al principio de** at the beginning of (16)
prisa haste, hurry; **tener** *(irreg.)* **prisa** to be in a hurry (3)
privado/a private
probar (ue) to taste, try
problema *m.* problem
proceso process
procurar to try; to produce
producción *f.* production
producir *(irreg.)* to produce
producto product
productor(a) producer
profesión *f.* profession (16)
profesional professional
profesor(a) professor (1)
profundidad *f.* depth
profundo/a deep
programa *(m.)* program
programador(a) programmer (16)
progresivo/a progressive

prohibir (prohíbo) to prohibit, forbid (12)
proliferación *f.* proliferation
promedio *n. m.* average
prometer to promise (7)
pronombre *m. gram.* pronoun
pronosticable predictable
pronto *adv.* soon; **tan pronto como** *conj.* as soon as (16)
pronunciación *f.* pronunciation
pronunciar to pronounce
propenso/a inclined, prone
propiedad *f.* property
propina tip *(to an employee)* (18)
propio/a *adj.* own (15)
proporcionar to provide; to adapt
propósito purpose
propuesto/a *p. p.* proposed
protagonista *m., f.* protagonist
protección *f.* protection
proteger (j) to protect (14)
protegido/a protected
protestar to protest
protocolo protocol
proveer (y) to provide
provincia province, region
provocar (qu) to provoke
proximidad *f.* proximity
próximo/a next (4)
proyectil *m.* projectile
proyecto project
prudente prudent, wise
prueba test; quiz (11)
psicología psychology
psicológico/a psychological
psíquico/a *adj.* psychic
publicación *f.* publication
publicar (qu) to publish
público/a *adj.* public (14)
pueblo small town
puerta door (1)
puerto (sea)port (7)
puertorriqueño/a *n., adj.* Puerto Rican
puesto place *(in line, etc.)* (7); job (16)
puesto/a *p.p.* put
pulmón *m.* lung (10)
pulpo octopus
punto point; **en punto** on the dot (AT); **punto de partida** point of departure; starting point; **punto de vista** point of view; **puntos cardinales** cardinal directions (5)
puntual punctual
puro/a pure (14)
púrpura purple

Q

que that, which; who (2)
¿qué? what? which? (AT); **¿a qué hora... ?** what time . . . ? (AT); **¿por qué?** why? (2); **¿qué hora es?** what time is it? (AT); **¿qué tal?** how are you (doing)? (AT)
¡qué... ! what . . . !; **¡qué lástima!** what a shame! (13); **¡qué mala suerte!** what bad luck! (11)
quechua *m., f.* Quechuan; *m.* Quechua

(language)
quedar(se) to stay, to remain *(in a place)* (5); to be left (11)
quehacer *m.* chore (9); **quehaceres domésticos** household chores (9)
quejarse (de) to complain (about) (8)
quemar to burn
querer *(irreg.)* to want (3); to love (15); **fue sin querer** it was unintentional (11); **quiere decir** it means
querido/a *n., adj.* dear (5)
queso cheese (6)
quetzal *m. monetary unit of Guatemala*
quiché *m.* Quiche *(language)*
quien(es) who, whom
¿quién(es)? who? whom? (AT); **¿de quién?** whose? (2)
química chemistry (1)
quince fifteen (AT); **menos quince** a quarter (fifteen minutes) to (the hour) (AT); **y quince** a quarter (fifteen minutes) past (the hour) (AT)
quinceañera *girl's fifteenth birthday party* (8)
quinientos/as five hundred (3)
quinto/a *adj.* fifth (13)
quiosco kiosk (18)
quitarse to take off *(clothing)* (4); **quitar la mesa** to clear the table (9); **quitarle** to get rid of
quizá(s) perhaps

R

rabino/a rabbi
racismo racism
radio *m.* radio *(set)*; **radio portátil** portable radio (12); *f.* radio *(medium)* (12)
radioyentes *m. pl.* radio audience
raíz *f. (pl.* **raíces***)* root
rama branch
ramo bouquet
ranchero/a farmhand
rancho ranch
rápido/a *adj.* fast (6)
ráquetbol *m.* racquetball
raro/a strange; rare (8)
rascacielos *m. s.* skyscraper (14)
rasgar (gu) to tear, rip
raso/a *adj.* flat
rato *n.* while, short time; **ratos libres** spare time (9)
ratón *m.* mouse (12)
raya: de rayas striped (3)
raza race; **Día** *(m.)* **de la Raza** Columbus Day (8)
razón *f.* reason (3); **(no) tener** *(irreg.)* **razón** to be right (wrong) (3)
razonable reasonable
reacción *f.* reaction
reaccionar to react (8)
real real; royal; **Real Academia Española** Royal Spanish Academy
realidad *f.* reality
realismo realism
realista *m., f.* realistic

realizar (c) to attain, achieve
rebaja reduction, sale (3)
rebasar to exceed, overflow
rebelde rebellious
rebelión *f.* rebellion
rebozo shawl
recado: dejar un recado to leave a
  message
recambio: llanta de recambio spare tire
recepción *f.* front desk (18)
recepcionista *m., f.* receptionist
receta prescription (10)
recetar to prescribe (*medicine*)
rechazar (c) to reject
recibir to receive (2)
reciclaje *m.* recycling
reciclar to recycle (14)
recién nacido/a newborn
reciente recent
reciprocidad *f.* reciprocity
recoger (j) to collect (11); to pick up (11)
recomendación *f.* recommendation
recomendar (ie) to recommend (7)
reconocer (zc) to recognize
recopilado/a compiled; abridged
recordar (ue) to remember (8)
recorte *m.* clipping
recreación *f.* recreation
recreativo/a entertaining
recto/a straight
rector(a) university president
recuerdo memory; souvenir
recuperación *f.* recovery
recurso resource; **recursos naturales**
  natural resources (14)
red *f.* Internet (12); **navegar (gu) la red**
  to surf the net (12)
redacción *f.*: **jefe/a de redacción** editor-
  in-chief
redecorar to redecorate
redondo/a round
reducción *f.* reduction
reducir (*irreg.*) to reduce
reembolsar to refund
reemplazar (c) to replace
referencia reference
referir (ie, i) to refer
reflejar to reflect
reflexivo/a *gram.* reflexive (4)
reformado/a reformed
refrán *m.* proverb
refresco soft drink (6); refreshment (8)
refrigerador *m.* refrigerator (9)
refugiar to take refuge
regalar to give (*as a gift*) (7)
regalo gift, present (2)
regatear to haggle, bargain (3)
régimen *m.* regimen
región *f.* region
registrar to search, examine (18)
registro register; record
regla rule
regresar to return (*to a place*) (1); **regresar
  a casa** to go home (1)
regular *adj.* OK (AT)
reina queen (17)

reírse (i, i) (de) to laugh (at) (8)
relación *f.* relationship (15)
relacionado/a related, associated
relacionar to relate, connect, associate
relajante relaxing
relajar to relax
religión *f.* religion
religioso/a religious
reloj *m.* watch (3)
remar to row (*a boat*)
remedio remedy
remoto distant, remote; **control** (*m.*)
  remoto remote control (12)
renunciar (a) to resign (from) (16)
repasar to review
repaso *n.* review
repente: de repente suddenly (10)
repertorio repertory
repetición *f.* repetition
reportaje *m.* report
reporte *m.* news, information, report
reportero/a reporter (17)
reposo rest
represa dam
representar to represent (13)
representativo/a *adj.* representative
reproducción *f.* reproduction
república republic
requerir (ie, i) to require
requisito requirement
resaltar to be evident, stand out
reserva *f.* reservation (18)
reservación *f.* reservation (18)
reservado/a reserved
reservar to reserve
resfriado cold (*illness*) (10)
resfriarse (me resfrío) to catch/get a
  cold (10)
residencia dormitory (1)
resolver (ue) (*p.p.* **resuelto/a**) to solve,
  resolve (14)
respecto respect, relation; **con respecto a**
  with regard to
respetar to respect
respeto respect, deference
respiración *f.* breathing
respirar to breathe (10)
respiratorio/a respiratory
responsabilidad *f.* responsibility (17)
responsable responsible
respuesta answer (5)
restaurante *m.* restaurant (6)
resto rest; *pl.* remains
restricción f. restriction
resuelto/a *p.p.* determined
resultado result
resultar to turn out, result
resumen *m.* summary
retablo *group of religious paintings*
retórica rhetoric; speech
retrato portrait
reunión *f.* meeting
reunir (reúno) to unite; **reunirse (con)** to
  get together (with) (8)
revelar to reveal
revisar to check (14)

revista magazine (2)
revolución *f.* revolution
revolucionario/a revolutionary
rey *m.* king (17); **Día** (*m.*) **de los Reyes
  Magos** Day of the Magi (8)
rico/a rich (2)
ridículo/a ridiculous
riesgo risk
riñón *m.* kidney
río river
riqueza *s.* riches, wealth
risa laugh, laughter; **muerto/a de risa**
  dying of laughter
ritmo rhythm, pace (14)
rivalidad *f.* rivalry
robar to rob
rodeado/a surrounded
rodilla knee
rojo/a red (3)
romano/a Roman
romántico/a romantic
romper (*p.p.* **roto/a**) to break (11);
  romper (con) to break up (with) (15)
ron *m.* rum
ropa clothing (3); **planchar la ropa** to
  iron clothes (9); **ropa interior**
  underwear (3)
rosa *n.* rose; **(de color) rosa** pink
rosado/a pink (3)
roto/a *p.p.* broken
rubio/a *n., adj.* blond(e) (2)
ruido noise (4)
ruidoso/a noisy
ruina ruin (13)
ruso/a *n., adj.* Russian
ruta route
rutina diaria daily routine (4)
rutinario/a *adj.* routine

S

sábado Saturday (4)
saber (*irreg.*) to know (6); to know how
  (6)
sabiduría wisdom, knowledge
sabor *m.* taste, flavor
sabroso/a savory
sacar (qu) to take out (11); to get (11); to
  extract (10); to take (photos) (7); **sacar
  buenas/malas notas** to get good/bad
  grades (11); **sacar el saldo** to balance a
  checkbook (16); **sacar la basura** to take
  out the trash (9); **sacar la lengua** to
  stick out one's tongue (10); **sacar una
  muela** to extract a tooth (10)
sacrificio sacrifice
sacudir los muebles (*m. pl.*) to dust the
  furniture (9)
Sagitario Sagitarius
sagrado/a sacred, holy
sal *f.* salt (5)
sala living room (4); **sala de
  emergencias/urgencia** emergency
  room (10); **sala de espera** waiting
  room (7)
salario salary (16)
salchicha sausage (6); hot dog (6)

salida departure (7)
saliente prominent
salir (*irreg.*) **(de)** to leave (4); to go out (4); **salir con** to go out with (15)
salmón *m.* salmon (6)
salón *m.* living room
salsa salsa (*music*); sauce
saltar to jump
salud *f.* health (10)
saludable healthful, healthy
saludarse to greet each other (10)
saludo greeting (AT); **saludos y expresiones de cortesía** greetings and everyday expressions of courtesy (AT)
salvadoreño/a *n., adj.* Salvadoran
sandalia sandal (3)
sándwich *m.* sandwich (6)
sangre *f.* blood (10)
sano/a healthy (10); **llevar una vida sana** to live a healthy life (10)
santo/a saint; **Día** (*m.*) **de Todos los Santos** All Saints' Day (8); **día** (*m.*) **del santo** saint's day (8)
satélite *m.* satellite
satirizar (c) to satirize
satisfacer (*like hacer*) to satisfy
saxofón *m.* saxophone
se (*impersonal*) one; *refl. pron.* yourself (*form.*) herself, himself, itself, themselves, yourselves (*form.*); **¿cómo se llama usted?** what's your name? (AT)
secadora clothes dryer (9)
sección (*f.*) **de (no) fumar** (non)smoking section (7)
seco/a dry
secretario/a secretary (1)
secreto *n.* secret
secuencia sequence; series
secundario/a secondary; **escuela secundaria** high school
sed *f.* thirst; **tener** (*irreg.*) **sed** to be thirsty (6)
seda silk (3); **es de seda** it is made of silk (3)
segmento segment, part
seguida: en seguida right away, immediately
seguir (i, i) (g) to continue (14)
según according to (2)
segundo/a *adj.* second (13)
seguridad *f.* safety
seguro/a *adj.* sure, certain (5); **es seguro** it's a sure thing (13)
seis six (AT)
seiscientos/as six hundred (3)
selección *f.* selection, choice
seleccionar to choose
sello stamp (*postage*) (18)
selva (tropical) (tropical) jungle (10)
semáforo traffic signal (14)
semana week (4); **fin** (*m.*) **de semana** weekend (4); **semana que viene** next week (4)
sembrar (ie) to sow, plant
semejanza similarity

semestre *m.* semester
senador(a) senator
sencillo/a simple
sendero path
sensación *f.* sensation
sensible sensitive, caring
sentarse (ie) to sit down (4)
sentido sense
sentimiento feeling
sentir (ie, i) to regret (13); to feel sorry (13); **sentirse** to feel (8); **lo siento (mucho)** I'm (very) sorry (11)
señor (Sr.) *m.* man; Mr., sir (AT)
señora (Sra.) woman; Mrs., lady (AT)
señorita (Srta.) young woman; Miss, Ms. (AT)
separado/a separated
separarse (de) to separate (from) (15)
septiembre *m.* September (5)
séptimo/a *adj.* seventh (13)
ser (*irreg.*) to be (2); **ser aburrido/a** to be boring (9); **ser aficionado/a (a)** to be a fan (of) (9); **ser descortés** to be impolite; **ser divertido/a** to be fun (9); **ser en** + *place* to take place in/at (*place*) (8); **ser flexible** to be flexible (11)
ser *m.* being
serie *f.* series
serio/a serious
serpenteante winding
serpiente *f.* serpent
servicio service (14); **cuarto de servicio** toilet; **servicio militar** military service (17); **servicio público** public service
servilleta (dinner) napkin
servir (i, i) to serve (4)
sesenta sixty
setecientos/as seven hundred (3)
setenta seventy (2)
sexo sex
sexto/a *adj.* sixth (13)
si if (1); **por si acaso** just in case (11)
sí yes (AT); **sí, me gusta...** yes, I like . . . (AT)
sicoanálisis *m.* psychoanalysis
sicología psychology (1)
sicólogo/a psychologist (16)
siempre always (2)
sierra mountain range (10)
siesta nap; **dormir (ue, u) la siesta** to take a nap (4)
siete seven (AT)
siglo century
significado *n.* meaning
significar (qu) to mean
significativo/a significant, meaningful
signo sign
siguiente *adj.* following (5)
sílaba syllable
silencio silence
silla chair (1)
sillón *m.* armchair (4)
simbólico/a symbolic
símbolo symbol
simpático/a nice (2); likeable (2)

sin without (4); **fue sin querer** it was unintentional (11); **sin duda** without doubt; **sin embargo** however; **sin falta** without fail
sincero/a sincere
sindicato (labor) union
sino but (rather)
sinónimo synonym
sintético/a synthetic
síntoma *m.* symptom (10)
siquiatra *m., f.* psychiatrist (16)
siquiera even; **ni siquiera** not even
sistema *m.* system; **analista** (*m., f.*) **de sistemas** systems analyst (16)
sitio place, location
situación *f.* situation
situado/a located
sobre *n. m.* envelope (18); *prep.* about; on, on top of; **sobre todo** above all, especially
sobredosis *f. s.* overdose
sobrepasar to exceed, surpass
sobrepoblación *f.* overpopulation
sobresaliente outstanding
sobrino/a nephew/niece (2)
social: trabajador(a) social social worker (16)
socialista *m., f.* socialist
socializar (c) to socialize
sociedad *f.* society
socio/a member
sociología sociology (1)
sociólogo/a sociologist
socorro *n.* help
sofá *m.* sofa (4)
sofisticado/a sophisticated
sol *m.* sun; **hace sol** it's sunny (5); **tomar el sol** to sunbathe (7)
solamente *adv.* only
solar solar (14)
soldado soldier (16); **mujer** (*f.*) **soldado** female soldier (16)
soleado/a sunny
soledad *f.* solitude
solicitar to request
solicitud *f.* application (form) (16)
solidaridad *f.* solidarity
solitario/a solitary
sólo *adv.* only (1)
solo/a *adj.* alone (7)
soltero/a single (*not married*) (2)
solución *f.* solution
solucionar to solve
sombra shadow; shade
sombrero hat (3)
sombrilla sunshade, umbrella
son las... it's . . . o'clock (AT)
sonar (ue) to sound (9); to ring (9)
sonreír(se) (i, i) to smile (8)
sopa soup (6)
sorprendente surprising
sorprender to surprise (13); **me (te, le,...) sorprende** it surprises me (you, him, . . .) (13)
sorpresa surprise (8)
sospechar to suspect

soy I am (AT)

su(s) *poss.* his, her, its, their, your (*form. s., pl.*) (2)

subir to go up (7); to get on/in (*a vehicle*) (7)

subjuntivo *gram.* subjunctive

subrayar to underline

subsistir to subsist

substituir (y) to substitute

subterráneo/a subterranean, underground

subtítulo subtitle

suburbio suburb (4)

subyugado/a subjugated

sucio/a dirty (5)

sucursal *f.* branch (*office*) (16)

sudafricano/a *n., adj.* South African

sudamericano/a *n., adj.* South American

Suecia Sweden

suegro/a father-in-law/mother-in-law

sueldo salary (12); **aumento de sueldo** raise in salary (16)

sueño dream; **tener** (*irreg.*) **sueño** to be sleepy (3)

suerte *f.* luck

suéter *m.* sweater (3)

suficiente sufficient, enough; **lo suficiente** enough (10)

sufijo *gram.* suffix

sufrir to suffer (11); **sufrir presiones** to be under pressure (11)

sugerencia suggestion

sugerir (ie, i) to suggest (8)

suicidio suicide

sujeto subject

suma sum, amount

sumamente extremely

superlativo/a *gram.* superlative

supermercado supermarket

superstición *f.* superstition

supervisión *f.* supervision

supervisor(a) supervisor

supuesto/a: por supuesto of course (11)

sur *m.* south (5)

surgir (j) to spring up, arise

suscribir (*p.p.* **suscrito/a**) to subscribe

suspender to cut off (*an allowance*)

sustantivo *gram.* noun (1)

sustituirse (y) to substitute

suyo/a(s) *poss. s., pl.* your, (of) yours (*form.*); his, (of) his; her, (of) hers; its; their, (of) theirs (17)

T

tabacalero/a related to tobacco

tabla table, chart

tal such, such a; **con tal de que** *conj.* provided that (15); **¿qué tal?** how are you (doing)? (AT); **tal como** just as; **tal vez** perhaps

talento talent

talentoso/a talented

talla size

tallado/a *p.p.* cut; carved

taller *m.* (repair) shop (14)

tamaño size

también also, too (AT)

tambor *m.* drum

tampoco neither, not either (6)

tan *adv.* as, so; **tan... como** as . . . as (5); **tan pronto como** *conj.* as soon as (16)

tanque *m.* tank (14)

tanto/a *adj.* so much; such; *pl.* so many; **tanto(s)/tanta(s)... como** as much/ many . . . as (5)

tapa snack

tarde *n. f.* afternoon, evening (1); **buenas tardes** good afternoon/evening (AT); **de la tarde** in the afternoon, evening (AT); **por la tarde** in the afternoon, evening (1); *adv.* late (1)

tarea homework (4); task (9)

tarjeta card (7); **tarjeta de crédito** credit card (6); **tarjeta de identificación** identification card (11); **tarjeta postal** postcard (7)

tasa rate, level; **tasa de alfabetización** literacy rate

tasca tavern

Tauro Taurus

taza cup

te *d.o. s.* you (*fam.*); *i.o. s.* to/for you (*fam.*); *refl. pron. s.* yourself (*fam.*); **¿cómo te llamas?** what's your (*fam.*) name? (AT); **te gusta...** you (*fam.*) like . . . (AT)

té *m.* tea (6)

teatral theatrical

teatro theater (9)

teclado keyboard

técnico/a *n.* technician (16); *adj.* technical

tecnología technology

tecnológico/a technological

tejano/a Texan

tejer to weave (13)

tejidos *m. pl.* woven goods (13)

telaraña web

tele *f.* television

telediario newscast

telefonear to telephone

telefónica telephone company office (10)

teléfono telephone; **hablar por teléfono** to talk on the phone (1); **teléfono celular / de coche** cellular/car phone (12)

telegrama *m.* telegram

telenovela soap opera (13)

televisión *f.* television; **mirar la televisión** to watch television (2)

televisor *m.* television set (4)

tema *m.* theme, topic

temblar (ie) to tremble

temer to fear (13)

temperatura temperature (10); **tomarle la temperatura** to take someone's temperature (10)

templado/a cool, temperate

templo temple

temporada season

temporal temporary

temprano *adv.* early (1)

tender (ie) to tend to; to make (*a bed*)

tener (*irreg.*) to have (3); **tener... años** to be . . . years old (2); **tener (mucho) calor/frío** to be (very) warm, hot/cold (5); **tener dolor de** to have a pain in (10); **tener ganas de** + *inf.* to feel like (*doing something*) (3); **tener (mucha) hambre/sed** to be (very) hungry/ thirsty (6); **tener miedo (de)** to be afraid (of) (3); **tener prisa** to be in a hurry (3); **tener que** + *inf.* to have to (*do something*) (3); **(no) tener razón** to be right (wrong) (3); **tener sueño** to be sleepy (3)

tenis *m. s.* tennis (9); **zapato de tenis** tennis shoe (3)

tensión *f.* tension; stress (11)

tenue faint; tenuous

teoría theory

tercer, tercero/a *adj.* third (13)

tercio/a *adj.* third

terco/a stubborn, obstinate

térmico/a thermal

terminación *f.* ending

terminar to finish

término term

termómetro thermometer

ternura tenderness

terraza terrace (4)

terremoto earthquake

terreno/a earthly; worldly

terrestre terrestrial, earthly

territorio territory

terrorista *m., f.* terrorist (17)

tertulia social gathering

testigo *m., f.* witness (17)

testimonio testimony

texto text (1); **libro de texto** textbook (1)

ti *obj.* (*of prep.*) you (*fam. s.*) (5)

tiempo time (5); weather; **a tiempo** on time (7); **hace buen/mal tiempo** it's good/bad weather (5); **llegar (gu) a tiempo** to arrive on time (11); **pasar tiempo (con)** to spend time (with) (15); **¿qué tiempo hace?** what's the weather like? (5); **trabajo a tiempo completo (parcial)** full-time (part-time) job (11)

tienda store (3); **tienda de campaña** tent (7)

tierra earth, land

timbre *m.* doorbell

tímido/a timid

tinta ink

tinto: vino tinto red wine (6)

tío/a uncle/aunt (2)

típico/a typical

tipo type

tira cómica comic strip

tirar to throw (out)

título title

toalla towel

tobillo ankle

tocar (qu) to touch; to play (*a musical instrument*) (1); **tocar música** to play music (8); **tocarle a uno** to be someone's turn (9)

todavía yet, still (5)

todo/a *n. m.* all; everything; **de todo** everything (3); **todo derecho** straight ahead (14)

todo(s)/a(s) *adj.* all (2); every (2); **de todas maneras** anyway; **por todas partes** everywhere (11); **todos los días** every day (1)

tomar to take (1); to drink (1); **tomar el sol** to sunbathe (7); **tomarle el pelo** to pull his/her leg; **tomarle la temperatura** to take someone's temperature (10)

tomate *m.* tomato (6)

tontería silly, foolish thing

tonto/a silly, foolish (2)

torcido/a twisted

toreo bullfighting

torno: en torno a about, regarding

toro bull; **plaza de toros** bullring

torpe clumsy (11)

tos *f.* cough (10)

toser to cough (10)

tostado/a toasted (6); **pan** (*m.*) **tostado** toast (6)

tostadora toaster (9)

total *n. m.* total; *adj.* total; **en total** in all

tóxico/a toxic

trabajador(a) *n.* worker; *adj.* hardworking (2); **trabajador(a) social** social worker (16)

trabajar to work (1)

trabajo job, work (11); report, (piece of) work (11); **trabajo de tiempo completo/parcial** full-time/part-time job (11)

trabalenguas *m. s., pl.* tongue-twister

tradición *f.* tradition (13)

tradicional traditional

traducir (*irreg.*) to translate

traductor(a) translator (16)

traer (*irreg.*) to bring (4)

tragedia tragedy

trágico/a tragic

trago (*alcoholic*) drink (18)

traje *m.* suit (3); **traje de baño** bathing suit (3)

trámite *m.* step, procedure

tranquilidad *f.* tranquility, calm

tranquilo/a calm, tranquil; **llevar una vida tranquila** to lead a calm life (10)

transbordador (*m.*) (**espacial**) (space) shuttle

transeúnte *m., f.* transient

transferir (ie, i) to transfer

tránsito traffic (14)

transmisión f. transmission

transmitir to transmit

transportación *f.* transportation

transporte *m.* (*means of*) transportation (14)

tras *prep.* after

trascendental important, far-reaching

trasladar to transfer, move

tratamiento treatment (10)

tratar to treat; **tratar de** + *inf.* to try to (*do something*) (13)

trauma *m.* trauma

través: a través de through, by means of

travieso/a mischievous

trece thirteen (AT)

treinta thirty (AT); **y treinta** thirty, half past (*with time*) (AT)

tremendo/a tremendous

tren *m.* train (7); **estación** (*f.*) **del tren** train station (7); **ir** (*irreg.*) **en tren** to go by train (7)

tres three (AT)

trescientos/as three hundred (3)

trimestre *m.* trimester; quarter

triste sad (5)

tristeza sadness

trofeo trophy

trompeta trumpet

tropa troop, group

tropezar (c) to run into

trozo piece, chunk

tu(s) *poss. s.* your (*fam.*) (2)

tú *sub. pron. s.* you (*fam.*) (1); **¿y tú?** and you? (AT)

tubería plumbing

tuberculosis plumbing

turbulento/a turbulent

turismo tourism

turista *n. m., f.* tourist

turístico/a *adj.* tourist; **clase** (*f.*) **turística** tourist class (7)

tuyo/a(s) *poss. s.* your, of yours (*fam.*) (17)

U

u or (*used instead of* **o** *before words beginning with stressed* **o** *or* **ho**)

ubicar (qu) to locate, place

último/a last (7); **de última moda** the latest style (3); latest (17)

ultravioleta *adj. m., f.* ultraviolet

un, uno/a one (AT); *indefinite article* a, an; **a la una** at one o'clock (AT); **una vez** once (10)

único/a *adj.* only; unique

unidad *f.* unity

unido/a close-knit

unificación *f.* unification

unificar (qu) to unify

unión *f.* union

unir to unite, join

universidad *f.* university (1)

universitario/a (of the) university (11)

unívoco/a univocal; of one voice

urbanismo city planning

urbano/a urban

urgencia: sala de urgencia emergency room (10)

urgente urgent (13)

usar to use (3); to wear (*clothing*) (3)

uso use

usted (**Ud., Vd.**) *sub. pron. s.* you (*form.*) (1); *obj.* (*of prep.*) *s.* you (*form.*) (1); **¿cómo es usted?** what are you like? (AT); **¿cómo se llama usted?** what's

your name? (AT); **¿y usted?** and you? (AT)

ustedes (**Uds., Vds.**) *sub. pron. pl.* you (*form.*) (1); *obj.* (*of prep.*) *pl.* you (*form.*) (1)

usualmente usually

útil useful (15)

utilización *f.* utilization

utilizar (c) to utilize, use

uva grape (5)

V

vaca cow

vacación *f.* vacation (7); **estar** (*irreg.*) **de vacaciones** to be on vacation (7); **ir** (*irreg.*) **de vacaciones** to go on vacation (7); **vacaciones de primavera** spring break (8)

vacuna shot, vaccination

vahído dizzy spell

Valentín: Día (*m.*) **de San Valentín** St. Valentine's Day (8)

válido/a valid

valle *m.* valley

valor *m.* value

variación *f.* variation

variado/a varied

variar (varío) to vary

variedad *f.* variety

varios/as *pl.* several

vaso (*drinking*) glass

vecindad *f.* neighborhood (12)

vecino/a neighbor (12)

vegetariano/a vegetarian

vehículo vehicle (12)

veinte twenty (AT)

veinticinco twenty-five (AT)

veinticuatro twenty-four (AT)

veintidós twenty-two (AT)

veintinueve twenty-nine (AT)

veintiocho twenty-eight (AT)

veintiséis twenty-six (AT)

veintisiete twenty-seven (AT)

veintitrés twenty-three (AT)

veintiún, veintiuno/a twenty-one (AT)

vejez *f.* old age (15)

velocidad *f.* speed (14); **límite** (*m.*) **de velocidad** speed limit (14)

vendedor(a) salesperson (16)

vender to sell (2)

venezolano/a *n., adj.* Venezuelan

venir (*irreg.*) to come (3)

venta sale

ventaja advantage (10)

ventana window (1)

ventilación f. ventilation

ver (*irreg.*) to see (4); **nos vemos** see you around (AT)

verano summer (5)

verbo *gram.* verb (1)

verdad *f.* truth; **¿verdad?** right? (3)

verdadero/a true

verde green (3)

verdura vegetable (6)

verificar (qu) to check

versión *f.* version

vestido dress (3)
vestirse (i, i) to get dressed (4)
veterinario/a veterinarian (16)
vez *f.* (*pl.* **veces**) time; **en vez de** instead of (16); **tal vez** perhaps; **por primera/última vez** for the first/last time (11); **una vez** once (10); **a veces** sometimes, at times (2); **dos veces** twice (10)
viajar to travel (7)
viaje *m.* trip (7); **agencia de viajes** travel agency (7); **agente** (*m., f.*) **de viajes** travel agent (7); **de viaje** on a trip (7); **hacer** (*irreg.*) **un viaje** to take a trip (4)
viajero/a traveler (18); **cheque** (*m.*) **de viajero** traveler's check (18)
víctima *m., f.* victim
vida life (11); **llevar una vida sana/tranquila** to lead a healthy/calm life (10)
vídeo video
videocasetera videocassette recorder (VCR) (12)
videoteca video library
viejo/a *adj.* old (2); **Noche** (*f.*) **Vieja** New Year's Eve (8)
viento wind (5); **hace viento** it's windy (5)
viernes *m. s., pl.* Friday (4)
vietnamita *n., adj. m., f.* Vietnamese
vínculo bond, tie, link
vinícola *adj., m., f.* wine, wine-making

vino (blanco, tinto) (white, red) wine (6)
viñedo vineyard
violencia violence (14)
violento/a violent
violeta violet
violín *m.* violin
visita *n.* visit
visitante *m., f.* visitor
visitar un museo to visit a museum (9)
vista view (12); **a primera vista** at first sight (15); **punto de vista** point of view
vitamina vitamin
viudo/a widower/widow
vivienda housing (12)
vivir to live (2)
vocabulario vocabulary
vocación *f.* vocation
vocal *f. gram.* vowel
volante *adj.* flying; **objeto volante no identificado (OVNI)** unidentified flying object (UFO)
volcán *m.* volcano
vólibol *m.* volleyball (9)
volumen *m.* volume
voluntario/a *n.* volunteer; *adj.* voluntary
volver (ue) (*p.p.* **vuelto/a**) to return (*to a place*) (4); **volver a** + *inf.* to (*do something*) again (4)
vosotros/as *Sp. sub. pron. pl.* you (*fam.*)

(1); *obj.* (*of prep.*) *pl.* you (*fam.*)
votar to vote
voz *f.* (*pl.* **voces**) voice; **en voz alta** out loud
vuelo flight (7); **asistente** (*m., f.*) **de vuelo** flight attendant (7)
vuelto/a *p.p.* returned; **billete** (*m.*)**/boleto de ida y vuelta** round-trip ticket (7)
vuestro/a(s) *Sp. poss. pl.* your (*fam.*) (2); yours, of yours (*fam.*) (17)

Y

y and (AT); **y cuarto (quince)** fifteen minutes, a quarter past (*the hour*) (AT); **y media (treinta)** thirty minutes, half past (*the hour*) (AT)
ya already (8); **ya no** no longer; **ya que** since
yacimiento deposit (*mineral*)
yerno son-in-law
yo *sub. pron.* I (1)
yogur *m.* yogurt (6)

Z

zanahoria carrot (6)
zapatería shoe store
zapato shoe (3); **zapato de tenis** tennis shoe (3)
zona zone

Vocabularies

English–Spanish Vocabulary

A

able: to be able **poder** (*irreg.*) (3)
abroad **extranjero** *n.* (18)
absence **falta** (14)
absent: to be absent **faltar** (8)
absentminded **distraído/a** (11)
accelerated **acelerado/a** (14)
accent **acento** (14)
according to **según** (2)
account **cuenta** (16); checking account **cuenta corriente** (16); savings account **cuenta de ahorros** (16)
accountant **contador(a)** (16)
ache **doler (ue)** *v.* (10)
ache **dolor** *n.m.* (10)
acquainted: to be acquainted with **conocer (zc)** (6)
actor **actor** *m.* (13)
actress **actriz** *f.* (*pl.* **actrices**) (13)
address **dirección** *f.* (12)
adjective **adjetivo** *gram.* (2)
administration: business administration **administración** (*f.*) **de empresas** (1)
adolescence **adolescencia** (15)
adult **adulto/a** (9);
advantage **ventaja** (10)
advice (piece of) **consejo** (6)
advisor **consejero/a** (1)
aerobic **aeróbico/a** (10); to do aerobics **hacer** (*irreg.*) **ejercicio aeróbico** (10)
affectionate **cariñoso/a** (5)
afraid: to be afraid (of) **tener** (*irreg.*) **miedo (de)** (11)
after *prep.* **después de** (4); *conj.* **después (de) que** (16)
afternoon **tarde** *n. f.* (1); good afternoon **buenas tardes** (AT); (a time) in the afternoon **de la tarde** (AT); in the afternoon **por la tarde** (1)
age: old age **vejez** *f.* (15)
agency: travel agency **agencia de viajes** (7)
agent: travel agent **agente** (*m., f.*) **de viajes** (7)
agree: I agree **estoy de acuerdo** (2)
ahead of time **con anticipación** (7); straight ahead **todo derecho** (14)
air **aire** *m.* (14)
airplane **avión** *m.* (7)
airport **aeropuerto** (7)
alarm clock **despertador** *m.* (11)
alike: to be alike **parecerse (zc)** (10)
all **todo(s)/a(s)** *adj.* (2)
allow **permitir** (12)
almost: almost never **casi nunca** (2)

alone **solo/a** *adj.* (7)
already **ya** (8)
also **también** (AT)
always **siempre** (2)
among **entre** *prep.* (5)
amusement **diversión** *f.* (9)
analyst: systems analyst **analista** (*m., f.*) **de sistemas** (16)
and **y** (AT)
angry **furioso/a** (5); to get angry (at) **enojarse (con)** (8)
announce **anunciar** (7)
another **otro/a** (2)
answer *v.* **contestar** (4); *n.* **respuesta** (5)
answering machine **contestador** (*m.*) **automático** (12)
antibiotic **antibiótico** (10)
any **algún, alguno/a** (6)
anyone **alguien** (6)
anything **algo** (3)
apartment **apartamento** (1); apartment building **bloque** (*m.*) **de apartamentos** (12); **casa de apartamentos** (12)
apologize **pedir (i, i) disculpas** (11)
apple **manzana** (6)
appliance: home appliance **aparato doméstico** (9)
applicant **aspirante** *m., f.* (16)
application (form) **solicitud** *f.* (16)
appreciate **apreciar** (13)
April **abril** *m.* (5)
architect **arquitecto/a** (13)
architecture **arquitectura** (13)
area **área** *f.* (*but* **el área**) (12)
argue (about) (with) **discutir (sobre) (con)** (8)
arm **brazo** (11)
armchair **sillón** *m.* (4)
army **ejército** (17)
arrival **llegada** (7)
arrive **llegar (gu)** (2); to arrive on time/late **llegar a tiempo/tarde** (11)
art **arte** *f.* (*but* **el arte**) (1); work of art **obra de arte** (13)
article **artículo** (1)
artist **artista** *m., f.* (13)
artistic **artístico/a** (13)
arts and crafts **artesanía** (13)
arts, letters **letras** *f. pl.* (2)
as . . . as **tan... como** (5); as much/many as **tanto/a... como** (5); as soon as **tan pronto como** *conj.*; **en cuanto** *conj.* (16)
ask: to ask for **pedir (i, i)** (4); to ask a question **hacer** (*irreg.*) **una pregunta** (4); **preguntar** (6)

asparagus **espárragos** *m. pl.* (6)
assassination **asesinato** (17)
at **en** (AT); **a** (*with time*) (AT); at . . . (hour) **a la(s)...** (AT); at home **en casa** (1); at last **por fin** (4); at least **por lo menos** (11); at once **ahora mismo**; at the beginning of **al principio de** (16); at times **a veces** (2)
attend (*a function*) **asistir (a)** (2)
attendant: flight attendant **asistente** (*m., f.*) **de vuelo** (7)
August **agosto** (5)
aunt **tía** (2)
automatic teller machine **cajero automático** (16)
autumn **otoño** (5)
avenue **avenida** (12)
avoid **evitar** (14)

B

baby-sitter **niñero/a** (9)
backpack **mochila** (1)
bad **mal, malo/a** *adj.* (2); it's bad weather **hace mal tiempo** (5); the bad thing, news **lo malo** (10)
baggage **equipaje** *m.* (7)
balance a checkbook **sacar (qu) el saldo** (16)
ball **pelota** (9)
ballet **ballet** *m.* (13)
ballpoint pen **bolígrafo** (1)
banana **banana** (6)
bank **banco** (16); (bank) check **cheque** *m.* (16)
bar **bar** *m.* (9)
bargain **ganga** (3)
baseball **béisbol** *m.* (9)
basketball **basquetbol** *m.* (9)
bath: to take a bath **bañarse** (4)
bathing suit **traje** (*m.*) **de baño** (3)
bathroom **baño** (4)
bathtub **bañera** (4)
battery **batería** (14)
be **estar** (*irreg.*) (1); **ser** (*irreg.*) (2); to be (feel) warm, hot **tener** (*irreg.*) **calor** (5); to be (very) hungry **tener** (*irreg.*) **(mucha) hambre** (6); to be . . . years old **tener** (*irreg.*)**... años** (2); to be a fan (of) **ser** (*irreg.*) **aficionado/a (a)** (9); to be able **poder** (*irreg.*) (3); to be afraid (of) **tener** (*irreg.*) **miedo (de)** (11); to be boring **ser** (*irreg.*) **aburrido/a** (9); to be cold **tener** (*irreg.*) **frío** (5); to be comfortable (*temperature*) **estar** (*irreg.*)

bien (5); to be flexible **ser** (*irreg.*) **flexible** (11); to be fun **ser** (*irreg.*) **divertido/a** (9); to be in a hurry **tener** (*irreg.*) **prisa** (3); to be late **estar** (*irreg.*) **atrasado/a** (7) to take place in/at (*place*) **ser** (*irreg.*) **en** + *place* (8)
beach **playa** (5)
bean **frijol** *m.* (6)
beautiful **bello/a** (14)
because **porque** (2)
become + *adj.* **ponerse** (*irreg.*) + *adj.* (8)
become accustomed to **acostumbrarse a** (10)
bed: to make the bed **hacer** (*irreg.*) **la cama** (9); to stay in bed **guardar cama** (10)
bedroom **alcoba** (4)
beer **cerveza** (1)
before *conj.* **antes (de) que** (15); *prep.* **antes de** (4)
begin **empezar (ie) (c)** (4)
beginning: at the beginning of **al principio de** (16)
behave **portarse** (8)
behind **detrás de** *prep.* (5)
believe (in) **creer (y) (en)** (2)
bellhop **mozo, botones** *m. s., pl.* (18)
below **debajo de** *prep.* (5)
belt **cinturón** *m.* (3)
bend **doblar** (14)
beside **al lado (de)** *prep.* (5)
best **mejor** (5)
better **mejor** (5)
between **entre** *prep.* (5)
beverage **bebida** (6)
bicycle **bicicleta** (12); to ride a bicycle **pasear en bicicleta** (9)
bicycling **ciclismo** (9)
big **gran, grande** (2)
bilingual **bilingüe** (11)
bill (*for service*) **cuenta** (6); **factura** (16)
biology **biología** (2)
bird **pájaro** (2)
birth **nacimiento** (15)
birthday **cumpleaños** *m. s., pl.* (5); birthday cake **pastel** (*m.*) **de cumpleaños** (8); to have a birthday **cumplir años** (8)
black **negro/a** (3)
blond(e) **rubio/a** *n., adj.* (2)
blood **sangre** *f.* (10)
blouse **blusa** (3)
blue **azul** (3)
boarding house **pensión** *f.* (18); room and full board **pensión completa** (18); room with breakfast and one other meal **media pensión** (18)
boat **barco** (7)
body **cuerpo** (10)
bookshelf **estante** *m.* (4)
bookstore **librería** (1)
boot **bota** (3)
border **frontera** (11)
bore **aburrir** (13)
bored **aburrido/a** (5); to get bored **aburrirse** (9)

boring: to be boring **ser** (*irreg.*) **aburrido/a** (9)
born: to be born **nacer (zc)** (15)
borrow **pedir (i, i) prestado/a** (16)
boss **jefe/a** (11)
bother **molestar** (13); it bothers me (you, him, . . .) **me (te, le, ...) molesta** (13)
boy **muchacho** (4); **niño** (2)
boyfriend **novio** (5)
brain **cerebro** (10)
brakes **frenos** (14)
branch (office) **sucursal** *f.* (16)
bread **pan** *m.* (6)
break **romper** (*p.p.* **roto/a**) (11); to break up (with) **romper (con)** (15)
breakfast **desayuno** (4); to have breakfast **desayunar** (6)
breathe **respirar** (10)
bring **traer** (*irreg.*) (4)
brother **hermano** (2)
brown **pardo/a** (3)
brunet(te) **moreno/a** *n., adj.* (2)
brush one's teeth **cepillarse los dientes** (4)
budget **presupuesto** (16)
build **construir (y)** (14)
building **edificio** *n.* (1); building manager **portero/a** (12)
bump into **pegarse (gu) en/contra** (11)
bureau (*furniture*) **cómoda** (4)
bus **autobús** *m.* (7); bus station **estación** (*f.*) **de autobuses** (7); bus stop **parada del autobús** (18)
business **empresa** (16); business administration **administración** (*f.*) **de empresas** (1)
businessperson **hombre** (*m.*)/**mujer** (*f.*) **de negocios** (2)
busy **ocupado/a** (5)
but **pero** *conj.* (AT)
butter **mantequilla** (6)
buy **comprar** (1)
by **por** *prep.* (4); in the morning (afternoon, evening) **por la mañana (tarde, noche)** (1); by check **con cheque** (16)

C

cabin **cabina** (*on a ship*) (7)
café **café** *m.* (18)
cafeteria **cafetería** (1)
cake **pastel** *m.* (6); birthday cake **pastel de cumpleaños** (8)
calculator **calculadora** (1)
calendar **calendario** (11)
call *v.* **llamar** (6); to be called **llamarse** (4)
campground *camping* *m.* (7)
camping: to go camping **hacer** (*irreg.*) *camping* (7)
can **poder** *v.* (/) *irreg.* (/) (3)
cancel a reservation **cancelar una reserva** to cancel (10)
candidate **aspirante** *m., f.* (16)
candy **dulces** *m. pl.* (6)
capital city **capital** *f.* (5)

car **coche** *m.* (2); car telephone **teléfono del coche** (12); convertible car **carro descapotable** (12)
card: identification card **tarjeta de identificación** (11); to play cards **jugar (ue) (gu) a las cartas** (9)
cardinal directions **puntos** (*m. pl.*) **cardinales** (5)
career **carrera** (2)
carrot **zanahoria** (6)
carry **llevar** (3)
case **caso**; in case **en caso de que** (15); just in case **por si acaso** (11)
cash (*a check*) **cobrar** (16); in cash **en efectivo** (16); to pay in cash **pagar (gu) al contado** (16)
cashier **cajero/a** (16)
cat **gato/a** (2)
catch a cold **resfriarse (me resfrío)** (10)
CD-ROM **CD-ROM** *m.* (12)
celebrate **celebrar** (5)
cellular telephone **teléfono celular** (12)
ceramics **cerámica** (13)
cereal **cereales** *m. pl.* (6)
certain **seguro/a** *adj.* (5); **cierto/a** (13)
chair **silla** (1); armchair **sillón** *m.* (4)
chalkboard **pizarra** (1)
change *v.* **cambiar (de)** (12)
channel **canal** *m.* (12)
charge (*to an account*) **cargar (gu)** (16); (*someone for an item or service*) **cobrar** (16)
cheap **barato/a** (3)
check (*bank*) **cheque** *m.* (16); by check **con cheque** (16); traveler's check **cheque de viajero** (18); to check **revisar** (14); to check into (*a hospital*) **internarse en** (10); to check one's bags **facturar el equipaje** (7)
check-up **chequeo** (10)
checking account **cuenta corriente** (16)
cheese **queso** (6)
chef **cocinero/a** (16)
chemistry **química** (1)
chess **ajedrez** *m.* (4); to play chess **jugar (ue) (gu) al ajedrez** (4)
chicken **pollo** (6)
chief **jefe/a** (11)
child **niño/a** (2); as a child **de niño** (9)
childhood **niñez** *f.*
children **hijos** *m. pl.* (2)
chop: **chuleta** (6) pork chop **chuleta de cerdo** (6)
chore: household chore **quehacer** *m.* **doméstico** (9)
Christmas Eve **Nochebuena** (8)
Christmas **Navidad** *f.* (8)
citizen **ciudadano/a** (17)
city **ciudad** *f.* (2)
class **clase** *f.* (1); first class **primera clase** (7); tourist class **clase turística** (7)
classical **clásico/a** (13)
classmate **compañero/a de clase** (1)
clean *adj.* **limpio/a** (5)
clean **limpiar** (9); to clean the (whole) house **limpiar la casa (entera)** (9)

clear the table **quitar la mesa** (9)
clerk **dependiente/a** (1)
clever **listo/a** (2)
client **cliente** *m., f.* (1)
climate **clima** *m.* (5)
close **cerrar (ie)** (4)
close to *prep.* **cerca de** (5)
closed **cerrado/a** (5)
closet **armario** (4)
clothes dryer **secadora** (9)
clothing **ropa** (3); to wear (*clothing*)
  llevar, usar (3)
cloudy: it's (very) cloudy, overcast **está**
  (muy) nublado (5)
clumsy **torpe** (11)
coffee **café** *m.* (1)
coffee pot **cafetera** (9)
cold (*illness*) **resfriado** (10); to be cold
  tener (*irreg.*) **frío** *n.* (5); it's cold
  (*weather*) **hace frío** (5)
collect **recoger (j)** (11)
collide (with) **chocar (qu) (con)** (14)
collision **choque** *m.* (17)
color **color** *m.* (5)
comb one's hair **peinarse** (4)
come **venir** (*irreg.*) (3)
comfortable **cómodo/a** (4); to be
  comfortable (*temperature*) **estar** (*irreg.*)
  bien (5)
communicate (with) **comunicarse (qu)**
  (con) (17)
communication (*major*) **comunicación** *f.*
  (1); means of communication **medio**
  de comunicación (17)
compact disc **disco compacto** (12)
comparison **comparación** *f.* (5)
complain (about) **quejarse (de)** (8)
composer **compositor(a)** (13)
computer **computadora** (L.A.) (12);
  ordenador *m.* (Sp.) (12); computer disk
  disco de computadora (12); computer
  file **archivo** (12); computer science
  computación *f.* (1); laptop computer
  computadora/ordenador portátil (12)
concert **concierto** (9); to go to a concert
  ir (*irreg.*) **a un concierto** (9)
confirm **confirmar** (18)
congested **congestionado/a** (10)
congratulations **felicitaciones** *f. pl.* (8)
conserve **conservar** (14)
contact lenses **lentes** (*m. pl.*) **de contacto**
  (10)
content *adj.* **contento/a** (5)
continue **seguir (i, i) (g)** (14); to continue
  straight ahead **seguir (i, i) derecho**
  (14)
control: remote control **control** (*m.*)
  remoto (12)
convertible (*car*) **descapotable** (12)
cook *v.* **cocinar** (6); *n.* cook **cocinero/a**
  (16)
cookie **galleta** (6)
cool: (6); it's cool (*weather*) **hace fresco**
  (5)
copy **copia** (12); to copy **hacer** (*irreg.*)
  copia (12)

corn **maíz** *m.* (5)
corner (street) **esquina** (14)
corporation **empresa** (16)
cotton **algodón** *m.* (3); it is made of
  cotton **es de algodón** (3)
cough **tos** *f.* (10); to cough **toser** (10);
  cough syrup **jarabe** *m.* (10)
count **contar (ue)** (17)
country **país** *m.* (2)
countryside **campo** (12)
course (*of a meal*) **plato** (6)
courtesy **cortesía** (AT)
cousin **primo/a** (2)
cover **cubrir** (*pp.* **cubierto/a**) (14)
crash (*computer*) **fallar** (12)
crazy **loco/a** (5)
create **crear** (13)
credit card **tarjeta de crédito** (16)
crime **delito, crimen** *m.* (14)
cross **cruzar (c)** (18)
cry **llorar** (8)
custard: baked custard **flan** *m.* (6)
custom **costumbre** *f.* (9)
customs **aduana** *s.* (18); (customs) duty
  derechos (*m. pl.*) **(de aduana)** (18);
  (customs) inspector **inspector(a) (de**
  aduanas) (18)

D

dad **papá** *m.* (2)
daily routine **rutina diaria** (4)
dance **baile** *m.* (8); **danza** (13); to dance
  bailar (1)
dancer **bailarín, bailarina** (13)
date (*calendar*) **fecha** (5); (*social*) **cita** (15)
daughter **hija** (2)
day **día** *m.* (1); day after tomorrow
  pasado mañana (4); every day **todos**
  los días (1)
deadline **fecha límite** (11)
dear **querido/a** *n., adj.* (5)
death **muerte** *f.* (15)
December **diciembre** *m.* (5)
declare **declarar** (18)
delay *n.* **demora** (7)
delighted **encantado/a** (AT)
deluxe **de lujo** (18)
dense **denso/a** (14)
dentist **dentista** *m., f.* (10)
deny **negar (ie) (gu)** (13)
department store **almacén** *m.* (3)
departure **salida** (7)
deposit **depositar** (16)
desirable **deseable** (12)
desk **escritorio** (1)
dessert **postre** *m.* (6)
destroy **destruir (y)** (14)
detail **detalle** *m.* (6)
develop **desarrollar** (14)
dictator **dictador(a)** (17)
dictatorship **dictadura** (17)
dictionary **diccionario** (1)
die **morir (ue, u)** (*p.p.* **muerto/a**) (15); to
  be dying **morir(se)** (8)
difficult **difícil** (5)
dining room **comedor** *m.* (4)

dinner **cena** (6); to have dinner **cenar** (6)
direction **orientación** *f.*
directions: cardinal directions **puntos** (*m.*
  pl.) **cardinales** (5)
director **director(a)** (13); personnel
  director **director(a) de personal** (16)
dirty **sucio/a** (5)
disadvantage **desventaja** (10)
disaster **desastre** *m.* (17)
disc: compact disc **disco compacto** (12)
discotheque **discoteca** (9)
discover **descubrir** (*pp.* **descubierto**) (14)
discrimination **discriminación** *f.* (17)
dish (prepared) **plato** (4)
dishwasher **lavaplatos** *m. s., pl.* (4)
disk: computer disk **disco de**
  computadora (12)
divorce **divorcio** (15)
divorced: to get divorced (from)
  divorciarse (de) (15)
dizzy **mareado/a** (10)
do **hacer** (*irreg.*) (4); (*do something*) again
  volver a + *inf.* (4); to do aerobics **hacer**
  (*irreg.*) **ejercicios aeróbicos** (10); to do
  exercise **hacer** (*irreg.*) **ejercicio** (4)
doctor (medical) **médico/a** (2)
dog **perro/a** (2)
door **puerta** (1)
doorman **portero/a** (12)
dormitory **residencia** (1)
double **doble** (18); double room
  habitación (*f.*) **doble** (18)
doubt **dudar** (12)
downtown **centro** (3)
drama **drama** *m.* (13)
draw **dibujar** (13)
dress **vestido** (3)
dressed: to get dressed **vestirse (i, i)** (4)
dresser (*furniture*) **cómoda** (4)
drink **bebida** (6); **copa, trago** (*alcoholic*)
  (18); *drink similar to a milkshake* **batido**
  (18); to drink **tomar** (1); **beber** (2)
drive (*a vehicle*) **conducir** (*irreg.*) (14);
  manejar (12)
driver **conductor(a)** (14)
during **durante** (4); **por** (4)
dust the furniture **sacudir los muebles**
  (9)
duty: (customs) duty **derechos** (*m. pl.*)
  (de aduana) (18)

E

each **cada** *inv.* (4)
ear (inner) **oído** (10); (outer) **oreja** (10)
early **temprano** *adv.* (1)
earn **ganar** (12)
earring **arete** *m.* (3)
east **este** *m.* (5)
Easter **Pascua (Florida)** (8)
easy **fácil** (5)
eat **comer** (2); eat breakfast **desayunar**
  (6); eat dinner **cenar** (6)
economize **economizar (c)** (16)
economy **economía** (1)
egg **huevo** (6)

eight **ocho** (AT)
eight hundred **ochocientos/as** (3)
eighteen **dieciocho** (AT)
eighth **octavo/a** *adj.* (13)
eighty **ochenta** (2)
electric **eléctrico/a** (14)
electrician **electricista** *m., f.* (16)
electricity **luz** *f.* (*pl.* **luces**) (11)
electronic mail **correo electrónico** (12)
eleven **once** (AT)
embarrassed **avergonzado/a** (8)
emergency room **sala de emergencias** (10)
emotion **emoción** *f.* (8)
energy **energía** (14)
engagement **noviazgo** (15)
engineer **ingeniero/a** (16)
English (*language*) **inglés** *m.* (1); *n., adj.* **inglés, inglesa** (2)
enjoy oneself, have a good time **divertirse (ie, i)** (4)
enough **bastante** *adv.* (15); **lo suficiente** (10)
entertainment **diversión** *f.* (9)
entire **entero/a** (9)
envelope **sobre** *m.* (18)
equality **igualdad** *f.* (17)
equipment: stereo equipment **equipo estereofónico** (12)
era **época** (9)
evening **tarde** *f.* (1); good evening **buenas tardes** (AT); in the afternoon, evening **de la tarde** (AT); in the evening **por la tarde** (1)
event **acontecimiento** (17); **hecho** (8)
every **cada** *inv.* (4); **todo(s)/a(s)** *adj.* (2); every day **todos los días** (1)
everything **de todo** (3)
everywhere **por todas partes** (11)
exactly, on the dot (*time*) **en punto** (AT)
exam **examen** *m.* (3)
examine **examinar** (10); **registrar** (18)
excuse me **con permiso, perdón** (AT); **discúlpeme** (11)
exercise **ejercicio** (3)
expect **esperar** (6)
expend **gastar** (8)
expense **gasto** (12)
expensive **caro/a** (3)
explain **explicar (qu)** (7)
expressions: greetings and expressions of courtesy **saludos** (*m. pl.*) **y expresiones** (*f. pl.*) **de cortesía** (AT)
extract **sacar (qu)** (10); extract a tooth **sacar una muela** (10)
eye **ojo** (10)
eyeglasses **gafas** *f. pl.* (10)

F

fact **hecho** *n.* (8); **de hecho** in fact (9)
factory **fábrica** (14)
faithful **fiel** (2)
fall (*season*) **otoño** (5)
fall *v.* **caer** (*irreg.*) (11); to fall asleep **dormirse** (4); to fall down **caerse** (11); to fall in love (with) **enamorarse (de)** (15)

fan **aficionado/a** (9); to be a fan (of) **ser** (*irreg.*) **aficionado/a (a)** (9)
far from **lejos de** *prep.* (5)
farm **finca** (14); farm worker **campesino/a** (14)
farmer **agricultor(a)** (14)
fashion **moda**; the latest fashion; style **de última moda** (3)
fast **rápido/a** *adj.* (6); **acelerado/a** (14)
fat **gordo/a** (2)
father **papá** *m.*, **padre** *m.* (2)
fax **fax** *m.* (12)
fear **miedo** (3); to fear **temer** (13)
February **febrero** (5)
feel **sentirse** (ie, i) (8); **encontrarse (ue)** (10); to feel like (*doing something*) **tener** (*irreg.*) **ganas de** + *inf.* (3); to feel sorry **sentir (ie, i)** (13); **lo siento (mucho)** I'm (very) sorry (11)
female soldier **mujer soldado** (16)
fever **fiebre** *f.* (10); have a fever **tener** (*irreg.*) **fiebre**
fifteen **quince** (AT); a quarter (fifteen minutes) to (the hour) **menos quince** (AT); a quarter (fifteen minutes) past (the hour) **y quince** (AT)
fifth **quinto/a** *adj.* (13)
fifty **cincuenta** (2)
fight **pelear** (9)
file: computer file **archivo** (12)
fill (up) **llenar** (14); to fill out (*a form*) **llenar** (16)
finally **por fin** (4)
find **encontrar (ue)** (8); to find out (about) **enterarse (de)** (17)
fine **muy bien** (AT)
fine *n.* **multa** (18)
finger **dedo (de la mano)** (11)
finish **acabar** (11)
first **primer, primero/a** *adj.* (4); at first sight **a primera vista** (15); first of (month) **el primero de (mes)** (5); first class **primera clase** (7)
fish (*cooked*) **pescado** (6)
five **cinco** (AT)
five hundred **quinientos/as** (3)
fix **arreglar** (12)
fixed price **precio fijo** (3)
flat (*tire*) **desinflado/a** (14)
fleeting **pasajero/a** *adj.* (10)
flexibility **flexibilidad** *f.* (11)
flexible **flexible** (11)
flight **vuelo** (7); flight attendant **asistente** (*m., f.*) **de vuelo** (7)
floor (*of a building*) **planta, piso** (12); ground floor **planta baja** (12); to sweep the floor **barrer el piso** (9)
flower **flor** *f.* (7)
folklore **folklore** *m.* (15)
folkloric **folklórico/a** (13)
following **siguiente** *adj.* (5)
food **comida** (6)
foolish **tonto/a** (2)
foot **pie** *m.* (11)
football **fútbol** (*m.*) **americano** (9)
for (intended) **por** *prep.* (1); **para** *prep.* (2);

for example **por ejemplo** (11); for God's sake **por Dios** (11); for the first/last time **por primera/última vez** (11)
forbid **prohibir (prohíbo)** (12)
foreign languages **lenguas** (*f. pl.*) **extranjeras** (1)
foreigner **extranjero/a** *n.* (1)
forest **bosque** *m.* (14)
forget (about) **olvidarse (de)** (8)
form (*to fill out*) **formulario** (18)
forty **cuarenta** (2)
four **cuatro** (AT)
four hundred **cuatrocientos/as** (3)
fourteen **catorce** (AT)
fourth **cuarto/a** *adj.* (13)
freedom **libertad** *f.* (17)
freeway **autopista** (14)
freezer **congelador** *m.* (9)
French (*language*) **francés** *n. m.* (1); **francés, francesa** *n., adj.* (2); (French-fried) potato **patata (frita)** (6)
frequently **con frecuencia** (1)
fresh **fresco/a** (6)
Friday **viernes** *m. s., pl.* (4)
fried **frito/a** (6); **patata frita** French-fried potato (6)
friend **amigo/a** (1)
friendly **amable** (2); **amistoso/a** (15)
friendship **amistad** *f.* (15)
from **de** (AT); from the **del** (*contraction of* **de** + **el**) (2)
front desk **recepción** *f.* (18)
front: in front of **delante de** *prep.* (5)
frozen; very cold **congelado/a** (5)
fruit **fruta** (6); **jugo de fruta** fruit juice (6)
full, no vacancy **completo/a** (18)
full-time job **trabajo de tiempo completo** (12); full-time workday **jornada (de tiempo completo)** (12)
fun: to be fun **ser** (*irreg.*) **divertido/a** (9)
function **funcionar** (12)
furious **furioso/a** (5)
furniture **muebles** *m. pl.* (4); to dust the furniture **sacudir los muebles** (9)
future **futuro** *n.* (12)

G

garage **garaje** *m.* (4)
garden **jardín** *m.* (4)
gas **gas** *m.s.* (12)
gas station **gasolinera** (14)
gasoline **gasolina** (14)
generally **por lo general** (4)
German (*language*) **alemán** *m.* (1); **alemán, alemana** *n., adj.* (2)
get **sacar (qu)** (11); to get along well/poorly (with) **llevarse bien/mal (con)** (15); to get down (from) **bajar (de)** (7); to get good/bad grades **sacar (qu) buenas/malas notas** (11); to get off (of) **bajar (de)** (7); to get on/in (*a vehicle*) **subir** (7); to get together (with) **reunirse (me reúno) (con)** (8); to get

up **levantarse** (4); to get up on the wrong side of the bed **levantarse con el pie izquierdo** (11); to get used to **acostumbrarse a** (10); to get, obtain **conseguir (i, i) (g)** (8); **obtener** (*like* **tener**) (12)

gift **regalo** (2)

girl **niña** (2); girl's fifteenth birthday party **quinceañera** (8)

girlfriend **novia** (5)

give **dar** (*irreg.*) (7); to give (*as a gift*) **regalar** (7); to give (someone) a shot, injection **poner(le)** (*irreg.*) **una inyección** (10); give a party **dar** (*irreg.*) **una fiesta** (8)

go **ir** (*irreg.*) (3); to be going to (*do something*) **ir a** + *inf.* (3); to go (to) (*a function*) **asistir (a)** (2); to go away, leave **irse**; to go by (train/airplane/bus/boat) **ir en (tren/avión/autobús/barco)** (7); to go home **regresar a casa** (1); to go out **salir** (*irreg.*) **(de)** (4); to go out with **salir** (*irreg.*) **con** (15); to go to bed **acostarse (ue)** (4); to go up **subir** (7)

golf **golf** *m.* (9)

good **buen, bueno/a** *adj.* (2); good morning **buenos días** (1); good night **buenas noches** (AT); the good thing, news **lo bueno** (10)

good-bye **adiós** (AT)

good-looking **guapo/a** (2)

govern **gobernar (ie)** (17)

government **gobierno** (14)

grade **calificación** *f.,* **nota** (11); **grado** (9)

graduate (from) **graduarse (me gradúo) (en)** (16)

grandchildren **nietos** *m. pl.* (2)

granddaughter **nieta** (2)

grandfather **abuelo** (2)

grandmother **abuela** (2)

grandparents **abuelos** *m. pl.* (2)

grandson **nieto** (2)

grape **uva** (5)

gray **gris** (3)

great **gran, grande** (2)

green pea **arveja** (6)

green **verde** (3)

greet each other **saludarse** (10)

greeting **saludo** (AT); greetings and expressions of courtesy **saludos y expresiones de cortesía** (AT)

ground floor **planta baja** (12)

grow **crecer (zc)** (15)

guest **invitado/a** *n.* (8); **huésped(a)** (18)

guide **guía** *m., f.* (13)

H

habit **costumbre** *f.* (9)

hairstylist **peluquero(a)** (16)

ham **jamón** *m.* (6)

hamburger **hamburguesa** (6)

hand in **entregar (gu)** (11)

hand **mano** *f.* (11)

handsome **guapo/a** (2)

happen **pasar** (5)

happening **acontecimiento** (17)

happy **alegre** (5); **feliz** (*pl.* **felices**) (8); **contento/a** (5); to be happy (about) **alegrarse (de)** (12)

hard **difícil** (5)

hard drive **disco duro** (12)

hat **sombrero** (3)

hate **odiar** (7)

have **tener** (*irreg.*) (3); **haber** (*irreg.*) auxiliary (12); to have a good/bad time **pasarlo bien/mal** (8); to have been (*doing something*) for (*a period of time*) **hace** + *time ago* (11); **hace** + *period of time* + **que** + *present tense* (11); to have just (*done something*) **acabar de** (+ *inf.*) (6)

he **él** (1)

head **cabeza** (10)

headache **dolor** (*m.*) **de cabeza** (10)

health **salud** *f.* (10)

healthy **sano/a** (10)

hear **oír** (*irreg.*) (4)

heart **corazón** *m.* (10)

heat **calor** *m.* (5); **gas** *m.s.* (12)

heavy (*meal, food*) **fuerte** (6)

Hebrew (*language*) **hebreo** (15)

hello **hola** (AT)

help **ayudar** (6)

her *obj.* (*of prep.*) **ella** (1)

her *poss.* **su(s)** (2)

here **aquí** (1)

highway **carretera** (14)

his *poss.* **su(s)** (2)

history **historia** (1)

hit **pegar (gu)** (9)

hobby **pasatiempo, afición** *f.* (9)

hockey **hockey** *m.* (9)

holiday **día** (*m.*) **festivo** (8)

home **casa** (2); at home **en casa** (1)

homework **tarea** (4)

honest **honesto/a** (15)

honeymoon **luna de miel** (15)

hope **esperanza** (17); to hope **esperar** (12); I hope, wish (that) **ojalá (que)** (13)

hors d'oeuvres **entremeses** *m. pl.* (8)

horseback: to ride horseback **montar a caballo** (9)

host **anfitrión** (8)

hostess **anfitriona** (8)

hot dog **salchicha** (6)

hot: to be (feel) hot **tener** (*irreg.*) **calor** (5); it's hot **hace calor** (5)

hotel **hotel** *m.* (18)

hotel guest **huésped(a)** (18)

hour **hora**; (at) what time? **¿a qué hora?** (AT); what time is it? **¿qué hora es?** (AT)

house **casa** (2)

household chore **quehacer** (*m.*) **doméstico** (9)

housing **vivienda** (14)

how? what? **¿cómo?** (AT); how are you (doing)? **¿qué tal?** (AT); how are you? **¿cómo está(s)?** (AT); how many? **¿cuántos/as?** (AT); how much does it

cost? **¿cuánto cuesta?** (3); how much is it? **¿cuánto es?** (3)

humanities **humanidades** *f. pl.* (1)

hunger **hambre** *f.* (*but* **el hambre**)

hungry: to be (very) hungry **tener** (*irreg.*) **(mucha) hambre** (6)

hurry: to be in a hurry **tener** (*irreg.*) **prisa** (3)

hurt **doler (ue)** (10)

hurt oneself **hacerse** (*irreg.*) **daño** (11)

husband **esposo** (2); **marido** (15)

hydraulic **hidráulico/a** (14)

I

I **yo** (1); I am **soy** (AT); I'm sorry **discúlpeme** (11), **lo siento** (11)

ice cream **helado** (6)

identification card **tarjeta de identificación** (11)

if **si** (1)

immigration **inmigración** *f.* (18)

in **en** (AT); (*the morning, evening, etc.*) **por** *prep.* (1); in a balanced way **equilibradamente** (10); in case **en caso de que** (15); in cash **efectivo: en efectivo** (16); in order to **para** *prep.* (2)

incredible: it's incredible **es increíble** (13)

inequality **desigualdad** *f.* (17)

inexpensive **barato/a** (3)

infancy **infancia** (15)

inform **informar** (17)

injection **inyección** *f.* (10)

injure oneself **lastimarse** (11)

inspector (customs) **inspector(a) (de aduanas)** (18)

installment: to pay in installments **pagar (gu) a plazos** (16)

instead of **en vez de** (16)

intelligent **inteligente** (2)

intend **pensar (ie)** (4)

Internet **red** *f.* (12)

interview **entrevistar** (16)

interviewer **entrevistador(a)** (16)

invite **invitar** (6)

invoice **factura** (16)

iron clothes **planchar la ropa** (9)

island **isla** (5)

isolation **aislamiento** (14)

Italian (*language*) **italiano** *m.* (1); **italiano/a** *n., adj.* (2)

its *poss.* **su(s)** (2)

J

jacket **chaqueta** (3)

January **enero** (5)

Japanese **japonés, japonesa** *n., adj.* (1)

jeans *jeans* *m. pl.* (3)

job **trabajo** (11); **puesto** (16); full-time/part-time job **trabajo de tiempo completo/parcial** (11)

jog **correr** (9)

joke **chiste** *m.* (8)

journalist **periodista** *m., f.* (16)

juice: (fruit) juice **jugo (de fruta)** (6)

July **julio** (5)

June **junio** (5)
jungle (tropical) **selva (tropical)** (10)
just in case **por si acaso** (11)

K

keep (*a place/documents*) **guardar** (7)
key **llave** *n. f.* (11)
king **rey** *m.* (17)
kitchen **cocina** (4)
know **conocer (zc)** (6); to know (how) **saber** (*irreg.*) (6)

L

lab, laboratory **laboratorio** (2)
laborer **obrero/a** (16)
lack **falta** (11); **escasez** *f.* (*pl.* **escaseces**) (14)
lacking: to be lacking **faltar** (8)
lady **señora (Sra.)** (AT)
lamp **lámpara** (4)
landlady **dueña** (12)
landlord **dueño** (12)
language: foreign languages **lenguas** (*f. pl.*) **extranjeras** (1)
laptop computer **computadora portátil** (12); **ordenador** (*m.*) **portátil** (12)
large **gran, grande** (2)
last **último/a** (7); to last **durar** (17)
late **tarde** *adv.* (1); to be late **estar** (*irreg.*) **atrasado/a** (7)
later: see you later **hasta luego** (AT)
latest: the latest style **de última moda** (3)
laugh (about) **reírse (i, i) (de)** (8)
law **ley** *f.* (17)
lawyer **abogado/a** (16)
lazy **perezoso/a** (2)
lead a healthy/calm life **llevar una vida sana/tranquila** (10)
learn **aprender** (2)
least **menos** (5); at least **por lo menos** (11)
leave **salir** (*irreg.*) **(de)** (4); (behind) (in, at) **dejar (en)** (9)
left: to the left (of) **a la izquierda (de)** (5); to be left **quedar(se)** (11)
leg **pierna** (11)
lemon **limón** *m.* (5)
lend **prestar** (7)
lenses: contact lenses **lentes** (*m. pl.*) **de contacto** (10)
less **menos** (5); less . . . than **menos... que** (5)
letter **carta** (2); (*of the alphabet*) **letra** (2)
lettuce **lechuga** (6)
level **nivel** *m.* (14)
liberty **libertad** *f.* (17)
librarian **bibliotecario/a** (1)
library **biblioteca** (1)
license **licencia** (1)
life **vida** (14); to lead a healthy/calm life **llevar una vida sana/tranquila** (10)
light **luz** *f.* (*pl.* **luces**) (11); *adj.* light, not heavy **ligero/a** (6)
like **gusto** (AT); do you (*form.*) like . . . ? **¿le gusta... ?** (AT); I (don't) like . . .

(no) me gusta(n)... (AT); I would like . . . **me gustaría...** (7); to like very much **encantar** (7)
likeable **simpático/a** (2)
likewise **igualmente** (AT)
limit **límite** *m.* (14); speed limit **límite de velocidad** (*f.*) (14)
line: to stand in line **hacer** (*irreg.*) **cola** (7)
listen (to) **escuchar** (1)
literature **literatura** (1)
little, few **poco/a** *adj.* (3); little bit **un poco** (1)
live **vivir** (2); to live a healthy life **llevar una vida sana** (10)
loan **préstamo** (16)
lobster **langosta** (6)
lodging **alojamiento** (18)
long **largo/a** (2)
look at **mirar** (2); to look for **buscar (qu)** (1)
lose **perder (ie)** (9)
loss **pérdida** (13)
love **amar** (15); **encantar** (7); **querer** (*irreg.*) (15); *n.* **amor** *m.* (15)
luggage **equipaje** *m.* (7)
lunch **almuerzo** (6); to have lunch **almorzar (ue) (c)** (4)
lung **pulmón** *m.* (10)
luxury *n.* **lujo** (12); luxury hotel **hotel** (*m.*) **de lujo** (18)

M

machine: answering machine **contestador** (*m.*) **automático** (12)
magazine **revista** (2)
maid **criada** (18)
mail **correo** (18); electronic mail **correo electrónico** (12)
major (*academic*) **carrera** (2)
majority **mayoría** (14)
make **hacer** (*irreg.*) (4); to make a good/bad impression on someone **caerle** (*irreg.*) **bien/mal a alguien** (16); to make plans to (*do something*) **hacer** (*irreg.*) **planes para** + *inf.* (9); to make stops **hacer** (*irreg.*) **escalas** (7); to make the bed **hacer** (*irreg.*) **la cama** (9)
mall: shopping mall **centro comercial** (3)
man **hombre** *m.* (1); **señor (Sr.)** *m.* (AT)
many: how many? **¿cuántos/as?** (AT)
March **marzo** (5)
market(place) **mercado** (3)
marriage **matrimonio** (15)
married **casado/a** (2); married couple **pareja** (15)
marry **casarse (con)** (15)
masterpiece **obra maestra** (13)
match **fósforo** (18)
material **material** *n. m.* (3)
mathematics **matemáticas** *f. pl.* (1)
mature **maduro/a** (5)
May **mayo** (5)
me *d.o., i.o.* **me**; *obj.* (*of prep.*) **mí** (5)
meal **comida** (6)
means of communication **medio de**

comunicación (17)
meat **carne** *f.* (6)
mechanic **mecánico/a** (14)
medical **médico/a** (10); medical office **consultorio** (10)
medicine **medicina** (10)
meet (*someone somewhere*) **encontrarse (con)** (10)
memory **memoria** (12)
menu **menú** *m.* (6)
merchant **comerciante** *m., f.* (16)
messy **desordenado/a** (5)
metro stop **estación** (*f.*) **del metro** (18)
Mexican **mexicano/a** *n., adj.* (2)
microwave oven **horno de microondas** *f. pl.* (9)
midday: at noon **a mediodía**
middle age **madurez** *f.* (15)
midnight **medianoche** *f.* (8)
military service **servicio militar** (17)
milk **leche** *f.* (6)
million **millón** *m.* (3)
mineral water **agua** *f.* (*but* **el agua**) **mineral** (6)
minus **menos** (5)
miss (*a function, bus, plane, etc.*) **perder (ie)** (4)
Miss **señorita (Srta.)** (AT)
mistake: to make a mistake **equivocarse (qu)** (11)
modem **módem** *m.* (12)
modern **moderno/a** (13)
molar **muela** (10)
mom **mamá** (2)
Monday **lunes** *m. s., pl.* (4)
money **dinero** (1)
month **mes** *m.* (5)
monument **monumento** (10)
moped **moto(cicleta)** *f.* (12)
more **más** *adv.* (1); **más... que** more . . . than (5)
morning **mañana** *n.* (AT); in the morning **de la mañana** (AT); during the morning **por la mañana** (1); good morning **buenos días** (AT)
mother **mamá, madre** *f.* (2)
motorcycle **moto(cicleta)** *f.* (12)
mountain **montaña** (7)
mountain range **sierra** (10)
mouse **ratón** (*m.*) (12)
mouth **boca** (10)
move (*residence*) **mudarse** (16)
movie **película** (4); **cine** *m.* (4); movie theater **cine** *m.* (4)
Mr. **señor (Sr.)** *m.* (AT)
Mrs. **señora (Sra.)** (AT)
Ms. **señorita (Srta.)** (AT)
much, a lot **mucho** *adv.* (1); how much does it cost? **¿cuánto cuesta?** (3); how much is it? **¿cuánto es?** (3)
museum **museo** (9); to visit a museum **visitar un museo** (9)
mushroom **champiñón** *m.* (6)
music **música** (13)
musician **músico/a** *n. m., f.* (13)
must (*do something*) **deber** (+ *inf.*) (2)

my *poss.* **mi(s).** (2); my, (of) mine *poss.*
mío/a(s) (17)

N

named: to be named **llamarse** (4); what's
your name? **¿cómo se llama usted?**
(*form.*) (AT); what's your name?
¿cómo te llamas? *fam.* (AT); my name
is . . . **me llamo...** (AT)
nap: to take a nap **dormir (ue, u) la
siesta** (4)
nationality **nacionalidad** *f.* (2)
natural resources **recursos** (*m. pl.*)
naturales (14)
nature **naturaleza** (14)
nauseated **mareado/a** (10)
neat **ordenado/a** (5)
necessary **necesario/a** (2); it is necessary
to (*do something*) **hay que** + *inf.* (13)
need *v.* **necesitar** (1)
neighbor **vecino/a** (12)
neighborhood **barrio, vecindad** *f.* (12)
neither, not either **tampoco** (6)
nephew **sobrino** (2)
nervous **nervioso/a** (5)
net: to surf the net **navegar (gu) la red**
(12)
never **nunca** (2); **jamás** (6); almost never
casi nunca (2)
new **nuevo/a** (2); New Year's Eve **Noche**
(*f.*) **Vieja** (8)
news **noticias** *f. pl.* (17); news media
prensa (17); news item **noticia** (8)
newscast **noticiero** (17)
newspaper **periódico** (2)
next **próximo/a** *adj.* (4); next to **al lado
de** *prep.* (5)
nice **simpático/a** (2)
niece **sobrina** (2)
night **noche** *f.*; good evening/night
buenas noches (AT); in the evening/at
night **de la noche** (AT); tonight **esta
noche** (5); in the night **por la noche**
(1); every night **todas las noches**
nine **nueve** (AT)
nine hundred **novecientos/as** (3)
nineteen **diecinueve** (AT)
ninety **noventa** (2)
ninth **noveno/a** (13)
no, not **no** (AT)
nobody, not anybody, no one **nadie** (6)
noise **ruido** (4)
none, not any **ningún, ninguno/a** (6)
noon: at noon **a mediodía**
North American **norteamericano/a** *n.,
adj.* (2)
north **norte** *m.* (5)
nose **nariz** *f.* (*pl.* **narices**) (10)
not ever **jamás** (6)
note **nota** (11)
notebook **cuaderno** (1)
nothing, not anything **nada** (6)
noun **sustantivo** *gram.* (1)
novel **novela** (3)
November **noviembre** *m.* (5)
now **ahora** (1)

nuclear **nuclear** (14)
number **número** (AT)
nurse **enfermero/a** (10)

O

obey **obedecer (zc)** (14)
obligation **deber** *m.* (17)
ocean **océano** (7)
October **octubre** *m.* (5)
of **de** *prep.* (AT); of the **del** (*contraction of*
de + **el**) (2); of course **por supuesto**
(11)
offer **oferta** (12); to offer **ofrecer (zc)** (7)
office **oficina** (1); personnel office
dirección *f.* **de personal** (16)
oil **aceite** *m.* (14)
OK **regular** *adj.* (AT)
old **viejo/a** *adj.* (AT); **anciano/a** (9); old
person **anciano/a** *n.* (9)
older **mayor** (5)
on **en** (AT); on the other hand **en
cambio** (10); on top of **encima de** *prep.*
(5)
once **una vez** (10)
one **un, uno/a** (AT)
one hundred **cien, ciento** (2)
one-way (*ticket*) **de ida** (7)
only **sólo** *adv.* (1)
open **abierto/a** (5); to open **abrir** (*p.p.*
abierto/a) (2)
opera **ópera** (13)
operate (*a machine*) **manejar** (12)
opportunity for advancement
oportunidad (*f.*) **de avanzar (c)** (12)
or **o** (AT)
oral **oral** (11)
orange (*color*) **anaranjado/a** *adj.* (3);
orange (*fruit*) **naranja** (6)
order (*in a restaurant*) **pedir (i, i)** (4);
(*someone to do something*) **mandar** (12)
organization **organización** *f.*
organize **organizar (c)**
orientation **orientación** *f.*
other **otro/a** (2); others **los/las demás**
(12)
ought to (*do something*) **deber** (+ *inf.*) (2)
our *poss.* **nuestro/a(s)** (2)
outdoors **afuera** *adv.* (5); **al aire libre** (9)
outskirts **afueras** *n. pl.* (12)
oven: microwave oven **horno de
microondas** (9)
overcoat **abrigo** (3)
own **propio/a** *adj.* (15)
owner **dueño/a** (6)
ozone layer **capa de ozono** (14)

P

pace **ritmo** (14)
pack one's suitcases **hacer** (*irreg.*) **las
maletas** (7)
package **paquete** *m.* (18)
pain **dolor** *m.* (10); to have a pain (in)
tener (*irreg.*) **dolor (de)** (10)
paint (the walls) **pintar (las paredes)** (9)
painter **pintor(a)** (13)
painting **cuadro, pintura** (13)

pair **par** *m.* (3)
pants **pantalón, pantalones** *m.* (3)
paper **papel** *m.* (1)
pardon me **(con) permiso, perdón** (AT);
discúlpeme
parents **padres** *m. pl.* (2)
park **parque** *m.* (5); to park **estacionar**
(11)
part-time job **trabajo de tiempo parcial**
(12)
participate (*in a sport*) **practicar (qu)** (9)
party **fiesta** (1); to have a party **hacer**
(*irreg.*) **una fiesta** (8)
passage **pasaje** *m.* (7)
passenger **pasajero/a** *n.* (7)
passing **pasajero/a** *adj.* (10)
passport **pasaporte** *m.* (18)
pastime **pasatiempo** (9)
pastry (small) **pastelito** (18); pastry shop
pastelería (18)
patient **paciente** *n., adj. m., f.* (10)
pay **pagar (gu)** (1); to pay cash **pagar al
contado/en efectivo** (16); to pay in
installments **pagar a plazos** (16)
pea: green pea **arveja** (6)
peace **paz** *f.* (*pl.* **paces**) (17)
peasant **campesino/a** (14)
pencil **lápiz** *m.* (*pl.* **lápices**) (1)
people **gente** *f. s.* (15)
percent **por ciento** (11)
perform (*a part*) **desempeñar** (13)
permit **permitir** (12)
person **persona** (1)
personnel director **director(a) de
personal** (16); personnel office
dirección (*f.*) **de personal** (16)
pet **mascota** (2)
pharmacist **farmacéutico/a** (10)
pharmacy **farmacia** (10)
philosophy **filosofía** (1)
phone: to talk on the phone **hablar por
teléfono** (1)
photo(graph) **foto(grafía)** *f.* (7)
photographer **fotógrafo/a** (15)
photos: to take photos **sacar (qu) fotos** *f.
pl.* (7)
physical **físico/a** (6)
physics **física** (1)
pick up **recoger (j)** (11)
picnic: to have a picnic **hacer** (*irreg.*) **un
picnic** (9)
pie **pastel** *m.* (6)
pill **pastilla** (10)
pink **rosado/a** (3)
place (*in line, etc.*) **puesto** (7); to place
poner (*irreg.*) (4)
plaid **de cuadros** (3)
plans: to make plans to (*do something*)
hacer (*irreg.*) **planes para** + *inf.* (9)
play (*a game, sport*) **jugar (ue) (gu) (a)**
(4); to play chess **jugar (ue) (gu) al
ajedrez** (4); to play cards **jugar (ue)
(gu) a las cartas** (9); to play (*a musical
instrument*) **tocar (qu)** (1); to play
music **tocar (qu) música** (8); to play (*a
part*) **desempeñar** (13)

player **jugador(a)** (9)
playwright **dramaturgo/a** (13)
please **por favor** (AT); pleased to meet you **mucho gusto** (AT); to please **agradar** (13)
pleased to meet you **encantado/a** (AT)
pleasing: to be pleasing **gustar** (7)
plumber **plomero/a** (16)
poet **poeta** *m., f.* (13)
point **punto**
police officer **policía** *m., f.* (14)
politician **político/a** (17)
politics **política** *s.* (17)
polka-dotted **de lunares** *m. pl.* (3)
pollute **contaminar** (14)
pollution: there's (lots of) pollution **hay (mucha) contaminación** *f.* (5)
poor **pobre** (2)
poorly **mal** *adv.* (1)
population **población** *f.* (14)
pork chop **chuleta de cerdo** (6)
porter **maletero** (7)
possible **posible** (2)
post office **correo; oficina de correos** (18)
postcard **tarjeta postal** (7)
potato **patata** (*Sp.*) (6); French fried potato **patata frita** (*Sp.*) (6)
pottery **cerámica** (13)
practical **práctico/a** (2)
practice **entrenar** (9)
practice **practicar (qu)** (1)
prefer **preferir (ie, i)** (3)
preferable **preferible** (13)
preference **gusto, preferencia** (AT)
prepare **preparar** (6)
prescription **receta** (10)
present (*gift*) **regalo** *n.* (2)
press *n.* **prensa** (17)
pressure: to be under pressure **sufrir presiones** *f. pl.* (11)
pretty **bonito/a** (2)
price **precio** (3); fixed price **precio fijo** (3)
print **imprimir** (12)
printer **impresora** (12)
profession **profesión** *f.* (16)
professor **profesor(a)** (1)
programmer **programador(a)** (16)
prohibit **prohibir (prohíbo)** (12)
promise *v.* **prometer** (7)
protect **proteger (j)** (14)
provided (that) **con tal (de) que** (15)
psychiatrist **siquiatra** *m., f.* (16)
psychologist **sicólogo/a** (16)
psychology **sicología** (1)
public **público/a** *adj.* (14)
punish **castigar (gu)** (17)
pure **puro/a** (14)
purple **morado/a** (3)
purse **bolsa** (3)
put **poner** (*irreg.*) (4); to put on (*clothing*) **ponerse** (*irreg.*) (4)

Q

quarter past (*with time*) **y cuarto** (AT)
queen **reina** (17)

quit **dejar** (16); (*doing something*) **dejar de** + *inf.* (10)
quiz **prueba** (11)

R

radio **radio** *m.* (*set*); portable radio **radio portátil** (12); **radio** *f.* radio (*medium*) (12)
rain **llover (ue)** (5); it's raining **llueve** (5)
raincoat **impermeable** *m.* (3)
raise **aumento** (12); (in salary) **aumento de sueldo** (16)
rare **raro/a** (8)
rather **bastante** *adv.* (15)
react **reaccionar** (8)
read **leer (y)** (2)
reader **lector(a)** (13)
reason **razón** *f.* (2)
receive **recibir** (2)
recommend **recomendar (ie)** (7)
record **grabar** (12)
recycle **reciclar** (14)
red **rojo/a** (3); red wine **vino tinto** (6)
reduction **rebaja** (3)
refreshment **refresco** (8)
refrigerator **refrigerador** *m.* (9)
regret **sentir (ie, i)** (13)
relative **pariente** *m., f.* (2)
remain (*in a place*) **quedar(se)** (5); to remain, stay (*as a guest*) **alojarse** (18)
remember **recordar (ue)** (8); **acordarse (ue) (de)** (11)
remote control **control** (*m.*) **remoto** (12)
rent **alquiler** *m.* (12); to rent *v.* **alquilar** (12)
renter **inquilino/a** (12)
repair **arreglar** (12); (repair) shop **taller** *m.* (14)
report **informe; trabajo** (11)
reporter **reportero/a** (17)
represent **representar** (13)
reservation **reserva, reservación** (*f.*) (18)
resign (from) **renunciar (a)** (16)
resolve **resolver (ue)** (*p.p.* **resuelto/a**) (14)
resource **recurso**; natural resources **recursos naturales** (14)
responsibility **responsabilidad** *f.*; **deber** *m.* (17)
rest **descansar** (4)
restaurant **restaurante** *m.* (6)
résumé **currículum** *m.* (16)
retire **jubilarse** (16)
return (*to a place*) **regresar** (1); **volver (ue)** (*p.p.* **vuelto/a**) (4); (*something*) **devolver (ue)** (*pp.* **devuelto/a**) (16)
rhythm **ritmo** (14)
rice **arroz** *m.* (6)
rich **rico/a** (2)
ride a bicycle **pasear en bicicleta** (9); to ride horseback **montar a caballo** (9)
right (*legal*) **derecho** *n.* (17); (*direction*) **derecha** *n.* (5); right? **¿verdad?** (3) to the right (of) **a la derecha (de)** (5); to be right **tener** (*irreg.*) **razón** (3)
ring **sonar (ue)** (9)
ripe **maduro/a** (5)

road **camino** (14)
role **papel** *m.* (13)
roller skates **patines** *m. pl.* (12)
rollerblade *v.* **patinar en línea** (9)
room **cuarto** (1); room (*in a hotel*) **habitación** *f.* (18); double room **habitación** (*f.*) **doble** (18); emergency room **sala de urgencia** (10); living room **sala** (4); room and full board (all meals) **pensión** (*f.*) **completa** (18); room with(out) bath/shower **habitación** (*f.*) **con/sin baño/ducha** (18); single room **habitación** (*f.*) **individual** (18); waiting room **sala de espera** (7)
roommate **compañero/a de cuarto** (1)
round-trip ticket **billete** (*m.*)/**boleto de ida y vuelta** (7)
rug **alfombra** (4)
ruin *n.* **ruina** (13)
rule **gobernar (ie)** (17)
run **correr** (9); (*machines*) **funcionar** (12); to run into **darse** (*irreg.*) **con, pegarse (gu) en/contra** (11); collide (with) **chocar (qu) (con)** (14); to run out of **acabar(se)** (11)

S

sad **triste** (5)
salad **ensalada** (6)
salary **sueldo** (12); **salario** (16); raise in salary **aumento de sueldo** (16)
sale **rebaja** (3)
salesperson **vendedor(a)** (16)
salmon **salmón** *m.* (6)
salt **sal** *f.* (5)
same **mismo/a** (10); same here **igualmente** (AT)
sandal **sandalia** (3)
sandwich **sándwich** *m.* (6)
Saturday **sábado** (4)
sausage **salchicha** (6)
save (*a place/documents*) **guardar** (7)
save **conservar** (14); (*money*) **ahorrar** (16)
savings **ahorros** *m. pl.*; savings account **cuenta de ahorros** (16)
say **decir** (*irreg.*) (7); to say good-bye (to) **despedirse (i, i) (de)** (8)
schedule **horario** (11)
school **escuela** (9)
schoolteacher **maestro/a** (16)
science **ciencia** (1); computer science **computación** *f.* (1)
script **guión** *m.* (13)
sculpt **esculpir** (13)
sculptor **escultor(a)** (13)
sculpture **escultura** (13)
sea **mar** *m., f.* (7)
seaport **puerto** (7)
search **registrar** (18)
season **estación** *f.* (5)
seat **asiento** (7)
second **segundo/a** *adj.* (13)
secretary **secretario/a** (1)
see **ver** (*irreg.*) (4); see you around **nos**

vemos (AT); see you later **hasta luego** (AT); see you tomorrow **hasta mañana** (AT)
seem **parecer (zc)** (13)
self **mismo/a** (10)
sell **vender** (2)
send **mandar** (7)
separate (from) *v.* **separarse (de)** (15)
September **septiembre** *m.* (5)
servant **criado/a** (16)
serve **servir (i, i)** (4)
service **servicio** (14); military service **servicio militar** (17)
set the table **poner** (*irreg.*) **la mesa** (9)
seven **siete** (AT)
seven hundred **setecientos/as** (3)
seventeen **diecisiete** (AT)
seventh **séptimo/a** *adj.* (13)
seventy **setenta** (2)
shame **lástima** (13); it is a shame **es lástima** (13); what a shame! **¡qué lástima!** (13)
shampoo **champú** *m.* (18)
shave oneself **afeitarse** (4)
she **ella** (1)
shellfish **marisco** (6)
ship **barco** (7)
shirt **camisa** (3)
shoe **zapato** (3); tennis shoe **zapato de tenis** (3)
shop (repair) **taller** *m.* (14)
shopkeeper **comerciante** *m., f.* (16)
shopping **de compras** (3); shopping mall **centro comercial** (3); to go shopping **ir** (*irreg.*) **de compras** (3)
short (*in height*) **bajo/a;** (*in length*) **corto/a** (2)
shortage **escasez** *f.* (*pl.* **escaseces**) (14)
shot **inyección** *f.* (10)
should (*do something*) **deber** (+ *inf.*) (2)
show **mostrar (ue)** (7)
shower **ducha** (18); to take a shower **ducharse** (4)
shrimp **camarón** *m.* (6)
sick **enfermo/a** *adj.* (5); to get sick **enfermarse** (8)
sickness **enfermedad** *f.* (10)
sight: at first sight **a primera vista** (15)
silk **seda** (3); it is made of silk **es de seda** (3)
silly **tonto/a** (2)
sincere **honesto/a** (15)
sing **cantar** (18)
singer **cantante** *m., f.* (13)
single (*not married*) **soltero/a** (2); single room **habitación** (*f.*) **individual** (18)
sink (bathroom) **lavabo** (4)
sir **señor (Sr.)** *m.* (AT)
sister **hermana** (2)
sit down **sentarse (ie)** (4)
six **seis** (AT)
six hundred **seiscientos/as** (3)
sixteen **dieciséis** (AT)
sixth **sexto/a** *adj.* (13)
sixty **sesenta** (2)
skate **patinar** (9)

skateboard **monopatín** *m.* (12)
ski **esquiar (esquío)** (9)
skirt **falda** (3)
skyscraper **rascacielos** *m. s.* (14)
sleep **dormir (ue, u)** (4)
sleepy: to be sleepy **tener** (*irreg.*) **sueño** (3)
slender **delgado/a** (2)
small **pequeño/a** (2)
smart **listo/a** (2)
smile **sonreír(se) (i, i)** (8)
smoke **fumar** (7)
smoking (nonsmoking) section **sección** (*f.*) **de (no) fumar** (7)
snorkle **bucear** (8)
snow **nevar (ie)** (5); it's snowing **nieva** (5)
so much; *pl.* so many **tanto/a** *adj.*
so that **para que** (15)
soap **jabón** *m.* (18)
soap opera **telenovela** (13)
soccer **fútbol** *m.* (9)
social worker **trabajador(a) social** (16)
sociology **sociología** (1)
sock **calcetín, calcetines** *m.* (3)
sofa **sofá** *m.* (4)
soft drink **refresco** (6)
solar **solar** (14)
soldier **soldado;** female soldier **mujer** (*f.*) **soldado** (16)
solve **resolver (ue)** (*p.p.* **resuelto/a**) (14)
some **algún, alguno/a** (6)
someone **alguien** (6)
something **algo** (3)
sometimes **a veces** (2)
son **hijo** (2)
song **canción** *f.* (13)
soon **pronto;** as soon as **tan pronto como** (16); *conj.* **en cuanto** (16)
sound *v.* **sonar (ue)** (9)
soup **sopa** (6)
south **sur** *m.* (5)
Spanish (*language*) **español** *m.* (1); **español(a)** *n., adj.* (1)
speak **hablar** (1)
speed **velocidad** *f.* (14); speed limit **límite** (*m.*) **de velocidad** (14)
spend (*money*) **gastar** (8); (*time*) **pasar** (5)
sport **deporte** *m.* (9)
sports player **deportista** *m., f.* (8)
sports-loving **deportivo/a** *adj.* (9)
spring **primavera** (5); spring break **vacaciones** (*f. pl.*) **de primavera** (8)
stage **escenario** (13)
stamp **sello** (*postage*) (18)
stand in line **hacer** (*irreg.*) **cola** (7); to stand up **levantarse** (4)
start (*a motor*) **arrancar (qu)** (12)
state **estado** (2)
station **estación** *f.* (7); bus station **estación de autobuses** (7); train station **estación del tren** (7); station wagon **camioneta** (7)
stationery **papel** (*m.*) **para cartas** (18); stationery store **papelería** (18)
stay *n.* (*in a hotel*) **estancia** (18); to stay

(*in a place*) **quedar(se)** (5); to stay in bed **guardar cama** (10)
steak **bistec** *m.* (6)
stereo equipment **equipo estereofónico** (12)
stick out one's tongue **sacar (qu) la lengua** (10)
still **todavía** (5)
stockings **medias** *f. pl.* (3)
stomach **estómago** (10)
stop **parar** (14); (*doing something*) **dejar de** + *inf.* (10); to make stops **hacer** (*irreg.*) **escalas** (7)
store **tienda** (3)
stove **estufa** (9)
straight ahead **todo derecho** (14)
straighten (up) **arreglar** (12)
strange **raro/a** (8); **extraño/a** (13); it's strange **es extraño** (13)
street **calle** *f.* (12); **camino** (14)
stress **estrés** *m.;* **tensión** *f.* (11)
strike (*labor*) **huelga** (17)
striped **de rayas** (3)
strong **fuerte** (6)
student **estudiante** *m., f.* (1)
study **estudiar** (1)
style: latest style **de última moda** (3)
subject (*school*) **materia** (2)
suburb **suburbio** (4); **afueras** *n. f. pl.* (12)
subway station **estación** (*f.*) **del metro** (18)
succeed in (*doing something*) **conseguir (i, i) (g)** + *inf.* (8)
such **tanto/a** (7)
suddenly **de repente** (10)
suffer **sufrir** (11)
sufficiently **bastante** *adv.* (15)
suggest **sugerir (ie, i)** (8)
suit **traje** *m.* (3); bathing suit **traje de baño** (37)
suitcase **maleta** (7); to pack one's suitcases **hacer** (*irreg.*) **las maletas** (7)
summer **verano** (5)
sun: it's sunny **hace sol** (5); sunbathe **tomar el sol** (7)
Sunday **domingo** (4)
supper **cena** (6)
support **apoyar** (17)
sure **seguro/a** *adj.* (5); it's a sure thing **es seguro** (13)
surf the net **navegar (gu) la red** (12)
surprise **sorpresa** (8); to surprise **sorprender;** it surprises me (you, him, . . .) **me (te, le, ...) sorprende** (13)
sweater **suéter** *m.* (3)
sweep (the floor) **barrer (el piso)** (9)
sweets **dulces** *m. pl.* (6)
swim **nadar** (7)
swimming **natación** *f.* (9); swimming pool **piscina** (4)
symptom **síntoma** *m.* (10)
systems analyst **analista** (*m., f.*) **de sistemas** (16)

T

T-shirt **camiseta** (3)
table **mesa** (1); table (end) **mesita** (4)

take **tomar** (1); to take (*a class*) **llevar** (3); to take (photos) **sacar (qu)** (7); to take care of oneself **cuidar(se)** (10); to take leave (of) **despedirse (i, i) (de)** (8); to take off (*clothing*) **quitarse** (4); to take out **sacar (qu)** (11); to take out the trash **sacar (qu) la basura** (9); to take someone's temperature **tomarle la temperatura** (10)

talk **hablar** (1); to talk on the phone **hablar por teléfono** (1)

tall **alto/a** (2)

tank **tanque** *m.* (14)

tape **cinta** (3); to tape **grabar** (12); tape recorder/player **grabadora** (12)

task **tarea** (9)

taste **gusto** (AT)

tea **té** *m.* (6)

teach **enseñar** (1)

technician **técnico/a** *n.* (16)

telephone company office **telefónica** (10)

telephone: cellular/car phone **teléfono celular / de coche** (12)

television set **televisor** *m.* (4); to watch television **mirar la televisión** (2)

tell **decir** (*irreg.*) (7); **contar (ue)** (17); to tell jokes **contar chistes** *m. pl.* (8)

teller **cajero/a** (16); automatic teller machine **cajero automático** (16)

temperature **temperatura** (10)

ten **diez** (AT)

tenant **inquilino/a** (12)

tennis **tenis** *m. s.* (9); tennis shoe **zapato de tenis** (3)

tension **tensión** *f.* (11)

tent **tienda de campaña** (7)

tenth **décimo/a** (13)

terrace **terraza** (4)

terrorist **terrorista** *m., f.* (17)

test **examen** *m.* (3); **prueba** (11)

text **texto** (1); textbook **libro de texto** (1)

thank you **gracias** (AT); thank you very much **muchas gracias** (AT); thanks for **gracias por** (8)

that *adj., that one pron.* **ese, esa** (3); that *adj., that one pron.* (*over there*) **aquel, aquella** (3); that *pron.* **eso** (3); that *pron.* (*over there*) **aquello** (4); *conj.* **que** (2)

theater **teatro** (13)

their *poss.* **sus** (2)

there is (not), there are (not) **(no) hay** (AT)

there: (over) there **allí** (3); **allá** (4)

therefore **por eso** (1)

these *adj.,* these (ones) *pron.* **estos/as** (2)

they **ellos/as** (1)

thin **delgado/a** (2)

thing **cosa** (1)

think **creer (y) (en)** (2); **pensar (ie)** (4)

third **tercer, tercero/a** *adj.* (13)

thirst **sed** *f.;* to be thirsty **tener** (*irreg.*) **sed** (6)

thirteen **trece** (AT)

thirty **treinta** (AT); thirty, half past (*with time*) **y treinta** (AT)

this *adj.* this one *pron.* **este, esta** (2); this *pron.* **esto** (3)

those *adj.* those (ones) *pron.* **esos/as** (3); those *adj.* (*over there*) those (ones) *pron.* (*over there*) **aquellos/as** (3)

three **tres** (AT); (three) thirty, half past (three) (*with time*) **media: (las tres) y media** (AT)

three hundred **trescientos/as** (3)

throat **garganta** (10)

through **por** *prep.* (1) (4)

Thursday **jueves** *m. s., pl.* (4)

ticket **boleto, billete** *m.* (7); **pasaje** *m.* (7); one-way ticket **billete de ida** (7); round trip ticket **billete** (*m.*)/**boleto de ida y vuelta**

tie **corbata** (3)

time **tiempo** (5); time (*period*) **época** (9); ahead of time **con anticipación** (7); on time **a tiempo** (7); spare time **ratos** (*m. pl.*) **libres** (9); to arrive on time **llegar (gu) a tiempo** (11); to spend time (with) **pasar tiempo (con)** (15); full-time (part-time) job **trabajo a tiempo completo (parcial)** (11)

tip (*to an employee*) **propina** (18)

tire *n.* **llanta** (14)

tired **cansado/a** (5); to be tired **estar** (*irreg.*) **cansado/a** (6)

to the **al** (*contraction of* **a** + **el**) (3)

toast **pan** (*m.*) **tostado** (6)

toasted **tostado/a** (6)

toaster **tostadora** (9)

tobacco stand/shop **estanco** (18)

today **hoy** (AT); **¿cuál es la fecha de hoy?** what's today's date? (5)

toe **dedo del pie** (11)

together **juntos/as** (15)

tomato **tomate** *m.* (6)

tomorrow **mañana** *adv.* (AT); **hasta mañana** until tomorrow (AT); **pasado mañana** day after tomorrow (4); see you tomorrow **hasta mañana** (AT)

tongue: to stick out one's tongue **sacar (qu) la lengua** (10)

too **también** (AT); too, too much **demasiado** *adv.* (9)

tooth **diente** *m.* (10)

toothpaste **pasta dental** (18)

tourist **turístico/a** *adj.;* tourist class **clase** (*f.*) **turística** (7)

trade **oficio** (16)

traffic **tránsito; circulación** *f.* (14); traffic signal **semáforo** (14)

train **tren** *m.* (7); train station **estación** (*f.*) **de trenes** (7); to go by train **ir** (*irreg.*) **en tren** (7); to train **entrenar** (9)

translator **traductor(a)** (16)

transportation (means of) transportation **transporte** *m.* (14)

trash: to take out the trash **sacar (qu) la basura** (9)

travel **viajar** (7); travel agency **agencia de viajes** (7); travel agent **agente** (*m. f.*) **de viajes** (7)

traveler **viajero/a** (18); traveler's check **cheque** (*m.*) **de viajero** (18)

treatment **tratamiento** (10)

tree **árbol** *m.* (14)

trip **viaje** *m.* (7); on a trip **de viaje** (7); round-trip ticket **billete** (*m.*)/**boleto de ida y vuelta** (7); to go on a trip **ir** (*irreg.*) **de viaje** (10); to take a trip **hacer** (*irreg.*) **un viaje** (4)

try **intentar** (13); try to (*do something*) **tratar de** + *inf.* (13)

Tuesday **martes** *m. s., pl.* (4)

tuition **matrícula** (1)

tuna **atún** *m.* (6)

turkey **pavo** (6)

turn **doblar** (14); to turn in **entregar (gu)** (11); to turn on (*machines*) **poner** (*irreg.*) (11); to be someone's turn **tocarle (qu) a uno** (9)

twelve **doce** (AT)

twenty **veinte** (AT)

twice **dos veces** (10)

two **dos** (AT)

two hundred **doscientos/as** (3)

type **escribir** (*pp.* **escrito/a**) **a máquina** (16)

U

ugly **feo/a** (2)

unbelievable **increíble** (13)

uncle **tío** (2)

understand **comprender** (2); **entender (ie)** (4)

underwear **ropa interior** (3)

unintentional: it was unintentional **fue sin querer** (11)

university **universidad** *f.* (1); (of the) university **universitario/a** (11); university campus *campus* *m. s.* (12)

unless **a menos que** (15)

unoccupied **desocupado/a** (18)

unpleasant **antipático/a** (2)

until **hasta** *prep.* (4); **hasta que** *conj.* (16); until tomorrow **hasta mañana** (AT)

upon + *verb form* **al** + *inf.* (3)

urgent **urgente** (13)

us **nos** *d.o.; i.o.* to/for us; *refl. pron.* ourselves; **nos vemos** see you around (AT)

use **usar** (3); **gastar** (8); to use up completely **acabar** (14)

V

vacant **desocupado/a** (18)

vacation **vacación** *f.* (7); to be on vacation **estar** (*irreg.*) **de vacaciones** (7); to go on vacation **ir** (*irreg.*) **de vacaciones** (7)

vacuum cleaner **aspiradora** (9); to vacuum **pasar la aspiradora** (9)

vegetable **verdura** (6)

vehicle **vehículo** (12)

verb **verbo** *gram.* (1)

very **muy** (1); very well **muy bien** (AT)

veterinarian **veterinario/a** (16)

videocassette recorder (VCR) **videocasetera** (12)

view **vista** (12)

violence **violencia** (14)

visit a museum **visitar un museo** (9)
volleyball **vólibol** *m.* (9)

W

wait (for) **esperar** (6)
waiter **camarero** (6)
waiting room **sala de espera** (7)
waitress **camarera** (6)
wake up **despertarse (ie)** (4)
walk **caminar** (10); to take a walk **dar**
  (*irreg.*) **un paseo** (9); to go on foot
  (walk) **ir** (*irreg.*) **a pie** (10)
wall **pared** *f.* (4)
wallet **cartera** (3)
want **desear** (1); **querer** (*irreg.*) (3)
war **guerra** (17)
warm: to be (feel) warm, hot **tener**
  (*irreg.*) **calor** (5)
wash **lavar** (9); to wash (the windows,
  the dishes, clothes) **lavar (las**
  ventanas, los platos, la ropa) (9); to
  wash (oneself) **lavar(se)**
washing machine **lavadora** (4)
waste **desperdiciar** (14)
watch **reloj** *m.* (3); to watch **mirar** (2); to
  watch television **mirar la televisión**
  (2)
water **agua** *f.* (*but* **el agua**); waterbed
  cama de agua (4); mineral water **agua**
  f. (*but* **el agua**) **mineral** (6)
we **nosotros/as** (1)
wear (clothing) **llevar, usar** (3)
weather **tiempo** (5); it's good/bad
  weather **hace buen/mal tiempo** (5);
  what's the weather like? **¿qué tiempo**
  hace? (5)
weave **tejer** (13)
wedding **boda** (15)
Wednesday **miércoles** *m. s., pl.* (4)
week **semana** (4); next week **la semana**
  que viene (4)
weekend **fin** (*m.*) **de semana** (4)
welcome: you're welcome **de nada, no**
  hay de qué (AT)

well **bien** *adv.* (AT); well . . . *interj.*
  bueno... (2)
well-being **bienestar** *m.* (10)
west **oeste** *m.* (5)
what . . . ! **¡qué... !;** what a shame! **¡qué**
  lástima! (13)
what? which? **¿qué? ¿cuál(es)?** (AT);
  what are you like? **¿cómo es usted?**
  (AT); what is the date today? **¿cuál es**
  la fecha de hoy? (5); what time is it?
  ¿qué hora es? (AT); what's your
  name? **¿cómo te llamas? / ¿cómo se**
  llama usted? (AT)
when + *verb form* **al** + *inf.* (3)
when? **¿cuándo?** (AT)
where (to)? **¿adónde?** (3)
where? **¿dónde?** (AT); where are you
  from? **¿de dónde es Ud.?** (2)
which **que** (2)
while + *verb form* **al** + *inf.* (3); **mientras**
  conj. (10); **rato** *n.* (9)
white **blanco/a** (3); white wine **vino**
  blanco (6)
who **que** (2)
who? whom? **¿quién(es)?** (AT)
whole **entero/a** (9)
whose? **¿de quién?** (2)
why? **¿por qué?** (2)
wife **esposa** (2); **mujer** *f.* (15)
win **ganar** (9)
wind *n.* **viento** (5); *adj.* **eólico/a** (14); it's
  windy **hace viento** (5)
window **ventana** (1)
windshield **parabrisas** *m. s.* (14)
wine (white, red) **vino (blanco, tinto)** (6)
winter **invierno** (5)
wish **deseo** (8); **esperanza** (17)
with **con** (1)
without **sin** (4)
witness **testigo** *m., f.* (17)
woman **señora (Sra.)** (AT); **mujer** *f.* (1)
wool **lana** (3); it is made of wool **es de**
  lana (3)
word **palabra** (1)
work (of art) **obra (de arte)** (13); *n.*

trabajo (11); to work **trabajar** (1);
  (*machine*) **funcionar** (12)
worker **obrero/a** (16); **trabajador(a)** *n.*
  (2); social worker **trabajador(a) social**
  (16)
world **mundo** (7)
worried **preocupado/a** (5)
worse **peor** (5)
woven goods **tejidos** *m. pl.* (13)
write **escribir** (*p.p.* **escrito/a**) (2)
writer **escritor(a)** (13)
written **escrito/a** *p.p.* (11)
wrong: to be wrong **no tener** (*irreg.*)
  razón (3); **equivocarse (qu)** (11)

Y

yard, patio **patio** (4)
year **año** (5); (*in school*) **grado** (9); to be
  . . . years old **tener** (*irreg.*)**... años** (2)
yellow **amarillo/a** (3)
yes **sí** (AT); yes, I like . . . **sí, me gusta...**
  (AT)
yesterday **ayer** (4)
yet **todavía** (5)
yogurt **yogur** *m.* (6)
you *sub. pron.* **tú** (*fam. s.*) (AT); **usted**
  (Ud., Vd.) (*form. s.*) (AT); **vosotros/as**
  (*fam. pl., Sp.*); **ustedes (Uds., Vds.)**
  (*pl.*); *d.o.* **te, os, lo/la, los, las;** to/for
  you *i.o.* **te, os, le, les;** *obj.* (*of prep.*) **ti**
  (5), **Ud., Uds., voso tros/as**
you're welcome **de nada, no hay de qué**
  (AT)
young woman **señorita (Srta.)** (AT)
younger **menor** (5)
your *poss.* **tu** (*fam. s.*) (2); **su(s)** (*form.*)
  (2); **vuestro/a(s)** (*fam. pl., Sp.*) (2); (of)
  yours **tuyo/a(s)** (2), **suyo/a(s)** (2),
  vuestro/a(s) (2)
youth **joven** *n. m., f.* (2); *adj.* young (2);
  as a youth **de joven** (9); (*young*
  adulthood) **juventud** *f.* (15)

Z

zero **cero** (AT)

Index

In this Index, cultural notes and vocabulary topic groups are listed by individual topic as well as under those headings.

Credits

Grateful acknowledgment is made for use of the following:

Photographs: *Page 2* © Ulrike Welsch; *4* Marty Granger; *9* (*from left*) Stephanie Cardinale/Corbis Sygma, Associated Press, Mitchell Gerber/Corbis, Gregory Pace/Corbis Sygma; *12* © Stuart Cohen/Comstock; *18* SuperStock; *26* (*left*) Marty Granger; *29* (*clockwise from top left*) PICTOR/Uniphoto, SuperStock, © Ulrike Welsch, © Peter Menzel, Antonio Mendoza/Stock Boston; *32* © Michael Newman/PhotoEdit; *37* A.G.E. FOTOSTOCK; *44* (*top*) Associated Press, (*bottom*) Susan Casarin; *53* (*left*) Marty Granger; *57* Bastone/Photoreporters, Inc.; *61* © Ulrike Welsch; *64* SuperStock; *77* Museo del Prado, Madrid, Spain/Giraudon, Paris/SuperStock; *80* © Llewellyn/Uniphoto; *84* (*clockwise from top left*) Associated Press, Gregory Pace/Corbis Sygma, Associated Press, Gregory Pace/Corbis/Sygma; *85* Susan Casarin; *89* Marty Granger; *93* Commissioned by the Trustees of Dartmouth College; *97* © Carmen Lomas Garza, 1987. Photo credit: Wolfgang Dietze, Collection of Leonila Ramirez, Don Ramon's Restaurant, San Francisco, California; *100* John Neubauer/PhotoEdit; *105* © Gonzalo Endara Crow; *106* Persson/Photoreporters, Inc.; *113* *Gregory Pace/Corbis* Sygma; *114* Marty Granger; *120* Marty Granger; *125* Corbis-Bettman; *130* Bonnie Kamin; *135* Suzanne L. Murphy/D. Donne Bryant Stock; *146* Vincente Wolf Associates, Inc.; *147* Susan Casarin; *152* © Bill Gentile/Corbis; *158* © Joe Viesti/The Viesti Collection; *175* (*top and bottom*) *A logo for America* by Alfredo Jaar; *176* (*top*) Uniphoto, (*bottom*) © Ulrike Welsch; *181* (*left*) Marty Granger; *185* © Rob Crandall/The Image Works; *189* Frans Lating/Tony Stone Images; *190* Robert Frerck/Odyssey/Chicago; *197* Marty Granger; *206* (*top*) photograph, Harold Naideau, cover design, Susanne Noli, (*bottom*) SuperStock; *212* (*top*) Marty Granger; *215* Courtesy of Oswaldo & Alice Arana; *218* V. Godoy/*Más*, Univisions Publications; *222* Jacques Pavlovsky/Corbis Sygma; *226* © Alex Ocampo/The Photoworks/DDB STOCK PHOTO; *227* © Stuart Cohen/Comstock; *233* SuperStock; *238* Marty Granger; *243* Marty Granger; *247* © Stephen and Donna O'Meara/Photo Researchers, Inc.; *251* SuperStock; *252* © H. Gans/The Image Works; *266* © Robert Fried/Stock Boston; *270* (*top*) Marty Granger; *274* © Prensa Latina; *278* © Ulrike Welsch; *281* Corbis-Bettmann; *290* (*from left*) Stephanie Cardinale/Corbis Sygma, Dana Fineman/Corbis Sygma, Associated Press; *294* Xavier Nunez/Antara Productions; *295* Susan Casarin; *300* © George Holton/Photo Researchers, Inc.; *304* Everett Collection; *306* © Ulrike Welsch; *312* Marty Granger; *319* Miami Herald Publishing Co.; *324* (*left*) Marty Granger; *329* © Ken Fisher/Tony Stone Images; *336* © Esbin-Anderson/Omni-Photo Communications, Inc.; *340* (*top*) Frederic de LaFosse, (*bottom*) Frank Trapper/Corbis Sygma; *349* Dalle Luche/Sestini/Grazia Neri/Corbis Sygma; *354* (*left*) Marty Granger; *358* © Ulrike Welsch; *362* PICTOR/Uniphoto; *364* © Ulrike Welsch; *375* Courtesy of C.S.E., Inc.; *376, 385* (*left*) Marty Granger; *389* © Michael Sewell/Peter Arnold, Inc.; *393* (*top*)

About the Authors

Marty Knorre was formerly Associate Professor of Romance Languages and Coordinator of basic Spanish courses at the University of Cincinnati, where she taught undergraduate and graduate courses in language, linguistics, and methodology. She received her Ph.D. in foreign language education from The Ohio State University in 1975. Dr. Knorre is coauthor of *Cara a cara* and *Reflejos* and has taught at several NEH Institutes for Language Instructors. She received a Master of Divinity at McCormick Theological Seminary in 1991.

Thalia Dorwick is Editor-in-Chief of Humanities, Social Sciences, and Languages for McGraw-Hill. She is in charge of the world languages college list in Spanish, French, Italian, German, Japanese, and Russian. She has taught at Allegheny College, California State University (Sacramento), and Case Western Reserve University, where she received her Ph.D. in Spanish in 1973. Dr. Dorwick is the coauthor of several textbooks and the author of several articles on language teaching issues. She was recognized as an Outstanding Foreign Language Teacher by the California Foreign Language Teachers Association in 1978.

Ana María Pérez-Gironés is an Adjunct Assistant Professor of Spanish at Wesleyan University, Middletown, Connecticut, where she teaches and coordinates Spanish language courses. She received a Licenciatura en Filología Anglogermánica from the Universidad de Sevilla in 1985, and her M.A. in General Linguistics from Cornell University in 1988. She is a coauthor of *¿Qué tal?*, Fourth Edition.

William R. Glass is the Executive Editor for Spanish at McGraw-Hill, and he is also in charge of the McGraw-Hill Second Language Professional Series. He s an Adjunct Professor of Spanish at The Pennsylvania State University, where he taught both undergraduate and graduate courses in language and applied linguistics. He received his Ph.D. from the University of Illinois at Urbana–Champaign in 1992 in Spanish Applied Linguistics with a concentration in Second Language Acquisition and Teacher Education (SLATE). Dr. Glass' research interests include second language reading theory and second language acquisition in tutored contexts. He is also a coauthor on *Manual que acompaña ¿Sabías que... ?*, another McGraw-Hill textbook series.

Hildebrando Villarreal is Professor of Spanish at California State University, Los Angeles, where he teaches undergraduate and graduate courses in language and linguistics. He received his Ph.D. in Spanish with an emphasis in Applied Linguistics from UCLA in 1976. Professor Villarreal is the author of several reviews and articles on language, language teaching, and Spanish for Native Speakers of Spanish. He is the author of *¡A leer! Un paso más*, an intermediate textbook that focuses on reading skills.

Los hispanos en los Estados Unidos	1500–1600	1700–1776	1835–1836	1846–1848
	Exploraciones españolas	Establecimiento de misiones en Arizona y California	Guerra de la independencia tejana	Guerra entre México y los Estados Unidos

México y Centroamérica	a.C.[a] 800–400	d.C.[b] 300–900	1200–1521	1821
	Civilización olmeca	Civilización maya	Civilización azteca florece hasta la conquista de Tenochtitlán por Hernán Cortés	Independencia de México y Centroamérica

[a]antes de Cristo [b]después de Cristo

Las naciones caribeñas	d.C. 25–600	1492–1498	1500–1512	1821
	Civilización igneri y fundación del pueblo de Tibes en Puerto Rico	Viajes de Cristóbal Colón al Caribe y a Venezuela	Colonización española de Venezuela, Puerto Rico y Cuba	Independencia de Venezuela y Colombia

Las naciones andinas	1000–1500	1200–1532	1532	1821
	Civilización nasca en el Perú	Imperio incaico	Francisco Pizarro conquista a los incas	Independencia del Perú

Las naciones del Cono Sur	1536	1724	1816	1818
	Primera fundación de Buenos Aires	Expulsión de los portugueses del Uruguay	Independencia de la Argentina, el Paraguay, el Uruguay	Independencia de Chile

España	a.C. 200	711–1492	1492	1500–1700
	Llegada de los romanos a la Península	Establecimiento del imperio moro en la Península	Reconquista de Granada; expulsión de los judíos de España; primer viaje de Cristóbal Colón	El Siglo de Oro

Los Estados Unidos y el Canadá	a.C. 800–d.C. 1600	1534	1600–1750	1776–1789
	Varias culturas indígenas	Jacques Cartier reclama el Canadá en nombre de Francia	Fundación de las colonias británicas	Guerra de la Independencia en los Estados Unidos